Thomas Harriot

Thomas Harriot:
A Biography

by

John W. Shirley

Clarendon Press · Oxford
1983

Oxford University Press, Walton Street, Oxford OX2 6DP
London Glasgow New York Toronto
Delhi Bombay Calcutta Madras Karachi
Kuala Lumpur Singapore Hong Kong Tokyo
Nairobi Dar es Salaam Cape Town
Melbourne Auckland
and associates in
Beirut Berlin Ibadan Mexico City Nicosia

Oxford is a trade mark of Oxford University Press

Published in the United States by
Oxford University Press, New York

British Library Cataloguing in Publication Data
Shirley, John W.
Thomas Harriot.
1. Harriot, Thomas   2. Science, Biography
I. Title
509'.2'4   Q143.H/
ISBN 0-19-822901-1

Library of Congress Cataloging in Publication Data
Shirley, John William, 1908-
Thomas Harriot, a biography.
Bibliography: p.
Includes index.
1. Hariot, Thomas, 1560-1621.   2. Scientists —
Great Britain — Biography.   3. Science — Great Britain —
History — Sources.   I. Title.
Q143.H36S46 1983   510'.92'4 [B]   83-3961
ISBN 0-19-822901-1

Set by Hope Services, Abingdon
and printed in Great Britain by
Redwood Burn Ltd., Trowbridge

Preface

It has been more than thirty-five years since I began seriously to study Thomas Harriot. Though most of these years have been occupied in more contemporary activities, this fascinating man has occupied a large portion of my waking thoughts during this period. Following his elusive genius has taken me to most of the places that Harriot himself visited during his sixty years, and has led me to view all or nearly all of the remaining records of his life and work. In this odyssey I have met literally hundreds of people who have taken pains to be of assistance in one way or another; among them I number a great many whom I have come to consider as personal friends. To give all credit in detail would require more space than the printer will allow, and, to be truthful, the infirmities of memory do not, at my present age, permit me to recall them all. So to those of you who are not here mentioned, I apologetically acknowledge my debt.

First, I must thank my family — Jerry, Jean, and Linda — for their patience in bearing with my interest. They have trundled hither to yon, living in trailers and castles, without complaint. They have joyed and suffered with me in finding, or not finding, what I sought. And Jerry has read the manuscript for these writings in many versions. Without them, this search would not have been so much fun.

Four particular institutions must be thanked for their help. When I was just starting, the John Simon Guggenheim Memorial Foundation generously awarded me a fellowship to spend more than a year in England to locate and photograph Harriot manuscripts, and Michigan State University granted a sabbatical to extend that study period at the Henry L. Huntington Library. The University of Delaware, particularly in the persons of President E. A. Trabant, Provost Leon L. Campbell, and Board Chairman J. Bruce Bredin, has done all in its power to assist my studies, including travel grants and a sabbatical for further English study. And the National Endowment for the Humanities helped by joining with the University to support the Thomas Harriot Symposium in 1971 which brought many Harriot scholars together to share their collective knowledge of the man whom they all admired.

From the outset I have enjoyed in many ways the assistance of the man who is undoubtedly the greatest scholar in the field of American exploration, David B. Quinn, and of Alison Quinn, his scholarly wife, who has graciously indexed the present volume. Never has either refused help when asked; David has corrected many of my howlers, and those that remain are because he did not see those sections. Another invaluable support has been His Grace, the Duke of Northumberland, direct descendant of Harriot's patron, the Wizard Earl. A man (like his ancestor) of wide and deep scholarly interests, His Grace has been generous beyond belief in giving me the keys to his archive and muniment rooms at both Syon House and Alnwick Castle, and has followed my research with personal interest. I cannot express the gratitude I feel for him. Three of the five latest Lords Leconfield and Egremont have also graciously permitted me full access to the Harriot manuscripts still remaining at Petworth House, Sussex, and I owe them a debt of gratitude. The estates agents and housekeepers at Alnwick, Syon, Petworth, and Sherborne have also been most helpful in locating and photographing manuscripts. The Reverend F. J. (Cousin John) Shirley, Residentiary Canon at Canterbury Cathedral and Headmaster of the venerable King's School, was able to get me access to many private libraries and gave me background in the religious controversies of Harriot's day. His untimely death was a great loss to us all.

Librarians and research staffs of many great libraries willingly and without complaint came to my assistance countless times. Though I cannot name them all, I remember kindly the staffs of the British Library (particularly the Manuscript and Photographic Departments), the Bodleian and the

Radcliffe at Oxford, the Public Record Office, the Sion College Library, the Victoria and Albert and the Warburg Institute in London (with special thanks to the late Frances Yates), the Folger Shakespeare Library and the Library of Congress in Washington, the Clements Library in Ann Arbor, and the Henry L. Huntington Library in San Marino. In my own institutions, Michigan State University, North Carolina State, and the University of Delaware, I have had full support, including inordinate inter-library loan service. The efforts of all these professionals make it clear that the academic community (in spite of its rivalry in many areas besides sports) is really unified in its search for truth.

Among others who deserve special mention for their participation in memorable aspects of photographing the Harriot manuscripts are Arundel Esdaile and David Wilson of the British Library, Eugene Powers and E. M. V. Glanville of University Microfilms, and Mr Tye of Rank-Xerox, London.

A most pleasant group of friendships has evolved among present-day scholars who are particularly interested in Harriot — Harrioteers, they call themselves — who meet annually in the Harriot seminars held alternately at Oxford and at Durham, with one visit to Delaware. R. C. H. (Cecily) Tanner is one of the founders of the group, which includes Alistair Crombie as host of the Oxford meetings and Gordon R. Batho as host at Durham. Members who have been active from the beginning include John D. North, David and Alison Quinn, John Roche, Jon V. Pepper, D. T. Whiteside, Ivor Grattan-Guinness. Among others who have joined the group on occasion and made important contributions must be mentioned Commander D. W. Waters, Alec Wallace, Jean Jacquot, F. R. Maddison, Muriel Ruykeyser, Christopher Hill, and Ernest Strathmann. Harriot's strong character welds such diverse scholars into a friendly community.

It is with some regret that I see this book in print; I have lived with it so long it has become a part of me. I realize how incomplete it is and how many errors it must contain. Had I another thirty-five years it would, I am sure, be a better biography than it is, but time has a way of insisting that a book be closed. Yet thoughts of Harriot and friendly associations he has generated will remain for me to enjoy in those years that lie ahead.

Contents

List of Illustrations   xi

  I. Harriot in History   1

 II. Harriot at Oxford, 1560–1580   38

III. Harriot with Ralegh, 1580–1585   70

 IV. New Horizons, 1585–1590   113

  V. Years of Transition, 1590–1600   175

 VI. The 1590s: Harriot Expands his Interests   241

VII. From the Court to the Tower — Ralegh   288

VIII. From the Court to the Tower — Northumberland   327

 IX. The Northumberland Circle   358

  X. The Mature Scholar   380

 XI. The Bitter End: Illness and Death   425

      Bibliography   476

      Index   491

Illustrations

1. Section of Robert Whittlesey's Engraving
   of the Plan of Oxford by Ralph Agas.
   Courtesy of the Bodleian Library   39
2. Harriot's Matriculation, Oxford Archives,
   KK9, f. 636
   Courtesy of the Bodleian Library   50
3. Harriot's Supplications, Oxford Archives,
   KK9, f. 296^r.
   Courtesy of the Bodleian Library   55
4. Notes on Officers and Watches, BL, Add.
   MSS 6788, f. 21.
   Courtesy of the British Library   98
5. Harriot's Phonetic Alphabet, Taken from
   BL, Add 6782, f. 337.
   Courtesy of the British Library   111
6. The Landing of the English.
   Courtesy of the British Library   130
7. Map of Ralegh's Virginia.
   Courtesy of the British Library   132
8. Indenture Granting Brampton Property
   to Harriot. Alnwick Castle: Syon MSS
   X.II.5.d.
   Courtesy of the Duke of Northumberland   213
9. Harriot's Release of Brampton. Alnwick
   Castle: Syon MSS X.II.5.d.
   Courtesy of the Duke of Northumberland   217
10a. Notes on Trajectories (1). BL, Add
    MSS 6789, f. 30^r.
    Courtesy of the British Library   256
10b. Notes on Trajectories (2). BL, Add MSS
    6789, f. 30^v.
    Courtesy of the British Library   257

xi

xii   *List of Illustrations*

11. Notes on Parabolic Motion. BL, Add MSS
    6789, f. 67.
    Courtesy of the British Library   260
12. Calculations of the Rate of Fall. BL, Add
    MSS 6788, f. 144.
    Courtesy of the British Library   264
13. The Imposition of Terra. Petworth 241/iv, f. 29^r.
    Courtesy of Lord Egremont   274
14. Waterworks at Syon. BL, Add MSS 6786,
    f. 369.
    Courtesy of the British Library   294
15. Pensions for the Three Magi. Petworth #600.
    The General Account, 1620.
    Courtesy of Lord Egremont   378
16a.b.c. Harriot to Mayerne. BL, Add MSS 6789,
    f. 446-7.
    Courtesy of the British Library   435-437

I. Harriot in History

On the twenty-ninth of June in the year of our Lord God
1621, Master Thomas Harriot 'of Syon in the County of
Middlesex, Gentleman, being troubled in [his] bodie with
infirmities. But of perfecte minde & memorie', lay on his
deathbed at the home of his friend, Thomas Buckner, Mercer,
in St. Christopher's parish, not far from the Royal Exchange
in London. As he itemized his personal possessions and made
careful disposition of his maps, his globes, his telescopes and
scientific instruments, Harriot naturally considered the mass
of unpublished mathematical and scientific papers which had
occupied the last forty years of his active life. He must have
considered his rightful place in history, and recognized all too
late that his failure to publish his discoveries jeopardized his
eternal reputation. He may have recalled that more than a
decade earlier his favourite student-friend, Sir William Lower,
MP for Lostwithiel in Cornwall, had strongly urged him to
mend his ways before it was too late. On 6 February 1610
Lower had written to his 'assured and true frind':[1]

Doe you not here startle, to see every day some of your inventions
taken from you; for I remember longe since you told me as much [as
Kepler has just published] that the motions of the planets were not
perfect circles. So you taught me the curious way to observe weight in
Water, and within a while after Ghetaldi comes out with it, in print.
A little before Vieta prevented you of the Gharland for the greate

---

[1] This important letter has been widely quoted. It was originally discovered
among the Petworth papers by von Zach in 1784 and extracted with others for
his proposed biography. Unfortunately, however, when the papers were returned
to Oxford, this part of Lower's letter was not included. As a result, it exists only
as reprinted in von Zach's publication of July 1803. See *Monatliche Correspondenz zur Beförderung der Erd-und-Himmels-Kunde, herausgegeben vom Freyherrn
von Zach*, Gotha, 28 bd., 1800–13, vol. VIII, pp. 49–54.

Invention of Algebra. al these were your deues and manie others that I could mention; and yet too great reservednesse hath rob'd you of these glories. but although the inventions be greate, the first and last I meane, yet when I survei your storehouse, I see they are the smallest things, and such as in Comparison of manie others are of smal or no value. Onlie let this remember you, that it is possible by to much procrastination to be prevented in the honor of some of your rarest inventions and speculations. Let your Countrie and frinds injoye the comforts they would have in the true and greate honor you would purchase your selfe by publishing some of your choise workes. but you know best what you have to doe. Onlie I, because I wish you all good, wish this, and sometimes the more longhinglie, because in one of your lettres you gave me some kind of hope thereof.

Too late, Harriot tried to make amends, leaving to his friends the task which for some reason he had found himself unable to do. Carefully he dictated to the scrivener who was writing down his last recorded words:[2]

Item. I ordayne and Constitute the aforesaid Nathaniell Thorperley first to be Ouerseer of my Mathematicall writinges to be received of my Executors to pervse and order and to separate the Cheife of them from my waste papers, to the end that after hee doth vnderstande them hee may make vse in penninge such doctrine that belonges vnto them for publique vses as it shall be thought Convenient by my Executors and him selfe. And if it happen that some manner of notacions or writinges of the said papers shall not be vnderstood by him then my desire is that it will please him to Conferre withe Master Warner or Master Hughes Attendants on the aforesaid Earle Concerning the aforesaid doubtes And if hee he not resolued by either of them That then hee Conferre with the aforesaid John Protheroe Esquior or the aforesaid Thomas Alesbury Esquior (I hoping that some or other of the aforesaid fower Last nominated can resolve him). And when hee hath had the vse of the said papers soe longe as my Executors and hee haue agreed for the vse aforesaid That then hee deliuer them againe vnto my Executors to be putt into a Convenient Truncke with a locke & key and to be placed in my Lord of Northumberlandes library and the key thereof to be deliuered into his Lordshipps hands And if at anie tyme after my Executors or the aforesaid Nathaniell Thorperley shall agayne desire the vse of some or all of the said Mathematicall papers That then it will please the said Earle to lett

[2] Harriot's will is now in the Guildhall in London in both the authentic copy for Probate proved in the Archdeaconry of London Court on 6 July 1621, and the Register Copy of the same Court. This quotation is from the Probate Copy. In this volume, customary manuscript abbreviations have been silently expanded in transcription.

anie of the aforesaid to haue them for theire vse so long as shall be thought Convenient, and afterwards to be restored agayne vnto the Truncke in the aforesaid Earles Lybrary Secondly my will & desire is that the said Nathaniell Thorperley be also Ouerseer of other written bookes & papers as my Executors and hee shall thincke Convenient.

But like other well-laid plans, this one, too, went awry, and Harriot's hope for the ordering of the papers of a lifetime of effort, the careful selection of 'the Cheife', and the uttering of them 'for publique vses' was never accomplished.

Nathaniel Torporley (1564–1632), named by Harriot as his literary executor, though a clergyman by profession, was qualified by experience for the publication of mathematical tracts. An amanuensis of François Vieta, Torporley had been engaged in transcribing his notes at the time of the publication of Vieta's great work on algebra, his *Algebra nova*, in 1591. A letter from Torporley to Harriot on the eve of his first meeting with Vieta shows that the two were close friends as early as 1586,[3] and at least one problem of Vieta was passed on to Harriot during the years while Torporley was in the service of the French mathematician.[4] On his return to England from France, however, Torporley had involved himself in ecclesiastical matters, though he undoubtedly kept his interest in new developments of mathematics through his English friendships. But by 1621 Torporley was ready to retire from active service as a clergyman and probably accepted the new editorial assignment willingly. The following year he gave up his ecclesiastical post at Salwarpe, accepted a pension from John Protheroe (1582–1624), one of Harriot's executors, and prepared to work on the Harriot manuscripts. A memorandum still remaining among the Harriot papers is headed:[5] 'Copyed from Master Protheroe. A note of the papers and bookes in Master Harriots truncke delivered to Master Torporley', and a subsequent list begins 'Notes of Papers of Master Harriots delivered to Master Torporley'.

---

[3] Jon. V. Pepper, 'A letter from Nathaniel Torporley to Thomas Harriot', *British Journal for the History of Science*, III.11 (1967), 285–90.

[4] BL Add. MS 6782, fo. 483.

[5] BL Add. MS 6789, fos. 448r&v, 449, 450. These lists have been published by Tanner, 'Nathaniel Torporley and the Harriot Manuscripts, *Annals of Science*, XXV.4 (1969), 339–49.

Just why Torporley did not follow through with the publication of Harriot's mathematical papers as he was asked to do is still subject to speculation. Torporley's study of Harriot's 'doctrine' was thorough, and by 1630 when he moved into Sion College, a home for retired clergy, his notes show that he had transcribed and understood most of Harriot's work on algebra.[6] One suggestion that has some supporting evidence is that in going through Harriot's non-mathematical papers Torporley had discovered Harriot's atomistic theories of light and matter, and as a clergyman was very upset by this unorthodox view of the nature of God's creations. Torporley may, as has been claimed, have turned his energies to the refutation of these erroneous views and lost interest in the development of Harriot's mathematical innovations.

Whatever the reason, Torporley did not fulfil the obligation placed on him by Harriot and this lack of action led the other literary executors to action. Lower and Protheroe had both died, so it was left to Harriot's long-time friend and associate in the household of the 9th Earl, Walter Warner (1550?-1636), to deal with the situation. Warner extracted from the voluminous notes of Harriot a small portion dealing with his method of solving algebraic equations, and ten years after Harriot's death he took them to press under the title *ARTIS ANALYTICAE PRAXIS, Ad æquationes Algebraicas nouâ, expeditâ, & generali methodo, resoluendas: TRACT-ATVS E posthumis THOMAE HARRIOTI Philosophi ac Mathematici celeberrimi schediasmatis summâ fide & diligentiâ descriptus:... LONDINI... Anno 1631.* This small volume of 180 pages, representing but a part of Harriot's innovative work on mathematics, was the only portion of Harriot's work to remain 'publique', and it is on this single work that his fame as a mathematician has rested in the centuries following his death.

The appearance of the *Artis Analyticæ Praxis* started the famous controversy over Harriot and his proper place in the history of mathematics. Harriot's own literary executor could be charged as responsible for starting the debate. Though

[6] R. C. H. Tanner, 'Nathaniel Torporley's "Congestor analyticus" and Thomas Harriot's 'De triangulis laterum rationalium"', *Annals of Science*, XXXIV (1977), 393-428.

there is evidence that Torporley had a hand in the selection of Harriot's papers to be printed by Warner and had some editorial prerogatives over some of the text, the sight of the final volume came as a shock to the old man. A manuscript fragment among Torporley's papers at Sion College severely criticizes the editors for the way in which they presented Harriot's solutions, for their failure to recognize some of his major accomplishments, and even for their inability to understand some of his notations.[7] He even went so far as to prepare a peevish title-page for a proposed work which he suggested he might write to rectify these errors. This title-page, translated from the original Latin by Henry Stevens,[8] reads as follows:

THE ANALYTICAL CORRECTOR
of the posthumous scientific writings
of THOMAS HARRIOT.

As an excellent Mathematician, one who very seldom ⎫
As a bold Philosopher, one who occasionally ⎬ erred.
As a frail Man, one who notably ⎭

For

the more trustworthy refutation of the pseudo-philosophic
atomic theory, revived by him and, outside his
other strange notions, deserving of
reprehension and anathema.

A Compendious Warning with specimens by the aged
and retired-from-active-life

Na: Torporley.

So that
The critic may know
The buyer may beware,
It is not safe to trust to the bank
The bell-wether himself is drying his fleece.

---

[7] Sion College MS L40. 2/E10. This MS is reprinted (with some inaccuracies) by James Orchard Halliwell in his *Collection of Letters Illustrative of the Progress of Science in England from the Reign of Queen Elizabeth to that of Charles the Second*, London, for the Historical Society of Science, 1841. See the Appendix, 109–16. See also Tanner's two articles on Torporley and Harriot.

[8] Henry Stevens, *Thomas Hariot, The Mathematician, the Philosopher, and the Scholar*, London, Privately Printed, 1900, p. 174. Stevens also gives the original Latin on p. 172.

The Revd. Torporley's rather peevish critical review adds little to an understanding of Harriot's contributions to algebra.[9]

Though the end note of the *Praxis* indicates that additional publication from Harriot's manuscripts was being considered, the cost of printing the volume had proved greater than anticipated so that any further works would require additional subsidy. Through his close friend, Thomas Aylesbury (1576–1657), another of Harriot's executors, Warner approached Harriot's patron, the 9th Earl of Northumberland, for more support. A letter, inscribed in Warner's hand as 'Sir Th. A. lettere about my busines' remains among the Warner manuscripts preserved in the Pell collection in the British Library.[10] It reads as follows:

Right Honorable:

May it please your Lordship: I presumed heretofore to moue your Lordship on the behalf of Master W[arner] for some consideracion to be had of his extraordinary expense in attending the publication of Master H[arriot's] book after the copy was finished. The same humble request I am induced to renew by reson of his present wants occasioned by that attendance.

For his literary labour and paines taken in forming the book and fitting it for the publik view he looks for no other reward then your Lordships acceptance thereof, as an honest discharge of his duty. But his long attendance through vnexpected difficulties in seeking to get the book freely printed, and after that was vndertaken the frivolous delais of the printers and slow proceding of the presse, which no intretees of his or myne could remedy, drew him to a gretter expence then his meanes would bere, including both your Lordships pension and the arbitrary help of his frends. It is this extraordinary expense which he cannot recouer which makes both him and me for him appele to your Lordships goodnes and bounty for some tollerable mitigation thereof.

I purpose god willing to set forth other peeces of Master H[arriot] wherin by reson of my owne incombrances I must of necessity desire the help of Master W[arner] rather than of any other. Whereto I find him redy enough because it tends to your Lordships service, and may the more freely trouble him, yf he receve some little encoragement

[9] According to Dr Tanner, Dr Landels is currently preparing a translation and analysis of this MS.

[10] This letter was first printed with some misreadings and ascribed to Nathaniel Torporley by J. O. Halliwell, *A Collection of Letters*, p. 71. It was also printed, correctly ascribed to Aylesbury by Stevens in his biography of Harriot (usually referred to by its originally proposed title, *Thomas Harriot and his Associates*), on pp. 189–90. This transcription is taken from the original, BL MS Birch 4396, fo. 90[r].

from your Lordship towards the repairing of the detriment that lies still vpon him by his last imploiment. But for the future my intention is to haue the impression at my owne charge and not depend on the curtesy of those mechaniks, making regard that that which may seeme to be saved by the other way will not countervaile this trouble and tedious prolongation of the busines. But the copies being made perfect and faire written for the presse they shall be sufficiently bound to deliver the books perfectly don out of their hands, and by this meanes the trouble and charge of attending the presse will be saved. Therefore my Lord What you do now will be but for this once, and in such proportion as shall best like you to favour the humble motion of him who is

July .5. 1632

Allway most redy at
your Lordships command
T. A.

Four months to the day after this letter was written, Henry Percy, 9th Earl of Northumberland, died quietly at Petworth House in Sussex, where he had retired following his release from the Tower shortly after Harriot's death. There is no evidence that he responded favourably to Aylesbury's request, and his oldest son, Algernon, who succeeded him as 10th Earl, seems even to have discontinued the pension which his father had given to Walter Warner. Any further publication of Harriot's works was out of the question, as a result, and either Warner or Aylesbury, in accordance with Harriot's last will and testament, 'putt [Harriot's papers] into a Convenient Truncke . . . in the aforesaid Earles Lybrary' in the country estate to which he had retired. There they remained, in Petworth House, Sussex, though the memory that they were there was lost following the deaths of Warner in 1636 and Aylesbury in 1657.

Though there was considerable discussion about the Harriot papers among English mathematicians of the time, like Pell and Wallis, the final disposition of the manuscripts remained unknown. Harriot's will, probated in Archdeaconry Court in London because of his death in the city, was not located, and the fact that Harriot had willed them to his patron Northumberland had been forgotten. The question of the retrieval of the papers was raised at one of the early meetings of the Royal Society of London where the Secretary, the Revd. Thomas Birch, recorded in the minutes of the meeting of 29 October 1662:[11]

Sir ROBERT MORAY mentioned, that there were some considerable papers of Mr. HARRIOT and Dr. HARVEY, which might be retrieved. And it was ordered, that those of Mr. HARRIOT being in the possession of the earl of CLARENDON, lord high chancellor, should be inquired after by Mr. MATTHEW WREN, and those of Dr. HARVEY by Dr. ENT and Dr. SCARBURGH.

A month later, on 19 November 1662, Mr Matthew Wren reported back:[12] 'Mr. MATTHEW WREN acquainted the society, that the lord chancellor, upon the intimation of their desire, had expressed his readiness to communicate to them several papers of Mr. HARRIOT, which he had in his custody; and that he would give Mr. WREN access to his trunks for them.' What papers the Earl of Clarendon might have had, or thought he had, cannot be determined, for they were evidently never produced for the scrutiny of Wren. After nearly a year had passed, on 30 September 1663, since no further information about the Harriot papers had been forthcoming, the Secretary introduced a reminder into the minutes:[13] 'It was ordered, that Mr. MATTHEW WREN be put in mind of procuring from the lord chancellor the papers of Mr. HARRIOT, who had also made considerable observations on the weather.'

There the matter rested for the next half-dozen years, with no further search recorded and no progress indicated in locating Harriot's mathematical manuscripts. Matthew Wren, Member of Parliament for St. Michael and secretary to Clarendon during early years, had transferred his position to that of secretary to James, Duke of York, in 1667, but still had not followed through on his charge. Again the matter was raised in the meeting of the Society on 2 December 1669:[14] 'Mr. COLLINS mentioned, that he had been informed, that many papers of the famous mathematician, Mr. THOMAS HARRIOT were in the hands of the son of the earl of Cherbury. Upon which Mr. OLDENBURG said,

[11] Thomas Birch, DD, Secretary to the Royal Society, *The History of the Royal Society for Improving of Natural Knowledge from its First Rise*, London, MDCCLVI. This important work has recently been reprinted in photocopy in The Sources of Science, no. 44, The Johnson Reprint Corporation, 1968. This extract is from vol. I, p. 120.
[12] Ibid. I. 126.
[13] Ibid. I. 309.   [14] Ibid. II. 410.

that he would endeavor to procure a sight and transcript of them, if they were in those hands.' If Mr Oldenburg did indeed seek the papers from Lord Herbert of Cherbury he would have been disappointed, for it is obvious that Dr Birch heard Mr Collins incorrectly. Collins must have been speaking not of Lord Cherbury, but of Lord Vaughan, son of the Earl of Carberry. In one of his letters to Vernon, undated, but apparently of about this time, Collins wrote as follows:[15]

As to Harriot, he was so learned, saith Dr. Pell, that had he published all he knew in algebra, he would have left little of the chief mysteries of that art unhandled. His papers fell into the hands of Sir Thomas Aylesbury, who was father to the late Lord Chancellor's [Clarendon's] Lady, by which means they fell into the Lord Chancellor's hands, to whom application was made by the members of the Royal Society to obtain them: his lordship (then in the height of his dignity and employments) gave orders for a search to be made, and in result the answer was, they could not be found. I am afraid the search was but perfunctory, and that, if his lordship (now at leisure) were solicited for them, he might write to his son the Lord Cornbury to make a diligent search for them. One Mr. Protheroe, in Wales, was executor to Mr. Harriot, and from him the Lord Vaughan, the Earl of Carbery's son, received more than a quire of Mr. Harriot's Analytics. The Lord Brounker has about two sheets of Harriot de Motu et Collisione Corporum, and more of his I know not of: there is nothing of Harriot's extant but that piece that Mons. Garibal hath.

Unfortunately for Harriot's reputation, lack of the primary evidence of his manuscripts did not prevent speculation about their contents nor development of firm opinions about what they must have contained. John Wallis (1616–1703), probably the most brilliant mathematician between Harriot and Newton, was somehow inspired to take up the cudgels on the behalf of his countrymen, Harriot and Oughtred. As Savilian Professor of Geometry at Oxford, President of the Oxford Philosophical Society, and a pioneer and close associate of the Royal Society of London, Wallis carried great influence. An early writer on the history and development of mathematics, Wallis became the leader of a great debate

[15] Stephen P. and Stephen J. Rigaud, *Correspondence of Scientific Men of the Seventeenth Century*, 2 vols. Oxford, 1841. Letter LIX, Collins to Vernon, undated, but about 1670. This extract is from I. 152-3.

between the English and the French mathematicians over the primacy of mathematical discovery between Vieta, Harriot, Oughtred, and Descartes. The first indication of Wallis's idolization of Harriot appears in a manuscript sheet in his hand in the Bodleian copy of Harriot's *Artis Analyticae Praxis*, the copy which Sir Charles Cavendish had presented to Robert Payne and which Wallis used to study for his elaborate analysis of Harriot's algebra in his own *A Treatise of Algebra, both Historical and Practical, Shewing, the Original, Progress, and Advancement thereof, from time to time; and by what Steps it hath attained to the Heighth at which now it is*.[16] Since this memorandum is so revealing about Wallis's general knowledge of Harriot and his manuscripts at this time and since it has never been reprinted, it is here included in full. Bearing the heading 'March .27. 1677: John Wallis. Geom. Prof. Oxon.', the note reads:[17]

The Author of this Book, Mr. Thomas Harriot, was contemporary with Mr Oughtred, but (it seemes) elder than he: For (as appears by this edition, being posthumous) that he was dead in ye year 1631 (how long before, I know not,) in which yeare (but somewhat earlyer (as I have been informed) than ye edition of this) Mr Oughtreds Clavis (but without ye Additions which are not joined with it) was first published: Mr Oughtred himself dying in ye month of May, 1660. (in a kind of suddaing extasy for joy, upon hearing of ye vote passed in ye Parliament then sitting, for restauration of ye King; which passed May .1. 1660, & ye King returned to London May 29, ye same year.) But he dyed very aged, about 87 years of age; as I learned partly from his own mouth in conversation with him some years before he dyed; & partly from a picture of him, which I have by me, graven in Copper & printed at Antwerp by William [unreadable] (who had a while before drawn it by ye life) where he is sayd to be Anno aetatis 73 in the year of our Lord 1646. Whether Mr Oughtred & Mr Harriot (though contemporaries) had any correspondence while they lived, I am not certain. But they were both very great men in this kind of knowledge; & scarce to be equalled (if at all) by any of that age.

Mr Harriot (as appears by ye dedication of this, & as I have otherwise heard) had some relation to ye family of ye then Earl of Northumberland; (as allso had the publisher Mr Warner, and Dr Pain also, sometime Canon of Christchurch Oxon, out of who's study (after his death) this book was bought.

[16] London, Printed by John Playford, for Richard Davis, Bookseller, in the University of Oxford, M. DC. LXXXV.
[17] Bodleian MS Savile 09.

That Mr Warner was the publisher of it (though his name be not put to it,) as I have otherwise heard, so it appears by that memorial, in the Title page, written by Dr Pains own hand; who could not be reasonably thought ignorant of it, being acquainted with the persons and having this presented to him (by Sir Charles Cavendish, of ye family of ye Earl of Devonshire) probably after its first publication; as appeares in the memorial written by Dr Pains own hand in ye page next before ye Title.

Dr Pain, (who was himself allso versed in these studies,) had (I perceive) carefully perused all or most part of it, as appears by some notes of his here & there in the boke, & by what is written by his hand in the two voyd leaves at the end of it. He had also amended with his pen all ye typographical faults mentioned in ye table of errata, & some others in ye book; and had very curiously reformed the pointings and other the like literall punctilios (to his own mind) especially toward ye beginning of the book. But he doth not seem to have gone over ye whole with ye like care.

For coming toward ye middle of ye book, & so onwards, I find many mistakes uncorrected: some of which I have amended with ye pen, & some I have noted in loose peeces of paper, put between ye leaves in their proper places, to avoid defacing ye book.

And, particularly, I have added what was wanting in the limitation of ye 19th, 20th, & 21th propositions of the Third section, pag. 45, 46. the want of which, made ye publisher to give us that note of his Hesitation, pag. 46.

There were divers other Mathematicall Books, at ye same time, bought out of Dr Pains study; (and now put into the Savilian Mathematick study as well as this) most of which have divers notes of his own hand writing in them: which may be known by comparing it with that of his writing in this book.

This treatise of Mr Harriots, was, (it seems) so well liked by Des Chartes, that he hath, in a manner, transcribed the whole of it for the substance (though in other order & words) into his Geometry (but without so much as ever naming ye Author,) which was first published in ye year 1637 (in French) six years after this was first extant.

There were many other very worthy pieces of Mr Harriots doing, left behind him, & well worth the publishing: as appears by Mr Warners Preface, & Title-page & some of them I have seen. But in who's hands they now are, or whether they be since perished, I cannot tell.

The idea that Descartes had borrowed from Harriot the basic algebraic doctrine on which his methods were derived without acknowledgement became fixed in Wallis's mind. And as he grew bitter over the injustice done to his English hero, the more certain he became that the plagiarism was intentional. In the absence of the manuscripts which could have revealed Harriot's true role in the development of algebraic theory,

Wallis became more and more certain that they would reveal Harriot's priority in their discovery. During the years that the Royal Society was seeking to locate the manuscripts, Wallis wrote to Collins making specific charges against Descartes:[18]

That which I most valued in [Descartes's] method, and which pleased me best, was his way of bringing over the whole equation to one side, making it equal to nothing, and thereby forming his compound equations by the multiplication of simples, from thence also determining the number of roots, real or imaginary, in each. This artifice, on which all the rest of his doctrine is grounded, was that which most made me set a value on him, presuming it had been properly his own; but afterwards I perceived that he had it from Harriot, whose Algebra was published after his death in the year 1631, six years before Des Cartes Geometry in French in the year 1637: and yet Des Cartes makes no mention at all of Harriot, whom he follows in designing his species by small letters, and the powers of them by the number of dimensions, without the characters of q, c, qq, &c.

By 1685, when he came to write his own *Treatise of Algebra* (Wallis's most widely read book which became the standard text of the eighteenth century),[19] his feeling about Descartes's injustice to Harriot's memory had grown to the point where he devoted twenty-five chapters (more than one-fifth of the total volume) to a reworking of Harriot's *Praxis*, and an elaborate analysis of Harriot's contributions to algebraic theory. Even in the *Preface* of this volume he stated his thesis:[20] 'In sum, [Harriot] hath taught (in a manner) all that which hath since passed for the *Cartesian* method of *Algebra*; there being scarce any thing of (pure) *Algebra* in *Des Cartes*, which was not before in *Harriot*; from whom *Des Cartes* seems to have taken what he hath (that is purely *Algebra*) but without naming him.' Again, in justifying his thorough analysis of Harriot's work, Wallis states:[21]

[Harriot] doth in divers things vary from the Method of *Vieta* and *Oughtred*. And hath made very many advantagious improvements in

___

[18] Rigaud, *Correspondence*, Letter CCCXXXV, vol. pp. 564-76. This passage is from p. 573.

[19] *Treatise of Algebra*, Ch. XXX-LIV, pp. 125-207.

[20] *Algebra*, 'Preface', p. [A4]ʳ. This passage is cited by J. F. Scott, *The Mathematical Work of John Wallis, DD., F.R.S. (1616-1703)*, London, 1938, p. 134. Scott gives a lucid and detailed account of the many controversies in which Wallis was involved.

[21] *Algebra*, p. 126; also cited in Scott, p. 134.

this Art; and hath laid the foundation on which *Des Cartes* (though without naming him,) hath built the greatest part (if not the whole) of his *Algebra* or *Geometry*. Without which, that whole Superstruction of *Des Cartes* (I doubt) had never been.

To conclude his eulogy, Wallis furnished 'A Recapitulation of Particulars' which listed twenty-five major innovations in mathematical theory and practice which he had found in the *Praxis* or inferred from what he 'knew' the lost manuscripts must have contained.[22]

Naturally, the French mathematicians, led by their distinguished Montucla, rose to the defence of their own Vieta and Descartes with a tenacity and dogmatism equal to that of their detractors, and for a century a heated dispute raged which had no possible solution.[23] It is difficult today to understand the violence of the debate or the intense feelings it generated. We can only agree with Cantor when, two centuries after the fact, he declared that these histories of mathematics were not histories at all, 'but rather an example of . . partisanship, inspired by excessive national pride.'[24] But it must be recognized that it was inability to see and to study Harriot's original manuscripts which made this long-drawn-out controversy possible, and made Harriot, as a result, a controversial figure whose place in the history of science, particularly mathematics, remained unresolved.

This long period of speculation about Harriot's actual work certainly heightened the scholarly interest when, in

[22] *Algebra*, Ch. LIII, 'A Recapitulation of Particulars in Harriot's *Algebra*; and the Estate to which had he reduced it', pp. 198-200.

[23] J. F. Montucla, *Histoire des mathématiques*, 4 vols., Paris, 1799-1802. In vol. II, pp. 110-11, Montucla comments on Wallis: 'Comment excuserons-nous M. Wallis, qui nous donnant un Traité historique de l'algèbre, semble avoir à peine jetté les yeux sur tout autre analyste que Harriot; qui après avoir traité Descartes de plagiaire, et avoir déprimé ses inventions autant qu'il l'a pu, forme en grande partie l'énumération de celles de son compatriote, de choses ou peu importantes, ou empruntées de ses prédécesseurs. Qui pourra même ne pas rire en voyant ce zélé restauranteur de la gloire d'Harriot, lui attribuer je ne dis pas seulement la résolution des équations du second degré, par l'évanouissement du second terme, invention de Viète, mais encore la méthode vulgaire qui procède, comme on sait, en ajoutant de part et d'autre de quoi faire un quarré parfait du membre où est l'inconnue. La partialité et l'aveuglement qui en est la suite ordinaire ne sauroient être portés plus loin.'

[24] This translation from Moritz Cantor, *Vorlesungen über Geschichte der Mathematik*, 4 vols., Leipzig, 1894-1908, from vol. III, p. 4, was made by Scott, op. cit., pp. 155-6.

1784, news started to circulate that the long-lost manuscripts had at last been found and that their contents were soon to be made public. It was an Austrian, Franz Xaver Zach (later to be created Baron von Zach), who made the discovery and began to build his own reputation by making sensational claims about their contents.[25] An arrogant young man of boundless ambition, following his required army service Zach had persuaded the Empress Maria Theresa to name him as a professor of engineering in a new training institution being established. This appointment was terminated by her son, Emperor Joseph II, and Zach was forced to wangle an appointment as the tutor to the young son of the Count de Bruhl. In 1783 de Bruhl was named Saxon minister to England and moved his family and retinue to London. Zach, characteristically aggressive, immediately involved himself in the current discussions about watches and timepieces in the solution of astronomical problems and became a staunch supporter of Mudge in his controversy with the Astronomer Royal, Nevil Maskelyne. Zach went so far as to claim that the extreme accuracy of Mudge's watches had enabled him to determine a number of errors in Maskelyne's *Nautical Almanac*. This claim so impressed Thomas Hornsby, Savilian Professor of Astronomy at Oxford and founder of the Radcliffe Observatory there, that in 1786 he obtained an honorary Doctor's degree for the young Austrian.[26] Pretentiously, Zach immediately began to style himself 'Dr. Zach' and arranged to have his name proposed as a Fellow of the Royal Society, but failed to gain election. Two years later he attempted to have his name listed as a foreign member of the Society, but was a second time blackballed.

While Zach was engaged in these controversies, his patron, the Count de Bruhl, married the dowager Lady Egremont,

[25] Much of this material on von Zach is extracted from the notes of Stephen P. Rigaud, one of the most valuable sources of information about Harriot for the interested student. Rigaud's MSS remain, nearly complete, in the Bodleian Library; the notes dealing with Harriot, his work, and his friends are primarily in MSS Rigaud 4, 35, and 50. Among Rigaud's notes remain many transcripts of records which have been lost elsewhere. Material on Zach is extracted primarily from MS Rigaud 35.

[26] Stephen P. Rigaud, *Supplement to Dr. Bradley's Miscellaneous Works: with an account of Harriot's Astronomical Papers*, Oxford, University Press, 1833, p. 53, n. c.

and in 1784 spent the summer at the Egremont estates at Petworth, Sussex. Lord Egremont, a descendant of a daughter of Josceline Percy, 11th Earl of Northumberland and grandson of Harriot's patron, the 9th Earl, had been granted title to Petworth House, the country estate to which the 9th Earl had retired after his release from the Tower in 1621. Visiting here, the Count de Bruhl found, hidden among the stable accounts, the long-lost manuscripts of Harriot, untouched since the death of the 9th Earl in 1632.[27] Recognizing their importance, de Bruhl pointed them out to young Zach, who immediately began to capitalize on their discovery by issuing public pronouncements about them, declaring the papers to possess supreme historical importance.

In 1786, taking advantage of his new association with Oxford University, Zach wrote a long Latin letter to the Delegates of the Oxford Press, proposing to prepare the more significant of the Harriot manuscripts for the press if Oxford would bear the expenses of publication.[28] His plans called for a life of Harriot written in imitation of Gassendi's lives of Purbachius, Regiomontanus, Copernicus, and Tycho Brahe, followed by some of Harriot's own astronomical observations with emphasis on the comets of 1607 and 1618. Sympathetic with Zach's publication plans, Lord Egremont gave authority for Zach to go through all the Harriot papers and to extract from the collection those parts which he felt most worthy of his publication. These selected papers Zach removed from the Petworth collection, retaining them in his own possession as he planned and discussed his proposed Oxford Press volume.

But 1786 saw a significant change in Zach's personal life which interfered with his immediate plans. Ernest II of Saxe-Coburg-Gotha appointed him as director of a proposed new astronomical observatory to be built on the Seeberg at Gotha. Shortly thereafter, 'Dr. Zach' was granted the title of Baron von Zach, another honour which Zach used to verify his scholarly authority. In his new post, Baron von Zach not only played a major role in the building of a modern new observatory and establishing a staff for it, but also assumed the role of editor of scientific correspondence from

[27] Ibid., Note A, p. 53.   [28] Ibid., Note B, pp. 53–7.

all over Europe in the fields of astronomy, geography, and hydrography. He became widely known as a lecturer and travelled throughout Europe, carrying a sextant with which he determined the exact geographic location of each city visited for the correction of the maps of his time. In many of these lectures he extolled the astronomical observations of Thomas Harriot, for whom he claimed priority over Galileo in many areas. But his proposed volume for the Oxford Press was not forthcoming, and his research on Harriot's actual manuscripts remained largely 'in progress'.

In 1788 the Baron wrote a full account of the importance of his discoveries from Harriot's manuscripts and published it in the *Astronomical Ephemeris of the Royal Society of Berlin*; he also translated this into English and published it for distribution in England.[29] In these writings there can be no question but that Baron Zach, to dramatize his discovery, made exaggerated claims for the priority of Harriot over Kepler and Galileo in his astronomical observations, and in their significance, both for their own time and in the time in which he wrote. For his mathematical innovations Zach indicated that Harriot's papers would put his French detractors to shame, and would even show that he had furnished the inspiration for many of the contributions they ascribed to Descartes. But as an astronomer himself, Zach especially stressed Harriot's role in that field:

... it has not hitherto been known that Harriot was an eminent astronomer, both theoretical and practical, which first appears by these manuscripts; amongst which, the most remarkable are 199 observations of the Sun's spots, with their drawings, calculations, and determinations of the sun's revolutions round its axis. There is the greatest probability of Harriot's being the first discoverer of these spots before Galileo Galilei, or Scheiner. . . .[30]

Of Jupiter's satellites — I found amongst his papers a great set of observations, with their drawing, position, and calculations of their revolutions and periods: his first observation of those discovered satellites I find to be of January the 16th, 1610, and they go till February the 26th, 1612. Galilei pretends to have discovered them January the 7th, 1610: there is then all probability of Harriot's being likewise the first discoverer of these attendants of Jupiter. [Zach is here confusing an observation with a calculation Harriot was making from Galileo's observations. According to his own account, Harriot's 'first observation of the new planets' was clearly dated 17 October 1610, a full nine months after Galileo's discovery.] [31]

Amongst his other observations of the moon, of some eclipses, of the planet Mars, of solstices, of refraction, of the declination of the needle, there are most remarkable ones of the famous comets of 1607 and of 1618, the later, for there were two this year: they were all observed with a cross staff, by measuring their distances to fixed stars, which makes these observations the more valuable, because they had but grossly been observed [before]; Kepler himself observed the comet of 1607, but with the naked eye, pointing out the place where it stood by a coarse estimation, without an instrument; and the elements of their orbits could, in defect of better observations, only be calculated by them. The observations of the comet of the year 1607, are the more of importance and consequence, even now for modern astronomy, as this is the same comet that fulfilled Dr. Halley's most wonderful prediction of its return in the year 1759. . . .[32]

Harriot's (and Lower's) observations of the comet of 1607 continued to intrigue Zach. In a supplementary volume of the *Berliner astronomisches Jahrbuch* he published Harriot's observations. This article, with its calculation of the comet's orbit, came to the attention of a young German, Friedrich Wilhelm Bessel,[33] who was just beginning the serious study of astronomy in anticipation of a nautical career. Bessel used Harriot's observations for a determination of the comet's orbit, and sent his results to the famous observer and author of comets, Heinrich William Mathias Olbers, for review. Olbers was impressed with the work of the young man, and quickly noted that the orbit as calculated agreed closely with the elliptical orbit of Halley's comet. He encouraged the young Bessel to continue his observations and to refine his method of calculating cometary orbits, which led Bessel to make important original contributions to astronomical mathematics. Bessel's article was in turn published by Baron Zach on the recommendation of Olbers, in his *Monatliche Correspondenz*, where it attracted so much attention that it turned Bessel away from navigation to the serious study

[31] Ibid., p. 59.
[32] Ibid., p. 59.
[33] See the article on Bessel in the *Dictionary of Scientific Biography* by Walter Fricke.

of celestial mechanics and astronomical mathematics. Late in life, Olbers remarked that he considered his enticement of Bessel into astronomy as his greatest contribution to astronomy. Thus Zach's exaggerated reports of Harriot's accomplishments did lead to the establishment of one of the fundamental physics tools of modern times — the Bessel function.

Naturally this continued publication created some stir in British circles which was augmented in 1796 when Charles Hutton reprinted much of the Zach account in his *Mathematical and Philosophical Dictionary*.[34] Hutton ended his account with the assurance that these important papers would shortly be in the hands of the public, since the work was already in the hands of the Oxford Press and further activity rested with them. But Hutton's assurance was quite inaccurate: Zach had not prepared any manuscripts for publication and had furnished Oxford with no copy of his proposed biography. Though claiming the glory of his discovery, he was leaving the blame for his real inactivity on the Oxford Delegates.

As a matter of fact, even before Hutton's declaration was made, Zach had given up any pretence of working on the manuscripts. In May 1794, after having carried the Harriot selections around with him for eight years, he sent the most important Harriot papers extracted from the Petworth collection to Bishop Cleaver, then Principal of Brasenose, asking him to submit them to the Oxford Press. The Press Delegates were in a quandary: they had agreed to publish an edited work and a biography, but they had received only a collection of unedited (and frequently disorganized) manuscripts with no explanatory text. Uncertain what to do, they divided the papers into two groups, mathematical and astronomical, and sent them for review in July of that year. The mathematical papers went to Dr Abraham Robertson (1751–1826), later Savilian Professor of Geometry and still later Savilian Professor of Astronomy; the astronomical papers went to Mr Powell of Balliol. Robertson was prompt in his assignment and in October he issued his report, listing

[34] 2 vols., London, 1796. The Zach account is included in the section on Harriot, vol. I, pp. 584–6.

the eleven bundles of Harriot's notes he had received, and concluding with his judgement that[35]

These papers, excepting the last [*De reflectione corporum rotundarum*], are in no point of view fit for publication. The greatest part of them consist of detached and unfinished explanations of the authors which he read; begun, according to all appearance, with the design of satisfying his own mind upon the subject before him, and dropped abruptly as soon as this satisfaction was obtained. . . . No first principles are laid down; due arrangement is overlooked; and the demonstrations, often defective, are expressed in a kind of algebraic shorthand . . . I offer these observations as reasons for my firm persuasion that he never intended the papers for publication; and that it would be injurious to his reputation to print them.

Powell was less prompt in his review; several years passed and he had still not replied, so the Delegates recovered the manuscripts and submitted the second group of astronomical observations to Robertson. In February 1798, Robertson made his second report, again indicating that the manuscripts were in no shape for publication of any kind.[36] Though he was undoubtedly correct in his general assessment, to the modern historian of science, his reasoning seems most unusual. Robertson appears to have viewed science as timeless and totally contemporary, without any recognition of the evolution of scientific ideas. He reported, for example, on Harriot's observations of sun spots without recognizing that they were the earliest known telescopic investigations of that phenomenon, contemporaneous with the observations of Galileo which exist only in printed form. These he did not consider worth publishing since 'I do not think that Harriot ever intended them for publication; nor do I think that the publication of them would either satisfy rational curiosity, or contribute, in the smallest degree, to the advancement of astronomy.' With regard to his observations of the Jovial planets, Robertson declared 'in my opinion, astronomy could not be advanced by the publication of any part of them.' And of the others, observations of the moon and the comets of 1607 and 1618, he felt the same, and dismissed them as insignificant. His final conclusion:[37] 'Upon the whole it is

---

[35] Rigaud, *Supplement*, Note D, pp. 61-3. This extract is from p. 62.
[36] Ibid., pp. 62-3.   [37] Ibid., p. 63.

my opinion that the publication of the papers mentioned in this report could only tend to prove that Harriot was very assiduous in his mathematical studies, and in his observations of the heavenly bodies; it could not contribute to the advancement of science.' In the light of these negative reviews, the Delegates withdrew from their agreement to publish the papers, and in 1799 they returned the Zach collection to Lord Egremont at Petworth House, Sussex.

In the meantime the bulk of the Harriot manuscripts had remained at Petworth where they had been left by Zach. Obviously, Zach had gone through them hurriedly, seeking sensational or exciting materials, and had been careless about retaining their original order. Much of the time he had turned the pages as he read them; at other times he piled the pages without turning them over, and in some instances he had gathered bundles without regard for top or bottom or had put together sections which did not belong together. As a result, following the extraction of the Oxford manuscripts, Harriot's papers were in almost chaotic condition. When the Oxford group were returned to Lord Egremont they were kept separate from the main group, probably considered the most valuable manuscripts since Zach had selected them for special consideration. In any case, about 1810 Lord Egremont made a presentation of the bulk of the Harriot papers to the British Museum, retaining the Zach collection at Petworth as his own. This separation, like the ransacking of Zach, made the whole collection much more difficult than before to work with, a difficulty which was compounded when the British Museum bound the non-Zach papers into eight tight volumes, with no attempt to order them before they were finally fixed in their disarray. The Oxford group, as viewed by Robertson, remained at Petworth House, buried in the vaults of the archives, once more forgotten.

Both the gift of the major collection of Harriot papers to the British Museum and the decision of the Oxford Press not to publish the Zach collection were generally unknown. As late as 1815 Hutton was still printing the Zach letters and blaming the Oxford Press for not printing them; Zach was still making capital of his great discovery of the unsung

British scientist, and other authors were taking up the story. In 1816 Professor Playfair, reviewing one of Baron von Zach's books in the *Edinburgh Review*, retold the Zach tale, concluding that the Harriot manuscripts had been 'consigned to the care of the University of Oxford; and are now, we have no doubt, in the progress toward publication.'[38] This aroused Robertson who was incensed at this continued attack on the Press, and he replied in an article in the *Edinburgh Philosophical Journal*, pointing out that the Harriot manuscripts had been reviewed, declined for publication, and returned to their owner sixteen years previously. To justify the actions of the Press once and for all, Robertson made public his review and analysis of the papers in his report to the Press.[39]

But even this publicity did not stop the rumours which continued even after the death of Robertson in 1826, and criticism of the Delegates for not bringing out the vaunted work of one of England's most distinguished scientists continued. As one of the Delegates, Stephen Peter Rigaud, felt strongly that these insinuations about the Press should be met head on. Rigaud had followed Robertson as Savilian Professor of Geometry in 1810, and on Robertson's death had succeeded him as Savilian Professor of Astronomy and Radcliffe Observer. As spokesman for Robertson, the Press, and the University, Rigaud counter-attacked. In a speech at the Ashmolean Society on 16 March 1832, Rigaud reviewed the criticisms of the Press, particularly emphasizing an attack in the *Journal of the Royal Institution* in which the author had 'expressly lamented that Harriot's papers & manuscripts are at present buried in one of the libraries of the University of Oxford.'[40] Rigaud's attempt at correction had not been printed in the next issue, so to defend his institution, Rigaud determined to reinvestigate the whole

[38] Ibid., Note H, p. 68.
[39] 'Art. XIV. — An Account of some Mistakes relating to Dr. Bradley's Astronomical Observations and Harriot's MSS. By Dr. Robertson, F.R.S., Savilian Professor of Astronomy in the University of Oxford. In a letter to Dr. Brewster', *Edinburgh Philosophical Journal*, VI (1822), 313–18.
[40] 'On Zach's account of Harriot's Astronomical Papers', Bodleian MS Rigaud 35, fos. 236–55. A preliminary draft of this same papers is in the same volume, fos. 256–85. This quotation is from fos. 243–4.

matter and, if necessary, to write a detailed account of the history of the papers. This led him to visit Petworth House, where the Earl of Egremont had not only generously allowed him access to his manuscripts, but permitted him to remove Harriot's papers to his Oxford study to review them at his leisure. As he reported to the members of the Ashmolean Society:[41]

... This enables me to understand, what could never have otherwise been made out, and by reference to records which are still extant in this place, I had the means of completely explaining the part, which the University had taken in the business. The particulars may be seen in the last number of the Journal — I do not like this kind of warfare, but I felt it a duty to defend our good name.

More importantly, this action which had led Rigaud to study Harriot's manuscripts also got him personally interested in what they really contained. A man of broad interests and extreme diligence, Rigaud was better equipped to study them than either Zach or Robertson had been. He could more accurately than they place Harriot's contributions against their historical background and assess their real worth. At the meeting of the British Association for the Advancement of Science held at Oxford in 1832, Rigaud displayed Harriot's actual astronomical observations to show where Zach had gone astray in his claims.[42] On 17 and 24 May of the same year, Rigaud read a long paper before the Royal Society of London entitled 'On Harriot's Astronomical Observations contained in his unpublished Manuscripts belonging to the Earl of Egremont'.[43] In these early speeches, Rigaud was bitter about Zach's distortion of Harriot's accomplishments, possibly inspired by his desire to justify the action of the press in rejecting their publication. One of his speeches of this year began:[44]

[41] Ibid., fo. 244.
[42] See the *Report of the First and Second Meetings of the British Association for the Advancement of Science; at York in 1831, and at Oxford in 1832*, London 1833. 'Transactions of the Sections, Miscellaneous', p. 602.
[43] *Abstracts of the Papers printed in the Philosophical Transactions of the Royal Society of London, Vol. III (1830–37)*, London, 1837, pp. 125–6. The original paper as delivered is to be found in Bodleian MS Rigaud 35, fos. 288–314.
[44] Bodleian MS Rigaud 35, fo. 256, 'Read at the Ashmolean Society, March 16, 1832'.

I have this evening to expose one of the grossest impositions which has for many years disgraced the annals of science. I have done much & I am doing more to make the truth generally known; but the story has been connected with Oxford: its success has given occasion for sneers of obloquy to those who are not friendly to our establishment. . . . I have now, likewise, the opportunity of submitting the original documents to all who will take the trouble of examining them, so that each from his own knowledge may become a substantive witness to the facts . . .

The death of Baron von Zach, on 2 September 1832, led Rigaud to soften his bitter attack though he still continued to reveal Zach's distortions. And as his notes (still remaining in the Bodleian) attest, Rigaud devoted much of his leisure time to seeking out new facts about Harriot and his friends. Rigaud seemed particularly impressed with the nobility or ties to nobility of Harriot's associates, and he spent many hours and days in seeking their tombs, recording their coats of arms or memorial verses, or noting anything which might add lustre to Harriot's reputation. It seems apparent from his well-indexed notebooks that Rigaud hoped and planned to do a more complete biography of Harriot than had yet been attempted and to edit some of his more significant papers for the use of the reading public. For the rest of his life, Rigaud took on the task which Zach had abandoned: he took notes on Harriot and his work, organizing and reorganizing his materials in preparation for a definitive work which, like Torporley's, Zach's, and like Harriot's own, was never published.

Rigaud's major contribution to the study of the Harriot papers rests in a small volume published in 1833 entitled *Supplement to Dr. Bradley's Miscellaneous Works: with an Account of Harriot's Astronomical Papers*. The 'Advertisement', dated March 1833, and printed on the reverse of the title-page, reads in part:

In the Appendix to Bradley's Miscellaneous Works (p. 522) I have ventured to say that no dependence was to be placed on the common account of Harriot's papers. That account, however, was given to the world by one, whose name has now been associated with the cause of astronomy for nearly half a century; it has in some quarters been very readily admitted, and unfounded accusations have been repeatedly derived from it against those, by whose fault it was supposed that the papers were withheld from the public. .... I have to regret that the scientific world has been deprived of the Baron de Zach before it was possible for me to complete the inquiry: but this has made me doubly careful not to overstate any thing. .... If I have been led on to a greater length than at first sight may appear necessary, it must be recollected that much more detail is requisite to efface a false impression than to satisfy unprejudiced minds.

Rigaud's *Account* makes it very clear to the reader that his major purpose in writing it was to justify the Oxford Press decision not to publish the Zach manuscripts. The greater portion of the text consists of citing the claims made by Zach followed by a careful review of Harriot's manuscripts to correct Zach's exaggerations or misinterpretations. By the nature of his enquiry, thus, Rigaud limited his investigation to the areas selected by Zach and to those special documents he had extracted from the main body of Harriot's papers. Rigaud's study of the bulk of Harriot's papers sent by Egremont to the British Museum was cursory in the extreme. As a result, Rigaud's report, like the one he was attempting to discredit, was partial and limited. And though Rigaud did make a serious effort to locate Harriot's will, like most other investigators he searched for it near Syon House in Isleworth, not knowing that Harriot had died in London. Consequently, he knew nothing of Harriot's manufacture of telescopes, his lens grinding and work with Christopher Tooke in the production of optical instruments. Though he was suspicious from Lower's letters that Harriot had been one of the first to use telescopes in astronomical observations, Rigaud was inclined to play this down, indicating that 'It is probable ... that Harriot had his [telescope] directly from the first inventor',[45] or that Lower's letter merely 'shews that telescopes were made in London as early as Feb. 1610.'[46] Rigaud must have merely glanced at Harriot's work on refraction since he did not observe Harriot's dating of observations which prove him well in advance of his contemporaries in these experiments.[47]

There is much on refraction in the British Museum, but it is generally confined to those cases in which the rays of light pass through a

---

[45] Rigaud, *Harriot's Astronomical Papers*, p. 20.
[46] Ibid., pp. 45–6.　　　　　　[47] Ibid., p. 41.

transparent medium of a regular shape: of astronomical refractions I was able to find very little, and in that little nothing of any importance. From these papers it is clear that Harriot was acquainted with the law which is deduced from the sines of the angles of incidence and refraction, but I did not mark any facts which could shew that he had used it before the time when it was discovered by Willebrord Snell. . . .

All in all, Rigaud seriously attempted to be scrupulously fair in his appraisal of Harriot's science. Though he felt it necessary to disparage the originality of Harriot's contributions in order to justify the Oxford failure to publish the papers and to discredit the exaggerated claims of Baron von Zach, Rigaud was still obviously impressed with what he saw in Harriot's handwritten notes and observations. He was fascinated by Harriot's Welsh friends, Lower and Protheroe, and went to considerable pains to trace their records in Cornwall and Carmarthenshire. He made numerous visits to London to clear up the Syon House/Sion College confusion which surrounded Harriot and Torporley, and he did monumental work in distinguishing between Harriot's own calculations and those he was collecting from others in his astronomical studies. But his other broad interests prevented him from following through with other publications on Harriot, and Rigaud died in 1839 while seeing his edition of the letters of the Collins collection from the library of Lord Macclesfield through the press.[48] His unpublished notebooks were willed to the Oxford library where most of them still remain. Rigaud's summary view of Harriot, with which he concludes his *Account*, serves (like Harriot's own will) as a posthumous apology for not completing the work which he intended to bring to press:[49]

To help in establishing the fair fame of Harriot would be a source of the highest gratification to me. He was not only a countryman, but a distinguished member of that university to which I have myself the honour of belonging. If truth hath obliged me to shew that his astronomical observations are not of that high character which they have been supposed to possess, he can well spare what does not belong to him. There is no degradation in being second to Galileo, and there is much praise to which he is most justly entitled. He certainly made a

[48] This work was completed and edited by his eldest son, Stephen Jordan Rigaud, and published in 1841. See n. 15 above.
[49] *Harriot's Astronomical Papers*, pp. 51–2.

very early use of the great invention of telescopes; he carefully examined some of the most curious phenomena, which they enabled him to
observe in the heavens; he took great pains to ascertain the laws of the
planetary motions, and was not deterred from the necessary calculations, even when, before the invention of logarithms, he was obliged
to work by methods of a more operose description. [It is difficult to
see how Rigaud missed Harriot's use of logarithms and his calculations
of his own tables.] Could I have continued the inquiry to an examination of his other pursuits, I probably should have met with results
more consonant with my wishes. Sir William Lower's letter encouraged
this hope very strongly: he appears to have shared in Harriot's studies,
and to have been intimately acquainted with them: his testimony
therefore is of great weight to the priority over Vieta, and I sincerely
hope that some one who has leisure, and to whom a residence in
London may give opportunities which I do not enjoy, will pursue this
part of the inquiry, by thoroughly examining the papers in the British
Museum.

So far as can be determined, no one rose to Rigaud's challenge,
and the Zach papers were returned to Petworth House,
unstudied.

The Petworth manuscripts of Harriot were again brought to
the attention of the public through the tremendous effort to
catalogue all manuscripts of historical importance undertaken
by the Royal Commission on Historical Manuscripts instigated
by Queen Victoria. Alfred J. Horwood of the Commission
visited Petworth House, Sussex, in 1877. His report, inven-
torying the manuscript holdings of Lord Leconfield was
published in *The Appendix to the Sixth Report* of that
year.[50] Near the end of his report, almost as an afterthought,
appears the following listing:[51]

A black leather box containing several hundred leaves of figures and
calculations by Harriot.

[50] *Sixth Report of the Royal Commission on Historical Manuscripts, Part I.
Report and Appendix*, London, HMSO, 1877. The report on the Manuscripts of
Lord Leconfield at Petworth House, Sussex, by Alfred J. Horwood is in the
Appendix, pp. 287-319.
[51] Ibid., p. 319. When I first viewed these MSS in the spring of 1948 and was
permitted to microfilm them through the kindness of Lord Leconfield, the
papers were in the exact order as left by Horwood, though the papers as arranged
by Rigaud were in the black leather box, and the calculations of rhumbs were in
a separate package. Since that time the rhumb calculations have been bound in
five volumes as HMC/240, and the other papers are bound in eight volumes, in
order quite different from the originals.

A large bundle of Harriot's papers.
(See Supplement to Dr. Bradley's Miscellaneous works with an account of Harriot's astronomical papers. 4to Oxford University Press 1833.)

They are arranged in packets by Professor Rigaud.

> Spots on the Sun.
> Comets of 1607 and 1618.
> The Moon.
> Jupiter's Satellites.
> Projectiles, Centre of Gravity, Reflexion of Bodies.
> Triangles.
> Snell's Eratosthenes Batavus.
> Geometry.
> Calendar.
> Conic Sections.
> De Stella Martis.
> Drawings of Constellations, papers on Chemistry and
>   Miscellaneous Calculations.
> Collections from the observations of Hannelius, Warner, Copernicus,
>   Tycho Brahe. On the vernal and autumnal equinoxes, the solstices,
>   orbit of the Earth, length of the year, &c.
> Algebra.

From all evidence available, these critical Harriot manuscripts remained in the Petworth vaults for more than seventy years, unexamined by anyone after Horwood. Though a cursory interest in Harriot remained in the late nineteenth and early twentieth centuries and at least two attempts were made to write his biography, no Harriot investigator looked at these papers. They remained as left by Rigaud and Horwood, with the astronomical and mathematical papers pinned together in bundles with seventeenth-century pins, and with the calculation of rhumbs tied in a bundle apart in a seventeenth-century black leather box.

Even though the Petworth manuscripts were not viewed for the seventy years following the Horwood listing, two biographies of Harriot by Henry Stevens and Agnes Clerke continued to stimulate popular interest and speculation about the man and his works. Henry Stevens, who styled himself 'Henry Stevens of Vermont, FSA, Student of American History, Bibliographer, and Lover of Books',[52]

[52] For a biographical account, see Wyman W. Parker, *Henry Stevens of Vermont, American Rare Book Dealer in London, 1945–1886*, Amsterdam, Israel, 1936. For Steven's researches on Harriot, see R. C. H. Tanner, 'Henry Stevens and the Associates of Thomas Harriot', in John W. Shirley, ed., *Thomas Harriot: Renaissance Scientist*, Oxford, Clarendon Press, 1974, pp. 91–106.

was neither a scientist nor a scholar, but a bookseller and bibliophile. This vigorous and attractive young man was first attracted to Harriot through his interest in early American history and the fact that Harriot had written the first English account of the New World. A collector of rare books on early America, Stevens considered Harriot's *A briefe and true report* to be one of the outstanding rare books of all time. In the same year that Horwood visited Petworth, 1877, when the great reprint series — the Early English Text Society, the Percy Society, the Camden Society — were in great vogue, Stevens initiated a literary association to be known as The Hercules Club, dedicated to 'thoroughly independent research into the materials of early Anglo-American history and literature', and to 'ferret out these materials, collate, edit, and reproduce them with extreme accuracy, but not in facsimile.'[53] Number 10 on his subscription list was to be the 1588 edition of Harriot's work on Virginia, and it was on this volume that Stevens began to work.

But Harriot the man began to engross Stevens as he had attracted Rigaud earlier. In the life of Harriot which Stevens was preparing to accompany the work, Stevens explained his increasing involvement:[54]

When I years ago undertook among other enterprises to compile a sketch of the life of THOMAS HARIOT the first historian of the new found land of Virginia and to trace the gradual geographical development of that country out of the unlimited 'Terra Florida' of Juan Ponce de Leon, through the French planting and the Spanish rooting out of the Huguenot colony down to the successful foothold of the English in Wingandacoa under Raleigh's patent, I little suspected either the extent of the research I was drifting into, or the success that awaited my investigations.

Stevens's small volume indicates the 'extent of the research'. Yet partly because of his business connections, Stevens confined his research to London. He did look through the Harriot manuscripts in the British Museum, transcribing most of the letters in the last volume, and making notes on a few other pages. But although he was aware of the Petworth

---

[53] From the 'Explanatory Headnote' to Stevens's biography by his son, Henry N. Stevens.

[54] Ibid., pp. 7–8.

papers both through the report of the Historical Manuscripts Commission and from Rigaud's published reports, both of which he cited, he made no effort to see them. Nor did he visit Oxford to see the Rigaud notebooks which he knew to be there. He retraced Rigaud's steps in ironing out the Syon House/Sion College confusion which had plagued early biographers. But his major 'success' was in locating Harriot's will in the records of the Archdeaconry Court of London, a gold-mine of information which had been missed by all previous searchers.

Stevens was quite confused by the Zach–Oxford controversy. He deplored the separation of the Harriot papers instigated by Zach, noting that this both depreciated their value and made research on their contents almost impossible. He praised Rigaud for 'working out the crooked and entangled history of the Zachian fiasco',[55] but he followed Zach in exaggerating Harriot's innovations and glorifying his contributions to the life and science of his day. As he wrote in his headnote:[56]

... From a concise bibliographical essay the work has grown into a biography of a philosopher and man of science with extraordinary surroundings, wherein the patient reader may trace the gradual development of Virginia from the earliest time to 1585; 'especially,' says Strachey, 'that which hath bene published by that true lover of vertue and great learned professor of all arts and knowledge, Mr Hariots, who lyved there in the tyme of the first colony, spake the Indian language, searcht the country,' etc; Hariot's nearly forty years' intimate connection with Sir Walter Raleigh; his long close companionship with Henry Percy; his correspondence with Kepler; his participation in Raleigh's 'History of the World'; his invention of the telescope and his consequent astronomical discoveries; his scientific disciples; his many friendships and no foeships; his blameless life; his beautiful epitaph in St. Christopher's Church, and his long slumber in the 'garden' of the Bank of England.

This sense of wonder about Harriot as a genius in his work and as a forerunner of the new science which was to follow might be expected of a man of historical and literary background like Stevens. But in his summaries of Harriot's correspondence with Kepler and in his interpretation of the Sion College notes of Nathaniel Torporley, he showed a

---

[55] Ibid., p. 187.   [56] Ibid., pp. 7–8.

better instinctive view of science and mathematics than one would expect. He recognized and cited many contemporary references to Harriot to bolster his admiration, but he was inclined to take casual references of testimonial or dedicatory verses at face value, ignoring the Elizabethan penchant for hyperbole on such occasions. But his discovery of Harriot's will did furnish Stevens with more information about Harriot's friends and associates than anyone up to his time had possessed and permitted him to place Harriot in his intellectual milieu. It led him to Harriot's friendship with Thomas Buckner and his death in his house, his burial at St. Christopher's and his memorial there (though he missed the point that Harriot was buried in the Chancel and not in the 'garden'). Through his interest in Harriot, Stevens also came to recognize the importance of John White in the Virginia ventures, and when the John White drawings came on the market, he was able (after they were turned down by Lenox) to obtain them for the British Museum,[57] where they still remain.

Stevens died as he was seeing his work on Harriot through the press, so though he had finished his text he had no opportunity to correct the proofs or to emend his original drafts. This was in the year 1885, the same year that Agnes M. Clerke was commissioned to write a life of Harriot for the *Dictionary of National Biography*. It is rather surprising that though they were working on the same project and using the same materials neither Stevens nor Clerke appears to have been aware of the activity of the other. Like Stevens, Miss Clerke covered most of the London sources and followed the secondary sources about Harriot, but did little with the information to be derived from Harriot's own manuscripts. Miss Clerke also discovered the record of Harriot's burial at St. Christophers, to which, she asserts (following the unsupported statement of Anthony à Wood) 'his body was removed with great ceremony'. With that clue, she also found the record of the memorial plaque placed in the church, later to be destroyed in the Great Fire of 1666. This plaque she ascribes to two of his executors, Robert Sidney (Viscount Lisle), and Sir Thomas Aylesbury, ignoring

---

[57] Parker, op. cit., p. 267.

the other two, John Protheroe and Thomas Buckner, in whose house Harriot died. This last executor she should have recognized, since it was he who was a member of the Parish of St. Christopher's and is mentioned in the burial record of Harriot on 3 July 1621, which Miss Clerke must have seen. But Miss Clerke was totally unaware that Stevens had found and copied Harriot's will: indeed, in her biography she declared that 'Harriot's will was not found' — an error which has been perpetuated in all the editions of the *DNB* issued to this time. This is particularly surprising since Stevens was very proud of his discovery, and it was discussed rather widely at the time she was preparing her brief life.

Though the plates for Stevens's book were complete at the time of his death in 1885, they remained unprinted and in the hands of his son, Henry N. Stevens (his literary executor) until 1900. Unfortunately for both the author and Harriot's reputation, printing, when it was ordered, was in a very limited edition of thirty-three large paper copies and 162 copies on small paper. As a result, though it was well known to students in the field, Stevens's biography made very little impact on the popular reputation of Harriot, and did little to stimulate others to continue the study of his life or works. Harriot's manuscripts remained largely unread, and historians of science and mathematics usually neglected his contributions to favour others who had published their scientific findings and were thus in the main stream of scientific development.

In the autumn of 1947 I was granted a Fellowship by the John Simon Guggenheim Memorial Foundation to collect materials for a new study of Thomas Harriot. Immediately I began negotiations to gain access to the Petworth collection of manuscripts, but without success. At that time the papers were under the control of Charles Henry Wyndham, 3rd Baron Leconfield, who had succeeded his father, Henry Wyndham, 2nd Baron Leconfield, in 1901. Charles, who had been a boy of five when Horwood catalogued the manuscripts under the supervision of his father in 1877, was uninterested in scholarship, lived the life of a semi-retired country gentleman, not at all congenial to requests for admission to his libraries. However I tried, I could not gain access to either the manuscripts or the old library where (according to Harriot's will now discovered) Harriot's manuscripts were originally kept and in which any artifacts left to the 9th Earl of Northumberland (such as telescopes, lenses, grinding equipment, and the like) might yet remain. My letters, along with others from the American Embassy and officials of the British Museum, remained unanswered. It was not until the spring of 1948, through the efforts of Sir Hugh Algernon Percy, 10th Duke of Northumberland and a distant cousin of Lord Leconfield and a British 'cousin', the Revd. (Frederick) John Shirley, Headmaster of King's School, Canterbury, and Senior Canon Residentiary of Canterbury Cathedral, both of whom were most interested in my research on Thomas Harriot, that Lord Leconfield agreed to receive me at Petworth House and to permit me to see the Harriot manuscripts. There through the kind offices of Lord Leconfield's estates agent, Mr J. H. Bennett, I was finally granted permission to photograph all of the Harriot materials for my study and that of other interested scholars, though restrictions were placed on the reproduction of the papers themselves. I was also permitted to go through the old library for any Harriot memorabilia that might remain, though none were found. Many of the books of the 9th Earl, bearing his crest and containing his marginal notes, remained on the shelves, but no notes or jottings by Harriot appeared in any of them.

When Charles Wyndham died in 1952 at the age of eighty, he was succeeded in turn by two brothers, the 4th and 5th Lords Leconfield, both of whom generally continued the restrictive practices of their elder brother. The succession of John Edward Reginald Wyndham as 6th Baron Leconfield (as well as 1st Baron Egremont) in October 1967, opened up the Petworth library considerably for serious Harriot scholars. Lord Egremont and Leconfield had been a secretary to Harold Macmillan during the Second World War and was himself an author and interested in publishing. Unlike his predecessors, he recognized that use of his manuscripts enhanced their value rather than detracted from it and felt a responsibility that the scientific and scholarly world be given access to such important intellectual source materials. This tradition has been carried on by his son, (John) Max Scawen Wyndham, the present Lord Egremont and Leconfield, who succeeded his father on his untimely death in 1972. Under his authority, copies of the Petworth Harriot manuscripts have been made available in microfilm and Xerox copies in three research libraries: the Bodleian Library in Oxford, the Science Museum, London, and in the History of Science Room at the University of Delaware Library. Here they may be studied, with only the restriction that any reproduction from these collections must have the approval of Lord Egremont and Leconfield.

During the last thirty years, interest in Harriot has grown steadily. A more widespread study of the history of science has brought more intense consideration of the science and mathematics of the sixteenth and seventeenth centuries when the new science was taking shape, with a consequent recognition of Harriot's central role in the English science of his time. Studies analysing the evolution of mathematical thought, like those of Cantor[58] and Cajori,[59] reviewed with unbiased eyes Harriot's contribution to the formation of modern algebra, though until recently such studies were based almost totally on the reading of the posthumous *Artis Analyticæ Praxis*. Recent studies of Lohne, Tanner, and Pepper[60] have brought fresh new light on Harriot's mathematical innovations through study of his actual mathematical papers and have begun to restore some of the lustre that was dimmed by the exaggerated claims of Wallis and Zach. Still a great deal remains to be done in this area comparing Harriot's working papers with those of his contemporaries, in England and abroad. Renewed interest in navigation and the perils of space travel have brought attention to similar problems for the early sea explorers.

---

[58] Moritz Cantor, *Vorlesungen über Geschichte der Mathematik*, 4 vols., Leipzig, 1880-1908, vol. II (1892), pp. 720-2.

[59] Florian Cajori, 'A Reevaluation of Harriot's *Artis Analyticæ Praxis*', *Isis*, XI (1928), 316-24. See also his *A History of Mathematical Notations*, 2 vols., Chicago, 1928; 'Thomas Harriot', I. 199-201; 'Signs in Theoretical Arithmetic', II. 115-17.

[60] All the recent studies here listed will be found in the bibliography. Some are also reprinted in John W. Shirley, ed., *A Source Book for the Study of Thomas Harriot*, New York, Arno Press, 1981.

This has focused attention to Harriot's activities as practical mathematician and as navigational instructor of Ralegh's sea captains. E. G. R. Taylor, Commander David Waters, and Jon Pepper have all made significant contributions by studying Harriot's navigational notes and calculations, though little has been done to assess his interest in the shipbuilding activities during the critical years surrounding the invasion of the Spanish Armada.

As America has begun to recognize the richness of its heritage, Harriot's role as an explorer and colonizer of the new world has received increasing attention. A number of reprints and facsimiles of his *A briefe and true report of the new found land of Virginia* have been issued,[61] and that work is now a firm part of American colonial history. Professor David Beers Quinn's monumental two-volume study of *The Roanoke Voyages*, published in 1955 under the auspices of the Hakluyt Society, has done more than any other work to put the American investigations of Harriot and White into sound perspective. Unlike many who have interested themselves in Harriot's account of the new world, Quinn has gone far beyond the printed sources and has thoroughly searched all of Harriot's manuscripts and canvassed all possible library sources for additional Harriot material to supplement his own accounts. This segment of Harriot's activities will not need to be done over again. And the interest generated by Quinn's studies has paralleled excavation and reconstruction of the original colony site at Roanoke Island under the direction of J. C. Harrington of the National Park Service,[62] and has led to the development of an Elizabethan garden at the site of the reconstructed fort, the building of a theatre for an outdoor presentation of a

[61] The history of the printing and reprinting of this volume may be found in D. B. Quinn's *The Roanoke Voyages*, 2 vols., London, The Hakluyt Society Publications (Second Series, CIV) 1952, vol. I, pp. 317-18. In this work, Quinn had again reprinted the work, this time with critical notes. Another photolithographic copy of the 1590 edition has been issued since Quinn's study by Dover Publications of New York, 1972, with an introduction by Paul Hulton.

[62] Jean C. Harrington, 'Archaeological Explorations at Fort Raleigh National Historical Site', *North Carolina Historical Review*, XXVI (April 1949), 127-49. See also his *Search for the Cittie of Ralegh; archaeological excavations at Fort Raleigh National Historic Site, North Carolina*, Washington, National Park Service, 1962.

drama presenting the story of the lost colony, and the establishment of a 'Harriot's walk' which leads the visitor through the underbush surrounding the fort to view many of the plants and trees originally identified by Harriot, bearing plaques containing Harriot's comments about them as he saw them in 1585–6.

But the major factor which has led to renewed activity in the study of Harriot as an instrumental figure in the new science has evolved from the spurt in scientific interest during the third quarter of the present century. The development of new and finer astronomical observatories, like that at Mt. Palomar, focused new attention on Harriot's early work on refraction and optical systems which culminated in his early use of the telescope. The work of Johannes Lohne in interpreting Harriot's working papers on refraction and light has taken us far toward a real understanding of his state of the art. The first landing of a man on the moon stimulated interest in Harriot as the first recorder of a telescopic observation of that body, seen by Strout and Moore as a link of Britain to the space programme, and by Shirley as one of the earliest scientific attempts to determine the size of the physical universe. New discoveries about the importance of sunspots in relation to the energy content of the solar radiation which initiates the photo-ionization of the ionosphere brings to Harriot's observation of sunspots a significance to modern scientific theory which belies the conclusions of Robertson. This has led to a study in modern terms and a comparison with the observations of Galileo as made by John North, and has led Richard Herr to put all of Harriot's drawings into the computer for their contribution to a modern study of the changing rate of rotation of the sun and its energy output. And growth of interest in modern atomic theory has led to new investigations of Harriot's atomism by Robert Kargon and new interpretations of his theory of impacts by both Jon Pepper and Martin Kalmar. These studies, and others like them, appear to show that in recent years Harriot is seen as a vital link between the exciting and expansive years of Elizabeth I and the equally exciting expanding universe of scientific knowledge of Elizabeth II.

Indicative of interest in Harriot as a focus of the intellectual activity surrounding the early days of modern science is the fact that for more than a decade an annual Thomas Harriot Seminar has been held at Oxford University under the auspices of the Oxford University Committee for the History and Philosophy of Science chaired by Alistair Crombie. This Seminar, originally designed to 'centralize information relevant to Harriot's life and work', has expanded somewhat over the years to place Harriot in the general background of sixteenth- and seventeenth-century science, covering Harriot predecessors, contemporaries, and followers from the period, roughly, from Copernicus to Boyle. Annual attendance has varied from thirty to fifty, with interested scholars attending and participating from France, Germany, Italy, Holland, Poland, and the Soviet Union, as well as from Great Britain and the United States. The continued success of the Oxford Harriot Seminar clearly shows the growing interest in, and respect for, Thomas Harriot as a mathematician and scientist.

A similar Thomas Harriot Symposium, organized by the present author and supported by the University of Delaware and the National Endowment for the Humanities, was held at the University of Delaware in April 1971. Its purpose was to inform American students of the history of science of the state of Harriot research, to outline some of the problems remaining to be resolved, and to indicate the resources for further study offered by the microfilm and Xerox collection of his manuscripts available for scholarly research in the History of Science Reading Room at the University of Delaware. More than thirty historians of science attended these sessions, a number of whom have continued their interest in Harriot's observations. The papers presented at the Delaware Symposium were published in 1974 by the Clarendon Press, Oxford, under the title of *Thomas Harriot: Renaissance Scientist*.

A second Harriot Seminar, patterned after the Oxford Seminar, was held at the University of Durham in December 1979, and again in 1981. These Seminars, under the aegis of Professor Gordon Batho, are planned as biennial affairs to alternate years with the Oxford Seminar. It has not yet been decided whether or not the proceedings will be published.

All these activities of the past quarter century, in addition to pointing up the need for more exact study of Harriot's actual papers in determining his place in the beginning of modern scientific thought, have also made such study much more feasible. Though the actual manuscripts are still scattered and are frequently out of order, their counterparts duplicated by modern copying facilities permit their restoration to their original order. It is now apparent that all or almost all of Harriot's manuscript notes are now available for study, and though they number nearly 9,000 folio pages in number, a large number are either blank or contain fragmentary figures only, so that the task of exhausting their contents on individual subjects is entirely possible. The originals, too, have been made somewhat more usable than they were previously. Seven of the eight volumes in the British Library (the exception is the very important eighth volume which badly needs similar treatment) have been rebound with the pages mounted so that they open more completely and marginal comments can be read more easily. The Petworth papers have also been collected into subject groups, and are now bound into ten small volumes, though not totally in the original order of Rigaud and Horwood, and not always properly sequenced within the groups. But again, the ease of working from photographic copies makes such reordering and sequences a simpler matter than it was before such copies were made available for research.

Given now, for the first time, both scholarly interest and available primary source materials, it seems assured that within the next few years what Rigaud called 'the fair fame of Thomas Harriot' will be fully established.

II. Harriot at Oxford, 1560–1580

Friday, 20 December 1577, was a ceremonial day at the University of Oxford, since it was matriculation day for the Hilary Term enrolment of new students. Nearly 250 aspiring young candidates gathered in the Church of St. Mary the Virgin that afternoon with their Principals for this first formal convocation, at the conclusion of which they would be duly inscribed undergraduate members of England's oldest and most revered university. Twenty colleges and halls were represented, with University College having the smallest number, two, and Magdalen the largest — twenty-two for the college and another twenty-two of the hall. St. Mary's Hall, escorted by the Principal, Richard Pygott, a fellow of Oriel and senior sponsor for that hall, was about average in size, with thirteen young men ranging in age from fifteen to twenty-nine standing ready to take their oaths.

With the full pomp and circumstance surrounding a formal assembly of the members of the University during the reign of Elizabeth I, the convocation, bringing together all the members of the University, assembled. Though the Chancellor, Robert Dudley, Earl of Leicester, who had held this post since 1564 at the appointment of the Queen, was not present, he was ably represented by the Vice-Chancellor, William Cole, doctor of divinity and president of Corpus Christi College, who had been appointed the previous July. First came the formal procession, the invocation and prayers, the announcements; then the ceremonies of matriculation began. The aspiring students stood to take formal oath that they both understood and would abide by all the statutes of the university — those that governed their studies, attendance at lectures, participation in disputations as required, their

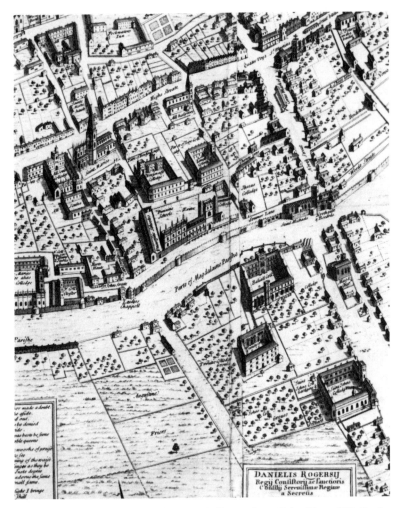

Fig. 1 Section of Robert Whittlesey's Engraving of the Plan of Oxford by Ralph Agas

personal conduct even to details of how they must dress for all occasions. Following this evidence of their compliance, they were led by their Principals one at a time before the Proctors, where each was called upon to give his Christian name and surname, the county in which he was born, the social status of his father (since tuition was based on ability

to pay), and his age. Pygott's boys in their turn filed past the
official recorder: 'Edward Ballam, Buckinghamshire, plebeian
father, age 18'; 'Thomas Beck, Salop [Shropshire], plebeian
father, age 16'; 'William Clarke, Dorset, plebeian, age 29.'
Sixth of the thirteen was 'Thomas Heriot, Oxon, plebeian
father, age 17.' These notes, inscribed by the Proctor on
this impressive occasion, furnish the full record of Harriot's
background, home, and date of birth.

It is indeed strange that for a man so widely known
throughout England for the remainder of his life, this single
entry in the Oxford Archives seems to be the only record to
shed light on his first twenty years. Though it indicates that
he had been reared and educated in the city in which he
sought further education, no confirmatory evidence, though
frequently sought, has been found. And beyond the fact that
he belonged to the social order of the common man in
Elizabethan England, no other record exists of Harriot's
father. In his will forty-odd years later, Harriot mentions
the son of a sister who had married a man named Yates and
the son of an uncle named John Harriot, but neither of
these names appears for certain in the Oxford parish or
court registers. Though there were, as we shall see, a number
of venerable traditions about his youth and early education,
so far as official records are concerned, Thomas Harriot
appears to spring full-blown as an Oxford student.

Though much smaller than the modern city in extent,
the Oxford where Harriot spent his youth and early man-
hood would not appear strange to a modern Oxonian. Many
of the landmarks, in fact many of the buildings, are essentially
the same as the ones Harriot knew. The Church of St. Mary the
Virgin, in which Harriot stood for matriculation into the
university, stood then as now 'in the middle almost of the
city, the chief consistory or basilica of the University.'
St. Mary's Hall, into which he was admitted, was likewise
centrally located just across the street from St. Mary's
Church between High Street and old Oriel College of Shed-
yard Street (now named Oriel Street). One tradition has it
that Harriot was born and educated in this same parish, and
if so it was perfectly natural for him to be attracted to what
was then the largest of the Oxford halls, in close proximity

and daily contact with the teachers and students of the surrounding colleges who were to be his lifetime friends and associates.

The streets that Harriot daily trod are also familiar in the present. In his day as now Catte (spelled c-a-t in the sixteenth century, but falsely expanded to 'Catherine Street' in the eighteenth) was a main cross walk across town, running as it now does east of St. Mary's Church through the old city wall at Smith Gate. What is now Radcliffe Street was then called School Street, going west of St. Mary's to the wall and Somnores Lane at about the point where the Old Ashmolean currently stands. In Harriot's day, School Street was lined on both sides with lecture halls and rooms for disputations and examinations, used by all the colleges and halls. What is now Broad Street was then the ruined remains of the old city walls and the Ditch, an extension of the moat which surrounded the Castle, with Horsemonger Street beyond the walls. St. Mary Magdalen and the Cross were landmarks in Harriot's day, though their street was called Fish Street rather than Magdalen or Cornmarket. Harriot, placed in modern Oxford, could still find many familiar haunts.

Unfortunately for one of Harriot's natural talents, the study of mathematics and the natural sciences, was in very low estate during his years at the University. As was pointed out by Anthony à Wood, Oxford's most famous antiquary, the Reformation had had a most deleterious effect on the scientific quality of Oxford education. Governmental commissioners, like those appointed to confiscate the properties of other monastic organizations, rummaged through the Oxford colleges, systematically weeding out and destroying books and manuscripts of medieval learning. As Wood recorded in his *Annals* of Oxford events for 1550:[1]

The works of the Schoolmen, namely P. Lombard, Th. Aquinas, Scotus and his followers ... they cast out of all College Libraries and private studies ... they brought it so to pass that certain rude young men

[1] Anthony à Wood, *The History and Antiquity of the Colleges and Halls in the University of Oxford*, ed. John Gutch, Oxford, Clarendon Press, 1796, vol. II, part i, p. 108. This passage is cited by Frances A. Yates in 'Giordano Bruno's Conflict with Oxford', *Journal of the Warburg Institute*, II. 3 (January 1939), 227–42.

should carry this great spoil of books about the city on biers, which being so done, to set them down in the common market place and there burn them . . .

Books which contained mathematical symbols or diagrams were particularly suspect and liable to destruction: 'Sure I am that such books wherein appeared Angles or Mathematical Diagrams, were thought sufficient to be destroyed, because accounted Popish, or diabolical, or both . . .' Many of the collections of the Good Duke Humphrey, nucleus of the University library and precursor to the Bodleian, were dispersed and lost. The major collections of manuscripts and books in England — those of the monasteries and the universities — were destroyed or dissipated.

In addition to this tragic loss of scholarly materials, the actual course of study had deteriorated as well. As Christopher Hill has pointed out, the purpose of the university declined from 1558 to 1642 to the place where it 'was twofold: to produce clerics for the state Church, and to give a veneer of polite learning to young gentlemen, few of whom had any intention of taking a degree.'[2] Giordano Bruno's diatribes against the English universities following his visit to Oxford three years after Harriot's graduation are well known. As translated by Frances Yates, Bruno complained that the Oxford professors were no longer Doctors of Philosophy, but were, instead:[3] 'doctors of grammar. A whole constellation of them reigns over this happy country, and their obstinate ignorance, pedantry and presumption are combined with a boorish incivility of manner which would provoke the patience of Job.' Instead of seeking truth, Bruno insisted, these 'blind asses' were merely pedants who spent their lives studying and playing with words:[4]

They examine every speech and discuss every phrase, saying this smacks of a poet, that of a comic writer, that of an orator. This passage is

---

[2] *Intellectual Origins of the English Revolution*, Oxford, Clarendon Press, 1969. An appendix, 'A Note on the Universities', pp. 301–14, refutes the more favourable position taken by Mark H. Curtis in his *Oxford and Cambridge in Transition, 1558–1642*, Oxford, 1959. Hill shows that of students from Somerset, excluding those studying for the clergy, only one in five of the matriculants graduated.
[3] Frances Yates, op. cit., p. 232.   [4] Ibid., p. 233.

serious, that light; this is sublime, that is *humile dicendi genus* . . . After these triumphs the self-satisfied pedant feels more pleased with his own prowess than with anything else in the world.

Bruno's British friends (Sir Fulke Greville and Sir Philip Sidney) were apologetic for the Oxford atmosphere, but begged Bruno[5]

not to take offense at the rudeness and ignorance of their doctors, but rather to pity the poverty of this country which is widowed of good learning in the fields of philosophy and pure mathematics, concerning which all are so blind that asses like these are able to pass themselves off as seers.

Though Bruno undoubtedly exaggerated the Oxford situation through pique at his poor reception there, it is still true that the reforms instituted by the 'New Statutes' of 1564–5 do indicate a turning away from the study of mathematics, science, and philosophy, and more emphasis on grammar, rhetoric, and dialectics. Under the influence of the Chancellor, Robert Dudley, Earl of Leicester, a detailed *Statuta pro Scholaribus* was issued which reviewed all aspects of the academic programmes and degree requirements. These statutes, designed to eliminate the Catholic schoolmen, put renewed emphasis on Aristotle; they also devoted more time to the studies of the trivium and pushed most of the quadrivial subjects into the Master of Arts degree. Fewer books were 'read' in lectures and more rote repetition of texts was required. According to these 'New Statutes' the actual course of study during Harriot's years at Oxford was as follows:[6]

GRAMMAR (two terms): Linacre, or Vergil, or Horace, or Priscian, or Cicero's *Epistles*.
RHETORIC (four terms): Cicero's *Orationes* or *Præceptiones*, or Aristotle's *Rhetoric*.
DIALECTIC (five terms): Porphyry's *Institutiones* or Aristotle's *Dialectic*.

[5] Ibid., p. 232.
[6] This curriculum is pieced together from numerous statutes included in Strickland Gibson, *Statuta Antiqua Universitatis Oxoniensis*, Oxford, Clarendon Press 1931. See particularly pp. xci, 378, 389–91. It might be pointed out that the 'Music' of Boethius was not music in its present sense, but was a mathematical study of ratios and proportions, much closer to arithmetic than to sounds.

ARITHMETIC (three terms): Boethius or Gemma Frisius.
MUSIC (two terms): Boethius.

The studies which would have appealed most to a student of Harriot's temperament, mathematics, astronomy, and the philosophies, were relegated at that time to the three years of post-baccalaureate study leading to the Master of Arts degree. But here, too, the curriculum was strongly based on Aristotle and his disciples. The prescribed texts for the Master's degree were as follows:[7]

GEOMETRY (two terms): Euclid.
ASTRONOMY (two terms): Orontius *de Sphaera* or Sacro Bosco.
NATURAL PHILOSOPHY (three terms): Aristotle *Physics*, or *De Caelo et Mundo*, or *de Meteoris*, or *de Parvis naturalibus*, or *de Anima*.
METAPHYSICS (two terms): Aristotle's *Metaphysics*.

From Harriot's early manuscripts, it is obvious that he was thoroughly familiar with at least the first three of these areas, and since he did not remain at the University for the Master's degree, he must have followed this reading as an undergraduate, going far beyond the requirements of the statutes.

William Harrison, writing about the British universities in the year that Harriot matriculated there, bears out the anti-scientific impact of the 'New Statutes' on the Oxford curriculum. Writing an appendix for the 1577 edition of Holinshed's *Chronicles of England, Scotland, and Irelande*, Harrison wrote:[8]

... in the publicke schooles of both the universities, there are found at the Princes charge (and that very largely) fiue professours and readers, that is to say, of diuinitie, of the ciuile lawe, Physicke [medicine], the Hebrue & the Greeke tongues: and for other publicke lectures as of Philosophie, Logicke, Rethoricke, & the Quadriuials. (Although the later I meane Arithmeticke, Musicke, Geometrie, and Astronomie, and with them all skill in perspectiues are now smally regarded in eyther of them) ...

The retrogressive nature of the 'New Statutes' is emphasized in a decree issued shortly after Harriot's graduation which modified the form to be maintained in the disputations.

[7] Ibid., p. 390.
[8] *The First Volume* ... London, 1577, Book II, Ch. 6, p. 79, col. 2.

As translated by Anthony à Wood, this reads:[9]

... it was ordered for the future that all Bachelaurs and Undergraduats in their Disputations should lay aside their various Authors, such that caused many dissentions and strifes in the Schools, and only follow Aristotle and those that defend him, and take their Questions from him, and that they exclude from the Schools all steril and inane Questions, disagreeing from the antient and true Philosophy ...

That these injunctions were enforced strictly may be inferred from the fact that there is no mention in any of the official statutes or records of the University of the works of any contemporary scientist or mathematician (including Copernicus, Kepler, or Galileo) until the establishment of the Savilian Professorship in Astronomy in 1619.[10]

From all the official decrees of the Chancellor, the Earl of Leicester, during the years surrounding Harriot's experience of Oxford, it appears that during these years there was more concern for the morals, social activities, and physical appearance of the student than there was for his intellectual stimulation. Evidently stung by the charges that students were dissolute, drunken, and licentious (as they were usually portrayed by the clergy), the officials filled the records with fresh injunctions governing all aspects of student life and conduct. The years that Harriot spent in Oxford seem to have been among those most narrowly prescribed and restricted.

The Convocations of 23 to 27 July 1576 passed a series of decrees and orders 'for the Reformation of Excesse, and some disorders in aparell'.[11] From this time hence, students were required to wear gowns and hoods whenever they appeared within the University. They were also required to wear 'a Square Capp', and after the first of October (three months before Harriot's matriculation) 'the Statute of the

---

[9] *History and Antiquity*, II. i. 226. The original statute is recorded in Gibson, op. cit., pp. 436–7.

[10] This is true in spite of the contentions of Francis R. Johnson, *Astronomical Thought in Renaissance England*, Baltimore, Johns Hopkins Press, 1937, that the universities exerted considerable indirect influence in promulgating the new astronomy. Johnson bases his 'must have had' philosophy on the recognition that the foremost English scholars of astronomy were university men. All remaining evidence shows, however, that their studies were performed *outside* the Universities and *not within*. The disputation subjects cited by Johnson on p. 181 are straight out of Aristotle and do not reflect Copernicanism as he claims.

[11] Gibson, op. cit., pp. 403–5.

Relme for Ruffs and hose shall be observed.' Even the colour
of the student's garb — black — was prescribed:

. . after the sayde 6 Day of July no Maister of Art nor Bachiler nor
Scholler of College nor Hall of what facultye somever he be shale weare
any Dublet or Jerkin of Blew, greene, Redd, white, or other lite colour
or layd with lace gard, welt, or Cutt or pincked except he weare a cote
with the sleeves on vppon the same and that none of the Persons
before saide shale make ether any such or any of Silcke or Velvett
in part or in all blackfacing . . .

. . . no Graduat or Scholler of any College shale weare when he is
abroad out of the vniuersitie any Hatt of any colour than blacke . . .

. . no Maister of Art nor other of lower degree shall wear any cloake of
other colour then Blacke . . .

All entering students were required to take formal oath that
they understood and would abide by all the University
statutes. And this strong emphasis on the requirement that
all students wear black (a part of the tradition of the *magus*)
must have made a profound impression on the young scholar.
There is some evidence that he abode by these dress injunctions for the remainder of his life, and appeared only in
garments of black.[12]

Harriot's undergraduate progress can be pieced out from
the official records, since the requirements for the BA degree
remain nearly unchanged between 1571 and 1622.[13] The
first step, Admission, as already described, called for the
student to present himself with his credentials to the head
of the College or Hall he wished to enter. If he was accepted,
his name was inscribed in the Buttery-book, he was assigned
a room and took up residence. At this time he chose (or was
assigned) a tutor who was responsible for his studies, for
seeing that he obeyed the regulations, and who oversaw
his dress and conduct. Once each week thereafter, University beadles visited the residence site, reviewed the
names of students in residence, and checked the entries in

---

[12] See below, p. 238.

[13] Details of Elizabethan University education are most clearly spelled out by
Andrew Clark in the Introduction, 'The Degree System of the University', vol. II,
part I, *Register of the University of Oxford, 1571–1622*, Oxford, for the Oxford
Historical Society, 1887. Much of the following section of this chapter is based on
Clark's work.

the Buttery-books. On the second Friday after the student's admission, he was taken by the Head or his representative to appear before the Vice-Chancellor (in his residence during vacations or at St. Mary's during term) for official entry into the University, a process known as Matriculation. At this time the student took his oath to observe for ever all the statutes of the University. After 1581 he was also required to subscribe formally to the thirty-nine articles of the Church, but this was not mandatory on 20 December 1577, when Harriot was formally matriculated. He also gave formal testimony as to his age, the place or county of his birth, and the social status of his father. All of these items were recorded in the Matriculation Register, and the student was given a Certificate of Admission by the Vice-Chancellor. At this time, too, the new student formally chose his faculty or course of study. In most cases (except for a very few colleges in which Law could be chosen from the start) the student became 'scholaris facultatis artium', an aspirant for the BA degree, the final degree for those not seeking advanced degrees, and the normal entry to the professions of teaching (with the terminal Master's or Doctor's degrees), theology, medicine, or law.

Having formally matriculated, the student began his study. He read the required texts and wrote the assigned analyses under the direction of his tutor. He also attended lectures and participated in disputations, both those required by his College and by the University. Attendance at all prescribed lectures was compulsory, and the interested student was permitted to attend some lectures which were not required. In each case, the students, properly garbed, awaited the lecturer at the gate of his College, escorted him to the lecture hall (usually in School Street) and remained in attendance for the one, two, or three hours assumed by the lecturer. The student could obtain permission to absent himself from a particular lecture by supplicating the Congregation, but without such special permission, each failure to attend required payment of a fine. And since the 'scholaris facultatis artium' had sworn adherence to all statutes, an absence without fine or dispensation could lay him open to the serious charge of perjury.

As important as attendance at lectures was the student's observation and participation in disputations. These were normally held at the School of Arts on Mondays, Wednesdays, and Fridays. Early in the morning on disputation day, three questions were posted with the names and colleges of the disputants who were to perform. During his first two years the student merely observed, but beginning with his ninth term he was expected 'respondere in parvis' — to respond to questions in grammatical and logical subjects. Three students participated in each; one as a respondent upholding the question, two as opponents refuting it. A Regent Master moderated the disputation, summarized the discussion with a short speech which invariably praised Aristotle and pure logic, announced his decision, and rewarded each student who had completed his disputation with a copy of Aristotle's *Logic* and a hood of plain black cloth. Students performing their required disputations each term were said to be disputing 'pro forma' and at the close of the exercises were created 'sophistae generales' in a sort of quasi-degree.

When the student was ready to apply for his degree, he performed in the major disputation which served as a sort of oral final examination of all he had learned. These disputations came during Lent, with each degree applicant serving as respondent twice. This was called 'respondere sub Baccalaureo in quadragesima'. Each student publicly debated the question with a Bachelor, and each disputation was expected to last for at least an hour and a half.

A third major requirement for graduation in addition to attending compulsory lectures and participating in disputations, was residence 'infra præcinctum Universitatis', generally interpreted to mean within a College or Hall. Throughout the reign of Elizabeth, the residential period was normally for sixteen terms for the BA, though special dispensation (usually for members of the gentry or nobility) could shorten this period from one to four terms. But as in the case of other requirements, the rigorous prescriptions of the official statutes could be mollified by special action of the Congregation to grant exceptions to the rules. As Andrew Clark pointed out in his extensive publication of the official records of the University, the Elizabethan University[14]

... possessed an elasticity which has now been lost, in the practice of granting 'dispensations'. When it was inconvenient for a student to fulfil the exact conditions of residence or exercises imposed by the Statutes, the governing body of the University (then a commonwealth, not, as now, an oligarchy) would grant an exception from the strict letter of the Statutes. Such exemptions were called 'dispensations'. These 'dispensations', accordingly, represent a very important element in the University life of the sixteenth and seventeenth centuries, and are in fact its most characteristic feature. They are, however, so multitudinous that a separate record of the date and nature of each of them would make a volume larger, I suppose, than the present, for few men passed through the University without benefit from dispensations . . .

Harriot, like most of his fellow students, took advantage of the generosity of the Congregation for dispensations which permitted him to take his degree.

Scholars have long tried to find official records regarding Harriot's parentage, home, or family life. John Aubrey, in the last quarter of the seventeenth century, sought information about Harriot, collecting notes for the lives of distinguished Englishmen. Enquiry among friends was fruitless: Dr John Pell was certain he was born in England, but knew not which county. Elias Ashmole thought he came from Lancashire. Local communities in Kent and Worcestershire bore the name Harriots or Harriotsham. Aubrey even located a coat of arms ('per pale, ermine and ermines, 3 crescents counterchanged') for the family 'Hariot', not recognizing that this Harriot was a different Thomas Harriot, a member of the Company of Skinners, born in Wollaston in the county of Northamptonshire on 2 November 1588, who died on 23 September 1653.[15] But Aubrey sought in vain for Harriot's memorial or any other record which might indicate his place of origin or parentage.

Anthony à Wood, the Oxford antiquary for whom Aubrey was collecting much of his information, was more successful, in that he found, for the first time, the Oxford matriculation record which gave 'Oxon' as the county of birth. Wood, on this clue, proceeded to seek additional verification. In his

[14] Ibid. II. i. 2.
[15] A copy of Fox's *Book of Martyrs* sold at Sotheby's on 26 Nov. 1939 (item 597) carries a copy of these arms on the back cover. Ownership and identity are inscribed on the inside of the front cover.

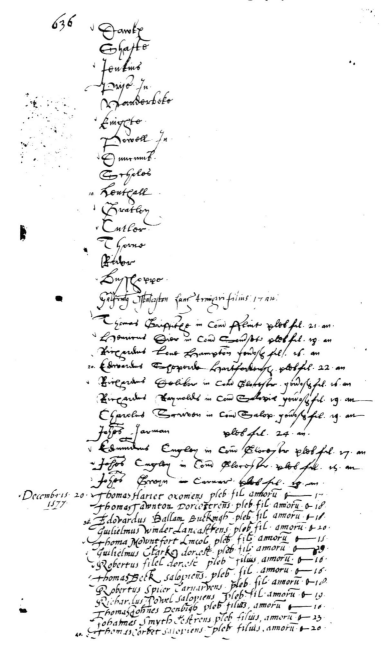

Fig. 2 Harriot's Matriculation Record

life of Harriot published in the 1691 account of Oxford 'greats', *Athenae Oxonienses*, he reports:[16]

THOMAS HARIOT, or *HARRIOT*, tumbled out of his Mother's Womb into the Lap of the *Oxonian* Muses, an. 1560, but in what Parish I cannot yet tell. All the Registers that begin before that time (namely that of S. *Ebbe*, S. *Aldate*, S. *Thomas*, which began that year, S. *Michael, All Saints,* and S. *Peter* in the *East*) I have searched, but cannot find his name. That of S. *Mary's* Parish, wherein I suppose this our Author was born, hath been lost several Years, and there is no Register remaining that goes above the Year 1599.

The Matriculation Record (Fig. 2), source of his data, still remains in the Oxford Archives, and reads:[17]

1577
20 Dec.   S. Mary H.   Hariet, Thomas;   Oxon.   pleb. f.,   17.

This record indicates that Harriot sought entrance and took up residence in Saint Mary's Hall sometime during the week beginning 30 November, 1577, since his matriculation was on the second Friday following his admission to the Hall (20 December 1577 was a Friday). Secondly it gives the fact that Aubrey missed, that Harriot was born in Oxford, or at least in Oxfordshire. Thirdly it establishes his birthdate at 1560 since he was seventeen in 1577. In this, Harriot matriculated at the median age for his class — of 259 matriculants in 1577 ranging from ten to over thirty, the median was seventeen. And lastly, it establishes the fact that, in spite of Aubrey's mistakenly giving him a family coat of arms, he was of a plebeian family, and, as a result, entitled to a fee payment of only 4 pence, the lowest of any social rank.

One bit of information that Wood missed about the existence of Harriots in Oxfordshire during these years is to be found in a will in the Bodleian of 'Thomas Harriotts of Clyfton in the county of Oxford, Smith' dated 20 May 1585.[18] In this will, Thomas Harriotts, a blacksmith who is obviously illiterate since he signs the will with an 'X', leaves all his properties and possessions, including leases in Nuneham

---

[16] This quotation is from the 1815 ed., re-edited by Andrew Clark, vol. II, pp. 299–300.
[17] Andrew Clark, *Register*, vol. II, part ii, 'Matriculations and Subscriptions', p. 79.
[18] Bodleian Library: MS Wills — Oxon.

Courtenay and 'the mayor farm' in Wallingford, to his wife
Joane and his daughter Alice. Apparently he left no living
sons since none is mentioned, though a brother, John
Harriots, is named as executor along with his wife's brother,
Henrie Amay. No further records appear to exist of any of
these members of the family, though the names might
furnish leads for further researches.

There is a bare possibility, however, that this Thomas
Harriots, illiterate though he was, might be related to the
more illustrious man of the same name. In his own will, the
mathematician Harriot mentions only two relatives. One of
them is 'John Harriotts, a servaunte to Mr. Doleman of Shaw
nere Newberry in Barkesheire ... but now married and
dwelling in Churchpeene about a Mile westward from the said
Shawe'. This John Harriotts, the will declares, is 'the sonne of
my uncle John Harriotts' who might conceivably have been
the brother of the Clifton blacksmith. Records of the
churches at Speen and Shaw, however, are of no help, since
the Speen Church records begin with 1629, and those of
Shaw Church with 1647. Neither of these shows any entries
of the name Harriot, except as a Christian name for young
ladies. It is still possible, however, that Oxford records still
unsearched might give additional information about Harriots
of the late sixteenth century, and reveal something about
Harriot's family and personal connections.

In choosing St. Mary's Hall for his education, Harriot made
a wise decision. As a Hall, St. Mary's offered greater academic
freedom during these years than did most of the more highly
organized Colleges. And as the largest and one of the oldest
of the Halls, it held standards of performance that were
eminently respectable. Part of this was due to its close connection with Oriel College. St. Mary's Hall, the former rectory
house of the Church of St. Mary the Virgin, had become
the property of Oriel when the church was appropriated by
Oriel in 1326. Bedel Hall was annexed in 1455, and St.
Martin's in 1503. By Harriot's time, all three Halls were
considered annexes to Oriel College, and their Principals
were traditionally fellows of Oriel. St. Mary's and Bedel
were united to house the St. Anthony and Dudley exhi-
bitioners of Oriel, and Martin Hall had become largely a

lecture hall with a few rooms for lodgers. Though records for this period are scanty, those that exist indicated that there were usually more members in St. Mary's Hall than in its senior foundation. In the year that 'Rawley's' name appears on the Oriel roster, 1572, Oriel recorded fifteen masters, four bachelors, and twenty-two undergraduate students. That same year, St. Mary's Hall listed two masters, ten bachelors, and thirty-four undergraduates.[19] Here, as in most similar cases, there seems a tendency for the members of the gentry and the sons of knights and nobles to be taken into the College, and the 'plebei filius' to be assimilated into the Hall.

Half a century after Harriot's death, Anthony à Wood attempted to explore Harriot's education. In 1671 he wrote:[20]

After he had been instructed in Grammar Learning within this City of his Birth, [Harriot] became either a Batler or Commoner in St. *Mary*'s Hall, wherein undergoing the severe Discipline then, and there, kept up by *Rich. Pygot* and *Thom. Philipson*, the Principals thereof, he took the degree of Bac. of Arts in 1579, and in the latter end of that Year did compleat it by *determination* in *Schoolstreet* . . .

At least in part, extant records bear out Wood's statements. Richard Pyggot and Thomas Philipson were the principals of St. Mary's Hall during Harriot's sojourn there, with Pyggot, the Principal who admitted him, and Philipson, the one who made recommendation for his degree. It may well have been one of these men, both of whom were at Oriel with Walter Ralegh, who introduced Harriot to his first patron. As C. S. Emden pointed out in his *Oriel Papers* in 1948:[21]

Richard Pigot, Fellow of Oriel, who is known to have been Henry Unton's tutor and who may have been Ralegh's too, was Principal of St. Mary Hall from 1570 to 1578, a period covering the residence of both the Untons and Ralegh at Oriel, and also the first year or two of Harriot's time at St. Mary Hall. What could be more natural than that Ralegh . . should turn to his old College, and in particular to one of its tutors, and ask who could be recommended as a resident tutor to improve his knowledge of mathematics and astronomy with a view to his qualifying himself to be a navigator? He may well have had further

[19] Clark, *Register*, II. ii. 39–40.
[20] *Athenae Oxonienses*, London, 1721 ed., cols. 459–60.
[21] *Oriel Papers*, Oxford, Clarendon Press, 1948, p. 19.

in mind the subsequent use of such a man of voyages of discovery. Pigot, or some other Oriel Fellow, would naturally reply: 'We have just had at St. Mary Hall the most brilliant young mathematician who has come our way for a long time. His name is Thomas Harriot.'

For this recommendation, Philipson might as well have served. Like Pyggot, he was Fellow in residence at Oriel during Ralegh's time there, and succeeded Pygott as Principal of St. Mary's Hall on Pyggot's retirement during Harriot's second year there. Whether either Pyggot or Philipson was tutor to Harriot cannot now be determined, since no records exist in the Oriel archives for this period. Nor do any records remain to attest to the academic interests or competencies of either of these Principals, since no books or manuscripts of the writings of either of them appear to have survived.

A little more of Harriot's undergraduate progress may be found in the Oxford Archives. Of the thirteen prospective scholars who were presented for matriculation with Harriot on 20 December 1579, only Harriot and two of his fellow students continued on to graduation. Like most of the students, Harriot resorted to 'supplications' to escape from the rigours of the statutory requirements for his degree. On 20 January 1579/80 Harriot submitted two supplications to 'the venerable congregation'.[22] The first (presenting the evidence that he had completed four years of studies of dialectics and was therefore among those created 'sophistæ generales') requested that he be permitted to serve as respondent during Lent only once rather than the mandatory two times, since a second response could not be done without great inconvenience ('causa est quia non sine maxima incommodo'). The second supplication, presented at the same time, requested that he be graduated with only one disputation in Lent (during the Hilary Term) in place of the required two. That these two supplications were approved by the congregation is shown by the entry of 12 February which lists 'Thomas Harriotes' as among those admitted to 'read in the faculty of arts' ('Admissiones ad lectionem alicuius libri facultatis artium'), which was the wording indicating candidacy for the bachelor's degree. 'Thomas Harriots' next appears on the list of candidates awarded the

---

[22] University of Oxford Archives, KK9, fo. 296^r (see Fig. 3).

Fig. 3 Harriot's Supplications

degree at the Easter Convocation. The actual ceremonies surrounding the issuing of the diplomas came, during these years, in mid July, in a day of gaiety, celebration, and homecoming which brought students, parents, and friends together in a mammoth celebration which taxed the housing and feeding services of the town. Since Harriot did not petition to be absent from this occasion, it must be assumed that he was in attendance to receive the degree which gave him the right to be called 'Master' Thomas Harriot for the rest of his life.

It is rather surprising that the only person we can be certain was one of Harriot's Oxford lecturers was the controversial Antonio Corano (or Antonius Coranus, or Antonio de Corro). Corano was 'lector catechismi' for St. Mary's Hall students during Harriot's residence there. The position of 'lector catechismi' had been established during the early 1570s by the Queen and Privy Council in an effort to stamp out Romanism in the Universities. Though formal subscription to the Thirty-Nine Articles was not required, emphasis on religious instruction had been strongly encouraged by the Chancellor for at least two decades.

Yet Harriot's 'lector catechismi' was noteworthy in that he was felt by the Oxford community to be himself of dubious orthodoxy. This was in part due to the unusual method of his appointment and may reflect a natural faculty reaction to administrative authority. But the story of Corano shows clearly that the Oxford of Harriot's day was close indeed to the universities of today.[23] Corano's Oxford connection began on 2 April 1576 when the Chancellor, Robert Dudley, Earl of Leicester, addressed a letter to the University Convocation in support of the application of a Spanish preacher of London for a doctor's degree in theology from Oxford. 'He is fit for the degree,' Leicester wrote, 'but he has not much money; and the degree is costly, expecially if he take the inferior degrees. Pray excuse him taking the degrees in order, and remit the fees of the Doctorate.'[24] This request aroused much discussion in the Convocation, and no action

---

[23] The story of Corano is told by Andrew Clark as an example of the animus existing against Catholics in the University of the time. See *Register*, I. ii. 153-7.

[24] Ibid. 153.

was taken at the meeting at which it was presented. A second meeting on the matter was held on 13 June and discussion centred on the question of the Anglican orthodoxy of a theologian educated on the Catholic continent, particularly one from Spain. This meeting concluded with the agreement that no degree could be considered unless Corano 'could bring testimonial letters [as to his orthodoxy] from Edmund Grindall, Archbishop of Canterbury and Edwin Sander, Bishop of London.'[25] These letters, if forthcoming, have been lost in the intervening centuries. But two years later, on 5 July 1578, the Convocation was still discussing the matter. At this session, Convocation named a committee to confer with Corano about his religious beliefs. Five days later Corano appeared in person before the Convocation, gave a statement of his beliefs, and offered to reside in the Oxford community for a period of up to six months so that they could observe by his life and actions that he was a sound and orthodox theologian.[26] It was at this time that Corano was given the post of 'lector catechismi' for his Oxford residency, and assigned to serve St. Mary's, Gloucester, and Hart Halls.

Four years later, after Harriot had graduated and left Oxford, Corano was still there, and still being ostracized by the University community. In May 1582 Leicester once more came to his defence. As summarized from the record by Andrew Clark:[27]

The Chancellor, writing from Court, 7 May 1582, said: —
'Rumours have been spread that Mr. Corano is detained prisoner. They are a mere slander. Corano wishes to purge himself of any charges against his doctrine or life, and I intend to hear him on 17 May. . . . Send here any charges you have against him, or any person who is willing to bring charges against him. If there is no clear accusation, let them bring even the cause why they suspect him. Send two or three of your body to hear his defence with me.'

To this letter, Dr. Withington, Vice-Chancellor, replied: — 'As regards Corano's doctrine, I never attended his lectures or disputations, and so have nothing to say. As regards his life and conversation, I know of no crime which can be charged against him or any of his family.

'On the advice of the heads of houses, I called a Convocation, read your letter, and asked any accuser or suspecter to come forward. Neither then nor since has any one appeared.'

[25] Ibid. 153–4.   [26] Ibid. 155.   [27] Ibid. 157.

Corano's name does not appear hereafter in the Oxford records.

Just what Harriot and his fellow students may have learned about theology from Antonio Corano remains open to conjecture. But it is highly possible that the ferment which surrounded his appointment as 'lector catechismi' during this formative period in these young men's lives may have contributed to their sensitivity to the religious scruples of the time, and may have made them more than normally reticent about discussing their private religious beliefs. Though Harriot, like both his patron-friends, Ralegh and Northumberland, later inspired gossip of unorthodox beliefs if not actual heresy, he carefully avoided any written philosophical pronouncements. Only once, late in life and suffering from his final illness, did he emulate his old 'lector' and express his 'articuli fidei orthodoxae' in a restrained and gentle fashion.[28]

Though there are no contemporary records to substantiate the fact, later evidence indicates a very high probability that Harriot's intellectual development was most influenced during his undergraduate years by two Oxford professors not members of St. Mary's Hall. These were two stimulating but slightly maverick members of the faculty, Richard Hakluyt of Christ Church and Thomas Allen of Gloucester Hall. As we shall see, from his graduation to his death Harriot remained close friends of both men.

Richard Hakluyt (1552–1616) was eight years older than Harriot, and was finishing his formal education about the time Harriot was starting his. But this end of his schooling was the beginning of his real career as a geographer and recorder of voyages and explorations, in which Harriot was an active collaborator. Undoubtedly this common interest brought the two together. According to his own account,

---

[28] In 1574 Corano published *Diologus Theologicus. Quo Epistola Divi Pauli Apostoli ad Romanos Explanatur*, London, Thomæ Purfætij ad Lucretiæ symbolum, 1574, which includes (pp. 96–107) a profession of his own beliefs: *ARTICVLI FIDEI Orthodoxæ quam Antonius CORRANVS HISPALENSIS SACRAE THEOLOGIAE STVDIOSAS profitur semperque professus est ...*

The rough draft of Harriot's letter to his physician, Mayerne, is to be found in BL Add. MS 6789, fo. 446[V]. It has been translated in part and reported in Jean Jacquot's 'Thomas Hariot's Reputation for Impiety', *Notes and Records of the Royal Society of London*, IX. 2 (May 1952), 169. See Ch. XI.

Hakluyt determined on a career in geography and exploration in the 1560's while still at school when he visited his elder cousin of the same name in his rooms in the Middle Temple. There the younger Richard saw his cousin's books on Cosmography, his collection of maps, and was led to reflect on the words of the 107th Psalm that those who go down to the sea in ships see the wonders of the Lord. As he reported:[29]

Which words of the Prophet together with my cousins discourse (things of high and rare delight to my young nature) tooke in me so deepe an impression, that I constantly resolued, if euer I were preferred to the Vniuersity, where better time, and more conuenient place might be ministred for these studies, I would by Gods assistance prosecute that knowledge and kinde of literature. . . . According to which my resolution, when, not long after, I was removed to Christ-church in Oxford, my exercises of duety first performed, I fell to my intended course, and by degrees read ouer whatsoeuer printed or written discoueries and voyages I found extant . . . and in my publike lectures was the first, that produced and shewed both the olde imperfectly composed, and the new lately reformed Mappes, Globes, Spheares, and other instruments of this Art for demonstration in the common schooles, to the singular pleasure and general contentment of my auditory. . . .

Though there has been a difference of opinion as to when Hakluyt lectured at Oxford and to whom the lectures were addressed,[30] Hakluyt's own comments above, taken with the Oxford practice of the time, make this matter clear. Hakluyt indicates that his 'publike lectures' followed his 'exercises of duety'. By long tradition at Oxford, all inceptors as Masters of Art were proclaimed regent-masters, and were committed to deliver the ordinary lectures ('Lectiones Ordinariae') for a two-year period thereafter. Before the establishment of the Regius Professorships, this was the only source for University lectures.[31] The regent-masters were also required to preside over the ordinary disputations in Arts, and though both the lectures and the disputations were normally held in the College of the regent-master, they were open to all members of the University at the proper state of academic development.

[29] Richard Hakluyt, *Principall Navigations*, 1589. Dedication 'To the Right Honorable Sir Francis Walsingham, Knight', sig. 2ʳ.

[30] See David B. Quinn, ed., *The Hakluyt Handbook*, London, The Hakluyt Society, 1974, vol. I, pp. 267–8, for a brief review of this question.

[31] Clark, *Register*, II. i. 95–101.

Hakluyt matriculated in Christ Church in 1570, probably during the Christmas term, and was determined BA at Easter 1574.[32] He immediately proceeded toward the MA, supplicated for the degree in May 1577, was licensed on 27 June, and incorporated during the ceremonies of the July 1577 Act. It was, then, at this time that Hakluyt had performed his 'exercises of duety' and became a senior member of his College and a regent-master. His teaching term as required (though it might be extended) would have started with the Michaelmas Term 1577 and extended through to the end of the Hilary Term 1579. His 'publike lectures' would have followed in the Michaelmas Term 1579, and these lectures involving the new geography would have coincided with the undergraduate years of Thomas Harriot.[33]

Just when Hakluyt's association with the practitioners of navigation and exploration began is not known. But by 1584 he had been engaged by Ralegh to write a prospectus for colonization in the new world, the manuscript of which has been since printed as *Discourse of Western Planting*.[34] Two years later, in early August 1586, he was present with Thomas Harriot to take the deposition of a sailor brought by Drake from Saint Augustine.[35] It was also Richard Hakluyt who first brought to public attention the mathematical role played by the young Harriot in navigation and exploration in 1587,[36] who reprinted his *Briefe and True Report* in his *Principall Navigations* in 1589, and who was instrumental in getting it published in several languages with the John

[32] From the Hakluyt Chronology, *Hakluyt Handbook*, I. 266–8.

[33] The materials existing for his instruction are detailed in G. R. Crone, 'Richard Hakluyt, Geographer', in *Hakluyt Handbook*, I. 8–14.

[34] For Hakluyt's associations with Ralegh and Harriot see D. B. Quinn, 'North America', in *The Hakluyt Handbook*, I. 224–53.

[35] David B. Quinn, *The Roanoke Voyages*, 2 vols., London, The Hakluyt Society, 1955, vol. II, pp. 763–6.

[36] In the Preface to the 1587 edition of *De Orbe Novo Petri Martyris Angleri Mediolanensis*, sig. Aiiij, Hakluyt wrote: 'By your experience in navigation you clearly saw that our highest glory as an insular kingdom would be built up to its greatest splendour on a firm foundation of the mathematical sciences, and so for a long time you have nourished in your household, with a most liberal salary, a young man well trained in those studies, Thomas Harriot; so that under his guidance you might in spare hours learn those noble sciences and your collaborating sea captains, who are many, might very profitably unite theory and practice, not without almost incredible results . . .'

White illustrations in the scholarly editions of 1590, to Harriot's obvious delight.[37]

According to all contemporary accounts, Hakluyt was an outgoing individual who developed wide acquaintanceships among the foremost persons in the world of navigation and exploration. He apparently gathered friends and disciples as avidly as he gathered maps and manuscripts. That he would have attracted an imaginative student like Harriot during these Oxford years seems an obvious probability. What Hakluyt, just beginning his professional career, lacked in experience he made up for by his enthusiasm and commitment, and some of this must have rubbed off on the impressionable young Harriot. Hakluyt, Ralegh, Harriot — it was inevitable that they would get together, and it is likely that the catalyst would have been Hakluyt. The chances that he brought Harriot to Ralegh's attention are at least as great as that the St. Mary's Principals, Pyggot or Philipson, may have done so.

A second faculty member who also undoubtedly influenced Harriot as an undergraduate was Thomas Allen of Gloucester Hall. In many ways, Allen is a puzzling character, quiet and retiring, withdrawn from the busyness that surrounds a University, but at the same time a popular teacher, a welcome guest on Gaudy Days, and a close personal friend of the Chancellor. Ten years older than Hakluyt and eighteen years Harriot's senior, Allen had left his Trinity fellowship to assume the retired quiet of individual study in Gloucester Hall the same year that Hakluyt arrived as a first-year student. In Gloucester Hall, Allen's duties were minimal and he was left free to follow his own inclination in mathematics, astronomy, and the new sciences, none of which was popular among the Oxford faculty of the day. He filled his lodgings with the latest scientific instruments, studied ancient and modern astronomy, cast horoscopes, and collected around him most of the aspiring young mathematicians of the University. As Anthony à Wood described him:[38] 'His sufficiencies in the Mathematical Sciences being generally

[37] See David B. Quinn and John W. Shirley, 'A Contemporary List of Hariot References', *Renaissance Quarterly*, XXII. 1 (Spring 1969), 9–26.

[38] *Athenæ Oxonienses, 1721*, col. 575.

noted, he was thereupon accounted another *Rog. Bacon*, which was the Reason why he became terrible to the Vulgar, especially those in Oxon., who took him to be a perfect Conjuerer.' It is likely that Wood got this view from John Aubrey, who wrote of Allen:[39]

In those dark times astrologer, mathematician, and conjurer, were accounted the same things; and the vulgar did verily beleeve [Allen] to be a conjurer. He had a great many mathematicall instruments and glasses in his chamber, which did also confirme the ignorant in their opinion, and his servitor (to impose on freshmen and simple people) would tell them that sometimes he should meet the spirits comeing up his staires like bees .

But Allen's reputation extended far beyond the gossip of the Oxford vulgar. Wood insists that Leicester offered him a bishopric which he declined to continue his life of retired contemplation in Oxford. He is also supposed to have taken Allen to court to explain to Elizabeth the new theories about the blazing star which had appeared in Cassiopeia in 1572. It was rumoured in 1583 that Count Albertus Laski had offered Allen a pension at his Polish estate at Sirade. And he is even supposed to have been offered by the scholarly 'Wizard' 9th Earl of Northumberland a pension similar to that later offered to Harriot. As Wood tells it, Allen[40]

... was also courted to live in the Family of that most noble and generous Count *Henry* Earl of *Northumberland*, a great Patron of Mathematicians; whereupon spending some time with him, he was infinitely beloved and admired not only by that Count, but by such Artists who then lived with, or often retired to him, as *Tho: Harriot, John Dee, Walt. Warner, Nath. Torporley,* Ec, the *Atlantes* of the Mathematical World . .

Certainly Allen made friends widely. Dr John Reynolds, President of Corpus Christi College who was at Gloucester Hall with Allen,[41]

... sayes that Mr. Allen was a very cheerful, facetious man, and that every body loved his company, and every howse of their *Gaudie-dayes*

[39] Andrew Clark, ed., *'Brief Lives,' chiefly of Contemporaries, set down by John Aubrey, between the Years 1669 & 1696,* 2 vols., Oxford, Clarendon Press, 1898. This passage from vol. I, p. 27.

[40] *Athenæ Oxonienses, 1721,* col. 575.

[41] Clark, *Brief Lives,* I. 27. This portrait is now in the Bodleian Annex.

were wont to invite him . . . His picture was drawne at the request of Dr. Ralph Kettle, and hangs in the dining roome of the President of Trin. Coll. Oxon . . . by which it appears that he was a handsome, sanguine man, and of an excellent habit of bodie . . .

Allen also attracted scholarly friends through his love for acquiring books and manuscripts. He had one of the outstanding collections of antiquarian and early mathematics books of his day, and furnished many books to young scholars which were not available in the formal libraries of the colleges or the university. Many of the notable manuscripts now in the Bodleian were gifts of Thomas Allen during his lifetime, or a posthumous gift from him through his executor, Sir Kenelm Digby. Allen also gave a large number of his books to Trinity College Library when it was renovated in 1624, and in his will left a large number more to that establishment.

When the University began to rebuild its collections through the efforts of Thomas Bodley, Thomas Allen was one of the stalwarts supporting the effort. He was a charter member of the Oxford committee first named as administrative overseers of the new venture, and when the committee was replaced by Delegates on 13 April 1602, Allen remained as a member, and was active for the remainder of his life. It is most likely that it was he who approached the 9th Earl of Northumberland and Sir Walter Ralegh for contributions in 1603, receiving donations of £100 and £50 respectively from them.[42] It was certainly he who solicited assistance from Thomas Harriot. A letter from Sir Thomas Bodley to Thomas James, the first Bodleian Keeper, dated 4 June 1601, includes the following:[43]

I thanke you for writing to those your other friendes whom you nominated: but Doctor Philip Bisse, among the rest, hath bestowed already ten poundes. Mr Heriot had been spoken withall by Mr Allen, before your letter came to me: and to day or to morrowe, I shall receaue his gifte: which I thinke will be greater for the qualitie then quantity . . .

[42] G. K. Wheeler, ed., *Letters of Sir Thomas Bodley to Thomas James, first Keeper of the Bodleian Library*, Oxford, Clarendon Press, 1926. Letter 78, dated London, 5 Apr. [1603].
[43] Ibid., Letter 3.

64 Thomas Harriot: A Biography

What that last phrase means can only be conjectured, but Bodleian records (which list only major gifts of money or books) do not indicate any contribution by Harriot of size or quantity deserving comment or commendation.

Another evidence of continued friendship between Allen and Harriot is contained in a letter to Harriot dated from Gloucester Hall on 27 July 1608. A student there, Alexander Lower, youngest brother of Harriot's close friend, Sir William Lower, Member of Parliament from Cornwall, wrote a letter of gratitude to his 'Clarissime Domine' in which he sends greetings from two of his best Oxford friends, 'Dominus Alesbury' (later to be one of Harriot's Executors) and 'Dominus Allen'.[44]

It might be argued that it was unlikely that Harriot, a student in St. Mary's Hall, and Allen, a scholar in Gloucester Hall, would be acquainted. But this ignores the fact that Oxford in the 1570s was still an intimate community. Though records are by no means complete, fortunately they appear to be almost totally available for the year in which Harriot matriculated. During December 1577 260 students matriculated in all the Halls and Colleges of Oxford. Between the first of the year and the following August, another 107 were enrolled. And in the Michaelmas term of 1578, ninety-one more entered. This gives a total of 458 students entered, and since the average tenure was much less than two years by all accounts, it is obvious that the total student enrolment at any one time was less than 1,000 undergraduates.[45] In a group of this size, it is most probable that a student of the acknowledged genius of young Harriot, even though he was a plebeian, would have quickly learned of the distinguished teachers on the faculty and would have sought their lectures and their company. The cheerful and gregarious Allen, too, was known to gather bright young students around him. Certainly the 'Roger Bacon' of his day and the young student called by Christopher Hill 'Oxford's solitary mathematician of eminence until the arrival of Briggs'[46] would have attracted each other like two of William Gilbert's magnets, and would

[44] Bodleian MS Clarendon 1, fo. 54r.
[45] These figures are compiled from Clark's *Register*, II. ii.
[46] *Intellectual Origins*, p. 310.

have clung together for the lives of their mathematical souls, as they apparently did.

Since Oxford University, though relatively small, attracted a large proportion of the extremely able or ambitious young men as well as those seeking culture and courtly manners, it is not surprising that Harriot probably became acquainted here with many of those whom he considered his close friends for the remainder of his life. Harriot's friends, naturally, were those primarily interested in mathematics and science as they applied to the expanded new world of his time, and they would, like Harriot, fall into the student circles surrounding Hakluyt and Allen, and would follow actions stemming from their lead in later life.

Two of Harriot's closest friends and associates — Robert Hues and Walter Warner — later to be associated with Harriot as the 'Three Magi' of the 'Wizard' 9th Earl of Northumberland, were already studying at Oxford when Harriot matriculated. Robert Hues, eldest of the three, was the first to enter the Oxford community, though he came in somewhat through the back door. As Anthony à Wood tells the story:[47]

... at his first coming to the University he was only a poor Scholar or Servitor of *Brazen-nose*, and among the *pauperes Scholares* is he numbered in the public *Matricula* under *Coll. Aenean.* about 1571. In that House he continued for some time a very sober and serious Student, and was countenanced by one or more of the Seniors thereof, but being sensible of the loss of time which he sustained there by constant attendance, he translated himself to *S. Mary's Hall*, and took the degree of Bac. of Arts at about 7 Years standing [c.1578], being then noted for a good *Grecian* ...

If this account is accurate, and there is no reason to doubt it, Hues was a student at St. Mary's Hall during Harriot's first two years there. They may even have shared the same tutor, since both were extremely interested in geography and navigation, and Harriot, like Hues, was known in his own time as 'a good Grecian'. As a matter of fact, it was to these two men that George Chapman submitted portions of his translation of Homer in 1611 for their review of his accuracy, though there is little evidence among the Harriot manuscripts that he maintained this early interest.

[47] *Athenæ Oxonienses, 1721*, I, col. 571.

In all probability, Hues, like his friends, was taken into the Ralegh–Hakluyt circle in the early 1580s. Certainly he knew Cavendish during the time of his travels to the New World in 1584 and 1585, worked with him in preparation for his circumnavigation of the globe, travelled with him around the world in 1586 to 1588, and was, from that time on, associated with Harriot and his mathematical and scientific friends.

Walter Warner, too, was a classmate of Hues at Oxford, and may have met Harriot there. Though John Pell, Warner's youthful collaborator in later years, thought that Warner was 'of no university',[48] and Anthony à Wood could find no record of him in the Oxford archives,[49] both men missed an item in the official records. Volume KK9 of the Archives shows that 'Gualterus Warner' was determinant in 1578/9 at the same convocation with Thomas Wright, Anthony Shirley, and Robert Hues. That this was the same Walter Warner who was later servant to Northumberland is not absolutely certain, but neither the name Walter nor Warner is especially common in Elizabethan times, and it would certainly be an odd coincidence if two men of this same combination were to appear as associates in a group of such close-knit interests. If Harriot did know Warner at Oxford, he must have found him to be, like Hues, almost a decade older, but this was not unusual with the wide divergence of ages in entering students in that day.

Another eminent Grecian, George Chapman, the poet, may have known both Harriot and Hues at Oxford, and may have shared their Greek tutor. Anthony à Wood was not certain whether Chapman was first at Cambridge or Oxford, though 'sure I am that he spent some time in Oxon, where he was observed to be most excellent in the Latin and Greek tongues',[50] though he evidently did not graduate. Warton, in his *History of English Poetry*, says (without giving any authority) that Chapman spent two years at Trinity College, Oxford.[51] But the fact that Chapman wrote dedicatory or

---

[48] Clark, *Brief Lives*, II. 293.
[49] *Athenæ Oxonienses, 1721*, I, col. 461.
[50] Ibid., col. 592.
[51] See the biography of Chapman in *DNB* IV. 27.

commendatory poems to Harriot, Keymis, and Royden, and was about the same age as all three gives some credence to the possibility that he, too, was an Oxford student during the same years.

Besides Chapman, two other men destined for literary success, were at Oxford when Harriot arrived, and were undoubtedly his friends during their undergraduate years. George Peele, who had been admitted BA in June 1577 continued on for the degree of MA, for which he was studying while Harriot was at St. Mary's Hall. Fourteen years later he was commissioned to write a poem on the occasion of the gartering of Henry Percy, 9th Earl of Northumberland. Walter Warner, Percy's servant, carried the 40s. reward to Peele. And Harriot, at this same time received his first grant of funds from the 'Wizard Earl' who was shortly to become his patron.

Matthew Royden, too, was a contemporary of Harriot at Oxford. Though details of his undergraduate college are missing from the records, he was studying for his MA while Harriot was in St. Mary's Hall. Royden supplicated for his Master's on 6 July 1580, was licensed the next day, and was incorporated at the midsummer convocation following the Easter Harriot received his degree. That Harriot, Warner, and Royden were friends is attested by the testimony in the trial of Christopher Marlowe for atheism in May 1593, just before his death. Richard Baines (who matriculated in St. John's three years after Harriot's graduation) is recorded as having testified that 'Moyses was but a Jugler, & that one Heriots being Sir W. Raleghs man can do more than he.' Baines also insisted that Marlowe not only held atheistic views himself, but in 'almost every company he cometh he perswades men to Atheism.'[52] Another poet, Thomas Kyd, was tarred by this brush, though he insisted that his friends could attest to the fact that it was Marlowe, not he, who preached atheism. As he wrote to Sir John Pickering, Keeper of the Great Seal:[53] '. . . for more assurance that I was not of that vile opinion, lett it but please your Lordship to enquire such as he conversed with all, that is (as I am geven

[52] BL Harley 6848, fos. 185-6.
[53] BL Harley 6849, fos. 218-19.

to vnderstand) with Harriot, Warner, Royden, and some stationers in Paules Churchyard.' Evidently Harriot did enjoy strolling in Paul's Churchyard for the gossip, for it was there in 1611 that John Chamberlain sought him out to get news of the 9th Earl.[54]

Nathaniel Torporley, the other mathematician frequently associated with the 'Three Magi' and Harriot's literary executor, just missed being at Oxford with Harriot. He matriculated at the age of seventeen in Christ Church on 17 November 1581, was determined BA at the Easter convocation of 1583/4, and continued on to the MA which he received on 8 July 1591. Torporley was a student at Oxford during all the years that Harriot was in Ralegh's household and most active in his navigational and explorational efforts.

Lawrence Keymis, who played such a tragic role in Ralegh's ill-fated voyage to Guiana in 1617/18, has long been thought to have been an Oxford student with Harriot. This is based on the account of Anthony à Wood:[55] 'LAWRENCE KEYMIS . . . became a Student in *Bal.* Coll. in 1579, aged sixteen or thereabouts . . . took the Degrees in Arts, that of Master being compleated in 1586, at which time he was well read in Geography and Mathematics . . .' This is, however, another case in which Wood failed to find the proper Oxford records. According to the Matriculation Register, 'Laurence Kemyshe of Wiltshire' enrolled at age 17 in Balliol College on 2 May 1581, more than a year after Harriot had graduated. Keymis received his BA during the Easter convocation of 1583/4, and his MA on 10 June 1586.[56] By the time that Keymis left Oxford, Harriot was well established in Ralegh's household, had spent his year in the New World, and was returning to England, and then to Ireland to become one of the colonists on Ralegh's Irish estates. Their friendship must have begun after this time, though it is probable that Keymis and Torporley, both students at the same time and of similar interests, were acquainted before joining the Ralegh-Northumberland circle.

[54] Norman E. McClure, ed., *The Letters of John Chamberlain*, 2 vols., Philadelphia, The American Philosophical Society, 1939. See vol. I, p. 318.

[55] *Athenæ Oxonienses, 1721*, col. 433.

[56] Clark, *Register*, II. ii. 97; II. iii. 116.

At the end of his life, on his deathbed dying of what must have been a most painful cancer of the inner passages of the nose, Harriot still had Oxford in his thoughts. As he drafted his final will and testament, he thought of his old Oxford friend, Thomas Allen of Gloucester Hall. He wrote:[57]

Item. I doe acknowledge that I have some written Coppies to the number of twelue or fowerteene (more or lesse) lent vnto mee by Thomas Allen of Gloster Hall in Oxford, Master of Artes vnto whom I desire my Executors hereafter named to restore them safely according to the noate that hee shall deliuer of them (I doubtinge whether I have anie true noate of them my selfe) . . .

It is probably this memory of Allen that recalled to Harriot the efforts to rebuild the Bodleian Library and his pledge of support for the venture. Following all other requests, he closes his will: 'Lastly my will and desire is that they [the executors] bestowe the value of the rest [of my estate] vppon Sir Thomas Bodleyes Library in Oxford, or imploy it to such Charitable and pious vses as they shall thincke best . . .' The memorial plaque which the 9th Earl of Northumberland caused to be placed near his grave in the chancel of the Parish Church of St. Christopher le Stocks (recently re-installed in the lobby of the Bank of England) again bears testimony to the affinity between Harriot and Oxford.

THOMAE HARRIOTI	THOMAS HARRIOT
Hic fuit Doctissimus ille Harriotus	He was that most learned man
de Syon ad Flumen Thamesin,	of Syon on the River Thames
Patria & educatione	By birth and by education
Oxoniensis.	An Oxonian.

[57] Two registered copies of Harriot's will are housed in the Guildhall Library, London.

III. Harriot with Ralegh, 1580–1585

Young Thomas Harriot had just turned twenty when he left Oxford to enter into the life of London. He was beginning the most exciting and eventful period of his life. Armed with the basic classical education of the gentleman of his age, a natural genius in mathematics, a native ingenuity and creative imagination, together with a warm personal attractiveness, Harriot was to move actively into the highest circles of politics and society of his day, to explore personally the uncharted lands of the new world and to move among savage peoples undreamed of by earlier generations, and to participate in the intellectually exciting realms of the dawn of scientific investigation and expanding commerce and industry.

London under Elizabeth I was a seething, dynamic society. Not only was it England's largest city, comparable in size and complexity with most other major European cities, but it was also the political, cultural, and intellectual centre of the island kingdom. Here was the brilliant Tudor court with the Virgin Queen and her sophisticated retinue of suitors and admirers on daily display; here were the officers of government, the lords and members of parliament; here were the Inns of Court — training ground for diplomatic or governmental functionaries, developers of gentlemen and hangers-on in courtly circles; here also were gathered the poets and historians, the actors and dramatists, the bear-baiters and goldsmiths, and at least 100,000 robust and hearty citizens supplying the services and necessities of life for England's humming metropolis.

Much of the bustle and activity of the city was centred on the river which dominated the heart of the London area. The Thames was the major thoroughfare for both people and material goods, the link between sections of the city, between London and England, and between London and the world. Into its waters came the wealth of nations, through commerce, or through piracy and plunder. On the banks of the Thames were concentrations of church and state, homes of the principal nobles, and the growing centres of commerce and industry which were for the first time in history beginning to make England a world power. Into this world of commerce, exploration, colonial expansion, piracy, and political intrigue in the early 1580s came Oxford-educated Harriot seeking his fortune. It is a real tribute to his memory to record that within a half-dozen years he had established himself there as one of the leaders in the programmes of expansion into the new world, and had become recognized by leading governmental figures as one of the most shrewd and knowledgeable members of the dynamic generation contemplating a whole new world of promise for the future, seeking unheard-of riches from the fabulous empires of the Indies and Cathay. Harriot had become a part of the day-to-day operating world of the pioneers of these grand dreams, a friend of the most advanced cartographers and geographers, associate of the most daring sea captains, involved with the most powerful and plotting members of Elizabeth's privy council, and the closest friend and associate of the most dashing courtier of the Queen's inner circle — young Walter Ralegh, guardian of her bed chamber and closest confidant of her hopes and aspirations for England. This was a heady life for a young man just out of his teens with a plebeian background so common that no record exists of his parentage or family background.

Just how Harriot came to move from Oxford to London remains a matter for conjecture. But certainly London, the hub of Elizabethan England, held an irresistible attraction for an ambitious young man. And it is almost certain that Richard Hakluyt, whose interests, friendships, and activities almost exactly paralleled Harriot's, had some part in his decision. More than most of the Oxford fellows, Hakluyt saw London as the focus of his interest in the navigation, exploration, and conquest of the seas which would fulfil his ambitions for his nation. He saw clearly that if England were to rival and outstrip Portugal and Spain for mastery of the sea lanes, she must move quickly to upgrade the competence of her seamen and bring their skills and tools up to the level already achieved by her continental rivals. The late E. G. R. Taylor suggested that Thomas Harriot might have been Hakluyt's companion when he met with Alderman Barnes, Governor of the Muscovy Company, to explore the establishment of a lectureship in London for the training of sea captains in the use of new and improved charts, instruments, and sailing methods. England's great naval hero, Sir Francis Drake, on his return in December 1580 from his three-year circumnavigation of the globe had declared such a training programme was essential; Drake had agreed to furnish the newest navigational instruments and to contribute £20 a year for the support of such a London lectureship. Perhaps Harriot was introduced to Drake as a candidate for such a post, but it has also been suggested that one of Harriot's Oxford friends (either Walter Warner or Nathaniel Torporley, though the latter had not yet graduated) may also have been considered.[1]

Professor Quinn has suggested that Harriot might have been taken into the household of a young gentleman aspiring to a career on the sea. As he has surmised:[2]

It is not unlikely that [Harriot] entered the household of some gentleman or merchant who had need of a tutor for his children. One might speculate on the possibility that wherever he settled it was in the company of men who were interested not in theory but in practice, in the problems of applying mathematics to such questions as navigation at sea, in the expansion of trade, and in the extension of knowledge about the world outside Europe. Such matters were being discussed in London in the years 1580 to 1583 and at the end of them Harriot emerges as a man who is vitally concerned with them.

Quinn even produces a candidate for this possible employer of young Harriot: a young man-about-town, Maurice Browne, who wrote of his plans, and those of his close friend John

[1] E. G. R. Taylor, *The Original Writings & Correspondence of the Two Richard Hakluyts*, 2 vols., London, The Hakluyt Society, 1935. For the account of this lectureship, see vol. I, pp. 23–5.

[2] David B. Quinn, 'Thomas Harriot and the New World', Ch. 3 in *Thomas Harriot, Renaissance Scientist*, ed. John W. Shirley, Oxford, Clarendon Press, 1974. This passage is from pp. 36–7.

Thynne, to seek such a tutor. It was Browne's idea to 'apply my time to the studdy of Cosmography, and the art of Navigatione', declaring that he and John Thynne 'will device to have somme convenient tyme ... to have an excellent fellow who dwelleth here at London to read Cosmography and to instruct us and to make us learned in the art of Navigation', in order that 'with the more easines we may come to the full knowledge thereof by experience.'[3] There is no evidence whether this 'excellent fellow' was Harriot or some other young man of similar quality, but certainly this declaration goes to show the kind of tutoring position that an Oxford graduate might have drifted into.

There is also a possibility that Harriot might have used his Oxford connections to open a private school in London for instruction in the theory and practice of mathematics. During these particular years a large number of such small schools were springing up to meet the demands of the rising merchant class and ambitious seamen for such instruction. Most of them were located in the vicinity of St. Paul's Cathedral. As early as 1543 one Hugh Oldcastle had settled in Mark Lane in Saint Olave's parish to teach arithmetic and the new and exciting casting of accounts.[4] Humphrey Baker, another self-taught arithmetician who dabbled in astrology and horoscopes on the side, had opened his house 'on the north side of the Royal Exchange, next adjoining to the sign of the Ship' to tutor children and apprentices in all aspects of the practical arts.[5] John Mellis soon followed suit, opening his home at 'Mayes gate nie Battle bridge in S. Ollaues parish in Short Southwarke, where, god to friend, they shall fine me readie to accomplish their desire [to learn handwriting, reading, arithmetic, and accounts] in as short time as may be.'[6] As a matter of fact, by 1580 such private instruction had become so popular that foreign teachers were settling in London, making claims of techniques and methods

---

[3] Ibid., p. 37.

[4] Hugh Oldcastle, *A briefe instruction how to keepe bookes of accompts* [London], 1588 (STC 18794), sig. A3r.

[5] Cited as from 'the edition of 1562' by Foster Watson, *Beginnings of the teaching of Modern Subjects in England*, London, 1909, p. 321.

[6] Hugh Oldcastle, *A Briefe Instruction and maner hovv to keepe bookes of Accompts*, Revised by John Mellis, London, 1588 (not in STC), sig. A3r.

superior to those of their British competitors and stirring up
nationalistic feelings. As Humphrey Baker wrote in 1580:[7]

I perceyued the importunitie of certayne straungers not borne within
this lande, at this present, and of later dayes so farre proceeding, that
they advanced and extolied [*sic*] them selues in open talke and
writinges, that they had attayned such knowledge and perfection in
Arithmetike, as no english man the like . . . For vnto this same effecte
they haue of late paynted the corners and postes in euery place within
this citie with their peeuishe billes, making promise and bearinge men
in hande that they could teache the summe of that Science in breefe
Methode and compendious rules such as before their arriuall hath not
been taughte within this Realme.

When Harriot graduated from Oxford, though competition
was keen in London among private schoolmen, the demand
for such instruction was growing even more rapidly. Had he
had the desire, Harriot could easily have established himself
among these private teachers; his Oxford degree granted him
better credentials for calling himself 'Master' (as he did
throughout his life) than the vast majority of such competition.[8]

Yet it seems to me that there is one other possible employment, not suggested heretofore, which may have taken Harriot
to London and into the thick of the mathematical application
to the growing complexities of navigation and cartography
which so concerned Richard Hakluyt. Just at this time
Hakluyt was recognizing the full impact of recent failures
arising from faulty navigation. The lack of success of three
of the voyages of Frobisher and of Sir Humphrey Gilbert's
enterprise of 1578-9, had convinced him that more serious
and systematic training must become part of the English
tradition if England were ever to achieve mastery of the
seas. It is at least possible that Hakluyt may have introduced
his young protégé to one of the most outstanding of his
friends, Sir Humphrey Gilbert, just as he had introduced
another young Oxford student, Stephen Parmenius, to him
during these years when he was working closely with Gilbert

[7] *The Well spring of Sciences*, 1580 edn. (STC 1211), sig. Avj^r-Avj^v.
[8] While Master John Dee did not teach in any such school directly, he did
'augment and improve' some of the texts used, particularly Robert Recorde's
Grounde of artes which went through at least fifteen editions in the century
following its first publication in 1542.

on the controversial north-west passage to the Orient.[9] Had he done so, there is no question but that they would immediately have been attracted to each other.

Sir Humphrey Gilbert (1539–83), elder half-brother of Walter Ralegh by fourteen years, was one of the most loyal and dynamic, though unpredictable, of Elizabeth's followers. Originally a royal ward of Princess Elizabeth before her accession and possibly, like her, a student of Roger Ascham,[10] following his education at Eton and Oxford, Gilbert had devoted his life and total resources to the study of navigation and the art of war. So loyal to the Queen and so protective of her rights was he that he frequently was an outspoken enemy of Spain, declaring her a national enemy, to the point where he was censured by his fellows in parliament. Two of his tracts, *A discourse of a discoverie for a new passage to Cataia [Cathay]* (published surreptitiously by George Gascoigne in 1576) and *A discourse how hir Majestie may annoy the king of Spayne* in 1577,[11] had established his reputation both as a proponent of the existence of a north-west passage and as a seaman willing to commit piracy on any Spanish vessel he might encounter. Though Gilbert repeatedly petitioned the Queen for a royal charter to seek the north-west passage during the 1560s, no such permission was granted. Frobisher and Michael Lok were granted permission to explore both the north-east and north-west passages instead, and it was not until 11 June 1578 that Gilbert was honoured with a charter for discovery, establishment of a colony, and base of operations in the new world for which he was authorized to be governor. The fact that no royal authority was given Gilbert until he had revealed his proposal to use a false colony for embarrassing Spain has led modern historians to suspect that his search for a passage to the orient was primarily a cover for his piracy. But the very real interest of both John Dee and Richard

[9] David B. Quinn and Neil M. Cheshire, eds., *The New Found Land of Stephen Parmenius*, University of Toronto Press, 1972, pp. 19–22.

[10] Donald B. Chidsey, *Sir Humphrey Gilbert: Elizabeth's Racketeer*, New York, Harpers, 1932. See Ch. III, pp. 10–18; also p. 95.

[11] David B. Quinn, ed., *The Voyages and Colonising Enterprises of Sir Humphrey Gilbert*, London, The Hakluyt Society, 1940. See Doc. 15 (I. 129–65); Doc. 22 (I. 170–5).

Hakluyt in these voyages gives more credence to the fact that Gilbert was seriously interested in the navigational exploration of the boundaries of the new world.[12]

Immediately upon receipt of his royal patent, Gilbert began to prepare for a large-scale expedition of discovery and the collection of men and materials to be used for colonization. Just what his plans were is not certain: his charter grant was vague and comprehensive. For six years it gave him full authority to[13] 'discover searche finde out and viewe such remote heathen and barbarous landes countries and territories not actually possessed of any Christian prince or people as to him . . . shall seme good And the same to have hould occupie and enjoye to him his heires and assignes forever. . .' But the Spanish ambassador, Don Bernardino de Mendoza, remained certain that this was merely another piratical expedition; he wrote to Philip II that he understood that Gilbert's 'design is to go and rob on the Indies route of your Majesty.'[14] As a good representative of his King, Mendoza did all he could to interfere with Gilbert's preparations. Though planned for late spring, it was not until late September that Gilbert had been able to assemble his fleet of eleven ships, 500 men, with their necessary supplies and provisions, ready for embarkation at Dartmouth. Gilbert himself commanded the *Anne Aucher* named after Lady Gilbert; the vice-admiral, the *Hope of Greenway*, was under the command of one half-brother, Carew Ralegh; and the vessel contributed to the expedition by Queen Elizabeth, the 100-ton *Falcon*, piloted by the Portuguese Simão Fernandez, was under the command of his younger half-brother, Walter Ralegh. The presence of Fernandez and the fact that Elizabeth was supporting the enterprise gave added support to the theory that the object was piracy, since it was well known that the Queen was always eager for Spanish gold, but not really interested in either exploration or colonial efforts.[15] Pessimists still were predicting failure since the admiral, Gilbert, and his two major commanders,

---

[12] Taylor, *Original Writings*, I. 12–13.
[13] Quinn, *Voyages . . . of Sir Humphrey Gilbert*, Doc. 28 (I. 188–94).
[14] Ibid., Doc. 25 (I. 186); see also Docs. 26 and 27.
[15] Chidsey, op. cit., p. 131.

his half-brothers, were all taking to sea together for the first time.

Difficulties there were. The late sailing, on 26 September took them to sea at a time of frightful gales. Before it really got under way, the fleet was dispersed, and it was nearly a month before it was able to reassemble at the Isle of Wight. Again it sailed on 29 October and again it was forced back — this time to the port at Plymouth. Once more it set sail; once more it proceeded to the Isle of Wight, thence to the coast of Ireland, and where it went from there is still not known. Richard Hakluyt, who spent most of his life recording the glorious navigational feats of British sailors, says only of Gilbert's voyage that 'it began, continued, and ended adversely.' Even the *Chronicles* of Holinshed record the voyage under the heading 'The viage hath not wished successe', reporting:[16]

But God not favoring his attempt, the journie took no good successe: for all his ships inforced by some occasion or mischance, made their present returne againe; that onelie excepted, wherein his brother Walter Raleigh was capteine, who being desirous to doo somewhat woorthie honor, tooke his course for the west Indies, but for want of vittels and other necessaries (needful in so long a viage) when he had sailed as far as the Ilands of Cape de Verde upon the coast of Affrica, was inforced to set saile and returne for England. In this his viage he passed manie dangerous adventures as well by tempests as fights on the sea; but lastlie he arrived safelie at Plimouth in the west countrie in Maie next following.

Though they undoubtedly had the conviction earlier, the total fiasco of this first voyage must have impressed on both Humphrey Gilbert and Walter Ralegh the need for more knowledgeable, trained, and experienced seamen; it must also have reinforced Richard Hakluyt's and John Dee's pleas that more accurate charts and globes, more carefully constructed navigational instruments, and better technological use of both were essential if British seamen were ever to bring the nation to the pre-eminence they sought.

These were not new aspirations for Gilbert. Nearly a decade earlier, in the early 1570s, he had given thought to

---

[16] Raphael Holinshed, *The first and second volumes of chronicles ... now newlie augmented ...*, 3 vols. [London], 1587. Vol. III, p. 1369.

the training he had received as a ward of the Queen and had concluded that it was social and superficial, inadequate for the education of men who would be leaders of the nation. As a result, he had prepared a memorandum for Queen Elizabeth in which he proposed 'The erection of an Achademy in London for education of her Maiesties Wardes, and others the youth of nobility and gentlemen'.[17] Gilbert's proposed academy was in many ways a most advanced and imaginative treatise on the education of a gentleman, and had it been established as he had hoped, would certainly have brought even greater lustre to her reign. Though instruction in what has become known as 'Queen Elizabeth's Academy' was in part traditional, with instruction in Latin, Greek, and Hebrew, as well as in logic and rhetoric, major emphasis throughout was on the practical application of learning to those professions which would be followed by England's future leaders. French, Italian, Spanish, and 'the highe duch toung' were to be mastered by these future diplomats, merchants, and travellers. Instruction was generally given in English instead of Latin; members of the faculty were to be required to conduct research and to produce scholarly works (one every three years if a translation; one every six years if original); and the 'Liberarie of the Achademy' was to be the precursor of the British Library. Not only were all books to be 'saffely kepte ... bownd in good sorte, made fast, and orderly set' but were to be recorded in a permanent register which the Keeper must make available to any aspiring reader. Furthermore, to ensure completeness, the Queen was to issue orders that[18] 'All Printers in England shall for ever be Charged to deliuer into the Liberary of the Achademy, at their owne Charges, one Copy, well bownde, of euery booke, proclamacion, or pamfletter, that they shall printe.'

Just what Gilbert felt was needed for the proper instruction of English seamen can be seen in his detailed notes of the instruction to be given by the mathematical lecturers of his Academy:[19]

[17] BL Lansdowne MS 98, art. 1, leaf 2. This was published by F. J. Furnivall in the Publication of the Early English Text Society, Extra Series, VIII, London, 1869, pp. 1–12.
[18] Ibid., p. 8.   [19] Ibid., pp. 4–5.

Also there shalbe placed two Mathematicians, And the one of them shall one day reade Arithmetick, and the other day Geometry, which shalbe onely employed to Imbattelinges, fortificacions, and matters of warre, with the practize of Artillery, and vse of all manner of Instruments belonging to the same. And shall once every moneth practize Canonrie (shewing the manner of vnderminienges) and trayne his Awditorie to draw in paper, make in modell, and stake owt all kindes of fortificacions, as well to preuent the mine and sappe, as the Canon, with all sortes of encampinges and Imbattelinges . . .

The other Mathematician shall reade one day Cosmographie and Astronomy, and the other day tend the practizes thereof, onely to the arte of Nauigacion, with the knowledge of necessary starres, making vse of Instrumentes apertaining to the same; and also shall haue in his Schole a shippe and gallye, made in modell, thoroughly rigged and furnished, to teache vnto his Awditory as well the knowledge and vse by name of euery parte thereof, as also the perfect arte of a Shipwright, and diversity of all sortes of moldes apertaining to the same. . . .

Also there shalbe one who shall teache to draw mappes, Sea chartes, &c., and to take by view of eye the platte of any thinge, and shall reade the growndes *and* rules of proportion and necessarie perspectiue and mensuration belonging to the same.

Gilbert's proposal appears to be the first call for practical instruction for the sons of gentlemen and nobles, and the first course designed for men of affairs. Though ignored by the Queen and resulting in no direct action, it was apparently widely circulated, and furnished an incentive for many more such proposals, both formal and informal, which led, ultimately to the establishment of the London lectures at the end of the century which expanded into Gresham College, and which led to the revision of curricula in the universities early in the next century. Significantly, too, the mathematical work outlined in Gilbert's proposal parallels almost exactly with the instruction of navigators to be given by Thomas Harriot during the next two decades. So close are they that it seems fairly certain that Harriot either had known and worked with Gilbert directly, or had access to a copy of his proposal when approached by Ralegh to assume that role for his own masters.

There is at least a good possibility that Harriot worked with Gilbert immediately after his graduation from Oxford, while Ralegh was once more in Ireland in the Queen's service. Gilbert was almost frenzied in preparing for a second expedition to the New World before his Charter expired in

1584 and he may well have recruited Harriot to assist in his preparations, as he had engaged the services of John Dee and Richard Hakluyt, both of whom knew and respected the young man. Such an assignment would surely have been attractive to Harriot, and from what is known of both men, they would have been kindred souls. The tragic end of the whole expedition, culminating in the death of Gilbert in a storm at sea south of the Azores on the ninth of September 1583, would have saddened Harriot, but would also have brought him to the attention of Gilbert's successor in the venture, Walter Ralegh.

The first actual testimony regarding Harriot in London places him in Ralegh's household, but does not indicate just when he entered such service. In late February 1587 Richard Hakluyt prepared for publication the *Decades* of Peter Martyr for the series of publications he was issuing for assistance to Britain's colonial efforts. For this volume he wrote an extended Preface, dedicated to Sir Walter Ralegh and praising him for his contributions to British navigational efforts.[20] In stressing Ralegh's contributions, Hakluyt included the following comment:[21]

Ever since you perceived that skill in the navigator's art, the chief ornament of an island kingdom, might attain its splendour amongst us if the aid of the mathematical sciences were enlisted, you have maintained in your household Thomas Hariot, a man pre-eminent in those studies, at a most liberal salary in order that by his aid you might acquire those noble sciences in your leisure hours, and that your own sea-captains, of whom there are not a few, might link theory with practice, not without almost incredible results. What will shortly be the outcome of this excellent and most prudent departure of yours, even those whose judgement is no more than moderate will undoubtedly be able to divine with ease. This one thing I know, and that is that you are entering upon the one and only method by which first the Portuguese and then the Spaniards at last carried out to their own satisfaction what they had previously attempted so often at no slight sacrifice. . . . There yet remain for you new lands, ample realms, unknown peoples; they wait, yet, I say, to be discovered and subdued, quickly and easily, under the happy auspices of your arms and enterprise, and the sceptre of our most serene Elizabeth, Empress — as even the Spaniard himself admits — of the Ocean. . . .

[20] Taylor, *Original Writings*. . . , publishes this dedicatory epistle as Document 56, in Latin, II. 356–62, and English, II. 362–9.
[21] Ibid., pp. 366–7.

The late E. G. R. Taylor made the assumption, since repeated by many, that this implied that Ralegh employed Harriot immediately upon his Oxford graduation. She wrote: 'He [Ralegh] brought the brilliant young mathematician Thomas Hariot, some eight years his junior, direct from Oxford to Durham House, his mansion in the Strand, where, setting his instruments up on the leads, Hariot laboured for years at improving observational technique and revising the Ephemerides.'[22] This is, however, impossible. Ralegh assumed his commission as Captain of Horse in Ireland in August of 1580 and did not return to court until the end of December 1581. He was not granted the use of Durham House by Elizabeth until 1583. And it was not until the death of Sir Humphrey Gilbert who perished on his return to England in September 1583 and finally vacated his expiring charter for exploration and discovery in the New World that Ralegh got really involved in his sea plans. Ever since his return from Ireland following his two years of battling the Irish insurgents, Ralegh had stayed close to court, establishing his reputation as an expert in Irish affairs, and climbing slowly in Elizabeth's favour. But with Gilbert's death he saw an opportunity to establish new channels to wealth and reputation, and began to enlist the support of the Queen for a new charter authorizing him to carry on the work begun by his half-brother. Though others were avidly seeking the same opportunity, Ralegh had high hopes for success because of his increasing familiarity with Elizabeth. And on 25 March 1584 he realized his ambition: Letters Patent, worded almost identically with those previously issued to Gilbert, gave and granted to 'our trusty and welbeloved servaunte Walter Raleighe Esquier' full rights 'to discover search fynde out and viewe such remote heathen and barbarous landes Contries and territories not actually possessed of any Christian Prynce' and 'the same to haue holde occupy and enioye to him his heyres and assignes for ever. . .'[23]

[22] 'Harriot's Instructions for Ralegh's Voyage to Guiana, 1595', *Journal of the Institute of Navigation*, V (1952), 345.

[23] David B. Quinn, *The Roanoke Voyages, 1584–1590; Documents to Illustrate the English Voyages to North American under the Patent granted to Walter Raleigh in 1584*, 2 vols., London, For the Hakluyt Society, 1955. Doc. I (I. 82–9).

It was almost certainly during this time, the autumn or winter of 1583 or at latest the spring of 1584 that Harriot must have joined Ralegh to help plan and prepare for his explorations in the New World, and to give instruction to his seamen as Hakluyt had proclaimed. Ralegh was just turning thirty, a handsome and extravagantly dressed young man who was beginning to make his presence felt in the court. He had been granted rights to Durham House by the Queen where he established his headquarters and where Harriot held adjoining rooms.[24] Nearly a century later, the antiquarian John Aubrey still recalled the place:[25]

Durham-house was a noble palace; after [Sir Walter] came to his greatness he lived there, or in some apartment of it. I well remember his study, which was a little turret that looked into and over the Thames, and had the prospect which is pleasant perhaps as any in the world, and which not only refreshes the eie-sight but cheeres the spirits, and (to speake my mind) I believe enlarges an ingeniose man's thoughts.

Harriot's chamber in Durham House, like that of Ralegh, was on the top floor, with entrance on to the 'leades' — the lead stripping which covered the roof — on which he stood to make astronomical observations and to perform some of his physical experiments. Now twenty-three or twenty-four, dressed in the simple black that he had apparently affected since his graduation from Oxford, Harriot lived in a room $21\frac{1}{2}$ ft. by $12\frac{1}{2}$ ft., spacious enough for him to conduct his classes and maintain his study there. This we know from a sheet of rough jottings among his manuscripts which shows how he occupied his time (and his enquiring mathematical mind) on one rainy day, estimating the volume of rain that would have occupied his room had it not been turned away by the leads and the spouts.[26] In a very early handwriting, probably dating from the early 1580s, Harriot wrote:

Ouer my Chamber at Durham house, the measured leuell square, (accountinge half the thickness of the wall which casteth in the rayne) within the which the rayne falleth to runne out of the spoute in the corner is, $268\frac{3}{4}$ foote square; after this manner: [Here is drawn a rough parallelogram indicated as being $21\frac{1}{2}$ ft. long, $12\frac{1}{4}$ ft. wide, and containing $268\frac{3}{4}$ sq. ft. or 38,700 sq. ins.]

[24] See the account of Ralegh's will of 1597, pp. 236 ff. below.
[25] Clark, *'Brief Lives'*, II. 183.
[26] BL Add. MS 6788, fo. 411ᵛ.

Since he had no watch or other instrument which would measure time intervals of seconds or minutes, Harriot made his measurements, as many experimenters of his time did, by counting his pulse, assuming that each beat represented a time of one second. For this experiment Harriot measured the water coming from the downspout in pints and with his 'cube' which held exactly 9 cubic inches,[27] and by rounding off his figures calculated that [had it continued at an average rate] it would have rained approximately $8\frac{1}{2}$ inches during a twenty-four-hour period.

But Harriot had far more serious things on his mind than measuring rainfall on a lazy afternoon. His major task was that of utilizing all that he had learned of mathematics and the physical sciences in improving the efficiency of deep-sea navigation. The problems which faced Ralegh (and consequently his man, Harriot) in entering the fields of exploration, piracy, and commercial exploitation of new lands were concrete and of vital importance. England was not yet a major sea power; she was trailing far behind Spain and Portugal in all matters of oceanic navigation and was only starting to solve the practical and scientific problems imposed by the expanding horizons of her activities. For generations, British seamanship had been limited to small coastal vessels of fishing or commerce; their sailing techniques had been based primarily on the sensory observation of water depth, tides, and coastlines, with the ship out of sight of land for only hours, or at most a day or so. To navigate safely, the master had to recognize the promontories, capes, steeples, and harbourage of the ports he was to visit. The tools of his trade were the rutter — a brief account of the

---

[27] Even in this very early experiment, Harriot gave full attention to the accuracy of his measurements and his instruments. On the other side of the same page on which he made his observations of rainfall he made the following notes about his 'cube':

'My cube of brasse whose internall side 3 inches. conteyneth of rayne water iust full by eye as it is euen by the sides & playned by a ruler ounces of troye. $14 \pm \frac{1}{2} \pm \frac{1}{16}$
Being filled more till it began to runne ouer the side being wet for it, it conteyned now $14 \pm \frac{1}{2} \pm \frac{1}{8} \pm \frac{1}{16}$
That experiment had error for I found after[wards] it had leaked & therefore I proued agayne the leakes being stopped. it is full with
iust   troy $14 \pm \frac{1}{2}$.'

profile of the coast (frequently illustrated by rough wood-
cuts) — an almanac, and a table of tides. For navigational
instruments he used a simple compass, housed in a binnacle
which may have held a candle for night observation, a lead
and line for measuring the depth of water, and an hour- or
half-hour-, minute- or half-minute-glass to measure the
watches and monitor the rate of progress through the water.
But primarily the art of the seaman was the art of pilotage,
learned by apprenticeship and experience — a relatively
simple craft.[28]

But the move from the shorelines to the ocean had changed
all of this. Though most ocean crossings utilized the shortest
possible jumps from island to island wherever they existed,
in the crossing from England to the New World ships were
out of sight of land for weeks, sometimes months, at a time.
The old sensory navigation was worthless and the ship's
master had to rely on instruments and observations with
which he was not familiar. Certainly he was most at home
when sailing east or west on the same latitude, since here
the magnetic compass and dead reckoning with lead and
line gave reasonable accuracy of the ship's location. But
crossings which contemplated a diagonal sailing across
latitude lines were infinitely more complicated. Since the
latitudinal circles grew shorter as one moved from the
equator to the pole, a ship sailing directly north-east by
compass would not move across the globe in that direction;
actually a translation from the plane map to a sphere shows
that such a ship would move in a spiral course. To avoid
this calamity, most pilots sailed directly west from England
to reach the coast of Newfoundland, following the coast to
a southerly site, or went south to the Canaries to sail west
to the West Indies. But not always was the true latitude of
the destination known. Maps and charts were notoriously
inaccurate, and it was not unusual in these days of intense
competition for an entrepreneur to record a false latitude on
his maps to mislead an opponent should he happen to obtain
copies by some nefarious means.

[28] For a more detailed account of the changes in the techniques of navigation
between 1550 and 1650 see D. W. Waters, *The Art of Navigation in England in
Elizabethan and Early Stuart Times*, New Haven, Yale University Press, 1958.

Once out of sight of land, the only fixed positions on which the master or pilot could rely were the sun, moon, and stars. To work with these with any confidence called for greater knowledge of astronomy and mathematics (including spherical trigonometry) and more precision in taking observations than they had ever used before. Ships, too, which had been reasonably safe when a port was only hours away, were frequently unable to survive when the sea turned savage and no port was within call. Trade with far-off lands, potentially so economically rewarding, could be truly profitable only if improvements in safety of vessels, improvements in the surety of sailing routes, and the sea abilities and confidence of the pilots and masters could be brought to a new and higher standard.

As Harriot assumed his duties in bringing mathematical order out of this navigational chaos to aid Ralegh in his plans for organization and development, he found it necessary to bring himself to the practical forefront of the art in a way that the University of Oxford could not take him. It was necessary for him to attack these problems on all fronts simultaneously. To this end, he proceeded, like the scholar he was, to read all the available writings of seamen and navigators, English, Portuguese, Spanish, classical, historical, and contemporary and to immerse himself in their lore. He became the familiar of the successful sea masters who arrived at the London docks, seeking information from them of their experiences, successes, and failures. He studied critically both the instruments available for astronomical and geographical observations, what corrections were needed to correct deficiencies in their use, and devised new charts and formulae for more accurate readings and calculations from those readings. He became involved in the collection of sailing rutters and maps of far-off places, and in the problems of stereographic projection, or translating the globe's surface on to a two-dimensional surface, and the reverse. He created new instruments for observation of celestial angles and distances, and made new observations of his own to check the tables of other astronomers which were available for the use of Ralegh's seamen. Though there is no evidence to ensure the fact, it seems almost certain to one who studies

Harriot's writings and jottings that in gathering his data and in clarifying his procedures, Harriot must have taken part in some of the voyages sponsored by Ralegh in his exploratory moves towards the exploration of the New World.

Unfortunately, among the Harriot papers there remain no notes that seem to date from his early period. We do know, from the evidence of Hakluyt and others, that he was conducting classes in navigation at Durham House in late 1583 and early 1584 in preparation for Ralegh's first expedition in search for a settlement site in the New World. To assist the seamen in these classes he wrote a text which he called *Arcticon*, of which no copy appears to exist. Lecture notes do exist, however, for the similar classes conducted by Harriot for the seamen preparing to take part with Ralegh in his visit to Guiana in 1595. These later notes are obviously, from internal evidence, only expansions of the basic text materials previously presented in the *Arcticon*. In one place where he is discussing accuracy in reading the cross-staff, Harriot notes:[29] 'How this error [in reading the cross staff] may be knowne & reformed I haue demonstrated & taught 11 yeares past [i.e. 1584] in my booke called Arcticon. Now only I will remember vnto you out of the same, that which I shewed you sometime too farr & sufficient for your vse.' Again, in noting the error that could easily creep into a reading of the altitude of the sun or a star, Harriot adds:[30] 'By truth of demonstration which I haue vttered in my Arcticon, which here for breuity sake I omit.' In yet another place, referring to a contemporary text on navigation dealing with the distance of Polaris from the true pole, Harriot comments:[31]

The which concepts to those that are ignorant of true arte, semeth very ingenious & artificiall [artful]; but to a Mathematician of iudgement it appeareth to be an ingenious sleyght, & sophisticate devise to make that seeme true which is not. The mathematicall demonstrations perticulerly to discover the errors of it, are not fit to be vttered in this manner of writing, in my Arcticon they are at length; for this place it shalbe sufficient to haue remembered the experimentes of there falsenes.

[29] BL Add. MS 6788, fo. 486.
[30] Ibid., fo. 487.
[31] Ibid., fo. 484*. This sheet was inserted on 13 Mar. 1952 from the Harriot papers remaining at Petworth as a gift from John Wyndham. It follows fo. 484.

Harriot worked on the problems of navigation for the remainder of his life. Stated in simplest terms, these problems implied knowing exactly where on the face of the earth the lands being sought were located (hence his interest in charts, maps, and the exact determination of latitude and longitude), how to get from where they were to where they wanted to be (which called for the location of the ship on the open sea through exact knowledge of the mathematics of the spheres of the earth and heavens) with the greatest efficiency in the use of time, ships and men (which led to careful analysis of the navigational tools available and the improvement of their accuracy). With his characteristic thoroughness, Harriot applied himself to all of these matters again and again, going at each stage of his own development as far as his mathematical and technical art would permit. Dr Jon Pepper, who has made the most intensive study of Harriot's navigational studies to date, summarizes his life's activities as follows:[32]

The stages of Harriot's work on navigation appear to be three. First, in the early fifteen eighties, he solved the problem of reconciling the sun and pole star observations for determining latitude, introduced the idea of using solar amplitude to determine magnetic variation, and, as well as improving methods and devices for observation of solar or stellar altitudes, he recalculated tables for the sun's declination on the basis of his own astronomical observations. Secondly, probably about the same time and certainly by about 1584, he produced a practical numerical solution of the mercator problem, most probably by the addition of secants, as Dee may have done earlier, and as Wright did about the same time. Thirdly, between 1594 and 1614, no doubt with considerable breaks in his efforts, he produced his great tables of meridional parts calculated (in effect) as logarithmic tangents. The first two stages applied traditional mathematics ingeniously but the third stage had to call into existence a whole new range of mathematical techniques, such as the conformality of stereographic projections, the rectification and quadrature of the logarithmic or equiangular spiral, the exponential series, and the derivation and use of interpolation formulae.

[32] 'Harriot's Earlier Work on Mathematical Navigation: Theory and Practice', pp. 54–90 of John W. Shirley, ed., *Thomas Harriot; Renaissance Scientist*, Oxford, Clarendon Press, 1974. This is from p. 54. See also Pepper's 'The Study of Thomas Harriot's Manuscripts: II. Harriot's Unpublished Papers', pp. 17–40 in *History of Science*, VI (1967); 'A Note on Harriot's Method of Obtaining Meridional Parts', *Journal of the History of Navigation*, XX (1967), 347–9; and 'Harriot's Calculation of the Meridional Parts as Logarithmic Tangents', *Archive for History of Exact Sciences*, IV (1968) 393–413.

The early navigational materials from which Pepper drew his conclusions about Harriot's work are those notes of lectures to Ralegh's sea captains in 1594 and 1595 in preparation for Ralegh's voyage to the Orinoco in search of the fabled city of Eldorado. Yet as has been previously indicated, these notes appear to be slightly augmented versions of the materials included in Harriot's *Arcticon*, and are hence placed at this phase of Harriot's life. Remaining are twenty-three folio pages in rough form with many deletions, additions, and interlinings numbered to indicate that they represent six lectures, which Harriot calls 'chapters';[33] a fragment of a seventh on the variation of the compass titled 'How to know your course to sayle to any place assigned';[34] a partially filled group of numbered sheets on the calculation of rhumbs labelled 'The Doctrine of Nauticall triangles Compendious';[35] and six diagrams or tables to go with the lectures.[36] The headings of the lectures remaining give a clear idea of the scope and contents of Harriot's instruction:

[Unnumbered] How to know your course to sayle to any place assigned; & in sayling to keep to [c.o.] make true recconing to find where you are at any time; & how farre from any place desired.
1. Some Remembrances of taking the altitudes of the Sonne by the Astrolabe and Sea Ringe.[37]
2. Of taking the altitudes of the Sonne or starres [c.o.] any starre by the crosse staffe with more exactenes then hath ben vsed heretofore. [Includes a table of 'Surplus of the Horizon in minutes' to correct for the 'Hight of the ey aboue the water in pases'.] [38]
3. How to find the declination of the Sonne for any time of the yeare & any place by a Speciall table called the Sonnes Regiment newly made according to late observations.[39]

[33] Harriot's using the nomenclature of books for his manuscripts may in part account for the confusion as to whether or not the *Arcticon* was a printed or a manuscript 'book'. Similarly, Harriot uses the title-page format for some sections of his mathematical notes, such as his 'Doctrine of Nauticall Triangles'.
[34] BL Add. MS 6788, fo. 491.
[35] Petworth House, Sussex: HMC 241/vi. b., fo. 1–22.
[36] These are all in BL Add. MS 6788, as follows:

(a) Surplus of the Horizon.	(fo. 488)
(b) Eleuation of the pole from meridian altitude of the Sonne.	(fo. 474)
(c) A figure shewing when the guardes are in rule.	(fo. 423)
(d) Allowances of the pole starre.	(fo. 423)
(e) Regiment of the Sonne.	(fos. 205^r–210^v)
(f) Amplitudes of the Sonne.	(fos. 211^v–220^v)

[37] Ibid., fo. 485.
[38] Ibid., fos. 486–9.   [39] Ibid., fos. 468–72.

4. How to find the elevation of the pole, by the Meridian altitude of the Sonne, & his declination. [Includes a table on 'Elevation of the pole. . .'.][40]
5. Of taking the altitude or elevation of the North pole by the north starre & a new rule of the guardes made and calculated according to praecise & late observations. [These 'late observations' are explained by Harriot as 'These thinges I spake vpon conference with these sortes of men as also vpon myne owne experience & triall at sea in sayling to the Indies, Virginia & homewards.'][41]
6. Of the manner to observe the variation of the compasse, or the wires of the same, by the Sonnes rising or setting.[42]

Reading these rather informal lecture notes gives the modern reader an unusual insight into the mind of Thomas Harriot. It is a clear mind, direct, straightforward, logical, and honest. It is obviously the mind of a scientist and mathematician. As E. G. R. Taylor has pointed out, these lectures show[43] 'how wide a gap there lay between [the scientists] and the practising sea-masters, a difference not only in mathematical knowledge and capacity, but in habit of mind. For the sailor worked by rule and by tradition, so that he was always likely to think the old way best.' And in spite of the fact that they were conducted in the social and informal atmosphere of Ralegh's (and Harriot's) home, Durham House, they are conducted in a serious and academic fashion that at times seems quite pedantic.

Most of the lectures have a traditional organization. They begin with a definition or statement of purpose. The history of the subject is then briefly outlined, together with a revelation of errors which have crept in because of faulty observations or calculations. Harriot next produces the results of his own more accurate observations, and furnishes the masters new charts or tables based on his own new figures. Then he goes through the procedure of making observations, pointing out simple errors in the use of instruments and corrections which must be made for greater accuracy. He concludes with problems or examples of calculations to fix the procedures in the minds of his hearers.

[40] Ibid., fos. 473–5.
[41] Ibid., fos. 476, 481–4, 423.
[42] BL Add. MS 6789, fos. 534–7.
[43] *The Haven-Finding Art*, augmented edn., New York, American Elsevier Publishing Co., 1971, p. 216.

The introductory lecture illustrates Harriot's lucid exposition. Entitled 'Some Remembrances of the taking of altitude of the sonne by the Astrolabe and Sea Ringe', it begins:[44] 'There are three instruments vsed at sea for taking of altitudes, the Astrolabe, the ring & the staffe. The Astrolabe hath ben the most auncient & is vsed commonly & only for the sonne. . .' Harriot is not, he says, partial to the astrolabe, though it is a favourite of astronomers, its readings are accurate, and it is valuable when the sun is high. But it hangs from a ring, and it tends to sway on a rolling ship so that the observer must adjust an index while the instrument is moving to align two holes so that the sun shines through them both. This is not only difficult to do, but since the light moves on the scale when properly adjusted, it is necessary to estimate the centre of the extreme readings. For these reasons, the sea-ring (also called the Nonius after its inventor) has advantages: it requires no index adjustment and has a scale twice as large as that of the astrolabe. But again, it hangs from a ring which permits it to swing with the moving ship, and the user must estimate the centre of a moving beam of light. The particular astrolabe and sea-ring used in this lecture demonstration had been obtained by Harriot for an earlier voyage, and there had proved too light to hang securely. But, he told Ralegh, 'by reason of yor speedy setting forth it cannot now be remidied.'

The second lecture treats of the cross staff: Harriot goes into detail on the proper use of that instrument and the corrections necessary for accurate results.[45] Different users of the cross staff have different habits as to where they place the base of the staff to make observations; this leads to different and unreliable readings. Harriot tells the captains to hold the staff always firmly against the 'vtmost corner of the seat of that ey which you mind to behold withall' for consistent readings. Again, some attempt to take the altitude of the sun by measuring from the centre or the bottom of the orb. This is folly and could lead to blindness. Harriot recommends that the sun be covered by the cross and that the observer then move the cross down until the top of the

---

[44] BL Add. MS 6788, fo. 485.   [45] Ibid., fos. 486–9.

cross just touches the upper edge of the sun while the bottom touches the horizon. True altitude could then be obtained by subtracting 16', the radius of the sun, from the observed altitude. Still another error needed to be corrected: in its construction, the staff was calibrated as though its end were at the 'center of sight' which would be at the centre of the lens of the eye. Since this was not the case, Harriot had measured the exact distance to be corrected for each captain's eye, and had marked each staff with the eye-staff distance which must be abated from the reading. This deviation, Harriot called the *Parallaxis of the staff*, and a correction must be made for each reading. And since the seaman took his reading from a deck above the surface of the water, an additional correction called the *Surplus of the Horizon* must be introduced for this. Once again Harriot furnished a chart to indicate the correction that should be made for deck elevations of from 5 to 50 feet. This session was closed by taking the seamen through two hypothetical readings as made from various longitudes to determine their corrected observations of solar altitudes. Here like a good teacher and to stimulate interest, Harriot used examples which approximated the locations where Ralegh's ships would actually be on their journey to the Spanish main. Ralegh's fleet sailed on 6 February 1595. The dates that Harriot used in his navigational classes for Ralegh's captains were 10 February, 'not a hundred leagues to the westwardes of England';[46] 18 March, 'to the westward of England 900 leagues or 3 houres [in time difference]';[47] and 6 May, 'to the westwardes of England 1000 leagues' and in the latitude of Trinidad.[48] Ralegh's fleet landed at Trinidad in early May.

Yet even with these corrections, Harriot was not satisfied with the cross-staff as currently made. In his manuscript on *Nauticall Triangles* he illustrates a different kind of staff,[49] a back-staff in which the observer turns his back on the sun, reading the position of the sun's shadow, and thus not taking the chance of blinding himself. Such an instrument was later devised by Captain John Davis, and credited to him, though it is likely that Harriot's invention came first. Harriot also

---

[46] Ibid., fo. 470.   [47] Ibid.   [48] Ibid., fo. 471.
[49] Petworth House, Sussex: HMC 241 VI/b, fo. 16ᵛ.

invented two back quadrants for observation of the sun and a quadrant for the stars, both anticipating the ultimate sextant.[50] But there is no evidence that these were actually constructed and put to use.

In his third lecture, 'How to find the declination of the sonne for any time of the yeare & in any place; by a speciall table called the sonnes regiment newly made according to late observations',[51] in reviewing the historical background, Harriot is at his scholarly best. New tables of declination are needed, Harriot asserts, because all current regiments are inaccurate. The old tables used primarily by Portuguese and Spaniards were 'calculated about some hundred years past' from the tables of Alphonsus, calculated in 1252 and published in the late fifteenth century. More modern regiments were made later from the Prutenic tables of Erasmus Reinhold, based on the observations of 'one Nicholaus Copernicus of Cracow in Poland'. Normally one would expect these later tables to be more accurate than the old, but 'it falleth out they are worse; our own men find faultes as sometimes the Spaniardes but know not where the fault is.' Better observations were made in 1577 when

Tycho Brahe, a noble gentleman of the Iland of Huaena in the sounde of Denmarke . . . By most diligent observations with large and praecise instruments . . . found Copernicus his tables, the prutenicles & all ephimerides made out of them to erre halfe a degree in the sonnes place & sometimes more; and the Alphonsine tables about one quarter of a degree. . .

Obviously impressed by Tycho's superior instruments, Harriot had created an enormous and ostensibly accurate instrument to make his own observations:[52]

I my self also haue ben an eye witness of the same in late years 1590. 1591. 1592. & 1593; by myne owne experiment with an instrument of

[50] Ibid.

[51] BL Add. MSS 6788, fos. 468–72.

[52] Ibid., fo. 469. In his doctoral dissertation on 'Thomas Harriot's Astronomy', Oxford, 1977, John Roche argues that Harriot's 12-foot instrument was most likely a *radius astronomicus* similar to the 10-foot instruments used by Digges and Dee, though perhaps mounted on a universal ball joint for easy handling. This seems to be highly probable. See also his 'The Radius Astronomicus in England', *Annals of Science*, XXXVIII (1981), 1–32, esp. sec. 7, 'The cross staff in England: Harriot to Greaves', pp. 23–8.

12 foote long vpon Duresme leades. Both there tables we find to erre in the greatest declination of the sonne. The Alphonsine haue 23. degrees & 33. min., 2 minutes too much & the copernicles 23. deg. 28 min., 3 minutes too little; for it is [by me] found to be 23 degrees & 31. minutes.

It is important to note that Harriot's figures are more accurate than those of any of his predecessors, though Pepper calculates that even his may have been a minute too high.[53] Harriot's 'Regiment of the Sonne' was, thus, an important tool for Ralegh's captains, and it was even more valuable for two additional reasons: in the first place, Harriot wrote the difference between the two calculations in red for easy and accurate interpolation, and as Commander Waters has pointed out, he also made corrections for longitude.[54]

In his next lecture, Harriot neatly and logically ties up the observations of the declination of the sun with the determination of latitude. Having shown that 'The elevation of the pole is always one in quantity with the distance of the Zenith from the aequinoctiall, which also is called the latitude of your place',[55] Harriot furnishes an elaborate table detailing each step to be taken in making such a determination, indicating whether corrections are to be added or subtracted. Once more he closes with two examples which knit together all the instructions he has given in his previous lectures.[56]

The fifth lecture, 'Of taking the altitude or elevation of the North pole by the north starre & a new view of the guardes made and calculated according to praecise and late observations',[57] is complete and complex. But in it Harriot discusses previous discrepancies in astronomers' estimations of the exact angular distance of Polaris from true north. From a study of all the known data from Hipparchus (130 BC) through Gemma Frisius (mid-sixteenth century) Harriot had concluded that the Pole star was moving 'nerer the pole by almost 24 minutes in that time whiles the starres moue one degree in longitude, which in our age falleth out to be nere the space of one hundred yeares.' Harriot's own observations

[53] Pepper, 'Harriot's Earlier Work. . .', p. 64.
[54] Waters, op. cit., p. 585.
[55] BL Add. MS 6788, fo. 473.
[56] Ibid., fo. 475.
[57] Ibid., fos. 476, 481–4, 423.

'with my instrument of 12 foote longe in the yeare 1591 & 1592' gave the true angular distance as 2° 56', and he calculated that it would be 2° 55' in the year 1598.

The sixth lecture, 'Of the manner to observe the Variation of the compasse, or of the wires of the same, by the Sonnes rising or setting',[58] is both innovative and very important. Here Harriot attacks the problem of determining the variation of the compass by a single observation of the sun. This he accomplishes by having the navigator observe the apparent direction of the sun at sunrise or sunset, and comparing this reading with the theoretical value which Harriot had calculated in a 'Table of Amplitudes' for each whole degree of declination up to 24° and for each degree of latitude up to 54°. This was a totally new method, and gave Ralegh's navigators an easier and more certain way of determining their true direction of sailing than had ever been available previously.

Just how valuable were these lectures in improving the technological proficiency of Ralegh's captains? Jon Pepper summarizes his estimate as follows:[59]

. . it may be said that they introduce valuable theoretical innovations as well as sound practical sense on observational techniques. The amplitude tables appear to be original and are of course accurate; they form a major contribution to the seaman's art. The Pole Star tables are based on sound principles, something not done before. In the absence of a full and certain knowledge of the observational parameters on which they are based, it is difficult to be sure about their accuracy, but one can have every confidence in Harriot's astronomical care and mathematical competence in calculating them. A similar remark applies to his new regiment of the Sun. The latitude algorith is unnecessarily involved, but is stated clearly and in quite a practicable form. Taken as a whole, the *Instructions* are a great improvement on the practice current until (and indeed after) their time, and give a very clear foretaste of the calibre and the later much wider attainments of the able young man of about 34 who produced them.

Another student of Harriot, Dr John Roche of Oxford University, is similarly impressed with Harriot's observations and mathematical analyses. Having reviewed Harriot's work against a background of the work of his contemporaries in

[58] BL Add. MS 6789, fos. 534-7.
[59] Pepper, 'Harriot's Earlier Work. . .', pp. 74-5.

England and abroad, and having noted what Harriot said he had covered in his *Arcticon* in the mid 1580s, Roche concludes:[60]

It is a great pity that Harriot never published his lost manuscript text-book *Arcticon*. He would surely have laboured to get even more accurate values for the astronomical distances needed. This book would have excelled even Nonius in rigour and would have been far superior to anything published to date in accuracy and clarity. It would have had an immediate impact on western navigation and established Harriot internationally as a navigational expert.

It is the lucid mind and clear expression inherent in Harriot that Pepper, Roche, and other Harriot scholars find attractive. This is again summed up by Roche when he says:[61]

Harriot's thinking was characterised by concentrated and extensive study, clarity and depth of thought, independence of mind, originality, and an economy of style. The contents of his manuscripts show that he preferred to deal with well-defined problems that could be treated mathematically. He stubbornly pursued problems until he solved them. He appears to have been more or less equally interested in pure mathematics, applied mathematics, and experimentation. Particularly important was Harriot's awareness of the need for systematic experimental and observational work and of the importance of checking earlier results. This is especially evident in his work on navigational astronomy, optics, specific weights, and in his studies of free fall. As a result, perhaps, of his early work on navigational instruments, Harriot was actively concerned all his life with the sensitivity and accuracy of his instruments, in reducing errors in their construction, and in the techniques of careful observation. Characteristic of him also is the accuracy and honesty with which he records his data, whether it be favourable or unfavourable. In doubtful cases he called in other observers to check his results. . .

It might be added that it was his concern for complete accuracy that led Harriot repeatedly to return to problems with more accurate data or more sophisticated mathematical solutions, sometimes after a period as long as two decades. And it might have been this perfectionism that kept him from publishing his great discoveries, considering that they were premature and might still be improved by additional labour.

Harriot's lectures, as we have seen, were serious and sober exercises, and leave the reader with the impression that he

---

[60] Roche, 'Thomas Harriot's Astronomy', p. 147.
[61] Ibid., pp. 28–30.

must have been a somewhat pedantic man with little sense of humour. It is pleasant to report, in this connection, that tucked in among his lecture notes is a rough draft of some doggerel, written in a moment of whimsy to serve as a fitting close to his last class. In essence, this briefly sums up the essence of his six lectures, alludes to the coming search for Indian gold, and expresses his best wishes for his hurriedly instructed class. Entitled 'Three Sea Marriadges', this bit of Renaissance verse reads as follows:[62]

Three Sea Marriadges.

Three new Marriadges here are made
one of the staff & sea Astrolabe.
Of the sonne & starre is an other
which now agree like sister & brother.
And charde and compasse which now at bate,
will now agree like master & mate.
If you vse them well in this your iourny
They will be the Kinge of Spaynes Atarny
To bring you to siluer & Indian Gold
which will keepe you in age from hunger & cold
God speed you well & send you fayre wether
And that agayne we may meet to gether.

But in addition to bringing his mathematics and science to bear on the navigational abilities of Ralegh's sea captains, Harriot was also expected to assist Ralegh with the selection of vessels and the improvement of shipbuilding. With the enthusiasm and self-assurance of youth, he entered this new venture. Yet once again, before mastering a new field of interest, Harriot, fresh from the theoretical training of the University, had to immerse himself in the practicalities of the craft. He began at the beginning, with the language of the sea. His navigational papers contain a number of pages of notes which are crude definitions of the words and phrases common to the sea. For example:

Whipping of ropes endes — with twyne to fasten the endes to keep him from fuzing out or riueling.

Kinking of a cable or stiffe rope — a fold that happens when the cable runneth out too fast & it doubles, for want of well ouer-setting the

---

[62] BL Add. MS 6788, fo. 490.

flukes in paying out of it, & then they say stopp stop to get out of the kink.[63]

A shot of cable is two cables bent together & wound one about an other & tied to make as one in length.

a splice. to splice is to ioyne two ropes or cables together by opening their endes & working one in an other with a fid.

a Fid is an iron about a foot longe & less, of the fashion of a bodkin.[64]

Harriot's logical and mathematical mind can be seen at work in his notes as he reviews the construction and operation of the various segments of the vessels of the Ralegh fleet.[65]

All ropes belonging to a ship serue to 4 vses

ffor mastes.				forestayes
yardes.		stayes		
sayles.				backestayes
ankers.		shroudes		
		top rope	to heaue vp the top mastes.	
		takles	one for euery top maste.	

mastes	sprite, bolesprite, boldsprite		
	fore maste	all haue top mastes	top
	mayne mast	vpon the top of the	gallantes
	Bonauenture mizen	mayne maste &	
		fore maste	
	after mizn	& hier flagstaues.	

Again, in making an analysis of the construction of a 100-ton vessel, Harriot wrote several pages of 'Notes', which include the following:[66]

The keele in a ship of (100^t), 12 ynches deep; 10 ynches broad.
The stern post & sterne are below as the keele but aloft the stern is thicker in & out, (& otherwise also)
it endes in a quadrant, & comes into the beake head as a stump.
the beake hed is 1/8 or 1/5 of the keele in length.
The timbers of 100^t of the midship bend, and 7 inches in & out
below & 8 inches brode & a lofte about 3 inches eueryway.
The lower wales are in thicknes 5 ynches & about 6 in bredth, the other are lesse. the planke between is 3 inches & so downe to the keele. vpward they are thinner in degrees.

One of Harriot's most interesting notes deals with the officers of the ship (Fig. 4).[67] This note is historically

---

[63] Ibid., fo. 35.   [64] Ibid., fo. 36.   [65] Ibid., fo. 28.
[66] Ibid., fo. 30.   [67] Ibid., fo. 21.

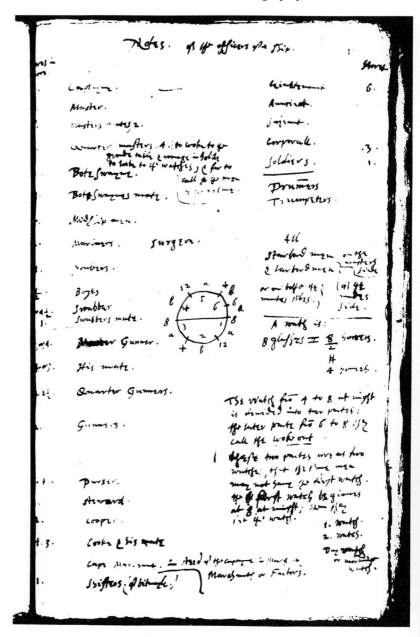

Fig. 4 Notes on Officers and Watches

important in that (1) it is one of the very rare listings of the personnel of an Elizabethan privateer giving the number of shares of loot to be assigned to each seaman and officer, and (2) it is the earliest known account of the ship's watches, their names, and the records of the 'bells' which timed each watch. Following a diagram of a twenty-four-hour clock divided into six four-hour watches, Harriot calls attention to the fact that 'A watch is: 8 [half-hour sand] glasses = 8/2 houres. = 4 houres.' The men are then divided up for duty:

All starbord men on the masters side & larbord men on the mates side. or on bothe mates sides [if there are two mates].

The watch from 4 to 8 at night is deuided into two partes: the later parte from 6 to 8 they call the *looke out*.

These two parts are as two watches, that the same men may not haue the first watch. the first watch beginnes at 8 at night; then they set the watch.

1. watch [8 to midnight]
2. watch [midnight to 4 a.m.]
Day watch
    or morning watch.

It is interesting that Harriot's notes show the same terminology as is current today.

Though Harriot's observations of ships begin by casual notes on what the current practice was, it is obvious that the importance of making improvements in present usage led Harriot to study carefully the purposes Ralegh's vessels were to serve and the optimum design which might render them more efficient. In this regard, one of Harriot's notes gives a valuable insight into how a British captain viewed the English ships he was called upon to sail. Headed 'Notes taken out of Captayne Edmund Marloe, his booke entituled: Ars Naupegica, or the art of ship building', these notes summarize the contents of an Elizabethan 'booke' which apparently was never published:[68]

The Easterling, Duch or Fleming build floty ships by reason those contryes ar subiect to flats and shoulds. And because they often bring them a ground they haue much flat flore to rest vpon. There sides also are vpright, and are built so for burthen & small draught of water. And they beare sayle not so much for there sides, but by reason of the great

[68] Ibid., fo. 39.

wayght that lyeth below vpon the flore (being so broad & long). But these for the most part are euill conditioned ships in the sea, being subject to rowle, tumble, & leape in a wrought sea; so that you must allwayes keep some sayle abrode.

Contrarywise the Spaniard (not accustomed to bring his ships a ground but allwayes to ride a flote, & also to trimme his ships vpon the carine [careen]. As you may se by there Carvells. And there Caractes likewise for the most part flare much of aloft. Now these hold a better wind & are easier in a wrought sea, and will commonly hull well, & wether quoyle. But they draw much water & are not well to be brought a ground without good shoring for feare they fall ouer.

The Frenchmen are nerest to perfection in bearing sayle & going well, being neat moulded ships. But they are not commonly so great in burthen as they loome for [appear]. They haue long rakes [projections of the upper part of the ship's hull and stern beyond the keel] & sharp forward on; and there decks steeue [incline upward] much forward. Where contrarywise the Easterling and Duch haue short vpright rakes, & are bloof [bluff] ships forward on [presenting a broad, flattened front, opposed to sharp or projecting, and having little rake or inclination]. Also there deckes steeue or hang backwardes on.

But our English ships are intended to haue such perfection, that (according to the intent of the builder) thcy hold burden with the Fleming; bearing with the Spaniard; going well with the French, &c.

Euery Nation aymeth at this: to haue there ships go well & steer well. Which proceedeth especially from the well weying of a ship fore & afte; for the Runne [that part of the ship's bottom which rises from the keel and bilge and narrows toward the stern] & Tuck [the gathering of the ends of the bottom planks under the stern].

These are the chief propertyes of a ship in the sea. To go well; to steer well, & beare a good sayle. As for the Burthen that belongeth to the owners profit, which some to much affecting hath made vs to haue so many furred ships. [In his own definitions[69] Harriot defines 'furring' which is not given in the *OED* as 'The Furring of a ship is when she will not beare sayle for want of bredth is to build her broader with [new] outsides with timber on the plumbes [vertical sides] & thin bord below & thicker vpward so far from below as is fit; & howsing it in vpward to agree with the vpper worke by thinner bordes agayne. Many marchantes shippes are fyne to be furred' though this was obviously a makeshift correction of poor ship design.]

These manuscripts of Harriot make it apparent that his duties for Sir Walter Ralegh went far beyond training sea captains in mathematical navigation; he was also called upon to assist in the selection, design, construction, and manning of the ships needed for all his enterprises. He was also helping

[69] Ibid., fo. 33.

Ralegh obtain financing for his voyages, and was directly responsible for the maintenance of his accounts. This personal involvement led Harriot to give over a long period full attention to the selection and construction of ships which, even under adverse conditions, would go well, steer well, and bear a good sail, while at the same time having proper depth and breadth for the stowing of merchandise or loot. To improve his grasp of the state of the art of ship construction, Harriot cultivated the acquaintance of one of the pre-eminent shipbuilders of the time, Matthew Baker.[70] Baker in 1572 had succeeded James Bull as the Queen's chartered shipwright, and was the first man to be titled 'Master Shipwright'. As early as 1573 Baker had built at his works in Deptford the 450-ton warship, *Dreadnought*, carrying 34 guns. In 1586 he completed the *Vanguard* of 561 tons and 36 guns, and in the naval build-up following the Armada, he produced the *Merhonour* (865 tons and 41 guns) in 1590, the *Adventure* (343 tons, 26 guns) in 1594, and the famous *Repulse* (777 tons and 50 guns) in 1596. Harriot, still in his mid-thirties, though obviously well informed of Baker's theories and principles, was in no way overawed by them, nor fearful of challenging the reasoning of the Master Shipwright.

Harriot began his criticism of Baker and his practices by considering the way in which Baker computed the tonnage of his vessels:[71]

It is knowne by experience that a ship whose depth .10. foote
is of burden a 100 tone   bredth .20.
                                     length .50. by the keele

Mr. Baker makes this rule & findes it lettle more or lesse then truth otherwise tried. He makes a solid nomber of 10. 20. & 50.; & then devides it by a hundred. the quotient is the tonnes of burden (in ye hold) as I take it. the sayd length bredth & depth must be in feet for this rule.

ffor tonnes & tonnage of the Kinges ships he multiplyes as before but deuides by 70. & the quotient is counted her tonnage. By these rules the Tonnage of shipps is measured for the King.

Tonnes & tonage is what a ship doth carry of ordinance master sayles & yardes together with that which she carry in hold.

[70] Philip Banbury, *Shipbuilders of the Thames and Medway*, Newton Abbot, 1971.
[71] BL Add. MS 6788, fo. 41.

Harriot's immediate reaction is that these calculations are much too crude for serious use. Baker, he complains, considers the bulk of the ship to represent a parallelopiped, which is in fact almost three times the actual bulk of a vessel of these dimensions. Much more accurate results could easily be found by dividing the 'solid number' or cubic feet of the parallelopiped by 3 and multiplying the result by 64 (the number of pounds in each cubic foot of water displaced by the vessel). But even greater accuracy could be obtained by simply determining the volume of the vessel's displacement — a feat which should easily be within the capability of the Queen's shipbuilder.

Harriot was also unimpressed by the almost linear proportions used by Baker in designing vessels of different displacements. For more than a dozen years Harriot kept notes on the dimensions of ships of various sizes which had proved to be efficient sailors. In some instances he took the measurements himself; in others he accepted the figures given by Hakluyt or other observers. Among others he noted were the detailed measurements of the East Indian Carrack, the *Madre de Deus*, the richest privateering prize captured by English sailors during Elizabeth's reign, in 1592.[72] He later noted the statistics of the highly controversial

---

[72] Robert Lacey, *Sir Walter Ralegh*, New York, 1974, p. 173. Waters, op. cit., pp. 233-4.

Harriot's notes on 'The caracte taken by Sir J. Bourros' round off the dimensions which he notes he obtained from Hakluyt, as he records 'See Voyages. 2. 198' (BL Add. MS 6788, fo. 41). Harriot gives the dimensions as 'length .100. foot. [by the heel] bredth 47. ft. depth .31.6.' and calculates 'by this recconing of 1457. tonnes but counted 1600. tons'. Hakluyt attributes the measurements 'by the exact rules of Geometricall observations' as by 'one M. Robert Adams, a man in his faculty of excellent skill' who 'found the length from the beak-head to the sterne (whereupon was erected a lanterne) to containe 165 foote. The breadth in the second close decke whereof she had three, this being the place where there was most extension of bredth, was 46 foot and 10 inches. She drew in water 31 foot at her departure from Chochin in India, but not above 26 at her arrivall in Dartmouth, being lightened in her voyage by divers meanes, some 5 foote. She caried in height 7 severall stories, one main Orlop, three close decks, one forecastle, and a spar decke of two floores a piece. The length of the keele was 100 foote, of the maine-mast 121 foot, and the circuite about at the partners 10 foote 7 inches, the maine-yard was 106 foote long. By which perfect commensuration of the parts appeareth the hugenes of the whole, farre beyond the mould of the biggest shipping used among us either for warre or receit.' Hakluyt, reprint of 1600 edn. of *Principall Navigations*, London, J. M. Dent, 1927, vol. V, p. 67.

Prince Royal, the largest English warship constructed up to the time of its launching in 1610, noting that estimates of its displacement ranged from 1,000 to 1,400 tons.[73] From all of these observations, Harriot drew some original quick conclusions of his own:[74] 'I am of [the] opinion that [the] depth is to be regarded with the bredth for [determining] the length of the mastes. . . The length of the ship in this reckoning I thinke also to be litle regarded because, when the mast is fitted in bredth & depth, it cannot be amisse for the longest dimension. . .' This quick estimate led Harriot to search for a mathematical solution which would correct the straight-line proportionality currently used by Baker and his fellow shipwrights. And in the tradition of the Renaissance scholar, Harriot began his search (working in Latin, naturally) among the classical mathematicians, finding his answer in Proposition XXI of Book I of the *Conics of Apollonius of Perga* in a geometrical construction which he proceeded to resolve into numerical proportions.[75] On the basis of this new solution, Harriot drew up a chart giving the proper length of the main mast for any vessel planned ranging from 12.5 to 1,562.5 tons, thus covering the whole range of Elizabethan merchant or war vessels. On the sheet of calculations in which Harriot derived his mathematical formulae, he records the event[76] 'Invented this Feb. 28 ♄ [his symbol for Saturday] $\frac{1607}{1608}$. & gaue it to: E. Marlow for Mr. Baker the Shipwrite.'

From other manuscripts of Harriot in the British Library, it is obvious that Harriot continued to work on improving shipbuilding techniques until the death of Ralegh in 1618. But most of these papers are in chaotic condition, and the drawings to which the calculations are keyed are missing, so that it is nearly impossible to determine just how precise Harriot's specifications really were. Other textual references

[73] BL Add. MS 6788, fo. 41.
[74] Ibid., fo. 4.
[75] Ibid., fos. 8, 10.
[76] Ibid., fo. 3. This is one of the very few dating errors to be found in Harriot's papers. 28 Feb. 1607/8 was a Sunday, not the Saturday that the astronomical symbol for Saturn indicates. 28 February 1606/7 was a Saturday, hence this note could have been either year.

show that he continued to work with Captain Marloe and Master Shipwright Baker, sharing with them his new information. This he did until his death. But during the period from the early 1580s until the late 1590s, work with ships, sailors, and navigation occupied most of his waking hours. Certainly he was intimately involved in every aspect of planning, preparing, and even performing in Ralegh's naval exploits, proving himself to be one of the most proficient of England's theorists and practitioners of the expansionist arts.

Ralegh sponsored a reconnaissance to America in 1584, designed to locate a site for future colonial efforts and to gain first-hand information about what was to be expected in such a venture. The first account of this voyage was that given by Raphael Holinshed in his 1587 edition of the *Chronicles*.[77] Though brief, this account gives most of the salient information:

In this yeare, 1584, euen at the prime of the yeare, namelie in Aprill, Maister Walter Raleigh esquier, a gentleman from his infancie brought vp and trained in martiall discipline, both by land and sea, and well inclined to all vertuous and honorable aduentures, hauing built a ship and a pinesse, set them to sea, furnished with all prouisions necessarie for a long viage, and commited the charge of them to two gentlemen (his own seruants) the one called Philip Amadis; the other Arthur Barlow, with direction to discouer that land which lieth between Norembega and Florida in the West Indies; who according to their commission, made as sufficient a discouerie thereof as so short a time would permit: for they returned in August next following, and brought with them two sauage men of that countrie, with sundrie other things, that did assure their maister of the goodnesse of the soile, and of great commodities that would arise to the realme of England, by traffique, if that the English had anie habitation, and were planted to liue there. Wherevpon, he immediatelie prepared for a second viage, which with all expedition (nothing at all regarding the charges that it would amount vnto) did presentlie set in hand.

Arthur Barlowe's discourse of this voyage, published by Hakluyt in his *Principall navigations* in 1589,[78] has been said by Professor Quinn to have 'had many attractions ... and well deserves its high reputation as one of the clearest contemporary pictures of the contact of Europeans with North

[77] *The Chronicles of England, Scotland, and Irelande, etc.*, vol. III (1587), col. 1369. This account is reprinted as Doc. 3 in *Roanoke Voyages* (I. 90–1).
[78] pp. 728–33; reprinted as Doc. 4, *Roanoke Voyages*, I. 91–116.

American Indians.' But, as Quinn continues, 'Its ethnological value is substantial, but for the historian its omissions are exasperating.'[79] One of these exasperating omissions is a list of the participants in this voyage, since Barlowe mentions only the two captains and eight other members of the company, who must have formed only a very small portion of the real crew and persons involved. Two vessels were employed: the flagship which was most likely the 200-ton *Bark Raleigh*, under the command of Amadas and with Simon Fernandez as pilot, the Portuguese who had sailed with Ralegh on the Gilbert expedition of 1578; the other, undoubtedly Ralegh's pinnace *Dorothy*. If, as Barlowe insisted, both vessels were 'well furnished with men and victuals', there must have been more than a hundred seamen, soldiers, and observers aboard. Knowing the role that Harriot had in Ralegh's household and his very close connection with Ralegh's naval activities, it is hard to believe that he was not one of the members of the Amadas–Barlowe expedition of 1584.

Quinn has mustered the evidence that probably both John White and Thomas Harriot (who played such primary roles in the 1585 voyage) were among those making this preliminary survey of Virginia. His case for John White is based primarily on his claim that his 1590 voyage was his fifth trip to Virginia,[80] which would have mandated that he have made the one in 1584. His case for Harriot's attendance is more subtle, but is equally logical and cogent. This is based primarily on the assumption that it was Harriot who took charge of 'the two sauage men of that countrie', Manteo and Wanchese, brought back to England on the return of the expedition. Quinn's arguments, though extended, bear repetition on this important matter:[81]

We might well ask, since White and Harriot were to be close partners in the newly named Virginia in the next year, whether they did not serve an apprenticeship together on the 1584 voyage; in other words whether Harriot's practical experience in America did not begin in 1584 rather than 1585.

[79] Ibid. I. 15.
[80] See White's letter to Hakluyt, 4 Feb. 1593, ibid., Doc. 107 (II. 715).
[81] 'Thomas Harriot and the New World', pp. 38–40.

This is not a matter on which we have any direct evidence, but there are some indications in the surviving materials which make it not improbable, though it must be stressed that his presence on the first Virginia voyage of 1584 is a conjecture rather than an established fact. It is at least probable that Arthur Barlowe and Philip Amadas (or one of them) had been Harriot's pupils before he set sail; Amadas was to sail again in 1585 as 'admiral of Virginia' and was something of an authority on maritime affairs. Hitherto it has been supposed that Harriot became involved with North America directly only after the return of the ships to England in September; that it was then he learnt to understand something of what the two Indians brought home had to say and was able to teach them some English. The narrative of Arthur Barlowe, as we have it in the form in which it was first published in 1589, was almost certainly prepared for circulation as promotional material for the 1585 venture as early as November or the beginning of December 1584. It contains geographical information which would seem to have required some linguistic bridge to be established before it could become intelligible. While the Indians brought back were reported on 18 October to be still unable to make themselves understood in English, but were referred to in mid-December as sources of information on the new land discovered by Amadas and Barlowe, it is clear that remarkable advances in contact with them were made during a very short period, so short as to raise serious doubts on whether it was possible in the time available. Nonetheless it was Harriot who was credited with making the bridge; it was he who by July 1585 had a working knowledge of Carolina Algonquian; and who was sent out then to take special note of everything concerning the Indians which was relevant to the English plans for settlement. It might seem much more possible for Harriot to have done what he did if he had indeed been able to go on the 1584 reconnaissance. This would have given him some practical knowledge of the problems of navigation on which he had been theorizing for some time; it would have given him six weeks of fairly intensive contact with the Indians in which to get some inkling of their language and of the topography of their tribal arrangements; he would, too, have had some weeks on the ship going back to England to begin the communication of English to the two Indians, Manteo and Wanchese, who were taken with the ship; there would then be a good possibility that, with his rapid capacity for learning new techniques, he had himself established some command over the language by the time of their return in the middle of September 1584. Even if the Indians were not able to make themselves understood by the middle of October, their English was probably sufficient, and Harriot's Algonquian adequate, for a good deal of information to be incorporated rapidly in the version of Barlowe's narrative which, it is suggested, was circulated, and for the statement in the bill put before the House of Commons on 14 December to confirm Ralegh's American rights to be justified on the basis that by 'some of the people borne in those parties brought home into this our realm of England . . .

singular great comodities of that Lande are revealed & made known
vnto vs.' Thus, though there is no direct evidence that Harriot was in
Virginia in 1584, if we accept him as the main (or sole) linguistic link
between the Algonquian-speaking Indians brought to England and the
English people, his employment on the 1584 voyage would appear to
be a necessary concomitant.

It is obvious through his writings about Virginia that
Harriot did master the Algonquian language and was the
main spokesman for the Ralegh expeditions in their early
years. This alone would set him aside as one of the most
advanced linguists of his time and the first Englishman to
master this highly complicated language. According to the
notes of John Aubrey, Harriot went even farther: he developed a special alphabet for the recording of the Indian
language:[82] 'Dr. Pell [John Pell the mathematician, later a
friend of Walter Warner] tells me that he finds amongst his
papers (which are now, 1684, in Dr. Busby's hands), an
alphabet that he had contrived for the American language,
like Devills.' It was undoubtedly his intent, as his writings
show, to compile a dictionary of Indian words and to record
them in such a way that their original sounds would be
preserved. But unfortunately, neither his 'alphabet. . .like
Devills' nor his dictionary which must have occupied much of
his time in the mid-1580s has survived. What papers might
have been in the hands of Dr Richard Busby, headmaster of
Westminster School, cannot now be known, since no Harriot
papers of any kind remain among his papers, though he is
known to have been interested in the Indians and their
language. There is some evidence in the registers of Sion
College that some of the Indian notes were in the possession
of Nathaniel Torporley and left in the Sion College library.
If so, these were destroyed in the fire that destroyed that
library in the late seventeenth century and have thus been
lost.[83]

---

[82] Clark edition, *'Brief Lives'*, I. 285. Clark suggests that the 'like Devills'
might reflect the use of symbols like tridents and pictures such a code message
in a volume in Queen's college, Oxford. (*Life and Times of Anthony à Wood*,
5 vols. Oxford, 1891, I. 498 and following facsimile. Unfortunately there is
nothing in Harriot's symbols like those shown here.)
[83] An Indian dictionary was indicated as having been burned in that fire,
according to records found in the index there by Wallace and Tanner.

There are, however, a few brief samples of a strange
writing scattered among Harriot's manuscripts and in the
Torporley papers remaining at Sion College. Though curious
and enigmatic, these remained generally unnoticed until
1956 when Miss Ethel Seaton collected a large number of
them and systematically studied them in an attempt to 'break
the code'. Beginning with the most frequently repeated
grouping, which she rightly assumed to be Thomas Harriot's
own name, followed by an identification of names of his
friends, she gradually evolved a series of letters which permitted her in general to 'translate' most of the fragments
remaining. But Miss Seaton missed the most important aspect
of Harriot's symbols. She saw this cryptic writing as a simple
transliteration code with cabalistic overtones. As she explained his efforts:[84]

Thomas Hariot's name is very nearly what he himself would probably
have recognized as a mystical circular name. It begins and ends with the
same letter, and it has the vowels o and a repeated in reverse order; the
frequent omission of i or y in the script (as here) may have been meant
to increase the palindromic effect. Harriot evidently then played the
school-boy trick (played also by Dr. Dee in his diary with Greek script)
of transliterating English words to disguise them. Several alphabets and
series of letters in this script occur in the manuscripts, but even in these
private papers Hariot was wary and did not provide the English alphabet
to de-code them.

Writers since this time have generally followed Miss Seaton's
lead, and have referred to Harriot's 'secret writing' or attempts
to conceal by means of a code. Unfortunately, this interpretation does Harriot a serious injustice.

A closer study of the extant samples of the writings which
exist has been made independently by the author and W. Alec

[84] See Ethel Seaton, 'Thomas Hariot's Secret Script', *Ambix*, V.4 (October
1956), 111–14. This is from p. 111. Though Miss Seaton was very ingenious in
arriving at a general understanding of Harriot's symbols, her failure to see them
as phonetic sometimes led her astray. For example, in one of the Sion College
examples, she mistakes 'llwt' — the phonetic for 'lute' — as 'pewt' which she
expands to 'pewter', which makes no sense. Mr Alec Wallace of Louisburgh,
County Mayo, Ireland, went farther, though he again felt that the writing was a
transliteration. He has used this writing to identify a map of Ralegh's Irish estates,
now in the National Maritime Museum at Greenwich, as having been copied by
Harriot while he was a resident of Ireland in 1589. I should like to thank Mr
Wallace for reporting his decisions, and Dr Louis Arena for transcribing Harriot's
symbols into the International phonetic alphabet.

Wallace of Louisburgh, County Mayo, Ireland. These studies
show that what Miss Seaton called 'Harriot's secret script'
was not an attempt to conceal, but a serious and scientific
attempt to reveal the true sound of the language — a phonetic
rendition of the words as pronounced, and not a transliteration of the words as spelled in English. It is evident that in
preparation for his year among the Virginia Indians, Harriot
prepared himself by creating a scientific kind of writing
which would enable him (and any other who held the key)
to reproduce the exact sound of the spoken words he had
heard in person. To create such a phonetic rendition, Harriot
had applied his analytical mind to the analysis of the manner
in which voice sounds were created, and had attempted to
create a symbol for each different vocal pattern. In this, he
was generations ahead of his time, developing, as he so often
did, a totally new and imaginative way to solve a problem
which had not been generally recognized as being a problem.

There was actually, in the 1580s, very little for Harriot
to draw on in searching for a sound transcription method
that would be constant and accurate. Because of the great
shifts in pronunciation in the century between Chaucer and
Shakespeare, many grammarians had become upset by the
inadequacies of English spelling. Men like Thomas Smith and
Richard Mulcaster had proposed simplified spelling to make
the written word more nearly conform to the spoken word.
But the classical influence was strong, and Latinisms were
generally to be preferred to the colloquial. Only one English
writer, John Hart, who has been referred to as 'the first
phonetician of modern times', had attempted, in a very
partial way to construct a phonetic spelling.[85] Hart recognized
the difference between voiced and unvoiced pairs (p–b; t–d;
f–v); for these sounds he used the ordinary arabic letters.
He did, however, create new letters to differentiate between
the sounds of initial sounds in *g*in (ʒ), *ch*in (ꙩ), *sh*in (ʃ),
*th*in (ꝼ), and *th*en (ð). But he oversimplified the vowel
sounds, indicating only two forms of each vowel — the 'long'

[85] John Hart, *An Orthographie, conteyning the due order and reason, howe to write or paint thimage of mannes voice, most like to the life or nature* [London] 1569. See also his *A Methode or comfortable beginning for all vnlearned, whereby they may bee taught to read English*, London, 1570.

vowel differentiated by a dot under the letter, and the 'short' vowel without. A brief look at some of Hart's simple passages will reveal how little his symbols actually show about the way in which they were actually pronounced.[86]

In developing his own phonetic alphabet, Harriot decided to discard the total alphabet used for writing or printing English. Instead, he developed a wholly new cursive script, patterned, it seems, on the kind of symbols which had evolved in the study of cossic numbers. Cossic (or algebraic) numbers were used widely, though not universally, to delineate powers and roots. In one of his mathematical sections where he is exploring how best to indicate powers and roots, Harriot shows his familiarity with the symbols popular with such algebraists as Diophantus, Vieta, Stifel, Clavius, and Stevin.[87] It was the notation of Stifel and Clavius that he occasionally used himself, and which furnished the model for his cursive phonetic script.

Obviously, Harriot studied carefully the mechanics of sound production in the use of the vocal cords, placement of the lips and tongue. Though he did not leave a treatise on phonetics nor a key to his symbols, there is one sheet of different size and texture, slightly crumpled, inserted among his mathematical papers, BL Add. MS 6782, fo. 337, which does give enough clues to unlock the meagre samples which remain. On the right half of the sheet are thirty-six symbols, six paired groups above the line representing twelve vowel sounds, and twenty-four grouped consonant symbols below the line. On the left half of the sheet are thirty-six words illustrating the sounds of the thirty-six letters. Figure 5 reproduces these phonetic sounds and words in the International Phonetic Alphabet to give, at last, a key to the interpretation of any passages now available or any that may appear in the future.

---

[86] A sample passage given in the *Orthographie* reads as follows: An exersiz or dat huile iz sed: huer-in iz declard, hou clerest ou de consonants ar mad bei dinstruments ou de mouth: huile uaz omited in depremisez, for dat ui did not mule abiuz In standard English, this would read: 'An exercise of that which is said, where-in is declared, how the rest of the consonants are made by the instruments of the mouth: which was omitted in the premises, for that we did not much abuse.'

[87] BL Add. MSS 6782, fo. 277.

VOWELS

POSITION	FRONT			CENTRAL			BACK	
HIGH	i (b<u>ee</u>t)	*ıℓ*	ai (b<u>i</u>te)		*ʒ*	u (b<u>oo</u>t)	U (b<u>oo</u>k)	*ℓ* *z*
	ı (b<u>i</u>t)	*ɛ*						
MID	e (b<u>ai</u>t)	*ℓ*	ə (b<u>u</u>t)		*z*	o (b<u>oa</u>t)		*ʒ*
	ɛ (b<u>e</u>t)	*ℓ*						
LOW	æ (b<u>a</u>t)	*2*	a (b<u>o</u>ther)		*ᴦ*	ɔ (b<u>a</u>ll)		*ᴦ*

CONSONANTS

		BILABIAL	LABIO-DENTAL	INTER-DENTAL	ALVEOLAR	ALVEO-PALATAL	VELAR	GLOTTAL
STOPS	Vl	p			t		k	
	Vd	b			d		g	
FRICATIVES	Vl		f	θ	s	š		h
	Vd		v	ẟ	z	ž		
AFFRICATES	Vl					č		
	Vd					ǰ		
NASALS		m			n		ŋ	
LATERAL					l			
GLIDES					r	y	w	

Fig. 5 Harriot's Phonetic Alphabet

Harriot's phonetic alphabet shows clearly that he was greatly in advance of any of the linguists of his day. He clearly understood the placement of the tongue on the roof of the mouth as it affects the issued sound; he paired these sounds as front, medial, and back sounds. He also paired the voiced and unvoiced consonants, and the quality as well as the quantity of the vowels. Altogether, Harriot had compiled a series of phonetic symbols which, because of his amazing care and insight, was fully capable of the task he had set for himself – that of recording for his fellow countrymen the true sound of the language spoken by Manteo, Wanchese, and their fellow Virginia savages. It is almost possible to see him practising his transcription and writing some sample words: Manteo,  ; Wanchese, 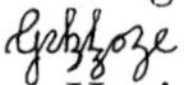 ; Virginia, .

Having prepared his linguistic tools, instructed the sea captains in the mathematics in which they were weak and supplied them with the most modern of observational tools, and having collected his own battery of scientific and technological artifacts for observations in the new world, Harriot must have felt thoroughly prepared for a year of totally new experiences among unknown peoples in an unexplored world, a great adventure for a twenty-five-year-old Englishman of that day.

IV. New Horizons, 1585–1590

The autumn of 1584 following the return of Amadas and Barlowe from their preliminary expedition to the New World was a busy one for all members of Ralegh's household. Harriot was active on many fronts — continuing to learn Algonquian from Manteo and Wanchese, refining his phonetic symbols for the accurate recording of Indian speech, gathering new navigational instruments and scientific instruments for use in his investigations on the voyage and during the year he was planning to spend in Virginia, in instructing Ralegh's sea captains for their ventures on the broad Atlantic, and such other miscellaneous duties as Ralegh assigned to him. Ralegh was mustering all his friends and associates to assist in preparing for a major colonization effort, and using all his influence and powers of persuasion to assemble the ships, supplies, and manpower he felt needed to establish a firm English colony in a savage land. Though there was much scepticism about the possible success of such a venture, there was a growing commercial interest, since the rewards of trade and piracy in England's growing naval force were beginning to be felt in the general economy. Elizabeth and many of her principal officers had profited immensely from successful forays against Spanish and Portuguese vessels, and growing dislike and distrust of Spain furnished even more impetus for continuing the undeclared naval warfare already generally acknowledged to exist.

At Ralegh's request, Richard Hakluyt attempted to divert the Queen to an interest in the possible profits to be realized from exploiting the resources of a whole new continent. He prepared a strongly worded manuscript which he hoped would enlist her personal and financial support of Ralegh's

113

venture: 'A particuler discourse concerninge the greate
necessitie and manifolde comodyties that are like to growe
to this Realme of Englande by the Westerne discoueries lately
attempted, written in the yere 1584. by Richarde Hakluyt
of Oxforde at the requeste and direction of the righte worshipfull Master Walter Raghly, nowe knight, before the
comynge home of his Two Barkes.'[1] This manuscript was
not widely circulated, but was, as Quinn points out,[2] 'regarded as a confidential study of English external relations
so far as the non-European world was concerned and as
Hakluyt was himself in the Queen's service in the diplomatic
sphere.' But it goes far beyond political propaganda; it shows
clearly the depth of thought and planning that was going into
Ralegh's preparations. The final chapter, 'A note of some
thinges to be prepared for the voyadge',[3] outlines various
areas that must be pre-planned: foods and spices necessary
for feeding the voyagers; seeds, birds, and animals that
should be carried for propagation for sustenance of the
settlers; expert soldiers and fortifications builders to ensure
protection against the savages; artisans for housing the
planters; artisans to produce articles of trade for the returning ships; and service employees to remain with the colony
as butchers, barbers, tailors, shoemakers, and bottlemakers.
All of these required advance effort, as Hakluyt pointed out
as 'divers thinges require preparation longe before the voyadge,
withoute the which the voyadge is maymed.'

Ralegh also called upon one of his professional soldier
friends[4] to advise him on the protection and governance
of a colony in a remote and savage land. An anonymous

[1] This is reprinted in E. G. R. Taylor, *The Original Writings & Correspondence
of the Two Richard Hakluyts*, 2 vols., London, Hakluyt Society (Second Series,
vols. LXXVI, LXXVIIO, 1935, Doc. 46ʳ (II. 211–326). The title-page is reproduced in David B. Quinn, *The Hakluyt Handbook*, 2 vols., London, Hakluyt
Society (Second Series, Nos. 144–5), I. 285. This title-page must have been for
a late draft of the work, since though it says that it had been composed in 1584
before the return of Amadas and Barlowe in mid-September, it also refers to the
recent knighting of Ralegh. Ralegh was knighted on Sunday, 6 Jan. 1585.
[2] *The Hakluyt Handbook*, I. 284.
[3] Taylor, *Original Writings. . .of the two Richard Hakluyts*, II. 320–6.
[4] This document is no. 8 in *The Roanoke Voyages*, I. 130–9. Though unable
finally to identify the author, Quinn proposes as possible Sir Roger Williams,
Sir John Smythe, or Thomas Digges, ibid., pp. 19–22.

manuscript recently found in the Essex Country Records
Office carries the heading 'For Master Rauleys Viage.' and
is endorsed as 'Notes geuen to Master Candishe'. It is obvious
from this document that early planning was for a much
larger and more complex settlement effort than finally came
about. For example, this study called for a defence force
for dealing both with the savages and protecting against
possible Spanish attacks of at least 800 soldiers, whereas
the actual expedition totalled 600, of whom not more than
200 were soldiers.[5] It was on this enlarged scale that an
administrative organization was proposed and a programme
of fortification and exploration was outlined. To maintain
close supervision of soldiers and workers one Captain was
to be named for each fifty men, an unusual concentration
of overseers. Constant guard of 100 sentinels was to be
maintained night and day, and it was planned that exploration and military preparation should proceed simultaneously:[6]

Whylst the forte is buldyng I would haue, 200, that should continually
goe a discoueryng, and returne euery eyght or tenthe day, and then
200, mor to do the lyke and that Companys that Com from discouery
to be iij days exempte from labor wache or ward after ther returne,
so as yow shall haue ,500, men to labor for the buldying of your forte.

Because of the danger of the situation, military discipline was
to be very strict throughout the colony. Disorders specifically
named and the penalties they should incur were listed as
follows:[7]

First that no Souldier do violat any woman [. . .death], 2 That no
Souldier do take any mans goods forcibly from hym [. . .a dubbell
restitution, if the souldier be not abell, to haue a years Imprisonment
the whype and bannishment or condemd to the gallys for vij years.
and the party to haue his restitution of the prince]. 3 That no Indian
be forced to labor vnwillyngly [. . .iij monthes Imprisonment]. 4. That
no Souldier shall defraud Her Maieste of her fyfte [. . .deathe or a
perpetuall Condemnation to the gallys or myns.]. 5 That no Souldier
abbandon his ensegne without leaue, of his Capten [deathe or vij
yeres Slauery]. 6 That non shall stryke or mysuse any Indian [. . .to
haue xx blows with a cuggell In the presentz of the Indian strucken.].
7 That non shall Enter any Indians howse without his leaue [vj monthes
imprisonment or slauery]. 8 That non shall stryke within the forte nor

[5] Ibid., no. 21 and n. 5, p. 173.   [6] Ibid., pp. 131-2.   [7] Ibid., pp. 138-9.

fytt within a myll of It [. . . lose of hand.]. 9 That non offer to draw
any weapon vppon any Conseler or his Captain, [present deathe without
remission.], 10 That no Souldier sleep in sentenell or abbandon his
sentenell or garde [present deathe without remission.].

Extreme and even brutal as these punishments seem to us
today, they are generally in line with the military and civil
punishments of their time, and in their recognition of the
rights of natives, reflect a more enlightened view than that
customary in the new world. In this, they reveal the very
enlightened view of both Hakluyts that such humane treatment was needed if the settlers were to win the Indians
away from their paganism and to embrace the enlightened
view of the Anglican church.[8]

Like Hakluyt, this anonymous Ralegh adviser felt it
important to discuss the special talents that the formation
of a new colony would require. The military specialists he
was leaving to the military commanders, since 'all men
know what ar nessesary', except that he would be sure that
they add[9] 'an Ingenyr and Cunynge trcucsc [traverse] Master
whos Iugment wer abell to know the places of Best aduantages
to buylde on, he to bulde, with Iugment that his forte be
not to byge, that his men may not be abell to defend It, not
to littell for that is more dangerus. . .' But other non-military
experts should also be included:[10]

Then I would haue a phisitien as well for the healthe of the souldier
as to discouer the simpels of earbs plantes trees roothes, and stons, [a]
good geographer to make discription of the landes discouerd, and with
hym an exilent paynter, potticaris and Surgiantes for low sycniss and
woundes.

An alcamist is not Impertinent, to trye the mettaylls that maybe
discouerd and an perfett lapidary not to be forgotten. Masons, Carpenters, makers of mudwals, su[m] of ye myners of Cornwell, Sume
excelent husband men, with all thinges appertayninge to husbandry. . .

Besides the military chain of command which he assumed
to be that of normal levels, an elaborate governmental
structure was suggested. A general was to be of total authority
in all matters, assisted by an advisory Council. A High

---

[8] Taylor, *Original Writings. . . of the two Richard Hakluyts*, II. 318, 334.
[9] *Roanoke Voyages*, I. 135.
[10] Ibid., I. 135–6.

Treasurer, especially charged with 'reseaue[ing] all apper-
taynynge vnto the Prince' would administer all petty
treasurers, auditors, customers, and other officers designated
as controllers, searchers, and such like. To this High Treasurer,
the Admiral was required to make quarterly reports giving
the treasures that had been accumulated, and especially
accounting for the fifth part of all which were reserved for
the Crown. From such listings in the preliminary planning,
it is obvious that Ralegh planned an expedition of considerable magnitude — one which would be a major endeavour in
any age.

Ralegh fully expected to be the leader of the fleet and
governor of England's first overseas colony. The rise in
fortune that had come to Sir Francis Drake following his
circumnavigation of the world in the years 1577 to 1580
furnished a model which Ralegh hoped to emulate. Most of
his accumulated resources were going into this venture, and
he was straining his credit in anticipation of vast returns. It
was a great shock to him when late in 1584 the Queen,
desiring him by her side, refused him permission to leave
England. What effect this decision had on the fate of the
venture is conjectural, but it is almost certain that had
Ralegh been in charge his enthusiasm, energy, unity of
purpose, and experience in leading people would have
brought the expedition to greater success than that achieved
by those who substituted for him.

It was not that the Queen was totally unmoved by Ralegh's
petitions. She was aware of the significance of the new
world's resources, and of the benefits to be had from maintaining a stronghold so near the Spanish shipping lanes. She
agreed to contribute the use of the *Tiger*, a galleass listed
variously as from 140 to 200 tons, which Ralegh immediately
named as flagship or 'admiral' of his expeditionary force.
But recruitment of other vessels was disappointing; though
there were rumours that a fleet of sixteen vessels had been
assembled, the shipping records from Plymouth indicated
that only 'vi shippes and barkes' carrying 'vi hundred men
or thereabowts' were in the final fleet.[11] Besides the *Tiger*,

---

[11] Ibid., no. 21 (I. 173).

carrying 160 men, two of Ralegh's own ships, the *Roebuck*, a flyboat of 140 tons, and the *Dorothy*, 50 tons; the *Elizabeth*, 50 tons, probably owned and provisioned by Thomas Cavendish; and the *Lion* (or *Red Lion*) of Chichester, 100 tons, owned at least in part by her captain, George Raymond. Two pinnaces, also owned by Ralegh, were towed by the *Tiger* and either the *Lion* or *Roebuck*. Of the 600 aboard, approximately half were sailors, 200 soldiers, and the rest settlers committed to remain in Virginia for at least a year in exchange for a promised grant of land in the new colony.

Unfortunately, though the expedition was but a fraction of that originally planned, it retained much of the over-elaborate administration and organization that had been arranged to satisfy all factions who were contributing to its support. Sir Richard Grenville, of an old Cornish family that dated back to the Norman Conquest,[12] was placed in charge of the sea portion of the expedition and given the dual title of General and Admiral. Grenville, not previously associated closely with Ralegh, as a Member of Parliament for Cornwall had been a member of the House committee called to confirm the Queen's Letters Patent for Ralegh's grants in the new world.[13] Thomas Cavendish, aged twenty-five and on his first sea assignment, was High Marshal, probably in repayment for his furnishing a vessel. Philip Amadas, a member of Ralegh's household who had at the age of nineteen the year before scouted the Virginia coast and located the island of Roanoke, was named Sir Richard's Vice-Admiral. Simon Fernandez, the Portuguese pilot with Amadas and Barlowe in 1584, was again Chief Pilot. Francis Brooke (not positively identified) was High Treasurer. And Ralph Lane, an equerry of the Queen's household, a soldier who had more than a decade of experience as a privateer and had been released from duty in Ireland by the Queen to go to Virginia, was Lieutenant to Sir Richard. Also gathered around Grenville as members of his Council on the *Tiger* were a number of young gentlemen of the west country:

[12] A. L. Rowse, *Sir Richard Grenville of the* Revenge: *an Elizabethan Hero*, Boston and New York, Houghton Mifflin Co., 1937.
[13] *Roanoke Voyages*, no. 6, I. 123.

Grenville's half-brother, John Arundell; his brother-in-law, John Stukeley; one of the Kendalls; a Prideaux.[14]

Once the expedition reached Virginia, however, to begin the activities of settling a colony, if Sir Richard Grenville was to return to England, a totally new administrative organization would take over. Ralph Lane became Governor of the colony. Amadas became Admiral of Virginia. Edward Stafford and John Vaughan were Captains of two of Lane's military companies. And because of Lane's penchant for high-sounding titles, he had *carte blanche* to create new positions. As a matter of fact, Lane's account of the expedition is full of pretentious titles, most of whom are not identified with any name: a Colonel of the Chesapians; Sergeant Major; Master of the Light Horsemen; Master of the Victuals; Keeper of the Store; and (to replace Francis Brooke who had returned with Grenville) a Vice-Treasurer.

The confusion inherent in these elaborate organizations seems compounded when the individuals involved are considered. Sir Richard Grenville, though he was to become an Elizabethan legend as a master of sea warfare in later years, was, so far as can be determined, on his first ocean voyage,[15] though he was in complete charge of every aspect of it. Lane, on the other hand, though put in a decidedly inferior role in the navigational part of the expedition, had had considerable experience in maritime affairs, having led marauding fleets to the coasts of Morocco and Spain, and served as an agent of the Queen in investigating unlawful imports as early as 1571.[16] Yet he was primarily a military man who had been called upon to build fortifications in Ireland, and who had created considerable unrest when he served as sheriff of County Kerry before he was released from those duties to

---

[14] A listing of the names of those colonists who remained with Lane in Virginia after the departure of Grenville is given in *Roanoke Voyages*, I. 194–7. Quinn, here and in other passages, identifies some of the settlers. William S. Powell of the University of North Carolina, on a Guggenheim grant, spent some time in England trying to identify as many as possible of the Roanoke colonists. Though I have not seen his final report, he has published some information in 'Roanoke Colonists and Explorers: an Attempt at Identification', *North Carolina Historical Review*, XXXIV (1957), 202–26.

[15] Rowse, op. cit., p. 203.

[16] *Calendar of State Papers, Domestic*, (1547–80), 418.

assume his responsibilities in Ralegh's voyage of exploration and settlement.[17] It seems inevitable that two such self-centred, strong-willed individuals as Grenville and Lane, placed in such a dual system of responsibility and leadership would come into conflict, and would generate friction among the seamen, soldiers, and settlers subject to such confused leadership.

Much too little is known of the settlers themselves to assess their potential or to show how carefully they were chosen for their task. Including Lane, there were evidently 108 soldiers and settlers who stayed the year in the new world; of most we know only their names. In his report on the colony, Hakluyt printed the list as 'The names of all those as well Gentlemen as others, that remained one whole yeere in Virginia, vnder the Gouernement of Master Ralfe Lane'.[18] Of the 107 names given, fourteen are designated as 'Master',[19] one is listed as 'Captain' (since the second Captain is given as a Master),[20] and three, probably boys, are given first names only — Daniel, Smolkin, and Robert. The remainder are listed by given and family names, nearly all of which are common English names and hence very difficult to identify or trace. The fact that spellings of the same name are so diverse in different accounts makes identification even more tenuous. Both Professor Quinn and Professor William S. Powell have spent much time in searching records for more information, but the results are by no means complete. Most of the accounts are general, and for this expedition a detailed chronicle which would outline just what was done and by whom is lacking. Nearly all the relevant documents are to be found in Professor Quinn's very thorough and scholarly two volumes on *The Roanoke Voyages*: they include an anonymous journal of the *Tiger* (possibly written by Barlowe),[21]

---

[17] John Knox Laughton in his biography of Lane in the *DNB* cites a letter of Sir Henry Wallop to Burghley in which he complains 'that Lane expected "to have the best and greatest things in Kerry, and to have the letting and setting of all the rest. . ."' This is dated 21 May 1585.

[18] *Roanoke Voyages*, no. 24 (I. 194–7).

[19] Masters Philip Amadas, Hariot, Acton, Edward Stafford, Maruyn, Gardyner, Thomas Haruie, Snelling, Anthony Russe, Allyne, Polyson, Kendall, Prideox, and Hugh Rogers.

[20] Captaine Vaughan.

[21] *Roanoke Voyages*, no. 23 (I. 178–93).

the account in the 1587 edition of Holinshed's *Chronicles*,[22] letters of Ralph Lane and Grenville,[23] Lane's discourse on the first colony as printed by Hakluyt,[24] annotations about John White's drawings,[25] and, most complete of all, Harriot's *A briefe and true report of the new found land of Virginia*.[26] Yet all of these were but a prelude for the major account of Ralegh's efforts in exploring and developing Virginia – this was to be a full account prepared by Harriot, one which apparently was completed but never published for some reason, and whose manuscript, though searched for by many over many years, has never come to light.[27]

Yet without the positive identifications which Harriot's chronicle would probably have furnished, certain observations are possible about the nature of the group and the friends and associates with whom Harriot spent his most exciting year. Undoubtedly the members of this expedition reflected a cross-section of English society of the day. Beyond the leaders who moved in high social and court circles in England, most of the gentlemen of the group were from London or from the old families of the west country. Undoubtedly, too, some were carefully selected specialists with specific tasks assigned to them. Many reports, including their own, show that Harriot was the 'good geographer to make description of the landes discouerd' and that John White was the 'excilent paynter' who was to accompany him. Both men had been in Ralegh's entourage previously, and both followed through on their obvious assignments. Quinn has identified the 'Alcamist' expected 'to trye the metayls that maybe discouered' as the one listed as 'Doughan Gannes' and called by Lane as 'Master Youghan' or 'Yougham'[28] as the Jochim Gaunse (Joachim Ganz) who was associated with George Nedham at the Keswick works of the Mines Royal Company in improving copper smelting methods in

[22] Ibid., no. 22 (I. 173–8).
[23] Ibid., nos. 25, 26, 27, 28, 29, 34 (I. 197–221).
[24] Ibid., no. 45 (I. 244–303).
[25] Ibid., no. 55 (I. 398–463).
[26] Ibid., no. 51 (I. 317–87). This is the text of the 1588 edn., collated with the 1589 Hakluyt and the 1590 de Bry.
[27] Cited from the 1588 edn., sig. [F-4$^{r\&v}$].
[28] *Roanoke Voyages*, I. 196, n. 1.

1581. In all likelihood this was the Joachim Ganz born in Prague as the son of David Ganz, astronomer and historian. As a Jew, Ganz's views of religion would have been of interest to Harriot who was already seeking ways to base beliefs on reason rather than faith, and it must be assumed that the two had more in common than their interest in the natural resources of the new land.

According to the possible identifications of William S. Powell, a number of the settlers were adventuresome young college graduates, mingled with young sons of gentle parents who anticipated university education following their return. Among those who remained with Lane for the year, Powell identifies Thomas Luddington[29] as a Fellow of Lincoln College, Oxford, later named as Preacher to the City of Lincoln. William White[30] he found as a graduate of Brasenose College, and suggests that he may have influenced Thomas Hulme[31] to enter 'the same college the year following his return home'.[32] Marmaduke Constable[33] was a young graduate (1581) of Caius College, Cambridge, and Thomas Harriot, of course, from St. Mary's Hall, Oxford, in 1580.[34] Other professional men identified as of common intellectual interest by Powell would include Robert Holecroft of Middlesex,[35] later a lawyer, and David Williams[36] a Welsh lawyer

[29] Though Luddington is not given the title 'Master' which a degree would have entitled him to, he is listed as no. 5 in Hakluyt's names in the midst of the highest-ranking gentlemen of the group. Powell's identification is in his 'Roanoke Colonists and Explorers', op. cit., p. 215.

[30] Ibid., p. 216. The difficulty in making identifications can be seen in the fact that the Register of the University of Oxford lists eight William Whites between 1565 and 1595. It is also possible that this is not properly a William White, but a misprint for John White, since his name is not on the list though we know he was among the settlers. Quinn suggests that (1) he may have drawn up the list for Hakluyt and forgot to put his name on the list; (2) he may have been listed as William White; or (3) he may have been given the name of John Twyt. *Roanoke Voyages*, I. 196, no. 7. White is no. 56 on Hakluyt's list; Twyt is no. 83.

[31] Ibid. Hakluyt lists Hulme as no. 63.

[32] This must be an erroneous identification. One Thomas Hulme graduated MA from Brasenose in July 1600, having completed his BA from Cambridge before February 1596/7. The Thomas Hulme who matriculated at Brasenose in 1586 did so on 13 May of that year, which would have been impossible for a colonist, since they were in Virginia during that month. See the Oxford Registers, II (1), p. 370; II (3), p. 201; II (2), p. 151.

[33] Ibid., p. 218, no. 45 on Hakluyt's list.

[34] Ibid., p. 219, Hakluyt no. 2.

[35] Ibid., p. 216, Hakluyt no. 20.   [36] Ibid., pp. 220-1, Hakluyt no. 99.

and Member of Parliament (1584 and 1586-9), who later became a London judge. Anthony Russe (or Rowse)[37] he identified with the Anthony Rowse who was MP for Cornwall, knighted in 1603. Though some of these identifications must be considered highly questionable, there can be no question but that the exciting attraction of a voyage to a new world and the opportunity to experience a totally new and primitive culture must have attracted some of the more venturesome young intellectuals to join the expedition. From all accounts, this was a young and hardy group, with an average age in the mid-twenties, so that Harriot would have much in common with many of them.

But many of the colonists came from the lowest social classes, too. Powell identifies John Brocke[38] as a shoemaker; John Fever[39] as a basketmaker; Christopher Marshall[40] as a customs official; and Rowland Griffin[41] as convicted of robbery and imprisoned in 1594. The commission granted to Ralegh by the Queen to take up shipping and mariners[42] was extremely broad, permitting the impressment of any ships, mariners, and soldiers to be found in the counties of Devon and Cornwall, or in Bristol. And that Ralegh would overlook the fruitful available manpower in the prisons is highly unlikely. As a matter of fact, Hakluyt, in his preparation of the *Discourse of Western Planting* for the Queen, specifically pointed out the benefits to England, and to the prisoners themselves, of impressing prisoners for the Virginia expedition:[43]

... the prisons and corners of London are full of decayed marchantes overthrown by losse at sea, by usurers, suertishippe[44] and by sondry other suche meanes, and dare or cannott for their debtes shewe their faces, and in truthe many excellent giftes be in many of these men, ... for that these men, schooled in the house of adversities ... may be employed to greate uses in this purposed voyadge, ... and to take of

[37] Ibid., p. 217, Hakluyt no. 11.
[38] Ibid., p. 214, Hakluyt no. 84.
[39] Ibid., Hakluyt no. 48.
[40] Ibid., p. 216, Hakluyt no. 98.
[41] Ibid., p. 215, Hakluyt no. 81.
[42] *Roanoke Voyages*, Doc. 1, 25 Mar. 1584 (I. 82-9). See also no. 10 (I. 144-5).
[43] Taylor, *Original Writings* ..., II. 326.
[44] Suretyship, i.e. imprisonment for having furnished surety for a defaulting debtor and not being able to pay.

them and of others that hide their heades and to employe them, for so they may be relieved and the enterprice furthered in many respectes.

There is inferential evidence that Ralegh was proceeding to recruit settlers by using the Queen's authority to take them from prison. When, for some unknown reason, he submitted the Queen's Letters Patent to Parliament for their confirmation, there was widespread discussion of the almost unlimited conscription authority he had been granted.[45] One of the amendments proposed in the House was designed to restrict Ralegh's ability to recruit debtors:[46] 'Provided allwayes that this Acte or anie thinge therein contayyned shall not in any wise be intended to geve any Licence power or Aucthority to any person or persons beinge in Prison either vppon Execucion at the sute of any person for debte or being imprisoned or vnder Arreste for any other cause whatsoever.' This restriction was not put into effect, however; though confirmation passed through the Commons and was presented to the House of Lords, it was withdrawn from there without action, probably at the request of the Queen who may have felt such a restriction on the scope of her royal Letters Patent would form a dangerous limitation of her prerogative. By her signet letter issued in June of 1585,[47] she renewed her blanket authorization for Ralegh to recruit for his Virginia activities.

The leaders, sailors, soldiers, colonists, and specialists that sailed from Plymouth on 9 April 1585 were a motley group, representing the cream and the dregs of Elizabethan society. But one thing they had in common: they were, in general, totally inexperienced in the roles and duties they were to perform. Except for Philip Amadas, Simon Fernandez, Arthur Barlowe (if he were on this second voyage), and possibly two of the masters, John Clarke and George Raymond, none had sailed on the broad Atlantic, and certainly none had experienced the difficulties of survival in primitive and savage lands, totally divorced from supplies or aid from a home base completely inaccessible in times of emergency. Even the most stout-hearted must have been prepared for trouble.

[45] *Roanoke Voyages*, no. 7 (I. 126–9).
[46] Ibid., p. 128.
[47] Ibid., no. 20 (I. 156–7).

Troubles there were, beginning with heavy seas and high winds shortly after leaving the southern shores of Britain. A storm in 'the Bay of Portingal' sank the *Tiger*'s pinnace and scattered the vessels. Sir Richard Grenville in the flagship continued on alone, reaching the Canaries on 14 April. There he tarried only long enough for fresh water and supplies, and headed for the West Indies without waiting for the other vessels, since a place for rendezvous had been established for Guayanilla Bay on the southern coast of Puerto Rico. Though records of the crossing are not adequate to determine the matter absolutely,[48] the evidence that does remain suggests that both Harriot and White were on board the major vessel of the expedition, the *Tiger*, carrying Grenville and most of the members of his council.

During the long sea voyage Harriot must have been very active. This was a practical opportunity for him to try out the navigational theories that he had been teaching. Undoubtedly he gained thorough experience in taking nautical observations, checking measurements of time against the stars. Ten days out of Plymouth, five days east of the Canaries, on 19 April, he made observations of the eclipse of the sun (which was not total in those waters[49]) though whether he attempted to use these observations to calculate longitude accurately is doubtful. But he was certainly able to test the traditional and crude dead reckoning of position by more accurate celestial observations than most pilots were capable of, probably using both the improved staff and back staff which he had developed for Ralegh's seamen. He noted the variation of the compass by measuring magnetic north against the position of the pole star, improving known charts of variation for future instructions in seamanship. And as

---

[48] The detailed logs being missing, the story of the voyage must be pieced together from the materials included by Quinn, ibid., Ch. III (I. 158-242). See S. E. Morison, *The European Discovery of America, the Northern Voyages, AD 500-1600*, New York, Oxford, 1971, pp. 633-5.

[49] Quinn (*Roanoke Voyages*, I. 380-1, n. 4) estimates the position of the *Tiger* on this day to have been approximately 20° N. latitude, 30° W. longitude. He cites Mr D. H. Sadler, Superintendent of HM Nautical Almanac Office, to the effect that at this position 'a partial eclipse would have been seen about sunset, but only the beginning would have been visible since the Sun would set about the time of greatest phase which at this point would be roughly one-quarter of the Sun obscured.'

they proceeded through the West Indies, Harriot gathered specimens of fruits and vegetables, sugar, ginger, tobacco, and pearls as samples of the richness possible through colonization or trade, to be returned to Ralegh along with John White's drawing of many of the same things. It was not in Harriot's nature to delay in beginning his work as Ralegh's scientific observer in the new world.

After leaving the Canaries, the *Tiger* continued to sail west, following the equatorial current, and made a rapid crossing. Land was signed at the island of Dominica in the Leeward Islands on 7 May. Dutifully, John White sketched the horizon as viewed from the ship.[50] Proceeding on past Santa Cruz (St. Croix) of the Virgin Islands,[51] they arrived at Puerto Rico, 10 May, and landed on a small island off the south coast for refreshment. They proceeded the next day to the Bay of Mosquetal (now Guayanilla Bay), their established rendezvous in the event the fleet had been scattered en route. While waiting for the other ships, Grenville put everyone to work: part of them, probably including Harriot and White, began an elaborate earthwork fortification for protection against the Spaniards;[52] the rest began construction of a new pinnace to replace the one that had been lost at the outset of the voyage.[53] On 19 May Cavendish arrived with the 50-ton *Elizabeth*, a great relief to Grenville, since he now felt strong enough to fight off any marauding Spaniards who might attack.

By 23 May the pinnace was finished. That same day the Spaniards had promised to deliver the needed supplies for which Grenville had negotiated. But when they did not come, Grenville went inland about 4 miles seeking them,

---

[50] All references to the John White drawings are to the definitive two-volume *The American Drawings of John White, 1577–1590, with drawings of European and Oriental Subjects*, by Paul Hulton and David Beers Quinn, published jointly by the British Museum and the University of North Carolina Press, 1964. The drawing of the horizon of Dominica is pl. 2 in the volume of plates, vol. II.

[51] Ibid., on the same plate as Dominica.

[52] Ibid., pl. 3.

[53] According to the anonymous *Tiger* journal (*Roanoke Voyages*, p. 181): 'The 13. day we began to builde a new pinnesse within the Fort, with the timber that we then felled in the countrye, some part whereof we fet[ched] three myle vp in the land, and brought it to our Fort vpon trucks, the Spaniards not daring to make or offer resistance.'

and, not finding them, fired the woods and returned to their fort.[54] Perhaps fearful of reprisal, Grenville decided to leave their rendezvous even though the rest of the fleet had not yet arrived. A message was cut into the trunk of a tree to inform them of the change in plans,[55] the fort was fired, and the following morning the *Tiger* and the *Elizabeth* withdrew from the mosquito-infested bay. Remaining near the coast, however, Grenville found himself in shipping lanes, and within a day of withdrawing had seized a small and a large Spanish frigate.[56] Grenville took the larger frigate with the Spanish captives to San German for ransom, and sent Lane with the smaller one to Roxo Bay on the south-west side of the island for a load of salt for future trade.[57] With which group Harriot travelled is not certain, but it is probable that he stayed with White who went with Ralph Lane. White's drawing of the loading of the salt[58] shows that a fortification was raised around the area to protect the workers from attack, and Harriot was well read and experienced in fortifications, as his manuscripts show.[59] But this salt venture had unfortunate consequences. While engaged in this assigned task, Lane found himself being observed by a force of Spanish horsemen and foot soldiers. In his excitement, Lane estimated the hostile force to be much larger than it was, and he felt that Grenville had without justification put his life, and those of his men, in danger. As he later wrote to Lord Burghley:[60]

My exceptione vnto him for which, and for his engaginge of me with onely squadre of .xxv. Souldiours and six Spanishe prisoners, with mattockes and Spades, (at Cape Rosso against the gouernour there

[54] Ibid., p. 183.

[55] Ibid., p. 161.

[56] Ibid.

[57] Ibid., pp. 184–5.

[58] *American Drawings of John White*, II, pl. 4.

[59] For Harriot's notes on the disposition of soldiers and earthwork fortifications, see BL Add. MS 6788, fos. 50–65. Harriot's drawings are remarkably like the earthworks here and at Roanoke, though they are conventional enough for that time that identification cannot be certain. Modern drawings of the archaeological excavations of the Roanoke fort are to be found in Jean Carl Harrington, *Search for the Cittie of Ralegh; archaeological excavations at Fort Ralegh, North Carolina*, Washington, National Park Service, 1962. The fort reconstruction is shown in Fig. 25, p. 30.

[60] *Roanoke Voyages*, Doc. 42 (I. 229).

Diego Melindes with fortye horse & -300- foote) to lade salte, where he
toulde me I shoulde fynde none to resiste, but findinge the contrary,
my tellinge him of it bred the grete vnkindnes afterwardes one his parte
towardes me.

It was at this point that the disaffection began between Lane
and Grenville which was to spread and divide the company.

On this same day, 29 May, The *Tiger* and *Elizabeth*,
strength augmented by the new pinnace and the captive
frigate, turned away from the West Indies and followed the
gulf stream up along the Spanish coast. According to the
unknown chronicler of the *Tiger*, several stops were made
along the way.[61] At Hispaniola, for instance, the reception
on both sides was most cordial: the English set up two
banqueting halls, one for gentlemen and the other for servants,
and enjoyed 'a sumptuous banquet. . .served. . .all in Plate,
with the sound of trumpets, and consort of musick', for
which the Spaniards reciprocated by furnishing horses for all
who would ride and releasing three of their fiercest bulls for
a hunt in which all three were slain. Gifts were exchanged
among the men, and supplies of all kinds were furnished
freely. Yet in spite of the 'great good will' with which they
parted, the English felt that it was their strength and ready
preparation that earned the respect they had enjoyed.

Both Harriot and White were fully occupied on their
voyage up the coast. One of their principal tasks was that
of observing the coastline and making any corrections they
felt significant in the charts of the area they possessed.[62]
In addition, White was collecting specimens of tropical flora
and fauna, making remarkably accurate water-colour drawings of crabs, scorpions, alligators, as well as fruits, birds,
and fish never before seen by Englishmen in general.[63]
According to Paul Hulton and David Quinn,[64] '[White]

[61] Ibid., Doc. 23 (I. 186-9).
[62] John White's map of eastern North America from Florida to Chesapeake
Bay is no. 110 (pl. 58) in *The American Drawings*, and the map of Ralegh's
Virginia is no. 111A (pl. 59). Both are reproduced in black and white in *Roanoke
Voyages* between pp. 460 and 461 of vol. I.
[63] See nos. 5A-32A in *The American Drawings*. The editors, Hulton and
Quinn, have arranged these illustrations as nearly chronologically as possible.
[64] Ibid., 'John White's Significance for Natural History', I. 47-52. This
quotation is from p. 47.

has some substantial claim to be the first to make a North American contribution to the great achievement of the Renaissance in exploring, identifying and recording the flora and fauna of the planet, an achievement which was a major element in the establishment of the scientific outlook and the making of modern man.' Harriot, whose notes have not had the good fortune to survive, must have taken the observations to determine longitude and latitude of the various sites and sought information about the native names and uses of the plants and animals being recorded by his scientific colleague.

Leaving the Spanish coastal waters, the Grenville fleet approached its destination in Virginia, on 23 June almost wrecking themselves 'on a breache called the Cape of Feare' (identified by Quinn as the modern Cape Lookout).[65] The following day, the 24th,[66] '. . . we came to anker in a harbor [probably Beaufort Harbor] where we caught in one tyde so much fishe as woulde haue yelded vs xx. pounds in London. . .' Two days later, on 26 June, they arrived at the island of Wococon in the Carolina outer banks (probably composed of parts of the present Portsmouth and Ocracoke Islands)[67] where they were able to land and establish a land base. On 29 June they suffered their first Virginia mishap: in attempting to bring the *Tiger* into the Wococon harbour, Simon Fernandez ran it aground on the shoals, and the vessel keeled over and sank.[68] A large portion of the supplies which had been accumulated for the colonists was destroyed, so that they were left without provisions to begin their long stay in this remote land.[69]

Undaunted by this accident, Grenville continued with the planned programme. Part of the men were assigned to the rescue and repair of the *Tiger*; others began to prepare for a programme of exploration.[70] On 3 July a small party was sent to Roanoke Island to announce their arrival to King Wingina; on the 5th John Arundell and Manteo made a

[65] *Roanoke Voyages*, I. 188; II. 868.
[66] Ibid. I. 188.
[67] Ibid. I. 189; II. 867.
[68] Ibid. I. 189.
[69] Ibid. I. 177.
[70] All these details are recorded in Doc. 23, *Roanoke Voyages*, I. 189-93.

The arriual of the Englifhemen   II.
in Virginia.

He fea coafts of Virginia arre full of Ilâds, wehr by the entrance into the mayne lâd is hard to finde. For although they bee feparated with diuers and fundrie large Diuifion, which feeme to yeeld conuenient entrance, yet to our great perill we proued that they wear fhallowe, and full of dangerous flatts, and could neuer perce opp into the mayne lâd, vntill wee made trialls in many places with or fmall pinnefſ. At lengthe wee fownd an entrance vppon our mens diligent ferche therof. Affter that wee had paffed opp, and fayled ther in for af hort fpace we difcouered a migthye riuer fallnige downe in to the fownde ouer againft thofe Ilands, which neuerthelesswee could not faile opp any thinge far by Reafon of the fhallewnes, the mouth ther of beinge annoyed with fands driuen in with the tyde therfore faylinge further, wee came vnto a Good bigg yland, the Inhabitante therof as foone as they faw vs began to make a great an horrible crye, as people which meuer befoer had feene men apparelled like vs, and camme a way makinge out crys like wild beafts or men out of their wyts. But beenge gentlye called backe, wee offred the of our wares, as glaffes, kniues, babies, and other trifles, which wee thougt they deligted in. Soe they ftood ftill, and perceuinge our Good will and courtefie came fawninge vppon vs, and bade us welcome. Then they brougt vs to their village in the iland called, Roanoac, and vnto their Weroans or Prince, which entertained vs with Reafonable curtefie, althoug the wear amafed at the firft fight of vs. Suche was our arriuall into the parte of the world, which we call Virginia, the ftature of bodee of wich people, they rattire, and maneer of lyuinge, their feafts, and bankctts, I will particullerlye declare vnto yow.

Fig. 6 The Landing of the English

preliminary voyage to the mainland, and Captains Aubrey and Boniten travelled up the outer banks. On Croatoan, the island just north of Wococon, they found two men who had been left there by Captain Raymond in June, and brought them back to the main party two days later. By 11 July preparations were completed for a full-scale survey of the mainland coast, and a large segment of the group was enlisted in this enterprise.

According to the unknown chronicler of the *Tiger*, four vessels were brought into this action, probably to impress the natives with the strength and the majesty of the Queen's emissaries. General Grenville, accompanied by Masters Arundel and Stukely and 'diuers other Gentlemen' led the procession in their 'Tilt boate' — a Thames boat covered with an awning to protect the passengers. They were followed in the new pinnace by Masters Ralph Lane, Thomas Cavendish, Thomas Harriot, and twenty others who are not named. Two ships' boats wound up the small fleet, one carrying Admiral Amadas, Captain Clark, and ten others, and a second with the Treasurer Francis Brooke, John White, and others. Obviously Harriot as a member of the Council held superior status and was an attendant of the Governor; White followed with the Admiral as second in command. But once ashore they worked together and shared their experiences and notes.

Provisioned for eight days, this voyage of exploration lasted just a week, starting on Sunday, 11 July, and returning to Wococon on the following Sunday, the 18th. Three Indian villages were visited: Pomeiok on Monday, Aquascocke on Tuesday, and Secotan, where they 'were well intertayned there of the Sauages' on Thursday. Undoubtedly, at each stop there were formal greetings from the Queen's emissaries to the native king, and the exchange of gifts.[71] It was, therefore, possibly a misunderstanding which led to the first of a series of hostilities with the savages. As reported by the *Tiger* observer:[72] 'The 16. we returned thence [to Secotan], and one of our boates withe the Admirall [Philip Amadas] was sent to Aquascococke to demaund a siluer cup which one of the Sauages had stolen from vs, and not receiuing it according to his promise, we burnt, and

---

[71] Among Harriot's MSS, BL Add. MS 6788, fo. 417ᵛ, is a listing of the various kinds of copper ornaments that should be taken as gifts for the natives on a later trip. This MSS is dated 29 Jan. 1601/2.

[72] *Roanoke Voyages*, I. 191.

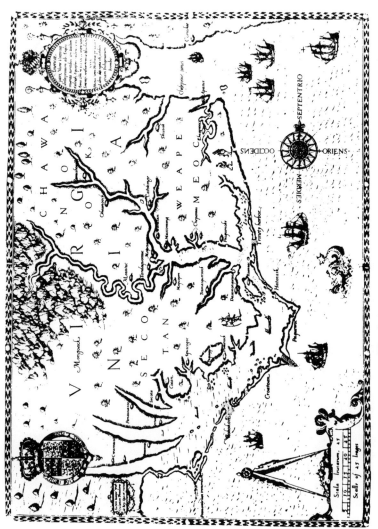

Fig. 7 Map of Ralegh's Virginia

spoyled their corne, and Towne, all the people beeing fledde.'
On Sunday, 18 July, they returned to Wococon where they
found that the *Tiger* had been refloated, newly caulked, and
was once more ready for service.

This week furnished both Harriot and White their first
experience of the native Indians with whom they would
spend the coming year. White made drawings of the two
villages of Pomeiok and Secotan,[73] their inhabitants,[74] and
some of their customs. Harriot continued his notes on the
Indian names for the things he saw, and gathered information
on their customs and beliefs.[75] As he wrote later of the
Indians of these southern cities:

This people therefore voyde of all couetousnes lyue cherfullye and att
their harts ease. . .[76]

And to confesse a truthe, I cannot remember that euer I saw a better
or quietter people than they. . .[77]

. . . as my selfe obserued and noted downe at by beinge amonge them.[78]

Obviously Harriot began his association with the Indians
with a favourable impression of them, and must have resented
the brutal burning of Aquascococke by the Admiral of
Virginia, Amadas.

On Thursday, 29 July, Manteo brought Granganimeo,
brother of King Wingina, on board the *Tiger* to meet with
the leaders of the expedition, and to offer them the hospitality
of his brother's island of Roanoke as the headquarters of
their colony. Granganimeo and Wingina had impressed
Amadas and Barlowe during their visit the year before, and
the tentative plans to make Roanoke their major base of
operations for the coming winter was probably formulated
at this time. On 5 August Master John Arundell was dis-
patched to England in the fastest of their vessels, probably
one of the prizes,[79] to carry news to Ralegh and the Court

---

[73] *The American Drawings*, no. 34A, pl. 31; no. 38A, pl. 35.
[74] Ibid., nos. 35A, 37A, 39A, pls. 32, 33, 36.
[75] Ibid., nos. 41A-53A, pls. 35-48.
[76] Harriot's headnotes to the de Bry engravings in Theodore de Bry's *America*,
part I, no. XX, 'The Towne of Secota'.
[77] Ibid., no. XXIII, 'The Marckes of sundrye of the Cheif mene of Virginia'.
[78] Ibid., no. XVII, 'Their manner of prainge with Rattels abowtte the fyer'.
[79] *Roanoke Voyages*, I. 192, n. 4.

of their safe arrival, of their decision to winter at Roanoke in spite of the loss of most of their provisions, and that Sir Richard Grenville would return with the remainder of the fleet to restock their supplies and to return with additional recruits. During the next three weeks the move was made; the colonists with their belongings and supplies were moved to Roanoke Island, a site was chosen, and work on Fort Ralegh was begun. On 25 August Sir Richard Grenville and his fleet 'wayed anker, and set saile for England.'[80]

With the departure of the fleet, Ralph Lane (now Governor of Virginia and in full control of the activities of the colony) and the 107 other men who remained with him were left totally isolated from further support from home. No news of their problems or successes could reach England; no help could come from there. Only the native people and the hostile Spaniards were near, the one a totally unknown element and the other always a possible threat. It is most unfortunate that so little evidence remains of just how they met the daily challenges that faced them, what natural leadership evolved from the heterogeneous collection of individuals thrown into such close fellowship. Just two accounts of this important year remain, both designed for special purposes and less complete and detailed than would be desired. First of these was the report on the first colony made by Governor Lane for inclusion in Richard Hakluyt's 1589 edition of *The Principall navigations*; the second was Thomas Harriot's *A briefe and true report*, written to quell adverse reports about Ralegh's efforts to settle Virginia and to encourage new recruits, published in February 1587/8 and republished by Hakluyt in the same edition with Lane's.[81] Though they agree in most of their details, they give very different impressions of the new world, differences which reflect the different personalities of the two observers.

Hakluyt's title to Lane's account spells out the exact period of his leadership of the colony:[82] 'An account of the

----

[80] Ibid. I. 192.

[81] Both of these are edited by Quinn in *Roanoke Voyages*; Lane's discourse as no. 45 (I. 255–94), Harriot's as no. 51 (I. 317–87). In Hakluyt's *The Principall navigations, voiages and discoveries of the English nation . . .*, London, 1589, Lane's account occupies pp. 737–47; Harriot's, pp. 748–64.

[82] Hakluyt, *Principall navigations*, 1589, p. 737.

particularities of the imployments of the English men left in
Virginia by Sir Richard Greeneuill vnder the charge of
Master Ralfe Lane Generall of the same, from the 17. of
August, 1585, vntill the 18. of June 1586, at which time
they departed the Countrie: sent, and directed to Sir Walter
Ralegh.' Obviously sensitive to the criticisms which had
been levelled at his handling of colonial affairs, Lane's
narrative alternates between apology and truculence. It is
divided into two sections: the first designed to[83] 'declare
the particularities of such partes of the Country within
the mayne, as our weake number, and supply of things
necessary did inable vs to enter into the discouery thereof.'
The second part was[84] 'touching the conspiracy of Pemisapan, the discouerie of the same, and at the last, of our
request to depart with S. Francis Drake for England.' Yet in
both of these, Lane reveals himself as a man greedy for
precious metals and pearls, and cruel and stern as a military
disciplinarian. To have retained the respect and esteem that
they held under his leadership must have been trying for men
as clearly understanding and sympathetic as Harriot and
White.

Giving no credit to Grenville for the explorations he had
conducted before his departure, Lane stressed the extent of
their investigations in an area approximately 100 miles in
radius from Roanoke. 'The vttermost place to the Southward
of any discouery was Secotan, being by estimation four score
miles [actually about 100 miles] distant from Roanoak';[85]
'To the Northwarde our furthest discouerie was to the
Chesepians, distant from Roanoak about 130. miles [slightly
over 100 miles]';[86] and 'To the Northwest the farthest place
of our discouerie was to Choanoke distant from Roanok
about 130. miles [really less than 100 miles.]'[87] Naturally,
all these explorations were carried out by water, since in
these virgin forests armed men and supplies could be transported only by boats. But this easy access by water brought
danger, too, and as a soldier Lane was not content with
Roanoke as a permanent site for his colony. In his view it
was much too restricted in scope and vulnerable to attack,

[83] Ibid.   [84] Ibid., p. 742.   [85] *Roanoke Voyages*, I. 256.
[86] Ibid. I. 257.   [87] Ibid. I. 258.

both from the Indians on land and the Spanish by sea. Lane also was distressed at the lack of quick wealth to be garnered in the Roanoke vicinity: there were no metals to be found, not even copper, and no precious stones or even pearls. So Lane early began to search for an interior location more wholesome, rich, and capable of development.

The local Indians carried rumours of a wealthy tribe dwelling in the vicinity of Chesapeake Bay, and Lane decided to divide his forces to send a winter encampment to the north. Though details of the locations of this site are intentionally vague to protect it from molestation, Lane records that access was difficult because 'the passage to it was very shalow and most dangerous, by reason of the breadth of the sound',[88] but once reached would be an ideal site for a colony:[89]

> ... the Territorie and soyle of the Chesepians (being distant fifteene miles from the shoare) was for pleasantnes of seate, for temperature of Climate, for fertilitie of soyle, and for the commoditie of the Sea, besides multitude of beares (being an excellent good victual, with great woods of Sassafras, and Wall nut trees) is not to be excelled by any other whatsoeuer.

These were cogent reasons for a possible move away from Roanoke, but probably a more persuasive one was the hope that the Chesapeake would furnish the quick wealth that had not been found on the more southerly waters. Rumours were afloat of an island in the Chesapeake where '[a] King had so great quantitie of Pearle, and doeth so ordinarily take the same, as that not onely his owne skins that he weareth, and the better sort of his gentlemen and followers, are full set with the sayd Pearle, but also his beds, and houses are garnished with them, and that hee hath such quantitie of them, that it is a wonder to see.'[90] John White's map of eastern North America from Cape Lookout to Chesapeake Bay[91] places this site on the southern shore, 6 or 7 miles

---

[88] Ibid. I. 257.

[89] Ibid.

[90] Ibid. I. 260.

[91] Printed as Illustration 7, ibid. I, facing p. 461 in black and white, and analysed in II. 847–48. It is reproduced in colour in *The American Drawings*, II, no. 110, pl. 58.

south-west of Cape Henry. Though no dates are given, it is probable that a group of settlers moved north about October, wintered in that area, returning to Roanoke about February. Quinn suggests that this party[92]

... was organized under a colonel who might have been any of Lane's leading assistants, Harriot, Amadas, Stafford or Vaughan being least unlikely... It certainly included either Harriot or White, or both, as the map indicates that some detailed survey work was done, including marking a shoal near the head of Currituck Sound, noting a final breach in the Banks, and tracing the coastline round Cape Henry to a fair depiction of Lynnhaven Bay, and a more conjectural drawing of the land and water distributions to the west and north...

Of the two, other evidence from Lane would place the presumption that it was White, not Harriot, who wintered away from Fort Ralegh. Lane mentions Harriot only twice in his narrative, but one of those calls attention to the fact that one of the few individual houses just outside the fort belonged to Harriot.[93] It seems highly unlikely that Harriot would have maintained a personal house at Roanoke during the winter of 1585-6 had he been leading a party in the environs of the Chesapeake Bay. Much more likely it was White who was there, charting the coastlines and visiting the Indian villages near by for inclusion on his maps, for the drawings he was preparing to take back to Walter Ralegh who was being knighted during the days the winter expedition was taking place.

Harriot did almost certainly accompany Lane and his men on their expedition of March 1586 to explore the Chowan and Roanoke rivers. Lane's original plans called for this party to proceed as far up the rivers as was easily navigable, and then to trek overland to the south bank of the Chesapeake to seek the wealth in pearls reputed to be there. But the Indians who had formerly been friendly were by this time beginning to show animosity. At Chawanoac he found himself engaged in skirmishes, and discovered that chief Wingina, long friendly to the English, was raising the natives for an assault on the expedition and the fort. A strong soldier and short-tempered, Lane entered the town; most of the chiefs fled into the

[92] *Roanoke Voyages*, I. 245.   [93] Ibid. I. 282.

forest, but Lane captured one of them, Menatonon, who was crippled. For two days Lane kept Menatonon in chains while he interrogated him about the lands and resources of the interior. From him he heard tales of precious metals (just what could not be determined since the Algonquian word for metal, copper, or gold was the same), and more rumours about the fabulous pearls on the Chesapeake, which excited the men greatly. Taking Menatonon's favourite son, Skiko, hostage, Lane sent him back to Fort Ralegh in the pinnace, and with about forty men and a number of friendly Indians including Manteo set out to travel further up the Roanoke river to seek the fabled gold and pearls.[94]

Wingina and his braves continued to harass the party; following them from the banks, they prevented them from obtaining any supplies to augment their diminished stocks. After three days of hard rowing upstream, reserves were exhausted to the point where Lane reported that they were reduced to eating cooked dog and boiled sassafras leaves. Obviously this hardship led finally to much criticism of Lane's leadership, since in his report Lane stresses that he was acting in a democratic manner throughout. As he tells the story,[95] it was he who suggested an immediate return to Fort Ralegh, but that the men, after a night of deliberation, voted to proceed:

Their resolution fully and wholly was (and not three found to be of the contrary opinion) that whiles there was left one halfe pinte of corne for a man, that we should not leaue the search of that Riuer... This resolution of theirs did not a little please mee, since it came of themselues, although for mistrust of that which afterwards did happen, I pretended to haue bene rather of the contrary opinion.

Two days later, however, after another skirmish with the Indians, though no one had been injured, the men were in more dire straits. Lane again suggested a return to Roanoke, and this time[96] '.. found my whole companie ready to assent vnto: for they were nowe come to their dogs porredge, that they had bespoken for themselves... wee had nothing

[94] This story is scattered through Lane's account, but is neatly pieced together by Quinn on pp. 246-7.
[95] Ibid. I. 267-8.
[96] Ibid. I. 272.

in the worlde to eate but pottage of sassafras leaues, the like wherof for a meate was neuer vsed before as I thinke.' The next day, Easter Sunday, 3 April, the men discovered Indian weirs holding fish and had their first real meal in a number of days. The following morning they were able, refreshed, to begin their return to Fort Ralegh, alive but disgruntled over their failure to find the fabled wealth they had sought.

On their return to the fort, they found more evidence of the Wingina plot to destroy the settlement. Skiko, Mena-tonon's son, had given favourable testimony of the plot, and other friendly Indians had reinforced his revelations. It appeared that Wingina was arousing all the neighbouring tribes for a concerted attack on Fort Ralegh and the adjacent settlement. It was in explaining this plot that Lane revealed that Harriot had a private house near his own:[97]

In the dead time of the night they would haue beset my house, and put fire in the reedes, that the same was couered with: meaning (as it was likelye) that my selfe would haue come running out of a sudden amazed in my shirt without armes, vpon the instant whereof they would haue knocked out my braynes.

The same order was giuen to certaine of his fellowes for Master Herriots: so for all the rest of our better sort, all our houses at one instant being set on fire as afore is sayde, and that as well for them of the forte, as for vs at the towne.

The day of assembly of the tribes was set for 31 May with the assault on the settlement ten days later, on Friday, 10 June. Again, however, Lane took firm action to forestall this attack. On the first of June, the day after their pre-liminary assembly, Lane, with about twenty-five men, including 'the Colonel of the Chesepians' (whom Quinn surmises was either Philip Amadas or Thomas Harriot) and the 'Serient maior' (also unnamed, but probably the other),[98] crossed the Sound to the Indian village of Dasemunkepeuc where the tribes were assembled. Lane tried first to im-mobilize the Indians by stealing all their canoes, but when that failed tried another ruse, claiming the escape of Skiko to gain access to King Pemisapan, as Wingina now called him-self,[99] so that

[97] Ibid. I. 282.   [98] Ibid. I. 287, notes 1 and 2.   [99] Ibid. I. 287.

...hereupon the king did abide my comming to him, and finding my selfe amidst 7. or 8. of his principal Weroances, & followers, (not regarding any of the common sort) I gaue the watchword agreed vpon (which was Christ our victory,) and immediatly those his chiefe men, and himselfe, had by the mercie of God for our deliuerance, that which they had proposed for vs.

During the ensuing fight Lane said the King himself, though apparently shot by the 'Colonel of the Chesepians', suddenly rose and fled, but was followed into the woods and slain by Edward Nugent and the deputy provost. With the King and his major supporting chiefs slain, the immediate danger to the settlement was dissipated, though the enduring hatred of the Indians was to remain.

It is almost certain that as Ralegh's geographer Harriot was an important member of these exploratory and military expeditions and must have participated in these forays. In discussing the fruitless voyages up the Chowan and Roanoke rivers Lane comments upon Harriot's information gathered from the natives:[100] 'For this riuer of Moratico promiseth great things, and by the opinion of Master Harriots the heade of it by the description of the country, either riseth from the bay of Mexico, or else from very neer vnto the same, that openeth out into the South sea...' But it seems highly unlikely that he could have been the 'Colonel of the Chesepians' who drew his pistol and shot King Wingina during the raid on their assembly headquarters. Rather, Harriot appears to have been repelled by Lane's brutality in dealing with the Indians — capture of Menatonon and his son, and his slaying of Wingina and his fellows. In his own account (discussed later in more detail) Harriot showed himself more sympathetic to the Indians than Lane appears to have been, believing them less treacherous and more helpful in general than did the impetuous soldier Lane. Though he seldom spoke a word against anyone in his account, Harriot did in this case:[101] '...some of our companie towardes the ende of the yeare, shewed themselues too fierce, in slaying some of the people, in some towns, vpon causes that on our part, might easily enough haue been borne withall...' These words also show Harriot to have had a close association with violent moments

[100] Ibid. I. 273-4.   [102] *Briefe and true report*, 1588, fo. F2ᵛ.

of the early settlement, and one whose counsel and advice was not always taken.

With the immediate Indian threat quelled and time for the early corn harvest approaching, Lane felt that the prospects for success of the Roanoke colony were good. There was still concern that the anticipated supplies to be brought by Sir Richard Grenville had not arrived, though the established day had long since past. Lane was still proceeding to see himself as the military leader of the Virginia venture; he was making plans for his new base on the Chesapeake with deep waters and a more healthful environment. To establish this he planned a two-pronged attack: a chain of small military posts across land from the Upper Chowan River to keep the land-route open, while the bark and two pinnaces moved by sea to convey the colonists and their supplies to their new headquarters.[102] But before this action could get under way, Sir Francis Drake arrived with his fleet, and the situation took on new dimensions.

Drake, who had been waging war on the Spaniards in the West Indies since September 1585, heard in Florida that the Spaniards were making plans to root out the British colony before it could establish a firm foothold.[103] This news had caused him to change his plans and to turn north to rescue Lane and his countrymen, or to give them what assistance they needed. Neither Drake nor Lane was aware that Sir Richard Grenville, with the anticipated supplies and reinforcements, was on the way. Had Grenville arrived first, the story of the English colonial undertaking might well have been totally different, and a strong foothold in the new world obtained at this first effort.

The accidents of Drake's prior arrival and the early mid-June hurricanes which led Lane and his colonists to abandon Roanoke and return to England before the arrival of Grenville's support brought much censure to Lane and his colony.

---

[102] This is the same plan that Lane suggested later for the defence of England in preparation for the Spanish invasion attempts of 1588.

[103] David B. Quinn, ed., *New American World: A Documentary History of North America to 1612*, 5 vols., New York, Arno Press, 1979, vol. III, pp. 307–10, gives the report of a foreign observer (probably German) who had talked with Drake in August 1586 after his return with the colonists, and who explained his reasons for visiting Virginia on his return to England.

It was to respond to this criticism that Lane devoted much of his report on his actions as Governor of Ralegh's Virginia settlement. Lane is particularly defensive about this action. Unlike his critical treatment of Grenville, Lane is unstinting in his praise of the generosity of Drake towards his fellows in distress. At their coming, Lane was still planning additional explorations, the moving of the colony headquarters to the Chesapeake Bay, and the securing of a deep-water base for future Virginia activities. His early requests to Drake were, thus, for the support that would strengthen these actions: 'not onely of victuals, munition and clothing, but also of barkes, pinnaces and boates, they also by him to be victualled, manned, and furnished to my contentation.'[104] He was also to exchange some of his experienced boatmen and artificers for some of the weak and unfit colonists whom Lane wanted to return to England. All these things were agreeable to Drake, and it was while supplies and boats were being transferred to Lane's command at Roanoke that 'there arose such an vnwonted storme, and continued foure dayes'[105] that threatened to drive Drake's fleet aground. Quickly the Admiral withdrew his ships to the safety of the open sea, while Lane and his men were lashed by the winds ashore.

It was following this latest danger and in ignorance that Ralegh's support was coming that the decision was made to abandon Roanoke and return to England immediately. But again, Lane protested, the decision was not his alone, but was a communal decision based on the best information at hand:[106]

Hereupon calling such Captaines and Gentlemen of my companie as then were at hand. . .their whole request was to mee, that considering the case that we stood in, the weaknesse of our companie, the small number of the same, the carying away of our first appointed barke, with those two especiall masters, with our principall prouisions in the same. . . Seeing furthermore, our hope for supplie with sir Richard Greenuill, so vndoubtedly promised vs before Easter, not yet come, neither then likely to come this yeere. . . that therefore I would resolue my selfe, with my companie to goe into England in that Fleete, and accordingly to make request to the Generall in all our names, that he would be pleased to giue vs present passage with him.

[104] *Roanoke Voyages*, I. 289.   [105] Ibid. I. 291.   [106] Ibid. I. 292.

But the storm and ill fortune continued to plague the Lane party. Obviously the departure of the settlers with the Drake fleet was frantic and dangerous, with the result that most of the things they had planned to take back to England with them were lost and the colonists were fortunate to escape with only their lives and the clothes they were in. As Lane describes their exodus:[107]

[Drake] most readily assented vnto [our request], and so hee sending immediately his pinnaces vnto our Island for the fetching away of [a] fewe that there were left with our baggage, the weather was so boysterous, and the pinnaces so often on ground, that the most of all wee had, with all our Cardes, Bookes and writings, were by the Saylers cast ouer boord, the greater number of the Fleete being much agrieued with their long and dangerous abode in that miserable road.

Three of the colonists, unnamed, away from the island on an inland mission, were left behind, the first abandoned or lost colonists of whom no later record was ever found.

The second account of the first English colony in the new world is that of Harriot — an account of much greater interest than Lane's because of its clear portrayal of how the colonists saw the land and viewed its aboriginal natives. Unfortunately, Harriot's brief forty-eight-page pamphlet is not the complete and well-documented account which Harriot and White were charged with making. It is, rather, a hurried and partial account, ordered by Ralegh for publicity purposes at a time when his colonizing ventures were in jeopardy. It was patently designed to counter the evil rumours surrounding Ralegh's Virginia projects, to attract new financial support for further colonization, and to reassure potential colonists that the new world was a rich and friendly place to explore and live in. Yet in spite of its brevity and controlled purpose, Harriot's treatise, cited by Randolph G. Adams as 'The first original English book describing the first English colony in America', and by David Quinn as 'the most delectable of Americana', has given him an important place in the early history of America.

Harriot's original publication was in a cheap paper edition selling for a few pennies, a timely but ephemeral kind of

107 Ibid. I. 293.

pamphlet which has survived in only six known copies.[108] It
bears the long (and typically Elizabethan) title:

A briefe and true re-/port of the new found land of Virginia: of / *the
commodities there found and to be raysed, as well mar-*/chantable, as
others for victuall, building and other necessa-/*rie vses for those that are
and shalbe the planters there; and of the na-*/ture and manners of the
naturall inhabitants: Discouered by the / *English Colony there seated
by* Sir Richard Greinuile *Knight in the* / yeere 1585, which remained
vnder the gouerment of Rafe Lane Esqui-/*er, one of her Maiesties
Equieres, during the space of twelue monethes: at* / the speciall charge
and direction of the Honourable SIR / WALTER RALEIGH Knight,
Lord Warden of / the stanneries; who therein hath beene fauou-/red
and authorised by her Maiestie and / her letters patents: / Directed to
the Aduenturers, Fauourers, / *and Welwillers of the action, for the
inhabi-*/*ting and planting there;* / By *Thomas Harriot*; seruant to the
abouenamed/ *Sir Walter, a member of the colony, and* / *there imployed
in discouering.*/ [Device] / Imprinted at London 1588.

Without the efforts of his friend Richard Hakluyt, it is
probable that Harriot's *A briefe and true report* would have
remained relatively unknown. But Hakluyt's efforts made
the book an immediate success: he printed the text in the
1589 edition of his *Principall navigations*, again in 1600, and
many subsequent editions. Hakluyt also persuaded Theodor
de Bry to publish Harriot's text along with some of the John
White drawings as a part of a series dealing with important
contributions dealing with the new world. This was accomplished with the publication in 1590 in Frankfurt of Part I
of a series bearing the name *America*.[109] Published in Latin,
English, French, and German, this work carried the full text
of *A briefe and true report*, illustrated by twenty-three de

[108] Though only six copies of the original quarto publication exist today, it
has been frequently reprinted. A facsimile of the 'Drake copy' now owned by the
Huntington Library was printed in 1903, and a facsimile of the Clements Library
copy was produced by Randolph G. Adams in the Ann Arbor Facsimile Series in
1931. Adams surveys the known copies as (1) the Bodleian Library copy, (2) the
University of Leiden Copy, (3) the 'Grenville copy' in the British Library, (4)
the so-called 'Drake copy' in the Huntington Library, (5) the 'Huth copy' in the
Clements Library, and (6) an incomplete 'Stevens-Lenox copy' now in the New
York Public Library. No further copies have been found.

[109] This 1590 edition has frequently been reprinted. It was reprinted in 1893
by Bernard Quaritch, London, under the title of *Harriot's Narrative of the First
Plantation of Virginia in 1585*. Modern facsimile reproductions are to be found
in *The American Drawings of John White*, 1964, vol. II, pls. 119–43, and in the
Rosenwald Collection Reprint Series, with an introduction by Paul Hulton,
Dover Publications, New York, 1972.

Bry engravings of John White drawings from the Virginia venture of 1585/6. For these illustrations Harriot was induced to write brief Latin notes giving details to explain their significance, notes which were translated into English for the English edition by Hakluyt himself. The Frankfurt edition of *America* was published in 1590 and was an immediate success, establishing young Harriot as one of the leading authorities on America and the American Indian.[110]

The original quarto edition of 1588 carried a brief preface by Governor Ralph Lane to attest to the accuracy of Harriot's account. In this preface, Lane calls Harriot 'an Actor in the Colony & a man no lesse for his honesty then learning commendable'.[111] Both these qualities are clearly evident in Harriot's account. In his own foreword to the volume, Harriot does not dodge the fact that much misinformation has been spread about the new world:[112]

There haue bin diuers and variable reportes with some slanderous and shamefull speeches bruited abroade by many that returned from [the new world]. Especially of that discouery which was made by the Colony transported by Sir Richard Greinuile in the yeare 1585 ... Which reports haue not done a little wrong to many that otherwise would haue also fauoured and aduentured in the action, to the honour and benefite of our nation... I haue therefore thought it good beeing one that haue beene in the discouerie and in dealing with the naturall inhabitantes specially imploied; and hauing therefore seene and knowne more then the ordinarie: to imparte so much vnto you of the fruites of our labours, as that you may knowe howe iniuriously the enterprise is slaundered.... that you ... may generally know & learne what the countrey is, & thervpon consider how your dealing therein if it proceede, may returne you profit and gaine; bee it either of inhabiting & planting or otherwise in furthering thereof.

[110] That these publications were a source of pride to Harriot is shown by the fact that about 1603, while listing published references to himself, Harriot listed as the tenth of twenty-seven references 'My discourse of Virginia in 4 languages.' See Quinn and Shirley, 'A Contemporary List of Hariot References', *Renaissance Quarterly*, XXII. 1 (Spring 1969), 9–26.
[111] *A briefe and true report*, 1588, sig. A2r&v reads in part as follows: 'Thus much vpon my credit I am to affirme: that things vniuersally are so truely set downe in this treatise by the author thereof, an Actor in the Colony & a man no lesse for his honesty then learning commendable: as that I dare boldely auouch it may very well passe with the credit of truth euen amongst the most true relations of this age. Which as for mine own part I am readie any way with my word to acknowledge, so also (of the certaintie thereof assured by mine owne experience) with this my publike assertion, I doe affirme the same.'
[112] Ibid., sig. A3r&v.

It is thus clearly to this dual purpose — to correct the prevalent rumours of the hardships of colonization and the cruelty
of the native Indians, and to attract more capital to the risks
of further ventures and more willing participants in later
colonies — that *A briefe and true report* was addressed.

Like the mathematical teacher he was, Harriot begins his
treatise with a clear statement of the organization of his
material to meet these purposes:[113]

The treatise whereof for your more readie view & easier vnderstanding
I will diuide into three speciall parts. In the first I will make declaration
of such commodities there alreadie found or to be raised . . . as by way
of trafficke and exchaunge with our owne nation of England, will
enrich your selues the prouiders; those that shal deal with you; the
enterprisers in general; and greatly profit our owne countrey men . . .
which commodities for distinction sake, I call *Merchantable*.

In the second, I will set downe all the commodities which wee know
the countrey by our experience doeth yeld of it selfe for victuall, and
sustenance of mans life. . .

In the last part I will make mention generally of such other commodities besides. . . as I shall thinke behoofull for those that shall
inhabite, and plant there to knowe of . . . with a brief description of
the nature and maners of the people of the countrey.

Obviously, this is neither the matter nor the organization that
Harriot would have chosen had he been writing an account
for the general audience of his day or for posterity. But
limited as this report is in its purpose and in the materials
selected for presentation, it offers valuable information
beyond that for which it was intended. Coupled with White's
drawings, it gives us a most effective introduction to the new
world as viewed through their eyes. It shows us something of
the character and mind of the author, his vitality and work
methods, and an insight into his personality which we look
for in vain in his mathematical and scientific manuscripts.

Especially noteworthy is the accuracy and completeness
of Harriot's observations and the thoroughness with which
he took notes of what he saw and heard. He objected
strenuously to the reports given out by some of the colonists
on their return, saying that they had 'spoken of more than
euer they saw or otherwise knew to bee there;' since they

[113] Ibid., sig. A4^v–B1^r.

'were neuer out of the Iland where wee were seated, or not farre, or at the leastwise in few places els, during the time of our aboade in the countrey.' Others were so imbued with desires for gold or silver that they paid little attention to the people, flora, or fauna, and 'had little or no care of any other thing but to pamper their bellies', or finding no 'soft beds of downe or fethers; the countrey was to them miserable, & their reports thereof according.'[114] In all these regards, Harriot's account is meticulous: he is careful always to separate what he himself observed from what had been reported to him by his fellow settlers or by the natives. For the commodities which he considered merchantable he used the common English names: alum, pitch, tar, resin, cedar, wine grapes, sweet gums, sassafras (as a medicine for syphilis), dyes, madder, and woad. For prospective colonists who would need to live off the local products, Harriot gave his information in the terms of the Algonquian Indians — *Pagatowr* for maize, *Wickonzowr* for wild peas, *Macocqwer* for 'Pompions, Mellions, and Gourdes', for example. One item of particular interest to Harriot, Ralegh, and their friends and of tremendous commercial importance in the establishment of colonies in the Virginia area was the Indian use of the smoking weed, tobacco:[115]

There is an herbe which is sowed a part by it selfe & is called by the inhabitants *vppówoc*. In the West Indies it hath diuers names, according to the seuerall places & countries where it groweth and is vsed: The Spaniardes generally call it *Tobacco*. The leaues thereof being dried and brought into powder: they vse to take the fume or smoke thereof by sucking it through pipes made of claie into their stomacke and heade; from whence it purgeth superfluous fleame & other grosse humors, openeth all the pores & passages of the body: by which meanes the vse thereof, not only preserueth the body from obstructions; but also if any be, so that they haue not beene of too long

[114] Ibid., sig. A4^v.
[115] Ibid., sig. C3$^{r\&v}$. Harriot, Ralegh, and Northumberland were all great smokers of tobacco and did much to popularize the habit at the court of Elizabeth. This habit may be in part responsible for the fact that King James I, who disliked and distrusted them all violently, wrote a vitriolic treatise against the tobacco habit. It has also been noted that Harriot, who died of cancer of the nose, was the first one on medical record to be officially recorded as a smoker by his physician. See p. 433 and Juraj Körbler, 'Thomas Harriot (1560-1621) fumeur de pipe, victime du cancer?', *Gesnarus*, IX (1952), 52-4.

continuance, in short time breaketh them: whereby their bodies are notably preserued in health, & know not many greeuous diseases where-withall wee in England are oftentimes afflicted.

This *Vppówoc* is of so precious estimation amongst them, that they thinke their gods are maruelously delighted therwith: Wherupon some-time they make hallowed fires & cast some of the pouder therein for a sacrifice: being in a storme vppon the waters, to pacifie their gods, they cast some vp into the aire and into the water; so a weare for fish being newly set vp, they cast some therein and into the aire: also after an escape from danger, they cast some into the aire likewise: but all done with strange gestures, stamping, sometime dauncing, clapping of hands, holding vp of hands, & staring vp into the heauens, vttering there-withal and chattering strange words & noises.

We our selues during the time we were there vsed to suck it after their maner, as also since our returne, & haue found manie rare and wonderful experiments of the vertues thereof; of which the relation woulde require a volume by it selfe: the vse of it by so manie of late, men & women of great calling as else, and some learned Phisitions also, is sufficient witnes.

All in all, Harriot's pamphlet contains thirty-three Indian names of native products, not counting place- and personal-names.[116] But from his parenthetical observations, it is apparent that these represent but a small part of the vocabu-lary he recorded during his year among the Indians, for example:

I haue the names of eight & twenty seuerall sortes of beasts which I haue heard of to be here and there dispersed in the countrie, especially in the maine[land]: of which there are only twelue kinds that we haue yet discouered . . .[117]

Of al sortes of foule I haue the names in the countrie language of fourescore and sixe . . . besides those that be named . . .[118]

There are many other strange trees whose names I knowe not but in the *Virginian* language . . .[119]

How Harriot and White worked together in their observations and their plans for future publication of a volume devoted to the flora and the fauna of the new world is also indicated by a casual aside in his catalogue. In discussing the 'Foule' to

[116] For a discussion of the Algonquian language and Harriot's Indian vocabulary, see Appendix II, 'The Language of the Carolina Algonkian Tribes', by the Revd. James A. Geary, in *Roanoke Voyages*, II. 873–900.
[117] *A briefe and true report*, 1588, sig. D2ᵛ.
[118] Ibid. sig. D2ᵛ.   [119] Ibid. sig. D4ᵛ.

be found in the Virginia wilds, he lists *Turkie cockes* and *Turkie hennes: Stockdoues: Partridges: Cranes: Her[o]nes:* & in winter great store of *Swannes* & *Geese.* This listing he follows with the statement that he has the names of eighty-six other fowl that[120]

...we haue taken, eaten, & haue the pictures as they were there drawne with the names of the inhabitants of seuerall strange sortes of water foule eight, and seuenteene kinds more of land foul, although wee haue seen and eaten of many more, which for want of leasure there for the purpose coulde not bee pictured: and after wee are better furnished and stored vpon further discouery, with their strange beastes, fishe, trees, plants, and hearbes, they shall bee also published.

For the sake of the scientific study of natural history, it is to be deplored that Harriot and White did not follow through on this original purpose. The exactness with which they presented their observations, even the most casual ones, and the simple and direct way in which they made the unknown known are almost unique in the descriptions and drawings of their contemporaries. It is no wonder that White rose to be the Governor of a later colony, and that Harriot earned the reputation of the most expert witness regarding the new world.

A briefe and true report also shows incidentally Harriot's deep interest in the technologies of the new science which was already occupying so much of his time and attention. Though his assignment in the new world was, in his own words 'in the discouerie and in dealing with the naturall inhabitantes', his personal commitment to scientific evidence continued even in the wilds of Virginia. Limited though space was on the colonists' ships, Harriot had carried with him the materials of a scientific laboratory to aid his observations. This is clearly revealed in a passage in which he records the impression the English colonists made on the savages they encountered:[121]

Most thinges they sawe with vs, as Mathematicall instruments, sea compasses, the vertue of the loadstone in drawing yron, a perspective glasse whereby was shewed manie strange sightes,[122] burning glasses,[123]

---

[120] Ibid. sig. D2^v–D3^r.

[121] Ibid. sig. E4^r.

[122] Because the early telescopes were called 'perspective glasses' this reference has often been interpreted to mean that Harriot brought telescopes or 'spy

wilde-fire woorkes, gunnes, bookes, writing and reading, spring clocks[124]
that seeme to goe of themselues, and manie other thinges that wee had,
were so strange vnto them, and so farre exceeded their capacities to
comprehend the reason and meanes how they should be made and
done, that they thought they were rather the works of gods then of
men, or at the leastwise they had bin giuen and taught vs of the gods.

Harriot's scientific interest in cause and effect is expressed
in another section of this tract where he discussed the deadly
sickness which the English brought to the natives. In some
way, Harriot associated this illness with the trickery of the
Indians, and called attention to the fact that in every instance
where they visited a native village where the Indians 'had
any subtile deuise practised against vs. . . within a few dayes
after our departure from euerie such towne, the people
began to die very fast, and many in short space; in some
townes about twentie, in some fourtie, in some sixtie, & in
one six score, which in trueth was very manie in respect of
their numbers. . . .'[125] This deadly disease, generally thought
to be small pox against which the natives had no immunity,
puzzled the Indians and caused much speculation among
them to explain it. According to Harriot, some decided that
the settlers were not mortal, but men returned from the
dead, who were supernaturally endowed. Some thought that

---

glasses' to the new world. Even so sophisticated a scholar as the late E G. R.
Taylor has made this suggestion in *The Geometrical Seaman*, Institute of Navigation, 1962, p. 87. But this name was also used for concave mirrors which
could also show 'manie strange sightes' as reported by Digges and Dee, and
there can be little doubt but this is what he carried with him in 1585. Harriot's
work on refraction and optics came nearly a decade after this, and it is through
these studies that the compound lens system undoubtedly evolved. I am convinced that Harriot's observation of the moon with a 6-power glass on 26 July
1609 (see p. 397) was his earliest telescopic observation.
[123] This was a simple convex or doubled convex lens designed to focus the
Sun's rays. Harriot was much intrigued with burning glasses; he knew the work
of Roger Bacon on this subject, and spent considerable time calculating the
maximum heat that could be generated optically through simple lenses. See
BL Add. MS 6789, esp. fos. 344–66. On fo. 361 Harriot indicates that 'The
greatest actuall heat vpon any material poynt is the heat of 84,525 sonnes,'
while the potential may be twice that.
[124] This is the earliest indication that Harriot was using mechanical time
pieces — these may have been used to attempt to determine longitude on the
voyage. But his watches, which he used in his astronomical observations, were
so inaccurate that they required constant correction by astronomical time, and
would have been useless for any such purpose.
[125] Ibid., sig. F1ʳ.

the colonists were shooting invisible bullets at them from distances beyond the line of vision. Others attributed it to the white man's God, 'as [Harriot adds] wee our selues haue cause in some sorte to thinke no less.'[126] One group attributed the sickness to celestial influences:[127] '. . . specially some Astrologers knowing of the Eclipse of the Sunne which wee saw the same yeere before in our voyage thytherward, which vnto them appeared very terrible. And also of a Comet which beganne to appeare but a few daies before the beginning of the said sicknesse.' This eclipse of the sun which Harriot had observed as a partial eclipse just ten days out of Plymouth, was total in the Chesapeake Bay area, and may have been construed by the natives as a forewarning of the visit of the white men. The comet mentioned here has been identified as one which appeared for about a month between mid-October and mid-November 1585 in the northern hemisphere,[128] which would date this sickness as of the fall of the settlers' arrival. But unfortunately Harriot does not comment on these Indian theories, though he confesses that he has some. Such expansion would belong in his more detailed formal treatise; in this propaganda tract he comments only that 'there are farther reasons then I thinke fit at this present to be alleadged.'[129]

It is in the sections of his report that deal with the Indians themselves that Harriot reveals his personal warmth and sympathy for men of a totally alien culture, and his willingness to accept their unorthodox beliefs with understanding. Here again, Harriot indicates that he is merely skimming the surface of his materials, and that he hopes later to publish a 'large discourse' at a time 'more conuenient hereafter'.[130] At this writing he is selecting only those materials designed to inform prospective colonists 'how that they in respect of troubling our inhabiting and planting, are not to be feared; but that they haue cause both to feare and loue vs, that shall inhabite with them.' To reassure such future settlers, Harriot stresses the vast superiority of English tools, clothes, housing, and weapons of warfare over those of the natives,

---

[126] Ibid., sig. F2^r.   [127] Ibid.   [128] *Roanoke Voyages*, I. 381, no. 1.
[129] Ibid. sig. F2^r.   [130] Ibid. sig. E1^v.

and considers the lurid tales of dangers told by returning colonists to be grossly exaggerated:[131]

If there fall out any warres between vs & them, what their fight is likely to bee, we hauing aduantages against them so many maner of waies, as by our discipline, our strange weapons and deuises els; especially by ordinance great and small, it may be easily imagined; by the experience we haue had in some places, the turning vp of their heeles against vs in running away was their best defence.

But as is obvious throughout, Harriot would avoid warfare and would strive to win their trust, affection, and support instead. He was critical of the members of his colony for their unnecessary cruelty toward the natives; he himself found them people of native intelligence and ingenuity in their own milieu:[132]

In respect of vs they are a people poore, and for want of skill and iudgement in the knowledge and vse of our things, doe esteeme our trifles before thinges of greater value: Notwithstanding in their proper manner considering the want of such meanes as we haue, they seeme very ingenious; For although they haue no such tooles, nor any such craftes, sciences and artes as wee; yet in those thinges they doe, they shewe excelencie of wit. And by howe much they vpon due consider- ation shall finde our manner of knowledges and craftes to exceede theirs in perfection, and speed for doing or execution, by so much the more it is probable that they shoulde desire our friendships & loue, and haue the greater respect for pleasing and obeying vs. Whereby may bee hoped if meanes of good gouernment bee vsed, that they may in short time be brought to ciuilitie, and the imbracing of true religion.

A true Elizabethan, though himself something of a free- thinker, Harriot felt strongly the necessity of bringing this 'true religion' — that is, of course, Anglican protestantism — to the misguided savages who had not had the opportunity to learn of Christianity. But in this effort, he expressed none of the militant zeal which the Catholic Spaniards had felt for this effort, and shows a humane and compassionate attitude towards them and their beliefs. It is obvious from this section that Harriot's grasp of the Algonquian language was well advanced, since he took great pleasure in conversations with the 'inhabitantes which were our friends & especially the *Wiroans Wingina*' on highly abstract subjects. Throughout,

[131] Ibid. sig. E2^r.   [132] Ibid. sig. E2^v.

Harriot seems as intensely interested in learning of their religious views as he was in sharing his Anglican beliefs with them. He learned 'the summe of their religion', he says, 'by hauing special familiarity with some of their priests,'[133] and was impressed by the similarity of their beliefs — one supreme god who created the universe, made woman first to conceive and bring forth children.

They beleeue also the immortalitie of the soule, that after this life as soone as the soule is departed from the bodie according to the workes it hath done, it is eyther carried to heauen the habitacle of gods, there to enioy perpetuall blisse and happinesse, or els to a great pitte or hole, which they thinke to bee in the furthest partes of their part of the worlde towards the sunne set, there to burne continually: the place they call *Popogusso.*[134]

But in sharing these similarities, Harriot used their conversations to lead them to recognize the deficiencies of their philosophy:[135] '. . .through conuersing with vs they were brought into great doubtes of their owne, and no small admiration of ours, with earnest desire in many to learne more than we had meanes for want of perfect vtterance in their language to expresse.'

Harriot was throughout impressed by the seriousness with which the Indians held their religion. In his description of the town of Secoton on their first expedition to the mainland, for instance, he discussed the special place reserved for 'their cheefe solemne feastes', 'wher they assemble themselues to make their solemne prayers', and remarks that 'This people therfore voyde of all couetousnes, lyue cherfullye and att their harts ease. Butt they solemnize their feasts in the nigt, and therefore they keepe verye great fyres to auoyde darknes, and to testifie their Ioye.'[136] The common points of their beliefs with Christianity and the seriousness of their religious purposes led Harriot to believe that they might easily be converted to the true religion of England:[137] 'Some religion they haue alreadie, which although it be farre from the truth, yet beying as it is, there is hope it may bee the easier and sooner reformed.' Harriot thus viewed the

---

[133] Ibid. sig. E3ᵛ.   [134] Ibid. sig. E3ʳ.   [135] Ibid. sig. E4ʳ.
[136] 1590 edn., headnote to engraving XX, 'The Tovvne of Secota'.
[137] 1588 edn., sig. E2ᵛ.

natives as untutored savages, recognizing in them the desire to assimilate the civilization which the settlers were able to bring to them. This was not a typical view for the times, and represents a tolerance for the views of others and a willingness to accept unusual premises of the same sort which permitted Harriot to discover innovative solutions to mathematical or scientific problems. It shows an open-mindedness about divergent ideas much greater than that shown by Harriot's own detractors when charges of heresy and atheism were brought against him for his unorthodox, though not extreme, beliefs.

One other aspect of Harriot's personal character is revealed incidentally through his commentary on the Indians. Harriot was much attracted to the moderate eating habits of the Indians, which must have been a great contrast to the overindulgence of the typical sixteenth-century Englishman. In his comments on the White drawings of the natives in the 1590 edition, Harriot uses the illustrations twice to express this view:

They are very sober in their eatinge, and trinkinge, and consequently verye longe luied because they doe not oppress nature.[138]

...Yet are they moderate in their eatinge wher by they auoide sicknes. I would to god wee would followe their example. For wee should be free from many kynes of diseasyes which wee fall into by sumptwous and vnseasonable banketts, continuallye deuisinge new sawces, and prouocation of gluttonnye to satisfie our vnsatiable appetite.[139]

Throughout history, Thomas Harriot has never been considered to have been either a Puritan or a reformer, but these passages reflect a belief in moderation and a respect for the material body which must have marked not only his own life habits, but may have been a part of his personality which influenced his friendships and his evaluation of others.

As we have seen from Ralph Lane's account, the hurried departures of the colonists during the severe storms of June 1586 cost us many of the drawings of John White and the notes of Harriot on the new world and its inhabitants. But many of the Harriot and White materials did survive. Some

[138] 1590 edn., Headnote to engraving XVI, 'Their sitting at meate'.
[139] Ibid., Headnote XV, 'Their seetheying of their meate in earthen pottes'.

of them may have been returned to England with Arundell or Grenville for presentation to Ralegh as preliminary evidence; others may have been retained even under the frantic conditions of the final flight with Drake. In any case, a year later Harriot was still planning to produce a much more complete report than the one he published. As a matter of fact, he says he had already prepared it:[140] 'I haue ready in a discourse by it self in maner of a Chronicle according to the course of times, and when time shall bee thought conuenient shall be also published.' This chronicle or detailed chronology of events in the colony, would include[141]

...what els [beyond that published in his *A briefe and true report*] concerneth the nature and manners of the inhabitants of *Virginia*: The number with the particularities of the voyages thither made; and of the actions of such that haue bene by *Sir Walter Raleigh* therein and there imployed, many worthy to bee remembred; as of the first discouerers of the Countrey: of our Generall for the time *Sir Richard Greinuile*; and after his departure, of our Gouernour there Master *Rafe Lane* with diuers other directed and imployed vnder theyr gouernement: of the Captaynes and Masters of the voyages made since for transportation; of the Gouernour and assistants of those alreadie transported, as of many persons, accidents, and thinges els...

This is the only reference to a chronicle by Harriot, which, had it really been issued, would have been the most valuable account of the first English colony. Its publication awaited an indefinite 'time...thought conuenient', probably by Ralegh, since its materials were gathered at Ralegh's request and written to bring additional credit to him and support for his ventures. But evidently no proper time in the affairs of Ralegh dictated its release, for it is obvious that it never reached the printer. Hakluyt carried this announcement of it in his *Chronicles*, and with his thoroughness would have included any subsequent report made by his friend Harriot, but there was none. Nor is any mention of the Chronicle made in Harriot's own listing of his printed notices. Thorough searches have been made in all possible places where the original manuscript might have been preserved, but these have proved fruitless. Nor is it likely that it will ever appear. As Quinn pointed out:[142]

---

[140] 1588 edn., sig., F4^r&v. [141] Ibid., sig. F4^r. [142] *Roanoke Voyages*, I. 387, n. 3.

No useful conjectures can yet be made on why the narrative was not published (if indeed it was completed as Hariot claimed) or how it disappeared, apart from suggesting that when Hariot moved over to the service of the earl of Northumberland about 1594 it, with the rest of the Virginia papers, remained with Raleigh and perished in the general loss of his muniments.

Another possible reason, however, was that it was no longer quite so important, since Ralegh's interests (and Harriot's as well) were shifting rapidly to other romantic and hopefully profitable ventures.

During the year that Harriot was in the new world on his first major assignment, Ralegh was seeking new outlets for his dreams of empire. Having received from the Queen his patents for the exploration and settlement of Virginia, he turned to another land of savages (in English eyes) to be exploited for profit. This country was Ireland, where during the late 1570s and early 1580s Ralegh had already earned a reputation, both as a ruthless warrior and as an expert in military and civil affairs. During the winter of 1585-6, while Harriot was with Lane in Virginia, the returned Sir Richard Grenville collaborated with Ralegh in plans for the colonization of Munster, where Catholic uprisings had been brutally suppressed and the land laid desolate between 1579 and 1583. Utilizing his new-found power in court to back his desires, Ralegh convinced the Queen that it would be to her advantage to establish colonies of English settlers in Ireland, and for his efforts, emerged with an illegally large grant of three and a half seignories (approximately 40,000 acres) assigned to his own use and development.[143] These estates were in the counties of Waterford and Cork, extending along the Blackwater River from Lismore Castle to the estuary at Youghal. In June of 1586, while Harriot and the Roanoke colonists were anxiously awaiting the relief ships from England, Ralegh was already listed as being a resident at Youghal[144] where tradition has it that he lived in the house called Myrtle Grove, still standing, and had been elected mayor of the town.[145]

[143] David B. Quinn, *The Elizabethans and the Irish*, Cornell University Press for the Folger Library, 1966, pp. 112-16.

[144] *Calendar of State Papers, Ireland, 1586-88*, CXXIV, Item 80, p. 77.

[145] Edward Edwards, *The Life of Sir Walter Ralegh*, 2 vols., Macmillan, 1868,

Though it cannot be determined with certainty, it is highly likely that Harriot and White, landing at Portsmouth with Drake's fleet in late July 1586, went directly to Youghal to bring Ralegh up to date on the details of the year at Fort Ralegh. But Harriot may, like Ralegh, have shuttled back and forth between Ireland, the west country, and London, to pursue the widespread interests of these years. In London, Ralegh was seeking to increase his stature with the Queen; in western England he was seeking ships, supplies, and settlers for the reinforcement of his new world explorations and colonizations; and in Ireland he was like all the 'undertakers', as they were called, recruiting workers for his large estates and overseeing the installation of improved farming methods to increase the returns from the use of land and to enrich himself and his Queen. In all of these, except the private wooing of Elizabeth, Harriot must have had a hand.

Details of Sir Walter Ralegh's years as an undertaker on his huge estates in Waterford and Cork have long remained sketchy, since historians have preferred to follow his affairs at court rather than the times spent in his periods of rustication. However, W. A. Wallace of Louisburgh, County Mayo, has recently uncovered a large number of Irish records which shed much light on the activities of Ralegh and his friends, Harriot, White, Mawle, and Floyer in Ireland.[146] From a study of copies of contemporary deeds still in the archives of Lismore Castle and from new identifications of contemporary survey maps, Wallace is able to show considerably more activity in the development of the Ralegh estates than has hitherto been possible. According to these new documents, Ralegh owned and was active in the management of his Irish properties for sixteen years before he lost favour and was forced to dispose of them. Thomas Harriot owned his estate at Molanna Abbey for ten years before selling it to William Floyer. John White, who has generally

---

I. 96. See also Lord Killanin and M. V. Duignan, *Shell Guide to Ireland*, 2nd edn., 1967, 'Youghal', pp. 462–5.

[146] Wallace revealed many of his findings in a paper, as yet unpublished, on 'White, Harriot, and Ralegh in Ireland: some new evidence' at the Thomas Harriot Seminar held in Durham, England, on 6–7 Dec. 1979. I am grateful to him for sending me a copy of this paper, together with many of the documents on which it was based. His recent death is greatly regretted.

been lost from sight after his many voyages to Virginia, lived in the Cork-Waterford area for at least a decade. And Ralegh's two local men who served as his agents through power of attorney, Robert Mawle and William Floyer, were housed in properties adjacent to those of Harriot and White, Mawle at the castle of Ballynetra and Floyer at the castle of Temple-michael. Obviously these men, located in a central position in Ralegh's estates, had a major role in the oversight and management of his Irish affairs.

Two other associates and close friends of Ralegh settled not too far away: Sir Richard Grenville and the poet Edmund Spenser. Grenville, though still active in naval affairs in Virginia and England, obtained through his Irish agent Sir Warham St. Leger a large tract of land in Kerrycurrihy, to the west and south of Cork.[147] By May 1589 Grenville had brought over nearly a hundred settlers, many of them his own relatives, and had stocked their farms with horses, cattle, and sheep from his Devon and Cornish estates. Like Ralegh, Grenville shuttled from Ireland to his west country homes and to the London court, and his letters are addressed sometimes from Bideford, sometimes Stowe, and sometimes from 'my poor house of Gilly abbey by Cork'. Like Ralegh, too, Grenville gradually increased his Irish land holdings, so that by 1590, when he spent almost the entire year there, he held two seignories, or 24,000 acres.[148] Undoubtedly the close friendship between Ralegh and Sir Richard continued during these years, as they worked closely on matters of Irish development and English defence.

In Ireland, too, the friendship between the two poets, Ralegh and Spenser, ripened. Undoubtedly they had met years earlier when they were both engaged in the early efforts of the English Anglicans to subdue the Irish Catholics. Ralegh as one of Elizabeth's Captains was actively engaged in fighting the insurgents; Spenser as a minor political functionary was active in the civil government. From his manuscript, *A View of the Present State of Ireland*, written

[147] The story of Grenville's Irish undertaking is told by A. L. Rowse in Ch. XV, 'Grenville in Ireland, 1588–90; the Plantation of Munster' in his biography of Grenville, op. cit., pp. 267–86.
[148] Ibid., p. 276.

in 1596, we learn that Spenser had been in Ireland to view the execution of Murrogh O'Brien in 1577. At that time he had been either a dispatch bearer for Leicester or an undersecretary to the Lord Deputy Henry Sidney. By the time Harriot was graduated from Oxford in 1580, Spenser was established in Ireland as secretary to Arthur Lord Grey of Wilton, who succeeded Sidney as Lord Deputy. From 1580 to 1588 Spenser lived in or near Dublin holding miscellaneous minor posts in government, and he may have renewed his friendship with Ralegh during these years. But with the granting of the forfeited lands of the Earl of Desmond in 1588, Spenser used his influence to obtain a small seignory of slightly over 3,000 acres. The centre of his estate was Kilcolman, midway between Limerick to the north and Cork to the south, and a little over 30 miles northwest of Ralegh's Irish headquarters. It was at Kilcolman that Ralegh paid a visit to Spenser in 1589, where in the midst of desolation and bloodshed they matched poems and discussed life at court. This visit Spenser commemorated with a pastoral poem, *Colin Clouts Come Home Againe*, in which the travelled rustic, Ralegh, called 'The Shepheard of the Ocean' from his sea exploits, was welcomed back by his friends and neighbours. As a result of this visit, Ralegh took Spenser back to London with the first three books of *The Fairie Queene* and introduced him to Elizabeth whom he induced to read this part of the proposed epic, and to give permission to use her as the co-ordinating central figure of the poem's allegory. When this work was published in 1596, it was dedicated to Elizabeth and contained 'A Letter of the Authors Expounding his whole intention in the course of this worke' designed to clarify the allegory. This letter Spenser addressed 'To the right noble, and Valorous, Sir Walter Raleigh, knight'.

It is possible that Spenser returned the visit to Ralegh at Youghal, too. During the late 1580s and early 1590s Spenser was courting Elizabeth Boyle, the young lady whom he later married. This courtship and marriage Spenser memorialized by his sequence of love sonnets, *Amoretti*, and his hymn to the wedding day, *Epithalamion*. Very little is known of Spenser's courtship or of his wife, but it is certain that the Boyle family lived in the environs of Youghal and present-day citizens of the town are quick to point out the very cottage where the courtship may have taken place — a cottage close to Myrtle Grove where Ralegh is reputed to have lived as Mayor of the city.[149]

Harriot's associate in the Roanoke expedition, the painter John White, also held lands in Ralegh's seignory. Though it has long been known that White, following his years support-ing Ralegh's colonies in Virginia, retired to Ireland, the place of his abode has been known only as 'Newtown in Kilmore',[150] a place not definitely located. But again Wallace's researches have finally established the location of White's Irish home, in Ireland as he had been in Virginia, a neighbour and associate of Harriot. As Wallace tells the story:[151]

...if White had wished to become a small tenant farmer in Ireland, he would surely have leased his farm from his former master. Ralegh had a reputation for loyalty to his family and his friends and his servants; and no one could have served his more faithfully than White, who, in the course of his service had lost not only his own small fortune in the 1587 expedition, but also his daughter and his grand daughter. So I thought that it was worth while looking for a sixteenth century site on Ralegh's estate which would fit in with the description 'Newtown in Kilmore', and I found one that fitted perfectly....

Many a Harriot scholar, on pilgrimage to Molanna, must have walked or driven through [a] village, without perhaps realizing that Ballynoe — Baile nua — is the Irish for Newtown! Ballynoe it was from the time of King John until 1450, and from the time of King James until the present day, and Newtown only when the English Church or the English undertakers were masters of Youghal. ... In the Annals of Youghal, the sale by Ralegh to Boyle of his Irish estate is recorded, and this particular section of it is described as 'the decayed town of Tallaghe, together with the lands and villages of Kilmore.' So here, in the Ralegh heartland, and only a few miles from Molanna Abbey is a 16th century Newtown in Kilmore, and it is here, I am sure you will agree, that White must have lived.

[149] Details about Spenser's activities in Ireland may be found in many critical editions of his work. See, e.g., H. S. V. Jones's *A Spenser Handbook*, New York, F. S. Crofts, 1930, especially Ch. II, 'The Life of Spenser', pp. 17–38. See also W. L. Renwick, ed., *A View of the Present State of Ireland by Edmund Spenser*, Oxford, Clarendon Press, 1970, pp. 171–90.

[150] On 4 Feb. 1593 White wrote to Hakluyt, dating his letter as 'from my house at Newtowne in Kylmore'. See *Roanoke Voyages*, Doc. 107 (II. 712–16). In n. 1 (II. 716) Quinn locates this 'with reasonable certainty' as about 'four miles east-south-east of Charleville, co. Cork'.

[151] Unpublished Durham Seminar speech, p. 2.

The task of developing their grants of Irish lands during these years was a most difficult one. In 1586, in bringing Holinshed's *Chronicles of Ireland* up to date, John Hooker wrote, in a dedicatory epistle to Sir Walter Ralegh:[152]

[Following the Desmond wars] The common people such as escaped the sword, al for the most part are perished with famine, or fled the countrie. The land it selfe being verie fertile, is waxed barren, yeelding nor corne nor fruits; the pasture without cattell, and the aire without fowles, and the whole prouince for the most part desolate and vninhabited, sauing townes and cities; and finallie, nothing there to be seene but miserie and desolation.

So desolated indeed was the land being offered to the undertakers that Hooker wrote:[153]

Finallie, euerie way the cursse of God was so great, and the land so barren both of man and beast, that whosoeuer did trauell from the one end vnto the other of all Mounster, euen from Waterford to the head of Smeereweeke, which is about six score miles, he should not meet anie man, woman, or child, sauing in townes and cities; not yet see anie beast, but the verie wooolues, the foxes, and the other like rauening beasts: manie of them laie dead being famished, and the residue gone elsewhere. . . .

In the late summer of 1586 a Commission was formed 'for meting and bounding into seignorities of Her Majesty's escheted and attainted lands.' On 2 September the members received their instructions, and on the 21st they moved to Dungarvan to survey the lands assigned to Sir Christopher Hatton, where they worked for eight days. Their report then continues:[154]

. . .from thence [we] departed to Lismore and Youghal, at both which places we have stayed there eight days more in meting and bounding such lands as we hear Sir Walter Rawley is to have, which hath been exceeding difficult and painful, by reason that the lands having been long waste are generally overgrown with deep grass, and in most places with heath, brambles, and furze, whereby and by the extremity of rain and foul weather, that hitherto we have found, we have been greatly hindred in our proceeding.

---

[152] Raphael Holinshed, *The Second Volume of the Chronicles*, 1587, 'The Irish historie', sig. Aij^v.

[153] Ibid., 'The Chronicle of Ireland', p. 183.

[154] *Calendar of State Papers, Ireland*, CXXVI, no. 52, pp. 167–8.

As a result of these difficulties, the commissioners decided to quit for the winter, leaving 'Mr. Robbyns and another meter with him to proceed in meting so well as they may during the winter time.'

It is probable that Ralegh was not in Ireland at the time of the official survey of his property, but later evidence shows it possible that he may have sent Harriot to keep an eye on the plotting of his lands. It is now certain that both Harriot and John White were interested in the surveys and served in Ireland, as they had in Virginia, as Ralegh's representatives in handling his charting and land measurements.

At least two maps surviving from the time of these surveys carry new information of the activities of Harriot and White. One of them, called the Inchiquin Map, is in the National Maritime Museum at Greenwich, and is one of a pair of maps dated on successive days in August 1589, both in the same hand, and both attributed to the well-known Irish cartographer, Francis Jobson. One of these maps is catalogued as 'a survey of the 22,719 acres surrounding the Abbey of Molanna on the Blackwater.' In his study of Harriot's Irish connections Wallace recently viewed this map, and to his surprise and pleasure discovered on the bottom right-hand corner a previously unrecorded example of Harriot's phonetic script. This he translates as follows:[155] 'COPID UWT OF DESCRIPTSHON OF ARTR ROBINS BY TOMAS HARYOTS OF YOHAL', followed by the date in English, '1589 AUGUST 28TH'.[156]

The other map dates from a decade later: it is known as the Mogeely Map, dated 1598, and if Wallace is correct in his analysis it ties both White and Harriot to the land surveys of Ralegh's properties. Working with Dr Rosalind Tanner, Wallace has compared the lettering on this map with the lettering done by John White on his Roanoke drawings, and has concluded that they are in the same hand. He therefore attributes the drawing of this map to John White. But in the cartouche which carries the acreage measurements

[155] Durham speech, p. 5.

[156] My own transliteration, based on Wallace's copy of the script does not vary significantly. It would read 'kopId Uwt of diskrIpsan of æ rtr robInz by tomæ s hæ ryots Iv yohæ l. 1589.'

is a different hand, and this he and Dr Tanner identify with Harriot.[157] Though handwriting identification is always somewhat hazardous, Wallace feels that the evidence is overwhelming that White and Harriot made the Mogeely Map for Sir Walter Ralegh. He concludes:[158]

So we now have proof for the first time that Harriot was engaged on the survey of the Lismore estate for Ralegh as early as 1589, and was still working on the survey side of the estate management as late as 1598. It is difficult to avoid the conclusion that he too worked for Ralegh in this capacity throughout the whole period of Ralegh's ownership of Lismore. We now know also that White was living on Ralegh's estate by at least February 1593, and probably from shortly after he returned from Virginia for the last time in 1590, and that he was working on farm surveys as late as 1598. It is hard to avoid the conclusion that he too worked for Ralegh in this capacity through the last ten or twelve years of Ralegh's ownership of Lismore. I would hazard a guess that, as each new farm lease arose on the estate, White, as the man on the spot, would prepare a map showing the boundaries of the new holding and an accurate survey of the fields enclosed, and that Ralegh's agent would take this to London, together with a draft lease, and that Harriot would then work out the acreage of the farm and fields and Ralegh would sign the lease and have his signature witnessed.

[157] On p. 4 of his paper Wallace writes: 'Here is one of the British Museum paintings entitled 'The flyer'. I have chosen this one because the letters happen to fit more neatly into the map than do some of the others, but almost any of the paintings would have suited as well. This capital 'T' is typical of White's hand, and he makes use of it constantly: — it is elegant and very free, but beautifully regular. One of the most noticeable features of White's hand is the unvarying nature of his letters. Once he had settled on the particular form of a letter which pleased him, he would use it thereafter without change, and he was, I think, one of the great masters of the italic hand of his day. The lower case letters here are also typical of his hand. And here, perhaps nine or ten years later, is the Mogeely Map with exactly the same "T" in 'TOWSES LAND', and exactly the same lower case letters in "Bryde flu."' Again, 'Dr. Tanner . . . agreed that the main body of the Mogeely Map was in White's hand, and she agreed that the cartouche and the acreage measurements of that map were in the same hand as the whole of the Inchiquin Map, but she maintained that this hand was not White's but Harriot's. Her evidence was completely convincing, and we were, therefore, at this stage, completely satisfied that the main body of the Mogeely Map was by White, and the acreage measurements and the cartouche there, and the whole of the Inchiquin Map were by Harriot. The occasional backward sloping "d" in the lower case, is a feature of Harriot's hand throughout his manuscript life. So also is the rather odd colon followed by a dash. In his folios of logarithmic tables you will often find it four times in a page. The slipping down from the upper case to the lower case in the middle of a word is also a feature of his hand, and there are many other points of identity. . .'

[158] Ibid., p. 5.

To attest this last statement Wallace has obtained copies of several leases made by Ralegh, copies of which are still preserved in the Lismore records in the National Library, Dublin, previously unnoticed. A number of these were signed by Ralegh, and witnessed by Harriot, and two of them, dated 10 February 1591 were witnessed by both Harriot and Sir Richard Grenville.[159]

Though there may still be some records about Ralegh, Harriot, and White in Ireland which are unavailable for public inspection,[160] we do have evidence that Harriot spent some time during the late 1580's as one of Ralegh's colonists. An official census, taken on 12 May 1589, 'A note or abstract of all such freeholders, fee farmers, lessees for years, copyholders, and cottagers, as are inhabiting upon the lands and possessions of Sir Walter Ralegh, Knight', is included in the *Calendar of State Papers, Ireland, 1588-92*.[161] Listed among the more than 150 English settlers is the intriguing entry: 'Upon the Abbeyhouse of Mollanna, Thomas Harriot, gent. and his family'.[162] The census addition 'and his family' is particularly interesting to Harriot devotees, since it is the only evidence anywhere

---

[159] Grenville signed these documents just a month before he was called to Court and given orders to sail with Drake as Vice-Admiral to attack the Spanish in the Azores. Ralegh had outfitted several ships in this attempt to follow up the Armada defeats, and had hoped to go himself, but he was again denied by Elizabeth, probably because it was felt that he was too hot-headed to serve under Drake. It was at the conclusion of this foray that the famous battle of the *Revenge* occurred which led to the death of Sir Richard and made him a national hero. It was Ralegh who wrote the tract which glorified this action: *A Report of the Truth of the Fight about the Iles of the Açores, this last Sommer. Betwixt the Reuenge, one of her Maiesties Shippes, And an Armada of the King of Spaine*, London, printed for William Ponsonbie, 1591 (STC no. 20651).

The evidence that Wallace gives for Harriot's making the land calculations (BL Add. MS 6787, fo. 476r&v) do not appear to me to be convincing. It is true that they are designed to show how to calculate irregular bodies, but appear elementary as if Harriot were giving instruction to a student, and there is no drawing which would appear to tie these figures to the island on which the Abbey of Molanna stands.

[160] Wallace has listed a number of items included in the National Library of Ireland Special List no. 15: (2) A list of Sir Walter Ralegh's tenants, with notes of the horse and footmen to be provided by each. 1595; (7) Memorandum about tithe corn belonging to the Abbey of Malanye, 1603; (10) List of Munster Undertakers, 1585; (11) Box of Estate Maps.

[161] PRO, *SP* 63 vol. XCLIV, no. 28, pp. 170-2.

[162] Ibid., p. 171.

to indicate that Harriot might have been married or at least lived with any member of his family. Lack of corroborating information, especially his will, has generally led to the belief, however, that this phrase indicated merely a household with servants adequate to run an establishment as large as Molanna Abbey and its surrounding fields, since no other property holders are listed for all these estates. It is even possible that the family was a fiction, added to the census by Ralegh to inflate his colonial efforts by padding the figures of residents on his seignory.

The Abbey of Molanna to which Harriot held a long-term grant, latterly an Augustinian priory, was originally founded in 501 by St. Mael-Anfaidh (or St. Molanfide, from which the name Molanna was derived) on the island of Dair-Inis in the Blackwater River, $2\frac{1}{2}$ miles north of Youghal.[163] From its founding to its dissolution, the Abbey was in constant use. And since the reformation movement came much later in Ireland than in England, the property was held by the Bishopric of Lismore until 3 February 1585/6 when, by warrant of privy seal, it was transferred to its first lay owner, Sir Walter Ralegh. Ralegh, in turn, assigned it to Thomas Harriot, perhaps as partial reward for his services in Virginia. Just how long Harriot lived there is not known, but a petition from William Floyer to King James in 1604,[164] indicates that Harriot relinquished title in 1597, when he sold the property to 'your Majesties orator for 200li'. This petition shows that Harriot entered and seized the property which means that he actually lived there, though there is no indication of how long he actually occupied it.

During Harriot's years of ownership Molanna would have been in much better condition than at any time since, since it had been released from the use of the church for only a few years. Now the Abbey remains as only a ruin, with the island connected to the main shore of the Blackwater by a causeway. The Abbey ruins are extensive and well-enough preserved that the organization of the establishment can be

---

[163] The Revd. Samuel Hayman, *Notes and Records of the Ancient Religious Foundations at Youghal, County Cork, and its Vicinity*, Youghal, 1855, p. 11.
[164] Hatfield House MS *196*.131.

determined, and lie in full view of Ballynatray House, home of the former owners, the Holroyd-Smyths.[165] Besides the church (of considerable interest as an original Irish choirless church), the sacristy, chapter rooms, refectory, kitchens, and gate house show the potential of housing at least a dozen families of colonists. Yet it is difficult to see how they might have supported themselves on the island; though fish weirs dating from times before Harriot's occupancy still exist (and still catch fish), the island is small, overgrown with oak trees, and to this day reflects the lack of fertility and the excessive undergrowth deplored by the surveying party in 1586. No evidence remains of Harriot's presence at Molanna; there are no American trees or shrubs which he might have brought back from Virginia, nor are there any records of his presence to be found in the extant records of Youghal. And considering the state of the countryside and the sixteenth-century modes of transportation, Molanna seems rather remote from Youghal and Lismore for Harriot to have been in close regular communication with Ralegh. Yet some evidence does exist which shows that he was, without question, intimately involved in handling Ralegh's financial and estate affairs. Unfortunately, what would undoubtedly have been the primary source of this information has not survived: Harriot's own papers dealing with his transactions on behalf of Ralegh in Ireland. In 1621, five years after the death of Ralegh, Harriot himself lay dying, putting his affairs in order. In his will, probated 6 July 1621, he finally disposed of his records of Ralegh's affairs:[166]

---

[165] For a detailed description of the ruins of the Abbey, see Patrick Power, *Waterford and Lismore: a Compendious History of the United Dioceses*, Dublin and Cork, Cork University Press, 1937, pp. 214–15. I should also like to express my gratitude to Mr Holroyd-Smyth for taking me over all the property in October 1968.

[166] Harriot's will, a most remarkable document, was first discovered in 1885 by Henry Stevens. Stevens printed it in an appendix to his brief biography, *Thomas Hariot and his Associates*, posthumously printed privately in 1900. For a fairly complete study of the will and Stevens's discovery, see Dr R. C. H. Tanner, 'The Study of Thomas Harriot's Manuscripts, I. Harriot's Will', *History of Science*, VI (1967), 1–16, where it is again printed in full. See also Ch. IX of this volume. This excerpt is from the certified copy of the Archdeaconry Court of London, currently housed in the Guildhall, London. A photographic reproduction of the probate copy of Harriot's will is included in the author's *A Source Book for the Study of Thomas Harriot*.

Item whereas I haue diuers waste papers (of which some are in a Canvas bagge) of my Accompts to Sir Walter Rawley for all which I haue discharges or acquitances lying in some boxes or other, my desire is that they may bee all burnte. Alsoe there is an other Canvas bagge of papers concerning Irishe Accompts (the persons whome they Concerne are dead many yeares since in the raigne of queene Elizabeth) which I desire alsoe may be burnte. . . .

Had Harriot not felt this last-minute urge to clear out his waste papers, we should know much more about his activities during these years than we now know. But their destruction tells us only that Harriot was in Ireland for a short time, and returned to London, leaving Lane and White living on Ralegh's Irish estates.

During the late 1580s another important friendship was developing in London between Ralegh and Harriot with one of the glamorous young nobles around the court, Henry Percy, 9th earl of Northumberland.[167] During these years Northumberland was in many ways the model of the popular conception of the young nobleman of his generation. Eldest son of Henry Percy, 8th earl, Henry was born at Tynemouth Castle in 1564, birth year of both Shakespeare and Galileo, four years after Harriot, and a dozen after Ralegh. Northumberland's uncle, Thomas Percy, the 7th earl who had assumed the title in the first year of Elizabeth, had been attainted in 1569 and beheaded at York in 1572. Since his only son had died shortly after birth, the title moved to Thomas's younger brother, Henry Percy, who became 8th earl in that year. A Catholic like his older brother, Henry was politically suspect under protestant Elizabeth (perhaps with some reason), and when he became involved in the Throgmorton conspiracy he was cast into the Tower, just as his eldest son, Henry, was reaching his majority. Shortly thereafter, the 8th earl was found dead in his bed, shot through the head and with a pistol by his side. Officially he was declared a suicide, though there were many rumours that he had been politically murdered. On 21 June 1585

---

[167] The most complete account of the Percy family is to be found in the family history by Edward Barrington de Fonblanque, *Annals of the House of Percy*, 2 vols., London, Privately Printed, 1887. Since de Fonblanque was commissioned by the Percy family, he had full access to all the family records, and gives some evidences which are not available anywhere else.

Henry Percy succeeded as 9th earl of Northumberland. At the age of twenty-one he was the titular head of a large Percy family. Besides the dowager Countess and an uncle, Thomas, Henry supported six brothers — William, Charles, Richard, Alan, Joceline, and George; and three sisters — Anne, who died in infancy, Lucy, and Eleanor. Naturally, in the light of the family history, life seemed precarious and demanding.

During the twenty-one years of his life to this time, Henry had followed the pattern expected of the heir in a wealthy and noble family. He had been broadly educated at home under private tutors (surprisingly enough under a protestant vicar), and had mastered not only the sports and skills demanded of Elizabethan gentlemen, but also the extremely sophisticated education in languages and humanistic studies that had come into vogue with the Renaissance. In the traditional manner, too, he had travelled abroad at the age of eighteen to polish his education, and had learned to sow his wild oats as the young cosmopolite was expected to do — to gamble heavily, to drink the spirits of wine and usquebaugh which were coming into fashion, and to 'drink' the new weed tobacco when it became available in England.[168] It was while he was in this period of youthful exuberance that the new young earl met and was attracted to the handsome and dashing Sir Walter Ralegh, and for the decade of what he called his profligacy before his marriage in 1592 the two men developed a close attraction that remained with them until they were parted by death.

In his prime in his early thirties, Ralegh was in these years the courtier *par excellence* — handsome, brilliant, recognized as a soldier and a poet, richly dressed, and

---

[168] Who was responsible for bringing tobacco to England is still a matter for dicussion, but whether it was true or not, Sir Walter Ralegh was certainly given credit for popularizing the fad of smoking in England. John Aubrey recites the common stories (Clark, *'Brief Lives'*, II. 181):

'[Sir Walter] was the first that brought tobacco into England, and into fashion ... I have heard my grandfather Lyte say that one pipe was handed from man to man round the table. They had silver pipes; the ordinary sort made use of a walnut and a straw.

It was sold for its wayte in silver. I have heard some of our old yeomen neightbours say that when they went to Malmesbury or Chippenham market, they culled out their biggest shillings to lay in the scales against the tobacco.'

welcome in many circles of courtesy and affairs, though also hated by many for his obvious pride and arrogance. To the young earl, however, he seemed a model of conduct, and Ralegh was not unwilling to court the wealthy young heir to one of the oldest noble families of England who could furnish him access to circles of nobility and who was no rival for the affection of the Queen. From the first days of his accession, the Northumberland records give evidence of their growing friendship.[169] In the first year of his earldom, Andrewe Yong, the earl's pursebearer, records:[170] '1585/6 Rewards: . . . to Sir Walter Rawley his man that brought your Lordship: a shert of maile xx^s'. The cofferer, Thomas Wycliffe, also recorded expenses for a similar gift, this one even more personal:[171] '1586/7 Rewards: . . . to the man that brought Sir Walter Rawleys Picher [picture] xx^s'. And as the friendship ripened, references became more and more numerous in the records:[172] '1586/7 Rewards: . . . To Sir Walter Rawleys Surgion for letting his Lordships bloud the 14th of March 1586 . . to Sir Walter Rawley a stroe [straw] coloured veluet saddle iiij^{li} iij^s . . . to Sir Walter Rawleys man that brought his Lordship a bed of Ceder or Cypresse [undoubtedly from the new world] x^s . . .' At this time it appears evident that as an affectation these two young

[169] The account records of the Percy family during this period are among the most complete and informative of details of the life of the time which are of great value to historians. Though there are some gaps in the records, the majority of the accounts exist in both rough and final form and are retained in the Northumberland archives. References to them in this volume are as follows: MSS described by the Historical Manuscripts Commission as located at Syon House (*HMC Appendix to the Sixth Report, 1877*, pp. 221-33) are referred to as 'Syon MSS' even though in most cases they have been moved to the Muniment Room at Alnwick Castle. Those originally reported as at Alnwick Castle (*HMC Third Report, 1872*, p. 45-125) are listed as 'Alnwick MSS'. Papers of the 9th earl classified as at Petworth House, Sussex, and called the 'Lord Leconfield' Papers (*HMC, Appendix to the Sixth Report, 1877*, pp. 287-319) are here listed as 'Petworth MSS'. Petworth MSS not classified by HMC are indicated here by the numbers assigned them in a new classification being made by Francis W. Steer and Noel H. Osborne, and issued by the West County Council as *The Petworth House Archives*, 1968 —.
[170] Alnwick MSS Household Accounts, I.I.1. In all these accounts, roman numerals are used to indicate expenditures, with superscript 'li' for pounds (*libra*), 's' for shillings (*solidi*), and 'd' for pence (*denarii*).
[171] Ibid. Another scroll in the same roll, Thomas Wycliffe, Coferer.
[172] Ibid., Jan. 1586/7.

bachelors, Lord Percy and Sir Walter, were appearing in similar equipage, for in addition to the straw-coloured velvet saddle which he gave to Ralegh, the earl bought for himself a new horse called Skelton, and fitted it out identically to match the one he had given to his friend:[173] 'Apparell: Item payd for a yeard & haulfe of straw couler veluet at xxjˢ the yeard for to couuer a saddel for scelton . . . A stroe colowred velvett sadle: Item paid for viij ounces of siluer freinge for the same saddle at vjˢ iiijᵈ the ounce. v feb. ljˢ vjᵈ . . .' Percy also began to ape Ralegh's affectation for jewels, and his accounts show him indebted to Ralegh for adornments he frequently purchased from him:[174] 'Payment of Debts: . . . to Sir Walter Rawleye in parte of payment of viij Cˡⁱ [£800 — a tremendous sum] for a Jewell of Diamonds the 17 of ffebruary 1586. ij Cˡⁱ [£200 paid] . . . to Sir Walter Rawley in part of payment of viij Cˡⁱ for the price of a Jewell 11 of Maij 1585. ij Cˡⁱ. . .' Northumberland's accounts even reveal constant drains on his privy purse for gambling for stakes that would have been considered high by most Elizabethans:[175] 'Money to his Lordship hands . . . lost in play to Sir Walter Rawley xˡⁱ . . . Lost in play . . money by his Lordship at sundry times within the tyme of the accompt lost in playe Cxxxxˡⁱ iiijˢ . . .' Though the records continue to record money lost in play to Ralegh, there is no record of any winnings: presumably these went directly into the Privy Purse. In early 1589 play was particularly heavy: Percy lost 40s. to Ralegh on 26 February, 15s. on 8 April, 5s. on the 16, 20s. more on the 28th. And so the friendship of the two men continued, as the Northumberland records bear evidence of their close relations for the rest of their lives. And this interlocking friendship was to lead to the unusual situation which was to bring Harriot to serve both men in different capacities, but with similar intimacy and friendship.

Of course, the major preoccupation and occupation of the English people during the last years of the 1580s was preparation for the defence of the realm from the anticipated

[173] Ibid., Roger Thorpe, Jan. 1586/7.
[174] Ibid., Thomas Wycliffe, Coferer.
[175] Ibid.

invasion by the Spanish. In some way, nearly every man in Elizabeth's kingdom was involved in preparing for warfare at sea and the subsequent landing on the island's shores. Like most members of the nobility, and in company of his friends the earls of Oxford and Cumberland, Henry Percy spent a large portion of his patrimony for aiding this cause. At his own cost he built, outfitted, and manned some sea vessels for the engagement, and offered his own personal services to serve under the command of Howard and Drake.[176] Though it is difficult to follow his activities on a day-to-day basis, Ralegh too was totally immersed in preparation for war. Early in the year, 1588, he was in Ireland, but as news of the massing of the Spanish fleet grew in intensity, he hurried to the West Country, to Devon and Cornwall, to recruit men from the Stanneries for the land forces on those shores, and to reinforce the defences of the Isle of Portland, of which he was then Governor.[177] And when the action started, he may have joined the fleet on 23 July when the sea battle was in the third day, and remained in the fray until the whole Spanish navy was out of action by shot or storm, though evidence of this is extremely tenuous.

In the preface to the tract which he wrote three years later about the heroic death of his friend and fellow Armada fighter, Sir Richard Grenville, *A Report of the Truth of the fight about the Iles of the Acores*,[178] later reprinted by Hakluyt, Ralegh described the battles:

[The Spanish navy] which they termed inuincible, consisting of 240. saile of ships, not onely of their own kingdom, but strengthened with the greatest Argosies, *Portugall* Caractes, Florentines and huge Hulkes of other countries: were by thirtie of her Maiesties owne shippes of warre, and a few of our owne Marchants, by the wise, valiant, and most aduantagious conduction of the L. *Charles Howard*, high Admirall of England, beaten and shuffeled togither; euen from the Lizard in *Cornwall*, where they shamefully left *Don Pedro de Valdes*, with his mighty shippe: from *Portland* to *Cales*, where they lost *Hugo de Moncado*, with the Gallias of which he was Captain, and from *Cales*, driuen with squibs from their anchors: were chased out of the sight of

---

[176] John Nichols, *The Progresses of Queen Elizabeth*, 2 vols., London, 1823, II. 532; de Fonblanque, op. cit. II. 193.

[177] Edwards, *Life*, I. 108–14.

[178] London, Printed for William Ponsonbie, 1591 (STC 20651), sig. A3ᵛ–A4ʳ.

England, round about *Scotland* and *Ireland*. Where for the sympathie of their barbarous religion, hoping to find succour and assistance: a great part of them were crusht against the rocks, and those other that landed, being verie manie in number, were notwithstanding broken, slaine, and taken, and so sent from village to village coupled in halters to be shipped into England. Where her Maiestie of her Princely & inuincible disposition, disdaining to put them to death, and scorning either to retaine or entertaine them: were all sent backe againe to their countries, to witnesse and recount the worthy achieuements of their inuincible and dreadfull Nauy. ... With all which so great and terrible an ostentation, they did not in all their sailing rounde about England, so much as sinke or take one ship, Barke, Pinees, or Cockbote: or euer burnt so much as one sheepcote of this land.

Though modern historians are inclined to credit the unusual summer storms of 1588 for the defeat of the naval forces of Spain, the Elizabethans were very willing to take credit for the astuteness of their fighting men. A quarter of a century after the fact, Sir Walter Ralegh was still glorying in the action, and implying that it might have been his advice and that of his associates which developed the strategy which saved England. In his *The History of the World*, published in 1614, he discussed the naval tactics of 1588:[179]

Certainly, hee that will happily performe a fight at Sea, must bee skilfull in making choice of Vessels to fight in: hee must beleeue, that there is more belonging to a good man of warre, vpon the waters, then great [en]during; and must know, that there is a great deale of difference, betweene fighting loose or at large, and grappling. The Gunnes of a slow ship pierce as well, and make as great holes, as those in a swift. To clap ships together, without consideration, belongs rather to a mad man, than to a man of warre: for by such an ignorant brauerie was *Peter Strosse*, lost at the *Azores*, when hee fought against the *Marquesse of Santa Cruz*. In like sort had the Lord *Charles Howard*, Admirall of *England*, been lost in the yeare 1588, if he had not beene better aduised, than a great many malignant fooles were, that found fault with his demeanour. The *Spaniards* had an Armie aboord them; and he had none: they had more ships than he had, and of higher building and charging; so that, had he intangled himselfe with those great and powerfull Vessells, he had greatly endangered his Kingdome of *England*. For twentie men vpon the defences, are equall to an hundred that boord and enter; whereas then, contrariwise, the *Spaniards* had an hundred, for twentie of ours, to defend themselues withall. But our Admirall knew his aduantage, and held it: which had he not

---

[179] 1614 edn., Book V, Ch. I, Section 6, pp. 350–1.

beene worthie to haue held his hed. Heere to speake in generall of Sea-
fight (for particulars are fitter for priuate hands, then for the Press) I
say, That a fleet of twenty ships, all good sailors, and good ships, haue
the aduantage, on the open Sea, of a hundred as good ships, and of
slower sailing. For if the fleet of an hundred saile keepe themselues
neere together, in a grosse squadron; the twentie ships, charging them
vpon any angle, shall force them to giue ground, and to fall back vpon
their next fellowes: of which so many as intangle, are made vnseruice-
able, or lost. Force them they may easily, because the twentie ships,
which giue themselues scope, after they haue giuen one broad side of
Artillerie, by clapping into the winde, and staying, they may giue them
the other: and so the twentie ships batter them in pieces with a
perpetuall vollie; whereas those, that fight in a troupe, haue no roome
to turne, and can alwaies vse but one and the same beaten side. If the
fleet of an hundred saile giue themselues any distance, then shall the
lesser fleet preuaile, either against those that are a-reare and hindmost,
or against those, that by aduantage of ouer sailing their fellowes keepe
the winde: and if vpon a Lee-shore, the ships next the winde be con-
strained to fall back into their own squadron, then it is all to nothing,
that the whole fleet must suffer shipwrack, or render it selfe. That
such aduantage may be taken vpon a fleet of vnequall speed, it hath
been wel enought conceiued in old time; as by that Oration of *Hermo-
crates*, in *Thucidides*, which he made to the *Syracusians*, when the
Athenians inuaded them, it may easily be obserued.

Of the Art of Warre by Sea, I had written a Treatise, for the Lord
HENRIE, *Prince of Wales*; a subject, to my knowledge, neuer handled
by any man, ancient or moderne; but God hath spared me the labour
of finishing it, by his losse; by the losse of that braue Prince; of which,
like an Eclipse of the Sunne, wee shall find the effects hereafter.
Impossible it is to equall words and sorrowes; I will therefore leaue him in
the hands of God that hath him. *Curæ leues loquuntur, ingentes stupent.*

No record exists to show what Harriot was doing to assist
Ralegh in the national defence, but it is certain that he was
involved in some way. It has frequently been assumed that he
continued his instruction in navigational techniques for the
newly recruited sea captains. But those navigational and shipbuilding notes that remain are from a later date, and give no
evidence of such activities. Most likely he was continuing his
regular duties in Ralegh's household — collecting information,
assembling maps and charts, maintaining liaison between
Ralegh and Elizabeth's officers, and keeping a close eye on
Ralegh's estates and business dealings while Ralegh was otherwise engaged. But whatever his role, we may be sure that
Harriot, like all free Englishmen, celebrated at the destruction

of the Spanish fleet and took great personal pride in rehearsing over and over all the details of the massive victory wrought by the valiant English men of the sea with the help given them by a Providence which proved the rightness of their cause.

V. Years of Transition, 1590–1600

Though the 1590s were in many ways less exciting for Harriot than the 1580s had been, they were, in other ways, more threatening and dangerous. England was in an age of transition, and with the ageing of the Queen, the race for power and place in the high circles of the court had accelerated. While Harriot himself was only a retiring member of the middle class, as a close friend and beneficiary of two of the principals of the courtly strife, he found himself unintentionally caught up in the turmoil and gossip which surrounded them, with the result that he appears to have withdrawn himself even more into the sheltered scholarly retreat of the semi-recluse.

Both Ralegh and his friend, Henry Percy, 9th Earl of Northumberland, felt the exuberance which marked the glorious defeat of the Spanish Armada. Ralegh, who for some unidentified reason had been in disgrace with the Queen and not welcome in her presence in the year following the Armada, had rusticated for a time in Ireland, and then returned again to court where he once more appeared in favour. Much of the cause of these vicissitudes lay in the mercurial nature of the Queen, her insistence on the complete fidelity of all around her to her own estimate of her youth, virtue, and loveliness, and the brutal fact of the difference in her age and that of her favourites. Elizabeth was, after all, nearing the age of sixty and her physical infirmities were beginning to show. Her most recent favourite, Robert Devereux, 2nd Earl of Essex, was in his mid-twenties, and Ralegh, who held a place in her affections unrivalled by anyone but Sir Christopher Hatton (who died in November 1591) was not yet forty. It was only natural that though rivalry for the Queen's affection was intense, the homage was more formal than real, and the constantly expressed love more metaphysical than human. And as the lively gossips of court affairs well knew, the handsome courtiers surrounding the ageing Queen found themselves attracted to the beautiful young ladies who were wards of the court to serve their Queen.

In 1590 Essex aroused the fierce wrath of Elizabeth by marrying, in secret and without her permission, Frances (Walsingham) Sidney, daughter of Sir Francis Walsingham and widow of that idealized knight, Sir Philip Sidney. Ralegh, too, was beginning to get a reputation for making advances to some of the court beauties, and there were rumours that he might be secretly married as well. The gossipy antiquary, John Aubrey, has left us one example of the sort of tale that was regaling the bawdy Elizabethan court:[1]

He [Sir Walter] loved a wench well; and one time getting up one of the Mayds of Honour up against a tree in a Wood ('twas his first Lady) who seemed at first boarding to be something fearfull of her Honour, and modest, she cryed, sweet Sir Walter, what doe you me ask? Will you undoe me? Nay, sweet Sir Walter! Sweet Sir Walter! Sir Walter! At last, as the danger and the pleasure at the same time grew higher, she cryed in the extasey, Swisser Swatter Swisser Swatter. She proved with child and I doubt not but this Hero took care of them both, as also that the Product was more than an ordinary mortal.

There was fire behind this verbal smoke. Ralegh was beginning to think in terms of settling down and appears to have been ready to retire from the limelight that marked London and Elizabeth's court. During early 1591 he searched the West Country for a possible estate where he could establish a seat for his own personal dynasty and had settled on Sherborne Castle in Dorset as a most congenial place to establish for his son. He immediately began a campaign to get the Queen to make a gift of the estate to him. But though he was at that time in high favour, Elizabeth, instinctively loath to part with landed property, refused to complete the

[1] This story is seriously cut by Andrew Clark in his edition of Aubrey as unfit for publication. It has, however, been published several times since. This quotation is from Oliver Lawson Dick, *Aubrey's Brief Lives, Edited from the Original Manuscripts*, London, Secker & Warburg, 1950, pp. 255–6.

grant, even though Ralegh had given her 'a jewell worth
£250 to make the Byshope' (Bishop Coldwell, who held
title to the land).[2]

Ralegh was also busy trying to increase his fortunes.
During the time he was seeking to increase his hold on
Sherborne he was also organizing a stock venture to raid
the Spanish ships carrying treasure from the New World back
to Spain, using as his rallying cry vengeance for the defeat
of Grenville and the *Revenge*. In this he was successful in
getting Elizabeth to contribute two vessels to the fleet, the
citizens of London another two, the Earl of Cumberland
six, his brother Carew one, and contributed one, the *Roebuck*, himself. In addition, Sir Walter stretched his credit
to borrow an additional £10,000 to man and and provision
the fleet, and obviously intended to participate most actively
and directly in the piratical venture.

Just when Ralegh formally married Elizabeth Throckmorton has long been a subject of controversy,[3] but there
is some evidence implying that it was in early 1588 and that
it was this marriage that drove him to consolidate his land
holdings and to attempt to build a fortune. On 19 November
1591 Elizabeth Throckmorton's brother, Arthur, wrote in
his diary that he had heard the two were married, but evidently
told no one of the fact.[4] On 24 February 1592 Sir Robert
Cecil was informed that Elizabeth Throckmorton was pregnant, and it is likely that he found the opportunity to inform
the Queen without delay.[5] But surprisingly Elizabeth took
no action, either disbelieving the report or waiting for Sir
Walter to inform her of the situation and to apologize for his

[2] Edward Edwards, *The Life of Walter Ralegh*, 1868, I. 464.

[3] Most of the discussion has centred upon the question of whether Ralegh's
marriage took place before or after his imprisonment by Elizabeth. But Pierre
Lefranc has uncovered evidence that the marriage actually took place more than
four years earlier, about 20 Feb. 1587/8, and that it was the fact that she had
been fooled for so long a time that made Queen Elizabeth bitter about his
deception and adamant in refusing to be reconciled about the match. See his
'La date du mariage de Sir Walter Ralegh: un document inédit', *Études anglaises*,
IX° Année, No. 3 (July–Sept. 1956), 193–211.

[4] Lefranc, *Sir Walter Ralegh écrivain*, Paris, Librairie Armand Colin, 1968,
p. 137, n. 10.

[5] Ibid. See also Robert Lacey, *Sir Walter Ralegh*, New York, Atheneum,
1974, pp. 165–72.

actions. On 29 March 1592 Lady Ralegh gave birth to a son, baptized on April 10 as Damerei Ralegh with Robert, Earl of Essex, and Arthur and Anna Throckmorton in attendance. Seventeen days later, Lady Ralegh returned to court to take her place among the Queen's ladies in waiting, and still the Queen did nothing. It was only when Elizabeth learned that Sir Walter was planning to leave the country on the expedition to the West Indies without obtaining her permission that Elizabeth acted: she ordered his immediate recall to the court, and in real anger, on 7 August 1592, without consulting the Council or any court, cast both Sir Walter and his now acknowledged wife into the Tower.[6] Ralegh's fears were realized, and he now found himself in despair and in danger for his life.

It is difficult to assess just what Ralegh's feelings for the Queen were. In late July, when the Queen left London because of the ravages of the plague, denying Ralegh the right to accompany her, Ralegh wrote to Sir Robert Cecil a letter which expressed his passion and desolation at the loss of the favour of the monarch he had so long served:[7]

My heart was never broken till this day, that I hear the Queen goes so far of[f], — whom I have followed so many years with so great love and desire, in so many journeys, and am now left behind her, in a dark prison all alone. While she was yet nire at hand, that I might hear of her once in two or three dayes, my sorrows were the less: but even now my heart is cast into the depth of all misery. I that was wont to behold her riding like *Alexander*, hunting like *Diana*, walking like *Venus*, the gentle wind blowing her fair hair about her pure cheeks, like a nymph; sometime siting in the shade like a Goddess; sometime singing like an angell; sometime playing like *Orpheus*. Behold the sorrow of this world! Once amiss, hath bereaved me of all. O Glory, that only shineth in misfortune, what is becum of thy assurance? All wounds have skares [scars], but that of fantasie; all affections their relenting, but that of womankind. Who is the judge of friendship, but adversity? or when is grace witnessed, but in offences? There were no divinety, but by reason of compassion; for revenges are brutish and mortall. All those times past, — the loves, the sythes, the sorrows, the desires, can they not way down one frail misfortune? Cannot one dropp of gall be hidden in so great heaps of sweetness? I may then conclude, *Spes et fortuna, valete.* She is gone, in whom I trusted, and of me hath not one thought of mercy, nor any respect of that that was.

[6] Edwards, *Life*, I. 135.   [7] Ibid. II, Letter XXV, pp. 51–2.

Do with me now, therefore, what you list. I am more weary of life then they are desirous I should perish; which if it had been for her, as it is by her, I had been too happily born.

Discounting from this declaration the natural exaggeration of the Elizabethan courtier, and subtracting the patent flattery expected of the followers of the vain Virgin Queen, there still remains some evidence of the depth of feeling that the now married, middle-aged courtier felt for his monarch.

Other gossips, too, were beginning to swirl around the head of Ralegh and his friends, gossips which were more directly related to the welfare and the future of Thomas Harriot. In November 1591, the Jesuit Robert Parsons, under the pseudonym of D. Andreas Philopater, licensed for publication a Latin tract entitled, *Elizabethæ, Angliæ Reginæ Hæresim Calvinianam Propugnantis, Sævissimum in Catholicos sui Regni edictum. . .cum Responsione. . .per D. Andream Philopatrum*, published in Augsburg in 1592.[8] Parsons's treatise was written in answer to a proclamation issued by the Queen on 18 October 1591 attacking the seminary priests and Jesuits who were secretly working to convert the English to Catholicism. In reply, Parsons attacked many of the court, particularly Cecil and Leicester, but spent much of his venom, too, on Sir Walter Ralegh. Ralegh was at this time seeking to be named to the Privy Council, and Parsons wished to discredit him. The tract branded both Cecil and Leicester as atheists, and in the case of Ralegh went even further, claiming that he maintained a school for the propagation of his atheism. The Catholic propaganda effort was so strong, and the reception of Parsons' book so popular that by the end of 1593 the *Responsio* had gone through at least five Latin editions, and had been translated into English, French, and German. The English version, shortened somewhat from the original, was published at Augsburg in 1592 under the title of *An Advertisement Written to a Secretarie of my L. Treasurers of England,*

---

[8] The most complete account of the Parsons attack on Ralegh and the Latin texts relating to this is to be found in Ernest A. Strathmann, *Sir Walter Ralegh: A Study in Elizabethan Skepticism*, New York, Columbia University Press, 1951, pp. 25 ff.

by an Inglishe Intelligencer. This work, widely circulated in England, digested the Philopatrus charges against 'Sir Walter Rawley' as follows:[9]

Of Sir VValter Rawley's Schoole of Atheisme by the waye, and of the Coniurer that is M. thereof,[10] and of the diligence vsed to get young gentlemen to this schoole, where in both Moyses, and our sauior, the olde, and the new Testamente are iested at, and the schollers taught amonge other thinges, to spell God backwarde.

Both John Dee and Harriot considered that Parsons was referring to themselves, and they quite possibly may have discussed the matter when they met at Dee's home at Mortlake shortly after the publication.[11]

The same religious zeal that led the orthodox Anglicans to search out Catholic subverters of the faith in the early 1590s led also to efforts to rout out atheists or other religious dissenters. Among the groups held highly suspect of atheism, freethinking, or even friendliness toward the Pope were the loose-living dramatists who took great pleasure in scandalizing the staid and puritanical Londoners. One of those most suspect was young Christopher Marlowe, who, since his student days at King's School, Canterbury, had been accused of being sympathetic to one Francis Kett who had been burned at the stake for his atheism.[12] Suspicion of Marlowe grew so strong that on 18 May 1593 it was decided to question

[9] STC 19885, listed under Philopatris, John, not under Parsons, sig. B[1]^v, p. 18.

[10] Though this idea is a gross exaggeration and could not have been taken seriously by the contemporary reader, it has been taken seriously and made as basic evidence against Ralegh and Harriot by Muriel C. Bradbrook in *The School of Night; A Study in the Literary Relationships of Sir Walter Ralegh*, Cambridge, University Press, 1936, p. 12 and *passim*.

[11] For the evidence that John Dee thought he was the one meant by the Master of the School of Atheism, see Ernest A. Strathmann, 'John Dee as Ralegh's "Conjurer"', *Huntington Library Quarterly*, X (1947), 365–72. That Harriot acknowledged himself to be the Master, see Quinn and Shirley, 'A Contemporary List', p. 21. The meeting of Dee and Harriot is attested to by Stephen P. Rigaud, who notes in Bodleian MS Rigaud 35, fo. 184 that 'In the Ashmole Library there is a copy of Manganin's Ephemerides, in the margin of which Dr. Dee has written many notices. 1592 August 27th Mr. Harriot 20°. 1594 March 18th Mr. Harriot came to me.'

[12] For a fairly complete discussion of the Marlowe affair, see John Bakeless, *The Tragicall History of Christopher Marlowe*, 2 vols., Cambridge, Harvard University Press, 1942, especially Ch. V, Marlowe's Monstrous Opinions' vol. I, pp. 105–40.

him formally and Her Majesty's Privy Council issued a 'warrant to Henry Maunder, one of the Messengers of her Majesty's Chamber, to repaire to the house of Mr. Thomas Walsingham in Kent, or to anie other place where he shall understand Christofer Marlow to be remayning, and by vertue thereof to apprehend and bring him to the Court.'[13] The testimony given in this investigation shows that Marlowe was suspected of being allied in his infamy with Ralegh and his Atheistic School; indeed, one modern author goes so far as to suspect that it was Ralegh who murdered Marlowe so that he could not testify against him.[14] Certainly, Marlowe was murdered under mysterious circumstances on 30 May 1593 before he could be brought before the Council, and the evidence gathered in preparation for the hearings continued to cast doubt on the orthodoxy of beliefs of both Sir Walter Ralegh and 'his man' Harriot.

The earliest document of the series still preserved is the so-called 'Baines libel', dated 12 May 1593, which may well be the original spy report which led the Privy Council to move against Marlowe. The author, Richard Baines, was a well-known investigator for the Council; his report is headed: 'A note containing the opinion of one Christopher Morly concerning his damnable Judgment of Religion, and scorn of Gods word'.[15] Though the testimony of Baines is well known and frequently quoted in part, it has never been printed in full.[16] Though scurrilous in tone and content, it furnishes a significant insight into the fears and beliefs of the Anglican of the day, and a background against which the orthodoxy of beliefs of Harriot and Ralegh may be measured. The complete text reads as follows:

---

[13] Ibid. I. 109.

[14] S. A. Tannenbaum, *The Assassination of Christopher Marlowe, a New View*, New York, 1928. See also Pierre Lefranc, *Sir Walter Ralegh écrivain*, p. 361.

[15] BL Harleian MS 6848, fos. 185–6. Another copy, which Bakeless believes was made for the Queen, is Harleian MS 6853, fos. 320–1. Quotations here are from the former.

[16] This was transcribed by F. S. Boas in his *Works of Thomas Kyd*, Oxford, Clarendon Press, 1901, pp. cxiii–xcvi, considerably excised. Boas excuses his deletions by saying (p. cxiii) that he has 'included here such portions of it as it is possible to reproduce.'

[1] That the Indians and many Authors of antiquity haue assuredly writen of aboue 16 thousand yeares agone wher ~~at Moyses~~ [c.o.] Adam is ~~said~~ [c.o.] proued to haue liued within 6 thowsand yeares.[17]

[2] He affirmeth that Moyses was but a Jugler, & that one Heriots being Sir W. Raleighs man can do more then he.

[3] That Moyses made the Jewes to travell xl yeares in the wildernes, (which Jorney might haue bin done in lesse then one yeare) ere they came to the promised land to th'intent that those who were priuy to most of his subtilties myght perishe and so an everlasting suporstition Remain in the harts of the people.

[4] That the first beginning of Religion was only to keep men in awe.

[5] That it was an easy matter for Moyses being brought vp in all the arte of the Egiptians to abuse the Jewes being a rude & grosse people.

[6] That Christ was a bastard and his mother dishonest.

[7] That he was the sonne of a carpenter, and that if the Jewes among whome he was borne did crucify him theie best knew him and whence he came.

[8] That Christ deserved better to dy then Barrabas and that the Jewes made a good choise, though Barrabas were both a theif and a murtherer.

[9] That if there be any god or any good Religion, then it is in the papists because the seruice of god is performed with more ceremonies, as Elevation of the mass, organs, singing men, shaven crownes, &c. that all protestants are Hypocriticall asses.

[10] That if he were put to write a new religion, he would vndertake both a more Excellent and Admirable methode and that all the new testament be filthily written.

[11] That the woman of Samaria & her sister were whores & that Christ knew them dishonestly.

[12] That Saint John the Evangelist was bed fellow to Christ and leaves alwaies in his bosome, that he vsed him as the sinners of Sodome.

[13] That all they that loue not Tobacco & Boies were fooles.

[14] That all the apostles were fishermen & base fellowes neyther of wit nor worth. that Paule only had wit but he was a timorous fellow in bidding men to be subject to magistrates against his conscience.

[15] That he had as good right to coine as the Queen of England, and that he was acquainted with one Poole a prisoner in Newgate who hath greate Skill in mixture of mettals and hauing learned some thinges of him he ment through help of a cuninge stamp maker to coin ffrench crownes pistolets and English shillings.

[16] That if Christ would have instituted the sacrament with more

---

[17] See Harriot's *Briefe and True Report*, 1588, sig. E3ʳ: 'But how manie yeres or ages haue passed since [the creation], they say they can make no relation, hauing no letters or other such meanes as we to keepe recordes of the particularities of times past...'

ceremoniall Reuerence it would haue bin had in more admiration, that it would haue bin much better being administered in a Tobacco pipe.

[17] That the Angell Gabriell was baud to the holy ghost because he brought the saluation to Mary.

[18] That one Richard Chomley hath confessed that he was perswaded by Marloe's Reasons to become an Atheist.

[19] These things, with many other shall by good & honest witnes be aproved to be his opinions and comon speeches and that this Marlow doth not only houlde them himself but almost into euery company he cometh he perswades men to Atheism willing them not to be afeard of bug beares and hobgoblins, and vtterly scorning both god and his ministers as I Richard Baines will Justify & approve both by mine oth and the testimony of many honest men, and almost al men with whome he hath conversed any time will testify the same, and as I think all men in Christianity ought to indevor that the mouth of so dangerous a member may be stopped. he saith likewise that he hath quoted a number of contrarieties oute of the Scripture which he hath giuen to some great men who in convenient time shalbe named. when those things shalbe called in question the witnes shalbe produced.

A second document, entitled 'Remembraunces of wordes & matter against Richard Cholmoley',[18] follows up on the accusation in 18 of the Baines Report. This document follows closely the Parsons line, scattering charges of atheism widely through the court. Members of the Privy Council are not only Atheists, but 'Machiavellians' as well; particularly the Lord Admiral. Sir Francis Drake, 'My Lord Threasour', and the Lord Chamberlain were all attacked. In all, eleven indictments are attributed to Cholmoley; one reinforces the case against Marlowe and involves Sir Walter, a second is against others of the Marlowe circle:

[7] That he saieth & verely beleueth that one Marlowe is able to shewe more sounde reasons for Atheisme then any devine in Englande is able to geue to prove devinitie & that Marloe tolde him that hee hath read the Atheist lecture to Sir Walter Raliege & others.

[8] That hee saith that hee hath certen men corrupted by his persuasions, who wilbe ready at all tymes & for all causes to sweare whatsoeuer seemeth good to him. Amonge whom is Master henry young & Jasper Borage & others.

By this time, Marlowe's room-mate and fellow dramatist,

---

[18] BL Harleian MS 6848, fo. 190 (old 175).

Thomas Kyd, had been imprisoned on the basis of three pages of a Unitarian tract devoted to proving that Jesus was not divine. This evidence is entitled: '12 May 1593. Vile hereticall coment denying the deity of Jhesus Christ our sauior fownd amongst the papers of thos Kydd prisoner which he affirmeth that he had ffrom Marlowe'.[19] This manuscript has been identified as a confession of faith made to Archbishop Cranmer in 1549 by a Unitarian heretic. It is written in a formal Roman hand which has been mistakenly attributed to Harriot.[20] It has, however, none of the identifying characteristics of Harriot's hand, and could serve as evidence only on the testimony of its owner.

In the meantime, Cholmoley (or Cholmley as he is sometimes called) had disappeared, and another court spy was sent to locate and question him. The report of the second spy also remains in the Marlowe–Kyd accounts.[21] This spy tried to insinuate himself into the 'dampnable crue' as spies of all ages have done, and he starts his report:

Ryghte worshipfull whereas I promised to sende you worde when Cholmeley was with mee; these are to lett you vnderstande that hee hath not yet bene with mee for hee doeth partely suspecte that I will bewray his villanye & his companye. But yesterday he sente two of his companions to mee to knowe if I would Joyne with him in familiaritie & becom of there dampnable crue. . .

Once insinuated, the spy 'soothed the villaynes with faire wordes in there follies', but obtained, in return, only the now conventional charges: they made 'sclaunderous reportes of most noble peeres & honourable counsailers, as the Lord Threasorer the Lord Chamberleyn the Lord Admirall, Sir Robert Cariee' and they enjoyed shocking their new member with vile and heretical statements such as

. . .that Jhesus christe was a bastarde Saint Mary a whore & the Aungell Gabriell a Bawde to the holy ghoste & that Christ was Justly persecuted by the Jewes for his owne foolishnes. that Moyses was a Jugler & Aaron a Cosoner the one for his miracles to the jewes to prove there was a god, & the other for taking the Earerings of the children of Israell to make a golden calfe with many other blasphemous speeches. . .which I feare to rehearse. . .

---

[19] Bakeless, op. cit. I. 114–15.   [20] Ibid., p. 115.
[21] BL Harleian MS 6848, fo. 191 (old 176).

On the obverse of this original letter are some rough notes, evidently written by one of the members of the investigating panel to indicate some actions already taken, and some remaining. It is evident from these jottings that the reputation of Harriot was being considered at this time. The notes read:

Ye athisme of ch[*olmoley*) [hole, doubtful reading]
   & others

_____

Young taken & made an instrument
   to take ye rest

_____

    hariet./

_____

borage dangerous
tippinges ij.

Certainly the 'taken' 'Yong' and the dangerous 'borage' are the Henry Young and Jasper Borage mentioned by the first spy as men converted to atheism by Cholmoley but willing to give evidence against him. The 'hariet' can be only the Thomas Harriot mentioned by Richard Baines as 'Sir W. Raleighs man' who was a better 'jugler' than Moses. This note would give credence to the idea that Harriot was called before the investigators to give evidence at this time, but if so, no evidence remains in the existing files.[22]

But other evidence of Harriot's involvements may be found in testimonies of the dramatists which could hardly have escaped notice. Still in prison after the death of Marlowe, Thomas Kyd wrote two letters to Sir John Puckering, Lord Keeper of the Great Seal of England, protesting his innocence and seeking release.[23] Kyd flatly denied the charges laid against him; the incriminating heretical papers found in his possession were there by accident, were the property of

---

[22] Testimony was given at the Cerne Abbas investigations by Nicholas Jeffreys that Harriot 'hath been convented before the Lords of the Counsell for denying the resurreccon of the bodye.' See below, p. 193.

[23] The first letter is BL Harleian 6849, fos. 218-19; the second Harleian 6848, fo. 154. In the first letter, in which he gives his own defence, Kyd speaks of Marlowe in the past tense; in the second, in which he makes accusations against Marlowe, he indicates that Marlowe had planned to go to Scotland to live, as Royden had done, 'if he had liued'. This may be why Kyd felt he could with impunity bring charges against his friend.

Marlowe, mixed with his own papers when they shared rooms together for their writing. Though it was not customary to speak evil of the dead, Kyd admitted that he found little to admire in Marlowe, since virtue 'neither was in him for person, quallities, or honestie, besides he was intemperate & of a cruel hart, the verie contraries to which my greatest enemies will saie by me.' To testify to his orthodoxy, Kyd suggested that some of his (and Marlowe's) friends be questioned:[24]

ffor more assurance that I was not of that vile opinion, lett it but please your Lordship to enquire of such as he conversed with all, that is (as I am geven to vnderstand) with [Thomas] Harriot, [Walter] Warner, [Matthew] Royden, and some stationers in Paules church-yard, whom I in no sort can accuse nor will excuse by reson of his companie. . .

This placed Thomas Harriot in something of an anomalous position: he had been pointed out as someone who was suspect and should be investigated, and at the same time was designated as a person of sufficient character that he could furnish references of respectability for an imprisoned suspect who declared his own innocence.

Another of the University-trained dramatists and pamphleteers, Thomas Nashe, took advantage of the popular hysteria about unorthodox beliefs to enter into the exposure of heretical thought in high places. Following up on the popularity of Parsons's work, he quickly wrote in 1592 a tract which he titled *Pierce Penilesse his supplication to the devill*. In this, among other charges, he levied the following veiled accusation:[25] 'I hear say there be Mathematicians abroad, that will proove men before Adam, and they are harbored in high places, who will maintain it to the death, that there are no divells. . .' This is a repetition of the slanderous charges that were going the rounds of London about Harriot and Ralegh. The following year he continued his attack in *Christs Teares over Jerusalem*, in which he exposed the iniquity of London. Here again he attacked the prevalent atheism with which he held the city to be riddled.[26] The English atheists, he claimed, 'followe the

---

[24] Harleian MSS 6849, fo. 218r.   [25] STC 18371, sig. C 4.
[26] STC 18336, sig. P 2v.

Pironicks, whose position and opinion it is, that there is no Hel or misery but opinion. Impudently they persist in it, that the late discouered Indians, are able to shew antiquities, thousands [of years] before Adam. . .' Harriot himself later acknowledged that the first reference was aimed at him,[27] and the second would certainly be recognized by the reader of the day as applicable to the young man who had so recently published the only English book dealing with the American Indians.

Charges like these were not unusual in the court of Elizabeth. Anyone who appeared to be rising in favour or rewarded by public office could expect to be subject to attacks from all sides, and in a time when the terms 'heretic' and 'atheist' were vague and tenuous at best, these were words which were likely to be hurled at even the most puritanical members of the court. But in the case of Ralegh and his servant friend, Harriot, they had more immediate significance, since Ralegh's most rapid rise to fame and fortune had created violent enemies, and his marriage to Elizabeth Throckmorton had made him vulnerable to the jealousy of the Queen, previously his staunchest supporter. And since Ralegh's fortune depended wholly on the favour of the monarch, such public accusations offered opportunity for his adversaries to wound him with trivia.

Yet fortune, characterized by the Elizabethans as a rolling wheel, once more turned to Ralegh's benefit. Not long after the court disgrace over his marriage and his consignment to the Tower by the Queen, one of his sea squadrons, waiting off the Azores, under the command of Sir John Borough, to way-lay the Spanish plate fleet returning from the West Indies, had the good fortune to encounter and capture a Portuguese carrack from the East Indies. Ralegh's own ship, the *Roebuck*, under Borough's command, took 'the Great Carrack', the *Madre de Deus*, the richest single prize so far taken in the Spanish war. The *Roebuck* brought the *Madre de Deus* to harbour in Dartmouth in early September, a little over a month after Ralegh's incarceration. Rumours about the fabulous wealth of the ship spread quickly throughout England; merchants

---

[27] Quinn and Shirley, 'A Contemporary List', p. 20.

and thieves hurried to Dartmouth to buy or steal the cargo. The sailors, too, began to pillage, and there was danger that the £180,000 cargo might be dissipated and the Queen's treasury despoiled of its share of the loot.

Sir John Hawkins and Lord Admiral Howard recognized that no man in England but Sir Walter could control the half-mutinous sailors of his own vessel, and on their recommendation Lord Burghley finally convinced the Queen that to save the cargoes at Dartmouth, Ralegh must be released from the Tower. Always ready to act in her own interest, Elizabeth ordered the release of Ralegh to proceed to the West Country, though he was to remain a state prisoner under the custody of an appointed keeper. And not trusting Ralegh himself, Lord Burghley sent his son, Robert Cecil, to Dartmouth to try to settle the matter before Ralegh could arrive. Cecil found things to be as bad as reported, with the treasures flowing away from Dartmouth like a flood, and in spite of everything he could do, the situation only got worse. The arrival of Ralegh worked like a miracle. In a letter to Sir Thomas Heneage, young Cecil reported:[28]

Within one half-hour, Sir Walter Ralegh arrived with his keeper, Mr. Blount. I assure you, Sir, his poor servants, to the number of one hundred and forty goodly men, and all the mariners, came to him with such shouts of joy, as I never saw a man more troubled to quiet them in my life. *But his heart is broken; for he is very extreme pensive longer than he is busied, in which he can toil terribly.* The meeting between him and Sir John Gilbert was with tears on Sir John's part. Whensoever he is saluted with congratulations for liberty, he doth answer, *No, I am still the Queen of England's poor captive.* I wished him to conceal it, because here it doth diminish his credit, which I vow to you before God, is greater amongst the mariners than I thought for. . .

By the strength of his popularity and his powers of persuasion, Ralegh did what no one else could have done: he stopped the looting, retrieved much of the stolen property, and saved the rewards for distribution among the investors.

Negotiations over the distribution of profits from such a large windfall were naturally long drawn out and somewhat acrimonious. Though the records are not clear, it was generally rumoured that the Queen took more than half (about £80,000) for her share, allotted about half that much to her current favourite, the Earl of Cumberland, and grudgingly allowed Sir Walter to keep a miserly £24,000 — which netted him a loss for all the effort he had put into organizing and underwriting the venture. But more important than the money at this crucial time, Ralegh's protection of the Queen's interest bought him his freedom from the Tower, and though he was technically still a prisoner of the state, freed him from the supervision of his keeper, Sir Christopher Blount. Still in partial disfavour, Ralegh again retired from the court to take up his life as a country gentleman with his wife and young son and a retinue which at times included Harriot at Sherborne Castle. Through continued negotiations he finally managed to execute a lease to hold Sherborne as a tenant, paying quarterly rent to the Dean and Chapter, an arrangement which held till the last years of Elizabeth's reign.[29] During the long years of his rustication, from late 1592 to 1597, Ralegh made Sherborne his base of operations, and most of his letters following his release from the Tower are dated 'from Sherborne Castell' or 'from my Castell'.

But Ralegh's enemies would not let him rest, and charges of irreligion, freethinking, and atheism followed him from London to Dorset. Following the accusations of Parsons and the testimony taken in the investigations of Christopher Marlowe and Thomas Kyd, an ecclesiastical commission was established to look into possible atheism in the County of Dorset. The commission hearings were held at Cerne Abbas, a small town about 10 miles south of Sherborne Castle, midway between Sherborne and Dorchester, during the week of 21 to 28 March 1594.[30] The report of this examination is entitled 'Examinacions taken at Cearne in the Countie of Dorset the xxjth daye of March in xxxvjth yeare of the raigne of our soueraigne Ladye Queene Elizabeth'. Members

---

[29] The fullest account of Sir Walter's holdings at Sherborne (though even this is not complete) is to be found in Joseph Fowler, *Mediaeval Sherborne: taken for the most part from original documents...*, Dorchester, Longmans, 1951, p. 372–405.

[30] The original documents of the Cerne Abbas investigations are to be found in BL Harleian MS 6849, fos. 183–90.

of the investigating team are also listed: 'Before vs Thomas
Lorde Howard Vicount Howarde of Bindon. Sir Raulfe
Horsey knight, ffrauncys James Chauncellor, John Willyams,
ffraunces Hawley, Esquiers, by verue of a Commission to vs
& others directed from some of her Majesties heighe Commissioners in Causes Ecclesiasticall &c.' That the entire
investigation was quite clearly for the purpose of exploring
the rumours that were going round about the religious
beliefs of Sir Walter Ralegh and 'his man' Harriot is evident
from the list of questions to be asked of each one called to
testify. This Interrogatory preserved with the transcript of
testimony taken reads as follows:[31]

Dorset   Interrogatory to be ministered vnto such as are to be
          examined in her majesties name by vertue of her
          heighnes Commission for Causes Ecclesiasticall.

1. Imprimis whome doe you knowe, or haue harde to be suspected of
   Atheisme; or Apostacye? And in what manner doe you knowe or
   haue harde the same? And what other notice can you giue thereof?
2. Item Whome doe you knowe, or haue harde, that haue argued or
   spoken againste? or as doubtinge the beinge of anye God? Or what
   or where God is? Or to sweare by God; adding if there be a god, or
   such like; and when & where was the same? And what other notice
   can you give of anye such offender?
3. Item Whome doe you knowe or haue harde that hath spoken against
   god his providence ouer the worlde? or of the worldes beginninge
   or endinge? or of predestinacion? or of heaven or hell? or of the
   Resurrecion in doubtfull or contenciouse manner? When & where
   was the same? And what other notices can you geive of any such
   offender?
4. Item Whome doe you knowe or haue harde that hath spoken
   againste the truthe of god his holye worde revealed to vs in the
   scriptures of the oulde & newe testament? or of some places thereof? or haue sayde those scriptures ar not to be beleived & defended
   by her Majestie for doctrine, & faith, and salvacion, but onlye of
   policye, or Civell government, and when & where was the same? And
   what other notice can you geive of any such offender?
5. Item Whome doe you knowe or haue harde hath blasphemouslie
   cursed god; as in sayinge one time (as it rayned when he was a
   hawkinge) if there be a god. A poxe on that god which sendeth such
   weather to marr our sporte? or such like. Or doe you knowe or have
   harde of anye that hath broken froth [*sic*] into anye other words of
   blasphemye and when? & where was the same?
6. Item Whome doe you knowe or have harde to have sayde, when he

was dead his soule shoulde be hanged on the topp of a poole; and ronne god, ronne devill, and fetch it that would haue it, or to like effecte? or that hath otherwise spoken against the beinge, or immortallitye of the soule of man? or that a mans soule shoulde dye & become like the soule of a beast, or such like; and when, & where was the same?

7. Item Whome doe you knowe or have harde hath counselled, pro-cured, ayded, comforted, or conferred with anye such offendor? when? where, & in what manner was the same?

8. Item doe you knowe or have harde of anye of those offenders to affirme, all these that were not of there opinions towchinge the premises to be schismatickes, and in error? And whome do you knowe hath soe affirmed? And when? & where was it spoken?

9. Item What can you saye more of anye of the premisses? or whome haue you knowne or harde can give anye notice of the same? And speake all your knowledge therein. /

Testimony on these questions was taken by the Com-mission from a large number of the ministers and church-wardens of the area. The ones chosen, though representing all segments of the country, were more concentrated from the area around Sherborne where Ralegh was currently in residence,[32] from Gillingham where Ralegh or his brother, Carew, had served as Grand Master for nearly a decade,[33] or from Portland, where he held the post of Governor of the Fort.[34] That the questions were pointed may be seen from the fact that of the twelve churchmen called to give testimony, only two did not in some way implicate Ralegh, Harriot, or some member of their intimate group. The two non-testifiers, John Hancocke and Richard Bryage, parson and church-warden respectively of South Parrot, swore that they had heard nothing on any of the questions raised by the Com-mission. John Jessop, minister of Gillingham, said that though 'he can say nothinge of his owne knowledge . . . he hath harde that one Herryott of Sir Walter Rawleigh his howse hath brought the godhedd in question, and the whole course of the scriptures, but of whome he so harde it he doth not remember. . .'[35] Jessop also indicated that Carew Ralegh

---

[32] With the exception of one letter from Dorchester, all of Ralegh's extant letters during May of this year were dated as from Sherborne. See Edwards, *Life*, II, Letters XL–XLV.

[33] Lefranc, op. cit., p. 382.

[34] Ibid.   [35] Harleian MS 6849, fo. 184r.

was inclined to be argumentative about the nature of God, and that in one instance of which he was aware, his brother Walter had attempted to soothe the matter over and to convince the Bishop of Worcester to present a convincing case to him, 'for sayed he, your Lordship shall heare him argue as like a pagan as euer you harde anye.' He concluded by adding that he had 'hard one Allen nowe of Portland Castle suspected of Atheisme, but of whom he harde it he remembereth not.' His churchwarden, William Hussey, had heard less; he only 'sayeth that he hath harde Sir Walter Rawleigh suspected of Atheisme. To the rest of the Interrogatory he can say nothinge.'[36]

John Davis, curate of Motcombe, in the north of Dorset just east of Gillingham, had heard the same rumours. Though he knew nothing of his own knowledge, he had 'harde Sir Walter Rawleigh by generall reporte hath had some reasoninge against the dietye of god, and his omnipotencye. And hath harde the like of Master Carewe Rawleighe, but not so directlye.'[37] But in response to question number 6, Davis introduced a new theme:[38]

. . .he hath harde that Sir Walter Rawleigh hath argued with one Master Ironsydes at Sir George Trenchards towchinge the beinge, or immortallitye of the soule, or such like: but the certaintye thereof he cannot saye further savinge askinge the sonne of Master Ironsydes vppon the report aforesaye, he hath aunswered that the matter was not as the voice of the Countess reported thereof, or to the like effects. . .

The story of the table conversation between Ralegh and Ironsides covered most of the County of Dorset evidently, for the next witness, Nicholas Jefferys, parson of Wyke Regis on the south coast, reported that not only had he heard of the argument, but that he had heard it from Ironsides himself. He was perfectly willing to give a second-hand account of the evening, but was quick to implicate Ralegh and his friends as suspect:[39] '. . .he hard by reporte of diuers that Sir Walter Rawleigh and his retinewe are generally suspected of Atheisme, and especially one Allen of Portland Castle [Ralegh's] Leiftenant, And that he is a great blasphemer & leight esteemer of Religion: and thereabouts

[36] Ibid.   [37] Ibid., fo. 184^v.   [38] Ibid.   [39] Ibid., fo. 185^r.

cometh not to Devine service or sermons.' Jeffreys also was quick to implicate Harriot. In answer to question three, 'he sayeth that he hath harde that one Herriott, Attendant ouer Sir Walter Rawleigh hath ben convented before the Lords of the Counsell for denyinge the resurreccion of the bodye.'[40] If this rumour is true, it furnishes the only evidence that Harriot was formally investigated for his religious orthodoxy outside the Cerne Abbas Commission hearings, and may have been a part of the Marlowe–Kyd enquiries of the previous year.

John Dench, churchwarden at Wyke Regis, answered only question 6 about the race for the soul. This he ascribed to Lieutenant Allen of Portland Castle:[41] 'he hath harde one Allen Leiftennant of Portland Castle when he was like to dye, beinge persuaded to make himselfe reddye to God for his soule, to aunswer that he woulde carrye his soule vp to the topp of an hill, and runne god, runne Devill, fetch it that will have it. . .' The Trenchard dinner had been bruited to the east of Dorset in a somewhat confused fashion. William Arnold, vicar of Blandford, reported that 'Master Ironsydes [had] deliuered some speach vnto him concerninge some disputacion had between him, & Master Carewe Rawleigh concerning the beinge or substaunce of the soule.'[42] This, he admitted, was only hearsay, 'And yet he remembereth he harde Master Carewe Rawleigh saye at Gillingham there was a god in nature', though he did not indicate whether or not this was commendable. He continued,[43] 'And further he sayeth he harde by an vncertain reporte of some strange opinions that should be defended by Sir Walter Rawleigh, but wheither the same be true or not certainlye he knoweth not.'

Thomas Norman, minister of Melcombe Regis, Weymouth, reported that a Master Jones and a Master Rogers had indicated that the Lieutenant of Portland Castle, Master Allen, had wanted to dispute religion with him but Master Jones had not felt that Allen was capable of reasoned disputation. Jones's son also reported that 'the sayd Allen spake as if he denyed the imortallity of the soule', and had gone so far as to 'teare twoe Leaves out of a Bible to dry Tobacco on. . . .

---

[40] Ibid.   [41] Ibid., fo. 186r.   [42] Ibid., fo. 185v.   [43] Ibid.

Also he sayeth that he harde of one Herryott of Sir Walter Rawleigh his howse to be suspected of Atheisme.'[44]

From Sherborne itself, it is interesting to note, no charges were laid against Sir Walter or 'his retenewe'. Francis Scarlett, minister of Sherborne, told in some detail of the blasphemies uttered by 'one Olliuer, seruant to Thomas Allen [of Portland Castle]', a story borne out by his churchwarden, Robert Asheborne. To attest these charges, he called upon three other Sherborne residents who were in turn called before the Commissioners to testify.[45] Surprisingly, their affidavits did not bear out the testimony of the Revd. Scarlett, as a marginal note alongside Scarlett's testimony indicates:[46] 'This relacion of Master Scarlett grounded vppon ye report of 2. women and one Robert Hyde is denyed by their oaths & found otherwise as appeareth by their particulars taken by Sir Rauf Horsey & Doctor James.'

This left only the story of the dinner party at the house of Sir George Trenchard to be investigated. They called the source of the story, the Revd. Raphe Ironside, minister of Winterborne Abbas near Dorchester, himself. Before the commissioners, Ironside appeared much more cautious than his colleagues had been. He prefaced his remarks by the warning that he could not answer any questions except those of which he had personal knowledge, since he had been 'persuaded by Counsell that he is in daunger to be punished, and therefore refuseth to saye any thinge vppon uncertaine reporte...'[47] As to the now famous dinner, however, he can speak, since he was a participant. His account, obviously well rehearsed from previous tellings, is somewhat verbose, but it is extremely valuable in that it shows much of the nature of philosophical discussions of the time, and gives insight into the quality of mind of both Ralegh and a typical clergyman of his day. For this reason, it is here reproduced in full.[48]

The relacion of the disputation had at Sir George Trenchards table betwene Sir Walter Rawleigh, Master Carewe Rawleigh &

[44] Ibid., fo. 186[r].

[45] The three affidavits of Robert Hyde, shoemaker, and Grace Brewer and Elizabeth Whetcomb, housewives, all of Sherborne, are appended to the Commission report: ibid., fos. 189[r], 189[v], 190[r].

[46] Ibid., fo. 186[v].　　[47] Ibid., fo. 187[v].　　[48] Ibid., fos. 187[v]–188[r].

Master Ironside hereafter followeth, written by him selfe & deliuered to the Commissioners vppon his oath.

Wednesday sevenight before the Assises summer Laste I came to Sir George Trenchards in the afternoon accompayned with a fellowe minister frind of myne Master Whittle viccar of fforthington. There were then with the knight, Sir Walter Rawleigh, Sir Raulfe Horsey Master Carewe Rawleigh Master John ffitziames &c./ Towards the end of supper some loose speeches of Master Carewe Rawleighes beinge gentlye reproved by Sir Raulfe Horsey in these words *Colloquia praua corrumpunt bones mores*./ Master Rawleigh demaunds of me, what daunger he might incurr by such speeches? wheruunto I aunswered, the wages of sinn is death, and he makinge leight of death as being common to all sinner and reightuous; I inferred further, that, as that liffe which is the gifte of god through Jesus Christ, is liffe eternall: so that death which is properly the wages of sinne, is death eternall, both of the bodye, and of the soule alsoe. Soule, quoth Master Carewe Rawleigh, What is that? Better it were (sayed I) that we would be carefull howe the Soules might be saved, then to be curiouse in findinge out ther essence. And soe keepinge silence Sir Walter requests me, that for there instruccion I woulde aunswere to the question that before by his brother was proposed vnto me. I have benn (saythe he) a scholler some tyme in Oxforde, I haue aunswered under a Bachelor of Arts, & had taulks with diuers; yet heither vnto in this pointe (to witt what the reasonable soule of man is) haue I not by anye benne resolved. They tell vs it is *primus motor* the first mover in a man &c. Vnto this, after I had replied that howsoeuer the soule were *fons et principuum*, the fountain, beginninge, and cawse of motion in vs, yet the first mover was the braine, or harte, I was againe vrged to showe my opinion, and hearinge Sir Walter Rawleigh tell of his dispute & schollership some time in Oxeforde, I cited the generall definicion of Anima out of Aristotle 2° de Anima cap 1°. & thence a *subito propris* deduced the speciall definicion of the soule reasonable, that it was *Actus primus corporis organici animantis humani vitam habentis in potentia*. It was misliked of Sir Walter as obscure & intricate: And I with all yealded that though it coulde not vnto him, as being lerned, yet it must seme obscure to the most present, and therefore had rather saye with devines plainly that the reasonable soule is a spirituall, & imortall substance breathed into man by god, whereby he lyves, & moves & vnderstandeth, & soe is distinguished from other Creatures: yea but what is that spirituall & imortall substance breathed into man &c. saieth Sir Walter; the soule quoth I. Naye then saith he you aunswer not like a scholler. herevppon I endevoured to prove, that it was schollerlike, naye in such disputes as these, vsuall, & necessary to runne *in circulum*, partlye because *definitio reicio* was *primum et imediatum principuum*, and beinge *primo non est prius*, a man must of necessitie come backwards & partlye because *definitio & definitum* be *nature reciproce* the one conuertiblie aunsweringe vnto the question made vppon the other. As for example, if one aske what is a man? you will saye he is a creature reasonable, & mortall; but if you aske againe what is a creature reasonable, & mortall, you must of force come backwarde, and aunswer, it is a man. *et sic de ceteris./* but we have principles in our mathematickes sayeth Sir Walter, as *totum est maius quamlibet [sic] sua parte.* and aske me of it, and I can showe it in the table, in the window, in a man, the whole being bigger than the partes of it. I replied first that showed *quod est,* not *quid est,* that it was but not what it was, secondlye, that such demonstracions as it was against the nature of a mans soule beinge a spirite for as his things beinge sensible were subiecte to the sence; soe mans soule being insensible was to be discerned by the sperite. nothinge more certaine in the worlde then that there is a god, yet beinge a sperite to subiecte him to the sense otherwise then perfection it is impossible./ Marrye quoth Sir Walter, these 2 be like, for neither coulde I lerne heitherto what god is. Master ffitziames aunswering that Aristotle shoulde saye he was *Ens, Encium.* I aunswered that whether Aristotle dyinge in a feaver shoulde crie *ens encium miserere mei* or drowninge himselfe in *Euripum* shoulde saye *quia ege te non capio tu me capies,* it was uncertaine, but that god was *ens entium* a thinge of thinges havinge beinge of him selfe, & geivinge beinge to all creatures it was most certaine, and confirmed by god him selfe vnto moyses. yea but what is this *ens entium* sayeth Sir Walter? I aunswered it is God. And being disliked as before Sir Walter wished that grace myght be sayd; for that quoth he is better than this disputacion. Thus supper ended and grace sayed, I departed to Dorchester with my fellowe minister. and this to my rememberance is the substance of that speach which Sir Walter & I had at Wolveton.

[Signed] Raphe Ironside

Theis examinacions before written are the trewe Copies taken at Cern the xxj[th] of March 1593 before the lord viscount Bindon, Sir Raufe Horsey knight, Master Doctor James Chancellor, John Williams, & francis Hawly, Esquiers./ what other Examinacions have ben taken by vertue of the Comysion, are vnknowen to vs./ [signed] Raufe Horse fra Hawley John Willyams

A number of matters remain unresolved about the Cerne Abbas investigation. In the first place, the composition of the commission appears suspiciously to have been drawn from people generally friendly to Ralegh. As Pierre Lefranc has pointed out,[49] though the ranking member of the commission, Lord Thomas Howard, Viscount Bindon, was one of Ralegh's greatest enemies,[50] the other four members were

---

[49] For Lefranc's analysis of the commission and its work, see *Sir Walter Ralegh écrivain,* pp. 379-93.

[50] Fowler, *Ancient Sherborne,* p. 392.

associates who would be as sympathetic a jury as he could have. Sir Ralph Horsey, deputy to the Lord Lieutenant, was not only a personal friend but even a remote cousin of Sir Walter. John Williams, sheriff of the county, was son-in-law to Sir George Trenchard, a close personal friend of Horsey, and who served along with him as deputy to the Lieutenant. Francis James, Doctor of Laws, previously Chancellor Of London, appears to have been neutral. But Francis Hawley who was Vice-Admiral of Dorset, held a position parallel to that held by Ralegh in Devon, and had worked closely with him in naval matters concerning the two counties. Though it is doubtful that the course of the investigations would be curtailed or modified by these associations, it seems certain (as was the case) that no charges would be levied against Ralegh or his associates unless evidence which was unequivocal and without doubt was produced. Even though the investigation was widely reported throughout Dorset and must have occasioned much speculation and gossip about the two Raleghs, Thomas Allen, and the mysterious Thomas Harriot, there was no tangible result from the inquest. No charges were laid against any of those suspected, and Ralegh's enemies at court must have been disappointed, and Ralegh (if he deigned to worry about the matter at all) relieved.

The testimony of the Revd. Ironside about the dinner conversation at Sir George Trenchards is illuminating about the personalities of the participants, though puzzling about what lay beneath the surface. It is difficult to believe, as Lefranc obviously does, that the whole performance was planned by Carewe and Sir Walter as a kind of 'priest-bating' designed to discredit the clergy and to furnish intellectual fun and games for the observers.[51] Rather, it seems to reflect just the kind of discourse to be expected when a highly intellectual, sceptical, anti-Aristotelian critic met up with the kind of unthinking acceptance of the status quo, bolstered by the sort of scholastic circular reasoning here adopted by Ironside. The fact that Ralegh stresses that he had 'been . . . a scholler some tyme in Oxforde . . . [had] aunswered under a Bachelor of Arts, & had taulks with diuers' is important in setting the

---

[51] *Sir Walter Ralegh écrivain*, p. 391.

tone and manner of the disputation. Ralegh was conducting
his table conversations with the kind of direct refutation
typical of the *respondere in parvisis* which was the final stage
in the formal Oxford education he attained; he was employing
the techniques of Aristotelian logic to refute Aristotelian
positions. As Ernest Strathmann sums up the discussion:[52]

The clue to the significance of Ralegh's impatience with Ironside's
definitions lies not in any fundamental disagreement in belief nor in
any irreverence in speech. Ralegh was dissatisfied, both temperamen-
tally and intellectually, with Ironside's logic. By shifting from faith to
logical argument and back to faith again, Ironside weakened his case,
all the more because Sir Walter was no respecter of Aristotle and even
on the definition of the soul gave his opinions only a qualified acceptance.... There is good reason to believe that Ralegh found such
speculations congenial (as many a passage from the *History* ... shows),
but no good reason to infer that it exceeded the bounds of religious
propriety.

In this discussion, Ralegh appears to have welcomed a divert-
ing philosophical discussion, seeking to explore the exact
nature of the soul and its relation to the body, even though
he knew full well that no such discussion could result in more
than a speculative basis for belief. But in Ironside he did not
find a suitable protagonist: Ironside preferred circular
definitions which led nowhere; he shifted his logical grounds
in a way that shed no light and made no progress. Naturally,
this disappointed Ralegh, so he terminated the discussion,
calling for the saying of grace, which, he said 'is better
than this disputacion'. Was this heretical? Strathmann
summarizes:[53]

If Ralegh were heretical in this colloquy, his heresy was philosophical,
not religious; as Ironside presented his case, Ralegh was rebellious
against Aristotle and school logic, not against Scripture or belief in
immortality. In that rebellion, from which the word of God is specifically exempt, lies the key to much of Ralegh's thought, to his sometimes unhealthy reputation with the churchmen, and to his contemporary influence.

It is unfortunate for the modern biographer that the Cerne
Abbas Commission did not follow up the suspicions directed

[52] *Sir Walter Ralegh, a Study in Elizabethan Skepticism*, pp. 145–7.
[53] Ibid., p. 147.

against the orthodoxy of Thomas Harriot. Had they included specific charges or testimony of his statements, his personal philosophy would be much clearer than it is, and would have denied or given substance to the somewhat vague speculations from the time of John Aubrey to the present. Gossipy Aubrey, gathering material for the work on famous Oxford graduates by the Oxford antiquary, Anthony à Wood, recorded some of the stories still going the rounds a half-century after Harriot's death:[54]

The Bishop of Sarum (Seth Ward) told me that one Mr. Haggar (a countryman of his), a gentleman and good mathematician, was well acquainted with Mr. Thomas Harriot, and was wont to say, that he did not like (or valued not) the old storie of the Creation of the World. He could not believe the old position; he would say *ex nihilo nihil fit.*[55] But sayd Mr. Haggar, a *nihilum* killed him at last; for in the top of his nose came a little red speck (exceeding small), which grew bigger and bigger, and at last killed him. I suppose it was that which the chirurgians call *noli me tangere.*[56]

In another note, Aubrey wrote:[57]

He made a philosophical theologie, wherein he cast-off the Old Testament, and then the New one would (consequently) have no foundation. He was a Deist. His doctrine he taught to Sir Walter Raleigh, Henry, earle of Northumberland, and some others. The devines of those times look't on his manner of death as a judgement upon him for nullifying the Scripture.

It is very likely that these were some of the rumours which were raising eyebrows in London, and in Dorset furnishing the basis for vague accusations in the Cerne Abbas enquiries. But from the records that survive they remain only rumours and hearsay, and the Commission called for no direct testimony

[54] Clark, *Brief Lives*, I. 286.
[55] Harriot did say 'ex nihilo nihil fit'; see BL Add. MSS 6788, fo. 493^r. For Ralegh's discussion of this, see his *History of the World*, Oldys and Birch edition, vol. II, 'Preface', pp. xlvii–lii. This statement of Harriot's belief has been confusing to later writers, since Anthony à Wood, who printed this material in his *Athenae Oxonienses*, omitted the semicolon and 'he would say' which completely reversed Harriot's position. Later historians, Jacquot, Strathman, and Lefranc have straightened this out.
[56] That Harriot died of cancer of the nose is correct, but the growth was inside, rather than outside, as legend has it. For an account of his illness and death, see Ch. XI.
[57] *Brief Lives*, I. 287.

on these matters. One reason probably was that during this time, Harriot was quite remote from the Dorset turmoils, only occasionally called to Sherborne by his rusticated patron. Newly discovered evidence shows that during this period Harriot was moving further from Ralegh, was remaining in London, keeping his rooms at Durham House and dining in the households of other London friends.

Ralegh soon began to chafe under his rustication and lack of favour. Though the enquiry at Cerne Abbas had not really harmed him, it had not helped him either. The Queen was still unwilling to receive him at court, and now some of his fellow West Country neighbours were suspicious of him. In looking for a way to regain the affection of the Queen and the respect of his neighbours, Ralegh turned, as he was to do all his life, to dreams of Spanish gold. He was convinced that the major source of the Inca gold which had rebuilt the coffers of Spain had originated in vast mines near the lost Empire of the Incas, in the fabled city of Manoa, home of the men who dressed in gold, the 'gilded man' Eldorado. This he located from Spanish accounts as between the Amazon and the Orinoco Rivers. Even as the Commission was at work at Cerne Abbas, Ralegh was making plans for a bold assault on this source of unlimited fortune. He was preparing ships, crews, and supplies for a voyage of exploration and discovery of the land he named Guiana and of the waters of the Orinoco River to question the natives about their lost city of gold.

During this time, while Ralegh was in Dorset and Harriot was relatively free from duties, Harriot continued to build his personal reputation, both as a leading exponent of navigational science and as a theoretical mathematician. Much of his time was spent in polishing his mathematical abilities, and some of his extant manuscripts dating from this period show him systematically working through the works of the great mathematicians from antiquity to his own time. It is probable that he was also in touch with many in the mathematical community in England, perhaps also on the continent, for though he published nothing, his fame as a 'profound mathematician' and innovator was becoming widely known. On 24 January 1590, for instance, he appears to have conferred

with the famous magus, Dr John Dee, since a book now in
the British Library,[58] a copy of *El Viaie que Hizo Antonio
de Espeio en el anno de ochenta y tres*, bears the inscription
in Dee's own hand: 'Johannes Dee: A° 1590. January 24. Ex
dono Thomæ Hariot, Amici mei'. And a list which Harriot
drew up about 1603 listing twenty-seven books which made
reference to his contributions and thought,[59] shows how
well known he was. From these citations, it is apparent that
Harriot was considered by his knowledgeable contemporaries
as having already established himself as a significant figure in
both practical and advanced mathematical theory. His work
is referred to in such works as the very popular *A briefe
treatise for the ready vse of the sphere*, 1592, by Robert
Tanner; Thomas Hood's *The vse of the two mathematicall
instruments, the crosse staffe and the Iacob's staff* of the
same year; and the 1594 edition of Robert Hues's *Tractatus
de globis et eorum vsu*. This last work resulted from the
collaboration of Hues and Harriot in the development of the
Wright–Molyneux globe of 1592, and refers to a publication
expected momentarily on the calculation of rhumb lines by
'Thoma Hariota Matheseos & vniuersæ Philosophiæ'. In
1593 Gabriel Harvey defended the mathematical practitioner
in his *Pierces supererogation*, placing Harriot in high company: 'what profound mathematician like Digges, Hariot, or
Dee, esteemeth not the pregnant Mechanician?' And even
the world-famous continental classical scholar, Joseph
Justus Scaliger, son of Julius Caesar Scaliger, knew of the
work of Harriot. In his treatise on the measurement of the
circle, *Cyclometria*, published in 1593, Scaliger made some
obvious errors which attracted considerable scorn from
professional mathematicians, and in one case, where he
sought the ratio between the diameter of the circle and its
circumference, he was accused of plagiarism. In a second
edition, 1594, Scaliger added an Appendix in which he
recognized this criticism: '*Quod dico, quia quidam hariolantur a nescio quo, (nomen enim perdidi,) me hanc rationem
furatum esse...*' (Translated freely, this reads: 'I say this

---

[58] BL b.32.a.32.
[59] For this list and the works it mentions, see Quinn and Shirley, 'A Contemporary List', loc. cit.

because certain persons are making the ridiculous allegation that I have plagiarized this ratio from someone or another (I have forgotten his name).') Harriot, and presumably others in the know, picked up this pun on his name in Scaliger's use of the unusual word *hariolantur* which might be missed by the modern reader except for Harriot's gleeful entry in his notes: 'Item Scaligers Appendix. Hariolantur Mee'. Harriot's identification of this back-handed reference is important in that it shows him already in the battleground of continental scholarship. From these years on, references to Harriot and his mathematical and scientific prowess are to be found in a great number of English and continental publications.

In the early 1590s while Ralegh's life was in constant turmoil, Harriot began to look for a more secure patronage. Quite naturally he turned to Ralegh's noble friend, Henry Percy 9th Earl of Northumberland. The Northumberland household account which had earlier shown the growing friendship of Percy and Ralegh, now began to contain the name of Harriot. The earliest account that I have found comes in one of the rare 'brevinge books' — kitchen accounts of the meals served, who was served, and the costs of supplying the table of the Earl, his retainers, and his guests. One of these labelled 'A common breevinge Booke Begun the xiiij of ffebruary 1590 [1591 NS]'[60] records that on Saturday, 20 February 1591, 'Sir Walter Rawleigh' dined at the Earl's table. Three weeks later, on 13 March 1591, again a Saturday, both Sir Walter and 'Master herriot' had supper with him. Details of this meal are typical of the breving-book entries and furnish a fair sample of the Earl's fare and hospitality. On this day, guests at the noon meal, dinner, included only Sir Charles Danvers, oldest son of Sir John Danvers (a decade later to be beheaded in the Tower for his major role in the Essex conspiracy) with one servant; and the Earl's younger brother, Master Richard Percy. At supper on that day the guest list was longer. Present with one servant was Henry Wriothesley, 3rd Earl of Southampton, neighbour and close friend of the Danvers (famous in history primarily because he was the only absolutely known patron of Shakespeare,

---

[60] Syon MS (now at Alnwick Castle) X.II.12.5.

his close friend, and generally thought to be the 'Mr. W. H.'
to whom Shakespeare dedicated his sonnets). Like Sir Charles,
Southampton was deeply involved in the Essex plot, was
tried with Essex on charges of treason, condemned to die,
but pardoned by the Queen on the intercession of Cecil. Sir
Walter Ralegh, with two servants, was there, along with
Master Richard Percy with one servant, a Master Cromwell,
and Master Harriot. The menu for supper (which cost a total
of 13*s*. 8*d*.) included 'Mutton, Lambes, hennes, wood cock,
plouers, carps, whitings, old lings, oisters, herrings, Butter,
eggs, [and] Buttered Beer'. Just where this simple meal was
held is not indicated, but it was in one of the several London
houses which the Earl was renting at this time. And though
this account covers more than a month's meals, no other
entry includes either Ralegh or Harriot.

The next extant breving book which has been preserved,
the one beginning 21 September 1591,[61] shows a very
different situation. The book opens with the statement that
'My lord came to London from Petworth. September xxj
.1591.', followed the next day by his brother, Richard, and
Master Lee. For most of the next seventy-seven days, this
breving book lists the Earl's attendant guests present for
dinner or supper, not including the Earl and his regular
retinue. Most regular in attendance was Richard Percy, since
he did not miss a single meal during this whole period. But
three others, Master Lee, Master Thinn, and, surprisingly,
Master Harriot also appear to have been regular diners at
the Earl's table. Of the seventy-four days on record (there is
no listing for some reason for 20, 21, or 22 October), Master
Thinn is present for seventy; Master Lee for fifty-six; and
Master Harriot for fifty-one. The presence of Masters Lee
and Thinn are explainable, since both are listed as attached
to the household for this period, though their names do not
appear elsewhere in the records. But no explanation is given
for Harriot. Nowhere is he listed among the officers, retainers,
or servants of the 9th Earl until several years later when he
was made a pensioner and listed as among the members of
the Percy family to receive his annual pension.

[61] Syon MS X.II.12.4.

Besides these regular diners, the special guests who appeared at Northumberland's table during this two-and-a-half month period comprise a very interesting group. Most frequent guest was 'Sir John Borrowes', obviously the Sir John Borough or Burgh, the bluff mariner friend of Ralegh who was, the following year, to be named Vice-Admiral of Ralegh's privateering fleet, and who had the good fortune to capture the Great Carrack. Sir John dined at the Earl's table on nineteen of the days listed. The 3rd Earl of Southampton's name appears again, this time for thirteen days. One of Ralegh's greatest enemies, Henry Howard, Earl of Northampton, seems to have been a house-guest of the 9th Earl for ten days at the end of November and early December. Howard was, at this time, in disfavour at court because of his involvement with the cause of Mary Queen of Scots and his open attendance at Catholic worship.[62] How Northumberland tolerated Howard as a welcome guest while still a close friend of Ralegh is difficult to understand, unless he was attempting a reconciliation between them.

Other occasional guests include a Master Slingsby, another temporary attendant of the Earl, for five days; a Master Mack Williams for three; a Master Cornwallis for two. Sir John Danvers, father of Sir Charles and Sir Henry, was present once. The younger son, Sir Henry Danvers was present once (not with his father). At an early age Sir Henry had been a page to Sir Philip Sidney and was probably in attendance on him at Zutphen when Sidney received the wound which later killed him. He took part in the siege of Rouen and was knighted there by the Earl of Essex for his

---

[62] Howard tried hard to gain the favour of the Queen by flattery and by seeking permission to fight against Spain, but was without success. He later attached himself to Essex, but retained the friendship of Cecil; he took no part in the Essex rebellion. Through Cecil, Howard entered into a long communication with James VI of Scotland, revealing clearly his enmity for Ralegh and poisoning James's mind against him. In these letters he made no secret of the fact that he would like to entrap Ralegh and Henry Brook, 8th Lord Cobham, by a charge of questionable negotiations with Spain. The gross flattery which had antagonized Elizabeth won him the favour of James, led to many honours and positions, and when the plot was fulfilled against Cobham and Ralegh, brought Howard to the position of one of the Commissioners appointed to judge the two of the false charges of high treason. Howard's role seems to have been consistent — vigorous enmity towards them both, with repeated demands for the death penalty for their reputed crimes.

valour. In 1594 Henry and Charles were involved in a feud with the neighbouring Long family; Henry murdered Henry Long, and was forced to take refuge on the continent.[63]

Certainly this is a strange collection of guests for the rather shy and retiring Earl of Northumberland — enemies of his closest friend, admitted Catholic sympathizers, hot-tempered swordsmen and admitted murderers, and later advocates of Essex in his rebellion against the Queen. It was certainly a more extrovert and less intellectual group than the associates Harriot had known in the household of Ralegh. But it probably reflects the personality of Northumberland: his own quick temper but willingness to take the part of an underdog; his tolerance of divergent points of view in matters of belief or dogma; his interest in exploring the implications of differing philosophical beliefs; and his personal warmth and attractiveness to those around him. Though the Earl's portraits (particularly the one by Van Dyke still on display at Petworth House) show him as somewhat aloof and mysterious, (saturnine, he was called, and it is likely that his dark and abstracted air was at least partially responsible for his nickname of 'The Wizard Earl'), he was neither in his relations to those around him. Yet he was proud and quick to anger, and, like Ralegh, ready to use the sword which was with him always, even in the Tower.

Much of the apparent withdrawal of the 9th Earl was undoubtedly due to the fact that he was fairly deaf and found conversations, particularly with strangers, difficult. In the mid-1590s Elizabeth sought to name Percy as her ambassador to the King of France, but he declined the honour. His letter of refusal, addressed to Sir Robert Cecil, tells us much of the man and his view of his estate:[64]

---

[63] Through the intercession of the French King, Sir Henry was pardoned by Elizabeth, and went with Essex into Ireland. Unlike his brother Charles, Henry did not take part in the Essex uprising, and in 1603 was created Baron Danvers by James. Two years later, in spite of the attainder of Charles, Henry was restored as blood heir of his father. It was this Sir Henry Danvers who gave the botanic gardens across from Magdalen College to the University of Oxford.

[64] HMC *Calendar of the Manuscripts of the Most Hon. the Marquis of Salisbury, K.G., preserved at Hatfield House, Hertfordshire*, London, 1895, vol. VI, pp. 260-1.

1596, July 13. — This present Tuesday [as dated] I received your letter
dated the 8th of July, and her Majesty's commandment for my preparation into France, and because I perceive that it demands haste, the
necessity of the cause how urgent I know not, and the late receipt of
your letter, I thought good by this to crave most humbly her Highness's
pardon for my dispense in this embassage, and withal to allege such
reasons for my excuse as I hope will both suit with her Highness's
liking, and obtain my desire. In the mean time with all speed I will
make my repair to Court.

The reasons I must bring forth to defend my demands to be reasonable must especially consist upon these two heads: the imperfection of
my hearing, and the consideration of my state.

The imperfection of my hearing, what absurdities of necessity it
must beget, as trouble to the King, evil performance of my part of her
Majesty's affairs, and disgrace to myself, I hope she will rightly understand when she shall remember how by the first I shall force a King to
speak with often repetitions, and to strain his voice above ordinary,
both which my secret conceit must needs hold as indecorum of good
manners, when I shall entreat him or force him to it out of my want:
besides, how slenderly I shall execute the performance of my charge
I must refer to her Majesty's judgment, when I shall not understand
distinctly by reason of the quickness of their pronunciation, and the
unacquaintedness of their accents, not being accustomed to it, which
defects how much it troubles me even in my own usual tongue with
strangers, none but myself and mine grief can best make witness of, or
they which have the condition of deafness. Further, how disgraceful the
end may be to me, considering the scoffing and scornful humours of
them to all of other nations in whom they discover the least imperfection, and how soon they may lay upon me the reputation of a fool,
and so by consequent and out of boldness grace me with some such
disgrace as hath happened to others before me, which in my opinion
would nothing fit with her Majesty's honour nor my contentment.

As his second excuse, the Earl declared that his income
would not permit him the luxury of serving as a royal ambassador to the court of a King:

...where most men's livings affords them a great overplus out of fines,
mine are so wasted for the most part, lying upon the borders, both out
of mine own absence, the Scot's incursions, my officers' knaveries, and
the small redress the poor people hath had of their wrongs, as not only
I make no further benefit then the rents, but also the rents themselves
are unanswered, and they greatly in my debts. . . .

These pleas of poverty (and possibly the pleas of deafness as
well) were greatly exaggerated to make his point, for though
the wealth of the 9th Earl had been considerably depreciated

by a decade of rather extravagant living, there is no question but that he was continuing to live in the luxury to which his birth and taste entitled him. And this richness of physical comfort was being shared by his retainers, knavish or not.

Another contemporary account furnishes us with a picture of the Earl's character and personality. In 1603, while Northumberland was in the Low Countries, his quick temper and injured pride led him to challenge his commander-in-chief, Sir Francis Vere, to a duel. Vere, evidently wanting to know the nature of the man who had challenged him, sought information from a mutual friend. A copy of this account, still preserved in the British Library, shows how he was presented to his self-confessed enemy:[65]

A Character of the most excellent Lord, the Earle of Northumberland./
He is, naturallye, a kynde of inward and reserued Man, and hee doth not easelye make the world such playe As to open him selfe, without much Observacion of their judgments: though since his Condicion hath produced, and planted him in the waye of the world, hee is ffounde to bee no such witch. Eyther this Man is very worthie, or such as knowe him best are deceyved most; ffor they whoe haue beheld him with more Curiositye and Care then with partiallitye and purpose to gyve Applause, haue ffounde much in him to prayse, and not soe much as a little to reprove.

This is soe true, that a Man whome I loue as my selfe is wonte to saye of this Person that hee hath but one quarrel to him, which is that hee cann ffinde nothinge in him to fforgiue. But yett I knowe not whether I ame ffullye of that mynde or noe, ffor I confesse I haue layde vpp a kynde of Quaere Concerninge him, which I keepe wholie to my selfe, and meane to watche the successe, And if hee Complye not with it As I thinke hee should (though I meane to leave the Circumstances of tyme and place to him selfe) it will lessen him much in somme respects with mee.

I hould the ffacultye of his mynde to bee verye Reallye good, and incomparablye better then they seame in such eyes As marke him not verye well. His Speeche is slowe and it deserves a Pardon of Course for many Reasons; for hee never speakes by Chaunce, never vppon varietye,

---

[65] BL MS Hargrave 226, fos. 241-3 (new), 256-8 (old). This MS is written in the same hand that wrote *The Copy of the Challenge by the Earl of Northumberland to Sir Francis Vere*, fos. 241-3 in the same volume. The Northumberland account carries the colophon: 'Examined with the Coppye, which Sir ffrauncis veere sent vnto mee; Att the verye ffirst daye, taken fforth of it; which was even vppon his departure, out of London ffor the Lowe Countryes, soe went all the waye by Land ffrom London, to: Thames, where hee tooke shippinge.' It should, therefore, be a true and accurate copy. I have taken the liberty of simplifying the punctuation.

never but with exact Truthe, and never, mee thincks, but with great Reason, and soe to shewe that hee is a very Temperate and prudent Man. And indeed he never seemes so much as to open his Mouth towardes speech tyll he haue ffirst asked Leave and Councell of his heart. His Apprehension is verye readye, and his judgments certainly sound, And all his Accions are such As not to ffeare a Censure; not to desire a Corner, But to bidd Men looke on, and doe their worst.

Behoulde him both att home and Abroade, and hee can Love and deffye yow both att once; ffor yow shalbe forced to esteeme him, and yow shall haue no Cause to Blame him.

Hee is a good Husband, a Noble Maister, a sweete Companyon, and though positivelye I can affyrme noothinge, yet I never hear otherwyse then that hee was a most generous and ffaithfull ffrinde.

When wee see him in Courte, his person and his Age gyve him verye good leave to seeme as greate a Man as hee is; and yet with all, hee is so Civill, modest, and quyett, as yf hee were byt Tennant by Courtesye to the very Cloathes hee weares. . . .

. . .as Concernes the Civill, and Constant, noble way of lyfe both in his Howses abroade and in the Capitall Cittye of the standing Courte where he is att home, whether wee Consider his Coaches, his Horses, his Trayne, his Liveryes, or his Table, which perhappes is (to speake modestlye) one of the best which for a doozin guests was ever kept in this kingdom; wherein I meane not onelye the dyett of fflesh and fishe, which Aunswers to the stuffe of our Clothes, But I Consider alsoe the Bread, Wyne, Salletts, Oyle, Vynegar, ffruite, Sweetmeats, Lynnen, Plate, and Lights, which at the Tables I accompt As the prettye Toyes of our Attyre. And indeed it is such, in all respects, as serveth to lett vs see whatt kynde of person he is, especiallye yf we take in the manner of this Attendaunce of his — Servants whoe looke as yf they were happie when they are Busye, and Lyve with that Intencion and Reverence in their Maisters sight as yf they were aboute somme great Affayer, which still Addes to his Lustre.

And, withall, yf wee dwell vppon the Consideracion of his owne person, there the Truth of this will best appeare, ffor he is both soe noble and so humble, that Obleiges and Conffoundes, and lookes fforth soe probably and effectuallye vppon yow that you will sweare your welcome though hee (whoe was onely Able to make it true) never spake a word of it. In the meane tyme, it is noe ffigure nor fflourish but a Reall truth, that he Beares him selfe soe As to seeme not the Man who gyves, but receyves all the honnor of the meetinge.

His society is easye and Agreeable att all tymes, his Moralists both for virtue and Conversacion great, and hee is never to be heard lowde or seeme in disorder, nor once to swear an oath, howe great sowever the occasion may eyther seeme or bee. And therefore wee owe him not onelye our affection, but our Admiration.

This description rounds out the picture of the person of the mature Henry Percy that Harriot was beginning to know. He was just starting to collect one of the finest scientific libraries of his time, was surrounding himself with distinguished gentlemen and scholars, particularly those versed in the new sciences and mathematics, and was beginning to be referred to as 'The Wizard Earl'. He was quiet, slow of speech, dedicated to reason and exact statement, pleasant to be with, generous to those around him, modest and retiring, but still enjoying the good life and the temperate pleasures of the flesh. He was a man generally quick to recognize quality in those about him, quick to respond with support and encouragement as well as with warm, personal friendship. The young man who had been a typical Renaissance noble-gentleman had developed into a model young noble-patron of the arts, sciences, and humanities.

During the years 1591 and 1592 only two items in the Northumberland household accounts record payments to Harriot: one in the foreign payments for the period from 5 June to 22 December 1591[66] reads simply 'To Master Herryotte for a glasse of Oyle . . . xˢ', a normal transaction involving a friend of scientific bent; and a second[67] 'Item payd to Master Heriot for a pounde of tobacco to viij of January 1591 [1592 NS]', a purchase which might be expected of a friend who had earlier brought tobacco back to England from the New World and introduced it to Sir Walter Ralegh who popularized it. Both of these entries represent the kind of trading back and forth that went on between Elizabethans and tell us nothing about the relationship existing between the two men involved.

The first significant grant of money from Northumberland to Thomas Harriot came on the occasion of Percy's installation into the Most Noble Order of the Garter at Windsor on 26 June 1593, as the author pointed out in 1949.[68] The accounts

[66] Syon MS X.II.12.6.
[67] Ibid., account of Roger Thorpe.
[68] See John W. Shirley 'The Scientific Experiments of Sir Walter Ralegh, the Wizard Earl, and the three Magi in the Tower, 1606–1617,' *Ambix*, IV (1948–51), 52–66. In this article I followed the statement first given by Sidney Lee in his article on Henry Percy in the *DNB* that the gartering occurred on the traditional day, St. George's Day, 23 April. In 1593, however, the ceremonies were held later, as is made clear by a poem on the event commissioned by the 9th Earl by the poet, George Peele. Syon MS U.I.2. 'Thomas Kelton Receyver' records a

of the Earl's 'foreign paymaster', Henry Forest, list the payments made on that occasion. The charge of his Lordship's 'Lodging at Winsore' is given as £6 5s.; expenses for his retinue as £101 4s.; and a number of gifts were recorded as having been dispensed on this happy occasion:[69]

Guyfts and Rewards/ Paid lykewyse by the said Accomptante as money by his Lordship given in rewards & guyfts, viz to the Lord Keper 2 guylte bell salts xxv^l [£25] to Mistris Ratcliffe a guylt Basen and Ewre xxj^l x^s vj^d to Master Gouldsbroughe xx^l to the Kinge at Armes for bringinge hir Majesties letter of the Gartier to his Lordship at Bathe xx^l to Master Nowell xx^l to Master heriat $\frac{xx}{iiij}$1 [£80] to Sir Thomas hennage man that brought an Agat salt to his Lordship xl^s to Master Moores man who brought your Lordship a mare xxxx^s and in dyuerse other Rewardes to dyuerse persones Cxxxij^l xvij^s vj^d — In all as by the bookes aforesaid may appeare: CCCxxij^l viij^s./

No evidence of any kind remains to show what Harriot had done to receive such a munificent reward. The sum of £80 was a very large amount in the 1590s: a handsomely paid teacher of Latin and Greek earned but half that sum for a year; a military captain earned only a sixth of that amount for a year's pay; and even the chief officers of the 9th Earl's household were paid only £10 or £20 for a full year's service. Possibly, if not probably, this reward represents the start of an annual patronage grant to Harriot. It is most unfortunate that both the rough drafts and final accounts of the Earl's chief disburser, the cofferer, who was responsible for payment of pensions to special retainers and members of the Earl's family, are missing for these critical years. But in the next one which does survive, the rough draft for February 1598 (1599 NS) is recorded:[70] 'Pencyon/ To Master herryot as parte of his pension being [blank in the original] by yeare the 12th of July by his Lordship commaundment xxxx^l more to

---

payment made by Walter Warner who was evidently charged with negotiating for 'Poeme gratulatorie': 'Rewards . . . to one Peele a poet by th'ands of Master Warner. .lx^s'. The poem itself, STC, no. 19539, carries the title: *THE HONOVR OF THE GARTER Displaid in a Poeme gratulatorie: Entitled to the worthie and renowned Earle of Northumberland. Created Knight of that Order, and installed at VVindsore, Anno Regni Elizabethæ. 35. Die Iunij .26. By George Peele, Maister of Artes in Oxenforde.*

[69] Syon MS U.I.2.t. Henry Forest, foreign payments.
[70] Syon MS U.I.2. Rough draft, Edmund Powton.

him the third of ffebr. as for his pencion due at Michaelmas last xxxx^l In all $\overset{xx}{iiij}$ l./ The fact that Powton, the Earl's cofferer, appears uncertain of the annual amount of Harriot's pension and records this as his Lordship's special order could be interpreted to indicate that this was a first pension payment. But it should be noted that this was the first accounting that Powton had done for the Earl, since he had just moved to the Earl's household from that of the dowager Duchess,[71] and he may have just been puzzled by what was (and remained) a most unusual item among a list of pensions for members of the Percy family. Later records show that Harriot received an annual pension for the remainder of his life.[72]

One other evidence of Northumberland's high esteem for Harriot can now be revealed for the first time. For some years, Harriot scholars have puzzled over several entries in the accounts of William Wycliff, the 9th Earl's 'Receiver General', responsible for the collection of rents in the northern counties. In the rough draft of his accounts for 1597 appears the cryptic entry[73] 'Received of Master Thomas heryott in part of the Rent of Brampton due at the tyme aforesaid xl^s'. The same accounts for Michaelmas 1598[74] give more detail: 'Bishoprick of Durham/ Received of Master Thomas herryot for the Rente in Brampton, due for one whole yeare ended at Michaelmas aforesaid lxxiij^s iiij^d.' The only Brampton listed in British gazetteers is a small market town in Cumberland which could in no way be considered under the Bishop of Durham. But that site is reasonably close to Percy holdings in Northumberland and the assignment could be faulty. The

---

[71] Gordon R. Batho, *The Household Papers of Henry Percy, Ninth Earl of Northumberland (1564–1632)*, Camden Third Series, vol. XCIII, London, 1962, p. 160.

[72] Entries in the pension accounts from 1599 to 1613 recording Harriot's pensions are as follows: Syon MS U.I.2.rr, to Michaelmas 1599; U.I.3.3.e, 'two whole years' to Michaelmas 1601; U.I.3.3.o, to Michaelmas 1602; U.I.3.l.x, to Michaelmas 1603; (here a gap of four years); U.I.3.2.ah, to Michaelmas 1607; U.I.3.3.ap, to Michaelmas 1608; U.I.3.3.ar, to Michaelmas 1609; U.I.3.3.ax, to Michaelmas 1610; U.I.4.f, to Michaelmas 1611; U.I.4.n, to Michaelmas 1612; U.I.4.z, to Michmaelmas 1613. All of these pensions were for the sum of £80 per year. Subsequent entries will be noted later.

[73] Syon MS U.I.2. Preliminary draft, William Wycliffe, Receiver General.

[74] Syon MS U.I.2.kk. William Wycliffe, Receiver General.

wording of the entry makes it appear that Harriot was renting property from the Earl, but all other evidence indicates that he was living in London during this period and would have no use for a holding in the north of England. As a result, the most likely explanation was that Harriot on these occasions made collections for his friend, turning the proceeds over to the receiver general. In 1949 I wrote that 'Hariot collected rents from Brampton, Bishoprick of Durham, in 1597 and 1598',[75] and later Batho indexed Harriot as a member of the Northumberland household by labelling his entry:[76] *Thomas Hariot, pensioner 1598–1621, collector of rents in Brampton, Cumberland, 1597–99, formerly servant to Sir Walter Ralegh.*

During the summer of 1975, however, while checking in detail the land holdings of the 9th Earl in the muniment room of Alnwick Castle, I found two very interesting indentures which not only solve this minor Brampton mystery, but more importantly shed new light on the relationship which existed between Harriot and his noble patron. Since these documents have not previously been seen, they are here reproduced through the kindness of the present Duke of Northumberland.[77] As can now be seen, Harriot was neither renting property from the 9th Earl nor collecting rents in his behalf. He was, instead, a recipient of the Earl's benefaction of a life interest in the total income from some of the entailed Percy property holdings in Durham, in exchange for which (and to indicate the Earl's retention of fee simple title in the property) Harriot was to return a token payment of rent, duly recorded by Wycliffe.

The first of these documents is an Indenture executed on 2 June 1595 in which 'the Righte honorable Henry Earle of Northumberland, Lorde of the honors of Cockermouthe and Petworthe, Lord Percy, Lucy, Poyninges, ffitzpaine & Brian, and Knight of the most Noble order of ye Garter' granted to 'Thomas Heryott of the Cyttie of London Gent.', 'for dyvers and soundrie good causes & considerations him there vnto especiallie movinge':

---

[75] 'Scientific Experiments', p. 28, n. 26.

[76] Batho, *Household Accounts*, p. 154.

[77] See Figs. 8 and 9. I should like to thank Mr David B. Graham of the Alnwick Estates Office for his kindness in making these copies for reproduction.

Fig. 8 Indenture Granting Brampton Property to Harriot

by theise presentes dothe demise graunt & to ferme lett vnto the sayde Thomas Heryott, all those his Landes, Tenementes & heriditamentes whatsoeuer lyinge & beinge in Brampton alias Barmeton within the County Palantyne of Durisme. That ys to saye, all the howses, edyfices, barnes, stables, backehowses, Dovecottes, orchardes, gardinges, with all & singuler the arable growndes, closes, moores, meadowes, pastures, feedinges, commons & common of pasture and all other the appurt-nances whatsoeuer thereunto belonginge or in any wise apperteyninge. ...To haue & to holde all the sayde Landes...to the sayde Thomas Heryott his executors or assignes from the day of the date thereof for & duringe the liffe naturall of the sayde Thomas Heryott. Yealdinge and payinge therefore yearely duringe the sayde tearme vnto the sayde Earle ... the some of fower poundes of lawfull money of England ... at the feaste of Saint Michael th'archangell, and th'annuntiacion of our blessed Ladye the Virgine Marie. . .

This generous act of Henry Percy changed Harriot's social status: it made him a lifetime member of the landed gentry, entitled to attach the title 'Gentleman' to his name (a right which he had already assumed on the basis of his Oxford degree), and gave him an independent source of income beyond his pension, in the use of which he need feel no restraint. Harriot under Northumberland had risen to a higher social rank than he could have done under Ralegh, or even by being pensioned by the 9th Earl. On the basis of this evidence, it is necessary to reassess his personal fortunes, raising them above even the lavish sums he was previously known to hold.

Location of the indentures led to the discovery of other papers respecting the Durham properties. One of them gives a clue as to the exact location of the property[78] 'the tenure or occupacion of George Ward gent or his Assignes situate lying & beinge in the Townes ffold & Territoryes of Barmeton alias Brampton in the parish of Hampton in the County Pallantyne of Durham. . .' This places the Brampton estate in the rural community just outside Darlington where the 9th Earl had other holdings. During the intervening years, the two names 'Barmeton alias Brampton' have grown welded, so that today this section carries the hybrid name of 'Barmpton'. And other lawsuits carry additional infor-mation about the property that Harriot had been given:[79]

[78] Syon MS X.II.5., 'Bills in Cancellar [Chancellory]'.
[79] Ibid. This file contains a number of lawsuits about northern properties, not further classified.

'Henry late Earle of Northumberland, great vncle of the said Henry now Earle of Northumberland was lawfully seized in fee or of some other estate of Inheritance of & in one Mesuage & Eleauen Oxganges of land medow and pasture in Barmeton alias Brampton . . .' Obviously, then, it was 'one Mesuage and Eleauen Oxganges of land' that were turned over to Harriot for his lifetime.

In the medieval village in the north of England, all land was held in common. The 'Messuage' consisted of both the household and its right to a portion of the adjoining properties. The portion of the commons holdings was based on the proportion of the arable land which was held. This arable land, called the *hide* or *ploughland*, was divided into *carucates*, each of which represented the amount of land which could be tilled by a single plough drawn by a team of eight oxen. The exact size of such a day's tillage varied widely according to the nature of the land and the customs of the village, and a *carucate* might range from 80 to 144 acres. One-eighth of each *carucate*, which required the tenant to furnish one ox, was known as an *oxgang* or *bovine*, and represented from 10 to 18 acres of tilled land. The other segments of the community, woodland, commons, and grazing land, were used by the tenants in proportion to the total segment of arable land they possessed.

Because of these local variations, it is impossible to determine exactly how large Harriot's holdings at Brampton were. 'One Mesuage & Eleauen Oxganges' would translate into the buildings, the tilled land, and the commons rights. The buildings, as enumerated in the indenture, include 'Tenementes, howses, edyfices, barnes, stables, backhowses, Dovecottes, orchardes, gardinges', the arable land as 'growndes closes moores meadows pastures, feedinges', as well as the allocated 'commons & common of pasture & all other ye appurtnances whatsoeuer'. Normally, by formula, these would figure out to include approximately 100 to 200 acres of arable land (for which Harriot would have to furnish eleven oxen during the growing season), and pasturage and wood rights would add another 500 to 1,000 acres. In the north of England during these years, this was a handsome property, and income from such an estate would make

Harriot independent in his own right. But with this income added to his equally handsome pension, he was certainly able to live comfortably, if not expensively, maintain his own staff of servants, and even give support to his own friends and associates when needed.

In the second indenture, dated 6 July 1615, Harriot relinquished his life rights to the Brampton property incomes which he had received for twenty years. But in taking rights to the property back from Harriot, Northumberland not only freed him from his obligation to pay £4 a year, but also added an additional £20 a year to his regular £80 pension. This for the first time explains the change in the pension accounts: from Michaelmas 1597 through 1613 the cofferer paid Harriot £80 annually, with a gap of two years at the point where the accounts are missing. But when they resume at Michaelmas of 1617, the pension has been raised to £100, showing the addition of the £20 of the second indenture. All subsequent accounts carry this amount.[80]

The fact that Harriot was considered by Northumberland to be an independent and free agent is reflected by the absence of many entries about him in the Northumberland household accounts. All of the Earl's servants or retainers, men like Powton, Wycliffe, or even Walter Warner, were considered charges of the Earl. Regular entries show them being furnished liveries, boardwages, transportation, or firewood. Harriot, like the Earl's other pensioners, his brothers or the dowager Duchess, paid all such expenses for his own household. Only one entry, 7 January 1596, lists payment '. . . for Master Herriottes horsmete ffor x dayes. . .',[81] but this is the exception which proves the rule. More in keeping with his place in the household are payments which show him as a companion or guest of the 9th Earl:[82]

---

[80] All extant General Accounts from 1616 to 1620 (only 1619 is missing) are for £100: Syon MS U.I.4.am, for 1616; Syon MS U.I.4.as., 1617; Syon MS U.I.4. ax., 1618; Petworth MS 600, 1620. The final entry, Petworth MS 601, is for £50, tacit recognition that Harriot died in the middle of that year.

[81] Syon MS X.II.12.6, 'a booke of riding charges beginning in December 1595. Master Edward Francis.'

[82] Syon MS X.II.12.6, Mr. Stapleton, foreign payments.

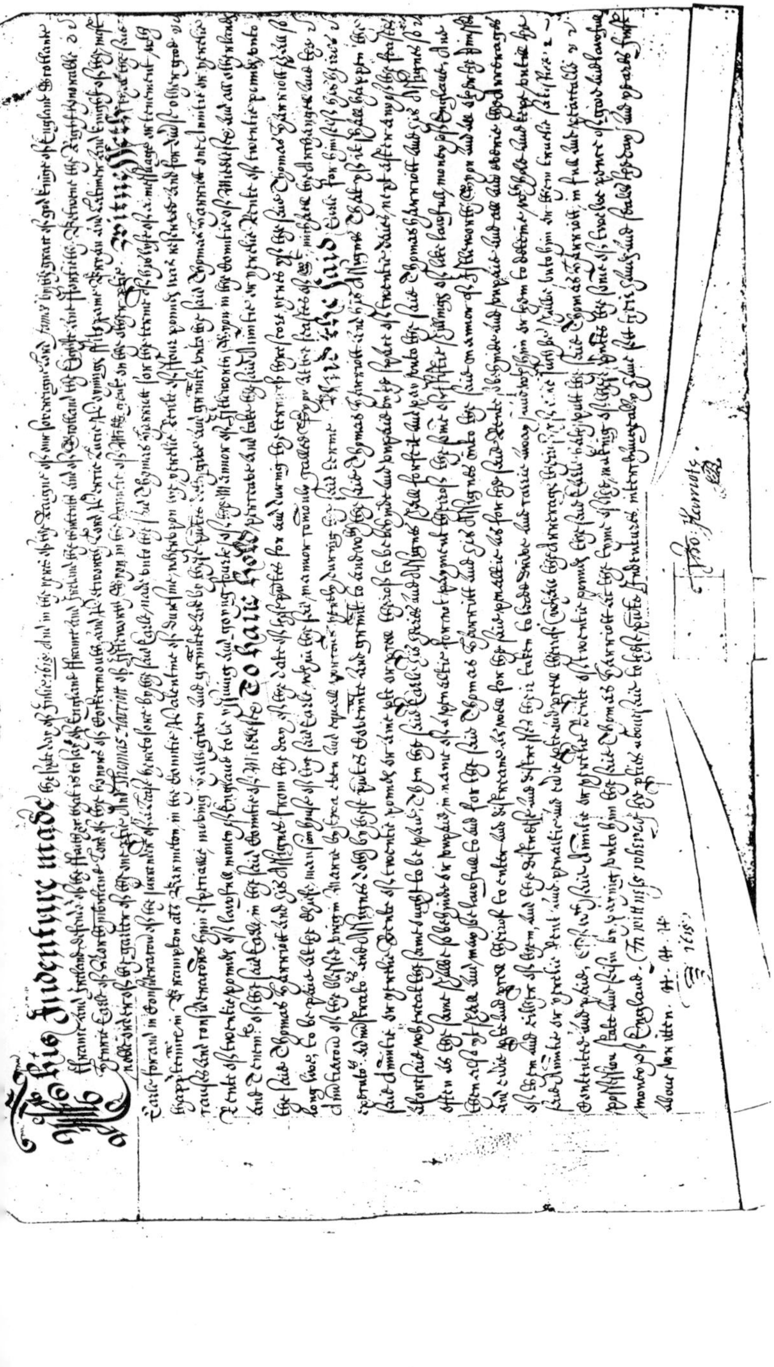

Fig. 9 Harriot's Release of Brampton

> Play./ To my lord which he lost att faysh to Master Heryott June ij [1596] xij^d. [Faish is an early card betting game, based on the drawing of cards.]
>
> or   To my lord which he lost at crosse and pile [tossing coins] Master Heryott and Master ffrainces plaiing October xiiij [1596] xij^d.

During the last half of the 1590s, though Northumberland's generosity to Harriot had made him really an independent gentleman in his own right, Harriot still remained in close association with Sir Walter Ralegh, active in his affairs. We know, for example, from a later lawsuit brought against Ralegh by the wealthy merchant, William Sanderson, over his financing of his Guiana voyage, how close the relationship of the two men really was.[83] Harriot admits in his own testimony that in late 1594 he was in Dorset and Devon, giving his services to Ralegh who was making preparations for his Guiana visit of exploration. He was with Ralegh and Lady Ralegh on the eve of Ralegh's departure, according to testimony of Ralegh's cousin, the London merchant who had a large share in some of his ventures, William Sanderson. According to Sanderson's testimony (as reflected by the interrogatory he prepared for the questioning of witnesses), Harriot had a principal role in Ralegh's record keeping and accounting. And Sanderson swears that, like Ralegh, Harriot was not above an occasional theft of documents or falsification of records.

The whole story of the financial manipulations is extremely complex and must be pieced together from Sanderson's petition and from the answers to the interrogatories which were presented for the review of the court. Out of these, a fairly coherent picture begins to evolve. This series of lawsuits began in February 1610 (1611 NS) when Ralegh's executors, John Shelbury and Robert Smith, operating on Ralegh's behalf, brought suit in the High Court of Chancery against William Sanderson, charging that he had dealt fraudulently with Sir Walter in the management of the finances of the Guiana voyages of 1594 and 1595. They held that Sanderson was accountable for £60,000 on which no final accounting or payment had been made. To explain the

[83] See John W. Shirley, 'Sir Walter Raleigh's Guiana Finances', *Huntington Library Quarterly*, XIII. 1 (Nov. 1949), 55–69.

absence of audited records in his behalf, Sanderson testified
that in January of 1594 (1595 NS) Sir Walter Ralegh and his
friends, Lawrence Keymis and Thomas Harriot, were in
Devonshire in final preparation for Ralegh's South American
voyage. William Sanderson, who according to his own testimony was a relative of Ralegh, since he[84] 'did marry and
take to wiffe Margaret Snedall the daughter of Hughe Snedall
and neece of Sir Walter Ralegh knight that is to say his sisters
daughter, by meanes of which intermarriadge your subject
and the sayd Sir Walter Ralegh became acquainted and grew
into inward love and frindship', had been responsible for
raising, either by furnishing bond or by direct solicitation,
the full sum of £80,000 which Ralegh put into the venture.
Quite naturally, Sanderson felt that he needed some surety for
his bonds and investments, since the Guiana venture was
obviously dangerous, and there was a chance that Ralegh
might not return. Consequently, some time before the
sailing date, he had presented Ralegh with statements of
account, indicating that he had collected and spent from
£44,000 to £45,000, towards which Ralegh owed £31 3s
$2\frac{1}{2}$ d. These accounts were given by Ralegh to Harriot for
audit, who[85] 'examininge the same sometimes demaunding of
[Sanderson] the warrants whereby he payed some of the
sommes sett downe in the sayde accompt, and at some other
times the receipts acquittances and cancelled bonds of them
to whom [he] had payed the same which [Sanderson protested, he] delivered to him accordinglie.' Later, further to
relieve Sanderson's anxieties, Ralegh drew up 'A Generall
Acquittance and Release' relieving him of any further
responsibility for Ralegh's debts.[86] Lady Ralegh, who had
come down to Devon from Sherborne to bid her husband
farewell, insisted that she, too, needed protection from
possible suits over these accounts. At her instigation, a
second document was executed by Sanderson, entitled 'A
Memorandum of Acquittance to Sir Walter Raleigh of dis-
chardge',[87] which was a general release, excepting only the

---

[84] PRO St. Ch. 8/260/4.
[85] Ibid.
[86] PRO C 24/372/126. Meeres's testimony to question 9.
[87] Ibid., testimony of both Meeres and Harriot to question 11.

slightly more than £30 still owing, and the interest on the money which had been borrowed under his bond, 'a very great somme of money indeed'. At this point Sanderson considered both men to be protected, but to his dismay he claimed to have found the crafty Ralegh had turned traitor, using his friend, Thomas Harriot, as his intermediary. As Sanderson claimed:[88]

Afterwards the sayd Sir Walter Ralegh the first [evidently a scribal error, since the sailing was the fifth] day of ffebruary *1594* [1595 NS] at the very instant upon his departure in his sayd intended voiage in the night time under the pretence of a desire he had to see the sayd Release so made by him which was sealed and delivered many dayes before unto your sayd subject as aforesaid; and your sayd subject nothing doubting of any ill meaning of his the sayd Sir Walter Ralegh gave the sayd release unto the sayd Sir Walter Raleghes hands who perusing the same a while presentlie gave the sayd release unto the sayd Thomas Herriots willing him not to deliver the same to your sayd subject unles he the sayd Sir Walter Ralegh should miscarry in his sayd voyage; but yf he should returne then to give it to himselfe againe with many more words to the same effect ... and so your subject being much grieved and discontented at his wicked doings turned from him without wishing or bidding him farewell the same being at the very instant of his departure and at midnight as he was about to take shipping as aforesayd. ...

Thus it was that at the time of the suit by Shelbury and Smith, Sanderson was without evidence for his defence, his accounts still being in the possession of Thomas Harriot. In righteous indignation, therefore, Sanderson filed a counter-suit against the whole group – Ralegh, Shelbury, Smith, and Harriot. Evidence in this suit is likewise difficult to assess, since many crucial documents are missing. Harriot's statements are unconvincing, since he refers mainly to previous testimony which is lacking, but he did admit that he still held the documents, and at the order of the court, he presented them for consideration.

At a third session, this time before Sir Edward Phillips, Master of the Rolls, the original documents were at last produced. All was as Sanderson had contended: the original accounts were presented, Sanderson's discharge or acquittance to Sir Walter, and Sir Walter's release of Sanderson.

[88] PRO St. Ch. 8/260/4.

But on the last of these, the one on which Sanderson relied
for his total exoneration, appeared a special endorsement.
Clearly written on the back, apparently in the hand of Sir
Walter, were the following words:[89]

Memorandum that it is agreed that the release to be sealed by the
honorable Sir Walter Ralegh to Master William Sanderson shalbe sealed
absolutely and without Condicion delivered, yet shalbe left with Master
Thomas Herriots to be by him kept vntill Sir Walter Raleghes returne
from his intended voiage of Gwyana. And that yf sayd Sir Walter
Ralegh should not returne in the sayd voyage but should dye therein,
it is then agreed that the sayd release shalbe delivered to Master Saunderson for his discharge against Sir Walter Raleghes executors for all
accions and accompts And that yf the sayd Sir Walter Ralegh retorne
from the sayd voyage then the sayd Master Herriotts shall redeliver the
sayd release to the sayd Sir Walter Ralegh; and the sayd Master Saunderson then to discharge himselfe of all accions and demaunds of the
sayd Sir Walter Ralegh by true accompt; and in the meane season by
like agreement Master Saunderson may have the release to shew to his
Creditors for their better satisfaction therein bringing in the same
againe to Master Harryotts. witnesses by us underwritten Chr: Harris
J: Meere [Walter Ralegh and William Sanderson].

This endorsement changed things greatly: Ralegh's release
was not a true release but a legal loop-hole for Sanderson to
use should Ralegh die. Should Ralegh return, Sanderson was
to be held to strict accounting, which was the purpose of
the original suit.

On seeing what he claimed was a document altered by
forgery, Sanderson flew into a rage. 'This is a false forged
and counterfeite note or writing for there never was any
such agreement betwene us, neither is this my name or my
handwriting that is subscribed to the same', he declared. He
demanded that all the supposed witnesses answer some more
specific questions about the endorsement, but all of them
were participants in the suit except Christopher Harris, who
unfortunately died before he could respond to Sanderson's
questions. Harriot's testimony regarding the endorsement
was as noncommittal as his previous answers had been:[90]

---

[89] The original of this document is not extant. This verbatim copy, excepting
the names of Ralegh and Sanderson, is quoted in St. Ch. 8/260/4.

[90] PRO C 24/372/126. Answer to questions 14 and 15.

...whilest the sayed acquitance or Release was in the hands and Custody of this deponent he did require no man to add any wrytinge to the same or to diminishe any thinge therein...That he taketh the sayd Acquitaunce and Release now presented vnto him to be the same that was delivered vnto him by Sir Walter Ralegh ... And is the same now, and as yt was when yt was deliuered vnto him (as he taketh yt) without any thinge done to yt by this deponent or by his knowledge consent request or procurement. . . .

Harriot was willing to swear that he did not forge any document; he did not swear that he was positive no one else had done so.

The trial dragged on. Sanderson accused John Meeres, bailiff of Sherborne, of doing the forgery,[91] indicating that he had evidence that Shelbury had paid him £19 16s. for doing the job. He also protested that the endorsement was patently after the fact, since it used the name 'Gwyana', which, he claimed, was never used until Ralegh used it on his return. However, since it was Ralegh who coined the name, he showed no reason why he could not have used it before he went, as well as after. But again, the official records record no outcome of all these proceedings. Whether Ralegh was devious in his handling of his finances, whether he would stoop to forgery and perjury as well as deceit was not settled by the court. Whether Sanderson was a victim of false practices, or was himself a conniving financier, bringing suit against those he owed in an attempt to avoid just payment, cannot be determined. Probably the truth lay somewhat in between with two sharp operators using the courts for their own purposes, and the go-between, Harriot, refusing clear statements about his own activities, avoiding personal trouble by verbal evasions.

The lawsuit does, however, reveal much about Harriot's relations with Ralegh during this period of transition in his patronage. While Ralegh was preparing for his Guiana voyage in 1594, and while he was absent from England in 1595, Harriot was still a close and confidential friend, responsible for auditing his accounts and preserving his precious papers.

[91] The evidence presented to this effect, and evidence that Meeres had been guilty of forgery of Ralegh's hand in the past, is presented in Shirley, 'Raleigh's Guiana Financing', pp. 66–9.

He was a trusted associate of Ralegh's Sherborne officers, privy to the private affairs of his patron friend and his wife, the Lady Elizabeth Ralegh. During Ralegh's absence, he seems to have served almost as steward to the Ralegh household. Yet during this same time, he was spending at least a part of his time in the Northumberland household, growing in intimacy with the 9th Earl, and beginning to receive munificent sums and grants from him. Undoubtedly, it was during the seven months from February to September 1595, when Ralegh was pursuing his chimerical dreams of gold through the rivers of the Orinoco delta, that Harriot changed his primary allegiance from Ralegh's household to that of the 9th Earl. Yet in spite of the fact that his support, his residence, and his responsibility had shifted focus, his interest and friendship remained centred in both whenever he was with them or either of them called on him for assistance.

True, Ralegh and Northumberland were themselves close friends, but there was a considerable difference in their life styles which must have made Harriot feel he was leading a divided life. With Ralegh, at Sherborne and Durham House, he was a friend, but a man of duties and responsibilities as well. He was subject to Ralegh's call, and could be assigned any task from an audit of accounts, preparation of a map or sailing rutter, calculations of proportions of a ship which might improve its efficiency, or even to serve as a special observer on a voyage of exploration. With Northumberland, Harriot was much freer; he appears to have had no formal duties or responsibilities. He was a pensioned gentleman, free to pursue his own interests, develop his own patterns of work and pleasure. Though considered a member of the Earl's household, he was neither a servant nor an officer of the household, he was an intellectual companion of an intellectually curious gentleman, and this association was built on pleasure and not on duty. In all the thousands of pages of Harriot's manuscripts which remain, though many have to do with the affairs of Ralegh, only one shows that Harriot did something at the request of the 9th Earl. This was late in life, when in June 1619 he was 'perfecting [his] auntient notes of the doctrin of reflections of bodyes' which he transmitted to Henry Percy 'whereby allso nowe at times of leasure when your minde is free from matters of greater waight you may think & consider of them, if you please.' A gentleman to a gentleman.

In 1594 Henry Percy decided to marry and produce an heir to carry on the Northumberland line. Speculation about his possible marriage alliances had been widespread; the Queen was visibly ageing, and the 9th Earl stood, by most contemporary calculations, eighth in line for the succession. According to one source,[92] sympathizers to the Catholic cause, feeling the Percys to be sympathetic, had agitated for him to marry the Lady Arabella Stuart. Lady Arabella stood second in line on the basis of her descent from Margaret, sister of Henry VIII, and a union between the two would strengthen both their claims. But Henry ignored this pressure, and instead chose to wed Dorothy (Devereux) Perrot, sister to Robert Devereux the 2nd Earl of Essex, and who had previously been married to Sir Thomas Perrot.[93] De Fonblanque, the official biographer of the Percys, holds that Elizabeth saw the danger of the match between Percy and Lady Arabella, arranged for her to be placed under restraint, and herself personally arranged the match with Dorothy Perrot.[94]

The marriage of Henry and Dorothy was not a particularly happy one, since Dorothy, like her brother Robert and her sister Penelope (the Stella of Sir Philip Sidney's *Astrophel and Stella* who later married Lord Rich) was inclined to be stubborn and self-centred, and the 9th Earl himself was strong minded and occasionally less than tactful. In addition to being sharp-tongued and too closely tied to the cause of her brother, the Earl of Essex, both of which Northumberland resented, Dorothy was having difficulty in furnishing him an heir. Two sons, both named Henry after their father, born in 1596 and 1597, died in infancy. A daughter born in 1598

---

[92] Thomas Wilson, 'The State of England, Anno Domini 1600,' MS in PRO. See *Calendar of State Papers, Domestic, 1601–1603*, p. 60. The table of popular succession is reprinted by Edward Barrington de Fonblanque, *Annals of the House of Percy*, 2 vols., London, 1887, II. 584.

[93] Sidney Lee in his biography of Henry Percy in the *DNB* indicates that Dorothy was the widow of Sir John Perrot and that the marriage took place in 1595. He was wrong on both counts.

[94] *Annals*, I. 203–4.

and named Dorothy after her mother, lived, as did a second daughter, born according to one of the household account records: 'Ladie Lucye Pearcye born this day [Sunday 2 September 1599] betwixe x and xj of the clocke at night',[95] who also survived. For some time Percy was seriously considering a separation and even offered Dorothy £1,000 a year as settlement for a divorce. But Dorothy, according to her own accounts, had brought estates to her new husband that she said brought in £1,500 annually, and she strenuously objected to his efforts to force her to a settlement for less than that, since she 'desired as much as she brought'.[96] It was not until 1602 when a third son, Algernon, was born strong enough to survive and become Lord Percy, the heir apparent, that Dorothy could feel secure as the mistress of the household, though gossip even at this time was that Northumberland was closer to Ralegh than he was to his wife.[97]

One of the major properties which Dorothy brought to her husband was the lease of the famous estate, Syon House, on the River Thames in Isleworth Hundred just across from Kew Gardens. Syon had been founded in 1415 by King Henry V as a monastery for the order of St. Bridget to expiate his father's reputation for his part in the murder of Richard II. It had prospered as a Catholic monastery until the Reformation, when it was confiscated by the crown. It had a long history of royal associations. One story about Syon is related in the current guidebook of the estate:[98]

After its suppression, Syon Abbey became Crown property, and here the unhappy Queen Catherine Howard was confined from November 1541 until she went to the block in February 1542. When Henry VIII died five years later his coffin lay for the night at Syon on its way from Westminster to Windsor. A curious prophecy was then fulfilled. Some years before, in 1535, a Franciscan friar named Peto, when preaching before the King, had declared that 'God's judgments were ready to fall upon his head . . . and that the dogs would lick his blood as they had

[95] Syon MS X.II.12.5, 1598–99. Mr. Ed: Metcalf Brevinge Booke — Petworth.
[96] G. B. Harrison, *A Last Elizabethan Journal, 1599–1603*, New York, 1933, item for 1 Dec. 1599.
[97] Arthur Collins, ed., *Letters and Memorials of State*, 2 vols., London, 1746, II. p. 59.
[98] *Syon House: The Story of a Great House*, Syon House Estate, 1950, p. 8.

done Ahab's.' During the night the coffin burst open, and in the morning the attendants found the dogs licking up certain remains which had fallen on to the floor. This was regarded as a divine judgment upon the King for his desecration of the monastery.

On the accession of the boy King Edward VI, the Lord Protector (1st Duke of Somerset), took the Syon property for himself and built the house which was the basis of the one that existed during the time of the 9th Earl — essentially the house remaining today. For Henry Percy, Syon House was an ideal residence near London: it was rich enough to furnish the luxury and comfort which always appealed to him, remote enough from the Court to serve his instinctive reserve; yet on the Thames close enough to the city and the Court that the trip there was an easy one. Though he held both house and land on lease only, Percy began at once to modernize the buildings and improve the gardens, and increased his efforts to obtain the estate as a freehold from the Queen. Though Elizabeth listened sympathetically, she could not bring herself to release such valuable property, even to her noble friend.

Some time during these years of the mid-nineties, Northumberland offered one of the estate houses as a residence and laboratory to Thomas Harriot. The house, only the foundations of which can now be located, stood just about a hundred yards north of Syon House, in the gardens of the present house occupied by the security guard, outside the wall and the present Muniment Room.[99] It was here that Harriot was to establish his laboratories as well as his residence. Just when this was done cannot now be determined, since during this period Harriot was not regularly dating his observations. But we do have his dating testimony to show that he was in Durham House in 1595 and was well along in his work on optics at Syon in August 1597. It is probable that he was living in Syon before that, since in late 1595 and 1596 he appears to have been an intermediary in a lawsuit

[99] In July 1971, working from contemporary maps and surveys now at Syon and the accounts of renovations in the house and walls, His Grace the Duke of Northumberland and I located these foundations. Ground level is currently about 3 feet higher than it was in Harriot's time, but many of the walls constructed by the 9th Earl are still perfectly intact.

centring on his friend, Walter Warner. In the accounts of William Wycliffe, the Earl's cofferer during these years, payment was recorded:[100] 'x° febr. 1596[/7] . . . Sutes in Law . . . to Master Haryot for the charges of the sute betwene Master Warner and ffletcher xviijˢ'. Though no record remains of the nature of this suit, more scattered references to the suit and Harriot's role in it remain:

Item . . . to Master Hariot for the charge of the sute betwene Master Warner and ffletcher viijˢ.[101]

Sewtes in Lawe / paid to Master Cavis man for ffletchers Sute agaynst Master Warner Cxˢ.[102]

. . . to Master Heryott for the charges of the Sute between Master Warner and ffletcher xviijˢ[103]

Sutes in Lawe . . . for the charges of Master Warner his sute in Lawe xiijˢ viijᵈ.[104]

followed by one cryptic entry which indicates that perhaps Warner lost his suit in spite of the support of the Earl and his friend Harriot:[105] 'Rewards & Guyftes/ . . . and to Master Warner towards the payment of his Debtes. lxxvjˡⁱ xiijˢ iijᵈ.' It was during these months, too, that Harriot had been furnished 'horsmete' for ten days, indicating that he was engaged in the Earl's business.

Other evidence shows Harriot continuing to give a large portion of his time and effort to the affairs of Ralegh. He was certainly engaged in bringing Ralegh's maps and rutters up to date, and as serving as his intermediary with members of the court. On 27 September 1595, Ralegh returned from Guiana and went immediately to Sherborne. Though he continued to put the best possible face on the value of his Guiana venture, it was by all realistic measures a fiasco. Ralegh had entered into his venture with the firm conviction that he could discover the source of Inca gold and recoup his fortune and regain the favour of the Queen. But the gold remained chimerical and the 'ore' he brought back proved under assay to be worthless. The money which he had

---

[100] Syon MS U.I.2. Preliminary draft: William Wyclife ac *1596*.
[101] Petworth MS 581, 3 July 1596.
[102] Petworth MS 577, 3 July 1597.
[103] Petworth MS 580a, 8 Feb. 1597/8.
[104] Syon MS U.I.2, Edward Fraunceys, Steward, Feb. 1597/8 – May 1598.
[105] Ibid.

invested (or tricked from Sanderson), and that which he had convinced his friends to invest, appeared hopelessly lost. Despondent, in November he wrote to Sir Robert Cecil:[106]

Sir. From this desolate place [Sherborne] I have little matter; from myself, less hope; and therefore I thinke the shorter the discourse, the better wellcum. . . .

What becumes of Guiana I miche desire to here, — whether it pass for a history or a fable. I here Mr. [Sir Robert] Dudley and others are sending thither; if it be so, farewell all good from thence. For although my sealf, — like a cockscome, — did rather preferr the future, in respect of others; and rather sought to wine the [native] kings to her Majesties service then to sack them, I know what others will do, when thos kings shall come simpely into their hands. . . .

In mid-October, while Harriot was playing cross and pile with the 9th Earl, Ralegh came up to London. On 15 October Rowland Whyte wrote to Sir Robert Mornay:[107] 'Sir Walter Rawley is here [in London], and goes daily to heare sermons, because he hath seen the wonders of the Lord in the deepe; 'tis much comended and spoken of. . . .' It is possible that while in London Ralegh again got in touch with Harriot, for a month later, on 13 November, three days after his despondent letter, he wrote again to Cecil:[108] 'I know the plott [map of Guiana] is by this tyme finished which yf yow pleas to cummand from Herriott that her Maiestye may see it, if it be thought of less importance then it deserveth, her Maiestye will shortly bewayle her negligence therein & the enemy, by the addition of so mich wealth weare vs out of all.'

How Harriot worked in maintaining Ralegh's file of rutters or sailing charts of the New World, especially of the coast of South America, can be seen from one interesting item of the collection which still remains. In the British Library collection is a book of rutters headed 'A Rutter or course to be kept for him that will sayle from Cabo Verde to the coast of Brasilie and all alongst the coast of Brasilia'. This rutter is heavily annotated in the hand of Harriot, and on the last page contains Harriot's working notes:[109]

---

[106] Edwards, *Life of Ralegh*, II, Letter LIV, pp. 107-9.
[107] HMC *Manuscripts of Lord de L'Isle and Dudley*, II. 173.
[108] HMC *Manuscripts of the Marquis of Salisbury*, V. 457-8. This quotation is checked with the original in Hatfield MS CP *36*. 9.
[109] BL Sloane MS 2292.

This whole rutter hath ben examined with a copy of John Douglas which was written out of Sir Walter Raleghes had of Captain Parker.

Those notes that are written on the blancke pages are diuerse [c.o.] such readinges as are in that copy & where lines are stroked without note of diuerse readings they are words of my copy more then in his. My copy was had of [Captain] E[dmund] M[arlow]. 1590. & this was examined .1595. & the last parte from page was 35 more then was in my copy. T[homas] H[arriot].

At the end of the copy, an inserted memorandum reminds Harriot of other copies he should peruse:

Master Soza in bull alley in Aldegate street nere the burres he hath a rutter of China coste & the east Indyes.
Timothy Shotton towardes Master Wattes hath also one now set [in type?]. it is pr. 1596.
Master Hacluit of Canada & some mappes of it. A rutter of the riuer Plate. A plot of the Caspian sea.
Master Hartewell a mappe of Africa & bok & map [c.o.] wherein Angola.

In addition to his work on maps, Harriot was still working on navigational problems, as he had done during Ralegh's absence from England. One of his rough draft studies, 'Of the manner to observe the variation of the compasse or of the wires of the same, by the sunnes rising or setting',[110] refers to an observation on 'the 10 of February next this yeare 1595 [NS 1596]'. This, like his work on rutters, makes it appear that he was still residing at Durham House where he was consulting with Ralegh's sea captains and managing many of Ralegh's London affairs while Sir Walter rusticated at Sherborne.

Again in July of 1596 Harriot appears as chief spokesman for Ralegh in London. Ralegh had joined up with Essex in a naval attack on Cadiz to forestall a new Armada. Ralegh commanded the *Warspite*, Essex the *Due Repulse*. In spite of bickering among the leaders (particularly between Ralegh and Sir Francis Vere whom Essex seemed to favour), the fleet sailed the first week of June. News of their tremendous victory over the Spanish fleet did much to raise the reputations of both Essex and Ralegh in England, both of whom needed such encouragement. On 5 July, before their

[110] BL Add. MS 6789, fos. 434–7.

return, Elizabeth named Sir Robert Cecil as her Principal Secretary (to the dismay of Essex who had nominated Thomas Bodley for the post). Within a week of the appointment, Harriot wrote to Cecil on Ralegh's behalf. Ralegh's second exploratory voyage to Guiana under the command of Lawrence Keymis had arrived back in England on 29 June, having spent five months charting the coast and rivers of Guiana. Though Keymis reported additional stories of 'headlesse men ... [whose] mouthes in their breasts are exceeding wide' and of other strange tribes who 'haue eminent heads like dogs, & liue all day time in the sea', he brought no gold, but only rumours of gold and the city of Manoa. More importantly, he felt, was his addition of new information about the rivers of navigable depth leading to the main water artery back into the interior which the natives called the 'Orinoque' but Ralegh's seamen renamed the 'Raleana'. It was to cover this event that Harriot hastened to inform Elizabeth's new Principal Secretary of Ralegh's efforts on England's claim to Guiana:[111]

To the right honorable Sir Robert Cicill Knight, Principall Secretary to Her Majesty, these.
[Endorsed] '11 July 1596. Master Harriot to my Master.'
Right Honorable Sir,
These are to let you vnderstand that whereas according to your honors direction I haue ben framing of a Charte out of some such of Sir Walters notes & writinges which he hath left behind him, his principall Charte being carried with him. If it may please you I do thinke most fit that the discovery of Captain Kemish be added in his due place before I finish it. It is of importance, & all Chartes which had that coast before be very imperfecte as in many thinges elce. And that of Sir Walters although it were better in that parte then any other, yet it was don but by intelligence from the Indians, and this voyadge was specially for the discouery of the same; which is as I find well & sufficiently performed. And because the secrecy of these matters doth much importe her maiesty & this state, I pray let me be so bould as to craue that the dispatch of the plotting & describing be don only by me for you, according to the order of trust that Sir Walter left with me before his departure in that behalf & as he hath vsually don heretofore. If your honor haue any notes from Sir Thomas Bastavile if it may please you to make me acquaynted with them, that which they will manifest of other particularytyes then that before Sir Walter hath described shall also be set downe.

[111] Hatfield MS CP 42/36.

Although Captain Kemish be not come home rich, yet he hath don the speciall thing which he was inioyned to do, as [that is] the discovery of the coast betwixt the river of Amasones and Orinoco where are many goodly harbors for the greatest ships her Majesty hath & any nomber: where there are great riuers & more then probability of great good to be don by them for Guiana as by any other way or to other rich contryes bordering vpon it: As also, the discovery of the mouth of Orinoco it selfe, a good harbor & free passage for ingresse & egresse of most of the ordinary ships of England, aboue 3 hundred miles into the contry. Insomuch that Berreo wondred much of our mens comming vp so far, so that it seemeth they know not of that passage; nether could they or can possibly find it from Trinitado from whence vsually they haue made there discoveryes. But if it be don by them the shortest way it must be don out of spayne. Now if it shall please her Majesty to vndertake the entreprise or permitte it in her subiectes by her order, countenance, & authority, for the supplanting of those that are now gotten thither, I thinke it of great importance to keepe that which is don as secretly as we may, lest the Spaniards learne to know those harbors & entrances, & worke to prevent vs.

And because I vnderstand that the master of the ship with Captain Kemish is somewhat carelesse of this, by geving & selling copyes of his travelles & plottes of discoveryes, I thought it my duty to remember it vnto your wisdome that some order might be taken for the prevention of such inconuenience as may thereby follow: By geuing authoryty to some Justice or the Mayor to call him before them & to take all his writinges & chartes or papers that concerne this discouery, or any elce, in other mens handes that he hath sold or conveyed them into: and to send them sealed to your honor as also to take bond for his further secrecy in that behalf. And the like order to be taken by those others as we shall further informe your honor of that haue any such plots which yet for myne owne parte I know not of: or any other order by sending for him vp, or otherwise as to your wisdome shall seeme best.

Concerning the Eldorado which hath been shewed your honor out of the Spanish booke of Acosta which you had from Wright & I haue seene when I shall haue that favour as but to speake with you, I shall shew you it is not ours that we meane there being three. Nether doth he say or meane that Amazones river & Orinoco is all one as some I feare do averre to your honor, as by good profe out of that booke alone I can make manifest: & by other meanes besides then this discovery I can put it out of all dout. To be breef, I am at your honors comaundement in love and duty farther then I can sodaynly expresse for haste. I will wayte vpon you at courte or here at London about any of these matter or any others, at any time, if I might haue but that favour as to heare so much. I dare not presume of my selfe for some former respectes. My fidelity hath never been impeached & I take that order that it never shall. I make no application. And I beseech your honor to pardon my boldnes because of haste. My meaning is all wayes good. And so I most humbly take my leave. This sonday, 11th of July, 1596.

> Your honors most ready at commandement
> in all services I may,
> Tho: Harriots.

In many respects this letter is very revealing. Not only does it show a relative intimacy between Harriot and Lord Burleigh's second son, Sir Robert Cecil, with an acknowledgement of favours previously received (a friendship most unusual for a young man of thirty-six with no position in the circles of the court and with no obvious authority of his own), but it also shows that of all Ralegh's servants, captains, and associates, it was Harriot to whom Ralegh had issued an 'order of trust' which put him in the position of analysing situations as they arose and giving him the authority to handle the political manoeuvering of his affairs, not only with the highest governmental officials, but with the Queen herself. That Harriot felt capable of accepting this responsibility may be seen both from his confidence in his own ability to compile all known information of Guiana for the Queen's use, and from his openness in revealing the evidences of indiscretion he saw in Keymis and his sea captain that might reveal Ralegh's (and the Queen's) secrets to the Spanish. He felt secure in handling a situation obviously beyond the capability of his friend, Lawrence Keymis.

That Keymis was not offended by Harriot's attempts to silence his captain and to preserve the secrecy of his findings on the second voyage to Guiana is seen from the fact that he returned Harriot's distrust with a handsome tribute to his friend. Shortly after his return in the summer of 1596, Keymis began to write for publication his account of the voyage, outlining the discoveries he had made, but (probably through Harriot's insistence) keeping his account vague enough that he gave nothing away to competing navigators. This account, *A Relation of the second Voyage to Guiana. Perfourmed and written in the yeare 1596*,[112] was dedicated

---

[112] 'Imprinted at London by *Thomas Dawson.* dwelling at the three Crosses in the Vinetree, and are there to be sold. 1596' (STC 14947). This whole work, including the dedication and commendatory poem was reprinted in Hakluyt's *Principall Nauigations*, III (1600), 631–71.

to Sir Walter Ralegh and designed to enhance his reputation as an explorer and expander of the colonial empire of Elizabeth. But it also carried a Latin poem signed 'Tui Amantissimus, L.K.', dedicated 'Ad *Thomam Hariotum* Matheseos, & vniuersæ Philosophiæ peritissimum, de *Guiana* Carmen. Dat. Anno. 1595. [To Thomas Harriot, skilled mathematician and universal philosopher, a poem of Guiana. 1595.]'. The poem itself, which has been translated by the American Poet, Muriel Rukeyser,[113] glorifies Guiana as a potential prize for England to seize and acquire, but it does little to glorify Harriot or to add lustre to Lawrence Keymis as a poet.

Though disappointed at the lack of treasure brought back by Keymis, Ralegh found his spirits cheered by the new reports of a city on an inland lake and rumours of gold statues weighing hundreds of pounds. The victory at Cadiz had helped him mend his fences with Essex and given him new credence in the Court. Sir Robert Cecil remained friendly and it became possible once again to extend his credit. Late in the year he fitted out the pinnace *Watts* and sent it back to explore the South American rivers which might furnish access to the inland lake. He also wrote his own account of his earlier visit to Guiana, naming it *The Discourse of the Large, Rich, and Bewtifull Empyre of Guiana, with a relation of the great and Golden Citie of Manoa (which the Spanyards call El Dorado) And of the Prouinces of Emeria, Arromaia, Amapaia, and other Countries, with their riuers, adioyning. Performed in the yeare 1595. by Sir W. Ralegh Knight . . . 1596.*[114] This account, though it did not attract the financial support Ralegh hoped for, was widely circulated, attracted much attention, and in large measure restored Ralegh's reputation in navigational circles. Elizabeth once more received him in court, and on 2 June 1597 she reinstated him as Captain of the Queen's Guard.

Ralegh's reconciliation with Essex, though somewhat superficial, led the two to consider another daring expedition to the Azores to intercept the Spanish vessels returning from the New World. Essex was to command the fleet; Ralegh was

---

[113] *The Traces of Thomas Hariot*, pp. 140–1.   [114] STC 20634 *et seq.*

to be rear admiral. Preparations were made for a sailing in
early July. On 3 July Ralegh asked Harriot to get the necessary papers from the Court to make the expedition official.
Harriot's letter of request still remains among the manuscripts
preserved at Hatfield House.[115] It reads:

[Addressed] To the right honorable Sir Robert Cicill Knight Principall
Secretary to her Majesty. [Endorsed] 3 Julij 1597 Master Harriot to
my Master. A writinge to be sente to Sir Walter Raleigh by the Run-
ninge poste. Right honorable Sir. Sir Walter hath sent vnto me in great
haste to send him a writing of importance to be vsed by him selfe
before his departure that was in my custody; his desire is that it wold
please your honor to set your seale & direction vpon the paper that
incloseth it, with your commaundement that it may come to him by
the running poste to Weymouth where he lyeth attending the comminge
of the fleet, hauing the soldiers there in a readines to be shipped as
soone as the Generall cometh. But if Sir Walter be gon before the
coming of the post that then it be returned vnto your honor & so
certayne to my self for his vse as he hath appoynted me. With my
duty remembred vnto your honor I most humbly take my leaue this
3 of July. Sonday night in haste Durham house.

Your honors in all services to be commanded
Tho: Harriots

One other last-minute piece of business remained for Sir
Walter. The renovations at Sherborne and the costs of his
voyages to the New World, his raising of forces for attacks
on the Spaniards in Cadiz, and his planned raids on the
Azores had strained his credit and all but depleted his resources. He now had a son and heir, the young Walter
Ralegh, to provide for, and estates which must be preserved
for him and his progeny. On 8 July 1597 on the eve of
sailing on the dangerous expedition with Essex, Sir Walter
executed a will which has only recently come to light.[116]
This document sheds much light on the estates of Sir Walter
at this time, and certainly shows the regard and friendship
he held for Thomas Harriot, already under the full patronage
of the Earl of Northumberland.

Though it may be merely legal tradition, Ralegh's will
begins with a statement of faith even more compelling than

[115] Hatfield MS 52. 101.
[116] MS of Simon Wingfield Digby, Sherborne Castle, Digby Estate Office,
Sherborne. A brief account of the will has also been given by A. M. C. Latham
in 'Sir Walter Ralegh's Will', *Review of English Studies*, XXII (1971), 129-36.

was customary. Certainly it seems to the modern reader to be out of character for a man whose orthodoxy had been questioned and who had even been charged with atheism.

In the name of god the ffather the sonne & the holye ghoste, Three persons and one god The eighth Daye of Julye Anno Domini .1597. I walter Raleghe of Colliton Raleghe in the Counteye of Deuon knighte Captaine of her Maiesties garde and Lord Warden of the Stanneryes in the Countyes of Devon and Cornewall acknowledginge that all fleshe ys grasse and that the Daye of our birthe ys the firste steppe to Death though the hower be vncertaine when the spiritt shall retorne to the lord that gave it doe ordeyne Declare & make this my laste will & Testament in manner & effecte followinge ffirste I humblye restore my sole to that most blessed & indivisible Trinitye one god most gloryous almightye & eternall on Whome by mercye & grace I firmelye relye by faithe for the remissyon of my sinnes And diligentlye attende by grace euerlastinge vnspeakable and most comfortable heavenlye blisse.

Leaving the disposition of his earthly body to the discretion of his overseers, Ralegh began his bequests. His first grant was to his older brother, Adrian Gilbert, to whom he left the income from his properties to the sum of £100 per year. All the rest of his land holdings he left to 'walter Ralegh esquire my sonne & heire apparant'. The major portion of the will then outlines the property holdings which Ralegh wishes to pepetuate with his desire that these shall all be vested first in his son, or following his demise, 'to the heires Males of my bodye lawfullye begotten And for Defaulte of such yssue to Dame Elizabeth my now Wiffe' for her lifetime. His son Walter is also to get some of Ralegh's other continuing sources of income, following payments of his current debts and the redemption of some 'great flagons of silver gilte' and 'twoe great silver pottes guilt of the same suite' which he had evidently pawned to finance his expedition. One 'suite of Porcelane sett in silver & gylt That is to saye two basons & Eweres with two flaggons and twoe boles sutable' he desired to go to 'my Right Honorable good ffrinde Sir Roberte Cecill'. His 'plate bedinge household stuffe furniture of house Jewels' (excepting his wife's pearls which he generously let her keep) were to be divided equally between Walter and his mother. Then Ralegh turned to other bequests:

Item I will ordeyne & apppointe that soe sone as my debtes are paid & dulye Discharged without fraude or Delayed practise which I specyallye Will & earnestlye Require be not attempted nor Vsed in anie sorte That then Thomas Harryott of London Gentleman shall yearlye at the feastes of St Michaell Th'arkangell & of Th'anunciacion of our ladye the virgin During my said tearme graunted for or in Respecte of the makeinge of licenses for the sale or Retayle of Wynes & keepinge of Tauernes aforesaid yf the said Thomas Herryott shall soe longe lyue haue & Receaue out of the said Rentes Revenues & paymentes touchinge the said Licenses one Anuitye or yearelye soome of one hundred pounds by the hands of such person & persons as by this my last will shall or ought to haue the rule estate & gouernment of the said tearme concerninge the said licenses according to the purporte and trewe meaninge hereof.

This is a most handsome and unusual grant: it is the same amount that Ralegh had devised for his favourite brother, Adrian Gilbert, and one-fifth the annuity he left his wife. It is very likely that at this particular time Ralegh felt under a special obligation to Harriot which led him to place this bequest at the head of the list, and it is probable that the sum here mentioned is a continuation of the amount he was then paying Harriot for his services. Though he was already accepting favours and grants from Northumberland, Harriot probably expected to continue to serve Ralegh as well. Certainly Ralegh appears to have very close ties to Harriot. The will continues: 'Moreover I geve to the said Thomas Harryott all my bookes & the furniture in his owne Chamber and in my bedchamber in Durham house Togeather with all such blacke suites of apparell as I haue in the same house.' In addition, Ralegh calls for the raising of further funds from the sale of 'the shippe called the Robucke with her Ancores Tackle & furniture & all my Artylerye and great ordinance'. From these proceeds, Ralegh decreed that 'my Reputed Daughter begotten on the bodye of Alice Goold now in Ireland shall haue the soome of ffiue hundreth Markes'. In the 1590s 1 mark was the equivalent of two-thirds of £1 sterling of 13s. 4d. Ralegh thus left his illegitimate daughter a bequest of £333 6s. 8d. From the sale of this ship Ralegh also ordered 'That Thomas Harryott shall haue twoe hundred poundes Allsoe Lawrence Kemishe one hundred poundes. . .'.

As executor of his will, Ralegh named his son Walter; or if he had died, his other children, male then female; or finally if none survived, his wife Elizabeth. During the minority of his son, however, Sir Walter felt the need to name some trusted overseers, and again he thought of Harriot:

> And I doe further ordeyne & make my trustye & faithfull frindes Arthur Throkemorton of Pawlersburye in the Countye of Northampton knight George Carewe of London knight Alexander Brett of Whitechurch in the Countye of Dorset esquire & Thomas Herryott of London gentleman aforesaid the ouerseers of this my last Will and Testament.

Only one other grant was left by Ralegh to any of his friends, retainers, or servants. That was to the man who was to give him so much trouble in the courts a few years later, the servant whom he inherited with Sherborne, and whom he called in 1592 the 'Keeper of the castle and overseer of all woods, and timber with the Hundred, and Collector of Rents'.[117]

> Item I geeve to my servant John Meere of Castletowne aforesaid one Annual or yearelye Rent of Twentye poundes of Currant english moneye to be paid him yearelye out of & from my mannors Landes & Tenementes in Sherborne aforesaid. . .Charginge & Requiringe him hereby That he Doe contynue like faithful & diligent serant to my said Wiffe & sonne as he hath byn to me. . .

This is the same John Mere that Sanderson accused of having forged Ralegh's name to the false endorsement on the acquittance he had left with Harriot in January two and a half years earlier.

Ralegh's will clearly shows that he considered Harriot not as a servant but as a 'trustye & faithfull frinde' to be given special affection and consideration. During the dozen or so years that he had served Sir Walter, Harriot had assumed a unique position in the household. Yet he remained as 'of London gentleman', not of Sherborne, associated closely with Durham House, where he was heir designate not only to 'all [Ralegh's] bookes & the furniture in his own Chamber' but to those in Sir Walter's bedchamber there as well, implying that these two rooms were probably adjoining, and formed the basic library collected for use of Ralegh's navigation and Harriot's instructions of sea captains. And, as has already been pointed out, the gift to Harriot of 'all such blacke suites

of apparell as I [Ralegh] haue in the same house' support the
assumption that Harriot took his Oxford vows seriously,
appeared in public in black only, in general striving to maintain the appearance of the Magister, the Magus, the master, or
the teacher.

Yet within a month of the time of the signing of this will,
Harriot was firmly established in Syon House, Isleworth, hard
at work in his own laboratories there pursuing his scientific
studies. Notes in the 1572 edition of the copy of *Opticæ
Thesaurvs, Alhazeni Arabis* now in the Universitetbibliotek in
Oslo, Norway, include many of Harriot's own holograph
corrections of Witelo's tables of the refraction of light. These
are dated:[118] 'Syon.1597. August .11.♃ [Thursday] et .12.
♀ [Friday].' These corrections are but a small portion of the
manuscript observations of refraction among Harriot's extant
manuscripts. They show clearly that by 1597 Harriot was
established in his laboratory in his Syon residence, engaged in
methodical observations of optics,[119] leaving only occasionally
to visit Durham House in London to continue there some of
his earlier experiments[120] or to perform special assignments
for his friend Ralegh. Exactly what proportion of his time he
spent in each place is difficult to determine, since the majority
of Harriot's mathematical papers (which constitute the
greatest proportion) are undated. During the months of May
and June 1599, however, while Harriot was engaged in a very
demanding series of chemical experiments dealing with the
Aristotelean elements,[121] he did keep a detailed log of his
activities.[122] From these we can determine that he was in his

---

[118] Some of Harriot's MS notes in this volume were reproduced by Lektor
Johannes Lohne in 'Thomas Harriot (1560-1621): The Tycho Brahe of Optics'
in *Centaurus*, VI.2 (1959), 113-21, pl. I. In this article Lohne apparently finds it
difficult to distinguish between Harriot's 1s and 2s. In dates, however, Harriot's
use of planetary symbols to designate days of the week as well as the date makes
such a determination simple. The observations shown from the Syon MSS are
clearly 1601, not 1602 as Lohne reads them.

[119] See particularly the optics papers in Add. MS 6789. Here, as a matter of
fact, are the original charts showing the tabulation of experimental results from
which Harriot extracted to correct Witelo. See especially fos. 406ʳ and 407ʳ.

[120] In his *Instructions* written for Ralegh's sea captains at the time of the 1595
Guiana voyage, Harriot says that he observed the obliquity of the ecliptic from
1590 to 1593 'by myne own experiment with an instrument of 12 foote long
vpon Duresme house leades'. Add. MSS 6788, fo. 469ʳ.

[121] For more details of these experiments, see Ch. VI.

Syon laboratory (many times for both day and night) for thirty-seven of the fifty-six days between Wednesday 2 May and Tuesday 26 June. During this time he spent at least three periods in London: Saturday to Monday, 5–7 May; Friday to Monday, 18–22 May; and Wednesday to Monday, 20–5 June. One week is unaccounted for: Thursday to Thursday, 31 May–6 June, since no entries are recorded for this week. There is no indication that he went to London then, but it is probable that he did. It would be very interesting to confirm that these dates coincided with visits of Sir Walter Ralegh to London on his duties as Lord Warden of the Stanneries, or his pursuit of his political effort to be made a member of the Privy Council, but it is impossible to follow his activities so closely.

One minor entry in the Northumberland accounts could be interpreted to indicate that Harriot was establishing his residence at Syon in early 1597. In the same account which records payment to Walter Warner 'towardes the payment of his Debtes'[123] is found an additional entry: 'Rewardes & Guyftes/ . . . to Master heryott in dyuerse pewther vessels and Pottes lxxvˢ iiijᵈ . . .', which might well indicate a kind of house-warming present for a new resident at Syon.

But by the turn of the century, Harriot must have felt secure in serving two important establishments with responsibilities for the estates of Sir Walter Ralegh and for the scientific interests of the 9th Earl of Northumberland. These dual duties were either simplified or complicated by his maintenance for a time of two residences. That he might have been making his observations from both sites to give continuity to his work, making necessary observational corrections is evident from one calculation (evidently made from astronomical observations) of the angular position between Syon House and Durham House (28° 8′ south of true east) and the exact distance (8 miles east and 4¼ miles south) which Harriot calculated from polar readings of 51° 33′ from Durham House and 51° 29′ for Syon House — probably read by means of his 'owne experiment with an instrument of 12 foote long vpon Duresme house leades'.[124] Both

[122] These MSS are somewhat scattered. Some are in BL Add. MS 6788, especially fos. 373–402; others are at Petworth: HMC 241/IV, pp. 25–9.
[123] Syon MS U.I.2, 'Edward ffraunceys Steward, 12 Feb. 1596/7 – May 1598'.

Harriot's computed angle and the distance (approximately
9$\frac{6}{10}$ miles as the crow flies) appear very accurate. Fortunately
both Syon and Durham were located on the Thames, approximately three hours by boat apart, so the shuttle was not
arduous. But it is certain that Master Harriot must have been
well known to the colourful boatmen plying their water
trade during these late years of the reign of Elizabeth, last
of the Tudors.

[124] Add. MS 6786, fo. 554^v. This instrument, used in 1590 and 1593 to
measure the obliquity of the ecliptic, was used in the 1600s at Syon in his various
astronomical observations of the moon and the comets.

VI. The 1590s: Harriot Expands his Interests

Unfortunately for a clear understanding of Harriot's development in his mathematical and scientific studies, Harriot did not see fit to date his early papers. Only nine items are dated before 1599, and none before 1591, of the thousand or so folio pages still extant which were written during these years. Moreover, it is evident from the mathematical portions of his manuscripts that Harriot found mathematics a continual preoccupation and development. From changes in his handwriting which can be fairly closely dated, it may be seen that he worked and reworked various problems and ideas over a period of years, frequently returning to earlier papers and improving his solutions on the basis of a more mature perspective. And since in most of his work he was considering matters stimulated by his own interest, and was not, in general, meeting obligatory deadlines, Harriot would frequently work on several investigations at the same time, or would find some interesting facet in the study in hand which would lead him to branch out in his research to follow the new interesting red herring.

This kind of intellectual evolution and shifting of ground may be seen in Harriot's researches during this period of transition between Ralegh and Northumberland. The earliest date he placed on any of his manuscripts during this decade was on 12 December 1591, on a large, two-sheet, triangular chart of numbers.[1] This chart carries the following explanatory note:

---

[1] BL Add. MS 6786, fos. 375^v–376^r.

241

There are three speciall groundplats vpon the which may be orderly piled bullets: The triangle: the square: and the oblonge. Concerning piling there are two questions: one; ~~whether~~ [c.o.] the number of bulletes to be piled being geven with the forme of the gound plat, to know how many must be placed in every ranke, with how many rankes in the sayd ground plat.

The second a pile being made to knowe the nomber of bulletes therein conteyned.

ffor the aunsweringe of which two questions this table I haue ~~set downe~~ [c.o.] calculated for ~~for~~ [c.o.] the purpose.

December .12. 1591.. [Sunday].

Obviously, this is a quick reference chart prepared for Ralegh to give information on the ground space required for the storage of cannon balls in connection with the stacking of armaments for his marauding vessels. The chart is ingeniously arranged so that it is possible to read directly the number of cannon balls on the ground or in a pyramidal pile with triangular, square, or oblong base. All of this Harriot had worked out by the laws of mathematical progression (not as Miss Rukeyser suggests by experiment),[2] as the rough calculations accompanying the chart make clear. It is interesting to note that on adjacent sheets, Harriot moved, as a mathematician naturally would, into the theory of the sums of the squares, and attempted to determine graphically all the possible configurations that discrete particles could assume — a study which led him inevitably to the corpuscular or atomic theory of matter originally deriving from Lucretius and Epicurus.[3] It appears that Harriot was expanding his horizons, seeking the potential of a union of experimental and mathematical theory in the explanation of natural phenomena.

The next assignment that Ralegh gave his young friend was much more challenging — to bring his science and mathematics to bear on improving the accuracy of fire of his

[2] *The Traces of Thomas Harriot*, pp. 117–18.

[3] Miss Rukeyser, evidently through consultation with Professor Cyril S. Smith, saw the relationship between Harriot's bullet chart and his mathematical and physical extrapolations from it. This was missed by Robert Kargon, and it seems evident that Kargon did not explore Harriot's own MSS thoroughly in his preparation of *Atomism in England from Harriot to Newton*, Oxford, Clarendon Press, 1966. Much scattered material remains in Harriot's papers which could expand on this significant part of Harriot's scientific theories.

heavy ordnance, particularly of the cannon on his ships at sea. Though the English had been building naval vessels for a hundred years, they had never proved themselves to be effective in battles at sea, and Ralegh had learned by experience in his sea fights with the Spaniards what was also borne out in the warfare of the Armada that the only effective cannon fire was that at point-blank range. Any shot fired at a range of more than 200 yards was almost certainly wasted. Ralegh correctly figures that greater knowledge of those factors that caused inconsistent results and a clearer understanding of the full trajectory of the cannon ball would greatly improve his chances for success in his raids against the Spanish and Portuguese vessels.

Other Englishmen were also beginning to see the need for more serious study of ballistics. In 1576 William Bourne, who had greatly improved the navigational tools of British seamen by the publication of his *A Regiment for the Sea*, wrote and prepared for publication another small practical volume entitled *The arte of shooting in great ordnaunce*. Somewhat self-conscious about bringing out the first English manual on the subject in which he had no practical experience, Bourne did not actually issue his book until 1587.[4] But even before the crisis of the Armada, Bourne had realized that British marksmanship was so poor that a text on the most elementary principles was necessary to combat the gross ignorance which existed. One of the most basic difficulties which Bourne recognized but did not feel free to comment on in such an elementary text was the lack of understanding of the physics of bodies in flight or even in free fall. Though Aristotle was being challenged in many areas, up to this time there had been no serious questioning of his ideas concerning the nature of matter and his concept of 'natural place' as accounting for weight and gravity. Bourne, who had early accepted the Copernican doctrine for celestial motion, was among the few who might question Aristotle's doctrine of terrestrial motion as well. And, as a matter of fact, Bourne did depict a somewhat more accurate

[4] STC 3420. Entered to H. Bynneman, 22 July 1578; printed by T. Dawson for T. Woodcocke, 1587.

course of a bullet's trajectory than would have been obtained from a strict adherence to Aristotle's rules.[5]

Disciples of Aristotle were still proclaiming that it was within the nature of matter to have a 'place' somewhere between the centre of the earth and the empyrean. Of the four elements, the element of earth was heaviest and its place was in the centre of the earth; water was somewhat lighter, and rested on earth; air was still lighter and rose by nature into the atmosphere above the water; and fire, lightest of all, rose by nature to seek the pure upper regions of the empyrean. Most substances known on earth were compounds of these elemental substances, and consequently had weights which would place them normally in some proper inter-mediate position in the vertical hierarchy. It was the action of natural place which led smoke to rise and cannon balls to fall. It was also the force of place which led, logically enough, heavier (more earthy) substances to fall at a more rapid rate than lighter (less earthy) substances, as experiments with lead bullets and feathers would readily show. According to these same disciples of Aristotle, matter had two natural motions: vertical straight line and circular. Matter moving from seeking its natural place was straight-line motion toward the centre of the earth; matter moving freely in space assumed a circular motion, since space was perfect, and the circle was the perfect geometric form.

From these basic postulates, the generally accepted course of a bullet or cannon ball was argued to consist of three parts. Through the force of the powder the shot would be driven in a straight line until that force was expended. Next it would move from its angle of ascent through a circular path until it was directly above the centre of the earth. In its final stage it would fall in a straight line, perpendicular to the earth's surface, toward the centre of the earth, to attain its natural place. Bourne, though his language is not easy to interpret, appears to have modified this Aristotelian trajectory, and to have accepted one, either on the basis of gunnery tradition or observation, closer to what could be observed

---

[5] For a more detailed discussion of most of these background studies, see A. Rupert Hall, *Ballistics in the Seventeenth Century*, Cambridge, University Press, 1952, Ch. II, pp. 29–59.

from the actual flight of the projectile. As he expressed it:[6]

As I suppose, it is very necessarye to know what manner of course or proportion the shotte flyeth in the ayre in his compas, that is to say, at any degree mounted that the peece is shotte as the Randare [Bourne calls the angle of elevation or 'random' the 'randar']. All those peeces that be shotte at the mountinge or any degree aboue poynte blancke, and under the beste of the Randare, hath .4. manner of courses in his dryuing or flying, by the vyolence of the blast of the powder, before the shotte come to the ground, so that the peece be shot against a leuelled ground. The first course is by a right line, and so long as the shot goeth violently. And the second course doth begin for to compasse, and yet flieth somewhat vpwards into the ayre, that is to say, further aboue the earth circularly. The third course is for a certain space or quantitie at the highest distance from the earth. And the fourth course is, it commeth downewards circularly towards the earth, and so stouping more and more, till it cometh downe to the grounde. . . .

The illustration following this verbal description shows the flight of the bullet to be a curving flight, neither straight line nor circular, though the woodcut is so rough that it cannot be accurately analysed. Bourne does point out, too, that the maximum range is achieved at a muzzle elevation of 45°. Below this elevation he assumes the range to be directly proportional to elevation; above 45°, increased elevation decreases range:[7] 'therefore they do neuer mount any manner of peece aboue the compasse of .45. degrees, except it be a Morter peece, and those be mounted alwayes aboue .45. degrees'. Bourne's treatise, however, did not have the impact of his navigational work, and was too elementary to contribute anything to the serious science of gunnery or of ballistics.

The most famous treatise on artillery when Harriot broached the subject was by the Italian Niccolo Tartaglia, first printed as part of his *La nova scientia* in 1537. This work was widely known throughout Europe and England and used by those who could read Italian, and was important enough that it was translated into English and published in London in the year of the Armada. The English title-page shows the scope of Tartaglia's treatise:[8]

[6] *The arte of shooting in great ordnaunce*, 1587, Ch. II: 'What manner of course the shot flyeth in the ayre', pp. 38–41.
[7] Ibid., p. 39.
[8] STC 23689.

Three Bookes of Colloquies Concerning the Arte of Schooting in Great and Small Peeces of Artillerie, variable randges, measure, and waight of leaden, yron, and marble stone pellets, mineral saltpeter, gunpowder of diuerse sortes, and the cause why some sortes of gunpowder are corned, and some sortes of gunpowder are not corned: written in Italian . . by Nicholas Tartaglia . . . And now translated into English by Cyprian Lucar, Gent. London, for Iohn Harrison, 1588.

This work, undoubtedly the most widely used book on gunnery of the century, was Aristotelian in theory throughout.[9] This may easily be seen in Tartaglia's discussion of the weight of the pellet:[10] 'Euery kinde of waight which being weyed departeth from the place of equalitie, is made thereby so much the more lighter, by howe much it is more departed from the said place of equalitie.' Or again:[11]

Euery peece lying leuell is intended to be in the place of equalitie. A pellet flyeth more heuily out of a peece lying leuell, than it will doe out of the same peece any whit eleuate. And a pellet shot out of a peece lying leuell rangeth in a more crooked line, and more sooner beginneth to decline downewards to the ground than it will do when it is shot out of a peece somewhat eleuated, & it striketh with lesse force than it wil do out of the same peece any whit eleuated.

The trajectory which Tartaglia constructs on these premises, as a result, gives the Aristotelian course of flight which had come to be generally accepted:[12]

A pellet goeth out of the mouth of a peece with great swiftnesse which is the cause why the pellet for a little time rangeth in an insensible crooked line, but after the force and swiftnesse thereof do any whitte abate, it then beginneth to flie more weakely and more slowlie, and afterwardes to decline towardes the ground and in that sorte continueth vntill it doth light vppon the ground.

With such a work the standard guide for training gunners, it is easy to see why marksmanship standards were so low during the sixteenth century, and it is obvious that Harriot had little to build on when he turned to the task of applying his mathematical knowledge and scientific instincts to the improvement of the art of gunnery.

One other British mathematician was also turning his attention to these problems. Thomas Digges, son of the

---

[9] See Hall, op. cit., pp. 37–42.　　[10] *Three Bookes of Colloquies*, p. 7.
[11] Ibid., pp. 8–9.　　　[12] Ibid., p. 12 (Third Colloquy, Margin).

mathematical almanac writer Leonard Digges and, like Harriot, a friend of John Dee, and leader of the English Copernicans, was interested in applying mathematics to practical problems. As a result, he turned early to matters of military fortifications, manœuvres, 'and for science in great ordinance especially to shoote exactly at Randons (a quality not unmeete for a Gentleman) [who] without rules Geometrical, and perfect skill in these mensurations, he shall never know anything.'[13] From these studies, Digges proposed to write a book on the firing of artillery. At the height of interest in the subject, 1591, when he again edited his father's treatise on practical geometry, Digges called attention to his plans on the title-page:[14]

A Geometrical Practical Treatize named Pantometria, diuided into three Bookes, Longimetria, Planimetria, and Stereometria . . . Lately Reviewed by the Author himselfe, and augmented with sundrie Additions, Diffinitions, Problemes, and rare Theoremes, to open the passage, and prepare a way to the vnderstanding of his Treatize of Martiall Pyrotechnie and great Artillerie, hereafter to be published. At London, Printed by Abell Jeffres, Anno .1591.

As a sort of preview of the work to come, in an appendix to this revised work, Digges included a series of 'Diffinitions taken out of my fyrst Booke of Martiall Pyrotechnye and Great Artillerie' followed by fifty-one 'Theoremes concerning the new Science of great Ordinance'. The theories of ballistics contained in these brief statements reflect a peculiar combination of Aristotelian concepts of mass and gravity and some of the new theories of celestial mechanics.[15] For example, in discussing the rate of fall of projectiles, Digges wrote:[16] 'If any two Bullets of equall quantitie, but vnequall waight, be let fall from anye loftie place to the Horizon, the more waightie shall euer fall the more swiftly: albeing not proportionally to their waighte, which Axiom is indeed erronious, albeit a great Philosopher haue auerred the same.' And again, Digges, in defining the terms he wished to use, described the trajectory of a bullet in the same three stages given by Tartaglia.[17]

---

[13] *Pantometria*, 1571, sig. Aiij (STC 6858).   [14] STC 6859.
[15] See Hall, op. cit., pp. 43–5.   [16] Theorem 5, p. 182..
[17] 'Diffinition' 1, p. 178.

Forasmuch as euery Bullet violently throwne out of any peece of Ordinance at any Angle of Random passeth a good distance directly without anye great variation from the right line pointed out by the Axis, and then falleth into a *Curve* Arke, and last of all finisheth either in a right line or in a *Curve*, approaching nighe a right line againe.

To explain the cause of the flight of a projectile, Digges once more reverts to the Aristotelian concept of mass and place:[18]

And because the Bullet violentlye throwne out of the Peece by the furie of the Poulder hath two motions, the one violent, which endeuoreth to carry the Bullet right out in his Line Diagonall, the other Naturall in the Bullet itselfe, which endeuoureth still to carrye the same directly downeward by a right line Perpendiculare to the Horizon.

But when he tried to describe the course of the bullet's flight in his 'Theoremes', Digges abandoned the straight-line/circle combination and sought a more suitable geometric curve to define the trajectory, though he found his mathematical skill inadequate for the task:[19]

These middle *Curve* Arkes of the Bullets Circuites, compounded of the violent and natural motions of the Bullet, albeit they be indeed meere Helicall, yet haue they a very great resemblance of the Arkes Conicall. And in Randoms aboue .45. [degrees] they doe much resemble the *Hyperbole*, and in all vnder, the *Ellipsis*: But exactlye they neuer accorde, being indeed *Spirall* mixte and *Helicall*.

But the practicality of Digges's observations about actual gunnery problems may be seen in the list of factors which he found might conspire against the hitting of the mark with consistency. Theorem 11 gives the gunners' excuses:[20]

There are also many other Accidental alterations happening by reason of the winde, the thicknesse or thinnesse of the Ayre, the heating or cooling of the Peece, the different manner of Raminge fast or loose of the Poulder, by close or loose rouling or lying of the bullet, by the vnequal Recule of the Peece, either by reason of the vnequality of the Platforme or Wheeles, or by the vneven lying of the Peece in his Carriadge, or deformitie of the Axtree, with diuers other such like, whereof no rules certaine can be prescribed, to reduce these vncertaine differences

[18] 'Diffinition' 14, p. 180.
[19] Theorem 24, p. 168. There is a printer's mistake in paging here. Sig. Aa4^V is numbered 182; sig. Bbl^r (which should be 183) is numbered 167, and the incorrect numbering continues on.
[20] Ibid., Theorem 11, p. 182.

to any certaine proportions: but all these are by Practice, Discretion, and Iudgement to be considered and vniformely guided and performed in their best perfection.

Though the observations and theories of Digges show him beginning to question the infallibility of Aristotelian concepts of mass and motion and reveal a shrewdness about practical matters of gunnery, it must be admitted that they form a very weak base on which to develop sound gunnery practices, or even for sound speculation about the flight of a projectile. As Rupert Hall sums up this background:[21]

[Charbonnier] has .. said of these writers of the late sixteenth and early seventeenth century that their works are of little interest, the implication being that they are now with justice utterly forgotten. Examined in the light of the knowledge to be given to the world within a very few years of their publication, contrasted with the great scientific achievements of the century, indeed these early works on artillery with their thoroughly medieval scientific background seem absurd and contemptible. How can their trifling arithmetical artifices compare with the imposing theorems of Galileo or the calculus of Newton and Leibniz? They reveal the fundamental uninventiveness of the mind, for during two generations at the height of the renaissance and of the rapid expansion of the use of artillery scarcely a useful footnote was added to the ballistic writings of Tartaglia, and make plain the barrenness in the field of technique, equal to the philosophical inadequacy of pre-Galilean mechanics, of the early manuals of gunnery. Although the art of shooting at long ranges was confessed to be the flower of gunnery, it was quite divorced from the physical speculations of the schools and there was no bridge between them until Galileo founded a new ballistics which derived nothing from Tartaglian doctrines expounded by the professional experts.

It is obvious from these remarks that Hall had not reviewed Harriot's manuscripts or he might have modified his comments about the inventiveness of mind and the mathematical sophistication of ballistic researches during this period.

Yet even with access to his remaining papers, definite conclusions about Harriot's studies of trajectories and falling bodies, his final tables of random and range, or the theoretical basis for many of his assumptions remain most difficult to establish. The papers which remain appear to be his rough notes, preliminary drafts, or mathematical explorations of

[21] Hall, op. cit., pp. 47-8.

possible solutions of problems not clearly designated. They
are not in any order, either from the fact that they were
unordered at the time of Harriot's death or have been ran-
sacked or thrown about since. But since no one appears to
have studied them in the intervening years, this latter seems
highly improbable. It seems almost certain that the existing
papers are the only ones among Harriot's manuscripts at the
time of his death. The formal listing headed 'A note of the
papers and bookes in Master Harriots truncke deliuered to
Master Torporley'[22] contains at the end of the first page
only two items devoted to these subjects:

Of velocities and randomes, 1. B[undle], = 11 pag.
Second experiments (for Ordnaunce), 1. b[undle], = p. 13.

Though not now collected into these distinct categories, it is
still possible to count more than this number of sheets on
these two topics.[23]

An additional entry, widely separated from the ballistics
sheets, may throw some light on the subject. One of the
personal jottings and remembrances which Harriot wrote
himself as reminders of things done or yet to be done reads
as follows:[24]

Memorandum
The properties of the four elementes.
Master Allens Book.
Varro.
My notes of ordinance. [Italics mine]
Proclus de moto.

This memorandum is in the handwriting characteristic of
Harriot during the period of 1590-5. What this undoubtedly
means is that Sir Walter Ralegh, to whom Harriot still owed
allegiance, had asked Harriot for the conclusions of his study
on the improvement of gunnery, possibly about the time he
was preparing for his voyage to Guiana where he expected to
meet the Spanish. If this were the case, Harriot would have,

[22] BL Add. MS 6789, fo. 448ʳ. This list has been translated and published by R. C. H. Tanner, 'Nathaniel Torporley and the Harriot Manuscripts', *Annals of Science*, XXV (1969), 339-49. These items are nos. 29 and 30.
[23] The ballistics papers are scattered (intermixed with other materials) in BL Add. MS 6789, fos. 2-86, and Petworth House, HMC 241/VIᵃ, fos. 1-13.
[24] BL Add. MS 6786, fo. 364ᵛ.

as he did in other cases for Ralegh and later for Northumberland, gathered up his observations, calculations, and conclusions, put them into good order, formally presented with
charts and diagrams, all written in a good hand for a final
or interim report of his scientific and mathematical study.
This would leave in his own custody only the rough notes
on which the study was made, with the more formal document the property of his patron who had requested the study
and supported its investigation. In this case, Harriot's final
word on trajectories, velocities, charts on range and elevation,
and the results of his 'Second Experiments' (of which more
later) would have been a part of Ralegh's books and manuscripts seized and destroyed at the time of his attainder in
1603, and never heard of since.

The rough papers remaining, however, still give some
insight into the successes and failures Harriot encountered
in analysing the problems of ballistics. Because of his habitual
thoroughness in researching both ancients and moderns in
any investigation he undertook, we may be sure that Harriot
was totally familiar with the writers and the theorists of his
own time. As a matter of fact, his notes contain information
and data from William Bourne, for example, that are not
covered in his published works,[25] showing that he did not
confine himself to the data in books. But with the observations and data in hand, Harriot approached each problem
as a totally fresh enquiry, not biased by the theoretical
explanation of others. As in all his researches, Harriot examined the data carefully, and sought out those mathematical
relationships which might be manipulated to derive simple
and effective formulae for use in solving other unknowns.
It was Harriot's combination of keen observation and instinctive mathematical feeling for the relationship between cause
and effect that set him apart from most of his contemporaries.

In what appears to be one of the earliest sheets of notes
dealing with the course of a projectile and the factors which
might affect its accuracy,[26] Harriot reflects both these
qualities. For some intuitive reason, the very first question

---

[25] See, e.g., Petworth House, HMC 241/VI[a], fos. 3[v], 4[r], 13[r].
[26] BL Add. MS 6789, fos. 3[v]–4[r].

he proposed to himself in the study of trajectory is one
which no one before had asked, and one truly critical for the
analysis of falling bodies of all kinds: 'Whether the time of
the bulletes ascendinge be aequall to the time of his descend-
ing in all oblique randoms as well as in the vpright.' To this
query, Harriot appends the correct answer, 'Yea'. Recognition
of this simple but not evident fact that the rise time and the
fall time were equal gave Harriot a tremendous advantage in
his further calculations of all aspects of trajectories.

Harriot's second observation on the same sheet reveals
the thoroughness with which he analysed his data. He would
make all the direct observations he could, but he might go
even farther. He wrote: 'That which is vnsensible by the
immediate iudgment of ye sense; may by consequence or
effecte be made very sensible', or, unobservable forces may
be determined by observing their effects. He then proceeded,
as had Digges, to list some of the observable variables which
might affect practical gunnery, as

The differences of sortes of powder.
The difference of the same sort at sundry times, dry moyste.
The difference of the quantity or wayte of euery charge [of powder].
Differences of the ramm[inge].
Difference of the wadd.

And so on through more than a dozen different differences,
including 'Movinge or ioggine of the peece af[ter] it is
charged; Recoylinge by inequality of the wheles, ground,
Axis; Diverse thicken[ess] of ye ayre be[ing] quiet, varying;
Windes direct[ion] & ligne; Asperity of the peece; Bow of the
peece; Heat of the peece; Fowlness of the peece.' A drawing
of trajectories accompanying this early text seems to be
patterned after the fashion of Tartaglia, with a nearly straight
line during ascent, circular motion at flight apex, and perpendicular entrance to the horizon at all but the lowest
elevations. Yet even in his first drawing, Harriot was seeking
numerical ratios between forward motion and vertical motion
at different randoms, and the margins of the paper are filled
with possible proportions.

Perhaps even more significantly, adjacent sheets show
Harriot grappling with geometric representations designed
to resolve the angular velocity of the projectile into vertical

and horizontal components.[27] Unfortunately, Harriot does not appear to have used this tool effectively in his calculations. Another sheet headed 'Of shotinge in ordinaunce' lists the items which need to be considered further:[28]

Considerations

Of one bullet out of one peece, shot at sundry times vpon seuerall angles of Random; the temper of the peece supposed to be one & the same quantity of powder and all other considerations alike.

Extra medium materiale.

1. In the motion of the bullet we are to consider it in the pece & also what it is out of the same.
2. In the pece it is vnequall & his poynte of swiftest motion is at the mouth of the pece in all angles.
3. This inequality riseth from two causes: if the force of the powder did continue to be one in the whole length of the pece; yet the motion of the bullet wold be vnequall, but the force of the powder beinge [c.o.] growinge greater & greater as it repeateth more [c.o.] accordinge as it taketh fire, not beinge all fired vntill it cometh to the mouth of the pece, then also is the lesse resistance of the medium whereby the 2 is manifest, the force of the last powder fired is greater because it is fired in motion.
4. In all angles of Random betwene the horizon & Zenith, the motion of the bullet is swiftest [c.o.] swifter the nerer the peece inclineth to the horizon; so that in the levell situation of the pece, the bullet emergeth the length of the sayd pece in the shortest time; & in the Zenith line in the longest. but the shortest time; absolutely is in his perpendicular situation downeward & so of the rest accordingly.

The carriages recoyle vnequally according to the angle of Random.

The Asperity of the bullet somewhat hindreth.

The vnequall wayt of the powder in severall charges. Ramminges. Ayre more dense &c.

Wind.

Still a third page of notes attempts to refine the nature of the flight of the projectile after it has left the muzzle of the cannon:[29]

The motion of a bullet by the violence of the powder to the hyest poynt above the horizon is perfourmed in aequall time to his motion downewardes to the poynt of beginninge his leuel, as well in any angle of random, as of the vpright. In the same time also a bullet of the same matter and mag[nitude] doth measure the perpendicular from the hyest poynt.

[27] Ibid., fo 2r.   [28] Ibid., fo. 19r.   [29] Ibid., fo. 62r.

The motion of any bullet downward from any poynt alofte naturall & free is still descendinge in euery poynt in continuall proportion, in such sake as if the line of his motion be devided into æquall partes, as the whole line hath to one of the partes with the rest from the beginninge; so hath the velocity at the end of the motion, to the velocity at the end of the sayd part. The which manner of ~~motion~~ [c.o.] proportion is expressed beinge the like, by a circle, a sector, the superficies of a cone, or a triangle of what kind soeuer.

Therefore a line of any random is devided by aequall time in the tropicke poynte.

This view of the trajectory of a projectile on the basis of the forces exerted on it by the explosion of the powder and the pull of gravity and an understanding of the time involved in each stage of the flight gave Harriot a much more accurate picture of what was happening than had been given by Tartaglia, Digges, Bourne, or any of the other students of the art of gunnery; it also furnished a sound base for the construction of tables of range and angle of impact. It would be most interesting to see just what charts Harriot did prepare for Ralegh, and how they would compare with similar pre-Galilean calculations.

In his first consideration of the range of a projectile, Harriot appears to have followed his contemporaries in considering range to be directly proportional to the random from point blank to the 'tropic point' of 45°. Yet having propounded this generalization, he immediately changed his position to refine the calculations:[30]

A peece shooting 1500 paces at the best of the random which is vnderstood at 45 degrees angle & 300 paces poynt blancke shall shoote at euery degree of mount $\frac{1}{45}$ of the difference, that is $26\frac{2}{3}$ paces.

or this more exactly:

It being knowne the range of poynt blancke, & of one degree mounte, the difference is the difference of euery degree mount to 10 degrees, then it somewhat descendeth in euery degree till 18 to 20 at which random it shot more ground then is left to the best of the random; & after 20 degrees the difference of the range do shorten more & more to the vtmost range of the greatest random.

Above the vtmost random, euery degree shorteneth his range the $\frac{1}{45}$ of the greatest range.

The vtmost range is quintuple to the range of poynt blancke or rather better.

[30] Ibid., fo. 47[r].

Harriot, however, was not content to leave the matter of projectile motion in such general terms. In his usual manner, he attempted to translate the relationship of time, motion, and distance into geometric terms, resolving the flight of the shot in terms of the force of the powder which gave it such violent motion, the inertia which a moving body was known to possess, the resistance to flight imposed by the medium through which it moved, and the attraction exerted on the bullet by gravity. All of these are expressed in a single sheet, more carefully prepared and better written than most of his other rough notes. It is very likely that this sheet is an early draft of the formal presentation of his ideas on the shooting of ordnance for Ralegh.[31] The sheet is reproduced as Figure 10a.

The gradus terminus [final stage] of motion I call ab, there is a time that ~~that~~ [c.o.] it moueth a space aequall to the line ac, so that in the same time it made a space abdc. In the same time if the motion be vniformiter crescent [constantly increasing], de is knowne which [I] propose to be aequall to cd. In ~~the time &~~ s [c.o.] space of ac the degree of motion is ce In the space of AF the degree is FH.

The question is what wold be the degree of motion if in the same time & the same space it shold moue equally.

Deuide fh in two aequall partes in the poynte i & make vp the parallelogramme akif, then ak shold be the degree in respecte of the first degree ab; to moue the space af in the same time as it did before diformiter.

If you will deuide the space moued diformiter by aequall time or accordinge to any other proportion of times you must devide ~~the you must devide~~ [c.o.] the trapeze or quadrangle bafh according to that proportion, by the doctrine of Bagdedimus, Comandinus, or Stevius.

I propose ac to be the line of leuell: the angle dac the angle of greatest random which is about 45 degrees so that the line abc would be continually crooked till it came to c; after if the motion did continue it wold be right as ce & perpendicular to ac the horizon. Now I say because of the bulletes gravity the crooked line is made. If the gravity be abstracted the motion wold be only in the right line ad; & if the resistance of the ayre or medium be abstracted, his motion would be infinitely onward.

On the obverse of this sheet (Fig. 10b), Harriot continued to wrestle with the problem of the various forces at work on the moving projectile:[32]

---

[31] Ibid., fo. 30[r].   [32] Ibid., fo. 30[v].

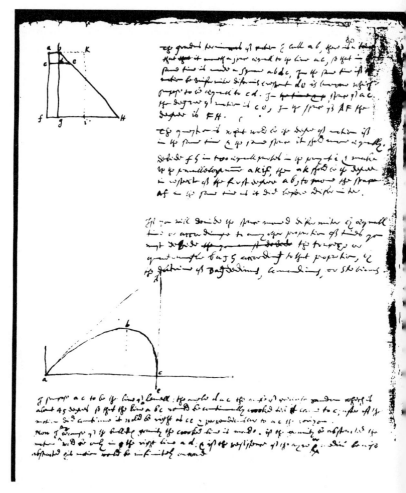

Fig. 10a Notes on Trajectories (1)

Any thinge being quiet when it begins to moue because if is moued by
a cause; that beginning is moued non gradua [not in equal steps]; but
the vis [moving force] be it material or immateriall ~~but~~ [c.o.] must be
of some degree; & the Mobile must beginne with the same degree;
which may be of diuerse quantities; in this diagram I mean it ab. & that
degree is aequall to same degree of the increase ab [cd] &c.

Two diagrams inserted here are apparently mathematical
explorations of the ratios between the *vis* or applied force

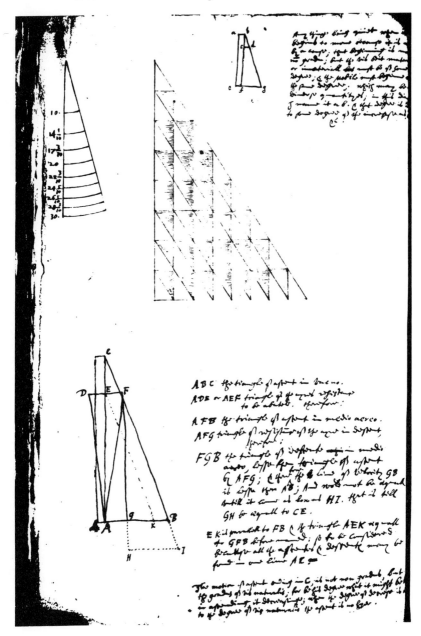

Fig. 10b Notes on Trajectories (2)

and the motion which it generates. One shows a straight-line progression between triangles, shaded for force and unshaded for motion. The other shows a relationship between force and motion in which the motion appears to be logarithmic. Neither is explained.

Yet Harriot is still intrigued to find a geometric explanation of the resolution of forces acting on the missile. The bottom of this sheet carries a further diagram and explanation:

ABC the triangle of ascent in vacuo
ADE of AEF triangle of ayres resistance to be abated. therefore:
AFB the triangle of ascent in medio aereo.
AFG triangle of resistance of the ayre in descent, therefore:
FGB the triangle of the descente this [c.o.] in medio aereo, lesse the triangle of ascent by AFG; and therefore the line of velocity GB is lesse then AB; And wold not be aequall vntill it come as low as HI. that is till GH be aequall to CE.
EK is parallell to FB & the triangle AEK aequall to GFB before named: so to be considered because all the ascentes & descentes may be found in one line AC

The motion of ascent ending in C. is not non gradus, but the gradus of vis naturalis; for be his degree what it might be [while] in ascending is decreasinge; when the degree of decrease is ae[quall] to the degree of vis naturalis the ascent is no hyer.

This is as close as he comes to the explanation of the forces at work on the moving projectile. Harriot recognized that the resistance of the medium operated to slow the bullet throughout its course, both in ascent and descent. The horizontal component of moving force gave it its forward motion; the vertical component its elevation. And the natural force of gravity gradually slowed the climb of the bullet until at the point where the vertical compound reached zero, the bullet was at its highest point in the trajectory. It was then obvious that in its fall, it was gravity which operated to accelerate the descent to the point of maximum force at impact.

With the completion of this report of his 'notes of ordinance', Harriot finished his work on ballistics in the 1590s. But the problems of projectile motion continued to intrigue him, and scattered among these early papers are a large number of later attempts to resolve these problems. Some of these later jottings are done on the earlier notes; others are on separate sheets or series of sheets interpolated among them. But it is easy to distinguish his early studies from the later ones: the writing is much darker, evidently done in India ink rather than gall, and the distinctive change in the form of his letter 'E' (which occurred in late 1606) makes separation simple.

In the intervening years, Harriot continued to keep abreast of new studies of projectiles. To the studies of range which he had earlier used from Bourne and the Spaniard Luys Collado,[33] he added the later studies of Alessandro Capo Bianco[34] which he probably procured in the 1602 edition. All of these furnished data for Harriot's consideration, a resolution of the forces acting on a projectile. One set of calculations dealt with the matter of velocity: in each Harriot used geometric methods to solve his problems. One[35] he heads: 'The velocity of a diagonall oblique, supposed aequall to the vpright'. A second[36] reads: 'Of velocities. The rate of two velocityes with there angles of random being geuen, to find the horizontall velocity & that of the vpright'. (In this instance, part of the 'E's are of the early sort, part of the later, which would indicate a probable date of 1606.) And another,[37] 'The rate of two velocityes geuen, to find the others, &c'. In all these, Harriot was groping with the problems of vector analysis, and very closely approaching the correct solution of the problems he had posed for himself.

Perhaps more importantly, in these additions to his early study, Harriot clearly came to the conclusion that the course of a projectile was parabolic. A series of rough notes headed 'To proue the perabola a speciall way. Good.'[38] or 'To proue

---

[33] Harriot's note on 'The experimentes of Luys Collado a spaniard' (with some interpolations from Bourne) are in Petworth House HMC 241/VIa, fo. 11. They are taken from either his *Practica manuale di arteglieria; nella quale si tratta della inuentione di essa, dell'ordine di condurla, & piantarla sotto a qualunque fortezza...* Venetia, 1586 (Thomas Digges's copy, dated 1588, is in the British Library), or his *Platical Manual de Artilleria, en la quae se tracta de la excelencia de el arte militar...* Milan, 1592.

[34] In his studies of velocities, Harriot compares the range statistics of Capo Bianco with those of Bourne in Petworth House HMC/VIa, fo. 4. The Capo Bianco work is undoubtedly the Alessandro Capo Bianco, *Corona e palma militare d'artiglieria, nella quale si tratto dell'inuentione di essa, e dell'operare nelle fettione di terra e mares...* Venice, 1598 and 1602.

[35] BL Add. MS 6789, fo. 31^r.

[36] Ibid., fo. 72^r.   [37] Ibid., fo. 32^r.   [38] Ibid., fo. 70^r.

the parabola vniuersally best.'[39] culminate in one sheet[40] with a diagram (Fig. 11) and text:

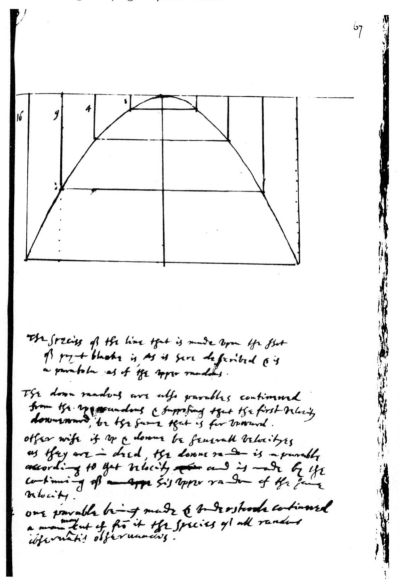

Fig. 11 Notes on Parabolic Motion

The species of the line that is made vpon the shot of poynt blanke is, as is here described & is a parabola as of the vpper randoms.

The down randoms are also parables continued from the vp randoms & supposing that the first velocity downeward, be the same that is for vpward.

Other wise if vp or downe be seuerall velocityes as they are in deed, the downe random is a parable according to that velocity and is made by the continuing of ~~an vppe~~ [c.o.] his vpper random of the same velocity. [See Fig. 11] One parable being made & vnderstood continued a man may cut of[f] from it the species of all randoms obseruatis obseruandos.

Like the velocity studies, these proofs of parabolic motion date from about 1607.

But Harriot was not content to deal wholly with theoretical consideration of these matters. During the 1590s it is apparent that he made a number of experiments in an attempt to solve some of the problems of mass, inertia, and gravity which in that day were almost totally clouded in mystery. Again, it is unfortunate that no text remains to explain just what he was doing, but from some of his rough drawings and sketches, it is possible to reconstruct at least some of his thinking, if not his actual procedures. One series of crude drawings[41] shows that he performed experiments involving the forces on weights resting on an inclined plane. These may well have been the practical experiments which led him to a consideration of the resolution of forces on a mass at different angles from the vertical.[42] Other drawings show him experimenting with the forces at work in centrifugal and centripetal forces in bullets connected to a rotating wheel by wires or threads.[43] One sheet, labelled 'Second Experimentes'[44] shows the great care with which Harriot used his troy balances to weigh his 'bullets', his 'wires', and his 'Thrids [threads]'. It was undoubtedly out of these experiments that Harriot became involved with the study of the resultant forces from the oblique impacts of elastic spheres which resulted in the only formal Latin explanation of theory completed by Harriot which remains for study, his *De reflexione corporum rotundorum, Poristica duo*.[45]

---

[39] Ibid., fo. 69^r.   [40] Ibid., fo. 67^r.   [41] Ibid., e.g. fos. 56^r and 83^r.
[42] Ibid., fo. 2^r.   [43] Ibid., fo. 83^r.   [44] Ibid., fo. 75^r.
[45] This study has been twice reprinted and analysed: first by Jon V. Pepper in 'Harriot's Manuscript on the Theory of Impacts', *Annals of Science*, XXXIII

But Harriot tried, also, to come to grips with the force exerted by the powder on the bullet to find some correlation between the *vis* and the *Mobile*. At the foot of the 'Second Experiments' sheet is the elementary data he obtained in a rough experiment to determine the force expended by the explosion of powder inside the cannon or musket. These notes read:

Experimented grossely, till better.

or $\frac{30}{32}$ graynes of powder in an inch.

2 graynes distant $\frac{1}{10}$ inch will fire one another, center from center.
2 graynes, at $\frac{1}{8}$ inch will not.
3 graynes less then $\frac{1}{10}$ distant do fire one $\frac{1}{8}$ inch distant.

My cube of 3 inches holdeth of corn powder) $13\frac{784}{1000}$ troy oz.

Pressed, it yeldeth but little in the pressing, not the $\frac{1}{20}$ parte by estimation.

A subsequent sheet, written perhaps a decade after these initial observations, carries on the calculations:[46]

A grayne of powder, $\frac{1}{30}$ of an inch.
It fyreth an other grayne laying $\frac{1}{10}$ ynch off, center from center.

The diameter of the sphere of fire $\frac{1}{30} + \frac{1}{60} = \frac{1}{60}$ [c.o.]

The semidiameter of the sphere of fire $\frac{1}{10} - \frac{1}{60}$

hoc est: $\frac{6}{60} - \frac{1}{60} = \frac{5}{60}$

The Diameter of fire. $\frac{10}{60}$.

(1976), 131–51; and secondly by Martin Kalmar, 'Thomas Hariot's De Reflexione Corporum Rotundorum: An Early Solution to the Problem of Impact', *Archive for History of Exact Sciences*, XVI (1977), 201–30. Kalmar gives a more complete analysis of the work than Pepper. Unfortunately, however, he did not work from Harriot's original MS, Petworth House, HMC 241/VIa, fos. 23–31, reprinted by Pepper. He used instead a copy made some years after Harriot's death, and now in BL Harley MS 6002, fos. 16v–21, which has some few additions, but is not, of course, as accurate as the original.
[46] BL Add. MS 6789, fo. 86v.

The Diameter of a
  grayne of powder) $\dfrac{2}{60}$.

Therefore:
  The rate of the sphere of fire to the sphere of powder as
  125, to: 1.

Another rough note at the foot of this second page shows that this was added at Syon House: 'The depth of the water in Syon Cestorne. $40\frac{1}{2}$ ynches'.

But in spite of his ingenuity and care in performing his experiments on bullets and trajectories, Harriot made an unimaginative mistake which caused him to waste several years of his life in futile experiments on mass and the nature of matter. Somehow, he could not force himself to abandon the Aristotelian position that heavier bodies fell at a faster rate than lighter ones. Though he was willing to assume that a body in motion would continue in motion indefinitely if there were not air resistance, he would not accept resistance of the medium as the cause of differing rates of fall. As Galileo was later to do, Harriot began his experiments by dropping bullets from a height. To solve his problem, he needed to know either the time it took for a falling body to traverse a known distance, or to measure the distance it would fall in an established time. Lack of a suitably accurate timing device made the former procedure difficult, though he could, as he had done in previous experiments utilize his own pulse as counting seconds. For the latter, he could attempt to measure differences in rate of fall by dropping two bodies simultaneously and measuring (or estimating) the distance between them at the moment of impact. Harriot used both means. One of his earliest experiments, in the very early 1590s, was with musket balls.[47] At this time he recorded the following data, probably from the leads of Durham House, London:

A musket ball of lead
  Semidiameter. $\frac{3}{4}$ inch. weyeth: 24 pennyweyt.
  Diameter. $\frac{11}{16}$ inch. weyt. $18\frac{1}{2}$ oz. 8 gr.
Pistol [ball].
  Diam. $\frac{1}{2}$ inch. weyt $7\frac{1}{2}$ penny.

[47] Ibid., fo. 76^r.

A bullet is falling $55\frac{1}{2}$ feet $2\frac{1}{2}''$.
   More then 2 pulses.
   Lesse then 3 pulses.
Tryed by 20 bullets one after an other.

Following this simple experiment, still in the 1590s after his move to Syon House, Harriot proceeded to test the difference of rates of fall, dropping different materials from the leads of the main house, a distance which he measured as 43 feet 3 inches from the ground. From the data he recorded, it is obvious that he was linking the rate of fall with the composition of the falling body, and was seeking a mathematical relationship between the mass of the material and the material's eagerness to seek its natural position in the Aristotelian scheme of place. Again, one of his earliest experiments in this was recorded as follows:[48]

> Experimentes in a cleare & calme day from the
> leades. of high. $43\frac{1}{4}$ foote. or 43 $\frac{25}{100}$ f.

In the fall:
lead & ~~cole~~ [c.o.] cherecole. 6 & 9 foote a sunder.)
lead & ~~wax~~ [c.o.] red wax. $\frac{1}{2}$ & 1 foote.   ) aboue 20 trialles.
lead & Iron. Scarce sensible difference.   )
lead & half empty tobacco box of firre. — 9 foote.

$\begin{matrix} 20 \\ 18. \end{matrix}$ cole = 1. leade.
8. wax = 1. leade.
3. iron = 1. leade.
   lead & water about a foote asunder for that high
   tried about 20 times though difficultly.
   remember to try agayne.

From these practical experiments, Harriot proceeded to seek a formula which would account for the difference in rate of fall and permit him to predict the falling rate of different materials. The standard against which he measured the rates of fall was the time required for a lead ball to drop the 43.25 feet from the Syon leads to the ground. Naturally, he was interested in discovering the ratio of the mass of other substances with that of his lead standard. This led Harriot to an elaborate experimental programme of determining the

[48] Ibid., fo. 75[r].

density of materials, which he started by weighing known volumes and comparing them against his standards. Shortly, however, Harriot saw the relationship between density and specific gravity, and used the short cut of the principles of Archimedes, weighing his substance in air, then in water, and from the difference in the two weighings, determining the specific gravity or density of the unknown. However, instead of using the density of water as 1 as is done today, Harriot used 1,000, so that his calculations give a modern specific gravity reading to three decimal places. The accuracy of his working can be seen by comparing modern readings with those of one of his earlier lists.[49]

[Harriot's Observations]		[Modern Readings]	
Aurum	19,135	Gold	19.3–19.4
Argentum Vivum	13,554	Quicksilver	14.193
Plumbum nigrum	11,351	Lead (black)	11.3437
Argentum	10,529	Silver	10.492
Bismutum	9,755	Bismuth	9.78–9.86
Aes	8,795	Bronze	8.80
Orichalcum	8,529–8,728	Brass	8.47–8.86
Ferrum	7,757	Iron	7.86
Chalbys	7,785	Steel	7.76–7.87
Stannum	7,297	Tin	7.30
Aqua	1,000	Water	1.00
Crystallum	2,650	Fuzed Quartz(?)	2.20

Harriot next attempted to find the mathematical formula which would explain their differing rates of fall, basing it on these relative specific gravities. In so doing, he recognized it necessary to compensate for the displacement of air by the falling bodies so as not to distort the relationship between matter and place. He started, therefore, with a geometric figure (see Fig. 12) which might illustrate the relationship between a mass of lead and a similar mass of another substance (here he began with red wax, which he determined to have a density one-eighth that of lead).[50]

The proportion of ayre to lead by red wax.
8 of red wax is aequall to 1 of leade.
In the same time that lead falleth 43 $\frac{25}{100}$ feet; (f)

---

[49] BL Add. MS 6788, fo. 113^r. Modern values are from a recent edition of *A Handbook of Physics and Chemistry*.
[50] BL Add. MS 6788, fo. 144^v.

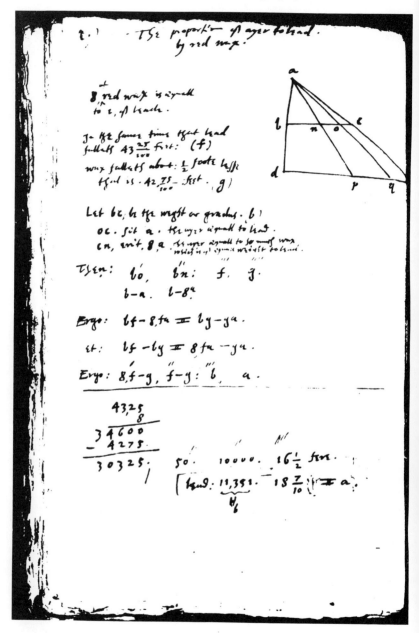

Fig. 12 Calculation of the Rate of Fall

Wax falleth about $\frac{1}{2}$ foote lesse, that is
$42\frac{75}{100}$ feet. (g)
Let bc. be the weght or gradus. (b)
   oc sit a. the ayre aequall to lead.
   cn. erit 8, a the ayre aequall to so much wax
        which is of aequall weight of lead.

	$'$	$''$	$'''$	$''\,''$
Then:	bo,	bn	:	f g.

      b − a. b − 8a
Ergo: bf − 8, fa = bg − ga.
Et   bf − by = 8, fa − ga.

        $'$ $''$ $'\,''$ $''\,''$
Ergo 8,f − g, f − g: b, a.

Translated into modern terms, these equations would read as
follows:

Let a = the density of air;
   b = the density of lead;
   c = the density of test material (red wax);
   f = the distance lead will fall in a certain time; and
   g = the distance the test material will fall in the same time.

Then, $b - a : b - \dfrac{b}{c} . a = f : g.$

Into this equation, Harriot substituted the densities he had
determined: 54.4 for a, the density of air; 11.351 for b,
density of lead; and for the unknowns c he substituted 7.757
for iron, 1.108 for red wax, and 2.650 for crystal. By these
equations, then, he calculated that iron would fall $\frac{1}{10}$ of a
foot behind the lead; red wax would fall $33\frac{24}{100}$ inches behind
lead; water would be $2\frac{16}{100}$ feet behind; ivory, $19\frac{9}{100}$ feet
behind lead in air, and $12\frac{4}{100}$ inches behind lead falling
through water.

The steps by which Harriot arrived at his equations are
not clear, but it is apparent that the distances he calculated
were close enough to those he observed that he felt confident
that he was close to the solution of the prediction of rate of
fall. A decade later, he was to return to these formulas in
determining theoretically the trajectories of bullets fired at
different randoms,[51] but for the time being he turned to the
study of even more fundamental matters.

   [51] These calculations are to be found in BL Add. MS 6788, fos. 145^V, 146^V,
147^V, and 148^V.

Obviously Harriot's study of densities led him back again to reconsider the basic theories of the nature of matter. The clue to his thinking is contained in the same memorandum to himself in which he mentioned his 'notes of ordinance'[52] as he reminds himself to study 'The properties of the four elementes'. Without a doubt this was taken by Harriot to be one of his most serious scientific explorations. He prepared himself meticulously for it; he gave his full time and attention to the investigation; and since he considered it a fundamental and critical exploration which might have permanent significance, he recorded, for the first time, the date and time of each step of his long investigation of the four Aristotelian elements of earth, water, air, and fire. But in delving into this new round of investigations, Harriot was entering a new kind of experimental world — the arcane and cabalistic intellectual morass of the early chemical world of alchemy.

It is very difficult for the modern student to respond sympathetically to the doctrines and philosophies of the early dabblers in chemistry, the alchemists and pharmacists in particular. Whereas we are concerned with the composition of substances and the transformations that they may undergo, the first students of the art were wholly taken up by consideration of three aspects of matter — the matter, form, and spirit. Yet these words had meanings different from ours today. We would hold iron and sulphur to be different kinds of matter, but to Aristotle and his followers they were of the same matter, but of different form. And each had a 'spirit' — a *pneuma* or breath — which still remained in it from the time of its original creation from the initial chaos (*massa confusa*) by the divine God as he separated light from darkness and the heavens from the earth. According to Aristotle, the act of creation brought forth four elemental substances, two visible and two invisible: the visible elements, earth and water, were heavy and tended by nature to fall; the invisible elements, air and fire, were light and by nature inclined to rise. All sublunary nature, the earth and the atmosphere below the moon, was composed of these four elements; all

[52] One of the simplest and clearest surveys of the history of alchemy is that of F. Sherwood Taylor, *The Alchemists, Founders of Modern Chemistry*, New York, Henry Shuman, 1949.

above the moon, the planets, stars, and celestial heavens were composed of an even more perfect fifth element called the *quintessence*, a bit of which remaining in all sublunary substances was the vital force or *pneuma* which was their active principle.

Since the creative act had subjected the original *massa confusa* to tremendous heats and pressures, it was natural that the four elements retained in their forms some of these qualities which had caused them. These qualities of form, again four in number and contrary in type, were hot and cold, moist and dry. These qualities were related to the four elements in a simple, logical way:

Element	Qualities	Natural Place	Symbol
Earth	cold and dry	centre of the earth	▽̵
Water	cold and moist	surface of the earth	▽
Air	hot and moist	above the earth	△̵
Fire	hot and dry	next to the heavens	△

Pure substances of these elements did not exist, at least within the range of earth and atmosphere in which man lived and worked. But all material things that man could observe contained some quantities of all of them, the difference in the proportion determining the physical characteristics which could be observed and tested. Colours, tastes, odours, degrees of hardness or fluidity — all of these were caused by interaction of the qualities of the elements involved in the material, the pure elements themselves being colourless, odourless, and as tasteless as rainwater (which was the closest to elemental form they knew) showed.

During the period between Aristotle and St. Thomas in the thirteenth century, a number of additions to these theories had been made. Most of these were logical extensions of the idea of symmetry and harmony in the universe. For example, it was logical to develop the association between the seven known planets and the seven identified metals:

Metal	Planet	Symbol
Gold	Sol	☉
Silver	Luna	☽
Copper	Venus	♀
Iron	Mars	♂
Quicksilver	Mercury	☿

Metal	Planet	Symbol
Lead	Saturn	♄
Tin	Jupiter	♃

Aristotle had theorized that all metals had been formed in the creation by two 'exhalations' or vapours — one moist, one dry or smokey — that come from the earth. Later alchemists associated these two vapours with specific substances: the dry vapour with sulphur and the moist vapour with quicksilver. Gradually this idea was expanded to embrace the theory that all metals were combinations of sulphur and quicksilver. This being deemed true, it seemed totally logical that by applying the same forces that had been in play during the creative process — heat, cold, pressure — the proportion of the qualities might be changed in the metal, the form of another metal superimposed, and the result would be the transmutation of one metal for another. It was just as logical that the use of proper chemical processes could transform mercury to gold or silver as that such processes could change metallic iron to a red, powdery substance.

Since such change in form would necessitate alteration of the vital principle or *pneuma* (which was, of course, related to the *quintessence* of the heavens), it logically evolved that the chemical processes which might be used in such transformation were related to the signs which marked the zodiac of heavenly bodies. And since there were a dozen zodiacal signs, it necessarily followed that there would be twelve chemical processes available in the search for either the transforming or perfecting of matter.

Process		Sign	Symbol
Calcination	Application of heat	Aries	♈
Congelation	Crystallizing, freezing	Taurus	♉
Fixation	Reducing volatile spirits to permanent form	Gemini	♊
Solution	Dissolving a solid by use of fluid or solvent	Cancer	♋
Digestion	Dissolving in gentle heat	Leo	♌
Distillation	Distillation	Virgo	♍
Sublimation	Converting solid substance to vapour by use of heat which resolidifies upon cooling	Libra	♎

Separation	Process of analysis or extraction	Scorpio	♍
Ceration	Softening of a hard substance	Sagittarius	♐
Fermentation	Fermentation	Capricornus	♉
Multiplication	Alchemical increase of volume	Aquarius	♒
Projection	Casting of the powder of the philosophers stone on a metal to effect its transmutation into gold	Pisces	♓

These, then, were the basic chemical theories and processes which were current at the time Harriot began his experimentation with the elements. Most unfortunately, the world of chemistry had evolved from and been dominated by the disciples of alchemy, most of whom were more interested in the search for gold for worldly riches rather than for scientific knowledge. These men considered the art of alchemy to be the recovery of a lost art of the ancients; they had not been interested in discovering new methods of investigation, but were attempting to reinterpret the writings of the great masters of the past. Most of these ancients and their followers had concealed their writings under false names, usually taking names of mystic antiquity, such as Democritus, Moses, Cleopatra, Hermes, Aquinas, Roger Bacon, or Raymond Lull. And in accordance with their traditions, usually called Hermetic, they expounded their doctrines not for clarity but by hidden allusion, symbolic pictures, intentionally vague poetry, mystic codes, or allegory. Almost never did they present a straightforward account of the materials or processes with which they performed their reputed miracles, nor did they attempt to share their findings openly with other alchemists. The stock in trade of the alchemist was mystery and deceit, and though there must have been in all ages a few clerks or scholars who were seeking knowledge, they remained hidden and unknown and, because of the economic importance of their craft, they were not interested in publishing their work for others to use. It is distressing to the student of the present age of relatively open science that Harriot, like his contemporaries, inherited the Hermetic traditions of secrecy and concealment along with their early chemistry.

Because he followed this tradition, Harriot's experiments on 'the properties of the four elementes' seem almost impossible to interpret. In all of his elaborate chemical experiments during 1599 and 1600 there is no place where he expresses his purpose or goal; nowhere does he summarize his progress, nowhere does he indicate why he is doing what he is doing; and nowhere does he give any conclusion as to what he has found or failed to find. And when these time-consuming experiments finally end, they terminate abruptly with no explanation of why, and Harriot turns to the studies which they had interrupted in the refraction of light. Yet it is obvious that Harriot took these experiments most seriously. They are clearly dated and the bare processes are listed with care and accuracy.[53]

If Harriot was trying to isolate the pure elements, as seems likely, he was actually involved in the processes of alchemy, since the alchemist, too, was attempting to purify metals which had become corrupted in order to bring them to full perfection. Details of their basic operations were fairly simple, though the recorded observations seem vague and confused. And since their reputed successes could never be repeated (since they were themselves imaginary or falsified), accounts of their methods and recorded observations were often highly imaginative. But essentially, the alchemist worked with the two substances believed to be basic to all metals, including the most perfect metal they sought, gold. These were mercury or quicksilver which they considered the essence of all metals, and whose mercurial form could most easily be changed, and sulphur, which gave its distinctive red colour to the quicksilver in the creation of pure gold. And since all metals, including the baser imperfect ones, were composed of these two basic substances and with differing qualities of heat, cold, moisture, or dryness, the laboratory process involved changing the lesser metals to the perfection of the perfect gold by adjusting their qualities

---

[53] Harriot's chemical notes are widely scattered and disorganized. Many are rough jottings of multiple weighings. But more than fifty observations are given dates and place of observation with enough detail that some indication of his activity may be obtained. The major Terra papers are among the MSS at Pet-

through the application of the known chemical processes. Most commonly, this began with the use of heat, starting with infrequent applications of low heats, and gradually increasing the frequency and intensity as the glowing metal came closer to perfection. It was in the final stages of intense heat, when success was almost achieved, and when the metal was glowing red in an almost golden hue, that most alchemical experiments failed — usually through failure of the imperfect glass vessels in which the 'distillation' or transmutation was taking place. But should the alchemical process work to destroy all the impurities in the base element and to restore the correct balance of the basic elements and qualities of the original creation, this newly refined 'gold' became the 'Philosopher's Stone', and by its perfection had the power to transform other base metals to the pristine perfection of itself.

To trace the changes in the purification process and its progress toward perfection, the alchemist closely observed every stage in the transformation of his materials. Any emanation of gas or liquid was carefully noted, and changes in colour were particularly important in the measurement of progress. Authorities, naturally, varied as to the exact details of the progression, but in general it was decreed that the most corrupt dross first to be eliminated lay in the range of black or gray, proceeded through a gamut of silver hues into a final rainbow effect generally referred to as the 'Peacock's tail', from which it emerged into the range of reds, culminating in the intense red marking the creation of the final perfect product. How Harriot felt that he might proceed through such transitional stages to the evolution of the even more basic elements of earth, water, air, and fire is difficult to imagine, but it may well be that such purification was felt to be within the power of the 'Philosopher's stone' to accomplish.

Harriot began his chemical studies in late April 1599, by getting his apparatus together for his experiments. By 1 May he had collected twenty-six glass vessels, had catalogued them by alphabetical letter, and had recorded accurate charts of their dimensions and the exact weight of water each would

---

worth, HMC 241/IV, pp. 25-9. The remainder are in BL Add. MS 6788, scattered between folios 368 and 413.

hold.[54] He even recorded data on the lamps he would use to inject heat for his trials:[55]

The content of my lampes.
The diameter of the base of the cylinder .3. inches.
The Hight [of] the cylinder .3$\frac{5}{8}$ vel. 3 $\frac{62}{100}$

and the placement of the lamps including their height from the earth.[56] To protect his glass vessels from breaking from continued exposure to heat, Harriot 'luted' the bases by smearing them with a kind of fire clay, taking them in order: A, B, C, D, E, F, first,[57] and H and I later.[58] With these preparations Harriot was ready to begin his experiments.

On Wednesday, 2 May 1599, having selected vessel H for the purpose, Harriot began his first experiment, starting with the heaviest element Terra. His account of this experiment is preserved among the manuscripts now at Petworth House,[59] (see Figure 13), and reads as follows:

The Nip [sealing and luting of the vessel] was at 12^h$\frac{1}{2}$ [12:30 p.m.]
The imposition was at 4^h$\frac{1}{4}$ after noone, the 2 of may being Wednesday .1599. at what time the matter lay as aboue.
As hy as the line a about the place where the glasse beginneth to narrow there were sweating drops at the imposition, but all clear aboue.
At 6^h there were some brode scales of dew & lay betwixte a and b.
At 7^h ther was a fine misty dew of siluer color vp to the line b. rounde about which is the very place that the copper pan did circulate or compresse, because I found it of the same measure.
At 8^h I found a sensible fine dewe as hy as c which is about an inch & a half hyer then b. with some of the hyest parte turning into some bigger drops.
At what time I noted two drops, one south, & the other west, within $\frac{1}{2}$ inch of the matter.
At 10^h the west drop was growne to be longe & parallele to the matter & now tuch.
Next ther was a drop within half an inch of the matter & an other h.11 East. NE ther was a drop bigger then his fellowes an inch & $\frac{1}{2}$

[54] See, e.g. BL Add. MS 6788, fo. 413^r (30 Apr. 1599) and fo. 391^r (4 May 1599).
[55] Ibid., fo. 380^r.
[56] Ibid., fo. 394^r. It is possible that this dates from 1600, since it shows four experiments, and all the remaining papers from 1599 cover only two. But the placement was undoubtedly the same or very similar.
[57] Ibid., fo. 380^v.   [58] Ibid., fo. 381^v.
[59] Petworth House, HMC 241/IV, fo. 29.

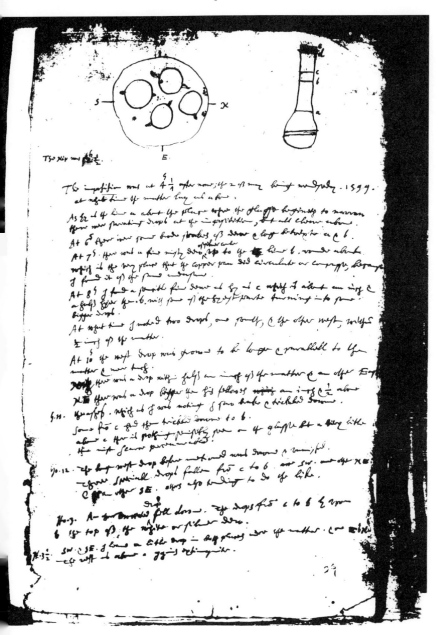

Fig. 13 The Imposition of Terra

aboue the ashes. which as I was noting I saw brake & trickled downe. some from c had then trickled downe to b.

aboue c ther is nothing sensibly seen on the glasse but a very little thin mist scarce perceivable.

h.12 The long west drop before mentioned was downe & running fell. Three speciall drops falled from c to b one SW and other NE. & an other SE. others also tending to do the like.

Ho.3 An other drop fell down. The drops from c to b ly vpon the top of the white or siluer dew.

Ho. $3\frac{1}{2}$ SW & SE. I found a litle drop in both places nere the matter. & one E b[y] N. The rest is aboue. Ignis extinguitus.

Though he had obviously been up most of the night watching the effect of heat on his Terra experiment, Harriot was up again in the morning, ready to continue.[60]

Terra. May 3 ♃.

At 10 of the clocke in the morning I found all in the same forme as I lefte it. The drops betwene c & b as before. The siluer or milky dew betwixt b & a also. but all the lower region vnder a which before was full of sprinkled great drops liying & sticking as it seemed vnapte to be vanished in any short time were now all gone. & a cleare glasse.

The afore sayd easterly drops were also cleare gone.

Now only appearing vnder the lute S a round drop like a buble.

SE 4 copper drops one hyer then an other. W. some small drops. NW a great drop. else all vnder the verge of the lute it is sene cleare.

The observations of these first two days are typical of the many that were to follow. Twenty-five such detailed notations remain, eighteen in May (4, 5, 8, 9, 11, 13 (2), 15, 18, 22, 24 (2), 25, 26, 27, 28, 29, and 30) and seven in June (7, 9, 13, 19, 20, and 25). It is obvious that the experimentation was being done at Syon, since Harriot twice indicates visits to London (5 to 8 May and 18 to 22 May). As was customary, the application of heat which started slowly and with low intensity gradually increased in pace. By 13 June it had reached the intense stage where from 13 to 17 June, Harriot alternated ten hours of intense heat with ten hours of cooling, day and night, without a break. Following this activity, Harriot left for London, with no indication that anyone at Syon continued the experiment. On his return on 25 June he noted no changes. His record reads:[61]

June 25 .☽. I returned. I saw no sensible difference.

[60] Ibid. fo. 27.   [61] Ibid., fo. 25.

> ho. 2pm I gave fire for an hour, in which time nothing did ascend.
> but two houres after a very sensible dew was in the lower region.

This is the last entry remaining, and since it appears in the middle of a sheet of notes, it is undoubtedly the last record of the Terra experiments in 1599. It is possible that Harriot had lost interest; it is more likely that he had come to the conclusion that this particular experiment had failed and further work on it would be fruitless, as all his work to this time had been.

The process itself, as we have seen, seems to have been relatively straightforward once it was started. But the evidence remaining leaves many interesting questions unresolved. What were the materials which were put into flask H before it was sealed? What significance did the orientation of the flask have, both in regard to its contents and to the observed drops and dews? Just what are the four circles shown on the surface and the small ears that protrude from them? What changes was Harriot looking for, and in which portions or in what matter in the flask?

From the wording of the observations, some clues can be obtained to some of these vexing questions. The four surface vessels are repeatedly referred to as lapis or lapides, the Latin 'stone'. This is a word sometimes used to represent the 'Philosopher's stone', or it may signify something with the qualities of a catalyst in the experiment. These four stones or dishes were evidently floating on a base of mercury or quicksilver, since on 18 May Harriot records:[62] 'I left the Northerly lapis appearing somewhat aboue the superficies of the ☿ [the symbol for mercury] & somewhat dry.' But, as might be expected from alchemical theory, it also appears that the lapides themselves were not stone, but were made of sulphur, the second essential base for all metals. On May 22, Harriot observed:[63] 'I found the Northerly sulphur to haue a reddish ring about that which appeared aboue the ☿ & within it somewhat whitish yellow.' Three days later he notes:[64] 'vpon this sublimation I found a ringe of whitish matter about the reddish verge of the sulphur in the ☿ ', with

---

[62] Ibid., fo. 28.   [63] Ibid., fo. 28.   [64] Ibid., fo. 28.

a marginal note that 'the other 3 lapides appeared aboue the superficies of the ☿ as the other had don.'

This conjunction of sulphur and mercury together with the processes which could affect the qualities which affected the form of metals shows Harriot to be working in the traditional way of the alchemists of his day. Like them, too, he was most interested in recording any changes which might indicate an alteration in the subjects of his experiments. He particularly notes changes in the mercury, the sulphur lapides, or any emanation which might deposit on the flask, its nature, extent, exact location, whether rising or falling, and especially its colour. Hence he records 'a fine misty dew' and '4 copper drops': (May 3); 'small springled drops' (May 5); 'I found the Northern sulphur to have a reddish ring about it which appeared aboue the ☿ & within in a somewhat whitish yellow' (May 22); 'A ringe of whitish matter about the reddish verge of the sulphur in the ☿' (May 25); 'all the lapides be closer together by much then at the imposition' and 'the lapides are sensibly bigger' (May 27). Even more drastic results were observed on 30 May:[65]

I find the NE side of the North ☉ [symbol for the sun or gold; possibly a lapis] a little condensed or solid white matter vpon the superficies but close to the sulphur which [c.o.] I thinke it to be one of the poles of the Sphaera ☉ because I cannot now descerne any other but if it be he is out of his place he was at first by farre.

It was probably this definite reaction which led Harriot to enter a period of intensive burning which congealed the mercury and cracked the sulphur before he gave up the experiment with a final negative observation on Monday, 25 June.

On Friday, 4 May 1599, two days after he began his experiment on Terra, Harriot started a second one labelled 'Aqua'.[66] This started off with the same enthusiasm and detail as did Terra. Like the earlier one, it began:

May .4. ☿ . [Friday] 1599   In Aqua F.
The just nip was $2^h\frac{1}{2}$
    The imposition into Aqua was hora $6\frac{1}{2}$. And because I found the
    solfer in terra worke so fast I tooke finer necke & prest also the
    ashes harder about the glasse.

[65] Ibid., fo. 26.   [66] BL Add. MS 6788, fo. 403ʳ.

h 7a   I was able sensibly to perceaue a litle thin mist in the region of ab. as for that of ag it was full of small drops as in the other but all the other regions cleare.

8a   It was then more sensible in the region of ab & also I might distinctly find the terme of the other region to c with a little thinner mist/

9a   The regions of cb & ba thicker of dew.

10a   The region of ba beginnes in diuers plases to appeare milky or siluer coloured. & vpon the line c diuerse greater drops round about aboue being nothing but cleareness in sense.

$11\frac{1}{2}$ The former regions somewhat thicker. I noted before some small drops in the verge of lute but set them not downe till now because they were but small.

West, one. N. 2. not far asonder. NE a big one. S a litle one. SW 2 greate ones nere to solfer redy to fall.

One of the greate drops fell which was SW & the other remayning, but seeming as though he wold fall.

Ignis extinguitus

I left all the flat wet drops lying in the line c hauing not fallen to the limbe of the next region as they did in Terra. The siluer mist is notable apparent but not so great as that was in terra.

The region of dc I left seeming cleare.

And before I departed the NE drop was also gone. The rest remayned.

Following the start of this second experiment, Harriot continued to observe the Aqua flask, recording evidences of dews and drops on 5 and 8 May. He recorded the date of 9 May, but made no notes and then left this experiment completely alone until the 9 June when he recorded:[67]

June .9. ♄ . I neuer gaue fire since the first time. I now espied the ☿ in diuerse places about the sulphurs to be congealed. The sulphurs are appearing aboue the superficies of the ☿, & all of them in notable appearance & evident; as it hath long before. The low region hath had a dew this 15 or 16 dayes past & doth continew.

On 13 June, forty days after imposition, Harriot 'gaue fire' for ten hours:[68] 'In which time the ☿ grew clearer and clearer & the sulphurs in the end palishe & the westerly some what dry at the top.' On the 19th he fired again for ten hours, and the next day reported that the sulphur lapides had risen above the surface of the mercury, the south-westerly somewhat flattened, the other three rounded. Once again he went to London for five days. On his return he 'found the coppes

[67] Ibid., fo. 402ʳ.   [68] Ibid.

shrunke away, else no difference',[69] and with seeming diffidence gave fire to both Aqua and Terra for one hour (his last record of the Terra experiment), but observed no sensible effect in either. The following day, Tuesday, 26 June, he records at noon that[70] 'I gaue fire till 8/ that is for 8 houres. There is no observation of any effect. . .' and this is the final entry regarding his experiments for 1599, which end not with a bang, but a whimper.

But Harriot did not give up easily. The following spring, at six o'clock in the morning of 15 April 1600, he was again at the task of weighing the same chemical flasks, recording weighings for A, B, C, D, E, F, G, H, I, K, L, M, N, O, P, Q, R, S, T, V, X, Y, Z, a, b, c, d, e, f, g, h, i, and k.[71] The next day he cryptically records the start of a new series of experiments:[72]

Terra.

Glasse. Q.

Coles. 7^h. 6'. mane. [in the morning]

Nipped hor. $7\frac{1}{2}$

Imposition in terram. hor. 11^h. 30'. AM.

The following day, Thursday, 17 April, he started another:

Aer.

Vas. C.

Imposition in Aerem.

hora. $11\frac{1}{4}$. A.

Sine aqua.

Nipped. ho. $7\frac{1}{4}$.

hora. 11^h. 0.

extracto.

With this experiment he began his record of observations:[73]

De aere.   I gaue no fire the first day. There were no drops nor dew at the imposition. Wer all dry till fire came as hereafter.

and proceeded to record firing from 9 a.m. to 4 p.m. on 18 April, noting dews and drops at noon, 2:00, 2:30, and 4:00 p.m.

On 22 April, Harriot began Aqua in vase E,[74] nipping at

[69] Ibid.

[70] BL Add. MS, fo. 401^r and Petworth 241/IV, fo. 25.

[71] BL Add. MS. 6788, fo. 393^r.

[72] Ibid., fo. 369^r.   [73] Ibid., fo. 368^r.   [74] Ibid., fo. 384^v.

7:30 a.m., making imposition at 12:10 p.m., but not firing. By this time, Harriot had all four elemental experiments under way at the same time — the first time for which a record remains. He then began to make his observational records only when he felt he saw significant changes, recording all four experiments on the same form, much more succinctly than in his earlier notes. On 25 April, however, Harriot began a new experiment on Aqua, which he labelled 'In plase of the other Aqua because cracked'.[75] On 30 April he recorded:[76] 'Bulla ♂ [sign of Mars or the metal iron] began in euery glasse to appeare. No fire since the first day', with a superimposed note that 'Aer had no fire in the first day but the second.' He then proceeded to give moderate heat for a quarter, half an hour, or an hour on 5, 6, 7, and 8 May and, since the lapides appeared to be drying, spared fire on the 9th. On 10 May he changed to intense heat on Terra for nine hours, and the other three for three four-hour firings with a thirty-minute interval between.[77] This more intense firing began to show results: on 21 May there appeared 'a blacke spot in the sulphur of the Southerly of Ignis', and one of Aer's sulphurs had 'a little of white remoued.'[78] On the 22nd he found the Easterly sulphur of Aer had broken, and the next day the black spot on Ignis had grown. On 29 May, a three-hour firing broke the vase of Aer, ending that experiment, and the next day, 30 May, Harriot wrote what is the final note on his alchemical experiments which has come down to us:[79] '[May] 30. ♀. I gaue fire at 7 morning. 4 houres, 3 times with an houres intermission to terra, aqua, & Ignis. The black of Ignis increased. The Terra grew cleaner, not yet broken. it hath ben white & tender many dayes before. & some cloudy matter forming.' Normally, such changes in form would call for more intense heat to bring more pressure on the balance of qualities in the generating matter. Still the 'tenderness' of the sulphur might call for the slackening off of the injection of heat. But no additional notes remain to indicate how Harriot reacted. In all probability he recognized, as he had the year before, that his experiments were leading nowhere, and that

[75] Ibid., fo. 370ʳ.   [76] Ibid., fo. 373ʳ.
[77] Ibid.   [78] Ibid.   [79] Ibid.

this effort to isolate or perfect the four basic Aristotelian elements was doomed to failure, and hence turned his attention to other activities which showed more promise of success. No more papers remain from 1600, so we can only surmise that he returned to his work on mechanics and optics which had engrossed him before he began to dabble in the morass of early alchemical chemistry.

It would be pleasant for the modern admirer of Harriot to find in these chemical experiments some new and promising innovations which might show him as contributing to the new scientific methods which were beginning to be developed. One change from the conventional technology of alchemy may be found in these notes and rough drawings of Harriot which at first glance appears promising. This is the positioning of the flasks in all of the drawings in accordance with the geographical directions, and the apparent orientation of the four lapides by the small ears always depicted on them. On first consideration, it might be reasoned that Harriot was adding the physical element of the Earth's gravitational field to the creative forces normally employed, that the outer recording of N, S, E, and W placed the flask in a definite position in the earth's magnetic field, and that the inner points showed the sulphur lapides floating on magnetized compass needles. This would at least be an imaginative and rational addition to chemical investigation, and particularly apt since this was during the period when the physician, William Gilbert, was preparing his famous work on magnetism in which he named Harriot as one who had made important contributions to that subject.[80] Yet a closer look at Harriot's drawing would eliminate this magnetic assumption; magnetic needles floating on mercury could not possibly remain in the orientation drawn by Harriot.

Another clue does exist, however, which may explain Harriot's orientation of his flasks, and perhaps even of the ears appearing on his floating sulphurs. Unfortunately, how-

---

[80] *G. Gilberti de magnete, 1600.* Licensed 7 Dec. 1599. Sig. A4 reads in part: 'Alli sunt viri docti que in longinquis navigationibus magneticae differentias observaverunt, Thomas Hariotus, Robertus Hues, Edouardus Wrightus, Abraham Kendallus Angli.' Harriot was certainly interested in the theories of the earth's magnetism, as his navigational notes clearly illustrate.

ever, it does not add to the scientific acumen of the man, but throws his experiments even more closely back to the mystical practices of the alchemists. But it should be presented.

Among the manuscript holdings of the Sion College Library on the Victoria Embankment are the seventeenth-century papers left by Harriot's friend and literary executor, the retired clergyman Nathaniel Torporley. Though Torporley ostensibly returned the Harriot manuscripts he borrowed from his executors after Harriot's death, a few of Harriot's own manuscripts and a few manuscripts from which Harriot had worked somehow got mixed up in Torporley's own notes, and there remain to this day. Among these fugitive papers from the Harriot collection are several papers on alchemy. One of these,[81] Dr Turner's recipe for making lute, is in the phonetic code occasionally used by Harriot, and gave Miss Seaton the key to its solution. Two others in the same hand, neither Harriot's nor Torporley's are purely alchemical. One is an extended poem, typically describing alchemical theory in highly abstract and figurative language; the other a graphic representation of the cosmos of the alchemist.[82] It closes with another typical verse:

> Our heavn this figure called is
> Our table also of the lower astronomy
> Which understood thou canst not misse
> To make our medicine perfectly
> On it therefore set thou thy study
> And vnto god both night and day
> For grace and for the author pray.

Largely traditional though this figure is, it does give some insight into the puzzling matter of Harriot's experiments: it explains the orientation, and also gives a clue to the significance of the four lapides. In this representation, four external circles give orientation to the 'heavn' of the alchemist. Each of these poles is associated with three signs of the zodiac, starting with Aries in the south, and proceeding in turn through west, east, and north. Each pole is also associated with a season of the year, one of the humours, one of the

---

[81] Sion College MSS: Arc. L. 40. 2/E.6. fo. 97^v; Ib, fo. 96^v.
[82] Ibid., fo. 87^r.

qualities of medicine, and one of the four elements. Charting this general orientation would give the following:

Direction	Zodiac	Season	Humour	Medical Quality	Element
SOUTH	♈ ♌ ♐	Summer	Choler	Attractive	FIRE
WEST	♉ ♍ ♑	Autumn	Melancholy	Retentive	EARTH
EAST	♊ ♒ ♎	Spring	Blood	Digestive	AIR
NORTH	♋ ♏ ♓	Winter	Phlegm	Expulsive	WATER

These apparently represent the characteristics and influences of the heavens, far beyond the realm of the planetary bodies.

A second group of circles, oriented within the outer four, are filled with allegorical poems about the sufferings of Christ, the creative process, the perfection of the quintessence, and the Philosopher's Stone as the quintessence of all of these. They read:

South
> As Christ from earth to heavn did ascend
> In cloudes of clearnes vp to his trhone
> And raigneth there shining without end:
> Right so our sonne now made our stone
> Vnto his glory agayne is gon
> His fier possessing here in ye south
> With power to heale leapres & to renew youth.

West
> As Christ the scripture making mention
> In the holy wombe descended of Mary
> From his high trone for our redemption
> Working the holy ghost to be incarnate:
> So here our stone descendeth from his estate
> Into the wombe of our virgin Mercurall
> To helpe his brethern from filth originall.

North
> As Christ his godhead from our sight
> When he our kind to him did take:
> Euen so our sonne his beames of light
> As for a time hath him forsake
> Vnder the winges of his make
> The mone he hideth his glory
> And bodily dieth in kind that he may multiply.

East
> As Christ our sauiour was tumulate
> After his passion and death on tree.
> And after his body was glorificate
> Vprose endued with mortality
> So here our stone buried after penalty
> Vpriseth from death darkens & colors variable
> Appearing in the east with clearnes incomparable.

Four intermediate circles dominate this realm of the stone.
Again they illustrate the alchemical symbols associated with
the four cardinal directions:

South   The altitude of the stone, fiery in quality, shining more
           then perfect quintessence, and end of ye practice, specu-
           lative, tenet ignem [gold holds fire].

West   The first or west Latitude of ye stone. And entring into the
           practice [practical] pole & earthly in quality occasionate.
           Saturne [lead] holdeth the earth.

North   The dark profundity of the stone in ye north purgatory all
           imperfect watry in quality, variable in colour ye eclipse of
           ye sonne. ☿ tenet aquam [mercury holds water].

East   The east latitude of ye stone and entring into ye speculatiue
           aier of ye full moone. Jupiter [tin] holdeth the ayer.

Immediately below this realm of the stone came the world of
the alchemist. Four verses included here expressed very
common and traditional alchemical symbolism:

> Here the red man [sulphur] & his white wife [mercury]
> Be spoused [united] with the spirity of life.
>
> Into paradise here we go
> There to be purged of payn and wo
>
> Here be they passed there payns all
> Shining briter then the Christall
>
> From paradise they go to heven to wonne [dwell]
> Shining brighter then doth the sonne.

Innermost are the planetary circles, earth in the centre, with
the seven known planets (whose signs also symbolized the
seven metals) in concentric circles around it. Added, too,
just below the sign of the cross which symbolized the perfection of the alchemical processes of purification, are the
symbols of the desirable end-products — ☉, ☽, and ☿ for
gold, silver, and mercury.

If this was (and it very well may have been) one of Harriot's
manuscripts giving alchemical clues to the processes of the
perfection of matter, it reinforces the view that Harriot had
abandoned his rational science in these chemical experiments.
All of the old clichés are here: the identification of the
process of purification with the expiation of the sins of man
in Christ; the alliance of the philosopher's stone with the

joys of heaven; the marriage of the red man with the white
wife — the union of sulphur and mercury to unite as gold.
None of these holds much promise for the isolation of pure
Aristotelian earth, water, air, or fire by the application of
known chemical processes.

But the manuscript gives some hint as to how Harriot set
up his experiments. It allies the four cardinal directions
directly with four of the fundamental metals and the Aristotelian elements:

North = Mercury holding water;
East   = Tin containing air;
South = Gold holding fire; and
West   = Lead holding earth.

It is likely, then, that Harriot's experiments, oriented as to
direction, were also employing the various metals which had
affinity with those directions. His flasks, then, contained
mercury on whose surface floated small dishes made of
sulphur. And it is probable that in each dish, perhaps considered something of a catalyst, was placed a portion of the
relevant metal. It might be that each of his experiments had
mercury in the north dish and gold in the south, for example.
Or it might have been the inserted metals which differentiated
between his experiments for the different elements, with his
flask for Terra containing Lead, Aqua holding mercury;
Aeris with tin; and Ignis containing gold. In this way, Harriot
would be putting together all the hypothetical alliances
which might unite to form, under ideal conditions, pure
samples of the basic elements of which all matter, animate
and inanimate, was formed.

That Harriot was diligent and assiduous in his experiments
is obvious from the evidence of his laboratory notes. He was
persistent for long periods of time. But when it became evident that the materials in the flask were not responding to
his chemical manipulations, that he was not making progress
toward the purification or isolation of matter, Harriot did
not hesitate to drop the whole experiment, which he did
finally and without warning at ten o'clock in the evening of
Friday 30 May 1600 after a full day of firing with no tangible
results. It is also interesting to note that though Harriot
customarily returned to his earlier investigations repeatedly,

in the case of his chemistry, he never looked back. There are no subsequent additions or jottings from later years, involving the use of chemical or alchemical theories or processes.[83] Harriot had learned his lesson well.

[83] In his DPhil thesis, 'Thomas Harriot's Astronomy' (Oxford, 1977), p. 19, John Roche indicates that Harriot's interest in alchemy is shown by his leaving his Executors in his will each 'a furnace with his appurtenances'. There can be little doubt, however, that these were not alchemical furnaces, but the furnaces used in his optical and lens making work, since he also leaves them samples of his optical glass and finished telescopes.

VII. From the Court to the Tower – Ralegh

The turn of the century found Ralegh and Northumberland, like their fellow Englishmen, somewhat uncertain about what the future would hold. The Queen, focus of the sensibilities and emotions of the Englishmen of a whole generation, was in her old age less effective in governing her country and her own feelings than she had been throughout her life. Her favourite tie to youth and vigour, the Earl of Essex, was out of favour, having wilfully flown in the face of her explicit commands, repeated his creation of large numbers of knights, entered into a compact with Tyrone, the rebel leader in Ireland, and returned to the Court to embrace the Queen against her strictest orders. As he languished in disgrace, barred from the Court and the presence of the Queen, the Queen too was in emotional turmoil and appeared for the first time in her life to be a vacillating woman, uncertain of what course of action she should take to chastise her youthful darling for failing to respect her royal authority.

Ralegh, rival to Essex for the favours of his monarch, could not seem to find advantage in the downfall of Essex. Though he continued to hold the offices given him by Elizabeth, he failed in his major effort to gain political advantage by becoming a member of her Privy Council. In spite of his most persuasive efforts, the Queen, though she did not flatly deny him, would not grant him his wish, and like the indecisive ruler she had become, actually took no action at all. In mid-March 1600 Ralegh, in despair, left the Court and returned to Sherborne to the life of a West Country gentleman, striving to consolidate his land holdings and to insure the future prosperity of his present and future heirs.

One of Sir Walter Ralegh's major concerns when he recognized the fickleness of the Queen was for the title of his Sherborne estates, on which he had based so much of his estate planning. For some reason, not now to be understood, Ralegh feared that the transfer of Sherborne to the Queen by the Bishop of Sarum had been faulty, and he entered into a number of involved transactions to attempt to clarify title. Later, in 1609 when the Crown was attempting to take over the properties as part of the actions of attainder, Ralegh made a formal statement to the Attorney-General regarding his negotiations with respect to his Dorset properties. As his account is reported by his biographer Edwards:[1]

'I conveyed the same estates to my son, ... twice, as I remember, by certain grants to certain persons and friends in trust. Those conveyances were revocable, and I did afterwards revoke them. ... For, finding my fortune at Court towards the end of her late Majesty's reign to be at a stand, and that I daily attended dangerous employments against her late Majesty's enemies, and had not in the said former grants made any provision for my wife, I made the former grants void; and then afterwards, for the natural love and affection which I bare to the said Walter Ralegh, then my only son, and still being desirous, as well to settle and establish some estate of and in the said castles and manors, and also some livelihood and provision for my wife, to be had thereout during her natural life, I made a new grant ... which last-mentioned deed was made not many months before the now Bishop [Cotton] was consecrated, as I verily believe. ... But by reason of my manifold troubles, I do not know where the said deed is, or in whose hands or custody.' Its purport, it is further said, was to convey the estates to his son, subject to a rent-charge of two hundred pounds a year for Lady Ralegh during her life. 'Her late Majesty,' proceeds Sir Walter, 'having afterwards procured from the said now Bishop the inheritance of the said lordship, castles, and manors, it pleased her to give me the same by a sufficient conveyance in law. ... And afterwards I did intend to settle the inheritance of the same upon my said son ...'

The 'certain persons and friends' to whom Ralegh placed his properties in trust can be identified as Sir George Carew, his kinsman John Meres, his estates agent; and Thomas Harriot, who appears to have served during this time as Steward of the Sherborne estates. A few of these documents still survive among the estate papers of Sherborne Castle in the records of

---

[1] Edward Edwards, *The Life of Sir Walter Ralegh*, 2 vols., Macmillan, 1868. This is from vol. I, pp 466–7.

the Digby Estate Office. The first of them, dated 1 August 1599, is typical of the negotiations, and shows the vagueness with which their purpose is described; it is a release from Harriot and Carew back to Ralegh of title and property rights which must previously have been granted to them:[2]

This Indenture made the first day of August in the one & fforteth yeare of the Raigne of our soueraigne ladie Elizabeth by the grace of god of England ffrance & Ireland Queen defendor of the faith &c Betweene the honorable Sir Walter Ralegh knight Captaine of her majesties gard & lo: warden of the Stanires in the Counties of Devon & Cornewall of the one party And Sir George Carew & Thomas Heriott gentleman of the other party Witnesseth that the said Sir George Carew & Thomas Heriott for diuerse good causes & consideracions them herevnto mouinge & especially for perfomance [of] the trust reposed in them haue deuised graunted assigned & sett over & by these presente doe demise graunte assigne & sett over vnto the said Sir Walter Ralegh All that ther Castle, mannors Lordshippes Landes Tenementes & hereditamentes Rentes Reuercions service aduousones patronages ffranchises liberties Royalties Jurisdicions & hereditamentes whatsoeuer within the hundred of Sherborne & yetminister in the County of Dorset To haue & to hold all & singuler the premisses with the appurtenances vnto the said Sir Walter Ralegh his Executors & assignes for all the tyme & tearme yett to Come & vnexpired which some tymes was graunted by John Gould-well late Bushoppe of Sarum vnto the Queens most Exelent Majestie In witnes wherof the parties first aboue haue to these present Indentures Interchangably sett ther names and seales the day & yeare first aboue written:/

[Signed]   George Carewe   [Signed]   Tho: Harriots

[Obverse]   Signed sealed & deliuered in the presence of
            Howard   Henry sothar   Welighe Elbert
                    'releas from Sir G. Carew
                            & T. Herriotts'

A second document represents the formal transfer of all property in trust to 'Sir Arthure Throgmorton of Paulers-perye in the Countie of Northampton, Knight, Alexander Brett of Whytestaunton in the Countie of Somersett, Esquier, and Thomas Heriottes of London, gentleman' for the use of Sir Walter and his heirs, subject to revocation by Sir Walter at any time. This must be the document which Ralegh indicates he drew up on 'the advice of a Counsellor-at-law,

---

[2] This document is released through the kindness of Mr P. A. Howe of the Digby Estate Office, Sherborne.

about the last year of her late Majesty's reign'.[3] Actually, this document is dated on 20 January 1603, just two months before the death of Elizabeth. And a third, executed on 14 June 1614 is a final revocation of the grant in trust, marking the end of Ralegh's fond hopes to leave a fruitful estate to his survivors. For this study, they are significant primarily because they show the high trust and regard that Sir Walter held for Thomas Harriot — numbering him among the most select group of his friends and relatives, even at a time when he was fully under the patronage of the 9th Earl, maintaining residences at Syon House, Isleworth, and Essex House, London, remote from Sherborne or Durham House. But these documents lead us further: they reveal something of the frame of Ralegh's mind during these last years of Elizabeth's life. Though Ralegh has often been cast as a political figure, he was really not concerned with political movements or events beyond what might influence him personally. And any intrigue that he might have engaged in was centred in the role of the Queen and in his association with her. Everything Ralegh possessed in the way of fame, fortune, or influence came about because the Queen willed them to be his; his success or failure, his existence even, was a reflection of their relationship. If she smiled on him, there was nothing he could not accomplish; if she frowned, he was, by his own admission, reduced to deepest despair. There is much evidence that he personally liked, for example, the Earl of Essex; it was only when Essex threatened Ralegh's affection in the eyes of the Queen, or worse, when his ambition led him to think of the possibility of supplanting her as monarch, that Ralegh became his implacable enemy.

This close tie with Elizabeth as a person as well as a Queen left Ralegh unable to participate in any significant way in the selection of her successor. Whoever was to be named as her successor, Ralegh knew he was finished. He recognized that Elizabeth's death meant the end of all those favours which had supported him. His efforts, as a result, were dedicated not to taking a major part in the succession, but in consolidating and making permanent those personal gifts

[3] Edwards, op. cit., I. 466.

and grants which the Queen had bestowed on him. This was why he spent his time away from Court to try to assure that his lands, his rights and licences, were maintained in good order, so that with the change in the ruler he could retire to the life of the West Country gentleman with an occasional adventure on the high seas.

Meanwhile, life in the Northumberland establishment pro-ceeded more serenely. The 9th Earl, through his noble rights and in his estates, felt much more secure than Ralegh, since he did not rely on his personal charm for this fortune. A noble of wealth and power in his own right, Henry Percy was firmly established at Syon House, planning the major repairs needed to make it a comfortable London residence. On New Year's day, like all his noble friends, he offered his gifts to the ageing Queen:[4]

her ma^{ties} New Year guifts	Paid by the said Accomptante for her Majesties newe yeres guyfte 1600 prouided by the lady newton and mistress Ratclif lxvj^{li} for her Majesties New yeres guift 1601 An ymbrodered petycote prouided by the lady Walsingham lx^{li} And for a Jewell gyven to her majestie & bought of Master Spillman her majesties Jeweller CC^{li} . . . . . . In all CCCxxvj^{li}

His own pensions were being paid at their regularly established rates:[5] 'to the right honorable the Countesse of Northumber-land [£500] the yere', 'to Sir Charles Percy, Knight . . . at [£66] by yere', 'to Sir Joceylyne Percy, Knight, at [£64 11*s*. 7*d*.] by yere', 'to Master Allen Percy for his Annuitie, viz in full payment for the yere ended at Michaelmas 1599 more for one Whole yere ended at Mychaelmas 1600 [£120]', and, in a separate pension section, 'Paid also by the said accomp-tante to Master herrate for his pencione at [£80] by yere for two whole yeres ended at mychaelmas 1601 [£160]'. The obvious regard of the 9th Earl for Harriot is revealed by the fact that this pension granted him more than any of the Earl's brothers, and was surpassed only by the grant to the Countess who was, during this latter year, pregnant with the child who was to be their son and heir apparent, Algernon, 10th Earl of Northumberland.

[4] Syon MSS U.I.3. Edmund Powton, Cofferer, rough draft, 1600–1.
[5] Ibid.

That Harriot was active in the Earl's affairs, as he was in Ralegh's, is also shown in the accounts of some of the repairs being made at Syon. According to the payments recorded between late February 1600 and late March 1602 by Thomas Wycliffe 'Payer & disburser of foreine paymentes'[6] for 'Reparacions' at Syon:

Paid likewise for certen Reparacions made & done about your Lordship's houses at Syon & London, viz. to ye plomber for mendinge the Condeyth pipes at Syon [34s. 4d.], to ye bricklayer for tylinge & mendinge the Cesterne Chamber ouer the water [13s. 10d.], & for other workes there by th'handes of Master Powton [9s. 4d.; 17s. 6d.]

Harriot was himself involved in these renovations as is shown, interestingly enough, by a drawing of the Syon waterworks remaining among his papers[7] which helps to locate his house. (See Illustration 14, where this diagram is reproduced.) The drawing shows the conduits covering the estate, originating at 'The Springhead', running to the house of 'S[ir] F[rancis] Darcy I thinck', to 'The farmes', to 'the pond' which seems to furnish the 'cesswell' for emptying the pipes, another to 'the Stables' with a mains junction at the entrance to the house, where it serves two cellar drains, a 'Cestern in the bathing room' (an interior bath installed for the comfort of the Countess), and to the 'Priuy' in the Kitchen. Just before the mains junction, a branch runs behind the house to serve the 'Laundry', and thence to Harriot's house, where it is shown as 'Priuy T.H.'. Other scratch drawings of about this same time show Harriot experimenting with water flow, probably to make a scientific determination of pressures. One sheet, labelled 'Concerning the Water Works'[8] gives a series of figures to show the rate of flow at various outlets, while another note,[9] in the midst of calculations concerning musket fire, records that 'The depth of the water in Syon Cestorne [is] $40\frac{1}{2}$ ynches.' Two other drawings of the Syon grounds, obviously drawn in rough scale,[10] show the main residence, and a second house, connected by a wall, at a distance approximately equal to the width of the main house, which must have been Harriot's house. That it was not

[6] Syon MS U.I.3.   [7] BL Add. MS 6786, fo. 369[r].
[8] BL Add. MS 6789, fo. 526[r].   [9] BL Add. MS 6789, fo. 86[v].
[10] BL Add'l MS 6789, fos. 263[v], 338[v].

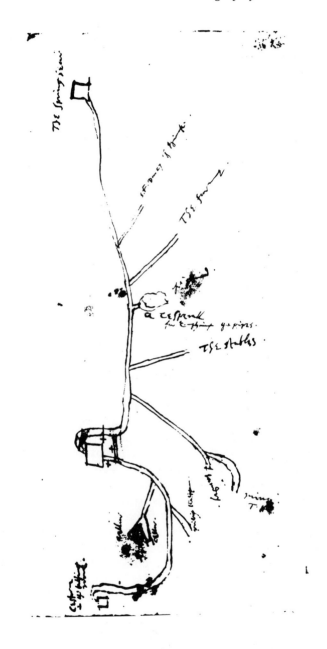

Fig. 14 The Waterworks at Syon

too far distant from the main house may be inferred also from an entry of 1607, in which Christopher Ingram, Clerk of the Works for Syon from 1599 to 1628, records repairs to the Countess's bath, followed (too closely to be casual) with notations regarding the construction 'for makinge a brick wall betweene the towre of her ladyship's lodginge and Master heryotts house';[11] augmented three years later by a higher wall:[12] 'the wall goeinge from her Lady-ship's Gardens to Master Herryotts house' given as 95 ft. long and 18 ft. high. This wall still exists, though the land level has now risen approximately 3 feet in the intervening centuries.

The spring of 1600 saw much of the 9th Earl's time and attention spent in making preparations for his visit to the Low Countries as a special emissary of the Queen to investi-gate the course of the war. The details of the preparation of the young noble soldier-ambassador are reflected in his personal expenditures:[13]

some necessary payments as for mending your Lordship's Armoure and for powther & shot vij^s . . . for mending your lordship's .2. pistols & for iiij moulds to them iij^s vij^d . . . almose [alms] to diuerse poore people & souldiers at seuerall tymes . . .

Crymsen velvett & taffatie to face your lordship's Armor . . . for makinge cleane of vij pistolls & for a new head for your lordship's pike . . . for a new sworde & dager guilt with gold . . . for a golden hatched Rapier . . . to Sir ffrancys Veres his players in Holland . . .

The accounts also give almost a day by day record of the progress of Percy and his retinue:

xxvj of August *1600* at Zerickzea
xxiij of October at ye Hage
xxviij of October at ye Hage
xxix of Januarie *1600* [1601] at ye Hage
ij of Februarye *1600* [1601] at Vtricke
xxiij of August *1601* at Rotterdam

[11] Syon MS U.I.3. Preliminary drafts, Audit of 1607.
[12] Syon MS U.I.4. Christopher Ingram, Clerk of Works.
[13] These are scattered through the rolls for 1600–1 in Syon MS U.I.3., particu-larly in those of Robert Delavale, 'Pursebearer and paier of his L: Rewardes', Christopher Ingram, 'Clarke of his lo: Workes', Raphe Burgeyne, 'gentleman of his Lp horse', and Edmunde Powton, 'Coferer and Steward of household', rough draft.

And they show, too, how carefully the ninth Earl followed the action, and how he was served by Walter Warner, Harriot's mathematical friend, who travelled with him as his literary secretary:

Bookes & mappes./ Paid also by the said Accomptante for diuerse bookes bought by master Warner & others for your lordship's vse at diuerse tymes and places aswell in England as in the lowe Countryes x^{li} to a Scryvener for Writinge ij discourses of warre x^s a discourse of the Armye of Cales iij^s paper papall for mappes xvj^s viij^d for iiij skinns of Velame to make ye mappes of Berke and Ostend x^s for ye sortinge & titlinge & cataloginge of your lordship's bookes at Syon xxv^s for binding the discourse of Ireland & other bookes xx^s v^d for coullers for mappes paintinge v^s for paper & coullours to make the leager of Berke ij^s to a painter that made the mappe of Berge in Collors xxvj^s for vj platts of Ostend & Berge ij^s for a mappe of Antwerpe vj^s for ij mappes of Netherland xviij^d for ye articles betweene the Archduke & the States generall v^s for ye pettigrue of Grave Morryes & a mapp of ye battell xx^s to ye painter at Hage for mappes xx^s and for a mappe bought by David Joanes ij^s In all as by his bookes & bills emengst other thinges examined may appere xvij^{li} xiiij^s vij^d . . .

This tour of duty in the name of the Queen, taken together with his serious responsibility to the state as one of her principal nobles, led Northumberland, unlike his friend Ralegh, seriously to consider the matter of succession. Though one avid claimant of the throne, Robert Devereux Earl of Essex, was by marriage Percy's brother-in-law (whose close followers and supporters were not only Northumberland's wife, Dorothy, but his two brothers, Sir Charles and Sir Jocelyn Percy), Henry Percy never took the Essex claims to the right of succession seriously. Nor did he ever give support to those few, mostly Catholic recusants, who favoured himself as a possible supporter of their cause. To him, the sense of ancestry was strong, and the claims of James VI of Scotland were compelling. So as Elizabeth's health began to fade, Northumberland, for apparently unselfish reasons, placed himself firmly in the camp of the supporters of James, though of course this had to be done surreptitiously. Elizabeth could not face the fact of death, and to talk openly of succession was treasonable in her eyes; nor could she bring herself to resolve the matter by a simple statement of her preference as to whom she would like to assume the throne on her demise. But as a friend in Court, Percy prepared to assist James in the transition, and for a short time he entered into a secret correspondence with him using his cousin, Thomas Percy, Constable of Alnwick, as his personal messenger.[14] His major purpose was to assure that James's assumption of the English throne would be peaceful, and that the impetuous Scottish king would not try to force his way to the crown of England before the people were ready to accept him. In addition, though he was not himself a Catholic, Percy did have many Catholic friends, and he apparently misread their strength in the selection of the new royal line, or their ability to use force, if necessary, to achieve their choice. It is obvious from the tone of his letters that Northumberland was not seeking personal gain, but was acting wholly from deeply patriotic motives in his advance counselling of the Scottish monarch. These motives are made clear in the first letter in which he approached the king:

O [Henry Earl of Northumberland] to 30 [King James].

. . . The two mane points that are most in question emongst ws, and that I thinke may giue your maiestie best satisfaction to wndirstand, are theas; the one, whither after her maiesties life your ryght will be yealded you peaceably, wythout blosse [blows] or not? the wther, whether it be lykely your maiestie befor your tyme will attempt to hasten it by force. . . .

. . . the world [he continues] assumeth a greater freedom since essex death to speake freely of your title, with the [greater] allouance of it then euer, nor can I marke our any one president [precedent] that any man is trubled for it. . . .

As for the warres of Ireland, [wars with which James was not sympathetic] . . . this being held for a maxime emongsst vs, that the Irishe will all comme and lay there swords at your feete quhen you s[h]all be our master. . . .

. . . For the papists, it is treue there faction is strong, there encrease is dayly, and there diffidence in your maiestie is not desperat . . . I will dare to say no more, bot it weare pittie to losse so good a kingdome for the not tollerating a messe in a cornere (if wppon that it resteth) so

[14] Copies of these letters are preserved among the Salisbury papers at Hatfield House. They were published in 1861 by the Camden Society, as Part III of John Bruce, ed., *Correspondence of King James VI. of Scotland with Sir Robert Cecil and Others in England, During the Reign of Queen Elizabeth*, vol. 78, pp. 53–76. Though there are many apparent misreadings of 'w' for 'u' and 'u' for 'v', these transcripts have followed the Camden version.

[15] Letter III, ibid., p. 64–70.

long as they s[h]all not be too busy disturbers of the guuernement of the state, nor seeke to make vs contributers to a peter prist. . . .

Northumberland must have been gratified by the warm reception which his letter received. James replied almost at once:

Ryght truistie cusing, I haue receeawed your most wyse plaine and honest letter from the hands of the gentilman berrar herof, and I haue conferred wyth hem at als great lentht as the oportunitie of the tyme could wyth saftie from the hasard of hes discouerie permite . . . yet am i infinitlie glaide, that you haue by so honorable a letter, and so weill a chosed messinger, maide the first discouerie thereof.

and signed himself 'Your louing and affectionat frynd'.

The correspondence that ensued was not particularly astute. James was friendly and kind in his responses, agreeing with whatever Northumberland suggested, amiably giving assurances that his rule would be benevolent and wise, his conduct acceptable to even his most severe critics. Northumberland took all this at face value, and spoke bluntly of affairs and people as he saw them in the English Court, trying always to be completely fair and objective:[15] '. . . since my opinion differs frome the wulgar, i will nether giwe more to my frynds then they deserue, nor conceale that i holde them faltie in concerning yow . . .' Most interesting of his comments are, thus, his impressions of his friends at Court. First, Northumberland attempted to set James straight on the real nature of the Earl of Essex. James had been greatly attracted by the dashing arrogance of Essex, and highly critical of the moves which led to his death, even though it worked to his own advantage. Northumberland wrote thus of his former brother-in-law:

. . . yowr maisties iwdgment of essex to be a noble gentilman, but that yow lost noe great frynd by hem, leades me on the rather to this discowrs; to conferme therefor yowr maiesties censour, I must say iustely, that although he was a man endeued wyth good gifts, yet was his losse the happiast chance for yowr maiestie and england that cowld befawle ws; for ether doe I feale in my iudgment, or he would hawe bene ane bloody scowrge to owr nation. Of this i can speake wery perticulary, as on whoe was as inward wyth hem as any lywing createur, the first two years i was matched wyth his sister. And could he then

[15] Letter III, ibid., p. 64–70.

dreame of any thinge but hawing the continowall pouar or ane army to dispose of, of being great constable of england, to the end that in an interregnum he might call parlaments to make laws for owr selwes? Did he not decree it, that it was scandalus to owr nation that a stranger sould be owr king? Was not his familiaritie wyth me quite cancellet when he had discowered my disposition leaning to yowr ryght, and that i was not to be leede by hes fortunes? Did he not secretly keepe me frome all preferments of the north parts wyth planting iealusies in the quens mynde of me, whiche are there stille freche when those maters come in dispute? Did he not euer prefer wthers of more facilitie to hes will then my selfe in any actions whereby i myght come any way to equall hem in the repwtation of a soldier? How often have I heard that he enweighed against yow emongest sutche as he conceawed to be birds of hes owen fortoune? Did hes soldiers followars dreme or speake any thing but of hes being king of england? . . . Well, to conclude, he woore the crowne of england in hes hart these many years, and therefor farre frome setting it wpone your head if it had beine in hes poware.

Obviously, the presumption of Essex rankled Northumberland and his ambition destroyed the natural affection which he might have had. And it is likely that the constant devotion of his sisters, Lady Rich and Northumberland's Countess, may have been basic to the antagonism which grew up between Henry and Dorothy Percy during these years.

Northumberland's statements with regard to his friend, Walter Ralegh, are also extremely interesting. As we have said, Ralegh was not really much concerned about the succession, since his whole fortune was vested in Elizabeth. But James had heard that Ralegh was opposing his rightful claims to the throne. What Northumberland did not know, and what James did not tell him, was that Sir Robert Cecil, the Queen's Principal Secretary, was also in private correspondence with James, and that Cecil, while professing friendship towards Ralegh and Northumberland, was really doing everything in his power to undermine them in the eyes of James. James was already suspicious of Ralegh, since Ralegh was obviously anxious to continue fighting Spain, and James wanted only peace. As a result of this predilection, he was willing, therefore, to believe the worst of any rumour about him that reached his ear. It was to ease this atmosphere of hostility that Northumberland rose to the defence of his friend:

. . . As for cobham and rawlieghe how thay bend towars yowr right this is my censowre, although thay be in faction contrary to somme

that howld wyth your title, yet in that point i can not deny but they
be of the same myndis, and to run the same cowrs. The first of theas
tuo i knowe not how his heart is affected; but by the latter, whome
sixtein years acquentance hathe confermed to me [this would date
their friendship as starting in 1587], I must needs affirme rawlieghs
ewer allowance of yowr ryght, and althowghte I knowe hem insolent,
extreamly heated, a man that desirs to seeme to be able to swaye all
mens fancies, all mens cowrses, and a man that owt of himselfe, when
your time sall come, will neuer be able to do yow muche good nor
hearme, yet mwst I needs confesse what i know, that there is excellent
good parts of natur in hem, a man whoes lowe is disawantaeus to me in
somme sort, which i cherise rather out of constancie than pollicie, and
one whome i wishe your maiestie not to loose, becaue I wowld not
that one haire of a man's head sowld be against yow that might be
for yow.

Northumberland, after a few more letters of general
advice and information, ended his correspondence with
James, shortly before Elizabeth's death, probably on 20
March 1603:[16]

I have laboured in your vynyard with all the industrie my poore vnderstanding would give me leave. If it shal happen, or pleas god to take
from ws oure mistres, you shal have instantly woord, and I think
newes of her departure will be no sooner with your Maiesty than
woord of your being proclamed amongst ws will ouertake it.

James replied:

Right trustie and wel belovit cousing, the more I heir from you the
more am I reioyced, and do think my selfe infinitely happye that one
of your place, endowed with suche sinceritie of loue towardes me, and
will all other partes of sufficientie, should be borne one daye to be a
subiect vnto me ... And thus I end, praying [you] for your owne pairt
to rest fully assured, that ye shall in the owne tyme have proofe in what
hye account ye are with

Your moast loving fryend,
JAMES R.

This letter was signed as from 'Halyrudous the 24 of Marche',
the day of the death of the Virgin Queen, Elizabeth I of
England.

The 9th Earl's correspondence with James had served him
well. In spite of the insinuations of Cecil, James was attracted

[16] Ibid., Letter V. In this letter Northumberland says that Elizabeth has not
slept for twenty days; according to Cecil, her final sleepless period began on
1 Mar. She died at 2 a.m. on 24 Mar.

to the blunt, northern personality which Percy's letters had revealed to him. On his progress to London, three days before the formal funeral of Elizabeth, James forwarded his orders to London that the Earls of Northumberland and Cumberland, Lord Mountjoy and Lord Thomas Howard, were to be admitted and sworn to his Privy Council.[17] Northumberland journeyed north to join the King's progress, and on Wednesday, 4 May, during a long day's hunt in the rain, Henry Percy rode on the King's right hand, with the Earl of Nottingham on the left.[18] And in the series of magnificent progresses with which James opened his reign, accompanied by most of his retainers and the members of the Court, James paid his homage to Northumberland by visiting him at Syon House on 8 June, 1603.

The extant household accounts of the Northumberlands are very revealing of the costs of such royal progresses, and explain why many fairly wealthy families went in debt when they were honoured by their monarch. They show, too, that in spite of all of Henry's protestations of having only a modest income, he did not stint in the style of his own living, or of spending what he wished for his personal comfort and convenience. Henry Taylor, 'Clarke of Kytchens', for example, shows expenses for 'diet' totalling £496 15s. 8d. in the audit of 1604, including charges for food:[19] 'at Syon [£90 3s. 6d.] . . . at London [£157. 14s. 11d.] . . . at Wyndsor [£48 5s. 0d] . . . and at Hampton Court [£200 12s. 3d.], not counting the 'Dyet in the Progres' totalling £283 17s. 6½ d., itemized

Paid also by the said Accomptante for the Expenses of your Lordship's dyet by the space of xviij wekes the kings majestie being in progres that is to say at Godlyman lxxvijs viijd at Basing Newberrye & Thrupton vijl vs iijd at Salisburye Cvijli iijs ixd ob. at Collingburne & Beddings viijli vijs Woodstocke xxvijl vijs jd Wynchester $\overset{xx}{iiij}$ xvl ixs iijd ob. and at Petworthe xxxiiijl xiijs xjd

Besides these charges, were the costs of boardwages and lodgings for the 'gentlemen yeomen & gromes . . . in the tyme

[17] J. R. Dasent, ed., *Acts of the Privy Council*, 1900-, xxxii, p. 495.
[18] J. Nichols, *The Progresses, Processions, and Magnificent Festivities of King James the First*, 4 vols., London, 1828. See vol. I, pp. 138-9.
[19] Syon MS U.I.3., expenses for 1603.

of the Kings majesties Progres' (including a St. George's
Day dinner, and lodgings in the Court) totalling £289 11s. 4d.,
and the 'diuerse houses and kytchens' that they had to rent
'at Grenewich for vj weeks ended the xxiij[th] of June 1603
. . . the house at Charing Crosse for iij weeks ended the xij
of Marche . . . [and] in the towre for iiij dayes.'

Gyles Grene, who had advanced from the Earl's 'Payer of
foreyn payments' to 'Steward of the Household' this year,
was responsible for preparing the house and guest accom-
modations for the King's party and presented receipts for the
one-day visit of £168 10s. 3d, itemized as follows:[20]

The kings majestie being at Syon./ Paid likewise by the said Accomptante for diuerse provisions bought and prouided by him against the
kings majesties cominge to Syon the viij[th] of June 1603, viz. for
diuerse wynes xlix[li] xvij[s] v[d] for Banqueting meate bought of madame
Crozier xxvj[li] x[s] for botle Ayle C[s] Runletts for Wyne & Vyniger xj[s]
iiij[d] iiij Doz of pypkins ix[s] vj[d] Wyne botles iiij[s] iiij[d] glasses lviij[s]
Cannes ix[s] flasketts & hampers vj[s] vj[d] for hire of plate taken vppe of
master Gossen the gold symthe vij[l] ix[s] ix[d] for hyre of Pewther vessels
and making restitucion for vessell glasses Trenchers & basketts that
were lost and stollen xxiij[li] ix[s] vij[d] for Rushes lxij[s] ij[d] mending of
matts hyre of hangings hanging them uppe making of tressells and
other necessarye Works in the Chambers & house ix[li] xix[s] iiij[d] for
mending the ranges in the kytchen xv[s] for the Caryage of your Lordship's stuffe & prouision to and from London to Syon lvij[s] In Rewardes
given to the Cookes in the kings majesties kytchen & to others that
brought presents xxvij[s] xvij[s] iiij[d] to Laborers in the kytchen & for
diuers necessaryes vj[li] xiiij[s] iiij[d] In all. Clxviij[li] x[s] iij[d].

Edmunde Metcalf, 'gentleman Clarke of his Lordship's
kytchen', was responsible for the purchase of the major food
supplies for the occasion. The Countess and the young Lord
Percy had been sent to Petworth for the period from 16 April
to 10 July so that they missed all the excitement. For their
kitchens there, Metcalf spent, during this period, £86 8s. 9d.[21]
But the major charges in his accounts, too, were occasioned
by 8 June when the official court of England centred at
Syon House. How many were in attendance is not known,
but unless appetites were unbelievably large, the number
must have been great to consume the foodstuffs served on
that day.

[20] Syon MS U.I.3. Giles Grene . . . Stewarde . . . 28 Mar. 1603–28 Mar. 1604.
[21] Syon MS U.I.3. Audit of 1604.

At the kings majesties being at Syon./ Paid more by the said Accomptante in diuerse prouisions maid and prouided for the kings majesties comynge to Syon the 8th of June 1603 viz in Beif vij^li xj^s. xxvj carcasses iij quarters of mutton xvj^li iiij^s ix^d xiij carcasses demi of veales ix^li viij^s vj^d xxv carcasses of lambe vij^li x^s in diuerse other Acates of fyshe & fowle Ciij^li iij^s iij^d in Oyles herbes Salletts fruits & Banqueting meats xiij^li x^s ix^d in Bread viij^li iiij^s in Butter & Egges viij^li xviij^s x^d . . . In all as by the bookes of the said Accomptante examined & cast vppe appeareth ≠ —C^{xx}_{iiij} xvj^li viij^s ix^d.

If Harriot was present on this occasion (and there is no reason to believe that he was not), his cholesterol level, like that of all the guests, must have been exceeding high when he finally crawled into bed (undoubtedly drunk). But Henry Percy, 9th Earl of Northumberland, must have slept well in the secure knowledge that the King had been pleased by the day and was his friend. He had chosen this occasion to knight Sir William Norton of Southampton, Sir Robert Worthe of Essex, Sir Marmaduke Wyvel of Yorkshire, and Sir Francis More of Buckinghamshire.[22] And he had let Percy know that he might make him a royal grant of Syon House, its properties, and the manor of Isleworth replacing the long-term lease granted by Elizabeth — a noble gesture which he did fulfil the following year.

Sir Walter Ralegh was not as happy as was Henry Percy with the coming of King James to the English throne. The undermining activities of Sir Robert Cecil, which had not been effective in the case of Northumberland, had destroyed Ralegh in the eyes of the suspicious James. Even before James arrived in London, Cecil brought before the Council the idea of removing Ralegh from his post as Captain of the Guard, using as his excuse the fact that Ralegh was remaining at Sherborne and was not in the Court to perform his duties. Lord Cobham, rising to Ralegh's defence, registered vigorous opposition to this move, and went personally to James to protest the move.[23] But Cobham's reputation, like that of Ralegh, had been undermined by Cecil, and he had no effect in his efforts to help Ralegh. On 8 May, the day after James

[22] Nichols, *Progresses . . . of King James the First*, I. 165.
[23] G. B. Harrison, *A Jacobean Journal, Being a Record of Those Things Most Talked Of During the Years 1603–1606*, London, George Routledge, 1941, p. 9.

arrived in London, Ralegh foresaw the personal impact that the new monarch would have on him. He was called before the Council and informed that the King had expressed his pleasure that the position of Captain of the Guard would henceforth be held by Sir Thomas Erskine, a decision which Ralegh accepted with humble submission. Less than a month later, James gave Durham House to the Bishop of Durham, and ordered Ralegh to have the property vacated by 24 June. Ralegh was, naturally, greatly upset by this move, but his pleas to the King had no effect on his decision.[24] But worse was yet to come.

James, always fearful of plots against his person, heard rumours that an attempt to murder him was being hatched by a group which had been involved in some of the Catholic controversies. A proclamation was issued calling for the apprehension of one Anthony Copley, said to be involved. Copley, arrested two days later on 5 July, was intensively questioned, perhaps tortured, and on 12 July was induced to confess to being part of a plot to assassinate the King. In his confession, Copley implicated five persons: Sir Griffin Markham; William Watson, a secular priest; George Brooke, brother to Henry Brooke, Lord Cobham; Sir Arthur Gorges, another friend of Ralegh's; and Lord Grey.[25] Recognition of the involvement of this group, all on the fringes of the Ralegh–Northumberland group, gave Sir Robert Cecil and Lord Henry Howard, both of whom had been vitriolic in their condemnation of Ralegh, Cobham, and Northumberland, access to the King in furtherance of their plots. As a result, two days later, when Gorges, Lord Grey, and George Brooke were taken into custody, Lord Cobham and Sir Walter Ralegh were arrested and taken to the Tower, though no formal charges were given them to account for the action.[26] Ralegh's appearance before the Council, where he was questioned by Cecil and the other members about all of his actions with the Catholic plotters, his relations with Cobham, and his dealings with the representatives of Spain, left Ralegh

[24] Ibid., pp. 35-6.
[25] SR 14/2, no. 46; HMC, *MSS of the Marquess of Salisbury at Hatfield House*, vol. xv, p. 157 [?].
[26] BL Richard Smith's *Diary*, Sloan 414.

confused and despondent. Though he protested his innocence and declared that any charges of his conniving with the Spanish king against James were entirely out of character with the actions of his entire life, his words fell on deaf ears. On 27 July, a special commission named to conduct the inquest went to the Tower to examine the prisoners. Sir Walter, recognizing that the commission included his most vigorous enemies and was apparently under the sway of Lord Henry Howard and Sir Robert Cecil, on learning that they were coming to question him, attempted suicide, as did his secretary, Edward Hancock. Hancock's attempt was successful, but Ralegh's was not: his knife made a great wound on his breast, but was deflected by a rib from entering his heart.[27]

This was undoubtedly the most anguished period of Ralegh's life. Before attempting suicide, he penned a letter to his wife in which he poured out his despair and proclaimed his innocence. It began:[28] 'Receive from thy unfortunate husband these his last lines; these the last words that ever thou shalt receive from him. That I can live never to see thee and my child more! — I cannot. . . .' After advising Elizabeth, still a young woman, to marry 'not to please sense, but to avoid poverty, and to preserve thy child', he continued:

For myself, I am left of all men that have done good to many. All my good turns forgotten; all my errors revived and expounded to all extremity of ill. All my services, hazards, and expenses for my country — plantings, discoveries, fights, councils, and whatsoever else — malice hath now covered over. I am now made an enemy and traitor by the word of an unworthy man . . .

This is obviously Lord Cobham, whom Ralegh had heard was the one who had accused him of complicity in the plots.

He hath proclaimed me to be a partaker of his vain imaginations, notwithstanding the whole course of my life hath approved the contrary, as my death shall approve it. Woe, woe, woe be unto him by whose falsehood we are lost. He hath separated us asunder. He hath slain my honor; my fortune. He hath robbed thee of thy husband, thy child of his father, and me of you both.

[27] Edwards, *Life*, vol. I, p. 375. *Calendar of State Papers, Venetian, 1603–07*, p. 82, no. 111.
[28] Edwards, *Life*, vol. II, pp. 383–7.

Ralegh then asks his wife to 'forgive thou all, as I do.' He singles out his ancient enemy, Lord Henry Howard, calling him 'my heavy enemy', but expresses surprise that Cecil had not supported him — 'I thought he would never forsake me in extremity. I would not have done it him, God knows.' And he closes with an emotional passage which foreshadows the famous poem that he is purported to have written on the night before his execution.

Oh intolerable infamy! O God! I cannot resist these thoughts. I cannot live to think how I am derided, to think of the expectation of my enemies, the scorns I shall receive, the cruel words of lawyers, the infamous taunts and despites, to be made a wonder and a spectacle!. . . O Death! destroy my memory which is my tormentor; my thoughts and my life cannot dwell in one body . . .

I bless my poor child, and let him know his father was no traitor. Be bold of my innocence, for God — to whom I offer life and soul — knows it. And whosoever thou choose again after me, let him be but thy politique husband. But let my son be thy beloved, for he is part of me and I live in him; and the difference is but in the number and not in the kind. And the Lord for ever keep thee and them, and give thee comfort in both worlds.

Naturally, this letter protesting his innocence was not released by his enemies, nor was word of his attempted suicide widely circulated. It is almost amazing that though the word got into the continental news, there was little publicity in English governmental circles, and of the death of Hancock none at all. When James heard of the attempt, he ordered the examination to continue, and ordered that 'some good preacher shall be present to make him known that it is his soul he must wound and not his body.'[29]

Life in London was particularly grim in the summer and fall of 1603; deaths from the plague were running from 1,500 to 2,500 per week, and in the first week of September passed the 3,000 mark. The King was on Progress, followed by most of the members of his Court. But the commissioners continued to try to extract incriminating admissions from the prisoners in the Tower in preparation for their trials for treason. A report on 11 September indicated that 'The judges of late met at Maidenhead to consider of the crime of

[29] Harrison, *Jacobean Journal*, p. 51.

the prisoners, and it is said they make no question of finding all culpable save only Sir Walter Ralegh, against whom the proofs are less pregnant.' But they continued their enquiries, keeping the prisoners isolated from each other, facing each in turn with charges and accusations which they had extracted (or claimed to have done) from the others. Under this intensive questioning, much conflicting testimony was taken, from which the commissioners could take whatever suited their purposes as they prepared for the trial, now set for early November at Winchester.

Since the evidence was totally based on hearsay, testimony of accused persons, and pure hypothesis, it was difficult for Ralegh to prepare a case for his defence. The case that was developing has been summarized by a modern jurist as follows:[30]

The indictment charged Raleigh with high treason by conspiring to deprive the King of his Government; to alter religion; to bring in the Roman superstition; and to procure foreign enemies to invade the kingdom. The facts alleged to support these charges were that Lord Cobham on June 11, 1603, the previous June that is, met Raleigh at Durham House, where the Adelphi now stands, and conferred with him as to advancing Lady Arabella Stuart to the throne; that it was there agreed that Cobham should bargain with Aremberg, the Ambassador of the Archduke of Austria, for a bribe of 600,000 crowns; that Cobham should go to the Archduke to procure his support from the King of Spain, and to the Duke of Savoy, promising to establish peace between England and Spain, to tolerate the Popish and Roman superstition, and to be ruled by them as to her marriage. Cobham was then to return to Jersey where he would find Raleigh and take counsel with him as to how to distribute Aremberg's bribe. On the same day Cobham told his brother [George] Brook of all these treasons and persuaded him to assent to them; afterwards Cobham and Brook spoke these words, 'that there never would be a good world in England till the King (meaning our sovereign lord) and his cubs (meaning his royal issue) were taken away.' Further Raleigh published a book to Cobham, written against the title of the King, and Cobham published the same book to Brook. Further Cobham, on June 14, at Raleigh's instigation, moved Brook to instigate Lady Arabella to write the letters as aforesaid. Also on June 17, Cobham, at Raleigh's instigation, wrote to Aremberg through one Matthew de Laurency, to obtain the 600,000

---

[30] Sir Harry L. Stephen, 'The Trial of Sir Walter Raleigh: a Lecture delivered in connection with the Raleigh Tercentenary Commemoration', *Transactions of the Royal Historical Society*, 4th ser. 2 (1919), pp. 172–87.

crowns, which were promised to him on June 18, and of which Cobham promised 8000 to Raleigh and 10,000 to Brook. To [all of] this Raleigh pleaded not guilty.

But Ralegh did what he could to bring direct confrontation in court with the witnesses involved. Evidently he asked Harriot to look into the matter of the Law of God in this matter, while he himself looked into the law of man. A series of rough notes remaining among Harriot's manuscripts shows the search he made, and the evidence he found in the holy scriptures. His notes read as follows:[31]

Numbers	35,30.
Deut.	17, 6.
*Deut.	19, 5.
Math.	18,15.
	16.
	17.
John.	8,16.
	17.
	18.
2 Cor.	13, 1.
Math.	7,12.
Luke.	6,13.
Tobit.	4,15.
Math.	7, 2.
prov.	26,27.
Eccus.	27,26.
prov.	19, 5.

The ordering of these references is evidence that in his search, Harriot was using a copy of the Geneva Bible, probably of the edition of 1583.[32] The first reference, Numbers 35:30, is on a page which had the headnote reading 'Lawes concerning murther' and reads as follows:

29.   So these things shalbe a law[1] of iudgement vnto you, throughout your generations in all your dwellings.

30.   Whosoeuer killeth any person, the iudge shall slay the murtherer,

[31] BL Add. MS 6787, fo. 119v.

[32] *THE BIBLE. Translated according to the Ebrew and Greeke, and conferred with the best translations in diuers languages. With most Profitable Annotations vpon all the hard places, ... And also a most profitable Concordance for the readie finding out of any thing in the same conteyned... Imprinted at London by Christopher Barker, printer to the Queenes most excellent Maiestie./ 1583./* (STC 2138).

through witnesses: but one witnesse shall not testifie against a
person to cause him to die.

A side note in the margin, alongside verse 29, served as a
concordance to refer the reader to other references on the
same subject. Obviously, Harriot, having located his first text
through either the headnote of the page or the sidenote on
the cited reference, got the further references which led him
on to the completion of his assignment in determining
Biblical law regarding the testimony of witnesses required
on a capital charge. The sidenote read:

1. A law to iudge murthers done, either of purpose or vnaduisedly.
    Deut. 17.6 and 19.15. Math. 18.16. 2 Cor. 13.1.

The second reference, Deuteronomy 17:6 repeated the
ancient Hebrew law:

6. At the mouth of two or three witnesses shall hee that is worthy
    of death dye: but at the mouth of one witnesse, hee shall not die.

with a sidenote concordance referring to the earlier reference
and the ones from Numbers, Deuteronomy, and Matthew.

The asterisk which Harriot has placed alongside his third
reference shows that upon checking this reference he found
he had made a mistake, or that there was a mistake in the
concordance. Deuteronomy 19:5 which he had copied in
error for 19:15, has nothing to do with testimony; it reads:

5. As he that goeth vnto the wood with his neighbor to hewe wood,
    and his hande striketh with the axe to cut downe a tree, if the
    head flip from the helue, and hit his neighbor that he dieth, the
    same shal flee vnto one of the cities, and liue.

The correct reference, which Harriot should have read was
the fifteenth verse instead of the fifth:

15. One witnesse shall not rise against a man for any trespasse, or
    for any sinne, or for any fault that he offendeth in, but at ye
    mouth of two witnesses or at the mouth of three witnesses shall
    the matter be stablished.

The same theme — that the testimony of at least two and
preferably three witnesses is essential for the condemnation
to death in Hebrew law — is repeated in the passages selected
in Matthew, John, and 2 Corinthians.

Matthew 7:12, Luke 6:13, and Tobit 4:15 are a second group of passages which Ralegh might use in his defence — restatements of 'The Golden Rule'. As expressed by Matthew, the statement read:

Matthew 7:12. Therefore whatsoeuer ye woulde that men should do to you, euen so do ye to them: for this is the Law and the Prophets.

and the next one, Matthew 7:1-2, issues a warning to false witnesses:

1. Iudge not, that ye be not iudged.
2. For with that iudgement yee iudge, ye shalbe iudged, and with what measure ye mete, it shalbe measured to you againe.

And for his peroration, Ralegh was prepared to cite the Bible as follows:

Proverbs 26:27. He that diggeth a pit, shall fall therein, and he that rolleth a stone, it shall returne vnto him.

Ecclesiasticus 27:26. Who so diggeth a pitte, shall fall therein [and he that layeth a stone in his neighbours way, shall stumble thereon,] and hee that layeth a snare for another, shall be taken in it himselfe.

And for a close, especially aimed at Cobham, was the serious warning:

Proverbs 19:5. A false witnesse shall not be vnpunished: and he that speaketh lyes, shall not escape.

During the first week of November, Ralegh was taken to Winchester by Sir William Waad, one of the men who had been heavily involved in preparing the case against Ralegh, and who had been named as one of the three special commissioners, along with Cecil and Ralegh's vitriolic enemy, Henry Howard, who were to sit as judges on him. Also on the bench were named Ralegh's old comrade Lord Thomas Howard, now Lord Chamberlain, Charles Blount, Lord Wotton of Morley, Sir John Stanhope the Vice-Chamberlain, and two Chief Justices — Sir John Popham and Sir Edmund Anderson — and their assistants. A jury of seven knights and nine gentlemen had been drawn. Ralegh was to conduct his own defence, and since the case involved treason against the King, the prosecution was conducted by the Attorney-General, Sir Edward Coke, and his assistant, John Hele,

Sergeant-at-law. The Indictment, which had been drawn from the examination at Staines on 21 August, was a complex one, consisting of ten points — each of which concerned an action of Sir Walter Ralegh which purported to link him with the treasonable plots of Cobham, Brooke, and Lord Grey. Because of the complications which existed between the items, Ralegh asked and was granted the right to make statements or to ask questions as the trial proceeded, rather than to follow the case of the prosecution with a unified statement of his defence. This procedure, while it may have been simpler for Ralegh, led to a personal interchange between the persons involved, including the members of the court and jury as well, which gives the whole proceeding an aura of drama and emotion usually barred from a court of law, particularly one in which the defendant's life is at stake. Perhaps no other case in British law has attracted so much judicial attention after the fact, with a general consensus by later jurists that justice or sound principles of jurisprudence had no part in the conviction of Ralegh. From the aspect of law, the 'trial' remains a travesty, since no witnesses were called, no evidence of any kind was produced, and the total case consisted of unsubstantiated accusations and charges — all of them made by persons themselves under charges of treason, and probably extracted through torture. But in spite of this, the reader must be impressed by the vigour and fortitude of Ralegh as he reacted boldly and without fear to every accusation brought against him.

Since no evidence was presented against him, there was little that Ralegh could do but protest his innocence, demand that he be faced in open court with his accusers, and insist that a man should not in justice be faced with the death penalty on the testimony of a single, unproduced witness. These basic legal tenets, based on ancient Hebrew law, were those developed and worked up by Harriot, after Ralegh was imprisoned and before the examinations began. After the results of the examination of Lord Cobham had been revealed which stated that Cobham laid all the blame for his actions on Ralegh, Ralegh brought forth his first defence on moral as well as legal grounds:[33]

My Lords, I claim to have my accuser brought here to speak face to face. Though I know not how to make my best defense by law; yet, since I was a prisoner, I have learned that by the Law and Statutes of this realm in case of treason a man ought to be convicted [the original reads 'convinced'] by the testimony of two witnesses. I will not take upon me to defend the matter upon the Statute of the twenty-fifth of Edward the Third, though that requires an overt act. But remember, I beseech your Lordships, the Statute of the first of Edward the Sixth which saith; 'No man shall be condemned of treason, unless he be accused by two lawful accusers.' And, by the Statute of the fifth and sixth of Edward the Sixth, those accusers 'must be brought in person before the party accused, at his arraignment, if they be living.' Remember also, my Lords, the Statute of the first and second of Philip and Mary which says, that 'at the arraignment of any man for treason every person who shall declare, confess, or depose anything against him shall, if living and within the realm, be brought forth in person before the party arraigned, if he require it, and object and say openly, in his hearing, what he can against him; unless the party arraigned shall willingly confess the same.

These laws, here cited by Ralegh, had been — as the Attorney-General would be certain to show in rebuttal — repealed, and Ralegh evidently knew it, as his next words show: 'Whether at this day these laws be in force I know not. But such was the wisdom of former times that any man accused must have, at the least, two lawful witnesses to be brought forth at the time of his arraignment.' It was at this point in his defence, that Ralegh turned to the scriptures, reminding the judges of the story of how Daniel took the judges to task for condemning Susannah without interrogating the witnesses against her, and how Daniel's questioning of their testimony uncovered their falsity. Daniel based his case then, as Ralegh was basing his now, on the ancient law of the Hebrews.

... the equity and reason of those laws still remains. They are still kept to illustrate how the Common Law was then taken and ought to be expounded. But, howsoever that may be, the law of God, I am sure, liveth for ever. And the Canon of God saith: '*At the mouth of two or three witnesses shall he that is worthy of death be put to death; but at*

---

[33] There are several accounts of Ralegh's trial in varying degrees of detail, but the official court records do not appear to exist. The best and apparently the most accurate account is one written about 1621 in a commonplace book of that time, now in the British Library in Harleian MS 39, fos. 265-312. This is the version cited most often by Edwards in his *Life*, vol. I, pp. 383-439. Citations here are taken from Edwards, pp. 407-8.

the mouth of one witness he shall not be put to death.'[34] And, again:
*'One witness shall not rise up against a man for any iniquity or any sin
that he sinneth. At the mouth of two or three witnesses shall the matter
be established.'* Divers other places of the Old Testament are to like
purpose, and the same is confirmed by our Savour, by Saint Paul, and
by the whole consent of the Scripture. By the law of God, therefore,
the life of man is of such price and value that no person, whatever his
offence is, ought to die, unless he be condemned on the testimony of
two or three witnesses.

As he had hoped it would, Ralegh's introduction of Canon
Law into a trial for treason led to considerable debate. Members of the bench and jury seemed split on the reasonableness
of Ralegh's demands that he be faced with his accuser,
Cobham, and permitted to question his testimony. But the
matter was resolved by the exposition of the law given by
the Lord Chief Justice, Sir John Popham, who replied:[35]

Sir Walter Ralegh, for the Statutes you have mentioned, none of them
help you. The Statutes you speak of in cases of treason were found to
be inconvenient, and were taken away by another law. . . . All is therefore put to the Common Law. And, by the Common Law, one witness
is sufficient, and the accusation of confederates, or the confession of
others, is full proof. Neither is subscription of the party so material to
the Confession, *if it be otherwise testified by credible persons.* [or, as
Edwards notes, by the 'credible testimony' of the Lord Chief Justice
himself.] And, of all other proofs, the accusation of one who by his
confession first accuseth himself is the strongest. It hath the force of
a verdict of twelve men.

The prosecutor, the Attorney General Sir Edward Coke, added
to the diatribe against Ralegh's interpretation of the law:
'You have read the letter of the law, but understand it not.
This dilemma of yours about two witnesses led you into
treason: for you thought with yourself, "Either Cobham
must accuse or not accuse me; if he accuses me, yet he is
but one witness; if he accuses me not, then I am clear."' On
this note, the trial continued, with more evidence brought

[34] Ibid., p. 409. The wording of these two quotations from Deuteronomy
15:6 and 19:15 cannot have been the words given by Ralegh, since they are taken
from the translation of the King James Bible which was first issued in 1611. I
have not been able to check this passage against the original BL MS to see if the
modernization was done by the original copier about 1621, or by Edwards himself. The wording current in both the Bishop's Bible and the Geneva Bible before
1611 is that cited in the notes about Harriot's search. See 308-10 above.

[35] Ibid., p. 411-12.

as to the testimony given by Cobham, and a very extended
discussion of how a book, purportedly advocating treason,
was obtained by Ralegh, and how he gave it to Cobham. But
Coke was still concerned about Ralegh's insistence that he
be faced by his accusers, and determined to disabuse the jury
of any significance to the Biblical law about witnesses, their
numbers, and their being heard. As the day drew to a close,
he introduced the matter again, bringing in this time additional
testimony attributed to Ralegh's long-time friend, Lawrence
Keymis.[37] 'Cobham saith that Kemishe came to him with a
letter, torn; and did wish him not to be dismayed, for one
witness could not hurt him.' Ralegh rose in anger: 'This
poor man [Keymis] hath been close prisoner these eighteen
weeks. He was offered the rack, to make him confess. I
never sent any such message by him. I only did write to
Cobham, to tell him what I had done with Mr. Attorney; I
having of his at that time the great pearl and a diamond.'
The commissioners all insisted that no one had threatened
Keymis with the rack, with Waad only remarking that when
he and the Solicitor had examined Keymis they had told
him that 'he deserved the rack' but did not threaten him
with it. Coke continued to present Cobham's charges on the
subject; Cobham had testified:

Kemishe brought him a letter from Ralegh, and that part which was
concerning the Lords of the Council was rent out, — 'that he was
examined and cleared him [i.e. Cobham] of all;' and that the Lord
Henry Howard said, 'Because he [Cobham] was discontented, he was
fit to be in on the action [i.e. his discontent led him to be a party to a
treasonable action].' And further, that Kemishe said to him, from
Ralegh, that he should 'be of good comfort, for one witness could not
condemn for treason.'

Again Ralegh denied that he had given any such message to
Keymis, or that Keymis had said any such thing to Cobham.
   This was the essence of the trial of Sir Walter Ralegh. No
evidence had been presented against him — only testimony as
to what others, particularly Cobham, had accused Ralegh of.
And Ralegh, on his part, could only deny the validity of the
accusations. As he indicated in his summary to the jury:[38]

[36] Ibid., p. 413.   [37] Ibid., pp. 422-3.   [38] Ibid., p. 428.

They prove nothing against me. Only they bring the accusation of my Lord Cobham, which he hath lamented and repented, as heartily as if it had been a horrible murder. For he knew that all this sorrow which should come to me is by his means. . . . I have spent £40,000 against the Spaniard. I have not purchased £40 a year. . . . I that have always condemned the Spanish faction — methinks it is a strange thing that now I should affect it! Remember what St. Austin saith: *'Sic judicatis tanquam ab alio mox judicandi.'* Now if you would be content, on presumptions, to be delivered to the slaughter; to have your wives and children turned into the streets to beg their bread; — if you would be contented to be so judged; judge so of me.

At this point, indicating that Ralegh had finally presented his case, the Attorney General read to the jury a final letter purporting to come from Cobham, making definite charges of treason against Ralegh. Interpolated with the reading were many phrases, such as 'Is not this a Spanish heart in an English body?' But throughout these concluding remarks it was apparent that Coke was riled by the fact that Ralegh had manoeuvred his case so that it was Ralegh who was quoting the scriptures, and Coke who was denying them. This was particularly bitter because of Ralegh's reputation as a free-thinker, perhaps even an atheist, and that his major defence had been worked up for him by Thomas Harriot, who was similarly suspect among the general public. To Coke and to Popham, the Chief Justice, this was clearly a case of the Devil quoting the scriptures for his own purposes. As a matter of fact, Coke, at the last, cited the quotation, and, to add insult to injury, taxed Ralegh with his antagonism to the Earl of Essex, whom Coke branded as a truly religious man.[39]

Coke: O damnable Atheist! He [Ralegh] hath learned some text of Scripture to serve his own purpose, but falsely alleged. He counsels him [Cobham] not to be led by the counsels of preachers, as Essex was. — He died the child of God. God honoured him at his death. [*Then to Ralegh*:] Thou was by. *'Et lupus et turpes instant morientibus ursæ.'* He died, indeed, for his offence against the law. The King himself spake these words: 'He that shall say that Essex died not for treason is punishable.'

The Chief Justice then gave judgement on Ralegh, in a long speech which has been variously recorded. Edwards, though

[39] Ibid., pp. 432-3.

he does not reproduce the final speech of Popham, indicates that in his judgement he 'used a brutality of language and a craftiness of insinuation which would have been not unworthy of the talents of Coke or of Waad. He knew that he could not be answered, and gave the reins to his coarse nature.'[40] Just what his words were cannot now be determined, but it is obvious that he picked up the animosity towards Ralegh's scripture quoting and the role that had been played by Harriot in the preparation of his defence. According to the manuscript copy in the Harleian collection, the one generally most accurate as far as can be determined, Popham taxed Ralegh as follows:[41]

To conclude other things there goes of you which are very atheisticall and prophane precepts said to be Sir Walter Ralegh's: if not yours you shall doe well to protest against them; if yours then renounce them and aske God forgivenesse for them as you hope for another life. And lett not Heriott nor any such Doctor perswade you there is no Eternity. one other thing stands confessed against you which is very irreligious perswading against all Confession to any preacher and reproving my Lord of Essex, that worthy Earle who no doubte died a good Christian and the Child of God and had he not bin intangled by some in his Closett had noe doubt submitted himselfe to the Queen and lived. . . .

Another version of Popham's judgement is to be found in the Public Record Office.[42] It varies in detail, but shows approximately the same theme:

Your case being thus, lett it not greive yow yf I speake a litle but of soule and love & your god. You haue byn taxed by the world with the defense of most heathenishe and blasphemous opinions which I lyst not repeate because Christian eares cannot endure to heere them, nor the authers and mayntainers of them suffered to liue in any Christian common wealth. Yow know what men say of *Hereiat*. You should doe well before yow goe out of the world to geue satisfaction heerein, and not to die with those imputations on yow. Lett not any devill perswade yow to thincke ther is no eternytie in hell fire. In the first accusation of my Lord Cobham, I observed his manner of speakinge. I protest before the hereing god I am perswaded, he spake nothinge but truth. You wrote that he should not in any case confesse any thinge to a preacher, telling him an example of my Lord of Esex, that noble earl. yf he had not byn careied away with others he had lived in honor this day amonge vs.

[40] Ibid. pp. 435–6.   [41] BL Harleian MS 39, fo. 312[r].
[42] PRO SP 14/4/83, fo. 36.

Popham then pronounced the official penalty for treason:[43]

Nowe it resteth to pronounce Judgment, which I wish you had not byn this day to receve, for yf the feare of God in yow had byn answerable to other your greatnes, you might have liued to have bine a singuler good subiect. I never sawe the licke triale and I hope I well never see the licke againe. But since yow haue bine fownd guilty of theise horable treasons, yowe shalbe had from hence to the place frome whence yow came, ther to abide till the day of execution, and from thence yow shalbe drawne vpon a hurdle through the streetes to the place of execution and ther to be hanged and cut down alive, and your body shalbe opened and your privye members cut of, and your hart and bowells pulled out and throwne into the fire before your eyes, then your head to be strecken of from your body, your body shalbe devided into fower quarters, to be disposed at the kinges pleasure. And God be mercyfull to your soule.

To have been singled out by the Lord Chief Justice as an atheist and an evil influence at the most sensational trial in England must have been a soul-searing experience for Thomas Harriot. There can be no doubt but that he had felt that he was helping his friend, Sir Walter, by preparing a defence based on Hebrew and Christian legal principles. But it was apparent from the trial itself that his efforts had harmed Ralegh rather than aided him. Invoking canon law for the defence of a man well known for his indifference to religion had antagonized and enraged both the prosecuting Attorney-General and the eminent justices on the bench. That Harriot was crushed may be gathered from the fact that among his existing manuscripts there is nothing indicating serious study or experimental research which carries a date between the period of 18 September 1603, shortly after Ralegh's imprisonment and two months before his arraignment, and 25 July 1604, nearly a year later, when he immersed himself in the problems of the specific gravities of various substances and their refractive indices, which had occupied him so broadly two years before.[44]

[43] Ibid., fo. 37.
[44] The date of 18 Sept. 1603 is found on a rough note dealing with the theory of calculation of the surface area of a spherical triangle, on fo. 106^r of BL Add. MS 6787. Just a few pages further on, at fo. 111^v is a rough note listing the names of some of those involved with Ralegh at the time of the Indictment or Arraignment of Ralegh. The names, listed in a column, are as follows: 'S.W.R. L. Grey. L. Cobham. M. G. Brooke. S. Ar. Gorge. S. Ar. Sandys. S. Griffin Marcum.'
The date of 25 July 1604 is on fos. 245^v, 246^v, and 247^v of Add. MS 6788.

It is very probable that it was the shock of thus being
publicly proclaimed an evil influence which led Harriot
seriously to consider how he might be viewed by posterity.
On the back of the final folio of a nearly finished mathematical work which he called 'The Doctrine of Nauticall
Triangles Compendious', Harriot jotted down a list of books
in which appeared some references to him or to his work.[45]
The list covered books published between 1587 and 1602,
and consisted of twenty-seven items, unnumbered, as
follows:[46]

[1]   Item a Theologicall discourse of Harveyes.
[2]   Item the Chronicle.
[3]   Item the Latin decades.
[4]   Item pierce penilesse, 1592.
[5]   Item a libellum intituled An advertisement &c. 1592.
[6]   Item Formans booke of longitudes.
[7]   Item Hoodes Answere to the same.
[8]   Item his staffe.
[9]   Booke of voyadges in master Lanes discourse.
[10] My discourse of Virginia in 4 languages.
[11] Item a latin discourse agaynst the state. 1593.
[12] Item Tanners booke of the sphere.
[13] Item a boke in Latin 1593 contra edictum Elizabethe.
[14] Item Master Hughes his booke. 1594.
[15] Item Gabriel Harveyes booke.
[16] Item plates booke, for a lanterne.
[17] Item a booke of carpentering Sir George More
                          Master More
[18] Item Scaligers Appendix. Hariolantur Mee.
[19] Item Iohn Davies seamans secretes.
[20] Captain Kemis of Guiana.

---

[45] For a more detailed account of this list and its significance, see the article
written by the author in collaboration with David B. Quinn, 'A Contemporary
List of Hariot References', *Renaissance Quarterly*, XXII. 1 (Spring 1969), 9–26.
[46] The list is to be found currently as fo. 22^r of Petworth House MSS: HMC
241/VI b. The books cited bear the following numbers in the *Short Title Catalogue, 1475–1640*: [1] STC 12915; [2] STC 13569; [3] Not represented; [4]
STC 18371; [5] STC 19885; [6] STC 11185; [7] Not extant; [8] STC 13699;
[9] STC 12625; [10] STC 12786; [11] Not identified; [12] STC 23671; [13]
Not represented; [14] STC 13906; [15] STC 12903; [16] STC 19991; [17] STC
18075 and STC 18071; [18] Not represented; [19] Not represented (copy in
British Museum); [20] STC 14947; [21] Not represented; [22] STC 1445; [23]
As [4] above; [24] STC 13635; [25] STC 24134; [26] STC 11883; [27] STC
12626.

[21] A Spaniard writing in latin of Virginia mappes & chartes.
                                     Dominus Sauile
                               Master Adrian Gilbert.
[22] Barlo tucheth me in his boke of Navigation.
[23] Master Hues de vsu Globorum.
[24] Master Chapmans Achilles.
[25] Master Torporly in valuis astronomicis.
[26] Doctor Gilbert on the Magnetes.
[27] Hacluit in his epistle to the Voyadges.

In considering the twenty-six printed references to his work or thought (no. 23 is an inadvertent duplication of no. 14, and is therefore crossed out in the original list), Harriot must have concluded that his reputation for history was more good than bad. Though there is no apparent organization in the order in which the works are listed, having probably been jotted down as he remembered them, when examined, they fall into three main categories. Seven of the references have to do with Harriot's work as an explorer in the new world, covering the period from 1587 to 1600, and noting the publication of many printings of his *Briefe and true report*. Ten of the references refer to Harriot's technological innovations, most of them in connection with navigation theory or practice, and include most of the works dealing with practical seamanship issued between 1592 and 1602. Negative to Harriot's reputation would be the books in the third group which exploited some of the unorthodoxies of Harriot's beliefs. These would include the works of the early 1590s which branded Harriot as Ralegh's 'Master' of his 'School of Atheism', his role in the controversial pamphlets of Richard Harvey, Thomas Nashe, and Gabriel Harvey, and, combining his science and unorthodoxy, his depiction as a 'Doubting Thomas' in the discussions about the computation of longitude in the works of Forman and Hood. But off-setting, to a large extent, the negative impact of these quarrel-some pamphleteers, were two long poems which had been dedicated to Harriot: one by Lawrence Keymis was a dedicatory Latin poem in flattering terms included in his *A relation of the second voyage to Guiana*, 1597, and re-printed in the 1600 edition of Hakluyt's *Principall Navigations, III*, addressed 'Ad Thomam Hariotum & vniuersae Philosophiae peritissimum'. The other, addressed 'To my admired and soule-loued friend Mayster of all essential and true knowledge, *M. Harriots.*' attached as a preface by George Chapman to the first portion of his famous translation of Homer's *Iliad*, in his *Achilles Shield* of 1598. Chapman, at least, found no lack of authority in Harriot; he portrayed him as the essence of reason and sound philosophy, the embodiment of wisdom:

> To you whose depth of soule measures the height,
> And all dimensions of all workes of weight,
> Reason being ground, structure and ornament,
> To all inuentions; graue and permanent,
> And your cleare eyes the Spheres where *Reason* moues . . .
>
> (sig. D–1ᵛ)

Harriot, Chapman insisted, did not follow most men in working for fame or riches, but sought only truth: '. . . who is he that may not learne of you, Whom learning doth with his lights throne endow?' And for the further propagation of this truth, Chapman had urged Harriot to publish and make known his findings:

> And when thy writings that now errors Night
> Chokes earth with mistes, breake forth like easterne light,
> Showing to euery comprehensive eye,
> High sectious brawles be calmde by vnitie,
> Nature made all transparent, and her hart
> Gripte in they hand, crushing digested Art
> In flames vnmeasurde, measurde out of it,
> On whose head for her crowne thy soule shall sitte . . .
>
> (sig. D–3)

What thoughts passed through Harriot's mind as he tried to reconcile such extreme evaluations of his character will never be known. 'Athiest', 'jugler', 'antichristian hellish Aristotelian', or 'Mayster of all essential and true knowledge' — sceptical and 'unbelieving S. Thomas' must have dismissed all such hyperbolic positions as unreal and exaggerated. But he must have taken pride and pleasure in the recognition that though he had not published, he was still known and recognized for his ideas and beliefs, both throughout England and on the Continent. He may even have shared some of Chapman's optimism about his future publication, and the impact his clear, mathematical mind might have in the new and emerging science of revealing the truths of nature and of rolling back the mists of 'error's Night'. In balance, he would have been justified in thinking that his contemporary assessment of his life and work, in spite of the tirades of Coke and Popham, was positive, and he must have taken heart at what the future still held for him, even though his patron and best friend, Sir Walter Ralegh, languished in prison under imminent threat of the horrible fate of a convicted traitor.

Whether or not James would have kingly mercy on the convicted traitors was for a long time uncertain. Certainly, following his trial, Ralegh was most concerned about getting his affairs in order, in assuring the legality of his claim to Sherborne, in settling his debts, and in making proper distribution of his few remaining sources of income for the use of his wife and heirs. In all of these he relied heavily on the advice and assistance of Thomas Harriot. On 4 December 1603, Lord Cecil wrote a memorandum to Sir Benjamin Tichbourne, the Sheriff who was to be in charge of the executions:[47] 'We have shewed the Kings Majesty your lettres, and he hath redd that of Sir W. Raleghs without superscription evry woord. he shall heare answer by Shelbury what shalbe don for Heriots coming about his Accompts which grace his Majesty intends to afford him.' This was evidently intended to be a final accounting. About this same date, the two priests, Watson and Clarke, were executed at Winchester, with the full provisions of the sentence of death for treason carried out by Tichbourne. The quarters of their bodies were displayed over the gates of the city, and their heads placed on one of the turrets of the Castle.[48] On 6 December George Brooke was also executed, though in his case some of the barbarities of the treason sentence were mitigated. Three other traitors were scheduled to die on Friday, 10 December — Markham, Grey, and Cobham. The execution of Ralegh was set for the following Monday, 13 December. But James, who had been tormented by the lack of evidence in all their trials, finally made up his mind to spare the lives of these four; on 7 December he signed the

---

[47] HMC: *Manuscripts of the Marquess of Salisbury at Hatfield House*, XV: 305 (Hatfield MS *102.*48.)
[48] Edwards, I. 441.

warrants which stayed their executions. But this knowledge he kept to himself, and on 8 December executed the death warrants just as if he planned to proceed with carrying out the sentences. In so doing, he played with the prisoners in a cat-mouse game, arranging matters so that the releases would arrive just at the point when the prisoners were on the scaffold awaiting death, releasing them for a short respite for prayer, and bringing them back to the scaffold for final release. Each prisoner in turn, thus, had to face death several times, before all were brought together on the scaffold to learn that they were not to die. What James hoped to accomplish by these manoeuvres is not to be determined; but actually they accomplished nothing more than the satisfaction the King derived from showing his complete control over the lives or deaths of his subjects.

Even the release from the immediate threat of death must have been somewhat bitter to Ralegh. In the month between the trial in October and the farce of the mock executions in December, Ralegh had shown his own true character. Either in abject fear for himself, or in a desire to save his family, Ralegh had written pleading letters to the King and Council and to many friends in Court. The nobility which he had shown in the court hearings was overshadowed by the lack of courage or weakness of spirit which he showed when truly facing death. Ralegh himself recognized this, and in an undated letter to his wife, sometime in early December, he wrote:[49]

Gett those letters (if it bee possible) which I writt to the Lords, wherein I sued for my lief, but God knoweth that itt was for you and yours that I desired it, but itt is true that I disdaine myself for begging itt. And know itt (deare wief) that your sonne is a childe of a true man, and who, in his own respect, despiseth Death, and all his misshapen and ouglie formes.

Harriot appears to have suffered some of the same agonies which marked the fall of Ralegh, since, as we have seen, there is nothing in his extant manuscripts to show any intellectual effort from the arrest of Ralegh until July of 1604. But no man can continue to live in such an extreme emotional state,

Edwards, Letter CXXIII, II. 286–7.

and there seems to have been a gradual relaxation of his anxiety as time slowly passed. Day by day the novelty of the King's prisoners in the Tower wore off, and the tensions which surrounded them relaxed. On their initial incarceration it had been decreed that each of the major prisoners, Grey, Cobham, and Ralegh, would be permitted to have two servants in attendance — one within the Tower as a personal servant, the other outside to run errands and assist in the management of affairs. But as time passed, even these restrictions were relaxed. In July 1604 the Lieutenant of the Tower, Sir George Harvey, protested to Lord Cecil that a large number of persons were being given access to the prisoners without warrant of authority, and that he had been forced to lock the garden gates to stop visiting between Sir Walter and Lord Grey.[50] Listed as having access to Ralegh without authority were: The Lady Ralegh, Sir Carew Ralegh, Sir George Carew, his physician (unnamed), Alexander Brett, Mr Peter van Lore, Mr Arthur Aston, Mr Charles Chewt, the Widow Morley, Mr Shelbury, and two servants, Peter Deane and John Talbot, the latter of whom shared Ralegh's life in the Tower to the end. Though Harriot is not mentioned in this list reviewed by Cecil, another list, undated, but sometime in late 1604 or early 1605 remains among the Cecil papers at Hatfield House.[51]

The Persons permitted to haue Access to Sir Walter Raleighe.

Sir Walter Rawleighe
- His Lady and his Sonne, and her wayting mayd.
- John Talbot / Peter Deane } Their to remaine in the Tower with him.
- John Talbot a boy
  Gilbert Hawthorne a Preacher
  Doctor Turner
  Doctor John a Surgion
  John Shelbury
  Thomas Herryot
  his Steward of Sherborne } To repaire to him at Convenient times

The fact that the surgeon, Doctor John, was granted access to Ralegh would appear to date this earlier rather than later, since there is no evidence of any need for surgery except that

[50] HMC MSS of the Cecils at Hatfield House, vol. XVI, 1933, pp. 192-3.
[51] MS 115.21. n.d.

following Ralegh's attempted suicide in July of 1603. More interesting, though, is the final entry 'his Steward for Sherborne', since there is no evidence that that title was ever formally employed. The closest such title was that of 'Bailiff' which had been held by John Mere when Ralegh assumed the estates. It is possible that this item may be an appositive, and that Ralegh considered Harriot as the one who was officially responsible for the management of Sherborne while he was absent. Several bits of evidence remain which reinforce the likelihood of this assignment. In Ralegh's will of 1597, Harriot had been named as one of the overseers of his fiscal affairs, along with Arthur Throckmorton, George Carew, and Alexander Brett. Again in 1599, in his legal manipulations regarding Sherborne, Harriot was named as trustee to Ralegh's estates, along with his cousin, George Carew. And even long after Ralegh's death, Harriot, in 1621 in his own will, showed that he had been responsible for managing Sir Walter Ralegh's accounts:[52] 'Item whereas I have divers wast papers (of which some are in a Canvas bagge) of my Accomptes to Sir Walter Rawley for all which I have discharges or acquitances lying in some boxes or other, my desire is that they may be all burnt.' In any event, whatever his formal position in the Ralegh household was, the evidence and traditions of the time tell us that Harriot was one of those who had ready access to the Tower for conferences with Ralegh, and that he exercised this prerogative freely during the thirteen years of Ralegh's residence there.

It is obvious from Harriot's manuscript notes of his activities, and from the reports on the activities of Sir Walter Ralegh that most of the terror and emotion surrounding the trial and sentencing had evaporated by the summer of 1605. Harvey was replaced as Lieutenant of the Tower on Monday, 12 August, by Sir William Waad. From his previous experience with Waad Ralegh might well have expected harsher treatment under him than he had had from Harvey. As a matter of fact, he expressed these concerns to Waad, since Waad wrote to Lord Salisbury that on the day before he was

[52] Guildhall Library, London, Register of the Archdeaconry Court of London, 1618–26/7, fo. 72^{v}.

sworn in to office,[53] 'Sir Walter Raleigh used some speaches of his dislike of me the day before, yet sithence he doth acknowledge his error, & seemeth to be very well satisfied.' Cobham, Waad indicated, was even worse:

My Lo. Cobham did forget himself toward me yesterday in the afternoone in such sort as I could doe noe less then shut hym up into his lodging. . . And if I should say to your Lordship privately what I think, his Passions when the fit takes him goeth beyond Choler & I wish that that he said unto me had ben private, & not so loud, as it was heard into the court.

Waad's report to Cecil of the condition in which he found the Tower prisoners gives us a fairly clear insight into the nature of their restraints.[54]

It may please your Honorable Lordship

I hold it my dewtie at my first entrance into this Chardg, to certifie your Lordship in what state I find the Prisoners, what liberty they have, & what warrants have been shewed me for the same. Sir Gawen Harvey hath delivered me only one cheif warrant limiting the liberty of access graunted them which passed in my time of waighting whereof I send your Lordship a copie The other warrants are only for commitment of Prisoners.

The Lord Cobham hath one Servant more than is allow'd in the warrant.

For access it is open, & there come ordinarily unto him many of all sorts, not warranted by any lettres I have seene.

For libertie, the dore of the Prison, where he is towards the leads, is not shut all the day, nor the dore at the other end of the Leads by which any may have access unto him: Besides there is another dore upon the Leades thorow the Lodgings of the Leiuetenants lately made, which stood open, by wich by a private staires many came & went untill it was observed.

The Prison dore to the leades, I leave open the day time, one of the other two dores out of the leads I have caused to be shut up, & the other I leave open, but appoint one to watch theire. There is another doore at the end of a paire of staires, to the hillwards which is at times oppen'd for bringing of victuals, & other necessary occasions for him.

Sir Walter Raleigh hath like accesse of divers to him, the doore of his chamber beinge alwais open all the day to the Garden, which indeed is the only Garden the Leiuetenant hath, & in the Garden he hath converted a little Hen house to a still house, where he doth spend his time all the day, in his distillations. I desire not to remove him, though I want by that meanes the Garden: But there beinge but a slendour

---

[53] BL Add. MS 6178, fo. 12r.   [54] Ibid., fos. 14r&v, 15r.

Pale on that side the Garden towards the Lieuetenants lodgings, & the other walles very low & broken downe, nothinge can be done in the House, none can come to the house, but he espieth them on all sides. Therefore if a brick wall were built w[h]ere the Pale now standeth & the walles raised very little which would not be above twenty markes charg, & which would be the more safe & convenient.

My Lord Grey is in the lodging my Lord Cobham lay in, when he was examined. he hath no access hitherto unto him, but he hath the liberty of all the kings lodgings, & the doore to those Gardens by which when the King was there, my Lord Chamberlane came to his lodgings is alwaies open, but he useth the same sparingly. He indicated to me he might she [miscopies for *see*?] the Lady Goring, & the Lady Fleetwood his neare kinswomen, if they came to visit him: which he saith was permitted to him formerly, but I see not by what warrant.

Morgan a Servant of the Lord Cobham by the connviency of his Keeper hath had access to Morgan the Prisoner, wherof I take as yet no knowledge neither think I it was for any purpose but in kindness, & yet I have appointed him another keeper.

The situation had stabilized. Ralegh's fears for immediate death had ended; life in the Tower had become routine; he felt free to pursue his own intellectual interests, to converse with his friends, to read and write and to continue his chemical experiments. Harriot, too, had adjusted to the new regimen. He was established in his new quarters at Syon House, secure financially with his pension from the 9th Earl, and the income from the Brampton estates which he held for life. He had acquired an assistant for his researches and calculations, Christopher Tooke, and servants to keep his household and make his physical life comfortable. He had access to Ralegh at the Tower, and could, when the urge seized either of them, visit there, riding in by the Great West Road, or taking the easier voyage down the Thames by boat. In the Tower he could inform Ralegh of the condition of his finances, help him with his researches, or take him books or manuscripts he needed for his studies. Life was still precarious, but life for an Elizabethan adventurer and pirate had always been full of danger and excitement, and neither Ralegh nor Harriot had ever feared quiet and solitude, so long as they had their active imaginations and acute perceptions. A major adjustment had been called for, but it had been accomplished, and life proceeded with a state almost normal for both men.

VIII. From the Court to the Tower – Northumberland

The lightning of James's displeasure which had struck Ralegh in the fall of 1603 and led to his conviction for treason struck a second time just two years later in November 1605. For reasons that are completely unexplainable from any evidence existing at the present time, the 9th Earl was caught up in the aftermath of that most publicized of all British political crimes, the infamous 'Gunpowder Plot' of 5 November 1605.

The very nature of the Gunpowder Plot itself is subject to much controversy among scholars. Some, following the lines of the official propaganda issued by King James and his officers, hold that the plot was in truth a serious attempt of the recusant Catholics to kill the King and his parliament and to return England to the Catholic religion.[1] Others, distrustful of the pat position upheld by the King and his principal Secretary, Robert Cecil (now the Earl of Salisbury), hold that the whole affair was part of the machinations of the Machiavellian Cecil to rid the country of potential enemies and to insure the continuation of the Anglican church with the King as its ultimate authority.[2] More moderate historians see elements of both; a spontaneous and frantic plot by a few Catholic sympathizers, most of whom had been followers of Essex a decade earlier, about which Cecil learned, and which he then manipulated to his own purposes to furnish an excuse for the destruction of his

[1] For the conventionally accepted view as expressed in official government documents, see John R. Green, *A Short History of the English People*, London, Macmillan & Co., 1909, pp. 482-3, cited hereafter.
[2] This view was originated by Father John Gerard, *What was the Gunpowder Plot?*, London, Osgood, McIlvaine & Co., 1897.

enemies.[3] But as the case of Ralegh was instigated and completed without any evidence of treasonable action in fact, the involvement of Northumberland in the Gunpowder Plot and his consequent conviction and imprisonment were, in the view of all historians, similarly without basis, stimulated and consummated by the craft and twisted mind and body of the King's leading counsellor, the implacable enemy of both Ralegh and Northumberland, Robert Cecil, Earl of Salisbury.

That a major national holiday should be devoted to an historical event so controversial seems most unusual, but it must be accepted that the bonfires and fireworks which mark Guy Fawkes Day on 5 November, and the children begging 'A penny for the Guy' are but a modern replacement of the traditional harvest festival of pagan times, and the celebration of 5 November just happens to come at a convenient time for such festivities. For most celebrants, little explanation is needed, and if one is asked, the traditional response is probably that expressed by J. R. Green in his *Short History of the English People*:[4]

The breach with the Puritans was followed by a breach with the Catholics. The increase in their numbers since the remission of fines had spread a general panic; and Parliament had re-enacted the penal laws. A rumour of his own conversion so angered the King that these were now put in force with even more severity than of old. The despair of the Catholics gave fresh life to a conspiracy which had long been ripening. Hopeless of aid from abroad, or of success in an open rising at home, a small knot of desperate men, with Robert Catesby, who had taken part in the rising of Essex, at their head, resolved to destroy at a blow both King and Parliament. Barrels of powder were placed in a cellar beneath the Parliament House; and while waiting for the fifth of November, when the Parliament was summoned to meet, the plans of the little group widened into a formidable conspiracy. Catholics of greater fortune, such as Sir Everard Digby and Francis Tresham, were admitted to their confidence, and supplied money for the larger projects they designed. Arms were bought in Flanders, horses were held in readiness, a meeting of Catholic gentlemen was brought about under

[3] Donald Carswell, *Trial of Guy Fawkes and Others*, Notable British Trial Series, Toronto, Canada Law Book Company, 1934; Paul Durst, *Intended Treason: What really happened in the Gunpowder Plot*, London and New York, W. H. Allen, 1970.

[4] Op. cit. (n. 1, p. 327 above), sec. II, 'The Gunpowder Plot'.

show of a hunting party to serve as the beginning of a rising. The destruction of the King was to be followed by the seizure of his children and an open revolt, in which aid might be called for from the Spaniards in Flanders. Wonderful as was the secrecy with which the plot was concealed, the family affection of Tresham at the last moment gave a clue to it by a letter to Lord Monteagle, his relative, which warned him to absent himself from the Parliament on the fatal day; and further information brought about the discovery of the cellar and of Guido Fawkes, a soldier of fortune, who was charged with the custody of it. The hunting party broke up in despair, the conspirators were chased from county to county, and either killed or sent to the block, and Garnet, the Provincial of the English Jesuits, was brought to trial and executed. He had shrunk from all part in the plot, but its existence had been made known to him by another Jesuit, Greenway, and horror-stricken as he represented himself to have been he had kept the secret and left the Parliament to its doom.

Actually, according to more recent reviews of the evidence, the Plot was much less formal and formidable than it was portrayed by the King and his agents. At this remote date, it is impossible to determine who of the men supposedly involved in the affair were actual participants, who were governmental spies, and who were innocent bystanders. Of the many detailed studies which have been made of the Gunpowder Plot, none has concentrated on the role played by Henry Percy, 9th Earl of Northumberland, and none has produced evidence of any sort to show that he was a part of or even informed about the plot, though it was to cost him all his governmental offices and favors, levy against him the largest fine ever imposed on an Englishman (£30,000, of which he ultimately paid £11,000), and keep him in close custody in the Tower for the sixteen years of his life between ages forty-one and fifty-seven, normally a man's most active and productive years. All of the chroniclers of these years report these punishments totally unjustified; nearly all attribute them almost solely to the malevolence of Cecil, who since he assumed his position at Court in July of 1596 had done everything in his power to undermine the two men whom he considered his enemies: Ralegh and Northumberland. Certainly there appears to be no other source which could have manoeuvred King James from his position of complete trust to that of complete distrust of one of the most stable members of his Privy Council.

The Gunpowder Plot furnished Cecil with one weapon he could use to force the downfall of his secret enemy. That weapon was the fact that one of the major conspirators was Thomas Percy, a remote cousin of the 9th Earl. Thomas Percy, as we have seen, was an agent of Northumberland for the collection of rents in the North, and had been named as Constable of Alnwick by the Earl. He had been Northumberland's emissary to James in Scotland before his coronation charged with finding out the King's feelings toward the Catholic gentry who were suffering under the persecutions of Elizabeth's last years. It is very likely that it was this assignment which led Thomas Percy, then in his early thirties and traditionally a protestant, to gain sympathy for the Catholic point of view, and which led him to rebel at James's acts of turning against the Catholics after he had assured Northumberland that he intended to pursue a moderate toleration of their religion.

In any event, without the knowledge of any of his Northumberland associates, Thomas Percy became involved with the young and rebellious plotters (being in fact the oldest of them), and went so far as to divert some of the funds he was collecting for his noble cousin to the cause of the uprising. It was Thomas Percy who, using the influence of the Percy name, induced the tenant of the Whinniard house to vacate in his favour — the house which the conspirators had decided was best located for their original plan to tunnel underground to place their gunpowder under the Houses of Parliament.[5] It was at this stage that Guy Fawkes, an expert in explosives, was called in to arrange for the final explosion — a minor figure, though the whole plot currently bears his name. Later, when the mining project had proved impossible, it was again Thomas Percy who arranged to lease the cellar underlying the Houses of Parliament themselves, ostensibly for the storage of his winter fuel. It was in this leased space that the conspirators stored their thirty-three barrels of gunpowder, covered with faggots and coal, ready for detonation on the morning of 5 November when the King was scheduled to open the Parliament session.

[5] For details, see Ch. IV, 'The House and Tunnel', in Durst's *Intended Treason*, pp. 49–67.

The plot was foiled at the last minute. A mysterious letter was delivered to William Parker, Lord Mounteagle (undoubtedly a government spy), on Saturday 26 October, warning him to stay away from the opening of Parliament, since those attending 'shall receyve a terrible blowe this parleament.'[6] Mounteagle immediately turned this warning over to Cecil, who, in a leisurely fashion, later showed it to King James. According to his own reports, James, with his keen, analytical mind immediately perceived the whole plot, and recognized that there was gunpowder placed in the cellars of Parliament, ready to be exploded when the Parliament was called into session.[7] Meantime, news of the disclosure had been leaked to the conspirators in the hopes that they would betray themselves. When they did not, the King ordered a search of the Parliament cellars, and at midnight on 5 November Guy Fawkes was arrested as he entered the cellars, with slow fuses on his person for the detonation of the gunpowder. He was immediately rushed to the Tower for questioning (with accompanying torture) to elicit all possible details of the conspiracy.

Two rumours began to circulate immediately, probably emanating from Cecil: one, that Henry Percy, 9th Earl of Northumberland, had received a note very similar to the one received by Mounteagle, but had not seen fit to notify either the King or his Secretary; and two, that Sir Walter Ralegh, still secure in the Tower for convicted treason, had some hand in the planning, through contacts with Captain Edmund Whitlock, a friend of both Ralegh and Northumberland who had received support and pensions from them both.[8] London was afire with gossip and speculation. On 7 November John Chamberlain wrote of the affair to Dudley

[6] This letter, so important to the discovery of the plot, was widely circulated. It has often been reprinted, as, e.g., in Henry Garnett, *Portrait of Guy Fawkes, an Experiment in Biography*, London, Robert Hale, Ltd., 1962, facing p. 80.

[7] King James's own account of the plot, the 'official' account, entitled *A True and Perfect Relation of the Whole Proceedings against the late most Barbarous Traitors*, London, Robert Barker, 1606, is generally conceded to be neither true nor perfect, but is a 'white paper' justifying government action.

[8] Though there is no evidence of regular support, the Northumberland accounts show sporadic payments to Whitlock, without any reason being given. See, e.g., Alnwick Castle, Syon MS U.I.3. for 1607 and 1608.

Carleton who had served as 'Controller of the Household' for the 9th Earl from September 1603 until March of 1605:[9]

Sir, Though I looked for you before this time, and have often wisht you here among your old schoolefellowes that are almost all come up to the Parliament: yet as matters are lately fallen out about your Lord,[1] I am well content you be absent. Not that your Lord (as I hope) can be any way toucht with this divelish conspiracie,[2] but that neerenes of name, bloude, longe and inward dependance, and familiaritie, cannot but leave some aspersion, that will not easilie or lightly be washt of without time: in which consideration I heare he is rather wisht then willed to kepe his house. I cannot but remember what you have divers times told me touching Thomas Percie,[3] that you suspected him to be a subtile flattering daungerous knave. He hath not only verefied your judgement, but exceeded all degrees of comparison, and gon beyond Nero and Caligula that wisht all Rome but one head that they might cut yt of at a stroke, for he at one blowe wold have ruined the whole realme. He had hired the house or lodging next to the Parliament, together with the seller or vault under the upper house: into which by the meanes of one Johnson[4] his man a superstitious papist, (or rather a priest as is thought) he hath conveyed any time this twelve-moneth as much pouder in sachells, as fowre or five and thirty barrells, hoggesheads, and firkins could contein, with intent the first day of the parlement when the King shold be in his speach to blowe them all up: and had so cunningly covered them with billets, faggots and such trash, that without long search they could not be discovered, and but that God blinded him or some of his, to send this inclosed[5] without name or date to the Lord Mountegle, yt was very like to take effect. But the carieng yt to the Lord of Salisberie and so to the King, yt gave such light, that watch being set, the fellowe was taken making his traines at midnight with a blinde lanterne, and presently confessed the plot, yet with such shew of resolution that he seemed to be chiefly greved that yt had wanted successe. The next day he was caried to the Towre, but what Sir William Waade (that is lieutenant) and other examiners have wrange out of him I cannot learne: only I heare Sir Edward Bainham come lately out of the Lowe Countries is sought for: and some five or sixe Jesuites and priests taken in a privie search. Percie comming up on a sleveles errand and before he was looked for to your Lord, durst not tarry to see the event, but went away that night that his man was taken. Curious folkes observe that this deliveraunce hapned to the King the fift of November aunswerable to the fift of August, both Tewsdayes, and this plot to be executed by Johnson as that at Johns-towne.[6] On Tewsday at night we had great ringing and as great store of bonfires as ever I thincke was seene. And this is all I can write or remember in this matter. . . .

[9] Batho, *Household Accounts*, p. xxviii. This letter is no. 75 in *The Letters of John Chamberlain*, vol. I, pp. 212-14.

¹ Henry Percy, 9th Earl of Northumberland.
² The Gunpowder Plot.
³ Thomas Percy, who took an active part in the Gunpowder Plot, was the great-grandson of Henry Percy, 4th Earl of Northumberland.
⁴ Guy Fawkes, for several days after his arrest, insisted that his name was John Johnson.
⁵ A copy of the famous warning handed to William Parker, 4th Lord Monteagle.
⁶ The Gowrie conspiracy, 1600.

On this same day, the 9th Earl, who had been requested by the King to remain in voluntary confinement in his London residence, Essex House, was committed to the charge of the Archbishop of Canterbury, and placed in house arrest at the Archbishop's home in Croydon.¹⁰ The following day he wrote to the Council from Croydon:¹¹

I shalbe gladde as matters falles out to store you with circumstances to the ende that the bare truth may appeare. . . . Friday [1 Nov.] was the day hee [Thomas Percy] came to London; I, neither anie of myne, did see him till Monday [the 4th] twelve of the clock, when he came to Sion to me; went away presentlie after dinner, after he had *Sawsed mee with a Gudgeon* [i.e. 'deceived me with a falsehood']; and then appeared to the rest of my people at Essex House, from whence hee was to passe as hee told me, and then told them, to Ware, that night; givinge them all the same gudgeon that hee had bestowed on me, before, as alsoe to my brother Charles, my brother Alan, Sir Edward Ffraunces [Steward of Petworth], Edmund Powton [the Earl's Cofferer], Giles Greene [his Steward], and Captain Whitlock [pensioner], as may appeare if they be examined. Soe as, my Lords, it is probable I should not have seen him at Sion uppon Monday [4 Nov.] if one accident had not happened; and that was this: A man of his came to the Court to my lodging uppon Sonday [3rd] to enquire of Thomas Percy [gossip had it that this man was Guy Fawkes, alias John Johnson]; this man was a stranger to all the Companie, and never seene before by anie of them; the fashion of the man your lordships shall understande, to the ende he may bee caught hereafter. If this man by this meanes had not discovered [i.e. divulged] that his master, Thomas Percy, had byne in towne by this Accidente; and that he fownde that my followers of necessity must knowe it, I thinke I should not have seene him uppon Monday at Syon, and the rest of my companie that afternoone at Essex Howse, one of the greatest arguments of suspition laid to my chardge. Though I be somewhat tedious in these triffles I say to your Lordships they be matters of moment to me, and I hope you will pardon me, for I saie still, *the more you knowe, the better it will be for me*.

¹⁰ Batho, op. cit., p. 6, no. 3.
¹¹ de Fonblanque, *Annals of the House of Percy*, vol. II, pp. 259-61.

A marginal note in Northumberland's handwriting on the copy of this letter still in Alnwick Castle,[12] indicates 'By this narrative I endeavoured to make probable that Thomas Percy would not have come uppon Monday to Sion, if by his man's enquiry for him at my lodginge at Courte, hee had not byne discovered to be in London.' A note, still preserved among the Percy papers at Alnwick Castle, carries the description of Thomas Percy that was being circulated for his arrest.[13]

Nov. 5. [1605] [Pencilled note: 'Description in proc. for his arrest'.]
The said Percy is a tall man with a great broad beard, a good Face, the colour of his Beard & Head myngeld with white haires, but the head more white then the beard. he stoopeth somewhat in the shoulders. well coloured in the Face. long footed, small legged.

On Saturday, 9 November, Ralegh was questioned in the Tower about the gossip that he had known of the Plot through Captain Edmund Whitlock. His testimony is terse, and (perhaps politically) reveals a coolness between him and his old friend, Northumberland:[14]

1605. Nov. 9. I have not had any other affair with Cap. Whitlock, then familiar & ordinarie discourse, neither do I know any other cause of his cumming unto me then to visite me, having not mich wherewith to busy himself. I haue sumetime spoken to him to finde the Earle of Northumberland's disposition towards me, from whom I never receiv'd other than a drie & frindless awnswere, from the Earle. I neither receiv'd letter or sent him any, either by Whitlock of any man since my troble.
With the French Imbasator I have no affaires, his wife came hither once with the Ladie of Essingham & the pale being then down, she saluted me & desired me to geve her a little Balscomum of Guiana, Whitlock being then in her companie, I sent it by him to her.
...I beseech you in charitie & for the love of God not to make more odious then ever the earth brought forth any by suspecting me to be knowing this unexampled & more then develishe invention...

The one hope that Northumberland had of being totally exonerated from any participation in the Gunpowder Plot was the testimony which might be given by Thomas Percy when he was caught. King James and Lord Salisbury both insisted that they had given order to capture Percy alive so

[12] Alnwick MSS, vol. CI, p. 4.
[13] Percy Family, Letters and Papers, vol. 7, 1600–7, p. 200.
[14] BL Add. MS 6178, fo. 22ʳ (old 469ʳ).

that he could give his own story of the innocence or guilt of Northumberland. But no record exists of any such order to the officers who were pursuing the scattered conspirators, and on Sunday, 10 November, news reached London that Percy had been shot. All of the details of the search and destroy mission are confused and the true facts will probably never be known. It is clear that Sir William Waad was putting Guy Fawkes 'to the test' in the Tower, but Fawkes had not even revealed his true identity and was thought to be John Johnson. And in spite of all torture, he had refused to reveal the names of other participants. Nevertheless, an official proclamation had been issued on 7 November by the King himself, declaring:[15]

Whereas Thomas Percy Gentleman, and some other his confederates, pesons knowen to be bitterly corrupted with the superstition of the Romish Religion, as seduced with the blindness thereof, and being otherwise of lewde life, insolent disposition, and for the most part of desperate estate, have been discovered to have contrived the most horrible treason that ever entered into the hearts of men, against our Person, our Children, the whole Nobilitie, Clergie, and Commons in Parliament assembled, which howsoever cloaked with zeale of Superstitious Religion, aymed indeed at the Subversion of the State, and to induce a horrible confusion in all things. . . .

The proclamation, then, commanded all of the King's 'Lieutenants, Deputy Lieutenants, Sheriffes, Justices of Peace, Mayors, Bayliffes, Constables, and all other our officers, Ministers, and loving Subjects' to 'employ themselves for the suppressing, apprehending, deterring, and discovering of all sorts of persons any wayes likely to be privie to a Treason so hatefull to God and man, and implying in it the utter subversion of the Realm, and dignitie thereof.' In the face of this declaration of the infamy of the Gunpowder Treason and the solemn avowal that frustrating this plot was essential to the preservation of the nation, it is not strange that, in spite of his insistence to Northumberland that he was seeking Percy to testify in his behalf, the King's orders to the pursuing constables were for his assassination. Clearly such orders must have been issued, since the man who fired the fatal shot at Thomas Percy, a man named John

---

[15] PRO State Papers 14, vol. 16, cited in Durst, op. cit., pp. 151-3.

Streete, was shortly thereafter granted a lifetime pension of
2s. a day, 'for that extraordinary service performed in killing
those two traitors, Piercie and Catesbie, with two bullets at
one shott out of his muskett.'[16] As a result, there was no way
in which Northumberland could prove his innocence of
complicity in the plot so ingeniously deduced by the King
himself.

Within a week of the death of Thomas Percy, a detailed
interrogatory was prepared for the 9th Earl. Prepared on
13 November, the questions were put to Northumberland
ten days later, on the 23rd. Both the original interrogatory
and Northumberland's answers (with his signature at the
bottom of each page) are still to be found in the Gunpowder
Plot Books[17] in the Public Record Office, where most of
the documents of the event are kept. These questions and
answers are so detailed in showing the action of Northumberland and his friends in these critical days and hours, that
they are here, for the first time given in some detail. Direct
extracts from the documents are given here in italics;
shortened paraphrases are reproduced in roman type.

Interrogations to be ministred to the Earle of Northumberland.

1. [Q] *Whither was not Thomas Percy with you by Monday the
   fourth of November last, what tyme of the daye cam he vnto you,
   and who dined with you that daye.*

   *At lambeth the declaration of the Earle of Northumberland the
   23 of november 1605.*

1. [A] *he Confesseth that his Cosin Thomas Percey cam to him on
   monday the fourth of this november about eleven of the clocke
   in the forenoone and there dined with him, Sir William Lowre,
   Thomas Percey his younge sonne and Heriot as his lo: thinketh.*

2. [Q] *Whether had not Thomas Percey private conference with you
   on that daye, was such conference within your house or without,
   who stood by or in the viewe when you so conferred, and when
   did Percy goe from your house at Sion that day.*

2. [A] *he sayth that betwene the said houre of eleven and twelve he
   had conference with Thomas Percey in the hall and in the parlor
   of his said house before dinner and had no other conference with
   him at any other time that day. and only after dinner Percy came
   to him, to knowe whether he would commaund him any service,*

[16] Durst, op. cit., p. 323.
[17] PRO State Papers 14/216. These are fos. 112, 113 r&v.

and sayth that Sir William lowre & others passed by as they were talking and about one of the clocke Thomas Percey went his waye.

3. [Q] *What was the conference that passed betwen Percey and you at your house at Sion on that day?*

3. [A] *the conference was concerning a prist, one Parkinson, his coming downe . . . the next sommer, and the entrance and taking possession of certen lands . . .*

4. [Q] *After your comming from Sion to Northumberland house on that day was not Percey there, and what tyme of the day did he goe from thence*

4. [A] *He knows not of his owne knowledge that percy was there after his lordship's coming to essex house, but the next morning he heard of fraunces* [Sir Edward Francis, Steward of Petworth] *that percey had bene there.*

5. [Q] *Who cam with you in your Companie from Sion*

5. [A] *He cam in his coatch and with him dalevell* [Robert Delaval, his Gentleman of the Horse] *& bargon* [Ralph Burgoyne or Burgen, former Gentleman of the Horse] *or one of them with Sir William Lowre as he remembreth.*

6. [Q] How often did Percy confer with or write or send to you between Saturday and Tuesday (the fifth of November) and by whom?

6. [A] Denies any message except for conference at Syon House.

7. [Q] What was the effect of this conference?

7. [A] This is already answered above.

8. [Q] Who brought the message that Percy was gone? When, where, and in whose presence was the message delivered?

8. [A] The Earl recalls no such message.

9. [Q] After Percy was gone, what moved you to send after him? Whom did you send after him, when, and how many?

9. [A] He had been advised by his Steward, Francis, to write to Percy about his affairs, so he had sent Wycliffe [three Wycliffe brothers, Francis, Thomas, and William, were engaged in handling Northumberland's fiscal affairs. This would undoubtedly be Francis, commissioner for the audits of the Northern properties, for which Percy collected] and later Fotherley [Thomas Fotherley, disburser for the privy purse and groom in chamber to Northumberland].

10. [Q] Why did you send after him?

10. [A] Answered above.

11. [Q] In what ways have you employed Thomas Percy in matters of trust?

11. [A] In many small ways initially; later his trust grew and he increased his duties. Finally made him Constable of Alnwick.

12. [Q] How have you benefited him or advanced him?

12. [A] Gave him a lease to a property called Wilby Park and certain demesne properties. When Percy returned from the Low Countries he had given him £200.

13. [Q] *Have you at any tyme affirmed that you had any power or meanes to despose of the Catholiques of England, or that they were to be directed by you?*

13. [A] Absolute denial of any such statement; says this is 'an old Scotch story'.

14. [Q] *Vppon what ground or warrant did you vse such speaches and when, where & to whom were they spoken.*

14. [A] See above.

15. [Q] *Did you euer saye or affirme to any catholique or any other, that if occasion served you would winne with that partie, or partake with them, to whome said you so, and when where and uppon what occasion.*

15. [A] Never said so.

16. [Q] *What iudgment was given to your knowledge vppon the figure* [horoscope] *that was cast vppon the kings natiuitie.*

16. [*A*] *Carleton* [Dudley Carleton who had just recently resigned from his position as secretary to the 9th Earl] *tould him that he receiued a letter (which he sawe) from St. Saveur of Paris that the kings natiuitie was cast in Paris, and that the kinge shuld live many yeres and this was since the king cam in, almost three yeares sense, and denieth that he knoweth or hath seene any other fygure touching the king's nativitie since his majesties came into England but had heard (but never seene any, and) Sir Robert Carewe had tould him of one about twoo yeres past & more But his lordship neuer sawe it.*

17. [Q] *By whom and by whose meanes, and when and where was the said figure so cast.*

17. [A] *He knoweth not of any that was cast otherwise than as is aforesaid.*

18. [Q] How long was Percy your 'Suter' in collecting rents?

18. [A] Six years; had done some collecting for sixteen.

19. [Q] Who was your former receiver, and why did you remove him?

19. [A] Felton was the former receiver; he had got into debt, first for £500, and later for £300 more.

20. [Q] Weren't you warned that Percy meant to deceive you about your rents and to flee beyond the seas? Who told you, and when?

20. [A] *He denieth that any man tould him any such matter.*

21. [Q] After being warned, why did you appoint him to collect rents?

21. [A] See answer to question above.

22. [Q] *Whether were not you acquainted with Whitlocks going to the tower on Wednesday morninge the sixt of November.*

22. [A] *He denieth that he was acquinted with his goinge.*

23. [Q] *Did not Whitlocke returne that day from the tower to you at Northumberland house, and what did he impart unto you ther.*

23. [A] *he sayeth that Whitlocke returned to him at Essex house his lordship ther being walking with his brother Allen, and tould his lordship that he was in the tower, and did see John Johnson* [the alias of Guido Fawkes] *ther newly sent to the tower and that one of the lieutenants menne required him to stay to attend on the lords of the council which he did a good space & no man calling for him he cam away, wherewith his lordship found fault, and said it was not well done, and the said Whitlocke said divell with him and then departed.*

24. [Q] *What moved you to lett him passe awaye, considering he tould you that he was ronne away, being comaunded to stay by order from the lords of the Councell. What was Whitlockes purpose in going that daye to the tower.*

24. [A] *for that Whitlocke said he stayed there a good space & was not called for by the lords* [in margin: 'and therefore thought the lords sent not for him'] *his lordship made no more of it, but confesseth it was an error in him.*

25. [Q] *After your Seruants Carleton* [Dudley Carleton], *Eppesley* [John Hippesley, later named Gentleman of the Horse, later in the service of the Duke of Buckingham] *and grene* [Giles Grene, Payer of Foreign Payments and Steward] *had been with ferrers* [Henry Ferrers had been tenant of the Whinniard house and was induced to move so that Percy could lease the house] *to persuade him to lett his house in Westminster to Percey, what relation made they to you thereof.*

25. [A] *he answereth that he never knew about it until after this matter was discovered.*

26. [Q] *When and by Whom did you first knowe that Percey had hyred the house and the Cellar in Westminster.*

27. [A] See Answer above; he had not known of these things until after the Plot was discovered.

That Northumberland was vigorously questioned, particularly about the references to a horoscope cast of the King, is seen from the fact that appended to the Interrogatory and its answers remains a holograph sheet dated '23 Nov: 1605' —

the same day — written by Northumberland for the record:[18]

That I had herd of the Kings natiuitie and also other princes at Vtricke by one Holecraft whoe told me he had sene it and that his fortunes were equally mixt good and bad, but they were things I neuer tooke motche hede to. That in a letter from Saint Sauveur he said they had bene busy in Paris about it, as scorning it: also Robert Carr told me that he had one and that it promised mutche good successe and happynes. But that I neuer saw any in my lyfe, I must afferme, and it is true of theas things I haue spoken in way of discours.

King James, who took credit for discovering the Plot, continued to give all aspects of the investigation his personal attention. Though undoubtedly Cecil and others were handling many of the back-stage matters, James himself dictated the direction of the investigations and accusations. Major attention was given to the Catholic side of the conspiracy, but the insidious accusations of involvement of Ralegh and Northumberland constituted a kind of minor plot which also occupied much of his time and attention. He was particularly interested in the rumours that they had been involved in casting horoscopes of him and his children, and it was undoubtedly he who inserted such questions into the interrogatories of suspects. Immediately Northumberland had testified about his contacts with Thomas Percy and that he had seen 'figures cast' in the Low Countries even before James came to the throne, a wide net was spread for the friends and associates of Northumberland. Many of them were imprisoned: Dudley Carleton was held for a time in the Tower; Thomas Harriot was confined to the Gatehouse. A hue and cry went out to find Harriot's mathematical friend, Nathaniel Torporley, who had been associating with Harriot at Syon House. Even Sir William Lower, Member of Parliament from Lostwithiel, Cornwall, who had married the daughter of Northumberland's wife by a previous marriage, and through these family connections had become one of Harriot's scientific disciples, was called to question. Obviously someone (Cecil undoubtedly) was feeding the King venomous slander about the whole group.

A note from James to the Earl of Salisbury at this time

[18] PRO State Papers 14/216, fo. 113ᵛ.

remains in the archives at Hatfield House.[19] Endorsed by Cecil, 'His Majesty to me/.', the note is entirely in James's handwriting, uses his normal Scottish recording of 'qu' for the letter 'w', and bears his royal seal. The note breaks into two parts: the first section apparently defends Northumberland from involvement in the Gunpowder Plot on the basis of private testimony; the second digs into the problem of the casting of his nativity. The note runs:

Sussexe sayeth that northumberlande prayed him to dyne with him that fatal tuesday & that thay being at dinner & discoursing of this great accident, northumberlande did aske some of his men hou & quehn percy gotte that house, quho telling him that percie had hyred it long agoe, northumberlande swaire that he neuer knew before that percie hadd it, so as ye maye nou see that it uas no lapsus memoriae that maid him denye to the counsall his knowledge of percies hauing that house, but only that purposlie he will not be thocht to haue had any knowledge of the hyring of that house, as for his purpose of not going to the parliament, he only saide at dinner that he was sleepie for his earlie rysing that daye, but soone after chainged his mynde & went.

Carleton wolde at his next examination be asked,

i   quho gaue him my natiuitie.
ii   quhen he sent it & by quhat meanes to his lorde.
iii   quhat his earande uas to spaine.
iiii   quhat paquettes he carried, quhose, & quhom to.
v   if euer he spake with crescuell [Cresswell] thaire.
vi   or with quhat other iesuites.
vii   & hou oft during his absence, & by quhat meanes he harde worde from his lorde.

i   herriote wolde be asked quhat purpose he hath haerde his lorde use anent my natiuitie.
ii   if euer his lorde desyred him to caste it, or tell him my fortune.
iii   if euer his lorde seemed to be discontented of the state.
iv   if euer he harde him talke, or aske him of my childrens fortune.
v   if euer his lorde desyred to knowe quhat should be his owin fortoune & ende.
vi   & if he did caste milorde, & his sonnes natiuitie by his owin comande & knowledge.

The answers to these questions appear to have been lost, but we may be sure that they were asked and signed testimony taken from both Carleton and Harriot. Harriot was probably already in prison on Saturday 25 November when Northumberland was interrogated at Lambeth, for the following

[19] Hatfield MS *134* 86. HMC, M. of Salisbury, vol. XVII, p. 530.

Monday, Cecil ordered a search of his house for possible incriminating documents. The search was carried out by Sir Thomas Smith:[20]

[Addressed] To the right Honorable my singular good L. the Earle of Salisburie.
[Endorsed]   25. Nouemb. 1605.   Sir Thomas Smith to my Lord.
Yt may please your Lordship.

I haue made as diligent search of Master Herriotts Lodging and studie at Sion as the time would permitt; And yet I stayed vntyll it was Late. To haue made an exact survey of all his papers there would have required many dayes; and I think it would not be to any purpose: because thes be all of an other sort then such as I shold finde. Lettres there are few, and almost none at all; And such as are, carrie an olde date; scarcely one written of Late. Bookes of all sorts of learning & many; of all sects and professions of religion: but neyther one place nor other (though I opened all his chests) hath afforded me any thing that I may thinke needfull to be brought vnto your Lordship. I haue therefore sealed vp his studie dore & his chests; to the end that there may be a more exact survey, if your Lordship shall think meete. My Lady of Northumberland did shew great respect vnto the warrant that I had, & with all willingnesse yeald to the making of the search. Thus much (though to little purpose) I thowght it my dutie to signifie to night; least your Lordship might expect more for the present; And so presuming on your favour to stay my self tyll to morrow morning I humbly take my leaue.

                    Your Lordships to do you all seruice
                                    Th: Smith
25. of 9ber

The willingness of Dorothy Percy to co-operate fully with the authorities at a time when her husband was in custody, and a number of her servants were in jail, speaks well for her conviction of the innocence of all concerned. As her husband had written to the King earlier, 'the more you know, the better it will be for me'.

On the next day, Tuesday, the dragnet had located Nathaniel Torporley. Sir Thomas Windebank wrote to the Earl of Salisbury a note dated '26 Nouemb. *1605*.' which reads:[21]

It may please your Lordship. Hauing employed a man of myne own in some little coulourable seruice this after noon. At last he hath found that this Topperley is lodged in the house of one Bankworthe in Bow Lane, a Skrivener. Whereof I wold not delaye to giue your Lordship

[20] Hatfield MS *113* 43. HMC, M. of Salisbury, vol. XVII, pp. 507–8.
[21] Hatfield MS *113* 45.

knowledge, to the end your Lordship may giue what furder direction it shall please yow. My self I feare shall not be able to attend any seruice in the morning, by reason of som phisicke allready taken, which I wish went not now. I humbly beseech your Lordship to pardon my rudeness heerin.

this 26. night of Nouember .1605.

Your Lordships most bound for euer

Tho: Windebank

The following morning Nathaniel Torporley was seized and questioned. And again it is obvious that it was the King's concern over the possible necromancy surrounding his horoscope that had led to his arrest. His signed testimony remains in the Gunpowder Book in the Public Record Office to commemorate the occasion:[22]

The Examinacion of Nathanial Topherley. ye 27 Nouember 1605.

A. Being asked whither were he euere acquaynted with the vtteringe or iudginge of any fygure concerninge the King's Natiuitye, he doth answer

> That he did sett once so farr as the positions without geuing any iudgement, which he brought to *Mr Heriot*. And in the beginninge of the King's raigne longe desyerous to know some sertayntye of the tyme of his byrth, *Mr Heriot* promised to learne what he could, and so vppon his cominge to him aboute the beginninge of the Parliament, *Mr Heriot* tould him, that the hower might be knowne more certayne bycause there was a cannon shott of at *Edenbrough* presently after his byrth. One reason why he sett yt, was his desyer to see how yt did agree with his happye fortune in cominge to the crowne. When *Heriot* had it he did putt it vpp in his lodgings at Essex House.

B. He confeseth: The end of Casting all Natiuityes is to see what iudgment is to be made of them.

C. He sayth when he had drawne yt, he did Looke vppon yt.

D. He sayth that *Heriot* sayd vnto him. That hauinge not an *Ephemerides* but Maginus which conteyned not the iournall of the Planetts, and being loth himself to take the paynes to work by *Tabulae Prutenicae*, willed me to bringe that which I did by Stadius, and I did deliuer yt vnto him.

E. Being asked why he would take all this paynes to worke by the precysest rules of arte to vnderstand the truth, yf ther were no other vse then puttinge yt vpp in his studye

F. He sayth, What vse *Mr Heriot* made he knoweth not, but he tould him none.

[22] PRO State Papers 14/216, fo. 122.

G.   Being asked how often he had talked with my Lord of Northumberland He answereth but once, which was at Syon before Queene
Elizabeth's death.

H.   He confesseth *Mr Heriot* acquainted him with my Lord of *North-
umberlands* sonns byrth that is deade: and this dignity did cast
his Natyuitye, but sayth he is not very suer of this.

I.   He will not say that he did yt with a pourpose not to iudge, but
sayth he did neuer iudge.

[Signed]   Nathanael: Torporley.

On this same day, Wednesday, 27 November, the 9th Earl
of Northumberland was removed from the custody of the
Archbishop of Canterbury at Lambeth, was made a prisoner
of the King, and taken to the Tower of London, which was
to be his home for the next sixteen years. One of Percy's
overseers, Sir William Lane, after his admission, wrote to
Cecil that 'My Lords first comminge hether was ffull of
passion, but now more reposed.'[23] But after he had regained
his composure, Northumberland sent for Lane to request
that he carry a petition to Cecil requesting that[24]

... Sir Edwarde ffrauncis may be permitted to haue acces vnto him to
confer off his lordships particular businesses; and ffurther desyreth
your lordships to admitte vnto him one Elks a skollar some halfe
yere agoe recommended to hym as a man ffitt hereafter to teache my
lord's yonge sonne, and ffor that purpos kepeth hym, to haue the
better experience of hym ...

This request puts to rest the tradition, still heard, that
Harriot lived in the Tower with Northumberland, both as
his scientific adviser and tutor to young Lord Percy.

On 30 November a second interrogatory was prepared,
probing the possible link of Northumberland to the Catholic
cause and the Gunpowder Plot.[25] This interrogatory is
endorsed 'Interrogatory which the Earle of Northumberland
is to answere in writing. 30 Nouember 1605', and reads as
follows:

1.   What Messages did you send to the king by Percy [in] the Late
Queenes time Concerning Catholicques, and what answere did he
bring back againe.

[23] Hatfield MS *113* 50. HMC, M. of Salisbury, vol. XVII, p. 518.
[24] Hatfield MS *114* 64. HMC, M. of Salisbury, vol. XVII, p. 608.
[25] PRO State Papers 14/216, fo. 125.

2. Whether did you euer affirme to the king that you had interest in the Catholiques, and that they made any Dependancie vpon you, or to such Effect, and When began the same first.

3. How often did you affirme in the Late queenes time, and how often since, that if occacion serued you would take the Catholicques part, and that you tooke vpon you to haue power and interest in them, and to whome.

4. When were you intreated to Joyne in a Peticion to the King for the Catholicques, and that you would subscribe the same, and whoe moued you ther vnto.

5. When did Percy or anie other, first moue you to giue the Catholicques hope or assurance of you, as a wise man to raise your fortunes with the King, when he should see that you had Power to doe good and Euil.

6. Of what matter of any importance did Percy discourse with you or anie other on the Monday at Dinner the 4th of Nouember Last at Sion.

Then, returning to his previous testimony, his involvement in the insurrection plans, came three final enigmatic questions:

7. Whether did you euer speak with Heriot about the figure of the Kinges Natiuity, and where, and how often, and with how manie others haue you Conferred about the same.

8. At what time did you increase your stable with great horses and when, and what moued you so to increase the same.

9. What was the Last time that your Lordship resolved to take Phisick and of whome, and to whome did you impart or giue Order for the same.

It is now, as it was then, obvious from these questions that they could not have been prepared by King James, since they were designed to search out facts that the King himself knew very well. They must, therefore, represent some more of the efforts of Cecil to ferret out information which he might use for his own purposes. As such, they enraged the volatile Northumberland, and he refused to submit his answers in writing as he had been asked to do. On 12 December the Venetian ambassador reported that[26]

The Earl of Northumberland's business stands where it did, for he will answer no questions upon examination, demanding that if there be any

[26] From the *Calendar of State Papers: Venetian*, as reported by G. B. Harrison, *A Jacobean Journal*, pp. 253–4.

charges against him a commission of his peers shall be appointed to try them. To this the Earl of Salisbury replied that he ought not to refuse that which others had done, naming my Lord of Essex who always answered what was asked of him. To which my Lord of Northumberland answered that Essex was a brave gentleman but in the later part of his life was not in his right mind, which brought him to his death. Last Sunday the Countess went to the King with a petition praying not for grace but for justice; that her Lord might have speedy trial; and that the king would not allow the ill will of a certain great one to ruin the Earl in fame, fortune and life. The King treated her gently; but those in Court reminded themselves that never a nobleman of his greatness committed to the Tower on such a charge came out alive.

About this time, Thomas Harriot, still languishing in the Gatehouse Prison, addressed a letter 'To the right honorable my very good Lord: the Earle of Salisbury, one of his Majestyes most honorable privy counsell, and principall secretary of State':[27]

Right honorable my very good Lord:

The fauour which I haue already receaued from your lordship, I shall alwayes, as I am bounden, faythfully acknowledge. And if it may please your honor to extend it farther for my release out of this dungeon of my many miseryes: the future seruice that you honor thereby shall enhable me vnto, shall declare an other manner of dutifull thankefulnes then wordes. What my hart acknowledgeth: my hand doth signe, & my future deedes, with the leaue of god & your lordships fauour, shall seale.

> Your lordships
> humbly euer at comaundement:
> a poore prisoner:
> Tho: Harriots

Dudley Carleton was also chafing under the suspicion and harassment which he was enduring from the inquisition surrounding his possible role in the plot. Salisbury, it appears, was the only one who could mitigate his situation, and, like Harriot, Carleton addressed a letter asking clemency.[28]

My Lord

I presume so much of your honorable fauor that vnless you thought I were well I should not lie by it thus long. and though for treatment I haue no cause to complaine, yet I make bold to write to your Lordship that I liue in great misery. for there can be no greater burden to an

[27] Hatfield MS *114* 40, HMC, M. of Salisbury, vol. XVII, p. 600.
[28] Hatfield MS *113* 142. This is endorsed only '1605'.

honest mind then to be long vnder suspicion of bearing part in so barbarous a villany. Wherfore I most humble beseach your Lordship and the rest of my most honorable Lords that you will please to take some speedy course for your satisfactions in my behalf. and whatsoeuer your Justice shall assigne me I shall not complayne of. The greatest punishment will be too little if the least fault be proued against me. and if nothing, I hope your Lordships in your fauorable Judgments will thinck sufficient of nine dayes restraint as a close prisoner and so I rest.

> Most humbly
> at your Lordships disposall
> Dudley Carleton.

Carleton's pleas seem to have been effective in getting him removed from prison where Harriot's were not. But they did not relieve him of suspicion, nor restore to him his offices of trust and his seat in the Parliament. In another letter he requests Cecil to intercede for him in these matters:[29] 'There rests one degree to which I would humbly pray to be restored, which is my attendance in Parlement. Where though my seruice can be of no great vse yet my absence is of much note. I would gladly be owt of the mouth of the multitude if your Lordship would so fauor me . . .' What response he received from these letters is not recorded, but it is not long after that Carleton found himself reinstated in the royal favour, and appears to have been completely exonerated from the royal disfavour which continued to plague Northumberland and his protégé, Harriot.

On Monday, 2 December, Sir William Lower was questioned about the much discussed dinner at Syon House on the fateful 4 November which had led to the suspicion of Northumberland and Harriot. His testimony remains in the Gunpowder Book at the Public Record Office:[30]

The Examinacion of Sir William Lower knight the 2 December .1605.

1. What companye dyned with my Lord of Northumberland at Syon on Monday before the Parliament should haue begonne

   He answereth Master Percye, Captaine Whytlock, and himselfe and he is not suer whither Master Heriot dyned ther or noe.

2. Wither was ther any speach at the table of any matters of Parliament.

   He answereth, Ther was a discourse, but he remembreth not the particulars.

[29] Hatfield MS *113* 141.   [30] PRO State Papers 14/216, fo. 137.

3. Was thir no speaches of the Articles agreed on the Commissioners for the Vnion.

He answereth. That all the discourse that was, was only vppon those articles of the vnion, which Percye shewed in a paper.

4. Whither do you know how Percye came by the Articles

He answereth he knoweth not

5. To whom did Master Percye showe the Articles besydes to your selff.

He answereth to no other bodye, but the Articles being in his hands, My Lord of Northumberland toke them from him, and reade them

6. What sayd the Earl of Northumberland when he had reade them.

He answereth. he remembereth that ther was a discourse but no particulars.

7. Betwene whom, and Percye, was the discourse

He answereth. That it was at the table in generall, by those that dyned ther.

[Signed] William Lowër.

From the nature of these questions, and the way they evolve, it seems certain that this was not a prepared interrogatory, but was a searching questioning, questions and answers of which were taken by a scribe and later presented for Lower's signature. It is likely that the questioner was His Majesty's Principal Secretary of State, the recently created Earl of Salisbury, who would find nothing in this testimony to incriminate Northumberland, Harriot, and Whitlock, but would see nothing to clear them of the suspicion which still surrounded them.

Two weeks later, on Monday, 16 December, Thomas Harriot addressed another letter requesting his release, this time not to Cecil, but to the Lords of the Privy Council. No evidence remains to indicate just what effect this letter had on its contemporary readers, but to the modern reader, it seems very revealing of the character and nature of its author. The letter, not in the official Gunpowder records, but in the files of Cecil at Hatfield House, reads as follows:[31]

[Addressed] To the right honorable my very good Lordes: The Lordes of his Majestyes most honorable privy councell.

[Endorsed] 1605 Master Heriot from ye Gatehowse Dec. 16

---

[31] Hatfield MS *114* 41. HMC, M. of Salisbury, vol. XVII, p. 554.

Right honorable my very good Lordes:

The present misry I feele being truly innocent in hart and thought presseth me to be an humble suter to your lordships for fauorable respect. All that know me can witnes that I was alwayes of honest conversation and life. I was neuer any busy medler in matters of state. I was neuer ambitious for preferments. But contented with a priuate life for the loue of learning that I might study freely. Wherein my labours & endeauours, if I may speak it without præsumption, haue ben paynfull & great. And I hoped & do yet hope by the grace of god & your Lordships fauour that the effects shall so shew themselues shortly, to the good liking & allowance of the state & common weale. But now this misery of close imprisonement happening vnto me at the time of my sicknes, which was more then three weekes old before; being great windenes in my stomack & fumings into my head rising from my spleen, besides other infirmityes, as my Doctor knoweth & some effectes my keeper can witnes. This I say without your honours fauour wilbe my vtter vndoing, not only in respect of great charges, greater then I am able to endure: but also of being in place where I am not likely to recouer health. Therefore the innocency of my hart feeling this misery of close imprisonement with sicknes & many wantes, besides the desire of proceeding in my studyes, maketh me an humble suter to your honors for liberty in what measure your wisedomes shall think fit. So shall I with faythfull acknowledgement spend the rest of my time so, that your honours shall not think any lawfull fauour ill bestowed. And I shall as my bounden duty is continue my dayly prayers to almighty god for the preservation of his Majesty and Royall progeny, and for the encrease of all honor and happines to your honors.

Your honors humble petitioner:
a poore prisoner in the Gatehouse

December 16 1605.   Tho: Harriots

The questioning of prisoners and the search for additional persons who might have been involved in the conspiracy continued on into 1606. On 10 January two of the plotters who had escaped the posse at Holbeach, Robert Winter and Stephen Littleton, were discovered at Hagley House, and removed to the Tower with their fellow suspects. Parliament began its meetings on 21 January, and immediately began discussing how it should proceed to punish the offenders and to prevent any similar attempt in the future. One action was taken: A Bill was introduced and passed that set aside 5 November as a day of public thanksgiving to Almighty God for each future year, to mark the occasion of God's sparing the King and the English nation.[32] On 25 January two more

[32] *A Jacobean Journal*, p. 265.

Jesuits were taken at Hendip, and on 27 January the eight
principal plotters, Thomas Bates, Sir Everard Digby, Guido
(or Guy) Fawkes (alias John Johnson), John Grant, Robert
Keyes, Ambrose Rookwood, and the two Winter brothers,
Robert and Thomas, were taken by boat from the Tower to
Westminster Hall, where they were tried by the Lords Commissioners in the Court of Star Chamber.[33] Though the trial
was closed, it was rumoured that the King was hidden in a
secret place to observe the prisoners, and the Queen and
Prince Henry were observing from another. Though the
prisoners had all given written confessions of their guilt
from their Tower 'questioning', they now pleaded 'Not
Guilty' of the long and involved charges levied against them.
But the outcome was never in doubt, and at the end of the
day the proceedings were ready to close. Sir Edward Coke,
the Attorney-General, summed up the nature of the plot,
assuming that the disclosure of the plot was, as it had proved
to be in the case of Ralegh, the evidence of the guilt of the
accused. And before presenting the case to the Jury for its
final verdict, he closed with a statement of the King's mercy,
which seems to have passed all understanding. As summarized by Professor Harrison, his remarks, just before reading the signed confessions of the accused, were as follows:[34]

In conclusion the Attorney spoke of the admirable clemency of the
King who, although these traitors have exceeded all others their predecessors in mischief, will not exceed the usual punishment of the law
nor invent any new torture or torment for them. 'And,' saith he,
'surely worthy of observation is the punishment by law provided and
appointed for high treasons; for first, after a traitor hath had his just
trial, and is convicted and attainted, he shall have his judgment, to be
drawn to the place of execution from his prison, as being not worthy
any more to tread upon the face of the earth whereof he was made:
also for that he hath been retrograde to nature, therefore is he drawn
backward at a horse-tail. And whereas God hath made the head of man
the highest and most supreme part, as being his chief grace and ornament, he must be drawn with his head declining downward, and lying
so near the ground as may be, being thought unfit to take benefit of
the common air; for which cause also he shall be strangled, being
hanged by the neck between heaven and earth, as deemed unworthy

[33] Details of the trial are to be found in D. Jardine, *Criminal Trials*, 1832,
pp. 115–81.
[34] *A Jacobean Journal*, p. 270.

of both or either; as likewise, that the eyes of men may behold, and their hearts contemn him. His bowels and inward parts taken out and burned, who inwardly had conceived and harboured in his heart such horrible treason. After, to have his head cut off, which had imagined the mischief. And lastly, his body to be quartered, and the quarters set up in some high and eminent place, to the view and detestation of men, and to become a prey for the fowls of the air. And this is a reward due to traitors, whose hearts be hardened; for that it is a physic of state and government, to let out corrupt blood from the heart.

The clemency and mercy of the king prevailed. The jury found all guilty. On 30 January four of the conspirators, Digby, Robert Winter, John Grant, and Thomas Bates were taken to St. Paul's Churchyard, where they were hanged, and the merciful treatment accorded convicted traitors was performed in the view of the general public. The next day the others — Guy Fawkes, Keyes, Rookwood, and Thomas Winter, were executed at Westminster. The heads of the traitors were set on London Bridge where they would be seen by the majority of citizens going about their daily tasks; the quarters of the bodies were placed over the various gates of the city; and the heads of Catesby and Thomas Percy, slain in the capture at Holbeach near Stourbridge in early November, nearly three months before, were set up to view on the top of the Parliament House which they had hoped to blow to kingdom come. The mercy of the King and his ministers was wide and deep.

The case of Northumberland continued to drag on without resolution. Though his final fate was not yet determined, he had resigned himself in the Tower to the best life available to one of England's greatest nobles. He paid an annual stipend of £100 to Sir William Waad, Lieutenant of the Tower, for the right to maintain his own kitchens and to supply his own table for himself and his friends and re-tainers.[35] He rented a stable in Milford Lane to keep his horses, which he rode in the Tower grounds (which he was permitted to do in Coldharbour Court) and for the use of his servants on their errands for him.[36] And he set up offices near the Martin Tower where he could meet with his attorneys,

---

[35] Alnwick Castle: Syon MS U.I.3 (2) G, Accounts for 1607–8 and thereafter.
[36] Batho, *Household Accounts*, p. 90, n. 1.

stewards, custodians, and agents in maintaining and improving his estates, and keep a close personal overview of the auditing of his account.[37]

On 25 June 1606 John Chamberlain penned one of his news letters to Dudley Carleton, with the news that[38]

... the Lordes [of the Council] sat much in counsaile about your Lorde [Northumberland] and on Monday morning [23 January] were with him in the Towre, but what passed I cannot learne, but only the common voyce goes the King wold have him to the Star-chamber. That day Sir Allen Percy [the Earl's brother] being as I take yt convented before them was committed to the custodie of the lieutenant of the Towre: I cannot learne the cause but some say yt is about the old matter of Percie that he was not sworne when he was admitted pensioner:[39] others, for conveyenge some letters lately to my Lord. Howsoever yt be the matter is not thought to be great, for your Lady [Dorothy, Countess of Northumberland] was yesterday with her Lorde, and Poulton hath still access to him, as before.

But the talk of the King and Council did presage action. Two days later, on 27 June, Northumberland was tried before the Star Chamber.

Though Star Chamber proceedings were traditionally secret, any activity involving so many people and affairs of such interest came to be subjects of common gossip. Certainly this was the case of the 9th Earl of Northumberland, who had been so high in the circles of the Court and country, and who maintained the haughty demeanour of the old gentry. The account of the charges against him was widely circulated. As cited by Edmund Howe, who edited and augmented John Stow's *Annals, or a Generall Chronicle of England*, for these years, they were:[40]

[37] Though the accounts for 1604 and 1605 are missing, those for 1606 and following show much greater detail than earlier ones on repairs and maintenance of all the Earl's properties. Surveys were made of all estates, most of which are still in the muniment room at Syon House. And the accounts record payments for the housing and feeding of the auditors near the Tower during these years, so that it is obvious that the accounts were being kept there.

[38] *Letters of John Chamberlain*, vol. I, p. 228.

[39] In June 1604 Thomas Percy had been admitted as one of the Gentlemen Pensioners. Northumberland, as Captain of the Pensioners, had admitted him to his post without requiring the Oath of Supremacy.

[40] *Annales, or a Generall Chronicle of England, Begun by John Stow: Continued and Augmented ... by Edmund Howes ...*, London, 1631, p. 884.

The 27. of June, *Henry* Earle of Northumberland was brought from the tower vnto the Star-chamber, before the great Lords and Judges afore-said, and ther conuicted of misprisions, contempts, and offences, that is to say.

1   For endeuoring to bee the head of the English Papists, and to procure them Tolleration.

2   For admitting and placing *Thomas Percie* to be one of the Kings Gentlemen Pentioners, without ministring vnto him the oath of Supremacie, knowing the said *Percie* to be a Recusant.

3   Whereas the said Earle being, and sitting in Councell with the other Lords, and saw apparent inducement, that the said *Thomas Percie* was a chiefe practiser and contriuer of the most horrible treason newly discouered, and the said Earle being by the good and iust reason of the King and Councell, restrained and commanded to keep his house; yet the said Earle wrote two seuerall letters into the North parts, vnto his friends and seruants, to haue a care of his money and reueneues, supposing the said *Thomas Percie* to be fled into those parts, negotiating them to preserue the same from the hands of *Thomas Percy*, and to bring the same treasure vp vnto him, and in the same Letters did vtterly neglect and forbeare to take any order, or giue any commaundement for apprehending the said *Thomas Percy*, being knowne for so damnable and dangerous a Traytor.

4   In presuming to write and send Letters abroad, after his restraint, without leaue of his Maiesty or his Priuie Councell.

5   That hee being a Priuie Councellour, sworne to preserue the Kings Maiestie and the State: to haue more care of his treasure, then of the King or State, without any endeuour to apprehend so dangerous a Traytor, as he knew the said *Percy* was.

6   Lastly, his letters into those parts where *Percy* was fled, the said Earle knowing at the Councell table how the state of all things stood against him: was to giue him a watch word and intelligence for his farther flight & escape, besides the Earle confessed, that since his Maiesties Raigne, hee had conference concerning the Kings Nobility, and how long, and in what manner he should raigne, &c.

For the which the said Earle was censured and adiudged to pay a fine to the vse of his Maiestie, the sum of thirty thousand pounds, and to be displaced and remoued from the place of a priuie Counceller, and from being Captaine of his Maiesties Pentioners, and from being Lieutenant of any of his Maiesties Counties, and from all and euery other Office which he held of his Maiesties grace and fauour, and hereafter to be disabled to take vpon him, or exercise any of the said Offices and Places, and to returne prisoner to the Tower of London from whence hee came, and there to remaine prisoner as before, during his life.

Still another account, probably one closer to the actual hearing of Northumberland before the Star Chamber, gives an account of the proceedings which links Harriot closer to the condemnation of the Wizard Earl than even John Chamberlain's gossiping account does. John Hawarde, a member of the Middle Temple who was interested in the activities of the Star Chamber, kept a notebook in which he recorded all of their activities. His account for the hearing of Northumberland on 27 June 1606, appears to be notes taken at the actual hearing, sometimes cryptic and difficult to interpret. He lists nineteen of the King's Lords of the Council present to hear the case of the King versus one of his greatest nobles:[41] The Lord Chancellor, the Archbishop of Canterbury, Lord Treasurer, Lord Admiral, Lord Chamberlain, the Lords Shrewsbury, Worcester, Northampton, Salisbury, Exeter, Zouche, Knolles, Wooton, Stanhope, the Bishop of London, the Lord Chief Justice, Lord Chief Baron, Sir John Fortescue, and Sir John Herbert. His report indicates that the secrecy of the Star Chamber proceedings was exaggerated, since Hawarde reports that 'A great scaffold was erected for the courtiers and other men of great account, and the side bar with a seat for the prisoners.' As in the case of Ralegh, the prosecution was handled by the Attorney-General, Sir Edward Coke, apparently with the same lack of moderation and restraint which marked the Ralegh trial. After Northumberland had been brought in from the Tower of London by Sir William Waad, Lieutenant of the Tower, and Sir William Lane, the Attorney-General began his case:[42] 'with very greate respecte, [Northumberland] beinge of highe and emynente place, & the greateste person & Cause that euer was broughte into that Courte.' Because of this, and from his own natural bent, Coke indicated that he would 'deale succinctlye & sincerelye, with protestacion of respecte of honor, & that truthe showlde be his Center & temperaunce his Circumference.' He would 'delyuer nothinge to preiudicate the partye nor preiudge ye Courte.' Then he proceeded

---

[41] Hawarde's notebook was edited by William Paley Baildon, and privately printed in 1894 under the title *Les Reportes del Cases in Camera Stellata, 1593 to 1609 from the Original MS. of John Hawarde*. The Northumberland trial is to be found on pp. 292-9.

[42] p. 293. This was Coke's last appearance as public prosecutor. Three days later he was rewarded for his efforts by being named as Lord Chief Justice of the Common Pleas.

to make flat statements of charges in matters which were totally without evidence.

In ye beginninge of the kinge's Raigne, & at the ende of ye Queene's Raigne, ye Lo. of Northumberlande became the heade of ye Catholikes, & a freinde to ye Catholique Cause. . . . the Spaniardes showlde lande in Milforde hauen, & in the righte of his wyfe he had Carewe Castle neere vnto it: & at that time he increasethe his stable, so that he tolde ye kinge his hole revenue would scarcelye mainteyne it.

. . . he sent [Thomas] Percie into Scotlande for a toleration, with 2 letters & a message pretendinge the more easye entraunce yf he woulde geue hopes of toleration . . . vpon Percie's retorne out of Scotlaunde, the Erle of Northumberland tolde the Catholykes that the kinge's Commaundemente was that they showlde be assured of ease of there persecutions: which the kinge himselfe *in verbo regio* saythe he neuer did promise or Commaunde.

. . . After this they plotted this pouder treason, & were all sworne & tooke the sacramente to effecte it, & to Conceall yt: & soone after this he [Thomas Percy] was made a pentioner, a fitte man to put an axe into his hande to carrye it ouer the kinge's head . . .

Though none of the evidence gathered in the case bore out these charges, there appears to have been no refutation of any kind permitted at this hearing, so that the King's Council heard only the accusations.

But in the Star Chamber proceedings, as in the original investigation of the Gunpowder Plot, it was in his supposed casting of a horoscope of the King's nativity that Harriot was involved. Again, though all the interrogations indicated that no such horoscope was cast, the Attorney-General went over the gossip previously investigated, and stated it as proved.

Dissimulation in religion had neuer goode ende; a fearfull thinge.

Simeon and Leuy meante fraude in there hartes. Dauid was a statesman, & yet it is sayde he Can not gouerne that can not dissemble. Northumberlande had neyther discontente, wante, nor disgrace: but he must Calculate the kinge's natiuitie by Sir Roberte Carre, & causeth him to wryte to Topperine[43] & to Herriotte:[44] *par le Canon ley* such persons are excommunicate.

[43] This is obviously a misreading of the name 'Torporley'. See pp. 342-3.
[44] Baildon notes and indexes the name 'Herriotte' as 'Probably George Heriot, the King's Jeweller, the founder of Heriot's Hospital, Edinburgh. See *DNB*'.

Obviously at this point in the charge Coke entered a diatribe
against astrologers in general and Northumberland's protégé,
Harriot, in particular, as both he and Popham, the Chief
Justice, had done in the trial of Ralegh. The brief and cryptic
jottings recorded by Hawarde were obviously designed only
to indicate the tenor of the discussion. Here they read:

Calculatinge [casting of horoscopes] *occupatissima vanitas et indocta
doctrina.*

　　Herriott is a funerall beaste. 13 Elizab.[45]

　　Inward essences are beste knowne by outwarde properties, as
great ryuers by litle springes, trees by there rootes or braunches.

A poll of the nineteen members of the Council showed
them to agree to the penalties suggested suitable for Northumberland's various offences: a fine of £30,000 to be paid
to the King; loss of his places as a member of the Privy
Council and as Captain of the Pensioners, and imprisonment
at the King's pleasure. Most significant of all the charges, was
Northumberland's failure to extract an oath of allegiance to
the King as Thomas Percy had been taken into the list of
Gentlemen Pensioners. No one appears to have commented
either on Northumberland's unorthodox beliefs, except the
Lord Chancellor. Condemning the plot as inspired by the
Devil, he was particularly incensed at the casting of the
King's horoscope: 'Theise figure flingers: a daungerous
thinge to raise a pryuate man's name aboue or neere the
kinge's name.' Most of the others were more subdued, and
Lord Salisbury even went out of his way to praise North-
umberland:

'I haue taken paines,' sayde hee, 'in my nowne harte to cleare my
lorde's offences, which now haue leade mee from the Contemplation
of his virtues; for I knowe him vertuous, wyse, valiaunte, & of vse &
ornamente to the state. The more perylous wyse men's actions be,
there the more industrye they vse to gouerne them.

But after this eulogy of the 9th Earl's character, 'He agreed
as to the fine with the Chief Justice, and imprisonment for
life during the Kings's pleasure.'

---

[45] Clearly a reference to Statute of Treasons, 13 Eliz. cap. 1, *Statutes of the
Realm*, IV, 525, especially the reference to intent in preamble.

Thus it was ended. Without ever having a chance to say a word in his behalf, with no evidence of any sort presented, and with no presentation of the elaborate testimony extracted during the long months of investigation into the Gunpowder Plot, Northumberland stood condemned of treason in one of the early actions which rendered the Star Chamber the synonym for trials which were a mockery of justice. Stripped of his honours at Court, he was led away from his former associates to return to the Martin Tower in the Tower of London which was to be his home for the next fifteen years.

IX. The Northumberland Circle

Probably no segment of English history has been more romanticized than the affairs centring in the Tower of London during the reign of James I. Even today, tours of the Tower focus on the period of Elizabeth and James, on such dramatic personages as Mary Queen of Scots, the Earls of Essex and Southampton, and the Lady Arabella Stuart, whose ghosts are paraded daily before visitors. The Bloody Tower, where Ralegh lived in cramped darkness while poring over his monumental *History of the World*, is a high point of the Tower tour, as is 'Ralegh's Walk' on the walls overlooking the Thames where Sir Walter is reported to have received the cheers of seamen and citizens when he took his morning stroll. Less dramatic, but still glamorous, is the sight of the Martin Tower, where Northumberland lived from late November 1605 to the end of summer 1621. There a sun-dial in the wall is pointed out as having been placed there by Northumberland's magus, Thomas Harriot, who was said to have lived there during the Earl's incarceration and to have tutored his eldest son, Algernon, later the 10th Earl. It was the inspiring tales told by Harriot of his exploits in the New World and the thrilling stories of Sir Walter Ralegh about his sea battles and his search for the fabulous treasure of the Orinoco that led Algernon to study the sea and to become later the Admiral of the British fleet. These are stirring and exciting accounts, and it is sad to relate that so little contemporary evidence bolsters them that they must be considered almost totally fictitious.

It is true that there was much contemporary interest in the affairs of the Tower during all these years, and a great deal of speculation was spent on the political intrigues which surrounded the King's prisoners. But local London gossip was much less romantic and certainly more realistic and prosaic than it has become in the minds of later historians. During the last three and a half centuries an artificial glow has surrounded Percy and Ralegh which has transformed the Tower into a kind of intellectual academy. The tradition of a 'Wizard' Earl and his 'Three Magi', first proposed by Read, Aubrey, and Wallis, has not only been accepted unquestioningly, but has grown by gradual accretion until it appears that Northumberland wittingly gathered around him a number of the greatest thinkers of his day, men trained in all aspects of the new science and philosophy, to discuss within those grim stone walls systematic solutions to intellectual problems of all kinds, in a sort of precursor to Bacon's New Atlantis. This pleasant concept has been embraced by historians of literature, as well as historians of science.

Literary historians have tended to downplay the science and to concentrate on the inclusion of literary figures in discussions which led to free-thinking, revolutionary, or heretical thought. Shakespearian scholars, in particular those dealing with *Love's Labour's Lost*, have constructed a formal organization called 'The School of Night' — a group which Shakespeare was satirizing in this play. In her volume of that name, Muriel Bradbrook summarizes this thesis:[1]

During the last ten or fifteen years there has been a growing interest in the literary activities of Ralegh, and in particular in the society founded by him and known now by Shakespeare's nickname 'The School of Night.' . . .
Ralegh was the patron of the school; Thomas Harriot, a mathematician of European reputation, was its master. It probably included the earls of Northumberland and Derby, and Sir George Carey, with the poets Marlowe, Chapman, Matthew Royden and William Warner. They studied theology, philosophy, geography and chemistry: and their reputations differed as widely as their studies. . . .
The three nobles were all of great family and all were eccentrics. Northumberland was known as the Wizard Earl: he was a moody man, interested in alchemy, a patron of the arts, and a scholar. After 1606 he was co-prisoner in the Tower with Ralegh, having been suspected of complicity in the Gunpowder Plot. There he collected a very large

[1] *The School of Night: a Study in the Literary Relationships of Sir Walter Ralegh*, Cambridge, 1936, pp. 7–10.

library. . . . These gentlemen, and the poets, whose lives are read sometimes with more interest than their poetry, were instructed by Thomas
Harriot, from whose work Descartes himself is said to have learned. . . .
Ralegh introduced Harriot to Northumberland, with whom he had
recently become friendly. The earl took to Harriot; in 1597 he granted
him a pension, and Harriot with Walter Warner and Robert Hughes were
known as the Earl's Three Magi. . . .

Though almost every statement in this thesis can be challenged,
much the same theme was repeated by Frances A. Yates in
her *Study of 'Love's Labour's Lost'*, published in the same
year, 1936.[2] Bringing together the literary allusions with the
science of the Renaissance, Miss Yates presented the Ralegh-
Northumberland-Harriot-Chapman group as disciples of
Giordano Bruno, and the chief proponents of Copernicanism
in England at the turn of the century.

Other historians of science and the history of ideas have
been inclined to see the Ralegh-Northumberland circle as
forerunners of the new science being advocated by Francis
Bacon. Christopher Hill, in his *Intellectual Origins of the
English Revolution*,[3] concisely summarizes these views:

Around Ralegh and Northumberland we can distinguish a literary and
scientific group. This consisted of the Earl's 'three Magi' — Hariot,
Robert Hues, and Walter Warner — together with the poet, mathematician and Hermeticist, Matthew Royden, a former friend of
Sidney's, who may have written *Willobie his Avisa* as a defence of the
Ralegh group, and George Chapman, who dedicated books to Ralegh
and Bacon. Chapman spoke warmly of Hariot and Hues in the Preface
to his translation of Homer. Hues had been an undergraduate at Brasenose College and then went to sea. He dedicated his first (Latin) edition
of his *Treatise on Globes* to Ralegh in 1592. . . . Hues was one of
Ralegh's executors. He also acted as tutor to Northumberland's eldest
son, the later Parliamentarian, and received a pension of £40 from the
Earl. He is said to have had connections with Gresham College. Warner,
pensioner of Northumberland's, friend of Hakluyt and Gorges, continued Briggs's work on logarithms, and claimed to have given Harvey
the idea which led to his discovery of the circulation of the blood. . . .

Even Robert Kargon, who ostensibly has studied the original
manuscripts, presents the view of an almost formal scientific
academy at work in the Northumberland-Ralegh circle in

---

[2] *A Study of 'Love's Labour's Lost'*, Cambridge, 1936. See especially pp. 7-9;
91-8; 137-51.
[3] Oxford, 1965, pp. 142-4.

his *Atomism in England from Hariot to Newton*, based solely
on hearsay evidence:[4]

The Wizard Earl's personality particularly fitted him for his role as
patron of the arts and sciences. . . . In his pursuit of knowledge, he kept
a splendid library, spending over £50 per annum on books alone. He
also gathered around him some of the most sparkling intellects of
England, including Thomas Hariot, mathematician, physicist, and
astonomer; Robert Hues, the author of *De globorum usu*; Walter
Warner, mathematician and physicist; Robert Norton, the translator
of Stevin; John Donne; and dramatists and poets, like Chapman and
Peel [sic]; Christopher Marlowe too is often included in this list. Sir
Walter Ralegh, a good friend of Percy, Ferdinando Stanley, and Lord
George Hunsdon likewise were among the men who, at various times,
gathered around the Earl of Northumberland. Other members of note
included Nathaniel Torporley, the mathematician Thomas Allen, and
Nicholas Hill.

Except from some small works of Torporley, Hill, and Hues, nothing
of scientific interest was published by the group while it was in existence.
To reconstruct the philosophical atmosphere and doctrines of the circle
is therefore difficult. Nevertheless, from the fragmentary information
which has filtered down to us, something about their views can be
established. First, the 'scientific' members of the group — Percy, Hariot,
Warner, Torporley, Hill, and Hues — were all Copernicans. Secondly,
with the exception of Torporley, they were also avowed atomists. The
two views are linked in one very important respect: both were phases
of a concerted attack upon Aristotelian natural philosophy. To be sure,
the members of the 'Northumberland Circle' were not the only critics
of Aristotle in the late sixteenth- and seventeenth-century England, but
they combine, as far as can be determined at present, the only English
school to combine Copernicanism with the complete rejections of
Aristotelianism which accompanies acceptance of the atomic philosophy
of Democritus, Epicurus, and Lucretius.

As we have seen, these accounts began almost immediately
following the death of the principals, starting with Dr Alexander Read's publications on cancer in 1635. Read stated
simply that[5]

This griefe hastened the end of that famous Mathematician, Mr.
Hariot . . . [who] at one time, together with Mr. *Hughes*, who wrote
of the Globes, Mr. *Warner*, and Mr. *Turperley*, the Noble Earle of

[4] Robert Hugh Kargon, *Atomism in England from Hariot to Newton*, Oxford,
1966. This passage is from pp. 6–7.
[5] *The Chirurgicall Lectures of Tumors and Vlcers. Delivered on Tuesdays . . .
in the Chirurgeans Hall these three yeares last past. . . by Alexander Read*, London,
1635 (STC 20781), p. 307.

Northumberland, the favourer of all good learning, and Mecaenas of learned men, maintained while he was in the Tower, for their worth and various literature. . .

An anonymous Roman Catholic, writing with more imagination than accuracy shortly after, put down some of the gossip still going the rounds, adding to the tradition of the traditional 'Three Magi':[6]

Henry the Earle of Northumberland, Brother to Thomas E: of Northumberland who was beheaded at York for the northern insurrection, was kept in the Tower of London a long time . . . where for better passing his time he got seauerall Learned persons to Live and Converse with him.

One of them was Mr. Heriot whose book De Algebra was not long ago printed at Paris, fol°. [This must be the *Artis Analyticae Praxis* published posthumously in London in 1631.] He presented Queene Anne with a viol of water which ebbed and flowed at the same time as the Thames. He allways carried about him a golden probe with which every day he tryed if a polipus he had in his nose yielded fresh blood. He said, that would give him at Least tenn dayes warning of his death by ceasing to bleed.

Another was Mr. Warrener, the Inventor probably of the circulation of the blood, of which subject he made a treatise consisting of two books which he sent to Dr. Harvey, who Epitomized them and printed them In his own name: he usually said that Dr. Harvey did not understand the motions of the Heart which was a perfect Hydraulick.

. . . Mr. Robert Hues, after he came out of the Tower, associated himself with Mr. Cauendish, and accompanied him round the world, [an obvious anachronism] purposely for taking the true Latitude of places which he put Into his booke de Globis: after his returne he setled himself in Christ Church: and there dyed and was buried in the Quire.

John Aubrey, a diligent and good-natured gossip, embellished the story to add more spurious details.[7]

When [Henry Percy, 9th] earle of Northumberland, and Sir Walter Ralegh were both prisoners in the Tower, they grew acquainted, and Sir Walter Raleigh recommended Mr. Hariot to him, and the earle setled an annuity of two hundred pounds a yeare on him for his life, which he enjoyed. But to Hues (who wrote *De Usu Globorum*) and to Mr. Warner he gave an annuity but of sixty pounds per annum. These 3

---

[6] Bodleian MS Rawlinson B 158, pp. 152-3.

[7] Bodleian MS Aubrey 6, fo. 35, as recorded in Andrew Clark's edition of *'Brief Lives,' chiefly of Contemporaries, set down by John Aubrey, between the Years 1669 & 1696*, 2 vols., Oxford, 1898. This from II. 285-6.

were usually called *the earle of Northumberland's three Magi*. They had a table at the earle's chardge, and the earle himselfe had them to converse with, singly or together.

Aubrey's account, somewhat fancifully augmented, was taken over by Anthony Wood for publication in his volumes on Oxford dignitaries, *Athenae Oxonienses*. Here Wood fixed the tale:[8]

After [Harriot's] return into *England*, [from his American sojourn of 1585-86] Sir *Walter* got him into the Aquaintance of that noble and generous Count *Henry* Earl of *Northumberland*, who finding him to be a Gentleman of an affable and peaceable Nature, and well read in the obscure Parts of Learning, he did allow him an yearly Pension of 120 *l*. About the same time *Rob. Hues* and *Walter Warner*, two other Mathematicians, who were known also to the said Count, did receive from him yearly Pensions also, but of less Value, as did afterwards *Nich. Toporley*, whom I shall mention elsewhere. So that when the said Earl was committed Prisoner to the *Tower* of *London* in 1606, to remain there during Life, [Harriot], *Hues*, and *Warner*, were his constant Companions, and were usually called the Earl of *Northumberland's* three *Magi*. They had a Table at the Earl's Charge, and the Earl himself did constantly converse with them either singly or all together, as Sir *Walter*, then in the *Tower*, did.

Naturally, this pleasant fiction was picked up by Harriot's great defender in the controversy over priority between English and French mathematicians in the development of algebra. John Wallis, the Oxford scholar, seized upon this view of a Tower academy when he wrote:[9]

Their prison was an academy where their thoughts were elevated above the common cares of life; where they explored science in all its pleasing forms, penetrated her most intricate recesses, and surveyed the whole globe till Sir Walter Raleigh's noble fabric arose, his *History of the World*, probably by the encouragement and persuasion of his noble friend.

So established, this story became gospel, repeated in nearly every biographical dictionary of the eighteenth and nineteenth centuries. It received its final accolade in the distinguished *Dictionary of National Biography* in the lives of Harriot and

[8] The original publication was in 2 volumes, London, 1691-2. This quotation is from the second enlarged edition, London, 1721, I, col. 460.
[9] This quotation from Wallis is cited by de Fonblanque, *Annals of the House of Percy*, II. 332.

Northumberland which remain unchanged to this day. On Harriot, Miss Agnes Clerke wrote:

About this time [1590] Ralegh introduced [Harriot] to Henry, earl of Northumberland, who admired his affability and learning, and allowed him to the end of his life a pension of 300 *l*. a year. After his committal to the Tower in 1606, the earl kept a handsome table there for Harriot and his mathematical friends, Walter Warner and Thomas Hughes, who became known as the 'three magi' of the Earl of Northumberland. The company was often joined by Raleigh.

Sidney Lee, writing on the 9th Earl, followed the same tradition:

Northumberland gathered about him in the Tower men of learning, to whom he paid salaries for assisting him in his studies. Thomas Harriot, Walter Warner, and Thomas Hughes, the mathematicians, were regular attendants and pensioners, and were known as the earl's 'three magi'. Nicholas Hill aided him in experiments in astrology and alchemy. He also saw something of his fellow prisoner, Sir Walter Raleigh.

A study of the remaining Northumberland records, however, presents a very different view of the Tower years than this romanticized and idealized picture. There was never a time when the 'Three Magi' lived in the Tower with Northumberland and Ralegh; there was never 'a handsome table' maintained for the advanced philosophical discussions which purportedly entertained the 'Wizard Earl'. And there is no evidence in any of the remaining papers that Harriot, Hues, Warner, Torporley, and Hill worked together in any mathematical studies or scientific experiments. In only one instance does Warner report an observation of a Harriot experiment, and that was done, apparently, at the home of Sir Thomas Aylesbury for his delectation.[10] In view of the widespread misinformation about the Northumberland circle, it might be well to review what the actual and official records of the Percy archives show about the role filled by the 'Three Magi' in that household.

Harriot's role in the Northumberland household was, as we have seen, more that of a friend than of a subordinate. Northumberland was his patron from the beginning of their

[10] John W. Shirley, 'An Early Experimental Determination of Snell's Law', *American Journal of Physics*, XIX (Dec. 1951), 507–8.

association, supplying him with a lavish pension (equal to that he gave his younger brothers) from the early 1590s until his death, and granting him income from entailed property 'for dyvers and soundrie good causes & considerations him there vnto especially movinge', as a mark of personal esteem. He furnished him a free house on his Syon estates, immediately adjacent to Syon House itself, and had it remodelled for use as a scientific study and laboratory. He gave Harriot access to his London town houses (Essex House during the Tower years, if he chose to stay there) whenever he visited London. And though Harriot is not listed as one of the Northumberland associates given regular access to the Martin Tower, he was certainly welcome there when he visited, as he frequently did, Ralegh in the Bloody Tower. But in all these activities, Harriot had no duties or responsibilities beyond those offered to a friend and patron; he was an independent scholar, following his own interests and concerns, entertaining his own friends and companions, and living like an Elizabethan gentleman in his own household and with his own servants. And certainly he was never considered a formal tutor for Northumberland's heir, Algernon Lord Percy, since the accounts show that this role was filled by Timothy Elks (his Lordship's Reader in the Tower) and special tutors who were imported to teach him to write, to draw, and to fence.[11] It was a Master Horsmanden who prepared young Percy for Cambridge, where he was under the general oversight of Robert Hues.[12]

According to these same accounts, the position of Walter Warner was far different. Warner entered the service of Northumberland as one of his retainers during the years that Harriot was in the household of Sir Walter Ralegh. Again, it was probably Ralegh who introduced Warner to Northumberland, since Warner was a member of the Ralegh-Hakluyt circle before Northumberland assumed his title,

---

[11] Alnwick MS, Household Accounts U.I.3. Audits of 1609, 1610, 1611.

[12] A letter from the 9th Earl to Mr Horsmanden outlining the duties Percy expected a tutor to do for Algernon is preserved at Alnwick Castle: Syon MS P. I. 3. x. and dated 6 Oct. 1615. The following year's accounts, General Accounts, 1616, Syon MS U. I. 4, lists Hues as receiving a pension of £40 per annum for the first time.

and, like Harriot, was known as an ingenious mathematician.[13] Again like Harriot, Warner never published any of his scientific papers, and details of his contributions must be gleaned from secondary reports, or from his own remaining manuscripts.[14] Most of the biographical details about Warner come from the distinguished seventeenth-century mathematician and diplomat, John Pell. Late in life, after Harriot's death, Warner befriended young John Pell and worked with him in developing and expanding his tables of logarithms. Pell, in turn, talked with John Aubrey about Warner, telling him what he had known of his background and life. Aubrey's notes on these conversations remain in the Bodleian Library:[15]

From Dr. John Pell:— Mr. Walter Warner:— his youngest brother was High Sheriff of Leicestershire, about 1642. He and his brother dyed both batchelors. Dr. Pell haz seen him that was sheriff; but was well acquainted with Walter. . . .

Walter had but one hand (borne so), he thinks a right hand; his mother was frighted, which caused this deformity, so that instead of a left hand, he had only a stump with five warts upon it, instead of a hand and fingers. He wore a cuffe on it like a pockett. The Doctor never sawe his stump, but Mr. Warner's man has told him so.

This Walter Warner was both mathematician and philosopher, and 'twas he that putt-out Thomas Hariot's Algebra, though he mentions it not.

Mr. Warner did tell Dr. Pell, that when Dr. Harvey came out with his Circulation of the Blood, he did wonder whence Dr. Harvey had it: but comeing one day to the earl of Leicester, he found Dr. Harvey in the hall, talking very familiarly with Mr. Prothero . . . to whom Mr. Warner had discoursed concerning this exercitation of his *De Circulatione Sanguinis*, and made no question but Dr. Harvey has his *hint* from Prothero. Memorandum:— Dr. Pell sayes that Mr. Warner rationated demonstratively by beates of the pulses that there must be a circulation of the blood.

When Mr. Hariot dyed, he made Sir Thomas Alesbury and Mr. Prothero his executors, by which meanes his papers came to be divided

[13] See p. 78 above.
[14] The majority of Warner's papers are in BL Add. MSS 4394-6 and 6754-6. For an account of these papers see Jean Jacquot, 'Harriot, Hill, Warner and the New Philosophy', in *Thomas Harriot, Renaissance Scientist*, John W. Shirley, ed., Oxford, 1974, pp. 107-28. The handwriting of many of these manuscripts classed as Warner's is very different from those receipts, book lists, etc., signed by Warner still retained among the Northumberland accounts, and this authorship may be open to question.
[15] MS Aubrey 6, fo. 32, reprinted in *Brief Lives*, II. 291-3.

into two hands. . . . none of them were printed, save that *Artis Analyticae Praxis*, which was printed by Mr. Warner . . . Sir Thomas Alesbury obtained of Algernon, earle of Northumberland (son to that earle, prisoner in the Tower), a continuation of the annuity, dureing Warner's life, upon condition that he should, out of Mr. Hariot's papers, drawe out some piece fitt to be published, which he did . . . but did not sett his name to it, and accordingly Warner had his money as long as he lived. . . .

The bishop [Seth Ward, bishop of Sarum] thinkes he was of Cambridge university, but is not certaine. Dr. Pell believes that he was of no university. . . .

Surprisingly, Anthony à Wood took Aubrey's statement about Warner's education as fact, and did not discover that Warner was in Oxford at the same time that Harriot and Hues studied there.

The Northumberland records show clearly that Walter Warner had entered the household of the 9th Earl some time before Harriot was given patronage. Though the records for the 1580s are somewhat spotty, it is easy to follow him from 1590 on. An entry in the accounts of John Mortymer[16] records an item 'to Mr Warner by his lordship's commandement when he went to London the xxijth of November 1590', and the 'Breevinge Booke' (a detailed accounting of the food and drink of the household and a list of the diners) 'Begun the xiiij° of ffebrij 1590'[17] lists Warner with one servant as a regular member of the Earl's household. During this period, Sir Walter Ralegh dined with them on Saturday, 20 February; Harriot dined on 13 of March. The roll of 'Disbursements at Petworth' beginning 16 May 1591,[18] which lists a complete roster of the Earl's entourage, gives 'Mr Warner . . . j°' (and one retainer or 'man' as he was usually called) among the fourteen gentlemen servitors, not counting their ten servants nor the thirty-one servants of Percy himself. This same list also includes a 'Mr hewes' (sans servant) who could possibly have been Thomas Hues, though the name Hewes, Hues, or Hughes were so common in Elizabethan England that this is by no means certain. The breving book for the period of 21 May 1591 to 26 June 1591[19] similarly

---

[16] Syon MS X.II.12.6.   [17] Syon MS X.II.12.5.
[18] Syon MS X.II.12.4   [19] Syon MS X.II.10.1.

included Warner and his man, as well as 'Mr hewes' as a regular diner. But the status of Walter Warner at this time is made clear by the accounts of 'fforeyne expenses . . . by . . . Roger Thorpe' from 25 December 1591 to 18 February 1591/2' with the entry:[20] 'Item payd to Mr Warner his waidge from th'annunciacion of our Ladye [25 Mar.] till Michelmas [29 Sept.] per Annuity . . . x^{li}'. This entry, showing that Warner's annuity of £20 per year was considered as 'waidges', places Warner in the category of a paid servitor or servant to the 9th Earl. But it also indicates that from the size of his stipend he was among the highest paid (and most respected) of the Earl's attendants. Remaining accounts show Warner's name on the rolls of paid servitors for the next twenty-seven years, though the name of 'Mr hewes' drops from the list after this initial entry.

As Professor Batho has pointed out,[21] Northumberland's retainers were a relatively small but select entourage by Elizabethan standards:

Analysis of wages lists and notes on accounting papers of the Earl suggest that the size and complement of household servants varied between just under 50 in the late 1580's and early 1590's and over 70 for the year 1603–04 . . . In the first year of his imprisonment the Earl's household was reduced to about 40 servants; thereafter a further period of expansion followed until in the 1620's the Earl was maintaining a household of eighty or so servants . . .

All of these members of the household were furnished lodging, board, and expenses in addition to their wages. How they were lodged and at which table they were served were functions of their status, and were jealously guarded perquisites. But all were, in accordance with the custom of the times, required to wear the special livery which marked them as the 9th Earl's men. This livery was easily identifiable; as Batho indicated:[22] 'Every man in the household, from the steward or cofferer down, was in the livery of the Earl — azure blue cloth with a cognizance of silver bearing the Percy moon. . . .'

[20] Syon MS X.II.12.6.
[21] Gordon R. Batho, *The Household Papers of Henry Percy, ninth Earl of Northumberland (1564–1632)*, London, 1962, p. xxi.
[22] Ibid., pp. xxxii–xxxiii.

Among this group, Warner held the highest status, dining with the Earl himself, along with the Earl's friends and associates. His travel and lodging charges show that he was very close to the Earl at all times: when the Earl was at Petworth, Warner was there; when at Syon, Warner had rooms in the main house;[23] and when Percy went to the Low Countries in 1600 and 1601 to participate in the military actions there, Warner went with him, shuttling back and forth to England as Northumberland's confidential messenger.[24] Later, during the Tower years (when Warner was supposed to have been a detached and philosophical companion) Warner was again the trusted messenger of the Earl and his chief contact with the world outside, maintaining rooms both at Syon House (where he roomed with Sir John Hippesley, Gentleman of the Horse),[25] and in the house on Tower Hill rented by Northumberland for the convenience of his auditors and visitors.[26]

According to the contemporary accounts, Warner appears as something of a literary assistant to the Earl, engaged in handling most of his affairs dealing with books and writing, maps, scholarly apparatus, and library activities. One early account indicates that it was he who negotiated with the poet, George Peele for composing the 'Poeme gratulatorie' on the occasion of the installation of the ninth Earl into the order of the Garter:[27] 'Rewards . . . to one Peele a poet by thands of Mr Warner. . .lx^s'. But the majority of payments to Warner (except for those dealing with his salary, expenses, or travel) deal with the purchase of books and supplies for the Earl's studies. For example, the 1596 accounts of Robert Stapleton, 'fforeyne Paymaister', now

[23] See, e.g., Syon MSS U.I.50.a.3.; X.II.12.6.; U.I.50.a.2.; U.I.3., and many others.
[24] Syon MS X.II.12.6. 'A booke of fforraine disbursements the 21st of October .1600. in the Low Countries'.
[25] Syon MS U.I.3. 'Henry Taylor'.
[26] Syon MS U.I.50.a.7. 1608.
[27] Syon MS U.I.2. 'Thomas Kelton Receyver'. This commissioned poem, honouring the 9th Earl, was published as *THE HONOUR OF THE GARTER Displaid in a Poeme gratulatorie: Entitled to the worthie and renowned Earle of Northumberland. Created Knight of that Order, and installed at VVindsore, Anno Regni Elizabethae, 35. Die Iunij .26. By George Peele, Maiser of Artes in Oxenforde* (STC 19539).

separated and scattered among Syon, Alnwick, and Petworth manuscripts, record the following items which are
typical:[28]

> ... to Mr Warner for bookes per bill July ij ... xxij^s
>
> ... to Mr Warner for glasses per bill Sept. last ... xj^s
>
> ... to Mr Warner for one sea compas which he bought for my lord
> December xxix ... vj^s
>
> ... sundry books and a Sea Compas as my bills thereto Remaining
> may Appeare ... xiij^{li} vj^s
>
> ... to Mr Warner for bookes by him bought the vj of Nouember
> 1596 of Paule Lynley to his Lordship's vse xxj^{li} ... a sea Carde xxx^s a
> Compas x^s and for new horixons to the globe vj^s.

During late 1600 and early 1601 Henry Percy visited the
Low Countries as a special emissary of the Queen to advise
the commander-in-chief Sir Francis Vere. On the continent,
Percy continued to build his library, collecting books, maps,
manuscripts, and other interesting documents of the campaign. Again, Walter Warner appears to have served as his
principal agent in these negotiations, and many expenditures
attest to his activities during these years.[29] Many of them
are summed up in the records of 'Rocke Churche ... Payer
and Disburser of fforeine payments aswell in England as in
the Low Countries' from 1 May 1600 to 27 May 1602:[30]

Bookes & mappes/ Paid also by the said Accomptante for diuerse
bookes bought by Mr Warner & others for your lordship's vse at diuerse
times and places aswell in England (xliiij^s vj^d) as in the lowe countreyes
(vj^{li} xv^s iv^d) ... to a Scryvener for Writing ij discourses of warre x^s a
discorse of the Armye of Cales [Cadiz] iij^s paper papall for mappes
xvj^s viij^d for iiij skinnes of velame to make ye mappes of Berke and
Ostend x^s for ye sortinge and titlinge & cataloginge of your lordship's
bookes at Syon xxxv^s for binding the discourse of Ireland & other
bookes xx^s v^d for coullers for mappes paintinge v^s for paper & coullours
to make the leager of Berke ij^s to a painter that made the mappe of
Berge in Collors xxvj^s for vj platts of Ostend and Berge ij^s for a mappe
of Antwerpe vj^s for ij mappes of Netherland xviij^d for ye articles
betwene the Archduke & the States generall v^s for ye pettigree of

---

[28] Syon MS U.I.2. 'fforein paments ... Mr Stapleton 1596.'; 'rough draft ...
Stapleton'; Petworth MS 580 'Robert Stapleton ... fforeyne Paymaister; 577
'William Wycliff'.

[29] Syon MSS X.II.12.6.; U.I.50.a.2.

[30] Syon MS U.I.3, already printed on p. 296.

Grave Morryce & a mapp of ye battell xx^s to ye painter at Hage for mappes xx^s and for a mappe bought by David Joanes ij^s In all as by his bookes and billes amongst other thinges examined may appeare/ xvij^{li} xiiij^s vij^d.

In the critical years preceding his incarceration in the Tower, Warner was active in the Earl's service. He was undoubtedly at Syon House on 8 June 1603 when James and his court visited there. He attended Percy in the progress of the King and his court to Winchester in October 1603, and was undoubtedly in attendance with the Earl in the trial of Sir Walter Ralegh at that time; it is even possible that he accompanied the Earl as he attempted to intercede with King James for the life of Ralegh. One account carries the item:[31] '...paid to Mr Warner the same daie [the last week in November, the sixteenth week of the royal progress] for boord wages as by a bill at Winchester...' It is even probable that Warner accompanied Percy on the fateful visit to London following his apprehension for complicity in the Gunpowder Plot in November 1605. An item signed by Warner in the board wages account for 1605 carries the following item in his own hand:[32]

For my botehire to Sion and back againe being sent thither by his Lordship the 6th of November about setting the Sycamore trees ... iij^s vj^d ... for the same going thither about the 24th of November [while Northumberland was still in the custody of the Archbishop of Canterbury] for books for his Lordship ... v^s.

When the salary accounts resume [after a gap of several years], Warner is found established at Syon, and his stipend (which had been £20) was doubled, to make him the highest-paid retainer of the Earl — the same £40 which was paid to Timothy Elks, his lordship's reader in the Tower, and twice that paid to Edmund Powton, steward of the Earl's estates.[33] From 1607 to 1615 Warner's stipend remains at this high level, and his duties appear to have remained the same.

[31] Syon MS U.I.50.a.3.
[32] Syon MS U.I.10. fo. 37. Another account (Syon MS U.I.8.b.11^v.) under 'Garden woorkes at Sion' contains an entry 'Paid to ye laborers for trenching to sett Sickamore trees in ye new garden' — a project on which Northumberland was working at the time of the Gunpowder Plot.

About 1615 the 9th Earl reviewed the status of his retainers and made some changes in their positions. In 1616 Warner's roommate at Syon, Sir John Hippesley, Master of the Horse, was removed from the salary list and placed in the more select group of pensioners which included the members of the Earl's own family. The following year, Warner, too, was removed from the list of those paid wages, and put on the pension list, though at exactly the same rate as he had been getting — £40 per annum. Though this was undoubtedly an increase in social status, the honour was a doubtful one, for as pensioner Warner no longer received the perquisites of housing, board, and expenses.[34] And from this time on it is likely that he had more freedom to follow his own interests, but his movements are more difficult to follow since his comings and goings are not reflected in the Northumberland accounts. He may even have left the Earl's active service entirely, since references in later correspondence indicate him as living mainly in London, 'at one Morgan's house, the hall of the Woolstable in Westminster',[35] except for periods spent at 'Cranborne Lodge near Windsore', home of his friend Sir Thomas Aylesbury when the plague raged in London.[36]

In later years, Warner found his pension inadequate to meet his needs. Publishing of Harriot's posthumous *Artis Analyticae Praxis* taxed his resources, and though Aylesbury did get some concessions over this, the alleviation was short lived.[37] During his declining years, Warner relied for support on gifts from his friends in the scientific community. On 2 May 1636 (when Warner was in his late seventies) Sir Charles Cavendish wrote him on a problem in optics on behalf of Hobbes. He closed his letter with the words: 'I haue sent you by this bearer Mr Butler Twentie pounds as

---

[33] Syon MS U.I.3. 'Edmund Powton . . . Steward . . . Michaelmas 1607'.

[34] Warner's pension remains at this figure in the few accounts remaining of the following years: Petworth MS 600 (1620), and for 1628–31 see Batho, *Household Papers*, p. 163. It is unaccountably missing for the year 1621 (Petworth MS 601) and was apparently discontinued by the tenth Earl on his succession in 1632.

[35] Letter from Walter Warner to Robert Payne, BL Birch MS 4279, fos. 307–8.

[36] Wood, *Athenae Oxonienses*, 1721, I, col. 460.

[37] See pp. 6–7 above.

an acknowledgement of your fauours.'[38] But in spite of all support, Warner died in poverty. After his death, Dr John Pell who was working with Cavendish to collect Warner's papers, wrote to Sir Charles on 7 August 1644:[39]

You remember that [Warner's] papers were giuen to his kinsman, a merchant in London, who sent his partner to bury the old man: himself being hindred by a politicke gout, which made him keep out of their sight that urged him to contribute to the Parliaments assistance, from which he was exceedingly averse. So he was looked upon as one that absented himselfe, out of Malignancy, and his partner managed the whole trade. Since my coming over, . . . both he and his partner are broken . and I am not a little afraid that all Mr Warners papers, and no small share of my labours therein, are seazed upon and most unmathematically divided between the Sequestrators and Creditors. . . .

From all these accounts, it appears that Walter Warner, though considered by his associates, as Aubrey tells us, 'harmless and quiet', led a generally harried and disappointing life. Undoubtedly his most gratifying years were those few from 1617 and 1631 when he was a pensioner and relatively free from his servant's duties, able to follow his own mathematical and scientific bent without too many financial worries. It is sad that he outlived so long his benefactors, and died in the want which had pursued him most of his life.

There is even less evidence in the Northumberland records that Robert Hues played a part in the life of the Tower circle than did Warner. His association with the 9th Earl was of shorter duration and much more tenuous in nature than that of either Warner or Harriot.

Undoubtedly, Hues was a friend of Harriot's from his college days. Several named Robert Hughes were registered at Oxford during these years, but Anthony à Wood identified the geographer Hues as the one who entered Brasenose about 1571, transferred to St. Mary's Hall, and was graduated there in 1578, As Wood tells the story, Hues was at that time:[40]

. . . noted for a good *Grecian*. Which Degree compleating by Determination, he afterwards travelled, and in fine became well skill'd in Geography and Mathematics. The last of which being the Faculty he

---

[38] BL Add. (Birch) MS 4407, fo. 186r.

[39] BL Add. (Birch) MS 4280, fos. 105r&v.

[40] Wood, *Athenae Oxonienses*, 1721, no. 658.

excelled in, made him respected by that generous Count *Henry* Earl of *Northumberland*, who allowed him an yearly Pension for the Encouragement of his Studies. . . .

If this is the proper identification, Hues would have been at St. Mary's Hall during Harriot's first two years there. If he was, it is almost certain that they knew each other, since they shared similar interests and would have followed the same studies. Both were primarily interested in mathematics, secondarily in geography and navigation, but they were also highly skilled in the classics as well. As a matter of fact, their mutual friend, George Chapman, insisted that it was to these two he turned when he sought a critical review of his major work, the translation of *The Whole Works of Homer*, in 1614.[41] In the preface to that work he wrote:

No conference had with any one living in al the nouelties I presume I haue found. Only some on or two places I haue shewed to my worthy and most learned friend, M. Harriots, *for his censure how much mine owne weighed: whose iudgement and knowledge in al kinds, I know to be incomparable, and bottomlesse: yea, to be admired as much, as his most blameless life, and the right sacred expence of his time, is to be honoured and reuerenced. . . . Another right learned, honest, and entirely loued friend of mine,* M. Robert Hews, *I must needs put into my confest conference touching* Homer, *though very little more then that I had with* M. Harriots. *Which two, are all, and preferred to all. . . .*

It is obvious, too, that Harriot and Hues continued to be friends, and there are many evidences that they were cognizant and appreciative of each other's activities. But there is no contemporary evidence to put them together in any formal circle around Northumberland.

Following their Oxford years the two worked independently. Harriot visited the New World; Hues circumnavigated the globe with Cavendish on his voyage beginning in 1586 and continuing to 1588, and as Harriot wrote the account of the newly settled Virginia, Hues has been credited with writing the account of Cavendish's voyage.[42] Harriot continued with Ralegh; Hues entered the service of Lord Grey

---

[41] 'Preface', Sig. iijv.

[42] See Richard Hakluyt, *Principall navigations (1589)*, ed. D. B. Quinn and R. A. Skelton, Hakluyt Society, 1965, I. xliv; also D. B. Quinn, *The Hakluyt Handbook*, Hakluyt Society, 1974, I. 229, n. 1: '. . .the suggestion that Hues

of Wilton on his return from his travels.[43] Both contributed their new-found knowledge and experience to Hakluyt and to Emery Molyneux who had been commissioned by William Sanderson (Ralegh's relative and supporter) to make new terrestrial and celestial globes for the widespread dissemination of new knowlege to the British people. These were issued in 1592, and two years later Hues published his *Tractatus de Globis et eorum vsu* to explain their proper use. This work he dedicated to Ralegh, and in it showed that he was familiar with Harriot's unpublished work on rhumbs.[44] But only after the death of Lord Grey in July 1614 can Hues be identified surely as having come under the patronage of the Earl of Northumberland. The General Accounts for 1616–17 and 1617–18 show Robert Hues receiving an annuity of £40 on the same pension rolls in which Harriot received his £100,[45] and he remains there on most of the remaining accounts until the death of Northumberland a decade after Harriot's death.[46]

The clue to Hues's role in the Northumberland household is to be found in the brief account of his life carved on his grave-stone in Christ Church, Oxford. As recorded by the antiquary, Anthony à Wood, this reads:[47]

In laminâ aeneâ, eidem parieti impactâ talem cernis inscriptionem.

Depositum Viri literatissimi, morum ac religionis integerrimi, Roberti Husii, ob eruditionem omnigenam, Theologicam, tum Historicam, tum Scholasticam, Philologicam, Philosophicam; praesertim vero Mathematicam (cujus insigne monumentum in typis reliquit;) Primum Thomae Candishio conjuntissimi; cujus in consortis, explorabundus velis ambivit orbem: deinde Domino Baroni Gray; cui solator accessit in arce Londinensi. Quo defuncto, ad studia Henrici Comitis Northumbriensis ibidem

---

might be the author of the narrative if N. H. is a misprint for M. H. (Master Hues) seems rather unlikely, especially in view of certain ambiguous geographical statements in the account.'

[43] See the evidence presented by Gordon Goodwin in the life in *DNB*.

[44] He writes, '*De Rumborum ortu, & usu, integrum fractatum expectamus a Thoma Hariota Matheaseos & universæ Philosophiæ peritissimo.*' See also Quinn and Shirley, '*A Contemporary List*', pp. 13–14. Hues' adjectives describing Harriot are identical with those used by Lawrence Keymis in his dedicatory poem on Harriot in his account of Ralegh's voyage to Guiana in 1596.

[45] Syon MS U.I.4. General Accounts, 1616, 1617.

[46] Batho, op. cit., p. 155.

[47] Anthony à Wood, *Historia et Antiquitates Universitatis Oxoniensis*, 2 vols., First edition, Latin, 1674, II. p. 288b.

vocatus est, cujus filio instruendo cum aliquot annorum operam in hac
Ecclesia dedisset, & Academiæ confinium locum valetudinariæ senectuti
commodum cemsuisset in ædibus Johannis Smith, corpore exhaustus,
sed animo vividus, expiravit die Maii 24, anno reparatæ salutis 1632.
ætatis suæ 79.

This contemporary evidence gives substance to the report of
Wood that[48] 'the said *R. Hues* the Mathematician . . . spent
one Year or two in the condition of a Tutor to *Algernon* son
of *Hen.* Earl of *Northumberland,* in *Ch. Ch.*' This statement
of Hues's service to Northumberland is borne out by the
official Oxford records which show Algernon's matriculation
as:[49]

15 July 1617 Ch. Ch. Percy, Aulgernoun; Cantabrigiensis (signs
among the 'nobiles' . . .).

This, then, explains the inclusion of Hues on the pension lists
of the 9th Earl. The indication of Algernon's residence as of
'Cantabrigiensis' might raise questions, but again the Percy
household records give explanation. A letter of Henry Percy
remaining at Alnwick Castle, dated 6 October 1615 and
addressed to a Mr Horsmanden,[50] commences: 'I thank you
for the charge you have undertaken to be tutor to my sonne;
I vnderstand yowr willingnes to apply your selfe wholy to
him and to dismisse somme of your puples that you may
follow the worke more soundly . . .' The letter continues to
give a thoughtful father's analysis of his son's physical and
intellectual needs, outlines the study he wishes implemented,
and concludes '. . .theas I wische his Cambridge dayes should
furnishe him with all.' Obviously Algernon's education came
not from association with scholars in the Tower circle, but in
three stages: Tower years of training in the arts and skills of
the gentleman, Cambridge preparation for study at Oxford
under a tutor Horsmanden, and Oxford study under the
scrutiny of Harriot's friend, Robert Hues, at Christ Church.

The ascription of Hues as an Oxford tutor to Northumberland's son rather than as a mathematical colleague of a
'Wizard' Earl in the Tower is further verified by the fact that

[48] Wood, *Athenæ Oxonienses,* 1721, II, col. 572.
[49] Clark, *Register of the University of Oxford,* 1877, Vol. II, Part 2, 'Matriculations and Subscriptions', p. 362.
[50] Syon MS P.I.3.x.

five years later, in 1622-3, this same Robert Hues was imprest for the charges of Algernon's younger brother, Henry Percy, at Oxford.[51] It is during this period, in the year before Harriot's death and during the period that Alexander Read formed his impressions, for one and only one year did the General Accounts for 1620 show pensions for Harriot, Warner, and Hues at the same time. The next year, though a half-year's pension is indicated for Harriot (since he died at midyear), for some reason neither Warner nor Hues appears to have received a stipend of any sort.

Hues may have spent some time with the Earl after Algernon left Oxford. In his will Harriot mentions 'Robert Hughes gentleman and nowe attendant vppon th'aforesaid Earle of Northumberland for matters of Learning', though his 'Learning' may have been the instruction of the younger sons instead of the Earl himself. Hues' pension continued for the next decade after the Earl had left the Tower, but there is no evidence that he was anywhere but at Oxford where the younger boys were being educated. But this is long after the time when the 'three Magi' were supposed to have formed an intimate circle surrounding the Earl, dealing with the philosophy and the science of the intellectual revolution which was then in ferment.

It is sad to undermine a tradition of more than three centuries and a half, particularly when the idea of such an enlightened philosophical group is intensely appealing to the historian of science. But from all the contemporary evidence which appears to remain, there is little real basis for such an association. Harriot, Warner, and Hues were scholarly men who were friends, who discussed their ideas with each other, and were in differing ways under the patronage of the 9th Earl of Northumberland. But they played different roles in the Northumberland household. Warner appears to have been for nearly all of his time with Northumberland, in the class of a gentleman servitor, charged with specific duties respecting the Earl's library and books. He was principally housed at Syon in the wing devoted to the other retainers and where the magnificent library of the

---

[51] Batho, op. cit., p. 155.

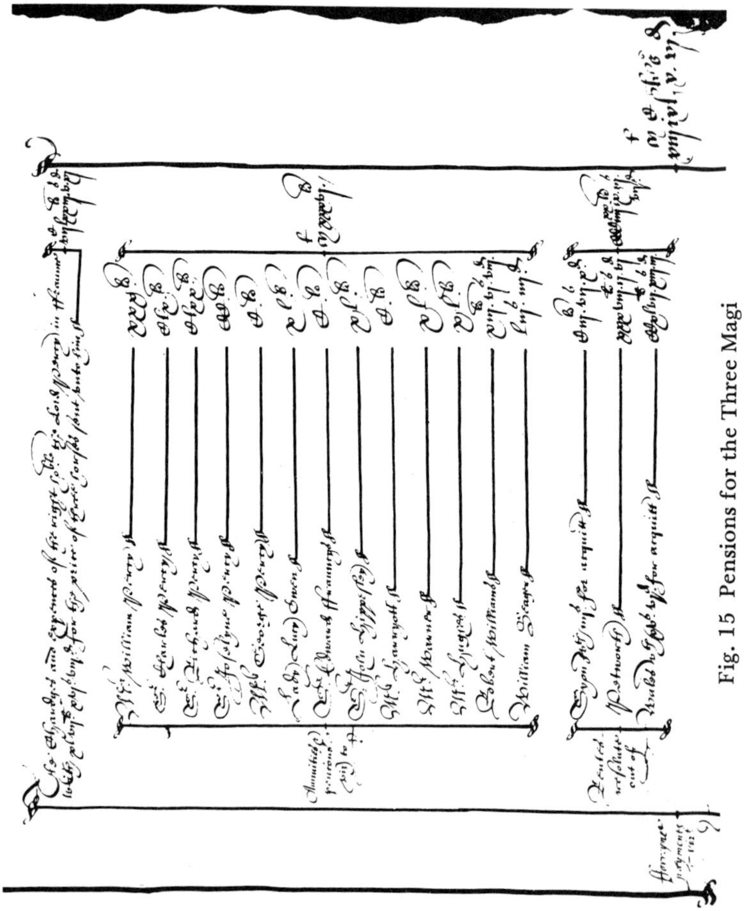

Fig. 15 Pensions for the Three Magi

Earl was kept. He did shuttle back and forth to the Earl in the Tower on occasions, carrying books, maps, globes, and other such materials for the use of the Earl in his Tower studies. But in those occasions when he remained in London, he stayed with the Earl's servants in a London house reserved for their use. Outside his editing of Harriot's *Praxis*, which he evidently undertook by default of Torporley and without the support and blessing of Northumberland, he seems to have made no studies at the behest of his patron. The role of Robert Hues was even more remote. From contemporary accounts and College records, he remained in residence at Christ Church, Oxford, where his major association with the 9th Earl was in educating his offspring. He did not appear to have lived at Syon, in the Tower, or in the Earl's rented London residences. Nor is there evidence located to this time to show that he had access to the Earl in the Tower, or that he accompanied him to Petworth on his release. And from all the manuscripts left by Harriot, it appears that his connections with the Earl directly were tenuous. He was occupied with his own concerns in science and mathematics which centred in his own house at Syon, though as a loyal friend he did on occasion visit his two friends, Henry Percy and Walter Ralegh, in the Tower, and undoubtedly did discuss his innovations with them, and did on at least one occasion compose a scientific treatise at the request of his patron.

But from all the evidence which diligent searches of contemporary source material can reveal, it appears certain that there was never a formal association surrounding either Ralegh or Northumberland; there were no meetings in the Tower where new ideas were openly discussed; there was no handsome table at which they regularly revealed to a presiding 'Wizard' their new ideas and startling discoveries about the evolving world of the English intellectual Renaissance. The Tower was not, as we should all like to imagine it, an extension of Gresham College or a Solomon's House. It was a prison where men and their hopes and ambitions were confined, where the shadow of death made each day an experience of fear and uncertainty, and where friends met on occasion to carry on the business of the day and to offer solace and consolation for the suffering which was the daily existence of those branded as enemies of the King.

X. The Mature Scholar

During the early years of the seventeenth century, when both Ralegh and Northumberland found their lives drastically altered by the new monarch, Harriot sensibly retired to the confines of his own study to pursue his private scholarship. No longer was Ralegh, in the Tower, asking him to serve as emissary among the ministers of the court; nor was Northumberland in direct contact with him since, seeking favours from the new Scottish king, he was spending more time with the court than with his familiars, until with the Gunpowder Plot he joined Sir Walter in the Tower. Harriot's papers clearly show that while Northumberland was progressing with James, Harriot remained at Syon, and, except for a few occasional visits to the city, his observations are almost invariably indicated as originating from 'Syon' at Isleworth on the river Thames.

Once he had discarded interest in the Aristotelian elements, Harriot turned to different studies of matter. Having stopped his final experiment at the end of May 1600, Harriot turned back again to the work on specific gravity and refraction which he had worked on earlier. The next dated manuscript is an interesting drawing of a complex collection of pipes through which water can work a devious course, labelled 'A water worke shewed before my lord chamberlayne at his house in blacke friers, the 23 of ffebruary $\frac{1600}{1601}$.', and endorsed 'The Lord Chamberlaynes water worke',[1] After a few sporadic efforts to explore rates and volumes of fluid flow,[2] problems which he found much too difficult for his

---

[1] BL Add. MS 6786, fo. 282r&v.

[2] Though most of Harriot's studies of hydraulics are much later (c.1612), a few are from this early period. See, e.g. BL Add. MS 6782, fo. 166r.

solution, Harriot returned in the summer of 1601 to the study of two phenomena which he felt he might be able to bring together: the specific gravity of liquid and translucent materials, and their refractive indexes. As we have said,[3] Harriot had learned before 1597 the law of sines of refraction — that the sine of the angle of incidence is proportional to the sine of the angle of refraction, both angles being measured from the normal — first published by Descartes in 1637 but attributed to Willebrord Snell who had made the discovery in 1621. Now he was trying to expand this finding by using mathematics to predict more difficult refractive situations. In one undated manuscript of about this time he posed himself the following question:[4]

> problema.
> Datis fractionibus ab aere ad aqua
> et ab aere ad vitrum: fractionem
> ab aqua ad vitrum invenire.
>
> [Given the refractive index from
> air to water and from air to glass,
> determine the refractive index from
> water to glass.]

which he then solved by developing a proportionality of sines.

Harriot's studies were interrupted by the trial of Ralegh in October of 1603, and while it is probable that he continued his investigations of refraction and specific gravities, no extant manuscripts are dated for the period of eight months following Ralegh's imprisonment in the Tower. When Harriot does return to more normal practice, it is July of 1604, and he shows himself to be deeply immersed in the study of the specific gravities of various liquids.[5] For the remainder of that year he was busy weighing, measuring, and using a hydrostatic balance to determine with extreme accuracy the specific gravity of such diverse substances as 'My crystall cone', 'Grey marble, octangle, hard', 'round

[3] See the author's 'An Early Experimental Determination of Snell's Law', *American Journal of Physics*, XIX (1951), 507-08.

[4] BL Add. MS 6789, fo. 252[r].

[5] These observations, scattered and out of all order, are mostly to be found in BL Add. MS 6788, between fos. 98 and 247, with some few in Add. MS 6789 (as fos. 327[v], 296[r], 190[n], and 331[r]).

loadstone of Ad[rian] Gilbertes mine',[6] 'stalkes of tobacco', 'ashes of egges without shelles',[7] 'Rubyes', 'Diamondes',[8] 'Browen Morter', 'white morter',[9] 'my square amber',[10] 'slag or Iron', 'copper ore', 'lead ore', 'shoing horne', and 'Brimstone.'[11] From the accuracy with which Harriot made his observation and from the great number and variety of substances with which he was working, it seems apparent that he was at this time planning to publish on a subject of great interest to the early chemists — the mass or density of all material things. It is highly probable that Harriot viewed these studies as an extension of his work on the Aristotelian elements and a possible source of data which would be helpful in developing his theories of the atomic structure of matter. Both of these, in turn, were being investigated for their relevance to the effect they might have on the refraction of light. Obviously there was some mathematical relationship between density, molecular structure, and refractive index in materials which were not opaque which might lead to a clarification of all three observable phenomena.

Sometime in late 1604 or early 1605, while he was turning his attention from simple refraction to the more complex movement of light through irregular shapes of glass, Harriot added a lens grinder to his staff. This man, Christopher Tooke, a very elusive person about whom almost nothing can be found, came to be a very close scientific assistant and companion to Harriot for the remainder of his life. The first reference to Tooke in the Harriot manuscripts is a casual one. In a rough sheet casually bound in the last volume of the British Library collection are some 'Remembrances',[12] in the handwriting of the early years of the seventeenth century, reminding Harriot of things he wanted to remember for a trip he was planning. Among such items as 'A riding cloke', 'My gerkin', 'Rapier', 'Hangers', 'shoes', 'bookes', 'A scarfe', 'A ribbon for my dagger', appears the

---

[6] BL Add. MS 6788, fo. 241^v (1604. Octob. 28. 30.)
[7] Ibid., fo. 242^v (June 28. 1605.).
[8] Ibid., fo. 240^v (Nouemb. 28. ☿. 1604.).
[9] Ibid., fo. 237^r (1604. Sept. 30.).
[10] Ibid.
[11] Ibid., fo. 237^v (1604. Octob. 20.).
[12] BL Add. MS 6789, fo. 514^r.

terse note of 'A horse for Kit'. Since there appears not to have been any other person named Christopher who was closely associated with Harriot during these years,[13] it must be assumed that this refers to Christopher Tooke.

That Tooke's work with Harriot was primarily associated with work in optics, lens grinding, and, later, telescope making is clearly shown in the bequests of Harriot's will. In this, his last record, Harriot's largest personal bequest, £100 (which is, as Pepper says, 'a generous legacy') and other perquisites go to his servant-friend:[14]

Item   I doe giue and bequeath vnto Christopher Tooke my foresaid seruante one hundred poundes. . . .

Item   I giue vnto my seruante Christopher Tooke one other furnace with his appurtenaunces out of the same Clossett [the North Closet of the Library of his Syon house from which he also gave furnaces to Protheroe and Torporley]. Alsoe I giue to him an other furnace out of the South Clossett of my said Lybrarie. . . .

[A bequest to the Earl of Northumberland of] my two perspectiue trunckes wherewith I vse espetially to see Venus horned like the Moone and the Spotts in the Sonne. The glasses of which trunckes, I desire to haue remooued into two other of the fayrest trunckes by my said seruante Christopher Tooke. . . .

[To each of his four Executors] One perspectiue truncke a peece of the best glasses, and ye fayrest trunckes as my said seruante Can best fitt to theire liking.

Item   I giue vnto my said servaunte Christopher Tooke the residue of my Cases of perspectiue trunckes with the other glasses of his owne making fitted for perspectiue trunckes (excepting two great longe trunckes Consisting of many partes which I giue vnto the said Earle of Northumberland to remayne in his Library for such vses as they may be put vnto). Also I bequeath the dishes of iron Called by the spectacle makers tooles to grinde spectacles, and other perspectiue glasses for trunckes vnto my foresaid servaunte Christopher Tooke.

By the early spring of 1605, Harriot, with Tooke's assistance, was beginning the study of the dispersion of light into

---

[13] John Bakeless in his *Tragicall History of Christopher Marlowe*, 2 vols., Cambridge, Mass., 1942, I. 135, assumes this to refer to Christopher Marlowe. But Harriot's handwriting on his sheet is much later than the death of Marlowe in 1593. Among other items on this sheet is 'Mr Willis booke, Bacon' which probably relates to Harriot's borrowing of *Sir Francis Bacon his apologie, in certaine imputations concerning the late Earle of Essex*, which appeared in 1604. This is probably the date of this particular sheet of notes.

[14] For more details of Harriot's will see Ch. XI below.

colours as it passed through prisms of glass or of crystal.[15] Using various of the instruments he had developed for his navigational observations and some which were specially constructed for this purpose,[16] Harriot made observations which permitted him to compute the different refractive indexes for light of different colours from green through orange to extremely red light.[17] By 1605 he was thoroughly immersed in studying the internal refraction of a crystal sphere, which he saw was the key to the understanding of the rainbow.[18] In all of these studies, Harriot showed a thoroughness and an understanding of sound experimental techniques which was unusual, if not unique, among scientists of his time. Johannes A. Lohne, who has studied Harriot's optical papers more than any other and who has attempted to duplicate many of his experiments, expressed his admiration for Harriot's methods as follows:[19]

What was the secret of Harriot's accuracy? Certainly not in any superiority of his measuring instruments, for though he had a deep familiarity with the *Great Optics*, where Alhazen in the seventh book described in detail an *organum refractionis*, Harriot himself preferred to employ simple measuring rods and graduated bronze disks. Even so Harriot's results were often better than Hooke's obtained sixty years later with the refined refractometer which we see depicted in the preface to his *Micrographia*. Was it that Harriot had sharper eyes and a steadier hand than most other men? It may be, but acuteness of vision and manual dexterity by themselves are not enough. If I may

[15] Harriot used prisms of his own making like that described in BL Add. MS 6789, fo. 184[r] and the pages before and after, and more complex prisms such as that he evidently borrowed from Mr W. Cope as described on fo. 148[r] in the same volume.

[16] In his early experiments in 1597 Harriot was using his staff, indicating 'partes of my staffe dobled', or 'partes of my staffe single' (BL Add. MS 6789, fo. 407[v]). On 2 Nov. 1604 Harriot was using his astrolabe for angular measurement but on 21 Dec. 1604 he replaced it with 'my new instrument of lynes from the center in brasse' ibid., fo. 327[v].

[17] See J. A. Lohne's biography of Harriot in the *Dictionary of Scientific Biography*. Lohne indicates that Harriot did not recognize the blue rays, but he does so at Add. MS 6789, fo. 142[r], where he describes 'An experiment of seeing colours by looking thorough a little hole lesse then pupilla vpon the moone at full'.

[18] These drawings and calculations are scattered throughout Harriot's optical papers, most important of which seem to be those surrounding the 'Pegium' drawing at Add. MS 6789, fo. 320[r].

[19] This is an extract from a paper of Lohne's read in his absence by Derek T. Whiteside at the Thomas Harriot Seminar held at Trinity College, Oxford, on 14 Dec. 1973. I am indebted to Dr Whiteside for this copy.

draw a general conclusion from his working papers, Harriot profited more by his ability to minimize random errors and by ruthless rejection of such results as might be vitiated by systematic errors. . . .

In experimental optics, certainly, Harriot was without peer in his own day. His still unpublished papers allow us to penetrate deep into the mind and methods of a pioneer physicist who measured refractions so finely that he from them deduced the sine-law of refraction, a theorem 'than which there exists none more noble and useful in the whole optics'. It was a major loss to the science of his day that his tables, formulas and geometrical schemes were little known even to colleagues and friends, and it was only after his death that certain of them had access to his papers. It is true that Kepler incorporated 13 of Harriot's specific weights into his *Visier Büchlein*, but who, apart from two or three surviving English friends, could know that they were only one very small offering from a vast storehouse of novel scientific findings? and that Harriot had been the finest experimental physicist of his time?

Harriot's care and diligence in seeking ever more accurate observations of refraction, though unpublished, did not go totally unnoticed. The report of his successes travelled at least as far as Prague, from whence on 2 October 1606, Johannes Kepler addressed a letter to Thomas Harriot in London. In this letter,[20] Kepler informed Harriot that he had heard of his remarkable achievements in Natural Philosophy, particularly in the field of optics. Like Harriot, he had been working with the refraction of light, and he would like to have Harriot's views on the origin and essential differences of colours, the causes of the Rainbow, and the haloes surrounding the Sun. Two months later, on 2 December, Harriot replied in a letter still preserved in the National Library at Vienna.[21] Though expressing gratitude at hearing from 'Domine Keplere', Harriot indicates that he must content himself with only a brief reply, since his health is so poor that he finds it difficult to write or even to think clearly. ('Ad singula respondere vna vice nimium est, praesertim hoc breui tempore quo responsum meum expectatur: sed maximè ob malam valetudinem qua nunc ita affectus sum, vt mihi

---

[20] This letter is preserved in Vienna, Nationalbibliothek, Cod. 10703, Bll. 378–380. It is accurately transcribed in Johannes Kepler, *Gesammelte Werke*, 17 vols. Munich, 1937–75, in Vol. XV, no. 394, pp. 348–51.

[21] Cod. 10703, Bll. 381–2. Eigenhändig. *Gesammelte Werke*, Vol. XV, no. 403, pp. 365–68.

molestum est vel scribere vel accuratè de aliqua re cogitare et argumentari.')

How accurate Harriot's account of his illness may be is difficult to assess. True, he was ill while imprisoned following the Gunpowder Plot in November of 1605, but that was a year past. It is also possible that though he was flattered to be recognized by so eminent a scientist as Johannes Kepler, Harriot was reluctant to reveal too much of his original experimental results, particularly since it appears that he had some plans for publishing them for his own credit. At any rate, he was somewhat vague in expressing his theories of refraction, did not mention calculation by the law of sines, and presented a table of refraction listing only ten liquids and five transparent solids, giving in each case the specific gravity and the angle of refraction in air for an incident ray of 30°. These, arranged in ascending order of refraction (from 11° 53' to 18° 0') included spring water, water, vinegar, Spanish and Rhine wines, spirits of wine (alcohol), salt water, petroleum oil, turpentine, and olive oil. The solids included rock salt, crystal, glass, amber, and resin, for all of which he reported the same refraction — 21° 4'. Harriot's discussion of the causes of refraction, like his tables of refraction, were too general to reveal much to Kepler. As a matter of fact, in his next letter, Kepler is forced to inquire just how Harriot defines his angles of incidence and refraction, as he is obviously not able to follow Harriot's argument. As for the rainbow about which Kepler had asked, Harriot replied that he did plan to write on the subject 'if God would grant him leïsure and health'. For the present he would say only that the cause of the rainbow lay in the action of light passing through a spherical drop of water, with reflection on the concave surfaces and refraction at the convex surfaces of each separate drop.

The Harriot-Kepler correspondence, which might have brought Harriot into international prominence for his work in optics, appears to have tapered off into generalities without really exciting the interest of either man. Kepler waited six months before replying to Harriot's second letter,[22] and

[22] Cod. 10703, Bl. 383. *Gesammelte Werke*, Vol. XVI, no. 439, pp. 31–2. This letter is dated from Prague, 2 Aug. 1607.

though he addressed him as 'Hariote celeberrime' and closed his letter as from 'T. Amicus', the tone of the letter is somewhat restrained and formal. Much shorter than his earlier letter, Kepler gave his thanks for the table Harriot had furnished, asked questions about his methods and materials, and after a brief comment on Harriot's theories, indicated that he was anxious to see more of his data and notebooks on the dispersion of colours and the refraction in single drops and multiple drops which would cause the phenomenon of the rainbow.

Again Harriot did not reply quickly to Kepler's requests. From 'Syon prope Londinum' on 'Julij 13. styl: vet: 1608' Harriot hastily penned a one-page reply.[23] The reason he gave for his brevity was that their mutual friend, John Ericksen, was waiting to depart for Prague. Briefly, then, Harriot commented upon the nature of his liquids: his turpentine was a purer and lighter substance than that used by Kepler, as were some of his other oils. Angles of incidence and refraction were the same as those used by Alhazen or Vitellio, though Harriot pointed out some errors in their observations, particularly those dealing with greater angles. As for the theories of refraction, Harriot in England was not so free to theorize on the doctrine of the vacuum as was Kepler, since here 'we still stick in the mud' (Haeremus adhuc in luto.), though he hopes God will soon put an end to such nonsense. Harriot was looking forward to receiving Kepler's astronomical commentaries, and requested that he also send him his meteorological observations for the past two years, in return for which he would send his own. He closed with the news that William Gilbert, who wrote on the magnet, had recently died, but he had left with his brother a treatise which defended the idea of the vacuum against the arguments of the peripatetics. This he hoped would be published shortly. And in a whimsical note, Harriot added that, to avoid leaving a vacuum at the bottom of the page he would like to note that gold, though a dense and opaque metal, when beaten out thinly as gold leaf

---

[23] Cod. 10703, Bll. 384-385. *Gesammelte Werke*, Vol. XVI, no. 497, pp. 172-73.

would pass the light of a candle, though it appeared as of a greenish colour. To make up for the brevity of this reply, Harriot increased the warmth of his salutation and close. The letter he addressed to 'Celeberrimo et doctissimo viro: D. Johanni Keplero, Mathematico Caesareo, amico suo plurimùm dilecto', signing it 'Tui amantissimus'.

Once again, more than a year passed before Kepler answered Harriot with what was to be the last letter in their brief correspondence.[24] After apologizing for his delay in replying, Kepler returned to the observation of refraction by Vitellio and Harriot, seeking to explain the discrepancy in their observations. But Kepler agreed with Harriot regarding the importance of the vacuum in explaining the bending of light rays and trusts that that matter may be resolved. For himself, he has published his *Astronomiae Novae* on celestial physics at Frankfurt; he is sorry he does not have a copy at hand. He is sorry to hear that Gilbert is dead, hopes to obtain copies of his work. He will send Harriot copies of his work on meteorology and would like to receive copies of Harriot's. Like Harriot's letter, Kepler's is but a single page on both sides, but unlike Harriot's it bears no florid address, no salutation, and no close. Obviously Kepler was not happy with the correspondence, and Harriot must have sensed it. For though Harriot continued to obtain Kepler's books and to follow his theories, there is no evidence that the correspondence was ever continued beyond this point.

It was probably slightly before his correspondence with Kepler that Harriot became acquainted with the man who appears to have been his closest personal friend and scientific associate, Sir William Lower. Though he was ten years Harriot's junior, Lower reveals in his letters that he was one of Harriot's greatest admirers and disciples. They also give more personal insight into Harriot's personal life and thought than any other of the meagre accounts which have been preserved.

William Lower, as Rigaud discovered in his extensive genealogical researches,[25] sprang from an old and respected

[24] Cod. 10703, Bl. 386. *Gesammelte Werke*, Vol. XVI, no. 536, pp. 250–1.
[25] See Note I appended to Stephen P. Rigaud, *Supplement to Dr. Bradley's Miscellaneous Works: with an account of Harriot's Astronomical Papers*, Oxford,

Cornwall family which could trace its pedigree for thirteen generations. The church epitaph of a younger brother, Sir Nicholas Lower, indicates that the father, Thomas Lower, 'descended of the house of St. Winnowe', had six sons: Sir William, John, Sir Nicholas, Sir Francis, Thomas, and Alexander. Though Rigaud could find no evidence as to just when Sir William was born, it was evidently about 1570, since the record of his matriculation into Exeter College, Oxford, dated 10 June 1586, reads:[26]

Lower, William; Cornwall, gen. f., 16.

indicating that he was the son of a Cornish gentleman, and sixteen at the time of matriculation. Rigaud also found that Lower's name appeared frequently in the Exeter College books until 1593, 'when it was removed without any indication of the individual's taking a degree.' On this basis, Lower would have been thirty-one when, in 1601, he was first sent to London as a member of Elizabeth's last parliament representing Bodmin. On the accession of James, Lower was returned to Parliament as the member for Lostwithiel, and was among those knighted by James in late March 1604. Since James did not dissolve this parliament for seven years, Lower was serving in this capacity during the years that he was familiar with Harriot. Sir William died at the age of forty-five in Carmarthenshire, six years before Harriot's final illness and death in 1621.

Harriot and Lower were undoubtedly brought together by their Northumberland connections. Probably about the time he first came to London on his parliamentary service, Lower married Penelope Perrot, daughter and heiress of Sir Thomas Perrot. Sir Thomas was the son of Sir John Perrot (1527?-1592), reputedly the illegitimate son of Henry VIII[27] who made his fame and fortune (if conviction of treason and death in the Tower can be considered fortune)

University Press, 1833, pp. 68-70. Rigaud's notes, including some information beyond that he published, are to be found in Bodleian Rigaud MS 35, from which much of this material is drawn.

[26] *Register of the University of Oxford*, II, Part 2, p. 151.

[27] Sir Robert Naunton, in his *Fragmenta Regalia*, 1641, p. 29, prints the contemporary gossip that Sir John 'was a Gentleman of the *Privy Chamber*, and in the Court married to a Lady of great Honour, which are presumptions in some

as one of the most cruel and uncompromising English officials in Ireland during their bloody wars of the 1580s. Much of his father's pride and belligerence evidently rubbed off on Sir Thomas, and it is recorded in the Council Book that on 7 February 1579/80 'Sir Thomas Parrott and Walter Rawley, Gentleman, being called before their Lordships for a fray made betwixt them, were, by their Lordships' order, committed prisoners to the Fleet,'[28] released only when they appeared before the Council to post bonds to keep the peace. Three years later, in July 1583, Sir Thomas was again in difficulty.[29] In a blunt and arrogant fashion he forced himself into the parish church of Broxburn in Hertfordshire with an armed party, a strange minister, and a willing young lady, demanding that they be permitted to wed without posting the required banns. It was over the vicar's protest and with the church secured with armed guards that a wedding was performed. The willing lady was Dorothy Devereux, daughter of Walter Devereux 1st Earl of Essex, and younger sister of the Queen's favourite, Robert Devereux, the 2nd Earl. When news of this reached the court, Elizabeth was furious, holding the upstart Thomas Perrot to be an unforgivable mismatch for the noble-born Dorothy. Once again Sir Thomas was thrown into the Fleet for his presumptuous action and the Lord Bishop of London, John Aylmer, was censured for the laxity of his marriage statutes.[30] Sir Thomas died shortly after, leaving his widow Dorothy, and a daughter of their hasty match, Penelope Perrot (Lower's wife), coheirs to the Perrot estates in Wales.[31]

---

implications, but if we goe a little further, and compare his pictures, his qualities, gesture, and voyce, with that of the King, which memory retaines yet amongst us, they will plead strongly, that he was a bubretitious Child of the *Blood Royall.*'
[28] Edwards, *Life of Ralegh*, I. 50.
[29] John Strype, *The Life and Acts of the Right Reverend Father in God, John Aylmer, Lord Bp. of London in the Reign of Queen Elizabeth*, Oxford, Clarendon Press, 1821, tells this story on p. 130 and Addition no. 8, pp. 217–19.
[30] Ibid. See also *Fragmenta Regalia*, 1641, p. 29; and Edwards, *Life of Ralegh*, I. 50–1.
[31] From a paper written by Francis Maddison on 'The Earliest Users of the Refracting Telescope in Britain: Thomas Harriot, Christopher Tooke, Sir William Lower, and John Protheroe' read at the Thomas Harriot Symposium at the University of Delaware, 5–7 Apr. 1971.

As we have seen,[32] the widow Dorothy (Devereux) Perrot married Henry Percy, 9th Earl of Northumberland, in 1594, so that her daughter Penelope (named for Dorothy's older sister, Sir Philip Sidney's 'Stella', later Lady Rich, and later still the lover and wife of the Earl of·Devonshire) became his stepdaughter. Lower's marriage to Penelope sometime in 1601 or 1602 brought him not only about 3,000 acres of land in Carmarthenshire near Llanfihangel Abercowan, including the farm called Tra'venti or Trefenti where they made their home, but also a family connection with Henry Percy and Syon House, where Thomas Harriot was already well established. Clearly, when Lower was in London to attend the meetings of the parliament, he would spend some time with his in-laws, and, because of his natural interest in science and mathematics, with their distinguished protégé in his near-by residence on the Syon grounds. Their friendship, once established, was continued by letter when Sir William returned to his home in Wales.

For some reason, probably sentiment, Harriot preserved nine of the letters he received from Sir William Lower[33] — a most unusual collection since Harriot preserved so few personal mementos. These letters are most revealing, not only of the personal relations between these two friends, but they also give a clear picture of their intellectual pursuits for the years between 1607 and 1611, the period in which their correspondence falls. Obviously the remaining letters

---

[32] See p. 225 above.

[33] Lower's letters are to be found collected in the last volume of the BL collection, Add. MS 6789, fos. 425–38 and 444, and in Petworth HMC 241/vii, fos. 1–6. Arranged chronologically they appear to be: (1) 30 Sept. 1607, Petworth HMC 241/vii, fos. 1–6; (2) 15 Jan. (no year), Add. MS 6789, fo. 444, Latin; (3) Undated note, ibid., fo. 435; (4) '12th day', fo. 437; (5) first half, printed von Zach, *Monatliche Correspondenz zur Beförderung der Erd-und-Himmels-Kunde*, 28 vols. Gotha, 1800–13, vol. VIII, p. 47; second half, Add. MS 6789, fos. 427–8; (6) 'the longest day of 1610' (11 June), fos. 425–6; (7) 4 Mar. 1611, fos. 429–30; (8) 3 Apr. 1611, fo. 431; (9) 19 July 1611, fo. 433. J. O. Halliwell in his *A Collection of Letters Illustrative of the Progress of Science in England*, London, 1841, published numbers 7, 8, and 9, pp. 38–42. Stephen P. Rigaud published with more care than Halliwell all of the letters except nos. 1 and 6 in his *Supplement to Dr. Bradley's Miscellaneous Works: with an account of Harriot's Astronomical Papers*, Oxford, University Press, 1833. This work is printed complete in the author's *A Source Book for the Study of Thomas Harriot*, New York, Arno Press, 1981.

are but a few of those which were written, and Harriot's side of the correspondence is totally missing. But internal references indicate their friendship must have begun before 1603[34] and possibly as early as 1601 or 1602,[35] and lasted until Lower's untimely death in 1615.

Lower's letters to Harriot reveal many aspects of their complex friendship. It is obvious that Lower is deferential to Harriot in matters mathematical and scientific, considering the older man to be his master and special adviser, infallible in his ability to direct his learning. But at the same time, the letters show a good-natured and high-spirited disciple ready to employ whimsy in expressing his learning difficulties, yet holding a respect and admiration for Harriot as a human being which leads him to confide in his master all his hopes, aspirations, and sorrows. Still this seems to be a somewhat one-sided confidence, since there is in his letters no reference to similar personal revelations of Harriot. Even in the absence of Harriot's responses, one is left with the impression that Lower is more outgoing than Harriot, Harriot more understanding and thoughtful than Lower.

Three of the letters cannot be accurately dated. One, the only one written in Latin, is signed merely as from 'Tra'uenti. Januar: 15' without an indication of the year. Obviously, however, this letter was written after Lower's marriage to Penelope Perrot, since only then did he become master of the Welsh farm which then, as now, bears this name, and which is still associated in local memories with the name of Lower and as the site of his astronomical observations. The tone of the letter, though, in which he addresses Harriot at 'Tresmegiste' and signs himself as 'tui amantissimus', is stilted and formal, lacking the cheerful friendliness of his English letters, and probably was written before the two were well acquainted. A second undated letter is a note written from London and addressed 'To his verie louing frind Mr Harriott att Sion' which begins 'when you were last

---

[34] In the letter of 6 Feb. 1610 Lower wrote '...you taught me the curious way to observe weight in Water, and within a while after Ghetaldi comes out with it in print.' Ghetaldi's *Promotus Archimedis* was published in 1603.

[35] In his letter of '12th day' Lower indicated that he had solved the equations for refraction. Harriot had solved these before 1601, and his later work was in refinement of his observations.

in towne you gaue me thes two following. . .' Then he proceeds with the observation that Harriot's formulas have given him new insights into the solution of cubic equations and requests similar 'shorte instructions (such as aboue which you gaue me once for Cubes)' for biquadrate equations, '. . .and then leaue me to pusle [puzzle] ouer. if you helpe mee not my three months speculation, will perish lamentablie.' The third, dated simply '12th day' is also a student's short note to his teacher, indicating his progress in his studies and what he needs to move on to. After indicating that he has mastered Harriot's equations for refraction (which probably places this before 1604) he concludes: [36]

I am so fresh now as me thinkes I can find out anie thinge. I am much in loue with the reason of construction of your table of proportionals; if when I come next vnto you; you would be pleased to make me vnderstand it, I should be much beholdinge vnto you.

Yours in all thinges that he is. . .

The rest of Lower's letters which are all dated are quite different in kind from these early notes of student to teacher. They show Lower as a friend and colleague of Harriot, secure in his close association and in many respects an equal contributor to knowledge as the two men entered the extra-terrestrial world of astronomy which was to occupy their major interests for the remainder of their active lives.

It was the blazing comet of 1607, later to be identified as Halley's Comet,[37] that focused the attention of Lower, Harriot, and, indeed, of all English and continental observers on this moving body in the skies. This was a time of earnest speculation and concern about the nature of the universe. The old belief in the Aristotelian and Ptolemaic system in which the earth formed the centre of the universe, around which the moon, sun, planets, and fixed stars revolved in perfect circles was breaking down.[38] Copernicus had returned to an older classic theory that the sun was the centre of the

---

[36] BL Add. MS 6789, fo. 437ʳ.

[37] See below, p. 396.

[38] For a brief account of this philosophical revolution see Alistair C. Crombie, *Augustine to Galileo, The History of Science A.D. 400–1650*, London, Falcon Press, 1952, Ch. VI, 'The Revolution in Scientific Thought in the 16th and 17th Centuries', especially pp. 307-28.

Thomas Harriot: A Biography

solar system, around which the earth and planets moved, with the earth's moon revolving around the earth as it moved around the sun. Tycho Brahe had concocted a hybrid system in which the moon, sun, and fixed stars revolved around a stationary earth and other planets revolved around the sun. One of the basic questions being argued was that of the nature of terrestrial and celestial matter, the traditional view being that the elemental substances of the earth, subject to change and decay, existed only from the centre of the earth to the orbit of the moon. The moon and all celestial bodies and space beyond were of a fifth element or essence which was perfect, unchangeable, and immutable. Central to this argument, naturally, came any celestial phenomena which might indicate a change in the superlunary space which could discredit the ideas of perfection and circular motion. In a sense, then, unusual astronomical phenomena were considered as critical matters, observations of which could have profound philosophical significance. This was the reason why the appearance of a new star in the constellation Cassiopeia in November of 1572 (lasting until early in 1574) created such a sensation throughout Europe, and why comets were being so thoroughly charted in an attempt to determine whether they were moving in the sublunary region in which change was normal and to be expected, or in the celestial space beyond the moon (or at the very least beyond the sun) which was held to be without possibility of such modification. Also being argued was the question of the solid celestial spheres: it was logically inconceivable that a comet could move through the sphere holding the sun or the moon's sphere without self-destructing.

For these reasons, it was with considerable excitement that Sir William Lower wrote to Harriot from 'Llanfihengel abercomen Cairmerthen' on 30 September 1607 about his observations of the spectacular comet which was coming into view. For 'his speciall good friend Mr Thomas Harriotte att Sion neere London' he enclosed his diary notes of his sighting, and a table of his measurement of its astronomical distance from various fixed stars.[39] His earliest journal entries read as follows:

[39] Petworth MS HMC 241/vii, pp. 1-7.

1607. Sept: 13. lookinge vpon the starres and especiallie aboue the greate beare, ther was no new phenomene./

17. passing ouer the sea into Wales aboute midnighte going abord I saw a Comete. it appeared vnder the greate beare in a line that might bee inagined issyinge from the vpper of the foure starres of the bodie, passinge between the two lower and opposite crossing the more westerlie of the two that were then vnder the beare and parrallell to the Horison and so forth till it cutt the said blasing starre in a point of that line, wher a perpendicle did fall from the vtmonst starre of his tayle.

his traine did reach to the saied more westerlie starre, but in lesse then an hower seemed to bee something declined from the saied starre westward. the starre was of the magnitude of thos of the greate beare & his traine was nubulous./

18. it was moued farre to the westward and was now come almost into a righte line of the Diagonall drawen from the former vpper starre of the greate beare. but thes obseruations were as I iournied without instruments. now I am come to my owne house and cross staffe that I sent downe for measuring of land. so the obseruations that follow are more artificiall.

Lower's log of observations continues on almost a daily basis until Tuesday, 6 October, with tabulations of his angular distances of the comet from 'bootes, vltima caude vrse maioris, lucida lyre, vespæstina', though recording four days when cloudy weather did not permit observations, and two nights when he did not observe because 'I was a gossipinge.'

Harriot studied Lower's letter carefully, as is shown from the notes he made on the backs of the sheets and on the margins of Lower's text. In a note on an observation of his own for 21 September he notes: 'Seen on fryday before [that would be 18 September] by Sir Allen P. [the first indication that the Earl's younger brother was interested in science] & 2 or 3 days before that by others.' In another note he comments that 'Mr Standish at Oxford saw it the 15th. at $10^h\frac{1}{2}$ pm.' And in another note 'Dee. 15. Sept. 1607. hora $10^a\frac{1}{2}$ pm [and] hora 2^a [unreadable] noctis' followed by 'Mr Standish at Oxford saw it & obserued it'. These are rough notes, and for some reason Harriot did not make a fair copy of his observations as he was later to do. All of his notes are in pencil, and have been incompletely overwritten in ink, probably by Zach, in a way which makes the observations difficult to read. But it is apparent that Harriot was more thorough in his observations than was Lower. On 22 September, for example, when Lower read three angular distances, he chose only one star less than 10° from the comet; the other two were 31° 40′ and 53° 10′ away — readings which would permit considerable error in translation. On the same day Harriot took nine observations ranging from 5° 0′ to 14° 35′, correcting one of Lower's readings by 4′. From these notes, it appears that Harriot used two different cross staffs, changing to get better accuracy, but, he adds there was 'no paralaxis considered'.

It should be noted that these Lower-Harriot observations of the Comet of 1607, though unpublished by them, did have an indirect impact on later astronomy. In 1784, to illustrate Harriot's proficiency in observation, von Zach published a few pages of these observations in his journal of astronomical correspondence. A young apprentice to an export-import firm, Friedrich Wilhelm Bessel,[40] found these observations intriguing, and for diversion proceeded to calculate the orbit of the comet by very ingenious mathematics. In 1804 he sent his calculations and his determined orbit to W. H. Olbers, an astronomer whom he knew. Olbers with surprise recognized that the Comet of 1607 was an earlier entry of Halley's Comet and saw the importance of Bessel's method of determining the orbit. He encouraged the young man to continue observations, and arranged for the publication of his work in *Monatliche Correspondenz*. Bessel's original work was so well received that he was offered the position of assistant in the astronomical observatory at Lilienthal; he left business to become one of the foremost astronomers of the nineteenth century. Strangely enough, Bessel's greatest contribution to modern science and mathematics came in 1817 while he was working through some of the unsolved problems of Johannes Kepler. To solve these, Bessel discovered the mathematics of the Bessel function, a basic tool in almost every segment of physics since his time. Certainly Lower and Harriot would have been amazed at this chance chain of events which followed their early ventures into astronomical observation.

[40] See the life of Bessel by Walter Fricke in *The Dictionary of Scientific Biography*, II. 97–102.

Undoubtedly it was the excitement generated by the appearance of the Comet of 1607 followed by his correspondence with Kepler that led Harriot to turn seriously to the application of his optical theories to the study of the heavens. For more than a decade, aided in recent years by Christopher Tooke, he had been studying refraction in plane surfaces, prisms, curved surfaces, and lenses. And there is ample evidence among his remaining manuscripts that the simple act of bringing lenses together into a compound system was certainly not beyond either his imagination or skill. Even though Galileo had not yet heard about the crude 'perspective glasses' that were being shown at continental fairs and carnivals, it is highly probable that, totally independently, Harriot and Tooke were refining the lens systems and leather tubes to contain them and permit focusing and internal adjustments. Though any notes and jottings he may have made during this process are now lost, one drawing still remains in the Petworth collection to show that their work was completed by mid-1609, and that Harriot had turned his new and powerful weapon of observation, as Galileo was later to do, on the moon.[41]

Dated '1609. July. 26. hor. 9. P.M.' in the left upper corner, and with a note reading 'The ☽ . 5 dayes old.', is the first astronomical drawing made with the benefit of a telescope to extend the capabilities of the human eye.[42] A notation on the lower right reads '$\frac{6}{1}$', Harriot's notation that this particular perspective glass magnified by six diameters, and the position of the moon and the outline of the lunar seas indicate that it was a terrestrial glass which did not invert the image, rather than the traditional celestial one which did. Harriot's excitement over the possibilities of this new instrument must have been great,

---

[41] A more detailed examination of Harriot's moon papers may be found in the author's 'Thomas Harriot's Lunar Observations', *Studies in Honor of Edward Rosen*, (Studia Copernica XVI) Ossolineum, 1978, 283–308.

[42] Petworth HMC 241/ix, fo. 26. That the date 1609 is correct is shown by the fact that on 26 July of that year, a Wednesday, the moon was actually five days old, since the new moon started on 21 July at 0:18; in 1610 the new moon commenced at 13:37 on 10 July. See Herman H. Goldstine, *New and Full Moons from 1001 B.C. to 1651 A.D.*. Philadelphia, American Philosophical Society, 1973.

and undoubtedly he exploited it in continued observations of the moon, and turned it to the other planets, the stars and constellations. But again, Harriot's reluctance to record his theories or his feelings kept him from recording or retaining these notes and jottings among his manuscripts, as did Galileo, who was prepared to rush to print with every new revelation of his 'cannons'. Or, it is possible, that what papers did exist got detached from the main body during the years they were in the possession of von Zach in the late eighteenth century. At any rate, it must be recorded that following this first observation in July of 1609, there are no further extant Harriot drawings made with his telescopes until nearly a year later – 17 July 1610[43] – when he indicates he is working with a ten-power glass.

The most frequently quoted of the Lower letters to Harriot is a long, rambling missive written at Tra'venti on 6 February 1610 new style. The first half of this letter, somehow detached from the second half, was taken by Zach from the Petworth collection in 1784 when he selected out of the mass of manuscripts the astronomical studies which impressed him so much and which he said he intended to publish. Since the half he extracted did not contain Lower's signature, Baron von Zach erroneously ascribed it to Harriot's patron, Henry Percy, rather than Lower, though the most superficial examination of the handwriting of the two men should have shown him his error. But in 1803, during his altercation with the Oxford Press of his proposed publications, Zach published the first half of the letter, using the section lamenting Harriot's lack of publication to give credence to his extravagant claims for Harriot's exceptional scientific priorities.[44] After this publication, the half letter got detached from the other Harriot papers so that when Zach returned the manuscripts to Oxford, this was not included. As a result, it was lost, and has never been recovered.

The second half of the letter, which must have been with the first half when Zach first saw them, was rediscovered

---

[43] Petworth HMC 241/ix, fo. 20.
[44] *Monatliche Correspondenz zur Beförderung der Erd-und-Himmels-Kunde, herausgegeben vom Freyherrn von Zach*, 28 vols., Gotha, 1800–13; VIII. 47–56.

and recognized by Stephen P. Rigaud in 1832 when he was in London following up on the Zach-Oxford controversy,[45] among the papers of Harriot which had been given to the British Museum by Lord Egremont in 1810.[46] In his brief account of Harriot's astronomical observations which he published in 1833[47] Rigaud brought the two halves together for the first time and printed the letter as a whole, using Zach's transcription for the first half. It is from this new union that the letter has had wide currency since that time.

This letter most clearly shows the intimate and friendly fashion in which Harriot and Lower worked together in their astronomical studies. At the outset, Lower thanks Harriot for the 'perspective Cylinder' he has sent him and asks for two or three more, though admitting that he had forgotten to pay 'the worke man', Christopher Tooke, for the one he had received. With whimsy he describes his first telescopic view of the Moon, which he describes as 'like the Description of Coasts in the dutch bookes of voyages', and says that at the full, it looks 'like a tarte that my Cooke made me the last Weeke — here a vaine of bright stuff, and there of darke, and so confusedlie all over.' And it is in this letter, too, that he introduces Harriot to a young neighbour friend of his who was later to become a close friend of Harriot:[48] 'I must confesse I can see none of this without my cylinder. Yet an ingenious younge man that accompanies me here often, and loves you, and these studies much, sees manie of these things even without the helpe of the instrument, but with it sees them most planielie. I mean the younge Mr. Protheröe.' John Protheroe lived a short way down the road from Tra'venti in a house called in Welsh Nantyrhebog (translated as Hawksbrook in English), and was later, as we shall see, one of Harriot's appointed executors, and a supporter of Nathaniel Torporley after Harriot's death.

Lower shows his solicitude for his master and friend in his personal concern for his future fame. His studies of

[45] See Rigaud's letter to the Revd. Thomas Sockett, 25 July 1832, in Petworth MS: HMC 241/x.
[46] BL Add. MS 6789, fos. 427-8.
[47] *Supplement to Dr. Bradley's Miscellaneous Works*, pp. 42-5.
[48] Zach, op. cit., p. 49; Rigaud, op. cit., p. 42.

Kepler, which bear out some of the theories he had earlier had from Harriot, cause him to reflect on the fact that Harriot has not left a permanent record of his scientific discoveries. Lower feels close enough to Harriot to remind him of his responsibility to posterity:[49]

Doe you not here startle, to see every day some of your inventions taken from you; for I remember longe since you told me as much, that the motions of the planets were not perfect circles. So you taught me the curious way to observe weight in Water, and within a while after Ghetaldi comes out with it, in print. a little before Vieta prevented you of the Gharland for the great Invention of Algebra. al these were your deues and manie others that I could mention; and yet too great reservednesse hath robd you of these glories. but although the inventions be greate, the first and last I meane, yet when I survei your storehouse, I see they are the smallest things, and such as in Comparison of manie others are of smal or no value. Onlie let this remember you, that it is possible by too much procrastination to be prevented in the honor of some of your rarest inventions and speculations. Let your Countrie and friends injoye the comforts they would have in the true and great honor you would purchase your selfe by publishing some of your choise works.

Belatedly, the scholar feels presumption for advising his master, so he adds:[50] '. . .but you know best what you have to doe. Onlie I, because I wish you all good, wish this, and sometimes the more longhinglie, because in one of your lettres you gave me some kind of hope thereof.'

The close, personal friendship existing between Harriot and Lower is clearly evident in the close of this letter which Zach did not see:[51]

After all this I must needes tell you my sorrowes. god that gaue him, hath taken from me my onlie sun, by continual & strange fits of epylepsie or Apolexie, when in appearence, as he was most pleasant & goodlie, he was most healthie, but amongst other things, I haue learnt of you to setle & submit my desires to the will of god; onlie my wife with more griefe beares this affliction, yet now againe she begins to be comforted./ let me here from you and according to your leasure & frindshippe haue directions in the course of studie I am in. aboue al things take care of your health. keepe correspondence with

---

[49] Zach, op. cit. pp. 50–3; Rigaud, op. cit., p. 43.
[50] Zach, op. cit., pp. 53–4; Rigaud, op. cit., p. 43.
[51] BL Add. MS 6789, fos. 427^v–428^r; Rigaud, op. cit., p. 45.

kepler. & wherinsoeuer you can haue vse of one, require it with all libertie, for I rest euer

Your assured & true frind to be
vsed in all things that you please

Lower's simple declaration that at the time he had lost his eldest son Harriot had taught him 'to setle & submit [his] desires to the will of god' paints a very different impression of the man than that left by Popham, the Lord Chief Justice, at the trial of Ralegh of a 'devill', 'atheist', and perverter of men's minds. So does the solicitude which Lower shows during his own time of grief for the health of a friend just turning fifty, but who has already begun to feel a mental and physical decline.

Four months later, on 11 June 1610, Lower was again writing to his Syon friend from his home on Mount Martin, Tra'venti. Here on the high ground near his house he had established his observatory, was studying Kepler, and was pleased to have Harriot's letter carrying news of Galileo's new discoveries. Lower was much impressed by the coincidence that just when Harriot's letter arrived, 'wee Trauentane Philosophers' — himself and Protheroe — were in the midst of a discussion of Kepler's theories regarding the size of the universe:[52]

... for sayd I (hauinge you say often as much) what if in that huge space betweene the stares and Saturne ther remaine euer fixed infinite nomber (which may supplie the apparence to the eyes & shalbe placed in ♋) which by reason of ther lesser magnitudes doe flee our sight. What if about ♄, ♃, ♂, &ct ther moue other planets also which appeare not. uist as I was saying this comes your letter.

These speculations engendered by the new telescopes were tremendously exciting.

We are here so on fire with thes things that I must renew my request and your promise to send mee of all sorts of thes Cylinders. my man shal deliuer you monie for anie charge requisite, and contente your man for his paines & skill. send me so manie as you thinke needfull vnto thes obseruations. and in requitall I will send you store of obseruations. send me also one of Galileus bookes if anie yet be come ouer...

The news which had reached Lower was undoubtedly that of the astronomical discoveries revealed in Galileo's *Siderius*

Nuncius, which had been published on 13 March of that year, and of which Harriot had received one of the first copies to reach England.[53] Here Galileo had printed some illustrations of the Moon as observed by his 'cannons', shown how the new telescopes had increased the number of stars in view, and reported on a third discovery (which set Lower and Protheroe 'on fire') of satellites of moons circling the planet Jupiter. These, Galileo reported, had been first seen on 7 December 1609 NS, with sixty-four sightings between then and March of the next year. Harriot and Lower were both excited by such a discovery and anxious to check them out for themselves; unfortunately, by the time the news reached England, Jupiter was too close to the Sun for direct observation (conjunction having occurred on 1 July 1610 OS) so they must wait until the two were separated.

Harriot made his first observation of the Jovial planets on Wednesday, 17 October 1610, an observation to which he gave the number 1 of the sequence of ninety-nine observations during the next year. This was not, as Zach had indicated, an independent discovery, since on his first sighting his record shows:[54]

1610.   My first observation of the new planets.   Octob. 17 . ☿. Syon.

In the inked copy of his series of observations, this is implemented by the addition:[55]

I saw but one, & that aboue.

Had this been an original discovery, Harriot's first pencilled observation would have used the singular 'planet' instead of the plural he did use. This heading, like Lower's letter, shows convincingly that Harriot was here following the footsteps of Galileo as he turned his perspective trunks toward the planet Jupiter.

Later that same year, Lower followed up their correspondence by a visit to Syon House where he observed with his master Harriot the Galilean planets. Meantime, Harriot

[53] See John D. North, 'Harriot and Galileo' in his 'Thomas Harriot and the First Telescopic Observations of Sunspots', loc. cit., pp. 136–9.
[54] Petworth MS HMC 241/iv, fo. 15ᵛ.
[55] Ibid., fo. 3ʳ.

had continued his observations. On 16 November he had
made his second observation from 'London at Neales in
black friers', this time seeing a second moon. Again on 19
November he observed one in London, and on his return to
Syon, saw a single orbiting moon on 28 and 30 November
and 4 December.[56] But on 7 December Sir William Lower
was present at Syon when Harriot took rough notes of
another observation. At 9 o'clock that night Harriot reported
but one planet seven or eight minutes from Jupiter, but at
5 o'clock the next morning, two were apparent. The original
notes record[57] 'two seen well & perfectly. S. W. Lower also
saw them.' In his fair copy Harriot split the observations:[58]

7/ Decemb. 7. ho. 9^a. $9^a\frac{1}{2}$.
I saw but one & aboue.

8/ Mane [morning]. ho. 17^a. Two seen on
the west side, a litle vnder.
S^r. W. Lower also saw them here.
The nerest fayrest. The farther
not well seen with in the reach of
my instrument of $\frac{20}{1}$ of $14'$ diameter.

This morning of Saturday, 8 December 1610, was a busy
one for both Harriot and Lower. Not only were they apparently up all night observing the moons of Jupiter, but for
a brief moment in the early morning when the sun was just
coming over the horizon, they made the original and independent observation that there were spots on the surface of the
rising sun.[59] This first observation, not numbered in the
series which was to start a year later, reads as follows:[60]

1610. Syon.

Decemb. 8. ♄. [Saturday] mane [morning] ho. [here the manuscript
is scratched over so that the hour is unreadable.]
That altitude of the sonne being 7 or 8 degrees. It being a frost & a
mist. I saw the sonne in this manner. Instrument . $\frac{10}{1}$ .B. I saw it twise or
thrise. once with the right ey & other time with the left. In the space
of a minutes time. after the sonne was too cleare.

To see actual imperfections in a celestial body ostensibly
composed of the perfect quintessence of extra-terrestrial

---

[56] Ibid., fo. 15^v. [57] Ibid. [58] Ibid., fo. 3^r.
[59] See John North's study of Harriot's sunspot observations.
[60] Petworth MS HMC 241/viii, fo. 1^r.

bodies was an almost unbelievable experience. Harriot checked to be sure that he was not seeing some defect in his vision, one eye, then the other. Then the sun was over-powering in its brilliance; Harriot could look no longer, and Lower evidently did not see, perhaps did not try to see. But like the 'Trauentane Philosophers' of Wales, the Syon Philosophers shared the excitement of a discovery which, of itself, spelled the doom of the doctrines of the perfection of the quintessence, of circular motion, cycles, and epi-cycles; and by showing the imperfections of a heavenly body showed the way for acceptance of more material explanations of the operation of the universe.

Three months later, on 4 March 1611 (using his own dating scheme in which he used date and month in the old style and year in the new style),[61] Lower wrote again 'To his singular good frind Mr Tho: Harriot at Sion./'[62] Although on the surface this appears to be a gay and whimsical letter, underneath it is sad and subdued. Lower begins with an ebullient and extended metaphor, comparing the use of his new logarithmic trigonometric tables to hunting dogs: 'Sir I neuer loued huntinge till you furnished mee with dogs. I will hence forward proue another Nemrode. . . . onlie your Curre dog Petiscus will not come into my sighte. . .' He goes on to say that his trouble had been caused by the fact that Mr Bill, the bookseller, had sent him a faulty copy of Pitiscus' *Trigonometriae sive de dimensione triangulorum libri quinqui*, sending the tables, but not the accompanying text. Lower continues to drag out the figure:

. . .your dog that hunts by the sines onlie and I, are growen familiar and he is an excellent dog: but your shee bitch hath no fellow for sureness, onlie she is slow. I had not lost hir, but knew hir goodnesse

---

[61] The internal references in these letters and details of sickness of his cattle shows clearly that Lower was using an unusual dating system. He was using the English day and month of the Julian calendar, but the year of the Gregorian. In 1582 the continental countries adopted a new calendar, starting the year on 1 Jan. instead of the traditional 25 Mar., and correcting for previous errors by moving the date ten days forward. Lower's letter, thus, would normally have been dated 4 Mar. 1610 (or 1610/11) in England, but 14 Mar. 1611 on the continent. But Lower appears consistent in his dating, using the continental year but the English date.

[62] BL Add. MS 6789, fo. 430ᵛ.

wel enough. . . . So that by the assistance of thes dogs of yours I grow
so confident as to vndertake to pursue in chace anie game; but then
onlie I shalbe sure that nothinge doe escape me, when you shall please
to imparte vnto me a brach of your triangular kinde. . . .

In a euphoric mood, Lower praises his teacher who has
taught him so well: 'My worke is crowned now you allow of
it, and indeed ther wanted in mee neither will nor industrie
to accomplish it, nor in you will nor skill to instruct mee in
the sacred wayes of arte. be you therefore euer of me incom-
parablie respected or be I not att all.' Lower laments that in
his pursuit of the study of astronomy neither he nor 'the
yonge Philosopher at Haukesbrooke' had been able to discover the 'Joueall starres' which he had seen with Harriot at
Syon: 'when wee I say haue often diligentlie obserued
iupiter wee could neuer see anie thinge. I impute it to the
dullness of my sighte, for onlie with your greate glasse I
could see them in London.' Then he closes his letter on a
sad, personal note.

my wiffe is well. now you know all my comfortes./ I haue lost my
second boy also and wel neere .80. cattle of the murraine & they die
still. now you know all my discomfortes and losses. farewell and lett
not the hugeness of this missiue discourage you from reedinge of it.
doe it at leasure and by peeces accordinge to your best opportunities.
and sometimes vse the power you haue in me, which is to dispose of
mee accordinge to the vtmost of all or anie of my abilities.

A month later, on 3 April 1611, Lower wrote a shorter
letter to Harriot, apologizing for the length of his earlier
one and promising to 'make you amends now with one as
shorte.'[63] Indeed, he confessed, he had considered not
writing at all, '(which perchance had bene best consideringe
the vse you haue of all your time) I could not consent vnto,
out of the addiction and delighte I haue to bee still con-
uersinge with you.' He concludes by asking some questions
about the solution of some of Vieta's problems, and once
more refers to the tragic loss of his cattle during the early
spring: 'all thes things stand well and so I thanke god doe we
also. Except my catle which haue al this winter bene persecuted with the Murraine. Since Christmas verie neer I haue
lost .100. beastes.'

[63] Ibid., fos. 531-2.

Only one more letter remains from Lower to Harriot and this is of a generally more sober tone; it is dated 19 July 1611.[64] For some reason, Lower appears to have turned away from the study of mathematics. He calls attention to the dullness of country life, saying 'indeed I haue here so much otium [leisure or vacant time] and therefore I may cast awaye some of it in vaine pursuites, chusing always rather to doe something worth nothinge then nothinge at all.' This search for time-consuming activity has led him to 'the .3. vexations of the scientificall mortals . . . to wit the squaring of the circle, the dubbinge of the Cube, and the Philosophers stone.' Apparently at the time of writing it was the last of these which was causing him the most trouble.

The fact that Sir William Lower, a highly intelligent devotee of the latest theories of the new astronomy should use his spare time in seeking, evidently seriously, the magic way to transmute base metals into gold, and that he does not hesitate to write to the man he considers England's greatest scientist for advice on the matter, startles the modern reader. But Sir William seriously wants Harriot to tell him:

1. first. whether . ☉. [gold] and . ☽. [silver] be bodies so difficult to be dissolued as alchemists affirme. I mean by dissolution (as I thinke they doe) that they must bee putrified and distilled.
2. if they may bee dissolued, whether with one simple alone or with many?
3. If they may bee dissolued and putrifyed, whether ther rectifyed partes being coniuoyned againe wilbe multiplied in virtue?
4. and lastlie that which should haue bene asked first, an sit [in what] Elixir?

Once again, Lower ends with a personal note: 'I am sorry to heare of the new troubles ther[65] and pray for a good issue of them especiallie for my Lady's sake and hir fiue little ones.'

---

[64] Ibid., fo. 433.

[65] Just what these troubles were is not clear. It may be that the Earl and his Lady were in another of their separations. More likely Lower was referring to the new gossip concerning Northumberland's participation in the Gunpowder Plot. Timothy Elks, his Lordship's reader, in the late summer of 1611 said he had learned from Captain Whitlock, one of the Earl's retainers now dead, that there was more than smoke in the meeting between the 9th Earl and his cousin Thomas Percy on the evening of 4 Nov. He wrote to a member of the Privy Council (State Papers Domestic, James I, vol. 66, nos. 28, 29) indicating that

In December 1611 Lower again visited Harriot at Syon, discussing his progress in mathematics and inquiring into Harriot's astronomical observations. There he found that though Harriot had been thorough and diligent in his recording of the orbits of Jupiter's moons, recording 103 observations between the start of his series on 16 November 1610 through the next 193 days before 28 May 1611, he had at that point (having determined to his satisfaction the radial distance of the four satellites from the mother planet and the periods of their orbits) ceased making further observations.[66] John Roche interprets this as due to the inadequacies of his telescopes, which were clearly of poorer resolution than those being used by Galileo.[67] But for some reason, Harriot appears to have been in the doldrums, suffering from listlessness or despondency, for except for a few efforts to correct his Moon map,[68] he has left no evidence of any additional study of the heavens.

It is probable that it was Lower who forced Harriot's attention back to the serious study of astronomy. Since he had been present[69] the year before when Harriot had first observed the phenomenon of a spotted sun, he must have been mystified why in the intervening year Harriot had made only one abortive effort to repeat the observation.[70] Now

friends of Whitlock should be reexamined. Among those he suggested be questioned were 'Henego Jhones', 'Mr Martin of the Temple', 'Sir Henry Godyer', 'Mr Ingram of the custome house', and 'Thomas Harriot' the mathematician. (See R. C. Bald, *John Donne: a Life*, Oxford, University Press, 1970, p. 190.) On 27 Nov. 1611 John Chamberlain wrote to Dudley Carleton: 'Three or fowre dayes since finding Master Heriot at great leysure in Powles I accosted him to see what I could learne of his great Lord. He told me that he had some inlargement and that any of his servants or frends might have accesse to him, that this last tempest was already blowne ouer, that Elkes and his accusations began to vanish. . .' *Letters of John Chamberlain*, I. 318.

[66] Harriot's observations of the Jovial planets are to be found in Petworth MS HMC 241/iv, fos. 1–46. The observations occupy fo. 3–16; the calculations, in almost complete muddle, occupy the remainder. The best effort to resolve these is that of John Roche in his Oxford thesis on 'Thomas Harriot's Astronomy' (1977), in Ch. V, 'Harriot's Jupiter Papers', pp. 247–303.

[67] Ibid., pp. 266–7.

[68] Petworth MS HMC 241/ix, fo. 27.

[69] See p. 403 above.

[70] Petworth MS HMC 241/iv, fo. 1. This is dated as Saturday, 19 Jan. 1610/11 and reads: 'a notable mist. I obserued diligently at sundry times when it was fit. I saw nothing but the cleare sonne both with right and left ey.'

a year after their initial sighting, Lower and Harriot, accompanied by Christopher Tooke, again turned their telescopes on the misty morning sun, and again saw the spectacle of an imperfect solar surface. Harriot recorded the experience as follows: [71]

Syon.   1611. Decemb. 1. ☉ mane [morning] horus. [hour] 10. 0$'$. per horologium solar [by the sundial].

I saw three blacke spots in such order as is here experessed as nere as I could iudge. observed by $\frac{10}{1}$ [ten-power telescope]. Sir W. Lower with Christopher also sawe the same. At sundry times all three seen & obserued at once for halfe an houre space. at which time and all the morning before it was misty.

The greatest was that which, appearing somewhat ragged, was most oriental & was of apparent angle about 2$'$. The other two, were nere of one bignes: & of 1$'$ magnitude. or there aboutes.

The next day, Monday, saw no observations, possibly from inclement weather, but on Tuesday, 3 December, much of the day was spent with the telescopes. On this occasion Harriot records as number two of a continuing series, observations made both morning and afternoon. [72]

Syon.   1611. Decemb. 3. ♂. hor. $8\frac{1}{2}$ [a.m.]. $5\frac{3}{4}$ [p.m.]

The sonne being 3 or 4 degrees hy. It was a frost & a litle mist. The position of the spots in the sonne we saw as is here set downe. They were 8 in all. The cluster of 4 orientall are the one great spot which appeared December the 1. That vnder the center with that at the top were seen also before. The two most occidentall we saw not before. The three occidental nere the limbe seeme not so darke as those orientall. The most orientall should be placed a little lower. The vppermost somewhat too big.

Sir William Lower and Christopher saw them with me, in seueral trunckes. $\frac{10}{1}$. $\frac{8}{1}$. $\frac{20}{1}$.

The next day observation three was made, but this time by Harriot alone: he records: 'I saw them twise in a short time. . .'[73]

After starting Harriot on his observation of sunspots, Lower apparently dropped out of active participation; there is no evidence of any further sightings by Lower in the 214 sunspot observations that follow. Christopher observed with

---

[71] Ibid., fo. 1^r.   [72] Ibid., fo. 2^r.   [73] Ibid.

Harriot a number of times, and there is some evidence that his sight was more sensitive than that of his master: once it is recorded that 'Chr. saw one more orientall sometimes as he sayd',[74] and another time it is noted that 'Chr. in a more temperate light with $\frac{20}{1}$ saw a dim one.'[75] But Harriot was conscientious in his viewing; during the good weather of the spring of 1612 he rose almost every morning before sunrise, to be in a position with his telescopes to view the sun through the early morning mist that was normal at the bend of the Thames where Syon House lay. On days when the mist was too dense or the sun too bright, he would return to his glasses in the late afternoon or at sunset to record any spots he might see. Obviously he was early experimenting with different perspective glasses, and he records observations using instruments of $\frac{8}{1}$, $\frac{10}{1}$, $\frac{10}{1}$ B (an improved glass with better resolution), $\frac{15}{1}$, $\frac{20}{1}$, $\frac{30}{1}$, and $\frac{50}{1}$. During December of 1611 he logged twenty sunspot readings; in January 1611/12, seventeen; February, twenty-two; and March, nineteen. Most of these observations were made at dawn. In April, May, and early June, Harriot continued to observe, usually in the late afternoon or early evening, making nineteen drawings for March, twenty-five for April, and eighteen for June. By this time he had almost completely settled on two telescopes, the better ten-power he labelled $\frac{10}{1}$ B, and a $\frac{20}{1}$. But he was finding less excitement in his viewing than he originally had, and on 7 June 1621 he ends his observation with the comment: 'I could see no more looking diligently as I vse to do.'[76] Two days later, when he moved from Syon to London for approximately seven weeks, he changed his recording format, enlarging the drawings, and simplifying the commentary, frequently recording only the number of spots observed, and not indicating at all what telescopes he was using. Obviously his interest was further waning, for though he made twenty observations in July, these dropped to fourteen for August and for September, twelve in October, seven in November and December, and fizzled out with the last four observations in January of 1612/13.

[74] Ibid., observation on 5 Dec. 1611.
[75] Ibid., fo. 10, observation 34, 26 Jan. 1611/12.
[76] Ibid., fo. 30, observation 112, 7 June 1612.

At this point, tangible evidence of the continuing friendship of Lower and Harriot ends. There are no further letters
and no indication in Harriot's manuscripts of visits of Lower
to his Syon laboratory. We do know that he continued to
live at his home in Tra'venti in Carmarthenshire, and that
from that base he served as something of an overseer of some
of the properties which 'My Lady' the Countess of Northumberland had inherited from the Perrots in the west country
nearby. A letter preserved in the Northumberland archives
in Alnwick Castle, dated from Tra'venti on 18 April 1613,[77]
shows him working with 'Mr Floid' and 'my cozen Protheroe'
in attempting to collect from a debtor who was, in his terms,
'a corrupt storehouse' of deceit in his dealings with the Lady
Northumberland.

Two years later, in 1615, Lower died suddenly at the untimely age of 45.[78] Whether he suffered, as did his sons, from
'Epylepsie or Apolexie' is unknown. But at the time of his
death he left a daughter, Dorothy, named after the Countess
of Northumberland, and his wife, Penelope, was again
pregnant. This second child, born posthumously late in 1615,
was named by his mother 'Thomas' — perhaps as recognition
of the close friendship between Sir William and Thomas
Harriot of Syon.[79] Lower's wife, Penelope, remarried, this
time to Sir Robert Naunton, an ambitious hanger-on at the
court of James, who had served as Member of Parliament
with Sir William,[80] and apparently left Tra'venti to reside in
London with her new husband, and shared with him the
pleasure of Buckingham and the preferments that followed
that association.[81] She helped with the establishment of
their luxurious home at Letheringham, Suffolk, while her

[77] Alnwick Castle MS Q.I.40.
[78] No will or burial record for Lower has been found. Rigaud, however transcribed the monument to the Lower family in Landulph Church at the burial
site of Sir William's younger brother, Sir Nicholas Lower of Clifton. This indicates
that 'Sir William Lower, Knight, deceased in Carmarthenshire' had preceded him
in death. See Bodleian MS Rigaud 35, fo. 1.
[79] Information about Thomas Lower was gathered by Rigaud and listed as
'Particulars collected at the Herald's Office.' Bodleian MS Rigaud 35, fo. 108.
[80] See the life of Sir Robert Naunton by Sidney Lee in the *DNB*.
[81] That the couple were close is attested to by the fact that Sir Robert arranged
to have Penelope buried with him and sharing a common memorial. This is
copied by Rigaud, loc. cit., p. 164.

husband rose from Master of Requests, Surveyor of the Court
of Wards, to be a member of the King's Commission to examine
Sir Walter Ralegh in August 1618. In this last, she would not
have pleased Thomas Harriot, since it was Sir Robert Naunton
who was credited with calling for the execution of Ralegh
and who occasioned the remark of one London citizen that
'Ralegh's head would do well on Naunton's shoulders.'[82]
Sir Robert died in March 1635, leaving Penelope with one
daughter, Penelope, of his own, and two children by Sir
William Lower — Thomas, who lived in London in a house
near Charing Cross, and Dorothy who married Maurice
Drummond who was knighted by King Charles I at Hampton
Court in July of 1625. Penelope the wife died in March
1654/5; she was followed by Thomas who died unmarried
on 5 February 1660 and daughter Penelope who survived
until November 1679, when she was buried with her brother
in St. Clement Dane's in London.[83] Thus ended the line of
Harriot's closest friend, Sir William Lower.[84]

Much less is known about Harriot's personal relationship
with that 'ingenious younge man' of Hawksbrook, John
Protheroe, the second of the 'Traventane Philosophers' and
introduced to Harriot by Lower. Unlike Lower, Protheroe
was a Carmarthenshire man by birth.[85] A summary of
existing records surrounding John Protheroe has been
gathered by Francis Maddison of the History of Science
Museum at Oxford as follows:[86]

[82] Cited by Sidney Lee. The story is also commented upon by Chamberlain in
his letter to Sir Dudley Carleton, no. 302, II. 177-8. The speaker was a Mr Wiemark, who was called before the Privy Council for his disrespect to the secretary
of state, but was dismissed upon apology.

[83] Bodleian MS Rigaud 35, fo. 109.

[84] The biography of Sir William Lower is not included in the *DNB* nor any
other of the standard reference works, hence this inclusion of some of the details,
not published, which Rigaud was able to gather together.

[85] See the very brief account of Protheroe and his connection with Lower in
Arthur Mee's 'Carmarthenshire and Early Telescopes', *Carmarthenshire Antiquarian Society*, IV (1908-9), 43-4. The former County Archivist of Carmarthenshire, Major Francis Jones, a descendant of one of the daughters of John Protheroe,
has published on the family in 'The Squires of Hawksbrook' and 'The Vaughans of
Golden Grove' in *Transactions of the honorable Society of Cymmrodorion*.

[86] Unpublished paper delivered at the Thomas Harriot Symposium at the
University of Delaware on 6 Apr. 1971.

John Protheroe, whose surname may also be found in the Welsh forms, Prydderch or Rytherch, was born about 1582, the son of James Rytherch, J.P., D.L., who became High Sheriff of the county in 1599, John Protheroe is probably the John Pretherch of county Carmarthen, armiger, who matriculated, aged 15, at Jesus College, Oxford, on 14 October 1597, and entered Lincoln's Inn on 7 April 1601. Although he was not James Rytherch's eldest son, John Protheroe succeeded to the estate at Nantyrhebog, probably because his elder brother, Rhys, owned extensive and valuable estates in Laugharne and was a very turbulent character, defying the King's writ, assaulting among others his own father, and generally acting as a feudal lord at Laugharne. John Protheroe married Elinor Vaughan, a sister of the first Earl of Carbery, by whom he had twelve children, becoming the grandfather 'of the lively Lucy Walter, a subsidized lady-friend of Charles II'. The Vaughan family, into which Protheroe married, occupied a dozen country houses, and, at the height of its affluence, the parent estate of Golden Grove in the Vale Tywi comprising over 50,000 acres, 25 extensive lordships, and six castles. If the possessions of the many branches are added to this, it may be said that nearly half Carmarthenshire owned a Vaughan for a landlord.

After the death of Sir William Lower in 1615, John Protheroe obviously took over his services for the 9th Earl and the Lady Dorothy in looking out for their Welsh estates. A letter, dated from 'Hawkesbrook. 28. October 1620', remains in the Northumberland archives,[87] endorsed 'Master Protheroe his lettre concerning his Lordship's affaires in the West Country and Wales' which reads:

Righte Honorable

I receued your lordship's letters and warrantes which I will execute with as litle noise as I canne that ye may pay in his money before he hears of it, and as gladly as any man, that hathe the best desir to doe your lordship service; I stay in the countrye purposly aboute it, for the Courte of wardes lookes for me euery day and I longe to see and speake with master Harriott. The 7. of this next Monethe I meane to make an entry from your lordship and the same day to beginne my iurney. I beleeue that Master Mansell will not oppose your lordship's pleasure whatsoeuer he say or giue out to the contrary and if he doe I dare bouldly promise that your lordship shall find your new tenantes more powerfull in this country to defende and possess themselues of your lordship's righte then Master Mansell to detayne it. I haue ben lately in Pembrockshyre and haue enformed my selfe of the valew of your

---

[87] Alnwick Castle: Syon MSS X.II.1.(2). Lady Percy had died on 3 Aug. 1619, so Protheroe was carrying on serving the 9th Earl for the estates of both.

lordship's landes there. Sir Iohn Stepnethy and Master Cannon meane
to vye for a part of it called Eliotts Gill, and giue out that to crosse one
another. each will giue much more then it is worthe if they soe bothe
deserue it and the best parte giues moste for those two respecte nothinge
soe much as money and therfore deserue noe respecte from others but
for their money. if they doe but bragge then I cann helpe your Lordship to such tenauntes as will giue your Lordship the full valew of those
landes either in rente or fine and shalbe in that place as able to doe
your Lordship seruice as either of them; if your Lordship please to
make noe graunte of any thinge vntill my comminge vp I hope you
shall not finde me vnprofitable in this seruice who am

your Lordship's seruante
Iohn Protheroe

The inclusion in this business letter of the declaration that
he 'longe[d] to see and speake with master Harriot' and was
looking forward to a visit with him in November, at a time
when Harriot was nearing the final stages of his terminal
illness, shows that Protheroe had assumed the close friendship which his mentor Lower had previously held. Though
there remains no letter addressed to Harriot, and no mention
of Protheroe in Harriot's own papers, the intimacy of their
friendship is borne out by the fact that the following year,
when dictating his will, Harriot named 'John Protheroe of
Hakesbrooke in the County of Carmarthen Esquier' as one of
his four executors. His estimation of Protheroe as an able
mathematician is attested to by the fact that Harriot also
suggests Protheroe as one who might assist in explaining the
mathematical notations used in his manuscripts.[88]

Protheroe did not survive his friend Harriot very long. His
own will, dated 22 August 1624, was probated by his executor
and brother-in-law, Walter Vaughan of Llanelly.[89] Like
Harriot's will, this one of Protheroe also shows the close-knit
nature of the Lower-Harriot-Protheroe circle of friends.
Protheroe admits indebtedness to the second husband of
Lower's wife, and provides for payment: 'I give and bequeath
unto ye R. Hon. Sir Robt. Naunton, Knt., and to his heirs
for ever the lands called Tir Eglwys, Hendre, Queen's Croft,

---

[88] See Ch. XI, p. 469.
[89] Protheroe's will was printed in abstract in 1908 by Walter Mee in his article
on 'Carmarthenshire and Early Telescopes, *Transactions of the Carmarthenshire Society*, IV (1908–09), 43–4.

and Cwrtbach in the parish of Llangunnocke in the occupation of John Pritchard, desiring him to accept these lands
in lieu of the £800 I owe him.' Similarly, Protheroe had
engaged in land dealings with another friend of the group,
Thomas Aylesbury, as his will records: 'And whereas he has
passed away to Mr Thomas Aylesbury the land of Mochau in
the parish of Llanstephan, for ye sum of £800, whereof there
is unpaid £400 which he allows the Executors towards the
payment of his debts.' Protheroe's major beneficiaries are his
son John, his daughter Margaret and his other unmarried
daughters, his son Charles, and his wife Elinor. His major
charge to his wife was that she continue a pension to
Nathaniel Torporley which Protheroe had evidently established, probably in memory of Harriot and his concern over
the publication of his papers. This is summarized by Arthur
Mee as:[90]

He gives to his wife during her life the herbage only of all those lands of
his on the north side of the Brook called Llethr-ach, adjoining his
demesne lands of Hawk'sbrook. He directs her to pay Nathaniel
Torperly, of London, Clerke, his yearly pension during life [amount
not given] the time unexpired, and if she should die before his son
Charles Protheroe come to full age.

Another mutual friend of Lower, Protheroe, Harriot, and
Torporley was Thomas Aylesbury. Possibly Aylesbury and
Protheroe became acquainted at Oxford, where, as we have
seen, Protheroe studied from the fall of 1597 to the spring
of 1601, though without receiving a degree. Aylesbury was
also studying there during that period, though his college was
Christ Church rather than Jesus. According to Oxford records,
Aylesbury, born in London and son of a gentleman, matriculated at Christ Church on 24 November 1598, aged eighteen,[91]
entering the class which the younger Richard Corbet had
joined that spring.[92] Both Aylesbury and Corbet proceeded
in an orderly fashion through the prescribed stages, both
admitted to candidacy as BA on 30 June 1602, determined
the next Easter, licensed MA on 9 June 1605, and incorporated

[90] Ibid., p. 44.
[91] *Register of the University of Oxford*, II. 2. 231.
[92] Ibid., II. 2. 226, reads: '1598. 7 Apr. Broadg[ate] H[all], Corbett (Corbet),
Richard; Surrey, gen. f . . , 15.'

in the same year.[93] Corbet stayed on at Oxford to study for the ministry, receiving his BD and DD degrees in 1617; Aylesbury left Oxford on receiving his Master's degree to become secretary to Charles Howard, Earl of Nottingham and Lord High Admiral,[94] remaining in this position until Howard relinquished this post in 1618. It was during this period that Aylesbury (possibly through their mutual friend Protheroe) became acquainted with Harriot to join the circle of his friends.

Among Harriot's extant papers, two letters from Aylesbury to Harriot remain. The first, addressed 'To my assured good frend Master Thomas Hariots at Sion' was sent from Margett [Margate] and dated '15 Apr. 1613' and noted in Harriot's hand as 'Rec. Aprill. 24.'[95] This is a short, friendly account of a rough sea crossing, noting 'the strange words [used] amonge our Mariners', and indicating that it serves the purpose only 'to lett you vnderstand, that wheresoeuer I am, I am bound to remember you'. The letter closes with what must have been a personal joke between the two: 'Your very loyteringe but lovinge schollar', adding the interesting postscript: 'I must not forgett to tell you, your glasses haue fitted my lord excellentlie well; and soe, as I feare, you will loose them both; but not without your owne consent, which I haue noe auctoritie to promise till you giue leave.' This makes it appear that Harriot was engaged in grinding spectacles as well as perspective glasses, and distributed them to his friends, including the Lord High Admiral, Charles Howard.

Aylesbury's second letter follows the furore that accompanied the Comet of 1618.[96] Addressed to Harriot from Newmarket and dated 19 January 1618/19, it reads:

Sir./
Though I haue bene yet soe little a while att new markett, that i haue not any thing of moment to ympart; yet I thinke it not amisse to write

---

[93] Ibid. Aylesbury's record is II. 2. 235; Corbet's, II. 2. 236.

[94] This is reported by Anthony à Wood in the brief life of Aylesbury included in *Athenae Oxonienses* (1721 edn.) under listing of MA's for 1605, 'Fasti', col. 168. Rigaud notes the same thing in Bodleian MS Rigaud 35, fo. 177.

[95] BL Add. MS 6789; the letter is fo. 439[r], and the address and note of receipt are fo. 440[v].

to beare salutacions, and let you know, that in these wearie iourneys I am oftentimes comforted with the remembraunce of your kind love and paynes bestowed on your loytering scholar, whose little credit in the way of learning is allwaies vnderpropped with the name of soe woorthie a Maister. The Comet being spent, the talke of it still runnes current here; The Kings Majesty before my cumming spake with one of Cambridge called Olarentia [Marginal note by Harriot: 'Oloren Shaw. Mr. Booth.'], (a name able to beget beleefe of some extraordinarie qualities) but what satisfaction he gaue, I cannot yet learne; here are papers out of Spayne about it, yea and from Roome, which I will endeauer to gett, and meane that you shall partake the newes as tyme serues. Cua vt valeas et me ames, who am euer trulie and vnfaynedly yours att commaund.

Tho: Aylesburie

Aylesbury's fellow student at Oxford, Richard Corbet, was also familiar with Harriot and his Syon House investigations into the new science. During the height of the excitement about the great comet, on 9 December 1618, Corbet addressed a verse letter, 'A letter sent from Doctor Corbet to Master Ailebury, Decem. 9. 1618.' which was published many years later in a volume entitled *Certain Elegant Poems, Written by Dr. Corbet, Bishop of Norwich.*[97] In this verse, Corbet stresses the attention the comet gets from all levels of society:

> Which Comet we discerne, though not so true
> As you at *Sion*, as long taild as you. . . [a possible
>   reference to 'that Devil Harriot'?]

He proceeds:

> Yet every morning when the starre doth rise,
> There is no blacke for three houres in our eyes;
> But like a Puritan dreames towards this light
> All eyes turne upward, all are zeale and white:
> More it is doubtfull that this prodigie
> Will turne ten Schooles to come Astronomie;
> And the Analysis we justly feare,
> Since every Art doth seeke for refeue [sic., refuge?] there,
> Physitians, Lawyers, Glovers on the stall,
> The Shopkeepers speake Mathematicks all,
> And though men read no Gospels in these signes,

[96] Ibid., fo. 443r.
[97] London, printed by R. Cotes for Andrew Crooke at the 'Green Dragon in Pauls Church-yard', 1647. This poem occupies pp. 31-33.

Yet all professions are become Divines,
All weapons from the Bodkin to the Pike,
The Masons Rule, and Tailors Yard alike,
Take altitudes, and th'early fidling knaves,
On Fluits and Hoboyes, made them *Jacobs* staves,
Lastly of fingers, glasses we contrive,
And every first [fist] is made a Prospective. . .

The philosophical interpretations arising from these confusing observations and the vigour with which they are propounded distress Bishop Corbet. Perhaps the knowledgeable philosophers of Syon House can bring order into this chaos:

Now for the peace of God and man advise
(Thou that has wherewithall to make us wise)
Thine owne rich studies, and deepe Harriots mine,
In which there is no drosse, but all refine,
O tell us what to trust to, lest we wax
All stiffe and stupid with his paralex. . .

Corbet then poses the major philosophical questions which were puzzling the serious thinker of the early seventeenth century, and which must have stirred Harriot from his lethargy to the study of the comet:

Say, shall the old Philosophy be true?
Or doth he ride aboue the Moone thinke you?
Is he a Meteor forced by the Sun?
Or a first body from Creation?
Hath the same starre beene object of the wonder
Of our forefathers? shall the same come under
The sentence of our Nephews?

and he concludes:

write and send
Or else this starre a quarrell doth pretend.

It is sad that a reply from Aylesbury to Corbet, even one in verse couplets like the letter itself, does not exist. Were it available, it would give some insight at least into how Harriot resolved these same questions in his own mind, none of which appears in his own observations and calculations which have been preserved. Once again Harriot's 'too great reservedness' or his fear of censure for his independent thought prevented him from philosophizing about his observations or their impact upon the celestial theories of his age. Yet as these were uppermost in the mind of Richard Corbet, so they must have dominated the discussions of Aylesbury and his friend, 'doubting Thomas', when they met and observed at Syon House that autumn.

A few occasional notes among Harriot's manuscripts reveal his association with a very prominent young man-about-court, John Harington, 2nd Baron Harington of Exton (1592-1614), the closest friend of the King's eldest son and heir, Prince Henry. It is obvious from Harriot's will that young Lord Harington studied under his tutelage for some time. To Sir Robert Sidney, Viscount Lisle, one of Harriot's four executors, Harriot made a bequest of[98] 'one Boxe of papers being nowe vppon the table in my Library at Syon, conteyning fiue quires of paper, more or less, which were written by the Last Lord Harrington, and Coppyed out of some of my Mathematicall papers for his instruccion. . .'

'The Last Lord Harington' was the second Baron Harington, eldest son of the John Harington who, as a distant cousin of King James, had been created first Baron Harington of Exton. The two families were close personal friends, and Lord Harington was given charge, under the royal seal, of the raising of James's eldest daughter, the Princess Elizabeth. It was natural that young John Harington and Prince Henry were thrown together, and it was this association that led to the creation of young John as Knight of the Bath when he was just thirteen years old.

Before he reached the age of eighteen, young John Harington was well known and respected, as was Prince Henry, throughout Europe as well as Great Britain. In Venice, the English ambassador eulogized young John to the Doge:[99]

He is a youth but little over sixteen, son of Lord Harington, a gentleman of the highest quality in our country and of great weight on account of the vast barony which he holds in England, where it is not the custom for the sons to bear their father's title during his lifetime. The sister of this young gentleman, the Countess of Bedford, is the

[98] See Ch. XI, p. 462.
[99] *Venetian Calendar, 1607-10*, pp. 215-16, as cited by Ian Grimble, *The Harington Family*, London, 1957, p. 162.

Queen's favourite maid-of-honour; and the Princess her Majesty's only daughter, is brought up at the house of Lord Harington, father of the youth, whose mother is governess to the Princess. Add to this that it is thought certain that the young man will marry Lord Salisbury's only daughter, and being the right eye of the Prince of Wales, the world holds that he will one day govern the kingdom.

According to all contemporary accounts, young Lord Harington was a paragon of all virtues. A Calvinist by conviction, he lived a devout and puritanical life, and though he travelled much in Catholic countries, he was unswayed by any attempts to influence his faith. His devotion to Prince Henry was one of the dominant forces of his life, and he gave up his foreign travels at age eighteen to devote his full time to his friendship with the Prince. The untimely death of Prince Henry on 6 November 1612 was a devastating blow to him (as it was to the hopes of Sir Walter Ralegh for whom Prince Henry had been a vocal advocate at court), and he never recovered. On the death of his father in August 1613, he became Lord Harington, but his life as a Baron was short: he died suddenly of a fever while visiting at Kew, just across the river from Harriot's residence at Syon, on 27 February 1613/14.

Just when Lord Harington studied with Harriot and how long their association existed cannot be accurately determined. Certainly it began before the death of Prince Henry, since a parenthetical note on one of Harriot's observations of sunspots (no. 26, taken on 11 January 1611/12)[100] indicates that this sighting was shared with S. J. H. — Harriot's usual notation for Sir John Harrington. This being true, it is likely that it was during the winter of 1611-12 that they were working together and that Lord Harington brought his close friend Prince Henry with him to meet his teacher.

Harriot's acquaintance with Prince Henry is much less documented than was that of Ralegh. But among the extant manuscripts remain two 'magic squares' which link Harriot with the Prince of Wales.[101] One, on a 21 × 21 format, links the letters *HENRICVS PRINCEPS FECIT* in a way that produces, according to Harriot's calculations, 739,024

---

[100] Petworth MS HMC 241/viii, fo. 8.
[101] BL Add. MS 6782, fos. 27, 28.

combinations of that reading.[102] The phrase *SILO PRINCEPS FECIT* is likewise worked into a 17 × 17 square to produce, Harriot notes, 51,480 combinations. It has been suggested that these letter squares might have been used as a basis for a cipher,[103] for which Harriot was known.[104] But it is far more likely that it was used merely as a pleasant afternoon's diversion, possibly as a way to illustrate the solution of a particular cubic equation.[105] Though these ciphers show some direct contact between Harriot and Prince Henry, they are not enough to suggest that the two were friends, as were Harriot and Harington.

Something of the nature of Harriot's instruction of young Lord Harington may be seen from one record of their association which remains among his manuscripts. On the back of the sheet bearing Harriot's observations of sunspots on 2 and 3 July 1612,[106] appears the following notation:

> Sir J[ohn]. H[arington].
> Opus Palatinum
> Andersoni Problemata
> Getaldi Apolonius
> Snellij Apolonius
> Theodosius de Sphæra græcolat.
> Euclidis Optica der Penam. Lat.

It is obvious that this is Harriot's memorandum recording a list of books which he had lent to his young scholar for study.[107] It indicates both the currency of Harriot's own

---

[102] This number is recorded on the bottom of fo. 27; it is also calculated ibid., fo. 57, along with the phrases: *Silo princeps fecit.* 17. 51,480; *Jacobus*; *Henricus princeps fecit.* (21) 739,024; *Carolus princeps fecit.* (20). This implies that Harriot may have made similar squares for the other members of the royal family as well.

[103] See Cecily Tanner, 'Henry Stevens', loc. cit.

[104] That Harriot was engaged in work on ciphers is shown from a letter of Sir Robert Cecil, writing to Sir George Carewe on 1 Oct. 1602, in which he said '. . . and for the Ciphre I like it better, a thousand tymes, then all Herriotts Lockes and keyes.' Lambeth Palace Library, Carew MS 604, p. 195.

[105] BL Add. MS, fo. 75, carries a marginal note of 'Henricus princeps' in Harriot's hand beside the solution of the cubic equation which applies.

[106] Petworth MS HMC 241/viii, fo. 36ᵛ.

[107] As listed in the BL catalogues, these volumes can be identified as follows: [Joachimus Georgius, *Rhaeticus*] Opus Palatinum de Triangulis, a G. J. R. coeptum, L. Valentinus Otho consummavit. Neostadii in Palatinatu, 1596.

library,[108] and the profundity of the mathematical study of
the serious young man. The first book, *Opus Palatinum*, was
the most complete table of trigonometric functions available
at the time. It was an expansion of the tables first compiled
by Rheticus for inclusion in Copernicus's *De revolutionibus*,
as later expanded by Rheticus himself and ultimately by
L. Valentin Otho on the orders of Frederic IV. The final
tables, bearing the title of *Opus Palatinum de Triangulis*, had
been published as early as 1596 and had proved an invaluable
aid to all who were solving trigonometric or astronomical
problems. It furnished young Harington with 'the hunting
dogs' which had so fascinated Sir William Lower when
Harriot furnished them to him. The volume of Euclid's
Optica et Catoptrica as edited by Joannes Pena, first published
in 1557, had gone through numerous editions, the latest in
1604, the one Harriot would probably have used, since it
coincided with his own work on optics about that time; and
since this edition was in Greek, it would furnish excellent
language training by one who was considered a Greek scholar
as well as a mathematician. Theodosius of Tripoli's book on
the sphere had also appeared in numerous editions since first
edited by Pena in 1558, but again it is interesting to note
that Harriot was using the Greek edition rather than one of
the numerous printings in Latin. The other three volumes

Alexandri Andersoni ... Supplementum Apollonij rediuiui, siue, analysis
problemantis hactenus desiderati ad Apollonij Pergaei doctrinam περι
νευρων, a Marino Ghetaldo ... hucusque, non ita pridem restitutam ...
Huic subnexa est variorum problematum practice, etc. Parisiio, 1612.

M. Ghetaldi Apollonius redivivus, seu restitutae Apollonii Pergaei de
inclinationibus geometriae liber secundus. 1613.

Willebordi Snellii Apollonius Batavus, seu, ex suscitata Apolloni Pergaei
περι διωρισμενης geometria. 1608.

Θεοδοωυ ὁπτικα και κατοπτκικα Theodosii Tripolitae Sphericorum libri
tres numquam antehoc Graece excusi ... latine redditi pro J. Penam.
Parisiis, 1558.

Εὐκλειδου ὁπτικα και κατοπτγικα Euclidis optica et catoptrica .. Eadem
Latine reddita per J. Penam ... His praeposita est ejusdem J. Penae de usu
optices praefatio. Parisiis, 1557. [or its latest edition]

Euclides optica et catoptrica e Graeco versa per I. Penam. 1604.

[108] Dr Tanner is currently studying all the references to mathematical authors
to be found in Harriot's MSS. When published it will be a very valuable insight
into what must have been one of the best scientific libraries of his time.

were very recent works: the *Getaldi Apolonius* obviously
refers to the attempt by Marino Ghetaldi to reconstruct the
lost book of Apollonius (*Inclinationum libri duo*) in a work
titled *Apollonius rediuiuus, seu restitutae Apollonii Pergaei
de inclinationibus geometriae* first published in Venice in 1607
(and augmented by further study in 1613). Willebrord
Snell's *Apollonius Batauus, seu, ex suscitata Apolloni Pergaei
geometria* had appeared in 1608. And the very remarkable
analysis of Ghetaldi's reconstruction of the lost work of
Apollonius by the brilliant young mathematician from
Aberdeen (who had been a friend to Vieta and was currently
a professor of mathematics at the University of Paris),
Alexander Anderson, had just appeared in Paris in 1612.
These last three books lent to young Sir John Harington
presented him with the latest and most scholarly works on
the classic Greek mathematical analysis which it would have
been possible to obtain, even during this time of intense
interest in the restoration of the classics.

All England mourned the untimely death of the 2nd Baron
Harington at the age of twenty-two, just sixteen weeks
following the shock of Prince Henry's death. Memorial
services were held in many churches; certainly Harriot would
have attended one of them. He may well have attended the
funeral service in London, where Richard Stock, Pastor of
All Hallows in Broad Street delivered the eulogy. Printed in
1614,[109] this gives some insight into the way young Baron
Harington was viewed by his contemporaries. Stock pointed
out that he had been

... of an excellent wit, firm memory, sweet nature, and prompt to
learning; so that in a short time he was able to read Greek authors,
and to make use of them in their own language. He spake Latin well,
wrote it with a pure and grave style; and was able to confer with any
stranger, readily and laudably, in the French and Italian tongues;
understood the authors which he read in Spanish, and for arts, was
well read in logic, philosophy, and the mathematics. He made a good
progress in the theoric part of the art military and navigation: so that
he wanted nothing but practice to make him perfect in both. His
understanding in heavenly matters, and the mysteries of salvation,

[109] *The Churches Lamentation for the losse of the Godly. A Sermon*, J. Beale,
1614 (STC 23273). This rare tract was reprinted in Sir John Harington's *Nugae
Antiquae*, ed. Thomas Park, London, 1804, vol. II, pp. 307-18.

was so admirable, that there was scarce any question could be propounded to him, about these matters, unto which he was not able to
give an understanding and quick answer.

Harriot must have mourned deeply for the loss of the young
scholar who had spent so many hours in his parlour, studying
the mathematical papers of his master and copying out of
them the essential doctrine 'for his instruccion' — five quires
of paper, roughly 120 foolscap sheets — so cherished by his
teacher that long after the pupil's death they were on display
on a table in his Syon library.

The deaths of Prince Henry and Lord Harington were the
first of a series of shocks which began to rock Harriot during
his mature years. They were followed two years later with
the sudden death of Sir William Lower; and, three years
later, by the execution of Sir Walter Ralegh himself. The
intense pleasure and excitement of learning had begun to
dim, overpowered by the grief and sad realization of the
essential misery inherent in the human condition. The
telescopic searches of the heavens to determine the nature
of the universe had tapered off with no firm conclusions.
The physical experiments to clarify the nature of terrestrial
matter had stopped. So far as the evidence from his manuscripts is concerned, he retired from his scientific experimentation and withdrew into tasks of routine reading and the
unimaginative calculation and recalculation of his navigational tables. Except for his observations of the comet
of 1618, Harriot dated only seven pages of manuscript
during the five years following Prince Henry's death. On 23
January 1613/14 Harriot wrote the date on a sheet of calculations that he and Christopher Tooke were making on his
tables of rhumbs;[110] this was five weeks before the death of
Lord Harington. That same month he drew a picture of a
child born with multiple deformities in Breynford.[111] In
April 1615 he took notes on a book he had borrowed from
M. T. Buck titled *Certayne briefe remembrances offered
for his Majesty &c. 1613*, sixteen quarto leaves written by
Sir Walter Cope.[112] He was evidently working on the calendar

---

[110] BL Add. MS 6786, fo. 99r.
[111] BL Add. MS 6789, fo. 488r.
[112] Ibid., fos. 527v&r (page bound reversed).

in 1616.[113] He wrote two letters to his physician about his illness.[114] And he settled a bookseller's bill in 1617, returning some of the volumes he had purchased.[115] It is obvious that his outlook on life had changed, and that he found himself in those years that should have been most productive, in the frame of mind that Carlyle was later to designate as 'The Centre of Indifference', unable to continue his physical experiments, follow up on his mathematical innovations, or even to prepare his accomplished work for presentation to the common weal as he had earlier planned to do. Like his closest friends he had died in spirit, though his physical body lived on.

[113] Petworth MS HMC 241/i, Harriot's treatise on the calendar though covering a number of years in determining the date of Easter, uses 1616 frequently for its reference point. These twelve sheets are not numbered.

[114] 4 Nov. 1615 and 5 Apr. 1616. BL Add. MS 6789, fos. 446[r], 447[r]. See detailed discussion in Ch. XI below.

[115] 31 Oct. 1618. Petworth MS HMC 241/iv, fos. 9[r&v].

XI. The Bitter End: Illness and Death

There is probably more detailed information about Harriot's final illness, death, and the testamentary disposition of his estate than about any other portion of his life. In part this is due to the sensational nature of the public view of the man himself — his prominence in the world of exploration and discovery, his tremendous reputation as a mathematician and scientist, his close association with many of the historical figures of his time, and, above all, his prominence as an unorthodox free-thinker in matters philosophical and theological. His death by cancer (a death which even then was linked to his smoking) was a source of wide gossip and generally considered a kind of retribution for his impiety. And among his own papers, too, remain some rough drafts of his letters to his physician (the only such drafts to exist) which furnish Harriot's own views of his disease, his symptoms, and his attitudes toward his final illness. Many of his doctors' medical records remain, and Harriot's will, as we have seen, gives much more detail about his intent for his worldly possessions and his accumulated mathematical and scientific information than was customary in his time, or, indeed, in most ages. By putting all this information together, we may get a fairly clear picture of the physical decline and death of one of the most illustrious Londoners of the early seventeenth century.

From available evidence, Harriot appears to have been of reasonably strong physique during the major portion of his life. His activities during his stay in the New World during his mid-twenties show that he had better-than-average stamina during this period of his life. In fact, Harriot seems to have been almost scornful of the four colonists who died during the trying year at Roanoke (not to mention the four who were killed by Indians, one who was hanged, and three abandoned when the colonists hurriedly left with Drake).[1] As Harriot described what he considered the remarkable achievement of this living through the trying winter:[2]

... for all the want of prouision, as first of English victuall; excepting for twentie daies, wee liued only by drinking water and by the victuall of the countrie, of which some sorts were very straunge vnto vs, and might have bene thought to haue altered our temperatures in such sort as to haue brought vs into greeuous and dangerous diseases: secondly the want of English meanes, for the taking of beastes, fishe, and foule, which by the helpe only of the inhabitants and their meanes, coulde not bee so suddenly and easily prouided for vs, nor in so great numbers & quantities, nor of that choise as otherwise might haue bene to our better satisfaction and contentment. Some want also wee had of clothes. Furthermore, in all out trauailes which were most speciall and often in the time of winter, our lodging was in the open aire vpon the grounde. And yet I say for all this, there were but foure of our whole company (being one hundred and eight) that died all the yeere and that but at the latter ende thereof and vpon none of the aforesaide causes. For all foure especially three were feeble, weake, and sickly persons before euer they came thither, and those that knewe them much marueyled that they liued so long beeing in that case, or had aduentured to trauaile.

During the years of his thirties and forties, Harriot appears to have remained strong and vigorous. Following the return from Virginia, he faced the rough life of an Irish colonist without hesitation. He was particularly active in Ralegh's naval activities and apparently worked tirelessly in his training of sea captains. During these years, too, he shows much physical endurance in his long and involved calculation of navigational tables; work which today is done in minutes by computers in Harriot's time required almost endless hours of multiplying and dividing extremely long numbers with great accuracy. During his experimental work with chemistry at the turn of the century, Harriot's working hours are depicted as unbelievably long as he continued repeated operations of heating, cooling, drying, agitating, day and night continuously

[1] Quinn, *Roanoke Voyages*, I, p. 384, n. 6.
[2] *A briefe and true report*, 1588 edn., sig. F3r&v.

for weeks at a time. Yet there appears to be no evidence of any kind that Harriot suffered from even the common maladies of his time until after the death of Elizabeth when Harriot was entering his mid-forties.

The first evidence of Harriot as an ill man comes during his forty-fifth year, at the time of the Gunpowder Plot in the autumn of the second year of James. As we have seen, because of his association with the 9th Earl and his consequent attendance at Henry Percy's dinner with his cousin Thomas Percy on the day before that infamous 5 November, Harriot was interrogated and imprisoned. It was from his prison cell in the Gatehouse, late in November, that Harriot wrote a plaintive account of an illness. In a letter to Robert Cecil, principal secretary of state, Harriot complained about 'this dungeon of my many miseryes'.[3] On 16 December, he went into greater detail:[4] 'But now this misery of close imprisonment happeninge vnto me at the time of my sicknes, which was more then three weekes old before; being great windeness in my stomack & fumings into my head rising from my spleen, besides other infirmityes, as my Doctor knoweth & some effectes my keeper can witnes.' Prison, Harriot protested, was a 'place where I am not likely to recouer health.' From this testimony it appears that Harriot was taken ill about the first of November (just about the time of the Gunpowder Plot) and by the time of this second letter had suffered nearly two months — a long illness for a man who had shown a rugged constitution under circumstances more trying than these. Yet from this time on, there appear indications of less-than-buoyant health which disrupt Harriot's thought and work.

Nearly a year later, in early December 1606, Harriot was apparently still handicapped by illness. On 2 October 1606 Johannes Kepler, having learned of Harriot's sophisticated work on optics from their mutual sea-captain friend, John Eriksen, wrote to Harriot from Prague,[5] asking his theories

[3] For the complete text of this letter, see p. 346 above.
[4] See pp. 349 above.
[5] The correspondence between Kepler and Harriot is preserved in the National-bibliothek in Vienna, Cod. 10703. Frequently cited, though never translated, the letters are accurately transcribed in Johannes Kepler, *Gesammelte Werke*, 17 vols.,

about the physical cause of colours, his methods of determining the refraction of light, and his theories of the rainbow.
On 2 December Harriot replied from Syon, expressing
pleasure at receiving a letter from so eminent a scientist
and extreme interest in the questions he raised, but indicating
that he would not be able to reply in depth because of his
poor health.[6] Freely translated his letter reads as follows:
'...To reply to your individual requests is not possible,
particularly in the brief time which I can hope to give your
response, especially because of the bad state of my general
health, which so affects me that it prevents either my writing
or even accurately thinking or mustering my arguments on
any subject.' Because of this, as Lohne has pointed out,[7]
Harriot did not put his best foot forward to reveal his significant optical discoveries, but merely sent a few elementary
tables of refraction. It is possible, of course, that Harriot
may have been withholding his scientific findings from a
rival observer, though this appears contrary to his nature,
and it is more likely that his pleas of illness were real and
not feigned. As a matter of fact, at the close of his letter,
Harriot indicates disappointment in not being able to answer
in detail about the rainbow, and promises to do so in the
future 'if God will give us the time and health to do so'
('si Deus det nobis otium and salutem').

No more is heard of this extended illness, and for some
time Harriot appears to have continued his work with normal
vigour. With his discovery of the telescope and the excitement
of exploring new astronomical horizons, he showed the
strength to work nearly through the night, night after night.
Yet his observations show that he suffered from normal
illnesses. For example, his observation of the Moon dated
10 September 1610 is noted as having been drawn from
memory ('memoriter') and the following day in recording

Munich, 1937–75. Letters 394 and 403 are in vol. 15 (1951), and 439, 497, and
536 in vol. 16 (1954).

  [6] The original reads: 'Ad singula respondere vna vice nimium est, praesertim
hoc breui tempore quo responsum meum expectatur: sed maxime ob malam
valetudinem qua nunc ita affectus sum, vt mihi molestum est vel scribere vel
accurate de aliqua re cogitare et argumentari.'

  [7] Johannes A. Lohne, 'Thomas Harriot, The Tycho Brahe of Optics', *Centaurus*,
VI (1959), p. 115.

his observation he notes:[8] 'I could not set downe the figure of all, nether this but by memory because I was troubled with the reume.' Four days later, on 15 September, his indisposition still remained, for though he conducted his observations, his drawings were made from memory later, as he noted: 'memoriter. The rume'.[9]

The following year Harriot was busy observing the planets about Jupiter. On 16 February 1610/11, a Saturday, he watched from London, seeing but one moon 'At D. Turners house in litle St Ellens'.[10] On Monday he observed again, still from London, but thereafter for a full week he made no observations at all. It is at least possible that this was another time of illness, and that his visit to Doctor Turner in London was a professional visit.

The 'D. Turner' at whose house Harriot was observing was Dr Peter Turner (1542-1614), a very popular London physician of the time. Son of the eminent botanist, William Turner, Peter was educated at Cambridge where he received his BA and MA, after which he studied medicine at Heidelberg, receiving his MD in 1571. In 1575 he was incorporated MD at Cambridge and in 1599 at Oxford. For a term he was physician to St. Bartholomew's Hospital; he also served several terms as a member of Elizabeth's parliaments. He served as principal physician to both of Harriot's patrons, Sir Walter Ralegh and the 9th Earl of Northumberland. According to the Percy accounts, he was retained on an annual basis by the 9th Earl. The accounts of Edward Francis, disburser of foreign payments for September 1594, contain the entry:[11]

Phisick.   Deliuered to Doctor Turner by your lordship's commaundement for his yearly fee. November xxix   xx*li*   [1593]

Dr Turner was also one of those persons (along with Dr John, 'a surgion') who was granted free access to Sir Walter Ralegh in the Tower in September 1605. Since it was obvious that he was a close intimate in the Ralegh–Northumberland

[8] Petworth MS HMC 241/IX, fo. 17.
[9] Ibid., fo. 14.
[10] Petworth MS HMC 241/IV, fo. 8, observations 48 and 49.
[11] Alnwick Castle, Syon MS X.II.12.6.

circle, it is only logical that during times of illness, Harriot would feel free to call on this eminent physician.

Some time before the death of Peter Turner, perhaps in 1611 or 1612, the affliction which was ultimately to lead to Harriot's death, cancer of the nose, began seriously to trouble him. It is probable that the early treatment of this ailment was at the hands of Dr Turner, since at his death it was his eldest son, Samuel, who interceded for Harriot in obtaining the services of the most eminent physician in London, the King's own physician, Theodore Turquet de Mayerne (1573-1655). Mayerne's detailed notes of his patients and his practice are still available and, coupled with Harriot's own letters to Mayerne about his illness, give us an unusually complete account of the course of his illness.

But even before his death, Harriot's prominence as a friend of Ralegh and Northumberland, his reputation for unorthodox beliefs, and his great reputation as a mathematician and scientist led to rumours and gossip about his illness and its causes. An anonymous Catholic gossip whose notes remain in the Bodleian, critical of the whole Northumberland circle, says of 'Master Harriot' that[12]

He presented Queen Anne [of Denmark] with a viol of water which ebbed and flowed at the same time as the Thames. He allwayes carried about him a golden probe with which every day he tryed if a polipus he had in his nose yeilded fresh blood. – he said that would give him at Least tenn days warning of his death by ceasing to bleed.

And, as we have seen,[13] members of the Anglican clergy also were inclined to read Harriot's fate as retribution for heretical views. As John Aubrey later reported:[14]

The Bishop of Sarum (Seth Ward) told me that one Mr. Haggar (a countryman of his), a gentleman and good mathematician, was well acquainted with Mr. Thomas Hariot, and was wont to say, that he did not like (or valued not) the old story of the Creation of the world. He could not believe the old position; he would say *ex nihilo nihil fit*. But sayd Mr. Haggar, a nihilum killed him at last; for in the top of his nose came a little red speck (exceeding small), which grew bigger and bigger, and at last killed him. I suppose it was that which the chirurgians call a *noli me tangere*.

---

[12] Bodleian MS Rawlinson B 158, fo. 152.   [13] See Ch. V.
[14] Andrew Clark, *'Brief Lives'*, 2 vols., I. pp. 284-7.

In printing Aubrey's materials, Anthony à Wood added some details which garbled the facts somewhat:[15]

This person [Harriot], tho' he was but little more than 60 years of age, when he died, yet had not an unusual and rare disease seized upon him, he might have attain'd, as 'tis thought, to the age of 80. The disease was an ulcer in the lip, and Dr. Alex. Rhead was his physician, who, tho' he had cured many of worser, and more malignant diseases, yet he could not save him.

Harriot's illness was exploited in political gossip as well as religious. A *sub rosa*, off-colour poem was evidently circulating in the court circles of James, linking Harriot's cancer of the nose with the Spanish Ambassador, Count Gondomar, who was largely responsible for Ralegh's final tragedy. As published a century later, the following doggerel verse was making the rounds:[16]

[Among some old MSS, (which by their *antique* aspect, could not have been written later than a whole Century since) I met with a *Stanza*, which tho' none of the *cleanliest*, may not unfitly claim a place after the foregoing, viz.]

To our English PHILOSOPHER, MR. T. HARRIOT, on his *Sympathy* with the *Spanish* Fox, Count GONDOMAR. N.B. *One had* a Fistula in Ano, *The other something like it* in Naso.

> TELL *me*, Philosopher, *what urges thee*
> *Still to commerce with* Statique *Policy?*
> *So far to sympathize, in sore Disaster,*
> *That both alike require the self-same Plaster?*
> *The* Nose of England's *deep* Philosophy
> *Lies* snuffling *with a* cancrous *Malady!*
> *An Omen dire: Since in a Night, or twain,*
> Infested *was the Pol'tique* A- *of* Spain!
> *Pray Heav'n, the* Madrid *Spell don't so benight us,*
> *But that our* Nose *may smell't e'er he besh—e us.*

Just what Harriot's sympathy with Count Gondomar may have been cannot now be determined (if it existed at all after his treatment of Ralegh), so it is impossible to tell what political significance he was supposed to have. More likely the simultaneous illness of two prominent figures of gossip

[15] *Athenae Oxonienses*, II, cols. 299–303.

[16] J. Morgan, ed., *Phoenix Brittanicus: Being a Miscellaneous collection of Scarce and Curious Tracts . . . Only to be found in the Cabinets of the Curious*, London, 1732, p. 368.

led to an imaginative linking which might have created a snicker or two as it was surreptitiously circulated around the knowing circles of the court.

A short note which Harriot retained among his miscellaneous papers shows that it was Samuel Turner who made the first approaches to Mayerne to accept Harriot as his patient. It is not dated, but must have been written after the death of Peter Turner, senior, on 27 May 1614, within a very few days. Endorsed 'To his very good frende Master Hariot give these', the letter reads as follows:[17]

Sir
          these shall request you to forgiue me my absence vntill tomorrowe. Thin I shall giue you more particular accounte of my discourse with Mayerne. in the meane time I shall lett you knowe that he cannot possibly com to London, thoughe he haue manny occasions to inuite him to it but he desires much to see you there: but betweene this and tuesday he will send you under his hand, the methode that he wolde aduise you in the cure: Tomorrowe I shall see you my selfe in the meane time I remaine.

your assured frende
Sam Turner.

Samuel Turner's intercessions were successful, and Dr Theodore Turquet de Mayerne, then at the height of his fame and with services much in demand, agreed to see Harriot when he was next in London. Mayerne, in earlier years on the continent, had been a controversial figure. In his lectures to physicians and surgeons he had openly advocated the use of chemical remedies abhorrent to the disciples of Galen. In December 1603 he was unanimously condemned by the College of Physicians of the University of Paris, and it was recommended that he be stripped of his position as royal district physician. But in spite of this criticism, Mayerne had continued his practice, and his popularity and favour grew. In 1606 he treated an English peer who had come to Paris for his services, and his chemical treatment resulted in a cure which spread his fame even further. He was induced to come to England, was presented to King James, and was appointed official physician to the

[17] BL Add. MS 6789, fo. 442.

King. In England, instead of being censured, Mayerne was lionized, endorsed by many prominent physicians, and sought after by many prominent members of the court circle. Among others who were under his care were Lord Rochester, the earl of Salisbury, and (in the final stages of his illness) Prince Henry. His English successes were so spectacular that many of the French physicians who had earlier scorned his practices crossed to London to consult with him on their more esoteric cases. Throughout his practice, Mayerne was meticulous about keeping records of his cases, recording in detail his observations about the patient, the nature and progress of the disease, and his recommended medicines and treatments. Among the twenty-three volumes of his manuscript notes in the Sloane collection in the British Library remain his notes of his observations of Harriot, his disease, and his treatment.[18]

The record of Harriot's initial visit with Mayerne is un-dated, though it immediately follows one dated 28 May 1615. A recapitulation in another notebook[19] indicates 'Maye 1615' for this interview, so that it seems most plausible that it appeared on Monday, Tuesday, or Wednesday – 29, 30, or 31 May of that year. Mayerne's initial notes, in some-what cryptic Latin, are as follows, with a rough translation:[20]

Mr Hariot

Vir admodum melancholicas.   Annorum circiter sexagint.
[A man somewhat melancholy.   In years about sixty (actually fifty-
   five.)]

Primus ex Virginia inuexit in Angliam vsum fumi tabaci.
[First introduced the use of tobacco smoke from Virginia into England.]

Vlcus καρκινῶδες in nare sinistra quod septum nasi
[A cancerous ulcer in the left nostril eats up the

depascitur et pro magnitudine sua haben labia
septum of his nose and in proportion to its size holds the lips

dura et inuersa.
hard and turned upwards.]

---

[18] Notes on Harriot's case are to be found in BL Sloane MS 1933, fos. 125ᵛ-126ʳ, 155ʳ&ᵛ-156ʳ, and 230ᵛ; 2065, fos. 133ʳ&ᵛ, 134ʳ&ᵛ, 135ʳ&ᵛ, and 136ʳ&ᵛ; and 2086, fos. 57ʳ&ᵛ and 58ʳ&ᵛ.
[19] BL Sloane MS 2065, fo. 133ʳ.
[20] BL Sloane MS 2086, fo. 57ʳ.

Non serpit multum intro narem.
[It has gradually crept well into the nose.]
Hoc malum patitur aeger a biennio.
[This evil the patient suffers the past two years.]

According to this account, Mayerne judged the onset of the cancer to have been in 1613. This information he may have had from Harriot himself, or he may (as he obviously did with Harriot's age) have made this as an estimate. But in any case, it shows clearly that by the spring of 1615, the cancer was well advanced and at this time, and for the rest of his life, Harriot must have been in constant (or as Mayerne indicated, 'calamitous') pain and suffering.

Probably more interesting than these technical details for the lay reader are two letters that Harriot himself composed to Mayerne in the periods between their appointments. These letters, preserved in rough draft among Harriot's miscellaneous papers, were first noted by Stevens, though he did not recognize them as addressed to Mayerne, but thought them written 'to a friend of distinction, name not mentioned, who had recently been appointed to some medical office at court'.[22] As a matter of fact, Stevens missed the whole Mayerne connection and for a misreading of the will indexed 'Mayorne (Mayornes), Mr., apothecary'. The part which impressed Stevens, and what has been quoted and requoted since, was the postscript which Harriot appended to his first letter. This has been used as evidence of the natural piety of the suffering Harriot and to refute the charges of atheism, deism, or free thinking which have plagued his reputation.[23]

The Harriot letters to Mayerne, written in a crabbed small hand in Latin, are evidently a first draft which he later copied, and were retained as a memento of what he had written. There are, therefore, many crossings out and many words written interlinearly, which make for difficult reading. They are so detailed and so illuminating as to the relationship between the patient and his physician, however, that a somewhat rough translation is included here. The first letter,

[21] BL Add. MS 6789, fos. 446r&v, 447r.
[22] *Thomas Hariot and his Associates*, p. 141.
[23] See, e.g., Jean Jacquot's 'Thomas Harriot's Reputation for Impiety', loc. cit., p. 169.

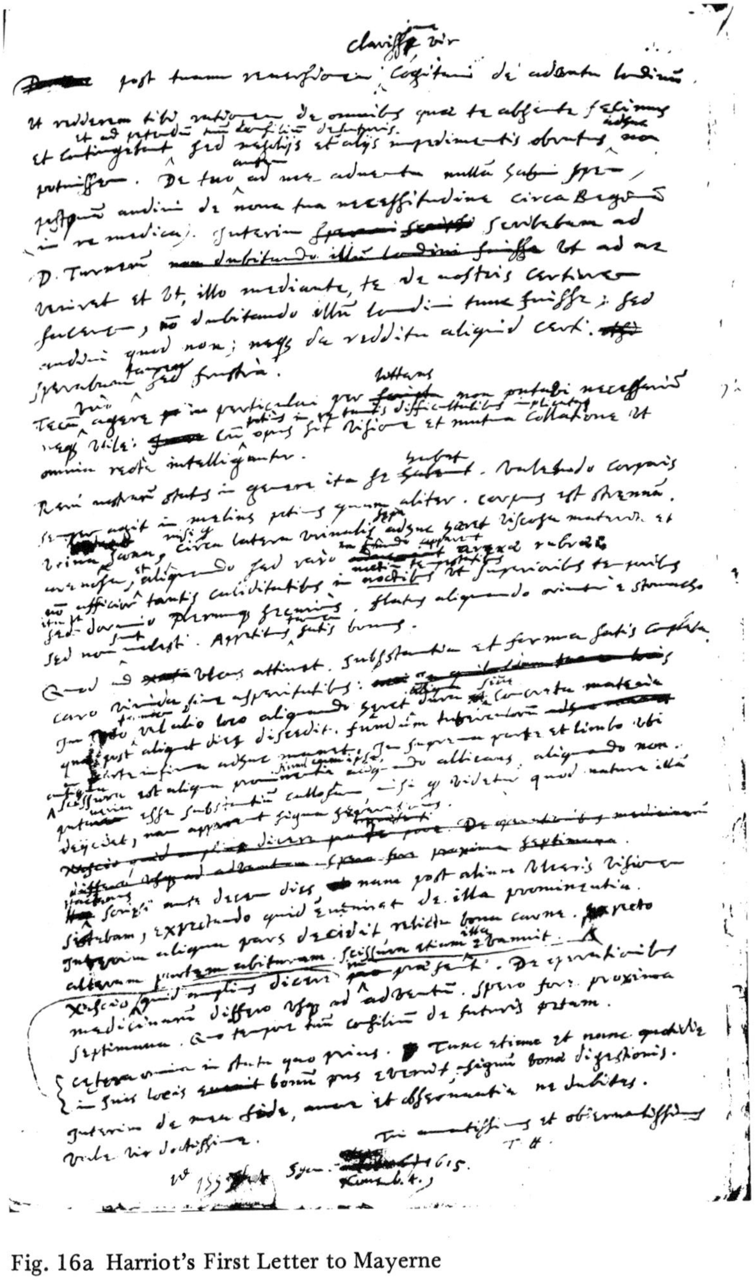

Fig. 16a Harriot's First Letter to Mayerne

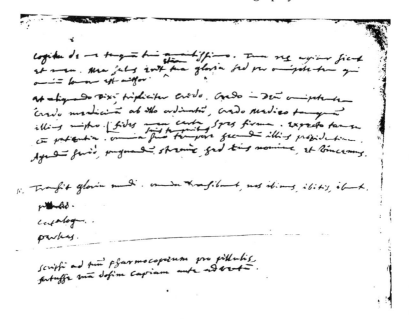

Fig. 16b Harriot's First Letter to Mayerne (cont.)

dated from Syon on 4 November 1615[24] (see Fig. 16), may
be rather freely translated thus:

After your return most illustrious Sir, I thought of going to London to
give you a report on all our doings during your absence and to ask your
advice on what to do now. But I was overwhelmed with business and
other impediments so that I was not able to do so. As for your letter
which I had previously received, I have not studied it in detail since I
learned of your new call to attend the Queen (on medical matters).[25]
In the meantime I wrote to Dr Turner so that he might come to see me
and so that by his mediation you might be better informed about my
case, for I did not doubt that he was that time in London; but I heard
he was not; nor anything precise about his return. I still hoped, but
in vain.

In any case, I thought it neither necessary nor useful to confer by
letter on the details in a case so bristling with difficulties, and it was

[24] BL Add. MS 6789, fos. 446r&v.
[25] Queen Anne (1574–1619), wife to James I, suffered from dropsy at least as
early as 1612 and it was from this that she died in 1619. Dr Mayerne, to whom
the Queen granted an annual pension of £400, was attending the Queen during
the period of Harriot's letters.

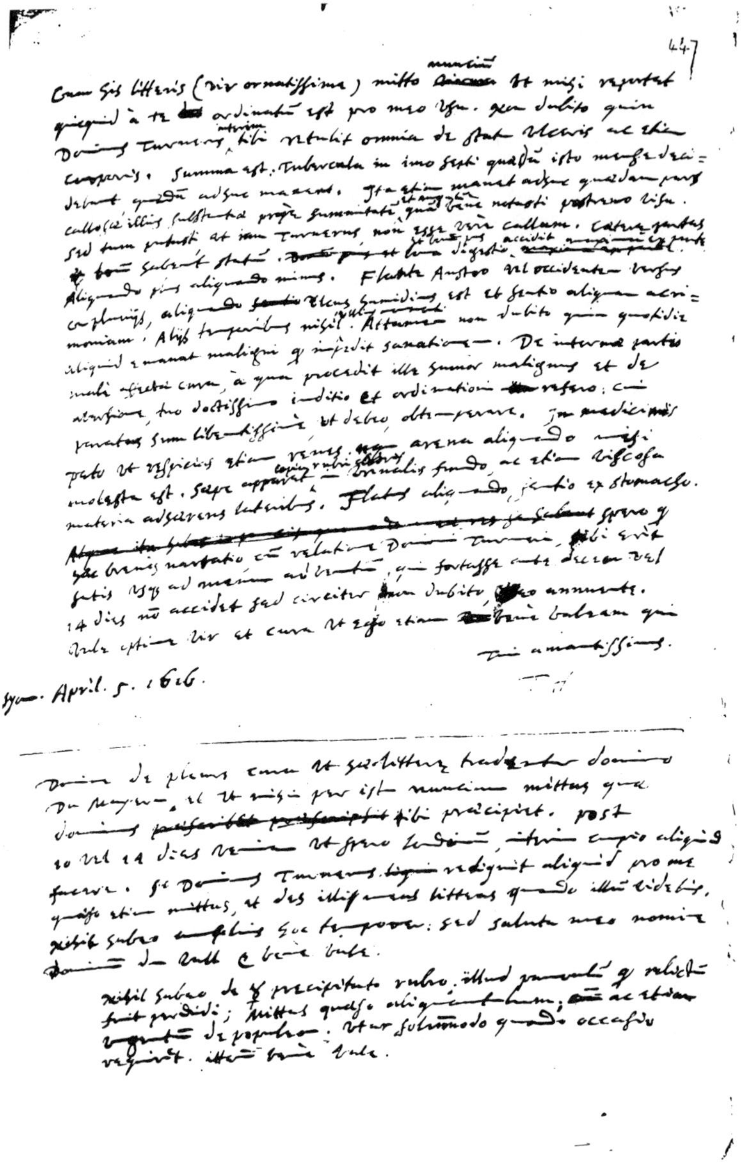

Fig. 16c Harriot's Second Letter to Mayerne

preferable to proceed from ocular examination and mutual consultation for all to be properly understood.

In a general way, this is the state of things with me. My bodily health continues rather to improve. My physique is vigorous. The urine appears healthy,[26] apart from a deposit of viscous and granular matter on the edges of the urinal,[27] and sometimes, though not at the bottom, the granules look red.[28] I am no longer so much afflicted with heats at night as I was, so that I usually sleep well.[29] Occasionally flatulencies rise from the stomach, but they are not bad.[30] Appetite is quite good all the same.

[26] In Tudor/Stuart times, the appearance of the urine was one of the primary bases for diagnoses of disease and would naturally be the primary aspect of his physical condition which the patient would report to his doctor. It is interesting to note that during these years the urinal was the symbol of the physician just as the Caduceus is today.

[27] Probably the most popular vernacular books on medicine written for the Elizabethan layman was Robert Recorde's *The Vrinall of Physick*, which went through at least four editions between 1547 and 1599 (STC 20816-19). Recorde describes the urinal as 'of pure clere glasse, not thyck nor greene in colour, without blottes or spottes in it, not flat in the bottom, nor too wyde in the necke, but widest in the myddel, and narrow styll towarde bothe the endes, like the facyon commenly of an egg, or of a very bladder being mesurably blowen (for the urinal shuld represent the bladder of a man).' This bladder shape divided the urinal into three different zones, the superior, the middle, and the inferior, each of which related to a different portion of the body. Discoloration or granular matter appearing in any of these zones indicated an unhealthy condition in (a) the head and brains, (b) the heart, lungs, kidneys, or stomach, or (c) the back or extremities. This is why Harriot so carefully described the appearance in such detail to help Dr Mayerne. For more general background material, see W. S. C. Copeman, *Doctors and Disease in Tudor Times*, London, 1960.

[28] According to Recorde, who held to the humour theory of medicine, '. . . yf the grounde be of claret coloure, ether red or blew, the token is nott good. for these blooddye coloures cum ether of too moche abundaunce of blood, other els by reason that the retentiue power is so feble, that ît can not kepe in the good humours, but suffreth them to run out.' For authority Recorde cites 'Hippocrates saith: In whose vryn there apperith grauell in the bottom, haue the stone in the bladder, or elles the raynes [kidneys], as Galen addith: but commonly if the stone be in the raynes, the grauell will be red.' A more modern interpretation would have Harriot excreting high levels of uric acid crystals or stones. Irritation might have caused slight bleeding which turned the 'granules' a red colour. Gout is often the culprit which can cause such excretion. It is highly unlikely that Harriot's cancer would have metastasized to the point where it could cause kidney problems, so this was really irrelevant.

[29] Fevers were also symptomatic in the humour theories, since the basic properties of the four humours were heat, cold, moisture, and dryness, and if any of these grew disproportionate the body was unhealthy. Cure of the disease could be achieved by normalizing the excess by prescribing the contrary, either by food, bleeding, purgation, or use of heat or cold.

[30] Flatulence appears to have been a chronic complaint of Harriot. His letter of December 1605 complained of 'great windeness in my stomack & fumings into my head rising from my spleen. . .'

As regards the ulcer. Substance and form are pretty full. The flesh is bright [vivid] without roughness. In one place or another are sometimes adhesions of hard matter which drop off after a few days. A rudiment of swellings persist at the base, too. Above and inside next to the old cleft, there is a sort of protuberance resembling flesh, sometimes whitish, sometimes not. I should have thought that it was callous matter, but for the fact that it seemed to detach itself naturally without any apparent signs of suppuration.

I wrote this ten days ago; now I have waited to make another examination of the ulcer to see what would happen to the protuberance. In the meantime, part of it has fallen off, leaving the flesh healthy. I wait to see whether the rest will come away, too. That crack is also disappearing. For the rest there is no change. As before and every day as requisite a healthy pus comes out, sign of a good suppurating process.[31]

I don't know what at the moment to say more. For the operation of the medicaments, I will defer till I come. I hope it will be next week. At which time I crave your advice for the future.

Meanwhile, do not doubt my confidence, my affection, nor my respect.
Farewell, most learned of men.

Your very affectionate and most respectful
T. H.

Syon. Novemb. 4. 1615 [Saturday]

[Added Postscript]

Think of me as your greatest of friends. Your welfare concerns me as much as mine. My health will be your glory, too, but through the Omnipotent who is the author of all good things.

As I have repeatedly said, my faith is threefold. I believe in one all-powerful God. I believe in the art of medicine to be ordained by Him. I believe in the physician as His minister. My faith is sure; my hope is firm. I look forward, however, with patience for all that may happen in its own time according to His providence. Let us drive on in earnest, battle strenuously, but in His name, and we shall overcome.

The world's glory passes away. Everything will pass away; we shall pass, you will pass, they will pass.[32]

[Additional jottings or notes]
>   pills
>   catalogues.
>   perkes.

I wrote to your pharmacist for pills. Perhaps I should take one dose before I come.

---

[31] Mayerne's notes give no mention of a discharge from Harriot's ulcerous nose.
[32] Jacquot, loc. cit., p. 169, translates this passage as follows: 'My cure will certainly be your glory, but by means of the Almighty who is the author of all good things. I believe in God Almighty. I believe in medicine as being ordained by Him. I believe in the doctor as His minister. My faith is sure, my hope is firm. Yet I wait with patience for all that may happen in its time according to His Providence. We must act earnestly, fight strenuously, but in His name, and we shall vanquish.'

Five months later, on 5 April 1616, Harriot addressed a
second letter to Mayerne through his pharmacist, Master de
Pleura, which was largely a recapitulation of the material
presented in the first. Since this letter appears on a new
sheet, it is possible that there were intermediate communi-
cations which have since been lost. Harriot's second letter
(see Fig. 16c), again roughly translated, reads as follows:[33]

With the present letter (most illustrious Sir), I send a messenger who
might report to me what you prescribe for my use. I do not doubt that
Master Turner in the meantime has told you all that concerns the state
of the ulcer and also of the body. To summarize: some of the tubercles
at the under side of the septum have disappeared during the month;
some remain. Also part of that callous matter still remains near the top
and in the angle, which you well observed at your last examination.
But at that time you thought, like Turner, that it was nòt really a
callosity. The lateral parts are in condition. A good and healthy pus
exudes largely from one part, sometimes more, sometimes less. Occasionally when the wind is in the south or west with rain some harm-
ful matter is produced which impedes cure. As for the treatment of
the internal ill-affected part from which this evil humour emanates
and how to remedy it, I rely on your most expert judgment and on
your advice, which I am ready most willingly to obey, as I must. As
regards medicines, I beg you to take into consideration the kidneys
as well, for the granules sometimes hurt. Often a reddish mass appears
at the bottom of the urinal, and also some viscous substance sticking
to the edges. Occasionally I suffer from stomach flatulence.

I hope this brief relation with Master Turner's report will suffice
you until my next visit which will probably be not sooner than in ten
or fourteen days, but about that time, no doubt, God willing. Keep
well, excellent man, and endeavour that I too be well.

Your very affectionate,
T. H.

Syon, 5 April 1616.

[Postscript for the Pharmacist]

Master de Pleura take care that this letter be conveyed to Master de
Mayerne, and by the same messenger send me whatever he prescribes.
In ten or fourteen days I hope to come to London: in the meantime I
wish to do something. If Master Turner leaves anything for me, I beg
you to send it as well, and to give him my letter when you see him.
That is all for the moment, but please greet Master de Valt in my name
and fare well.

I have no red mercury precipitate;[34] the lot I was left has been lost.

---

[33] BL Add. MS 6789, fo. 447r.

[34] Precipitate of red mercury was one of the medicines prescibed for Harriot
by Mayerne.

Please send me a small quantity, as well as some ointment of poplar.[35]
I shall use it only if the occasion should require it. Once more, fare well.

Harriot's letters to Mayerne give us some insight into the
beliefs of the two men. Harriot's descriptions of his symptoms
show that Harriot, like his physician, was relatively free from
the Galenic concern for the balance of humours and the
Aristotelian system of qualities which dictated their traditional
treatments. True, Harriot does produce details of the appearance of his urine so important to the Galenical followers, but
he does so in concrete chemical terms rather than by the
traditional locating of spots in the urinal, or in the direct
relation of his urine with the course of his illness. He seems
more concerned with the physical development of the
tumour itself, its changes, its conditions, and the apparent
effect of the chemical medications which have been applied.
In this view of his disease, Harriot like Mayerne, was ahead
of his time, utilizing an outlook which was to flower in the
last half of the seventeenth century and gradually to replace
the cabalistic and astrological view of disease among the
enlightened class of doctors.

Harriot's profession of faith, attached to his letter of
November 1615, has been seized upon by his modern friends
as at least a partial refutation of his contemporary reputation
for unorthodoxy.[36] And it is possible that it was a sincere
and heartful expression of pious belief in the divine nature
of physical cures and true honour and respect for God's
ministers through whom He operated. But it cannot be
considered as a spontaneous outpouring of faith and must,
at best, be taken with several grains of salt. Theodore Turquet
de Mayerne was a dedicated Huguenot and a devout Calvinist,
and in the light of Harriot's reputation he may well have
demanded some assurance of faith from Harriot before he
would accept his case. If so, the assurance which Harriot
produced was most conventional; it is practically a plagiarism
of the 38th chapter of Ecclesiasticus from the books of the

---

[35] Ointment of poplar (*Unguenteum populeum*) was a very old remedy used to
soothe local inflammation and in particular, skin cancer. See Robley Dunglison,
A Dictionary of Medical Science, Philadelphia, 1847, p. 1076.

[36] It has been used particularly by Stevens, Jacquot, and Strathmann, whose
works have been cited.

Apocrypha included in all Tudor and Stuart translations of the Bible. This book of proverbial wisdom concentrated on the honour due to physicians and the divine nature of their calling as they served as God's ministers on earth. Ministers of the church used this chapter widely as an argument for retaining the profession of medicine for members of the ordained clergy, as it had been during the middle ages and during the early Renaissance in England, and still remained, largely on the continent. And in those places where the Reformation had limited the authority of the clergy, these same Biblical passages were used by lay physicians as a substitute for the Hippocratic oath which many held to be a statement of pagan belief. Harriot's threefold faith – his belief in God, in God's ordination of the art of medicine, and of the physician as a minister of God – was only a recapitulation of the creed which aspiring and expanding professional organizations of physicians were attempting to foster. As such, it may well be recognized as a statement of the position which his physician would expect him to adopt rather than a freely given or original statement of personal belief.

During the period of his treatment by Mayerne, Harriot's illness, though undoubtedly painful and debilitating, apparently did not affect his ability to live an almost normal life. Though he had been branded by Mayerne as 'exceedingly melancholy', this imbalance of his humorous fluids with the excessive cold and dry of black bile (which according to the Galenical principles indicated an affinity with the element earth and a symbol of the nature of the autumn of life) did not necessarily reflect itself in his personality. Yet had it done so, this might have been only a natural reaction to the sadness and tragedy which marked this portion of his life.

On 8 August 1618 Harriot's closest friend, Sir Walter Ralegh, returned home from his tragic voyage to Guiana. Whereas he had left London in high hopes of redeeming his fortune and had promised the King to bring back the gold of the Incas, he returned in chains after a series of misfortunes which had cost him his son and heir, Walter, the loss of his ships, and the fortune he had put into the venture, and had led to the suicide of another close friend — Lawrence Keymis. On 10 August Ralegh was escorted back to the Tower, sick and racked with fever, and on the 18th he was brought before a special commission appointed to review his case. The trial was merely a formality with the outcome obvious from the first. As John Chamberlain wrote to Sir Dudley Carleton:[37] 'Yt is generally thought that Sir Walter Raleigh shall pay this new reckoning upon the old score' — his treason conviction of fifteen years earlier.

On 28 October 1618 Sir Walter was led by the Lieutenant of the Tower to the bar of the King's Bench at Westminster, where Sir Henry Yelverton, the Attorney-General, read to the Lord Chief Justice the sentence of death which had been imposed on him at Winchester in 1603 but held in abeyance at the King's pleasure. It was the King's pleasure, he indicated, that this sentence should now be carried out. There was nothing that Montague, the Lord Chief Justice, could do but accede to the King's desire, but in doing so he expressed much more sympathy and a higher regard for Ralegh than his predecessor had done at the original trial in Winchester. Addressing Ralegh he concluded:[38] 'I knowe you have bin both valiant & wise and I doubt not but you retaine both these virtues for now you shall have occascion to use them. Your faith hath hitherto bin questioned but I am resolved you are a good Christian for your booke which is an admirable worke doth testify as much.' The King's clemency being withdrawn, there was no delay in proceeding to carry out the sentence; Ralegh was beheaded early the next morning. On 31 October, John Chamberlain gave a graphic and detailed account of these events in a letter to Sir Dudley Carleton which may still give some of the atmosphere of those days:[39]

I remember that in my last letter I saide that Sir Walter Raleigh was not secure, but now he is past all peradventure for upon Thursday morning he was beheaded in the old palace at Westminster twixt the Parlement House and the church. On Wensday he was brought from the Tower to

---

[37] *The Letters of John Chamberlain*, no. 299, II, p. 167.
[38] A contemporary transcript of the proceedings is to be found in BL Harleian MS 39, fos. 360r&v, from which this is taken. Another account, nearly the same though seemingly in a later hand is included in Harleian MS 1576, fos. 212r&v.
[39] *The Letters of John Chamberlain*, no. 302, II, pp. 175–8.

the Kings-bench barre, (as they say the manner is when a man lives above a yeare and a day after he is condemned) and there demaunded what he could say for himself why the sentence pronounced against him at Winchester shold not be put in execution. The summe of his aunswer was, that the King had imployed him in his service and geven him a commission wherin he stiled him his loyall subject, and withall geven him *potestatem vitæ et necis*,which did amount to a pardon, for in all reason he must be master of his owne life that hath power over other mens: the judges replied that there is no pardon for treason by implication, wherefore he must find a better plea or undergo the sentence. Then he spake of his triall at Winchester and avowed that all or the far greater part of those that were present did acquit him in theyre conscience, and that the Kings gracious forbearing him so long, (and by for this late accident longer wold have don, even to an hundred yeares yf nature could have drawne out his life so long), did shew that his Majestie approved his innocence. But in conclusion he was willed to prepare himself, and so was delivered to the sheriffes of London and conveyed to the Gatehouse, where he spent the rest of that day in writing letters to the King and others, and in prayer with the Deane of Westminster,[40] who came the next morning at five a clocke and ministred to him the communion and when he had broken his fast about eight a clocke came to the scaffold, where he found the earles of Arundell, Oxford, Northampton, the Lord of Doncaster and divers others. He made a speach of more then halfe an howre, wherin he cleered himself of having any intelligence with Fraunce, (which had ben objected to him,) more then to save his life and hide himself from the Kinges indignation: then that he never had any yll intent towards his Majestie not so much as in thought, that he had no other pretence nor end in his last viage then the inriching of the King, the realme, himself and his followers: that he never had any undutifull speach concerning his Majestie with the runagate French phisician,[41] nor ever offered to Sir Lewes Stukeley 10000*li* to go with him into Fraunce, nor told him that the Lord Carew had geven him advise to be gon, and that he and the Lord of Doncaster wold maintain him in Fraunce, of which points he had ben accused by them, and though he protested not only to forgeve them but to pray God to forgeve them, yet he thought fit to geve men warning of such persons. To all this and much more he tooke God so often and so solemnly to witnes, that he was beleved of all that heard him. He spake somewhat of the death of the earle of Essex and how sorry he was for him, for though he was of a contrarie faction, yet he fore-saw that those who esteemed him then in that respect, wold cast him of as they did afterward. He confessed himself the greatest

[40] The Dean of Westminster was Dr Robert Tounson (or Townson), who wrote his own account of his conversations with Ralegh in a letter to Sir John Isham on 9 November. That letter is published as Appendix III in Edwards's *The Life of Sir Walter Ralegh*, II, pp. 489–92.

[41] This was Sir Lewes Stukeley's physician, a Frenchman named Mannourie, undoubtedly the 'a french man' of Harriot's note — see below.

sinner that he knew, and no marvayle as having ben a souldier, a seaman and a courtier: he excused the disfiguring of himself by the example of David who fained himself mad to avoide daunger: and never
heard yt imputed to him for a sinne. In conclusion he spake and behaved
himself so, without any shew of feare or affectation that he moved
much commiseration, and all that saw him confesse that his end was
omnibus numeris absolutus, and as far as man can discern every way
perfect. Yt will not be amisse to set downe some few passages of divers
that I have heard. The morning that he went to execution there was a
cup of excellent sacke brought him and beeing asked how he like yt,
as the fellow (saide he) that drincking of St Giles bowle[42] as he went
to Tiburn, saide yt was a goode drincke yf a man might tarrie by yt.
As he went from Westminster Hall to the Gatehouse, he espied Sir
Hugh Beeston in the throng and calling to him prayed he wold see
him to moorow: Sir Hugh to make sure worke got a letter from
Secretarie Lake to the sheriffe to see him placed conveniently, and
meeting them as they came nere to the scaffold delivered his letter
but the sheriffe by mishap had left his spectacles at home and put
the letter in his pocket. In the mean time Sir Hugh beeing thrust by,
Sir Walter bad him farewell and saide I know not what shift you will
make, but I am sure to have a place. When the hangman asked him
forgivenes he desired to see the axe, and feeling the edge he saide that
yt was a fayre sharpe medicine to cure him of all his diseases and
miseries. When he was laide downe some found fault that his face was
west-ward, and wold have his turned, whereupon rising he saide yt was
no great matter which way a mans head stoode so his heart lay right.
He had geven order to the executioner that after some short meditation
when he stretcht forth his handes he shold dispatch him. After once or
twise putting foorth his handes, the fellow out of timerousnes (or what
other cause) forbearing, he was faine to bid him strike, and so at two
blowes he tooke of his head, though he stirred not a whit after the first.
The people were much affected at the sight insomuch that one was
heard say that we had not such another head to cut of. Another wisht
the head and braines to be upon S. N. shoulders.[43] . . . Yt is saide we

---

[42] McClure adds the explanatory footnote: 'At St. Giles in the Fields, 'prisoners
convayed from the City of London towardes Teyborne, there to be executed for
treasons, fellonies, or other trespasses, were presented with a great Bowle of Ale,
thereof to drinke at theyr pleasure, as to be theyr last refreshing in this life'
(Stow, *Survey of London*, ii, p. 91.)

[43] This is augmented by Fuller in his *Worthies of England*, III. 175-6, where
he says 'One Mr. Wiemark, a wealthy man, great novellant, and constant Pauls-
walker, hearing the news that day of the beheading of Sir Walter Ralegh, "His
head," said he, "would do very well on the shoulders of Sir Robert Naunton,
secretary of state." These words were complained of, and Wiemark summoned
to the privy council, where he pleaded for himself, that he intended no disrespect
to Mr. Secretary, whose known worth was above all detraction; only he spake in
reference to an old proverb, "Two heads are better than one." And so for the
present he was dismissed. Not long after, when rich men were called on for a

shold have some declaration set out touching the causes of his execution at this time, but whether his protestations and manner of dieng may alter the case God knowes: for he died very religiously, and every way like a Christian, insomuch that the Deane of Westminster (they say) commends him excedingly and sayes he was as redy and as able to geve as take instruction. His execution was the more remarkeable for that yt fell out the day of the Lord Maiors triumph, though yt began with a tragedie, and being a reasonable fayre morning grew very fowle all the day after.

Ralegh's heroic conduct at his execution not only impressed those present to see it, but quickly became the talk not only of London but of all of England. As I have written elsewhere, on this day 'Sir Walter Ralegh the man was beheaded and Sir Walter Ralegh the legend was born.'[44]

Thomas Harriot was among those present in Westminster yard on the October morning of Ralegh's execution, probably at the back of the crowd as Ralegh had been at the execution of Essex. This fact is attested to by a half-sheet of wrinkled and battered foolscap which he kept among his miscellaneous papers, and which remains in the collection now in the British Library.[45] Obviously torn from another sheet and carrying writing that is scratched and blurred as though written while being held in his hand, this paper greatly excited Henry Stevens who first noted it and published a fairly accurate version of it.[46] But Stevens erroneously interpreted Harriot's notes as those to be used by Ralegh for his speech:

[Ralegh] had prepared himself, and is said to have consulted a *'Note of Remembrance'* which he held in his hand while speaking. it is possible, nay, probable that this very same *'Note'* still survives in 'paper saving' Harriot's 'waste' ....It is thought to possess internal evidence of having been drawn out *before* the speech, and is not therefore Hariot's jottings of remembrance *after* it. But positive proof is wanting.

It is beyond all doubt, however, in the well-known handwriting of

---

contribution to St Paul's, Wiemark at the council-table subscribed a hundred pounds; but Mr. Secretary told him two hundred were better than one; which betwixt fear and charity, Wiemark was fain to subscribe.'

[44] See the author's 'Sir Walter Ralegh and Thomas Harriot', in *Thomas Harriot, Renaissance Scientist*, p. 16.

[45] BL Add. MS fo. 533ʳ.

[46] *Thomas Hariot and his Associates*, pp. 134–5.

Hariot, and is presumed to be the 'note of remembrance' *for* the speech, made in the Gate House, probably from dictation, during the night before the execution. It appears as if hurriedly penned with a blunt quill, and is on a narrow strip of thin foolscap paper such as Harriot used. It is about twelve inches long and nearly four inches wide, about one-third of the lower part of the paper being blank. There is no heading, date, or anything else on the paper. . . .

With some minor differences from Stevens's readings, Harriot's note reads as follows:

> Two fits of an agew.
> Thankes to god.
> of calling god to witnes.
>   note
> His pa [c.o.]
> That
>   He speake iustly & truely.
>   Touchinge his [c.o.]
>   that
>   1). Concerning his loyalty to the
>   King.   French agent.
>   & commission from the
>   french King.
>   2). of slanderous speeches touching
>   his maᵗʸ.   a french man
>   Sʳ. L. Stukeley.
>   3). Sʳ L. Stukely.   My lo: carewe
>   4). Sʳ L. Stukely.   My lo: of Danchaster
>   5). S. L. St: Sʳ Edward perham.
> 6.)
>   S. L.: St. A letter on London hy way.
>   10,000ˡⁱ.
>   7.) Mine of Guiana.
>   8.) Came back by constreynt.
>   9.) My L. of Arundell.
>   10.) Company vsed ill in the voyadge.
>   11.) Spotting of his face & conter-
>   fetting sicknes.
>   12.) The E. of Essex.
> _____
>   Lastly. he desired the company
>   to ioyne with him in prayer. &c.

It is difficult to see how Stevens could reason that these notes were prepared before the speech 'from internal evidence'. Both the fourth line ('That He speake iustly & truely') and the final two lines ('Lastly. he desired the company to ioyne with him in prayer. &c.') show Harriot writing of Ralegh in the third person as an outside viewer of the scene. Nor is there any reason why Ralegh should have dictated his 'Note of Remembrance' to Harriot; he had ample paper and supplies with him in the Gatehouse, and he spent much of the evening before the execution in writing letters, some of which still survive. No contemporary evidence shows Harriot spending any time with Ralegh during these final hours, though many accounts of those hours remain. Rather the note shows that Harriot was present during Ralegh's final moments, and that he was moved by the scene is evidenced by his retention of this memento, even though he destroyed most of his papers dealing with Ralegh and his affairs.

Though this Harriot note cannot be reviewed romantically as 'the note' which Ralegh carried to his execution as Stevens portrayed it, it nevertheless does have real value for the historian.[47] As has been frequently pointed out, many reconstructions have been made of Ralegh's final speech from contemporary accounts, such as those of Thomas Lorkin, Dean Townson, Archbishop Sancroft, and John Chamberlain, down to the present biographers of Ralegh from Edwards to Lacey, so that the historical event has become a matter of folklore. Comparison of all these versions show that nearly all contain the same subject materials. But no two agree in the exact wording of any subject, nor in the exact order in which these subjects were presented. No account indicates major points which are not listed by Harriot. Harriot's notes, therefore, taken at the speech instead of reconstructed from memory later as were the other accounts, though not detailed enough to give any information about the exact words used by Ralegh, do establish the exact order in which he presented his various arguments. They do, furthermore, by giving eye-witness testimony to the event, establish that the stories which have come down by tradition are a relatively accurate account of what actually transpired in that fateful Thursday in October 1618.

[47] 'Sir Walter Ralegh and Thomas Harriot', loc. cit. See also Barnett J. Sokol, 'Thomas Hariot's Notes on Sir Walter Raleigh's Address from the Scaffold', *Manuscripts* (Summer 1974), pp. 198–206.

The excitement in London about the fall of Ralegh's star was superseded, both at court and at Syon House, by new excitement caused by the sighting of the great 'blazing star' (the Comet of 1618) in November, less than a month after Ralegh's execution. John Chamberlain, writing from London on 21 November to Sir Dudley Carleton, linked the two together:[48]

We are so full still of Sir Walter Raleigh that almost every day brings foorth somewhat in this kind, besides divers ballets whereof some are called in, and the rest such poore stuffe as are not worth the over-looking. But when this heat is somewhat allayed, we shall have a declaration touching him, that shall contradict much of that he pro-tested with so great asserveration,[49] but the proofes had neede be very pregnant and demonstrative, or els they will hardly prevaile. . . .On Wensday [18 November] we had no Star-chamber by reason of the Lord Chauncellors indisposition. That was the first day we tooke notice here of the great blasing-star, though yt was observed at Oxford a full weeke before: yt is now the only subject almost of our discourse, and not so much as litle children but as they go to schoole talke in the streets that yt foreshewes the death of a king or a quene or some great warre towards. Upon which occasion (I thincke) yt was geven out all this towne over that the Quene was dead on Thursday: but yesterday I heard for certain that she is in a fayre way of amendment: and looked out of her window to see the hunting of a foxe.

Harriot had seen the Comet earlier. Among his manu-scripts is a chart showing the course of the Comet in which he indicates a first sighting at 'London and Syon' on Sunday, 15 November.[50] And, as we have seen earlier,[51] Harriot immediately immersed himself in this study to escape from the pain of the loss of his oldest and dearest friend.

There was much illness in court during the winter of 1618/19, and Theodore Turquet de Mayerne was so busy attending his noble patients that he could give Harriot scant attention. Though she refused to accept her disease as serious, Queen Anne was wasting away from the dropsy, and the

---

[48] *The Letters of John Chamberlain*, no. 305, II, p. 185.

[49] Chamberlain in undoubtedly referring to Sir Lewes Stukeley's defence of himself against Ralegh's attacks: *To the Kings most excellent maiestie, the humble petition of Sir L. Stucley touching the bringing up of Sir W. Raleigh*, 1618 (STC 23401).

[50] Petworth MSS HMC 241/VII, fo. 20.   [51] See Ch. X, p. 423.

King was suffering from what Chamberlain called 'a shrewde fit of the stone.'[52] The Queen finally succumbed on 2 March 1618/19, and her body was transported to Denmark House to await burial. This was handled badly and in exceedingly poor taste. James was insistent that there would be no funeral until arrangements could be made which would equal or surpass the lavish funeral that had been accorded to Queen Elizabeth. This called for raising considerable money, and James remained in his bed in New Market, collecting revenues wherever he could find them. He decided to hold off ceremonies until after Easter which came on 28 March that year. This decision caused some consternation in the city, particularly among London entertainers and 'to the great hindrance of our players, which are forbidden to play so long as the body is above ground.'[53] Further delays followed, and the funeral was not held until 13 May, by which time the nation was weary of grief. Chamberlain, who attended and reported the affair to Sir Dudley Carleton, thought it was a poor show:[54]

Yt were to no purpose to make any long description of the funerall which was but a drawling tedious sight, more remarqueable for number then for any other singularitie, there beeing 280 poore women besides an army of meane fellowes that were servants to the Lordes and others of the traine, and though the number of Lordes and Ladies were very great, yet me thought altogether they made but a poore shew, which perhaps was because they were apparrelled all alike, or that they came laggering all along even tired with the length of the way and waight of theyre clothes, every Lady having twelve yardes of broade cloth about her and the countesses sixteen. . , . The Prince came after the arch-bishop of Caunterburie (who was to make the sermon) and next before the corps, that was drawne by sixe horses. Yt was full sixe a clocke at night before all the solemnitie was don at church, where the herse is to continue till the next terme, the fairest and stateliest that I thincke was ever seene there.

During the spring of 1619 Harriot occupied his time in organizing his mathematical papers and consolidating some of his scientific observations. It is probable that he sensed that the end was near, and he wished to put some of his affairs in order. Among his concerns were his observations on the

[52] *The Letters of John Chamberlain*, no. 320, II, p. 220.
[53] Ibid. no. 321, p. 222.   [54] Ibid., no. 327, p. 237.

theory of the oblique impact of elastic spheres which had occupied his attention a dozen years before.[55] The original manuscript of nine pages, meticulously written in India ink in Latin and with careful illustrations, is still preserved among the Harriot papers retained at Petworth House. It bears the title *De reflexione corporum rotundorum Poristica duo*, and was apparently written at the request of Henry Percy, Harriot's patron. A copy of this paper is preserved among the Harley manuscripts in the British Library, to which is attached a letter now missing from the original. This letter reads:[56]

Sir: when Master Warner & Master Hues were last at Syon, it happened that I was perfecting my auntient ~~papers~~ [c.o.] notes of the doctrin of reflections of bodyes. Vnto whom I imparted the Magisteryes ~~of~~ [c.o.] thereof, to the end to make your Lordship acquainted with them as occasion serued. And least that some perticulars might be mistaken or forgotten, I thought best since to set them downe in writing, whereby allso nowe at times of leasure when your minde is free from matters of greater waight you may thinke & consider of them, if you please. Yt had bin verie conuenient I confesse to haue written of this doctrine more at large & particularlie to haue set downe the first principles with such other of elementall propositions, as all doubtes might haue bin ~~cleered~~ [c.o.] preuented; but my infirmitie is yet so troublesome that I am forced, as well that, as other tracts to let alone till time of better abilitie. / In the meane time I haue made choyce of two propositions in whose explication you shall finde I hope the summe of all, that of this argument is reasonable to be deriued.

---

[55] Because this is one of the few finished documents by Harriot, it has received more attention by modern historians of science than most of his papers. For transcripts of this document and different evaluations of it, see Jon V. Pepper's 'Harriot's Manuscript on the Theory of Impacts,' *Annals of Science*, XXXIII (1976), pp. 131-51, Martin Kalmar's 'Thomas Harriot's *De Reflectione Corporum Rotundorum*: an Early Solution of the Problem of Impact', *Archive for History of Exact Sciences*, XVI (January 1977), 201-30, and Johannes Lohne, 'Essays on Thomas Harriot', Part I, 'Billiard Balls and Laws of Collision', pp. 189-229, *Archive for History of Exact Sciences*, XX (1979), 189-312. Texts and interpretations of these differ. Pepper takes his text from the Petworth copy — Petworth MS HMC 241/VI^a, fos. 23-31; Kalmar used the copy in BL Harley MS 6002, fos. 16^v-21. Lohne assumes that Harriot was working with billiard balls, working out the way in which impact worked on balls rolling on a flat surface. He indicates that Northumberland was an avid billiards fan, but gives no evidence for this assertion. Both Pepper and Kalmar consider Harriot's work to be more general and theoretical than this.

[56] BL Harley MS 6002, fo. 21. An inaccurate copy of this was published by Halliwell in his *A Collection of Letters*, 1841, p. 45.

And if any doubtes doe arise either of the hypotheses therin vsed, or of the concomitantes and contengenses [contingencies?] therein allso intimated; allthough vpon due consideration onely thay may be resolued: yet because I am before hand in consideration of these matters, I shall be ready when I haue notice of them, to giue your Lordship full satisfaction for your ease. / And seeing that my purpose, god willing, is within a few dayes to see your Lordship, I cease from more wordes resting, &c.

Syon. June 13. 1619.

Not only does the internal evidence of this letter attest to its authenticity (Harriot's illness was well advanced and painful by June 1619 and he found work extremely difficult), but the subscript also gives testimony to its probable correctness. Whoever the penman was who made this copy, he added the following note: 'Master Hariots letter to my Lord Northumberland: annexed to his treatise of Reflections: lent me to transcribe by Sir Thomas Alesburie.' Certainly Alesbury was one of the very few who would have had access to this manuscript, and permission to copy it.

But Northumberland, too, had more serious matters on his mind than the theory of impacts. His wife, Dorothy, strong-minded sister of the Earl of Essex, was very ill. Though their marriage had frequently been stormy, the imprisonment of Percy had brought the two closer together, and they had learned to respect each other's virtues more. On 3 August 1619 Dorothy Percy died, and she was buried at Petworth on the 14th of the same month. John Chamberlain passed the story on to Carleton:[57]

As we came from Ditton we passed along by Thistleworth where Mistris Jones related the whole storie of the Lady of Northumberlands siknes and death in such pittifull termes as might rather make us laugh then weepe, as that the furie of the feaver debated much the day before she died, insomuch that the phisicians were confident of her recoverie, that she went away like the snuffe of a candle, and that there was never so fayer a corps seene for white and red, with a number of suchlike phrase that I cannot remember, but the truth is she is much lamented: and her Lord takes the losse so impatiently as is not credible but to those that see yt, specially and continually condemning himself of ingratitude towards her that had deserved so well and worthilie of him, insomuch that those about him are put to an yll

[57] *The Letters of John Chamberlain*, no. 334, II, p. 334.

office, and are faine to remember and rip up the thwartings and crosses between them thereby to counterbalance and lessen his grief; but no doubt *dies minuet dolorem*, yf nothing els will. . .

Harriot at Syon, and not at the Tower with the Earl, was probably spared most of this passion of the moment, but because the two were such close friends and communication was so direct, it is most likely that he did forget his own illness to visit the Tower to console his madly grieving patron.

Harriot's illness was growing progressively worse during this year, to the point where he was prevented from further scientific investigations or even serious review of his past activities. There is no calculation, reading note, or observation among his manuscripts dated after the 15 December 1618 observations of the Comet of 1618, and his letter to Northumberland the following June (if only a copy). Yet he did apparently maintain some interest and activity about his library. A bill for the purchase of forty-two books at a total cost of £13 15s., dated 31 October 1617,[58] shows that he paid £5 on 29 July 1618 and returned the folio volume 'Alexander de Alexandro fo. 269' on 13 July 1619. This entry is the last record of Harriot's activity until he appears in June 1621 on his deathbed, composing his last will and testament.

In his final illness, probably in 1620, a new physician was enlisted to the service of the dying Harriot. Dr Alexander Read (or Reid, or Rhead) (1586?–1641) was a much younger man than Mayerne, but one who had already considerable fame as a distinguished anatomist and surgeon. A Scot in both birth and disposition, Read received his education at the University of Aberdeen, graduating MA in 1600. Like most medical men of his day, he continued his studies abroad, studying surgery in France before returning to England in 1618 to practise medicine at Holt on the Welsh border. According to the account of his life in the *DNB* by D'Arcy Power (indexed under 'Reid'):

On one occasion he was asked by Lord Gerard, near Newport, to see his tailor, whose leg had been injured, and he cut it off above the knee with a joiner's whip-saw, stopping haemorrhage with a mixture of

---

[58] Petworth MS 241/IV, fos. 9r&v.

unslaked lime, umber, whites of eggs, and hare's fur. The man lived as a pensioner of Lord Gerard for many years, and the success of this operation, performed with no instruments of medicine but what the place afforded, increased Reid's fame as a surgeon. . .

But Dr Read was already well known as an anatomist and had written at least two very advanced treatises on dissection and the human body. The first, *The Manuall of the anatomy; or Dissection of the body of man*,[59] had been published in 1612, and had given the commentary which would normally accompany the dissection of a corpse for the instruction of physicians. A second book, entitled Σωματογραφια ἀνθρωπινη, *or a description of the Body of Man*,[60] followed in 1616. This second volume contained a large collection of woodcut illustrations to accompany the text of his first, with detailed pictures of all the bones, muscles, veins, arteries, nerves, sense and digestive organs, together with the Greek and Latin names, to aid the physician to do his own dissection or to follow the dissection of others.

About the time he was called upon to treat Harriot, Read was at the height of his fame. On 28 May 1620 he was incorporated MA at Oxford, and the following day King James created him Doctor of Physic by Royal decree. Though his case notebooks do not remain, it is possible to follow some of his ideas and the treatment he would have accorded Harriot, who by now was willing to entrust himself to a doctor known for his daring and drastic cures. Read's understanding of the nose and its functions can be gathered from his description of it in his *Manuall of the anatomy*:[61]

CAP. XXI. *Of the Nose.*

The skin cleaveth so fast to the muscles and cartilages, that it can hardly be severed without renting.

The muscles are seven: wherof one is common and six proper.

---

[59] *. . .containing the enumeration and description of the parts of the same, which usually are shewed in the publick anatomicall exercises*, London, printed by R. Bishop for Francis Constable, 1612 (not in STC). This was reprinted in 1638 (STC 20784).

[60] *. . .By Artificiall Figures representing the members, and fit termes expressing the same. Set forth either to pleasure or to profite those who are addicted to this Study*, [London] Printed by W. Iaggard dwelling in Barbican, and are there to be sold. 1616 (STC 20782).

[61] This is taken from the 1638 edn., pp. 461–5.

They only move the cartilages of the nose. The veins come from the external jugular. The arteries from the saporals, and the sinews from the third paire. The bones of the nose are in number foure: the cartilage fiue: the inner membrane which covereth the sides of the nose proceedeth from the *dura mater*, passing thorow the holes of the *ethmoides*. The muscle membrane, draweth in the nostrils. The haires straine (as it were) the aire, and keepe out insects.

From the red and spongius fleshy portions, with the which the distances of the spongius bones are filled, the *polypus* springeth. The upper part of the nose which is bony, is called *dorsam nasi*: the ridge, *spine*: the laterall parts, where the cartilages are, are called *allae* or *pinnae*: The tip of the nose, *globulus*, *orbiculus* and *pyrula*: The fleshy part next to the upper lip, *columna*.

The uses of the nose are eight. 1. By it the aire is taken into the braine, for the generation of animal spirits. 2. The lungs draw in by it the aire, for the refreshing of the heart, and the generation of the vitall spirits. 3. That by it smels might be carried to *processus mammillares*. 4. By it the braine dischargeth excrements. 5. It furthereth the speech. 6. It beautifieth the face. 7. It parteth the eyes, that one should not see the other: which would have hindred the sight. It is a defense unto them also, and staieth the visible *species*. By fleering up it expresseth anger: and in the Hebrew tongue is taken for anger.

Shortly after Harriot's death, Read was named a candidate to the College of Physicians, and the following year was made a member. He was appointed as a lecturer on anatomy at Barber-Surgeon's Hall on 28 December 1632 and lectured there for a number of years. These lectures he published in 1635, and it is in this work that he preserved the account of his treatment of Harriot. Read's lectures, sent to the printer in August 1634 as he was leaving this post (according to his dedication of the work), had the elaborate title:[62] *THE Chirurgicall Lectures of Tumors and Vlcers. DELIVERED on Tusedayes* [sic] *appointed for these Exercises, and keeping of their Courts in the Chirurgeons Hall these three yeeres past, viz. 1632, 1633, and 1634. By ALEXANDER READ Doctor of Physick, and one of the Fellowes of the Physitians College of LONDON.*

Harriot's illness is commented upon in Treatise 2, 'A treatise of Vlcers', Lecture 26. This section Read heads: 'Lect. XXVI. *Of Ozaena*.',[63] and comments 'Of all the ulcers

---

[62] *. . . LONDON. Printed by I. H. for Francis Constable and E. B. and are to be sold at the signe of the Crane in Pauls Churchyard. 1635* (STC 20781).

of the nose, I will onely speake of Ozaena, omitting the rest.'[64] Later on in his discussion he continues:[65]

Cancerous ulcers also seaze upon this part [i.e. in the nostrils, about the holes of the *ethmoides*]. This grief hastened the end of that famous Mathematician, Mr. *Hariot*, which whom I was acquainted but a short time before his death; whom at one time, together with Mr. *Hughes*, who wrote of the Globes, Mr. *Warner*, and Mr. *Turperley*, the Noble Earle of *Northumberland*, the favourer of all good learning, and Maecenas of learned men, maintained while he was in the Tower, for their worth and various literature. But seeing those documents which I delivered for the curation of cancers already, may suffice, I will only set down the description of an effectual water in this griefe. . . .

The lotion which Read gives as his prescription for this ailment[66] is only a soothing lotion with much less palliative or curative powers than those previously used by Dr Mayerne. It is quite probable, however, that Read recognized the hopelessness of Harriot's situation, since his general 'Prognosticks' for Ozaena were anything but optimistic.[67]

    I. All sorts of Ozaena are of a maligne nature, because such is the humor which produceth each one of them.
    II. All such ulcers are of hard curation: First because the braine doth still afford plentie of these corrupt humors. Secondly because the part affected is of a moyst temperature. Thirdly because the facultie of internall medicaments, which are prescribed for correcting of the of the malignitie of the humors, is much abated before it come to the heart.

---

[63] This use of the term precedes by more than twenty years the earliest use recorded in the *New English Dictionary on a Historical Basis*. There the word is defined as '1. *Path.* A fetid muco-purulent discharge from the nose, due to ulcerative disease of the mucous membrane, frequently with necrosis of the bone.' The word derives from the Greek, based on the evil odour given off by the discharge.

[64] Ibid., p. 299.

[65] Ibid., p. 307.

[66] Ibid., p. 307. Read's prescription is:

R_x *spermat. ranar. et limacum, an. 1b. ii.*
    gemmar. quercus, et hedera terrest. an iiii.
    Extilletur aqua e stillatorio communi, unde prolici solet
      aquarosacea in recipiens, cui immissae sint caphurae
      calcinate ii.
    Inject this water into the nose, and lay to the sores either double clouts, or lint moystned in this water, as you shall think most fit, morning and evening.

[67] Ibid., p. 301.

III. An Ozaena, a symptome of the Pox is more easily cured, than that which is a disease it selfe: First, because the last commeth neerer to a cancerous qualitie than the first: Secondly, because we have more sure medicaments against the first than we have against the second: if this kind of ulcer continue long, it taketh away the sense of smelling.

IV. That which is apparent is of an easier curation than that which is hid or latent: seeing then the ancient Authors, with an unanimous consent, pronounce the curation of an Ozaena to be difficult, in setting down the method of curing this griefe, my part is to shew unto you what meanes moderne practicers by their industrie have found out to remove this doubt of hardnesse of curing. . . .

By the time that Read saw Harriot, then, he found a malignant cancer giving off a fetid discharge and eroding away the bony structure of the face. To him it was apparent that a positive cure was remote if not impossible.

According to his discourse, however, treatment fell into two classes — the physical treatment and, as a last resort, the surgical (or chirurgical) excision of the cancer. Physical treatment fell into three types. First were those of diet. The patient suffering from Ozaena must 'shun all meats, which are either of an hard concoction, or afford a corrupt and evill juyce.'[68] He must 'use great moderation in the use of wholesome and convenient food', which (if we believe Harriot's comments about moderation of the Virginia Indians) should not have been difficult for the abstemious Harriot. Even total fasting was to be encouraged, since this 'dries the habit of the body . . . furthers concoction . . . [and] digests vapors that otherwise would mount to the head.' These remedies should relieve the flow, but if they did not, the second stage of phlebotomy or bleeding should be attempted.

Phlebotomy, or opening a vein to let the blood flow, was a practice of the Galenists treating imbalance in the bodily humours. Though Mayerne and others of the iatro-chemical school did not favour the practice, obviously in this Read was traditional. Bleeding, he argued, was necessary since[69]

Phlebotomie impaireth the quantitie of the humours contained in the masse of the bloud: secondly, it maketh way for the receiving of better

[68] These treatments are described in pp. 301-4, ibid.   [69] Ibid., p. 304.

bloud into the vessels, which of a necessitie must ensue after the appointing of a convenient diet, and exquisite purging of the body, which immediately after Phlebotomie is to be performed.

To accomplish these desirable goals, 'If the body be plethorick: First open the Cephalica of the right arme in the Spring and Summer; but of the left, in the Harvest and Winter: Then three or foure dayes afterward, open the veines under the tongue, which will serve for derivation of the humor, as the former die for revulsion of the same.' Purgation, to expel further the undesirable humours was next to follow. In a case involving a disease of the head, as in Harriot's case, this must be achieved by 'catharticall medicaments', since 'vomitive medicaments are not so convenient as the catharticall in the diseases of the head . . . [since] Vomitions . . . send up vapors to the head.' Purgatives used were many: either the vegetable variety of which Read recommended 'Agarick, Turpentum, Coloquint, Scammonie, the black Ellabore' to be given in pills or potions (recipes for which he gave), or mineral emetics 'mostly commonly taken from Antimonie and Mercurie.' Once this series had been completed (and repeated, if it appeared helpful) the physician had exhausted his remedies. Further treatment depended upon the physician's friend, the surgeon.

Though he had himself achieved fame as a surgeon, Read was noticeably reticent about the effectiveness of this art in a case like Harriot's. But though he was dealing with a malign disease whose cure was doubtful at best, it was the duty of the doctor, as a last resort, to employ every possible strategy. Read quoted Hippocrates as his defence that 'Against extreme griefes, extreme remedies are best.'[70] And Read's surgical treatments were extreme by any standard. Again, Read outlined two stages: cauterization and excision. Cauterization called for the application of caustics to burn away the tissue; this was helpful in curing an Ozaena but 'this mean is only used when the sore is rebellious to powerful ordinary meanes.' Two ways were proposed for the application

---

[70] Ibid., p. 308. This section on cauterization and surgery follows immediately on Read's introduction of Harriot as his example, so there can be little doubt but that in these final steps Read was outlining his last treatment of Harriot just before his death.

of the lye to the sore: to apply the lye directly or in an unguent form:[71]

... the first is made of the strongest soap lees [the old spelling of 'lyes'] boyled to the consistency of a soft stone. The second is made of the like lee, and unslaked lime, boyled to the forme of a firm unguent. The first is best in Tumors which possesse the convex part. The second is most convenient, if they be in parts concave...

Purpose of the introduction of caustic lye to the sore was either 'to cause an eschar [scar] by impressing it upon the ulcer' or 'to dry the ulcer, by often applying of it, still desisting before the party feele any paine, by reason of extreme heat.' The lye was applied with a glass pipe. If the pipe end by which the lye was applied was closed, it would dry the ulcer only. If the pipe end were open, so that the raw lye would coat the wound, a scar would be formed.

The last resort of the surgeon if all else failed was to turn to the surgeon's knife for removal of the diseased parts. In that time, with no means of deadening the patient's pain and with no knowledge of antisepsis chances of success were minimal, and the operation was hard on the patient and on the doctor as well. As Read pointed out:[72] 'The Chirurgeon who is to doe this, ought to be resolute, cheerful in countenance and speeches, and no wayes scrupulous: otherwise he shall make the Patient dismayed, and fearful "Which [here he quotes Galen] doth much weaken and abate the courage of the Patient."' Undoubtedly Harriot's suffering was great under the ministrations of the resolute and cheerful Scottish physician and surgeon who took over in the absence of the less drastic and more modern Mayerne. But as Read pointed out, real knowledge about the cause and treatment of carcinoma of the nose had advanced but little since the time of the ancient and classic doctors. Hopes for a cure were slight by both doctor and patient, and the patient, like the doctor, could do no more than bear his suffering with fortitude and express his faith in the righteous cause of any heavenly spirit who might look after him.

Although Read indicated that Harriot's cancer 'hastened

[71] This whole process is discussed in the general section on treatment, ibid., p. 42.
[72] Ibid.

the end', it is difficult to assess the actual cause of his death. Certainly the evidence of his will shows that his brain was not affected and that he remained to the end alert and in possession of all his rational faculties. More likely, a long and painful decline took its toll of a vital organ, or infection caused fatal complications. But his decline was rapid, and the end came on 2 July 1621, not, as was long supposed, at his home at Syon in Isleworth, but in the heart of London, where he may have gone for treatment from his doctors, as a visitor in the home of a long-time friend, Thomas Buckner, who lived on Threadneedle Street near the Royal Exchange.

Three days before his death on 'ye nine and twentieth daie of June, in the years of our Lord God 1621' Harriot dictated, with unusual logic and clear-headed detail, his last will and testament. This document is undoubtedly one of the most valuable documents he has left, giving as it does specific information about his personal affairs and his own wishes regarding the use and disposition of his lifelong accumulation of manuscripts. A large number of scholars interested in Harriot and his work had sought this document over the centuries, but because of the place of his death and the manner of filing of wills, no one found it. Stephen Rigaud made a vigorous search, but found no trace, and Miss Agnes Clerke, preparing the biography of Harriot for the *Dictionary of National Biography* in 1885 wrote that 'Harriot's will was not found', a statement which remains in later editions uncorrected. But the will was found, even before Miss Clerke wrote, by Henry Stevens, and a copy of the certified copy was appended to his manuscript of *Thomas Hariot, the Mathematician, the Philosopher, and the Scholar*, printed in 1900 after his death by his son and literary executor, Henry N. Stevens.[73]

[73] Harriot's will, one of the most valuable documents remaining for details of his life and work, was vigorously sought after before it was finally discovered by Stevens. For though records of his burial at St. Christopher's existed, they had not been found by the members of the Royal Society, S. P. Rigaud, Agnes Clerke, and the others, who assumed Harriot to have died at Syon House, Isleworth. When finally located, in the Archdeaconry Court of London, two copies were found – a probated copy which was on file, and a copy of this in the *Registry of the Archdeaconry Court of London, 1618–1626/7*, fos. 71$^{r&v}$, 72$^{r&v}$. Stevens

Harriot's will commences with a typical testamentary identification:[74]

In the name of God Amen   ye nine and twentieth daie of June, in the year of our Lord God 1621 And in ye yeares of the raigne of our soueraigne Lord James by the grace of God of England Scotland ffraunce & Ireland the nineteenth And of Scotland the fower and fiftieth I *Thomas Harriotts* of Syon in the County of Middlesex gentleman being troubled in bodie with informitie. But of perfecte minde & memorie Laude & praise be giuen to Almight God ~~my maker~~ [c.o.] for the same doe make & ordayne this my last will and testament. In manner and forme following (viz[t]) . . .

The deletion of the two words, 'my maker' in the certified copy — not included in the register copy — could be interpreted as a hesitation of the dying Harriot to accept the full doctrine of orthodox Anglican belief. But it is much more likely that this is only a scribal misplacement of words for the will proceeds into the traditional commitment of his soul in words which go beyond the essential in terms of explicit doctrine:

First & principally I Committe my Soule in to the hands of Almighty God my maker [here is where those words belong] and of his sonne Jesus Christe my Redeemer, of whose merritts by his grace wrought in mee by the holy Ghoste I doubte not but that I am made partaker, to th'end that I may enioye the kingdome of heauen prepared for the electe.

Just how much of this piety must be attributed to the conventions of the last testament of a Jacobean gentleman cannot be determined, since the form varies widely in

---

made a copy of the probated copy and this was published in 1900. The will was rediscovered in 1906 by Henry R. Plomer who evidently had not found Stevens's book, and he printed it a second time in 'The Will of Thomas Harriot, Mathematician and Astronomer (1580-1621)', in *The Home Counties Magazine*, VIII (1906), 240-7. It was published for the third time in 1967 by Rosalind Tanner in her article 'Thomas Harriot as Mathematician, a Legacy of Hearsay', in *Physis*, IX (1967), 235-47. A photo-reproduction of the probated copy is included in the author's *A Source Book for the Study of Thomas Harriot*, New York, Arno Press, 1981. Dr Tanner has made additional comments on the will in 'The Study of Thomas Harriot's Manuscripts, I. Harriot's Will', a paper which she gave at the first Thomas Harriot Seminar at Oxford on Friday, 10 Nov. 1967. This was published in *History of Science*, VI (1968 for 1967), 1-16.

[74] Quotations from the will are taken from the probated copy, as being closest to the original.

different wills. But 'doubting Thomas' or 'that Devil Harriot' did not object to the inclusion of this doctrine at any rate, and thus puts a conventional front on his final message on earth.

Next Harriot disposed of his earthly remains. If he were to die in London his will was 'that my bodie ~~may~~ [c.o.] bee interred in the same parishe Churche of the house where I lye', that is St. Christopher's parish, where, indeed, it was finally buried. But cautiously Harriot deferred to the wishes and good judgment of his executors or his patron, 'the right honorable my very good Lord the Earle of Northumberland if it bee his pleasure to haue me buryed at Isleworth in ye County of Middlesex.' Should he leave his sick bed and return to Syon House, 'I doe ordayne that my buriall be at ye said Church of Ilseworth [*sic*] without question.'

Harriot next turned to the disposition of his property. Naturally, he first thought of Northumberland, his patron:

Item   I will & bequeath vnto the aforesaid Earle One woodden Boxe full or neere full of drawne Mappes standing nowe at the Northeast windowe of that Roome which is Called the parlor of my house in Syon, And if it pleaseth his Lordship to haue anie other Mappes or Chartes drawne by hand or printed Or anie Bookes or other thinges that I haue I desire my Executors that hee maue haue them according to his pleasure at reasonable rates excepte my Mathematicall papers in anie other sorte then is hereafter menccioned. Excepting alsoe some other thinges giuen away in Legacies hereafter alsoe specified.

Recollection of the box of maps and charts in his library brought to mind other valuable items borrowed or having especial value for one of his friends. To his friend Sir Robert Sidney, Viscount Lisle he bequeathed:

One Boxe of papers being nowe vppon the table in my Library at Syon, conteyning fiue quires of paper, more or lesse which were written by the Last Lord Harrington, and Coppyed out of some of my Mathematicall papers for his instruccion *Alsoe* I doe acknowledge that I haue two newe great globes which haue Couers of Leather the which I borrowed of the said Lord Lisle And my will is that they bee restored vnto him againe. . . .

To John Protheroe, Nathaniel Torporley, and his servant Christopher Tooke he gave each 'One furnace with his appurtenances out of the North Clossett of my Library at

Syon'. To each of his four executors, to be named later, he bequeathed 'One perspective truncke, a peece of the best glasse, and ye fayrest trunckes, as my said servaunte Can best fitt to theire likeing'. His most prized telescopes he reserved for the Earl of Northumberland: '*Item*   I giue vnto the afore-said Earle of Northumberland my two perspectiue trunckes wherewith I vse espeatially to see Venus horned like the Moone and the Spotts in the Sonne The glasses of which trunckes I desire to haue removed into two other of the fayrest trunckes by my said servaunte Christopher Tooke.' Christopher Tooke, obviously the craftsman who had made Harriot's glasses, was to receive the balance of the optical instruments and supplies:

Item   I giue vnto my said servaunte Christopher Tooke the residue of my Cases of perspective trunckes with the other glasses of his owne making fitted for perspective trunckes (excepting two great longe trunckes Consisting of many partes which I giue vnto the said Earle of Northumberland to remayne in his library for such vses as they may be put vnto).[75]

Later on in the dictation of his special bequests and payment of his debts, Harriot recalled a library item which he had previously forgotten:

Item   I doe acknowledge that I haue some written Coppies to the num-ber of twelue or fowerteene (more or lesse) lent vnto mee by Thomas Allen of Gloster Hall in Oxford Mr of Artes vnto whome I desire my Executors hereafter named to restore them safely according to the noate that hee shall deliuer of them (I doubting whether I haue anie true noate of them my selfe) . . .

One of the most intriguing sections of the will deals with miscellaneous bequests which Harriot makes to friends, relatives, and servants, for whom no other record exists among extant Harriot materials. Harriot first thinks of the mistress of the house in which he lies dying: 'I giue and bequeath vnto Mistris Buckner wife vnto Thomas Buckner Mercer of whose house being in St Christophers parishe I nowe lye, and hereafter nominated one of my Executors the

---

[75] Diligent searches of both archives and libraries of Petworth House, Syon House, and Alnwick Castle have failed to turn up any such contemporary 'per-spective trunks', so it must be presumed that they have been lost.

some of fifteene poundes towards the reparacions of some damages that I haue made, or for such other vses as shee shall thincke Convenient. . .' One cannot help but speculate upon what damages to the house or furnishings of Mistress Buckner the critically ill Harriot could have wrought, or of the pleasure afforded him by the Buckners' eldest son, to whom he left a magnificent grant of five pounds. But perhaps this was a gift in lieu of a grant to the father, Thomas Buckner, who must have been one of Harriot's oldest friends. Buckner was one of the colonists who spent the year 1585-6 with Harriot in Virginia, being listed among 'The names of all those as well gentlemen as others, that remained one whole yeere in Virginia vnder the gouernement of Master Ralfe Lane'[76] as number 93 of the 107 settlers.

Harriot's will gives the only remaining testimony of the household he maintained at Syon and the retainers kept by a gentleman of some means in Elizabethan and Jacobean times. When compared with the lavish life style maintained by Sir Walter Ralegh or the 9th Earl of Northumberland, the retinue of Harriot seems trivial. But in comparison with that of most gentlemen without inheritance or title, it shows him as having enjoyed reasonable comfort, with adequate service to free him from the drudgery of day-to-day living. Harriot makes bequests to six household servants — four currently in his service, and two who had retired:

Item   I doe giue and bequeathe vnto Christopher Tooke my foresaid servaunte one hundred poundes. [This is the largest monetary grant given by Harriot, and is in addition to the other grants made in the will, indicating that the two men must have been close indeed.] *Item*   I giue & bequeath vnto my servaunte John Sheller fiue poundes more then the forty shillinges which I haue of his in Custodie (being money giuen vnto him at seuerall tymes by my frends) which in all is seauen poundes to be imployed for his vse according to the discrecion of my Executors for ye placing of him with an other Master. *Item* I giue and bequeath ~~vnto Joh~~ [c.o.] Joane my servaunte fiue poundes more then her wages. *Item*   I giue and bequeath vnto my servaunte Jane which serveth vnder the said Jone fortie shillinges more then her wages which wages is twenty shillinges by yeare [this gives some indication of the current value of the pound.] *Item*   I giue and bequeath

[76] David B. Quinn, *Roanoke Voyages*, I, p. 197. Quinn did not identify Buckner as the 'Thomas Bookener' listed.

to my auncient servaunte Christopher Kellett a Lymning paynter [originally an illuminator of manuscripts, but by this time extended to mean a book illustrator or painter] dwelling neare Petty ffraunce in Westminster fiue poundes. *Item* to my ancient servaunte Joanne wife to Paule Chapmen dwelling in Brayneford end I bequeathe fortie shillinges.

A personal servant, John Sheller; two house servants, Joan the housekeeper and Jane, her assistant; and a scientific assistant and associate who worked with him in his calculations, made observations for him when Harriot was incapacitated or away from home — Christopher Tooke who ground lenses, made telescopes and glasses for Harriot and his friends; and two former servants, one personal, Christopher Kellet, and a housekeeper who had married and moved away, another Joanne — these were the household retainers who served Harriot during his active life, and whom he, dying, recalled with affection.

It is in personal details of family that the will is most disappointing. The fact that here is no mention of wife or children, coupled with the fact that there is no mention of any of these in any other letter or document of the time, makes it as certain as negative evidence can do that Harriot remained a bachelor throughout life. Only two bequests are made to relatives:

Item I giue & bequeath vnto my Cozen Thomas Yates my sisters sonne fifty poundes towardes the paiement of his debts but not otherwise. But if his debts doe fall out to be lesse then fifty poundes then the residue to remayne to him selfe. *Item* to John Harriottes Late servaunte to Mr Doleman of Shawe neere Newberry in Barkeshire and being the sonne of my Vnckles John Harriotts but nowe married and dwelling in Churche peene about a Myle westward from the said Shawe I doe giue and bequeath fifty poundes.

This generous allotment for each of two cousins, one of whose fiscal responsibility appears questioned, indicates that Harriot held in high regard the claims of blood relationship. The fact that no other relative is even mentioned forces us to assume that these were the only family members who remained at the time of his death.

No trace has been found of a Thomas Yates during the years of the 1620s and a search through the probated wills in London and Oxford shows no one of that name during the ensuing years. Identification of Yates as 'my sisters sonne' gives the only evidence extant that Harriot had a sister, no mention of whom remains in any other document. There is only one mention of the name 'Yates' in the Harriot manuscripts: on one sheet, while testing the writing of a pen, Harriot wrote 'William Yates' twice followed by 'Christopher Tooke' once. It is, of course, possible that William Yates was the one who married Harriot's sister, and that Thomas was his son. In any case, Thomas Yates would have been Harriot's nephew, not his cousin according to modern usage, though Elizabethan and Jacobean usage was much looser than ours.

The second item also gives meagre information: Harriot's father had a brother named John Harriot, who had a son of the same name. But this information does little to furnish clues as to Harriot's immediate family. According to Stow's *Survey of London*,[77] there was a John Hariot living in London about this time as parson of Fenchurch, but this John Hariot had earlier been knighted, and with his meticulous observance of matters of gentility and nobility, Harriot would certainly have given him the 'Sir' he deserved. It is interesting to note, however, that, as previously pointed out,[78] the illiterate blacksmith named Thomas Harriotts 'of Clyfton in the County of Oxford' who signed his will with an 'X' six weeks after young Harriot had sailed for the New World, named his brother John Harriotts as his executor. It is at least possible that this is the 'Vnckle John Harriotts' who had fathered the 'John Harriottes Late servaunte of Mr Doleman of Shawe neere Newberry in Barkeshire and being the sonne of my Vnckles John Harriotts but now married and dwelling in Church peene about a Myle westward from the said Shawe.'[79] But, alas, all of these leads appear to have come to a dead end.[80]

---

[77] John Stow, *A Survey of London, reprinted from the text of 1603*, Charles L. Kingsford, ed., Oxford, Clarendon Press, 1908, 2 vols. This is from I, p. 200.

[78] See Ch. II, 'Harriot at Oxford'.

[79] Though the servant John Harriotts has left no trace, the Dolemans of 'Shawe neere Newberry' were distinguished and are well recorded. Newbury was early the centre of the textile industry during the reigns of Henry VIII and

Harriot next turned to his debts: according to his reckoning he owed but little:

Item   Concerninge my debts, I doe acknowledg that at this presente I doe owe moneyes to Monseir Mayernes a Potycarie More to Mr Wheately a Potticary dwelling neare the Stockes at the East end of Cheapeside *Item*   to my Brewer dwelling at Braynford end. *Item*   To Mr John Bill Stacioner for Bookes The somme of the debts to all fower before mencioned I thincke and Iudge not to bee much more or lesse then forty poundes. *Item*   I doe acknowledge to owe vnto Mr Christopher Ingram keeper of the house of Syon for the aforesaid Earle of Northumberland Three thousand sixe hundred of Billetts which I desire to be repayed vnto him.

Harriot next turned to the naming of his executors. His closest friends, Sir Walter Ralegh and Sir William Lower, were dead. Lower's young friend, 'John Protheroe of Hawkesbrooke in the County of Caermarthen Esquior' was chosen, as was 'Thomas Alesbury of Westminster Esquior' and 'Thomas Buckner Mercer dwelling in St Xophors parishe in London not farre from ye Royalle Exchange' in whose house Harriot lay dying. His fourth executor shows his intimacy with the members of the Northumberland family as he named 'Sir Robert Sidney knight viscount Lysle' for that role. In making this request, Harriot was properly deferential, indicating that he would like the young viscount

---

Elizabeth, and the Charter of Weavers was granted there by Elizabeth. Leader of the industrialization of the industry was the famous 'Jack of Newberry' whose exploits were chronicled in the novella of that name by Thomas Dekker. After the death of Jack of Newberry, William Dolman, who had been his manager, took over the business. His son, Thomas Dolman, continued to build the family fortunes in the weaving business, and in 1554 bought the manor of Shaw, just outside Newbury. Late in life he spent much time and money in building the Shaw estates on a grand scale, and on his death in 1575 his son, John, continued that work, completing the manor house in 1581. Shaw remains one of the finest Elizabethan mansions in the country, now forming part of a Secondary Modern School for girls. It was during the heyday of the Dolmans at Shaw that John Harriotts the second served as servant to the family. Later he moved to the older centre, Speen, about 2 miles west of the centre of modern Newbury. For information on Shaw, Newbury, and the Dolman family, see R. Neville Hadcock, *Borough of Newbury Official Guide*, London, various editions.

[80] No will exists for a John Harriot in Berkshire; see the *Index to Wills Proved and Administrations granted in the Court of the Archdeacon of Berks, 1508 to 1652*, Oxford, 1893. Records of the Speen Church (Burials from 1629, Baptisms from 1630, and Marriages from 1635) reveal no entries in any of the variant spellings of Harriot. Records for the Shaw Church begin much later in 1647, but likewise reveal nothing more of any Harriot.

to serve '(if his Lordshipp may take soe much paynes in my behalfe)'. But this request also indicates that his relationship with Sidney was not as close as that of the other three executors, about whom he expressed no hesitation. The Viscount Lisle was at this time but twenty-six years old — younger than Harriot's favourite students, Lord Harington and Prince Henry would have been. He was the son of Robert Sidney, younger brother of the legendary Sir Philip. Robert Sidney the elder had been created Earl of Leicester in 1618, and his son, Robert had assumed his father's second title, Viscount Lisle, as a courtesy title. Before this, in 1616, at age twenty-one, young Robert had married Dorothy Percy, eldest daughter of the ninth Earl of Northumberland, and it was undoubtedly through this family connection that Harriot and the young Viscount became acquainted. Harriot's bequest to Sidney of the five quires of mathematical notes of the 'Last Lord Harrington' was a proper assignment, since Lord Harrington's grandmother had been a Sidney and the two families had always remained close. That Viscount Lisle accepted the executorship is shown by the fact that the probated will is presented as coming from all four men, though presented by only two: Alesbury and Buckner.

Harriot's executors were given responsibility for the disposition of his worldly goods. After paying his debts and bequests, from the remainder £20 was set aside for the poor: those of 'the hospitall in Christes Churche in London, Some parte vnto the said parishe of St Xophers where I nowe lye, and some parte (which I would haue the greater) vnto the poore of the parishe of Isleworth neere Syon'. This £20 Harriot estimated would come from the sale of his books, and the balance would cover expenses of the executors with a remainder which he wished them to bestow 'vppon Sir Thomas Bodleyes Lybrary in Oxford'.[81] To ensure that the books were sold at proper figures, Harriot called on the expertise of his old friend Hues: '*Item*   my will and desire is that Robert Hughes gentleman and nowe attendant vppon th'aforesaid Earle of Northumberland for matters of Learning

---

[81] A search of the Donation Register for this period, kindly made for me by Mr D. H. Merrry, revealed no gift recorded as from Thomas Harriot.

bee an ouerseer at the prizing of my Books, and some other thinges as my Executors and hee shall agree vnto.'

But the major concern of the dying scholar was his final responsibility to the learned world. He was acutely aware that in his avid search for new knowledge he had not left published works for the preservation of what he had learned. His manuscripts he knew to be valuable in themselves, but he hoped for more, and in his last requests he left to his friends to do what he had been unable to force himself to do, to order his notes, organize them, and see them through the press.

Item I ordayne and Constitute the aforesaid Nathaniell Thorperley first to be Ouerseer of my Mathematicall Writinges to be received of my Executors to pervse and order and to separate the Cheife of them from my waste papers, to the end that after hee doth vnderstande them hee may make vse in penninge such doctrine that belonges vnto them for publique vses as it [c.o.] it shall be thought Convenient by my Executors and him selfe. And if it happen that some manner of Notacions or writinges of the said papers shall not be vnderstood by him then my desire is that it will please him to Conferre with Mr Warner or Mr Hughes Attendants on the aforesaid Earle Concerning the aforesaid doubtes. And if hee be not resolued by either of them That then hee Conferre with the aforesaid John Protheroe, Esquior or the aforesaid Thomas Alesbury Esquior (I hoping that some or other of the aforesaid fower Last nominated can resolue him).

Then, evidently torn between his desire to have his work published and the safekeeping of his manuscripts for posterity, Harriot continued:

And when hee hath had the vse of the said papers soe longe as my Executors and hee haue agreed for the vse aforesaid That then hee deliuer them againe vnto my Executors to be putt into a Conuenient Truncke with a locke & key and to be placed in my Lord of North-umberlands Library and the key thereof to bee deliuered into his Lordshipps hands. And if at any time after my Executors or the afore-said Nathaniell Thorperley shall agayne desire the vse of some or all of the said Mathematicall papers That then it will please the said Earle to lett anie of the aforesaid to haue them for theire vse soe long as shall be thought Convenient.

Harriot here began a new section: '*Item* whereas I haue diuerse waste papers', then remembered that he had left his papers unsecured in the hands of Torporley, had the scribe strike out those words, and continued: 'and afterwards to be restored agayne vnto the Truncke in the afore said Earles Lybrary. Secondly my will & desire is that the said Nathaniell Thorperley be also Ouerseer of other written bookes & papers as my Executors and hee shall thincke Convenient.'

Having satisfied himself that he had done what he could to preserve the knowledge attained in a lifetime of intense labour, Harriot thought of some of his other activities. These he appeared to denigrate, and in so doing requested his executors to perform an unforgiveable act – to destroy materials of historical value.

Item   whereas I haue diuers waste papers (of which some are in a Canvas bagge) of my Accompts to Sir Walter Rawley for all which I haue discharges or acquitances Lying in some boxes or other my desire is that they may bee all burnte. Alsoe there is an other Canvas bagge of papers concerning Irishe Accompts (the persons whome they Concerne are dead many yeares since in the raigne of queene Elizabeth which I desire alsoe may be burnte as likewise many Idle papers and Cancelled Deedes which are good for noe vse.

With this injunction, Harriot closed his will with the standard formulas:

Item   I revoake all former wills by mee heretofore made saue onely this my presente last will and Testament which I will shalbe in all thinges effectually and truely performed according to the tenor and true meaning of the same. *In witnes* wherof I the aforesaid Thomas Harriotts haue to this my present Last will & Testament put my hand & seale yeouen [obsolete past participle of 'give'] the daie and yeare first above written [signed Tho: Harriotts].

This document was signed, sealed, and delivered in the presence of its witnesses: 'Immanuell Bowrne Will: ffitter: Scrivener & Tho: Alford, servante to the said scrivener.'

On the Monday following the Friday on which Harriot dictated this will, Harriot died. Evidently his patron, Henry Percy, 9th Earl of Northumberland, who was in the final stages of arranging for his release from the Tower after sixteen years of incarceration at the King's pleasure, did not feel it necessary to change Harriot's burial plans to place his remains in the local Syon parish church at Isleworth instead of the suggested church of St. Christopher's parish in London. As a matter of fact, the King's release from the Tower (along with the release of the Earls of Oxford and Southampton) as celebration for the royal fifty-seventh birthday, carried the injunction that Northumberland abandon residence at Syon House near the Court, and confine himself to an area within 30 miles of his country estate at Petworth in Sussex.[82] It was to Petworth that he was preparing to ride when he left the Tower in great style on July 18th, about two weeks after Harriot's death. John Chamberlain, as usual, described the scene in a letter to Sir Dudley Carleton:[83]

That afternoon [Wednesday, 18 July 1621] the earle of Northumberland was released from his long imprisonment in the Towre, whence the Lord of Doncaster[84] went to fetch him, and brought him home to his house with a coach and sixe horses. Yt was my chaunce to see him in Paules church-yard, and in my judgement he is nothing altered from what he was more than fifteen yeares ago that he was committed. He hath libertie to lie at Petworth, or in any place within thirtie miles compasse of yt, within which circuit I take Sion to be.[85] The warders of the Towre make greate moane that they have lost such a benefactor... The earle of Northumberland continues at Sion for ten dayes, and then goes to Petworth, from whence to Penshurst to see his daughter Lile[86] and so where he thincks goode within his precinct.

Northumberland's passage through London in a coach drawn by six horses caused much attention and was variously construed by those who saw him. Most contemporary Londoners saw this as a gesture of contempt for the King's favourite, the Duke of Buckingham, who had introduced the luxury of using four horses to draw his coach.[87]

---

[82] See G. R. Batho, *The Household Papers of Henry Percy, Ninth Earl of Northumberland* (London, 1962), p. xix. See also letter of John Chamberlain below. Batho indicates that the Earl visited Syon House infrequently after this, but I have found no evidence that he did so.

[83] *Letters of John Chamberlain*, Letter 387 (II. 389–91).

[84] The Viscount Doncaster was James Hay, who had married the 9th Earl's daughter.

[85] Syon House is more than 30 miles from Petworth House, though the restrictions may not have been meticulously applied.

[86] This is Dorothy (Percy) Sidney who married Viscount Lisle.

[87] A play on the life of the Wizard Earl entitled *Eight Horses for My Coach*, written by Grant Uden, was performed in the Coach house at Alnwick Castle in the spring of 1948. Performance was by the students and staff of the teacher's training college housed in the Castle following World War II, and the final performance was attended by the present Duke and Duchess of Northumberland. This play, for example, focuses on the pride of Henry Percy, undiminished by his imprisonment, still disdainful of the King and his favourites.

Chamberlain inclined to the idea that this was a gesture of his son-in-law James Hay, Viscount Doncaster, who was trying to honour his wife's father. But in any case, it is obvious that Henry Percy had more concerns on his mind in July 1621 than the disposition of the body of his associate, Harriot.

The day after his death, Harriot was buried on 3 July 1621 in the church of the parish in which the Buckner family lived. According to the brief biography of Harriot written by Agnes M. Clerke for the *Dictionary of National Biography*, 'His body was removed with much ceremony' though there appears to be little evidence to substantiate this.[88] The official Registers for St. Christopher's parish, 1588–1653, carry the following entry:[89]

	Buryalls 1621.	1621.
. . . 5.	Mr Thomas Hariots Sojourner	July
	at Mr Buckners was bu-	3
	ried in the Quire —	1621
	The Chancell July 3, 1621	

Three days later, on Friday, 6 July, two of Harriot's executors, Thomas Alesbury and Thomas Buckner, attesting the fact that they spoke also for the other two executors, Sir Robert Sidney and John Protheroe, probated Harriot's will. Sometime later, a memorial plaque was erected in the choir of the chancel east of the nave perhaps (as Stevens assumed) 'at the expense, it is understood, of his noble friend the Earl

---

[88] Miss Clerke got this story from Anthony à Wood. In his *Athenae Oxonienses*, 1721, I. col. 461, he wrote: 'As for our Author *Hariot*, who for some time lived in *Sion* Coll. near to *London*, he died 2 *July* in sixteen twenty and one; whereupon his body was convey'd to S. *Christopher's* Ch. in *London*, by the brethren of the Mathematical Faculty, and there by them committed to the Earth with Solemnity.' Nearly everything is wrong with this statement: Sion College was not a teaching college with a staff, but was a home for retired clergymen; Harriot never went there, since it was founded after his death. Wood was confused or imaginative, and Miss Clerke followed.

[89] Guild hall: MS 4421/1. The full title reads: 'The Register Booke of all the xpeninges [christenings] mariages and Burialles in the parrishe churche of St. Christophers nere the Stockes in London from the .9. of Nouember In the fyrst yere of the raigne of our soueraigne Ladye Queene Elizabeth.' This has been published as *The Register Book of the Parish of St. Christopher le Stocks in the City of London*, Edwin Freshfield, editor, 3 vols. (London, 1882). The Harriot item in in vol. I, p. 39.

of Northumberland',[90] or (as Miss Clerke held) 'by his executors Robert Sidney, Viscount Lisle, and Sir Thomas Alesbury.'[91] Much more likely than these suppositions, however, was that it was his non-scientific friend, Thomas Buckner, who made these final arrangements. Not only was it in his parish that Harriot was buried, but Buckner was himself a vestryman of the parish church which received his body.[92]

Though St. Christopher's was totally destroyed in the Great Fire of 1666, the wording of Harriot's memorial has been preserved. A dozen years after his burial, Anthony Munday and Henry Dyson, editing a new edition of the popular *The Survey of London* by John Stow, searched out and recorded memorial materials in London churches. Their new edition, the third of the antiquarian history of the city from its beginning, was printed in 1633.[93] During their search, Munday, Dyson, or one of the 'others' visited St. Christopher's near the Royal Exchange. In their new records, they preserved the wording of the Harriot memorial which had been added after the 1618 edition. Their account reads:[94]

[90] Stevens, op. cit., p. 142.

[91] *DNB* s.v. 'Harriot, Thomas'.

[92] This is reported in Muriel Rukeyser, *The Traces of Thomas Hariot*, p. 287, but she did not give the source of this record.

[93] This exceedingly rare edition carries the impressive title-page: 'THE / SURVEY / OF / LONDON: / Contayning / The Originall, Increase, Modern / Estate, and Government of that City, / Methodically set downe. / *With a memoriall of those famouser Acts of Charity, which for / Publicke and Pious Vses have beene bestowed by many Worshipfull / Citizens and Benefactors.* / As also all the Ancient and Moderne Monuments erected in the / Churches, not onely of those two famous Cities, LONDON and / WESTMINSTER, but (now newly added) / Foure miles compasse. / — / Begunne first by the paines and industry of Iohn Stovv, / in the yeere 1598. / Afterwards inlarged by the care and diligence of A. M. / in the yeere 1618. / And now completely finished by the study and labour of A. M. H. D. / and others, this present yeere 1633. ... / LONDON, / Printed by ELIZABETH PVRSLOVV, and are to be sold by / NICHOLAS BOVRNE, at his Shop at the South Entrance of / the ROYALL EXCHANGE. 1633. /' (STC 23345).

[94] This entry regarding Harriot's memorial has not previously been noted. Stevens and Clerke both found the entry in the John Strype edition of 1720 and later. Fortunately, the Stevens and Strype transcriptions are correct. The portion here quoted (all dealing with St. Christopher's) appears on pp. 821–2 of the 1633 edition.

S. Christophers.

This Church was repaired and beautified at the proper cost of the Parish, in the yeere of our Lord 1621.

But is now very shortly to be repaired and beautified againe, with a great deale of cost intended.

In the same Church is the following Epitaph.

Siste viator, leviter preme,
Iacet hîc juxta, Quod mortale fuit,

C. V.

THOMAE HARRIOTI.

Hic fuit Doctissimus ille Harriotus
de Syon ad Flumen Thamesin,
Patria & educatione,

Oxoniensis,

Qui omnes scientias Caluit,
Qui in omnibus excelluit,
Mathematicis, Philosophicis, Theologicis.

Veritatis indagator studiosissimus,
Dei Trini-unius cultor piissimus,
Sexagenarius, aut eo circiter,
Mortalitati valedixit, Non vitæ,
Anno Christi M.DC.XXI. Iulii 2.

Harriot's final earthly memorial may be rather freely translated as follows:[95]

Stay, traveller, lightly tread;
Near this spot lies all that was mortal
Of that most celebrated man
THOMAS HARRIOT.
He was that most learned Harriot
Of Syon on the River Thames;
By birth and education
An Oxonian
Who cultivated all the sciences
And excelled in all —
In Mathematics, Natural Philosophy, Theology,
A most studious searcher after truth,
A most devout worshipper of the Triune God,
At the age of sixty, or thereabouts,
He bade farewell to mortality, not to life.
The Year of our Lord 1621, July 2.

[95] Slightly different translations have been given by Henry Stevens (op. cit., p. 145) and Muriel Rukeyser (op. cit., pp. 296–7).

Three hundred and fifty years to the day after Harriot's death, on 2 July 1971, a group of Harriot admirers from both sides of the Atlantic and from Europe, gathered in the Entrance Hall of the Bank of England, as close to the site of Harriot's grave as could be determined, to pay tribute to Thomas Harriot's memory and to unveil a bronze plaque carrying the original Latin of his monument destroyed by the Great Fire. Through the kindness of the Governor and Deputy-Governor of the Bank of England, a niche in the marble walls, originally designed for a piece of sculpture, had been allocated for this purpose, and a bronze plaque designed by their architects to put the Harriot memorial into the decor of the Hall. Brief memorials were given by David Beers Quinn, Andrew Geddes and John Rankin, Professor of Modern History in the University of Liverpool, speaking for the British scholars and admirers, and by the author, representing American friends from the New World which Harriot had done so much to publicize and explain. Following these official ceremonies on Threadneedle Street, the present Duke of Northumberland gave a small dinner in Harriot's honour at Syon House, where Harriot himself had frequently been a guest of the 9th Earl of the same Percy family.

As his memorial still reminds us: Harriot bade farewell to all mortal things, but he still lives in memory and, as we have seen, in influence, in the world of living men.

Bibliography

I. 1580-1700

A. PRIMARY HARRIOT MANUSCRIPTS AND SIGNATURES

Alnwick Castle, Northumberland
    Syon House MSS
        G.II.1.a.   Signature of Harriot on lease, 7 July 1600.
        X.II.5.d.   Grant of income from Brampton, signed, 2 June 1595.
                 Release of Brampton Grant, signed, 6 July 1615.

Bodleian Library, Oxford
    University of Oxford Archives, KK9.

British Library
    Harriot's mathematical and scientific papers:
        Add. MS 6782, fos. 1-504.
        Add. MS 6783, fos. 1-426.
        Add. MS 6784, fos. 1-413.
        Add. MS 6785, fos. 1-441.
        Add. MS 6786, fos. 1-561.
        Add. MS 6787, fos. 1-578.
        Add. MS 6788, fos. 1-567.
        Add. MS 6789, fos. 1-538.
        Sloane MS 2292, A book of rutters with notes by Harriot.

Guildhall Library, London
    Harriot's Will:
        Certified Copy: Archdeaconry Court of London.
        Register Copy: Archdeaconry Court of London, 1618-26/27,
            fos. 71-2.

Hatfield House
    CP 42/36   11 July 1596. Letter, Harriot to Sir Robert Cecil, on up-
              dating of maps.
    CP 52/101 3 July 1597. Letter, Harriot to Sir Robert Cecil, request-
              ing his signature on a paper for Ralegh.
    CP 114/40 Nov. or Dec. 1605. Letter, Harriot to Salisbury request-
              ing release from prison.

CP 114/61   16 Dec. 1605. Petition from Harriot to Privy Council for release from Gatehouse Prison.

National Library, Vienna

Cod. 10703. Bll. 381-2.   2 Dec. 1606, London. Letter from Harriot to Johannes Kepler in Prague.

Bll. 384-5.   13 July 1608, Syon near London. Letter from Harriot to Johannes Kepler in Prague.

Oslo University Library

The copy of *Opticæ Thesavrvs* containing the *Optica* of Witelo and the *Perspectiva* of Ibn al-Haytham, ed. Friedrich Risner, Basel, 1572, contains tables of refraction written by Harriot and dated from Syon 11-12 Aug. 1597 and 23 Feb. 1597/8.

Petworth House, Sussex

The 'black box full of papers of rhumbs', now bound into five volumes:

HMC 240/i, fos. 1-170.

HMC 240/ii, fos. 171-253.

HMC 240/iii, fos. 254-321.

HMC 240/iv, fos. 322-402.

HMC 240/v, fos. 403-53.

The other Harriot papers selected out by Baron von Zach:

HMC 241/i, fos. 1-135. Algebra, Geometry, Calendar, Conic sections.

HMC 241/ii, fos. 1-94. Calculations from observations of Hannelius, Copernicus, Brahe, the vernal and autumnal equinoxes, solstices, orbit of the earth, length of year.

HMC 241/iii, fos. 1-88. Kepler, *de Stella Martis*; Snelii, *Eratosthenes Batavus*.

HMC 241/iv, fos. 1-80. Constellations, chemical papers, miscellaneous calculations, Jupiter's satellites.

HMC 241/v, fos. 1-17. Triangles.

HMC 241/vi, fos. 1-54. Projectiles, centre of gravity, reflexion of bodies. *Doctrine of Nauticall triangles Compendious*.

HMC 241/vii, 1-41. Comets of 1607 and 1618.

HMC 241/viii, fos. 1-78. Observations of sunspots.

HMC 241/ix, fos. 1-46. The moon.

HMC 241/x, fos. 1-84. Letters.

Public Record Office

Lawsuits against Ralegh with testimony by Harriot: C 24/372/125; C 24/372/126; St. Ch. 8/260/4.

B. SECONDARY MANUSCRIPT REFERENCES TO HARRIOT

Alnwick Castle, Northumberland

Alnwick MSS   7, fo. 286, 288.

9, fo. 122.

Leconfield MSS 1620-1629.

Syon House MSS   U. I. 2: t, gg, kk, hh, rr.

　　　　　　　　U. I. 3: e, o, x, ah, ap, ar, ax.

　　　　　　　　U. I. 4: f, n, z, am, as, ax.

　　　　　　　　U. I. 50: a5, a7.

　　　　　　　　X. II. 12. 4.　Breving book starting 21 Sept. 1591, Harriot regular diner.

　　　　　　　　X. II. 12. 5.　Breving book starting 14 Feb. 1590/ 1. Harriot occasional diner.

　　　　　　　　X. II. 12. 6.

Bodleian Library, Oxford

Aubrey MSS 13, fo. 342, 20 July 1683, Wallis letters to Aubrey.

Clarendon I, fo. 54, 27 July 1608, Latin letter to Harriot from Alexander Lower.

Rawlinson B 158, fos. 152-3. Gossip about Harriot and his friends.

Savile 09, 22 Mar. 1677. Manuscript notes of John Wallis on Harriot prefixed to his copy of *Artis Analyticae Praxis*, 1631.

British Library

Add. MS 38170, F. 92. Harriot Ralegh's agent to settle compensation for loss of Sherborne.

Birch MS 4394-6. Papers of Walter Warner contain Harriot material.

　　　　　　　　4395, fo. 92. Original draft of Preface to *Artis Analyticae Praxis* by Torporley.

　　　　　　　　4396, fo. 87. Letter, Aylesbury to Northumberland about costs of publishing the *Praxis*. Reprinted in Stevens, q. v., pp. 189-90.

　　　　　　　　4458, fos. 6-8. Copy of Torporley's 'A Synopsis of the Controversy of Atoms'. Reprinted in J. Jacquot's 'Thomas Harriot's Reputation for Impiety', q. v., pp. 183-7.

Harley MS 6001, fos. 1-40; 6002, fos. 1-57; 6083, fos. 1-455; 6848, fos. 185-6. Manuscript mathematics notes, containing some notes from Harriot's papers.

Sloane MS 1993, pp. 230, 260-1, 319-21. A copy of Mayerne's notes on the treatment of Harriot's cancer.

2065, fos. 133-6. Mayerne's original notes.

2086, fos. 57-9. Another copy of the above.

C. 32. a. 32. *El Viaie que hizo Antonio de Espeio en el Anno de ochenta y tres*. . . Madrid, 1583, reprinted by Hakluyt in Paris, 1586. Title page carries inscription in hand of John Dee indicating book was a gift from Thomas Harriot, 'Amici mei'.

Guildhall, London

MSS 4221-1. Register of St. Christopher-le-Stocks, 1558-1653. Harriot's burial; the Chancel, 3 July 1621.

Hatfield House

CP 196/131　Petition of William Floyer for title to Abbey of Molana.

CP 115/21　Persons to have access to Ralegh in the Tower.

CP 134/86   Interrogatory of Dudley Carleton on Harriot and the Gunpowder Plot, Nov. 1605.

CP 113/63   Sir Thomas Smith to Salisbury on search of Harriot's lodgings and study at Syon.

Lambeth Palace Library
Carew MS 604, fos. 195-6. Cecil to Carew, 1 Oct. 1602.

National Library, Vienna
Cod. 10703, Bl. 378-80; 383; 386. Letters from Kepler in Prague to Harriot in London, October 1606; 2 Aug. 1607; 1 Sept. 1609.

Petworth House, Sussex
MS Accounts, nos. 429, 581, 600, and 601 contain references to Harriot and his pension.

Public Record Office
SP/ 216 [Gunpowder Book]: Interrogatories:
    fos. 112, 113, 113x, Northumberland, 23 Nov. 1605.
    fo. 122, Nathaniel Torporley, 27 Nov. 1605.
    fo. 125, Northumberland (second), 30 Nov. 1605.
    fo. 137, Sir William Lower, 2 Dec. 1605.

Sherborne House, Dorset
Digby Estate Papers. 8 July 1597, Will of Sir Walter Ralegh. Harriot both a beneficiary and an overseer.

Syon House, London
Archives: B. XIII. 1 a, b, c. Early maps of Syon House property, some showing Mr Harriot's house.

C. BOOKS AND PRINTED REFERENCES TO HARRIOT

1. Acknowledged by Harriot *c.*1603 (see Quinn and Shirley, 'A contemporary list of Harriot References', *Renaissance Quarterly*, XXII (1969), 9-26.
  [1] HARVEY, RICHARD, *A theological discourse of the Lamb of God* (London, 1590).
  [2] HOLINSHED, RAPHAEL, *Chronicles* (London, 1587).
  [3] ANGLERIUS (PETRUS MARTYR), *De orbo nouo decades, octo*, ed. Richard Hakluyt (Paris, 1587).
  [4] NASHE, THOMAS, *Pierce Penilesse his supplication to the deuil* (London, 1592).
  [5] PARSONS, ROBERT, *Elizabethae ... edictum ... cum Responsione* (Antwerp?, 1592; Lyons, 1592; Rome, 1593).
  [6] FORMAN, SIMON, *The groundes of longitude* (London, 1591).
  [7] HOOD, THOMAS, a lost book on longitude.
  [8] ——, *The vse of the two mathematicall instrumentes, the cross staffe and the Jacobs staff* (London, 1592).
  [9] HAKLUYT, RICHARD, *Principall nauigations*, 1st ed. (London, 1589) reprints Harriot's *Briefe and true report*.
  [10] HARRIOT, THOMAS, *A briefe and true report of the new*

found land of Virginia (London, 1588). Also published (Frankfurt, 1590) with the White illustrations (captioned by Harriot) engraved by Theodor de Bry. Also in Latin, French, and German.
[11] Unidentified.
[12] TANNER, ROBERT, *A briefe treatise for the ready vse of the sphere* (London, 1592).
[13] PARSONS, ROBERT (John Philopatris, pseudonym), *An advertisement written to a secretarie of my L. Treasurers of Ingland* (1592).
[14] HUES, ROBERT, *Tractatus de Globis et eorum Vsu* (London, 1594).
[15] HARVEY, GABRIEL, *Pierces supererogation* (London, 1593).
[16] PLAT, SIR HUGH, *The jewell house of art and nature* (London, 1594).
[17] MORE, RICHARD, *The carpenters rule* (London, 1602).
[18] SCALIGER,JOSEPH JUSTUS, *Cyclometria*, 2nd edn., (Leiden, 1594).
[19] DAVIS,JOHN, *The seamans secrets* (London, 1595).
[20] KEYMIS, LAWRENCE, *A relation of the second voyage to Guiana* (London, 1596). Includes dedicatory Latin poem, 'Ad Thomam Hariotum & universae philosophiae peritissimum' which was also reproduced in Hakluyt's *Principall nauigations*, III (1600).
[21] WYFLIET, CORNELIS VAN, *Descriptionis Ptolemaicae augmentum sive Occidentalis notitia breuis commentario* (Louvain, 1597).
[22] BARLOW, WILLIAM, *The nauigators supply* (London, 1597).
[23] A repetition of number [14], crossed through.
[24] CHAPMAN, GEORGE, *Achilles Shield* (London, 1598). Prefatory poem, 'To my admited and soule-loved friend Mayster of all essential and true knowledge, M. Harriots'.
[25] TORPORLEY, NATHANIEL, *Diclides coelometricae seu valuae astronomicae vniuersales* (London, 1602).
[26] GILBERT, WILLIAM, *De Magnete* (London, 1600).
[27] HAKLUYT, RICHARD, *Principall nauigations*, 2nd edn. (London, 1598–1600). Dedicatory epistle, vol. II (1599).

2. Others
  CHAPMAN, GEORGE, *Translation of the whole works of Homer* (London, 1611). Preface says he conferred only with Harriot and Hues in making his translation.
  CORBET, RICHARD, *Certain Elegant Poems* (London, 1647). Contains 'A poetic letter sent from Dr Corbet to Sir Thomas Aylesbury, Dec. 9, 1618, on the occasion of a Blazing Star', which praises Aylesbury and Harriot.
  GIBSON, THOMAS, *Syntaxes Mathematica* (London, 1655).
  HALLEY, EDMOND, 'De numero radicum, in aequationibus solidis ac biquadraticis', *Phil. Trans. Royal Society*, XVI (1686–87) 391.

Bibliography 481

READ, ALEXANDER, *The chirurgical lectures of tumours and vlcers: Deliuered . . . in the Chirurgeans Hall these three years last past, viz. 1632, 1633, and 1634* (London, 1635). For Harriot's death see p. 307.

STOW, JOHN, *The suruey of London . . . inlarged by the care and diligence of A[nthony] M[unday]* (London, 1633). Contains, p. 821, the record of the monument erected to Harriot in St. Christopher's Church (reprinted in Stevens, q.v., p. 142).

WALLIS, JOHN, *A treatise of algebra, both historical and practical* (London, 1685). Chs. 30–54 (pp. 125–207) devoted to Harriot's *Artis Analyticae Praxis*.

——, *Opera Mathematica* (Oxford, 1693), II, Preface, 206, 207–13.

II. 1700–1900

A. MANUSCRIPTS

Bodleian Library, Oxford
Rigaud MS 9, fos. 1–6.
Rigaud MS 35, fos. 100–329.
Rigaud MS 50, fos. 49–69.

B. BOOKS

AUBREY, *'Brief lives', chiefly of Contemporaries, set down by John Aubrey, between the Years 1669 & 1696*, ed. Andrew Clark, 2 vols. (Oxford, 1898). Includes:
'Thomas Hariot (1560–1621)', I. 284–7.
'Robert Hues (1553–1632)', I. 426.
'Sir Walter Raleigh (1552–1618)', II. 177–94.
'Nathaniel Torporley (1563–1632)', II. 263.
'Walter Warner (15—–1640)', II. 291–3; 15–16.

BALL, WALTER W. ROUSE, *A Short Account of the History of Mathematics* (London, 1888), pp. 210–11.

BIRCH, THOMAS, *The History of the Royal Society*, 4 vols. (London, 1756–7). Reprinted by Johnson Reprint Company (New York, 1968). Search for Harriot papers, see 29 October 1662, I. 120; 19 Nov. 1662, I. 126; 30 Sept. 1663, I. 309; 2 Dec. 1669, II. 410.

BOSSUT, CHARLES, *Histoire générale des mathématiques origine jusqua l'année 1808* (Paris, 1810). See Période III, Ch. I, pp. 285–6.

CANTOR, MORITZ, *Vorlesungen über Geschichte der Mathematik*, 4 vols. (Leipzig, 1880–1908). See vol. II (1892), pp. 720–2.

CLERKE, AGNES M., 'Thomas Harriot (1560–1621)', in *DNB* 1885 et. seq.

DE FONBLANQUE, EDWARD B., *Annals of the House of Percy*, 2 vols. (London, 1887).

EDWARDS, EDWARD, *The Life of Sir Walter Raleigh*, 2 vols (London, 1868). Important correspondence throughout.

GLANVILL, JOSEPH, *Plus Ultra, or the Progress and Advancement of Knowledge since the days of Aristotle*, (London, 1668). See ch. IV.

HALLIWELL, JAMES ORCHARD, *A Collection of Letters Illustrative of the Progress of Science in England from the reign of Queen Elizabeth to that of Charles II* (London, 1841). A very valuable collection, though not always accurate in transcription.

HUTTON, CHARLES, *A Mathematical and Philosophical Dictionary*, 2 vols. (London, 1796). Reprints Baron von Zach's account of the Harriot papers. I, pp. 584-6.

LAGRANGE, COUNT JOSEPH LOUIS, *Oeuvres de Lagrange*, 14 vols. (Paris, 1867-92). See IV, p. 539.

MARIE, M. MAXILIAN, *Histoire de sciences mathématique et physiques*, 12 vols (Paris, 1883-8). See Tome III (1884), pp. 92-3.

MICHAUD, *Biographie universelle ancienne et moderne ... Nouvelle Édition* (Paris, 1857). See Tome XVIII, p. 492.

MONTUCLA, JEAN ÉTIENNE, *Histoire des mathématiques* (Paris, 1799-1802), Harriot, Wallis, Vieta, and Descartes, II. 105-20.

MORGAN, JOSEPH, *Phoenix Britannicus: Being a Collection of Scarce and Curious Tracts* (London, 1732). Obscene poem on Harriot, p. 368.

Nouvelle biographie générale depuis les temps le plus reculés jusqu'à nos jours, 46 vols. (Paris, 1853-66). See vol. 23, pp. 450-1.

OLDYS, WILLIAM, 'Life of Sir Walter Raleigh', in the 11th edn. of the Oldys and Birch edn. of *History of the World* (London, 1736). Starts report that Harriot and Ben Jonson worked with Ralegh on his *History*, p. 185.

RIGAUD, STEPHEN P., 'Account of Harriot's Astronomical Papers', included in *Supplement to Dr. Bradley's Miscellaneous Works: with an Account of Harriot's Astronomical Papers* (Oxford, 1833). Reprinted in the Sources of Science Series, No. 97, of the Johnson Reprint Corporation (New York, 1972).

WOOD, ANTHONY à, *Athenæ Oxonienses* (London, 1721). 'Thomas Hariot, or Harriot', Life no. 543, cols. 459-62.

——, *Athenæ Oxonienses and Fasti Oxonienses*, 2 vols. (London, 1815).

C. PERIODICALS

BESSEL, FRIEDRICH WILHELM, 'Berechnung der *Harriot*schen und *Torporley*schen Beobachtungen des Cometen von 1607', *Monatliche Correspondenz*, X (1804), 425-40.

RIGAUD, STEPHEN P., 'On Harriot's Papers', *Royal Institution of Great Britain Journal*, II (1831), 267-71.

——, 'On Harriot's astronomical observations contained in his unpublished manuscripts belonging to the Earl of Egremont', *Proceedings of the Royal Society*, III (1830-7), 125-6.

ROBERTSON, A., 'An account of some mistakes relating to Dr. Bradley's astronomical observations and Harriot's MSS', *Edinburgh Philosophical Journal*, VI (1822), 313-18.

VON ZACH, FRANZ XAVER (Baron), April 1786 Latin letter to Delegates of Oxford University Press proposing publication of Harriot's papers and a biography. Reprinted by Rigaud in his 'Account of Harriot's Astronomical Papers', note B, pp. 53-7.

——, Announcement of discovery of Harriot manuscripts: 'Mémoire sur la nouvelle planète Ouranus', *Mémoires de l'Académie de Bruxelles*, V (1788), 22-48.

——, Preliminary report on Harriot and his work: 'Beobachtungen des Uranus; . . . und Anzeige von den in England aufgefunden Harriotschen Manuscripten', *Astronomisches Jahrbuch für das Jahr 1788*, Berlin. Reprinted in translation in part in Hutton's *Mathematical and Scientific Dictionary*, 1796, and in full in Rigaud, 1833, note C, pp. 57-61.

——, 'Etwas aus den, von Herrn von Zach in Jahr 1784 in England aufgefunden Harriotschen Manuscripten, vormemlich Original-Beobachtungen der beyden Kometen von 1607 und 1618', *Astronomischen Jahrbuchern, erster Supplement-Band*, 1793, pp. 1-41.

——, *Allgemeine geographische Ephemeriden* (Weimar, 1798), pp. 1, 230, 484, 635.

——, 'Bruchstück eines Briefes *Henry Percy's Earl of Northumberland* an den berühmten Analysten *Thomas Harriot* in London', *Monatliche Correspondenz zur Beförderung der Erd-und Himmels-Kunde*, VIII (1803), 47-60.

——, 'Lettre v. De M. le Baron de Zach sur les Manuscrits de Thomas Harriot . . . 1er Août 1822', *Correspondence astronomique, géographique et statistique du Baron de Zach*, VII (1822), 105-38.

III. SINCE 1900

A. BOOKS

BAKELESS, JOHN, *The Tragicall History of Christopher Marlowe*, 2 vols. (Cambridge, Mass., 1942), I. 105, 111, 128-30, 134-37. Many allusions to Harriot are incorrect.

BATHO, GORDON R., *The Household Papers of Henry Percy, Ninth Earl of Northumberland (1564-1632)* (London, 1962), *passim*.

BRADBROOK, MURIEL C., *The School of Night*, (Cambridge, Engl., 1936). Harriot references throughout; see esp. pp. 9-11. Not generally accepted today.

CAJORI, FLORIAN, *A History of Mathematical Notations*, 2 vols. (Chicago, 1928). I. 199-201; II. 115-17.

COOLIDGE, JULIAN LOWELL, *A History of Geometrical Methods*, (Oxford, 1940), Cites a widely quoted letter of 28 Nov. 1934 from David Eugene Smith with the erroneous information that the mathematical papers in the British Library are not by Harriot but of a much later date. How Smith reached this conclusion cannot be conceived.

CORBITT, DAVID L., *Explorations, Descriptions, and attempted Settlements of Carolina, 1584–1590* (Raleigh, 1948).

DURANT, DAVID N., *Ralegh's Lost Colony*, London, Weidenfeld & Nicolson, 1981.

EIFERT, VIRGINIA L. S., *Tall Trees and Far Horizons: Adventures and Discoveries of Early Botanists in America* (New York, 1965), pp. 1–22.

EMERSON, EVERETT, 'Thomas Hariot, John White, and Ould Virginia', in *Essays in Early Virginia History Honoring Richard Beale Davis* (ed. J. A. Leo Lemay) (New York, 1977), pp. 1–11.

GLASER, ANTON, *History of Binary and other Nondecimal Numeration* (Privately Printed, 1971), pp. 10–13.

GUNTHER, ROBERT W. T., *Early Science in Oxford*, 10 vols. (Oxford, 1923–35). See II. 293–4 for Harriot and his telescopes.

HILL, CHRISTOPHER, *Intellectual Origins of the English Revolution* (Oxford, 1965). See esp. Ch. VI: 'Ralegh – Science, History and Politics', pp. 131–224; pp. 139–45 devoted to Harriot.

HULTON, PAUL, and QUINN, DAVID B., *The American Drawings of John White, 1577, 1590*, 2 vols. (London and Chapel Hill, 1964).

JAFFE, BERNARD, *Men of Science in America* (New York, 1944). Ch. I, 'Thomas Harriot (1560–1621): Bringing the Seeds of Science to America', pp. 1–22.

JOHNSON, FRANCIS R., *Astronomical Thought in Renaissance England*, (Baltimore, 1937), *passim*; main entry, pp. 226–9.

KARGON, ROBERT H., *Atomism in England from Harriot to Newton* (Oxford, 1966). See esp. pp. 5–42.

LEFRANC, PIERRE, *Sir Walter Ralegh écrivain: l'oeuvre et les idées*, (Paris, 1968), *passim*; main entry, pp. 344–52.

MCLEAN, ANTONIA, *Humanism and the Rise of Science in Tudor England* (New York, 1972).

MERSENNE, P. MARIN, *Correspondence de P. Marin Mersenne*, ed. Cornelis de Waard and others, 12 vols. to date (Paris, 1932–).

NICHOLSON, MARJORIE, *Science and Imagination* (London and Ithaca, 1956). Sees Harriot as a possible link between Kepler and Donne.

PEPPER, JON V., 'Studies in the Mathematical and Scientific Work of Thomas Harriot' (1979, unpublished PhD dissertation, University College London).

QUINN, DAVID B., *The Discovery of America* (with W. P. Cummings and R. A. Skelton) (New York, 1972).

——, *The Elizabethans and the Irish* (Ithaca, 1966). Harriot at Molanna, pp. 115–16.

——, *The Hakluyt Handbook*, 2 vols. (London, 1974).

——, *North America from Earliest Discovery to First Settlements* (New York, 1975).

——, *Raleigh and the British Empire* (London, 1947).

——, *The Roanoke Voyages, 1584–1590. Documents to Illustrate the English voyages to North America under the patent granted to*

Walter Ralegh in 1584, 2 vols. (London, 1955). Reprints Harriot's *Briefe and True Report*, with notes, I. 317-87. See also 'Thomas Harriot and John White', I. 35-60.

——, *Virginia Voyages from Hakluyt* (London, 1973).

ROCHE, JOHN J., 'Thomas Harriot's Astronomy' (1977, unpublished DPhil dissertation, Oxford University).

RUKEYSER, MURIEL, *The Traces of Thomas Harriot* (New York, 1971). A poetic and literary account, but sensitive in developing a sympathetic understanding of Harriot.

SCOTT, J. F., *The Mathematical Work of John Wallis* (London, 1938). References throughout; see esp. Appendix I, pp. 195-6, and pp. 133-65.

SHIRLEY, JOHN W., ed., *Thomas Harriot, Renaissance Scientist* (Oxford, 1974). A symposium volume which includes:

Rosen, Edward, 'Harriot's Science, the Intellectual Background', pp. 1-15.

Shirley, John W., 'Sir Walter Ralegh and Thomas Harriot', pp. 16-35.

Quinn, David, B., 'Thomas Harriot and the New World', pp. 36-53.

Pepper, Jon V., 'Harriot's Earlier Work on Mathematical Navigation: Theory and Practice', pp. 54-90.

Tanner, Rosalind C. H., 'Henry Stevens and the Associates of Thomas Harriot', pp. 91-106.

Jacquot, Jean, 'Harriot, Hill, Warner and the New Philosophy', pp. 107-28.

North, John, 'Thomas Harriot and the First Telescopic Observations of Sunspots', pp. 129-65.

——, 'Thomas Harriot's Lunar Observations', *Science and History: Studies in Honor of Edward Rosen* (Ossolineum, 1978), pp. 283-308.

——, ed., *A Source Book for the Study of Thomas Harriot*, New York, Arno Press, 1981. Introduction and Bibliography.

SMITH, DAVID EUGENE, *History of Mathematics*, 2 vols. (Boston, 1923). See esp. I. 388-9.

STEVENS, HENRY, *Thomas Hariot, the Mathematician, the Philosopher, and the Scholar, Developed Chiefly from Dormant Materials, with Notices of his Associates . . .* (London, 1900). This important volume was printed in limited edition: 162 copies in small paper and 33 in large. It has been reprinted in the Burt Franklin Science Classics Series, No. 10 (New York, 1972).

STRATHMANN, ERNEST A., *Sir Walter Ralegh: A Study in Elizabethan Skepticism* (New York, 1951). See esp. pp. 43-60.

TAYLOR, E. G. R., *The Haven-Finding Art: A History of Navigation from Odysseus to Captain Cook* (New York, 1971). See pp. 218-25.

——, *Late Tudor and Early Stuart Geography, 1583-1650* (London, 1934). References throughout.

——, *The Mathematical Practitioners of Tudor and Stuart England* (Cambridge, Engl., 1954). Biography of Harriot, No. 55, pp. 182-3.

WATERS, DAVID W., *The Art of Navigation in England in Elizabethan and Early Stuart Times* (New Haven, 1958). See 'Appendix No. 30. Thomas Hariot's Contribution to the Art of Navigation', pp. 584-91.

YATES, FRANCES A., *A Study of 'Love's Labour's Lost'* (Cambridge, 1936). Harriot a member of the Northumberland group satirized in this play.

B. PERIODICALS

BATHO, GORDON, R., 'The Finances of an Elizabethan Nobleman: Henry Percy, Ninth Earl of Northumberland (1564-1632)', *Economic History Review*, IX (1957), 433-50.

—, 'The Library of the Wizard Earl: Henry Percy, Ninth Earl of Northumberland (1564-1632)', *Library*, XV (1960), 246-61.

—, 'The Wizard Earl in the Tower, 1605-1621', *History Today*, VI (1956), 344-51.

BLOOM, TERRIE F., 'Borrowed Perceptions, Harriot's Maps of the Moon', *Journal of the History of Astronomy*, IX (1979), 117-22.

BREMER, FRANCIS J., 'Thomas Hariot, American Adventurer and Renaissance Scientist', *History Today*, XXIX (1979), 639-47.

CAJORI, FLORIAN, 'A Reevaluation of Harriot's *Artis Analyticae Praxis*', *Isis*, XI (1928), 316-24.

CROMBIE, ALISTAIR C.; PEPPER, JON V.; QUINN, DAVID B.; SHIRLEY, JOHN W.; and TANNER, R. C. H., 'Thomas Harriot (1560-1621): an original practitioner in the scientific art', London *Times Literary Supplement* (23 Oct. 1969), pp. 1237-8.

CUNNINGHAM, DOLORA G., 'The Ralegh Group and the History of Elizabethan Skeptical Thought', *American Philosophical Society Yearbook* (1968), pp. 551-2.

GEORGE, F., 'On Harriot's Meridional Parts, *Journal of the Institute of Navigation*, IX (1956), 560-9.

GLASER, ANTON, 'Binary Numeration from Hariot to the Computer Age', a paper delivered at the Second International Congress of Mathematical Education, 29 Aug.-2 Sept. 1972, University of Exeter.

HARRINGTON, JEAN C., 'Archaeological Explorations at Fort Raleigh National Historic Site', *North Carolina Historical Review*, XXVI (1949), 127-49.

HERR, RICHARD, 'Solar Rotation Determined from Thomas Harriot's Sunspots Observations of 1611-1613', *Science*, CCII (8 Dec. 1978), Cover and pp. 1079-81.

JACQUOT, JEAN, 'Thomas Harriot's Reputation for Impiety', *Notes and Records of the Royal Society*, IX (1952), 164-87.

JONES, PHILLIP S., 'Historically Speaking: the Binary System', *Mathematics Teacher*, XLVI (1953), 575-7.

KALMAR, MARTIN, 'Thomas Harriot s 'De Reflexione Corporum Rotundorum'; an Early Solution to the Problem of Impact', *Archive for History of Exact Sciences*, XVI (1977), 201-30.

KARGON, ROBERT H., 'Thomas Hariot, the Northumberland Circle, and early Atomism in England', *Journal of the History of Ideas*, XXVII (1966), 128-36.

KÖRBLER, JURAJ, Thomas Harriot (1560-1621), fumeur de pipe, victime du cancer?', *Gesnarus*, IX (1952), 52-4.

LOHNE, JOHANNES A., 'Dokumente zur Revalidierung von Thomas Harriot als Algebraiker', *Archive for History of Exact Sciences*, III (1966-67), 185-205.

——, 'Essays on Thomas Harriot', *Archive for History of Exact Sciences*, XX (1979), 189-312. Includes: 'Billiard Balls and Laws of Collision', pp. 189-229; 'Ballistic Parabolas', pp. 230-64; 'A Survey of Harriot's Scientific Writings', pp. 265-312.

——, 'The Fair Fame of Thomas Harriott. Rigaud *versus* Baron von Zach', *Centaurus*, VIII (1963), 69-84.

——, 'The Increasing Corruption of Newton's Diagrams', *History of Science*, VI (1967), p. 69-89. Discusses Harriot's theory of trajectories, pp. 76-7.

——, 'Kepler und Harriot, Ihre wege zum Brechungsgesetz', *Internationales Kepler-Symposium Weil du Stadt, 1971*, (1973), pp. 187-214.

——, 'A Note on Harriott's Scientific Works', *Centaurus*, VII (1961), 220-1.

——, 'Regenbogen und Brechzahl', *Sudhoff's Archiv*, XLIV (1965), 401-15.

——, 'Thomas Harriot als Mathematiker', *Centaurus*, XI (1965), 19-45.

——, 'Thomas Harriott (1560-1621), the Tycho Brahe of Optics', *Centaurus*, VI (1959), 113-21, + 5 plates.

——, 'Thomas Harriot', *Dictionary of Scientific Biography*, VI (1972), 124-9.

——, 'Zur Geschichte de Brechungsgesetzes', *Sudhoff's Archiv*, XLII (1963), 152-72.

MEE, ARTHUR, 'Carmarthenshire and Early Telescopes', *Transactions of the Carmarthenshire Society*, IV (1908-09), 43-4. More on Lower than on Harriot.

MORLEY, FRANK VIGAR, 'Thomas Hariot — 1560-1621', *Scientific Monthly*, XIV (1922), 60-6.

NICHOLSON, MARJORIE, 'The "New Astronomy" and English Literary Imagination', *Studies in Philology*, XXXII (1935), 425-62. References *passim*; see esp. pp. 431-4.

PEPPER, JON V., 'Harriot's Calculation of the Meridional Parts as Logarithmic Tangents', *Archive for History of Exact Sciences*, IV (1968), 359-413.

——, 'Harriot's Manuscript on the Theory of Impacts', *Annals of Science*, XXXIII (1976), 131-51.

——, 'Harriot's Work on the True Sea-Chart', *Actes du XIIe Congrès International d'Histoire des Sciences, Paris 1968*, IV (1971), 135-8.

——, 'A Letter from Nathanial Torporley to Thomas Harriot', *British Journal for the History of Science*, III (1967), 285-90.

——, 'A Note on Hariot's Method of Obtaining Meridional Parts', *Journal of the History of Navigation*, XX (1967), 347-9.

——, 'Some Clarification of Harriot's Solution of Mercator's Problem', *History of Science*, XIV (1976), 235-44.

——, 'The Study of Thomas Harriot's Manuscripts: Harriot's Unpublished Papers, *History of Science*, VI (1967), 17-40.

PLOMER, HENRY R., 'The Will of Thomas Harriot, Mathematician and Astronomer (1560-1621)', *Home Counties Magazine*, VIII (1908), 240-7.

QUINN, DAVID B., 'The Failure of Raleigh's American Colonies', *Essays in Honour of James Eadie Todd* (London, 1949) pp. 61-85.

——, 'The Munster Plantation: Problems and Opportunities', *Journal of the Cork Historical and Archaeological Society*, LXXI (1966), 19-40.

——, 'Thomas Hariot and the Virginia Voyages of 1602', *William and Mary Quarterly*, 3rd Series, XXVIII (1970), 268-81.

—— and SHIRLEY, JOHN W., 'A Contemporary List of Hariot References', *Renaissance Quarterly*, XXII (1969), 9-26.

REINHOLD, ROBERT, 'Twentieth Century Discovers an Elizabethan Genius', New York *Times* (8 Apr. 1971), p. 39.

——, 'Rediscovering an Elizabethan Genius', *International Herald Tribune*, (13 Apr. 1971), p. 14.

ROBERTSON, JEAN, 'Some Additional Poems of George Chapman', *Library*, 2nd Series, XXII (1941), 168-76. Identifies two portraits as possibly those of Thomas Harriot.

ROCHE, JOHN J., 'The Radius Astronomicus in England', *Annals of Science*, XXXVIII (1981), 1-32, esp. sec. 7, 'The cross staff in England: Harriot to Greaves', 23-8.

SADLER, D. H., Calculating the Meridonal Parts', *Journal of the Institute of Navigation*, VI (1953), 141-7.

SANDISON, H. E. 'Arthur Gorges, Spenser's Alcyon and Ralegh's Friend', *Publications of the Modern Language Association of America*, XLIII (1928), 645-71.

SCRIBA, CHRISTOPH J., 'Wallis und Harriot', *Centaurus*, X (1964-65), 248-57.

SEATON, ETHEL, 'Thomas Hariot's Secret Script', *Ambix*, V (1953-65), 111-14.

SHIRLEY, JOHN W., 'An Early Experimental Determination of Snell's Law', *American Journal of Physics*, XIX (1951), 507-8.

——, 'Binary Numeration Before Leibniz', *American Journal of Physics*, XIX (1951), 452-4.

——, 'George Percy at Jamestown, 1607-1612', *Virginia Magazine of History and Biography*, LVII (1949), 227-44.

——, 'Improvements in Techniques of Navigation in Elizabethan England', Tekniska Museet Symposia, *Transport Technology and Social Change*, II (1980), 117-30.

——, 'The Scientific Experiments of Sir Walter Ralegh, the Wizard Earl, and the Three Magi in the Tower, 1603-1617', *Ambix*, IV (1949-51), 52-66.

—, 'Sir Walter Ralegh's Guiana Finances', *Huntington Library Quarterly*, XIX (1949) 55–69.
— and QUINN, see Quinn and Shirley, above.
SOKOL, BARNETT J., 'Thomas Hariot's Notes on Sir Walter Raleigh's Address from the Scaffold', *Manuscripts* (Summer 1974), 198–206.
—, 'Thomas Harriot – Sir Walter Ralegh's Tutor – on Population', *Annals of Science*, XXXI (1974), 205–12.
STROUT, EUGENY and MOORE, P., 'The Very First Maps and Drawings of the Moon', *Journal of the British Astronomical Association*, LXXV (1964–65), 100–5.
TANNER, ROSALIND C. H., 'Nathaniel Torporley and the Harriot Manuscripts', *Annals of Science*, XXV (1969), 339–49.
—, 'Nathaniel Torporley's 'Congestor analyticus', and Thomas Harriot's 'De triangulis laterum rationalium''', *Annals of Science*, XXXIV (1977), 393–428.
—, 'La place de Thomas Harriot dans l'histoire de la médecine et de l'astronomie', *Gesnarus*, XXIV (1967), 75–7.
—, 'On the Role of Equality and Inequality in the History of Mathematics', *British Journal for the History of Science*, I (1952), 159–69.
—, 'The Ordered Regiment of the Minus Sign: Off-beat Mathematics in Harriot's Manuscripts', *Annals of Science*, XXXVII (1980), 127–58.
—, 'The Study of Thomas Harriot's Manuscripts: Harriot's Will', *History of Science*, VI (1967), 1–16.
—, 'Thomas Harriot (1560–1621)', *Medunarodi Simpozij 'Geometrija i Algebra Pocetkom XVII Stoljeća' povodom 400-godisnjice rodenja Marina Getaldića, Dubrovnik, 1968.* (Proceedings of the International Symposium on 'Geometry and Algebra at the beginning of the 17th century' on the 400th anniversary of the birth of Marino Ghetaldi) (Zagreb, 1969), pp. 161–70.
—, 'Thomas Harriot as Mathematician: a Legacy of Hearsay', *Physis, Rivista Internazionale di Storia della Scienza*, Part I, IX (1967), 235–47; Part II, IX (1967), 257–92.
—, 'Un mathématicien à son médecin: Lettres de Thomas Harriot à Théodore de Mayerne', *Actes de la Société helvétique des Sciences naturelles* (1970), pp. 161–70.
TAYLOR, E. G. R., '"The Doctrine of Nauticall triangles Compendious": Thomas Hariot's Manuscript', *Journal of the Institute of Navigation*, VI (1953), 131–40.
—, 'Hariot's Instructions for Ralegh's Voyage to Guiana, 1595', *Journal of the Institute of Navigation*, V (1952), 345–51.
VACCA, G., Sui Manoscritti Inediti di Thomas Harriot', *Bollettino di Bibliografia e storia delle scienze matematiche*, VI (Turin, 1902), 1–6.
WALLIS, HELEN M., 'The first English globe; a recent discovery', *Geographical Journal*, CXVII (1951), 275–90. Describes the Molyneux globe discovered at Petworth on which Harriot may have worked and which he certainly knew and used.

WEBB, SUZANNE S., 'Raleigh, Hariot, and Atheism in Elizabethan and early Stuart England', *Albion*, I (1969), 10–19. A negative report.

WHITE, GEORGE, 'Thomas Hariot's Observations on American Geology in 1588', *Illinois Academy of Science Transactions*, XLV (1952), 116–21.

Index

Abbot, George, archbishop of Canterbury, 450
Acosta, José de, *Historia natural de las Indias* (1590), 231
Adams, Randolph G., 143, 144n
Adams, Robert, 102n
Aeris experiment, 286
Africa, map of, 229
Agas, Ralph, *Plan of Oxford*, 39 (fig.)
Albert of Habsburg, archduke of Austria, 307
alchemy, 268, 272-3, 278, 283, 406; heaven of, 284-6; symbolism, 285
algebra, 2, 4-5, 11-13, 27, 33, 400
Alhazen, *Treasury of Optics*, 384, 387
Allen, Thomas, lieut. of Portland Castle, 192-3, 194, 197
Allen, Thomas, mathematician, 58, 61-2, 64, 69, 361, 463; portrait, 63
almanac, 84
Alnwick Castle, 471n; Percy archives at, 169n, 212
Alphonsine Tables, 92, 93
altitudes of sun or star, 86, 88, 89, 90-1
Amadas, Philip, at Roanoke, 131, 133, 139; voyages to Virginia, (1584) 104-5, 113; (1585), 106, 118, 119, 120n, 124
Amay, Henrie, 52
Amazon River, 200, 231
amplitudes, table of, 94
An advertisement written to a secretarie of my l. treasurers of Ingland (1592), 318
Anderson, Alexander, mathematician,

Problemata (1612), 420, 421n, 422
Anderson, Sir Edmund, chief justice of common pleas, 310
Anglican church, 152-3
Anne of Denmark, queen of James I, 362, 430, 436; illness, 449; funeral, 450
Apollonius of Perga, *Conics*, 103; 'Inclinationum', 422
Aqua experiments, 278-81, 286
Aquascococke, Indian village, 131, 133
Archdeaconry Court, Diocese of London, 7, 29, 410n
Archimedes, 265
Arena, Louis, 108n
Arenberg, Count, ambassador, 307
Aristotle, 43, 44, 45, 48, 195-6, 361, 380, 441; theory of matter, 268-71, 286; theory of terrestrial motion, 243-4, 246-8, 393; rate of fall, 263
arithmetic, 44
Armada (1588), 34, 141n, 243; English preparations for, 170-1; naval tactics, 172-3
Arnold, William, vicar of Blandford, 193
Arundel, Thomas Howard, earl of, 444, 447
Arundell, John, Roanoke colonist, 119, 129, 131; return to England, 133-4, 155
Asheborne, Robert, churchwarden, 194
Ashmole, Elias, 49
Ashmolean Society, 21
Aston, Arthur, 323
astrolabe, 88; use of, 90
astronomical observations, 16, 19, 22, 407; *see also* Jupiter; moon; sun

491

astronomy, 394-6; in navigation, 85, 87; at Oxford, 44, 45
atheism, 67, 154, 179-85; *see also* Cerne Abbas
atomic theory of matter, 242
atomism, 35, 361
Aubrey, Captain –, at Roanoke, 130
Aubrey, John, *Brief Lives*, 49, 51, 107; extracts, 62, 82, 168n, 176, 199, 362-3, 430; notes on Pell, 366-7
Aylesbury, Thomas (d. 1657), 64, 364, 367, 372, 452; biography, 414-15; correspondence with 9th earl, 6-7; with Harriot, 415-16; executor, 2, 9, 30, 467-9, 472
Aylmer, John, bishop of London, 390
Azores, battle of (1591), 164n, 171; expedition to (1597), 177, 233-4

back-staff, 91, 125
Bacon, Francis, 360, 383n
Bacon, Roger, philosopher, 150n
Baines, Richard, 67, 181, 185
Baines libel, 181, 182-3
Bainham, Sir Edward, 332
Baker, Humphrey, astrologer, 73; *Well spring of sciences* (1580), 74
Baker, Matthew, shipwright, 101-2, 103, 104
Ballam, Edward, at Oxford, 40
Balliol College, Oxford, 68
ballistics, 243-9; Harriot's work on, 249-55, 256(fig), 257(fig.), 258-9
Ballynetra Castle, Co. Cork, 158
Ballynoe (Baile nua), Kilmore, 160
Bancroft, Richard, archbishop of Canterbury, 333, 345, 354, 371
Bank of England, London, 29, 474-5; Harriot plaque in, 69
Barlow, William, *The navigators supply* (1597), 319
Barlowe, Arthur, voyage to Virginia (1584), 104-6, 112, 120; (1585?), 124
Barmeton, *see* Brampton, Durham
Barnes, George (d. 1592), governor of Muscovy Co., 72

Baskerville (Bastavile), Sir Thomas, 230
Bates, Thomas, conspirator, 350; executed, 351
Beaufort, N. Car., 129
Beck, Thomas, at Oxford, 40
Beeston, Sir Hugh, 445
Bennett, J.H., agent at Petworth, 32
Berliner astronomisches Jahrbuch, 17
Berreo, Antonio de, 231
Bessel, Friedrich W., astronomer, 17-18, 396
Bessel function, 18, 396
Bible, 441-2; Bishop's, 313n; Geneva, 308, 313n
Bideford, Devon, 158
Bill, John, stationer, 467
Birch, Thomas, secretary Royal Society, 7, 8, 9
Blount, Charles, Lord Mountjoy, earl of Devonshire, 301, 310, 391
Blount, Sir Christopher, 188, 189
Bodleian Library, 10, 23, 430; Allen's gifts to, 63; Harriot's bequest to, 69, 468; copies of MSS in, 33; Rigaud notebooks in, 25
Bodley, Thomas, 63, 230
Boniten, Captain –, at Roanoke, 130
Borage, Jasper, 183, 185
Borough, Sir John, 102n, 187, 204
Bourne, William, 251, 259; *Arte of shooting in great ordnaunce*, 243, 244; extract, 245; *Regiment for the sea*, 243
Boyle, Elizabeth, wife of Spenser, 159-60
Boyle, Richard, earl of Cork, 160
Bradbrooke, Muriel, *School of Night*, 359
Bradley, James (d. 1762), astronomer, 23, 27
Brahe, Tycho, 15, 27, 92; theory of planetary motion, 394
Brampton, Cumberland, 211, 212
Brampton (Barmeton), Durham: indenture of grant to Harriot, 212, 213(fig.), 214-15; release, 216, 217(fig.); rents, 211, 212, 326
Brasenose College, Oxford, 373
Brazil, rutter of, 229
Brett, Alexander, 237, 290, 323, 324

Brewer, Grace, housewife of Sherborne, 194n
Briggs, Henry, mathematician, 64, 360
British Association for the Advancement of Science, 22
British Library (formerly British Museum), 78; Harriot MSS in, 20, 24, 26, 28, 37, 399; Mayerne notes in, 433; Pell collection in, 6; White drawings in, 30
Broad Street, Oxford, 41
Brocke, John, shoemaker, 123
Brooke, Francis, Roanoke colonist, 118, 119, 131
Brooke, George, 304, 307-8, 311, 317n; executed, 321
Brooke, Henry, Lord Cobham, 204n, 299, 303, 305; arrested (1603), 304; case against, 307-8; reprieved, 321-2; in Tower, 325-6; and Ralegh trial, 310-14, 317n
Brouncker, William, president Royal Society, 9
Browne, Maurice, with Gilbert (1583), 72-3
Bruhl, Count de, 14-15
Bruno, Giordano, 360; remarks on Oxford, 42-3
Bry, Theodor de, *America* pt. I (1590), 144-5, 318
Bryage, Richard, churchwarden, 191
Buckingham, George Villiers, 1st duke of, 471
Buckner, Thomas, mercer, 464; Harriot dies in house of, 30, 31, 460; bequests to, 463-4; executor, 1, 467, 468, 472, 475
Bull, James, shipwright, 101
Burghley, Lord, *see* Cecil, William
Burgoyne, Ralph, gentleman of the horse, 295n, 337
burning glasses, 149, 150n
Busby, Richard, headmaster Westminster, 107

Cadiz, 229, 233, 234, 370
Cajori, Florian, studies of Harriot, 33
Calais, 171
calendar, 27, 423-4
Cambridge University, 365, 376
Camden Society, 28

Canada, map of, 229
Canary Is., 125
cannon balls, piling of, 242
Canon Law (Law of God), 308-13, 315, 317, 355
Canterbury, archbishops of, *see* Abbot; Bancroft; Cranmer; Sancroft
Cantor, Moritz, Harriot studies, 13, 33
Capo Bianco, Alessandro, *Corona e palma militare d'artigliera* (1602), 259
Carbery, earls of, *see* Vaughan
Carew, George, earl of Totnes, 444, 447
Carew, Sir George, 237, 289, 290, 323, 324
Carey, Henry, Lord Hunsdon, lord chamberlain, 183, 184
Carey, Sir Robert, 184
Carleton, Dudley, controller of household, 9th earl, 338-41; correspondence, *see* Cecil, Robert; Chamberlain, John
Carmarthenshire, 25
Carolina Algonquian language, 106-7, 113, 147, 148; alphabet for, 107-10, 111(fig.), 112; dictionary, 107
Carolina Outer Banks, 129, 137
Carr, Robert, Viscount Rochester, 340, 355, 433
Caspian Sea, map of, 229
Cassiopeia (constellation), 62, 394
Catesby, Robert, conspirator, 328; death, 336, 351
Catherine Howard, Queen, 225
Catte Street, Oxford, 41
cauterization, 458-9
Cavendish, Sir Charles (d. 1654), mathematician, 10, 11, 372-3
Cavendish, Thomas, 66, 115, 118; voyages: (1585), 126, 131; (1586-8), 362, 374
Cecil, Robert, earl of Salisbury, 203, 204n, 230, 235, 304-5, 310, 321, 354, 356, 433; and Gunpowder Plot, 327-9, 332, 345-6
correspondence: with D. Carleton, 346-7; with Harriot, 230-2, 234; with T. Heneage, 188; with James I, 299, 341; with Northumberland (9th earl), 206;

Cecil, Robert (*cont.*)
  with Ralegh, 178-9; with
  W. Waad, 325
Cecil, Thomas, 1st earl of Exeter, 354
Cecil, William, Lord Burghley, 120n,
  127, 179, 188
celestial observations, 197-8, 401-2
celestial spheres, 394
census (1589), in Ireland, 164
Cerne Abbas, Dorset, investigation
  into atheism, 185n, 199-200;
  rumours about Ralegh, 191-7;
  see also Commission (1594)
Chamberlain, John, letter writer, 68;
  letters to Dudley Carleton,
  (1605), 331-3; (1606), 352,
  354; (1618), 443-6, 448, 449;
  (1619), 450, 452-3; (1621), 471
Chancery, High Court of: Ralegh v.
  Sanderson (1610), 218-22
Chapman, George, poet, 66-7, 359,
  360; *Achilles Shield* (1598),
  319; 320; trs. Homer (1611),
  65, 320, 374
Chapmen, Joanne, servant, 465
Charles II, king of England, 10
Chauncellor, Francis James, commis-
  sioner, 190
chemistry, 27, 238, 272; apparatus,
  273-4, 275(fig.); experiments,
  276-82; *see also* alchemy
Chesapeake Bay, 136, 137, 141-2,
  151
Chesepians, (Chesapeake Indians), 135,
  136
Chewt, Charles, 323
China, rutter of, 229
Cholmoly, Richard, 183, 184, 185
Chowanoke (Choanoke), Indian village,
  135, 137-8
Chowan River, N. Car., 137, 140, 141
Christ Church, Oxford, 362, 375, 414
ciphers, 420
Clarendon, earl of, *see* Hyde, Edward
Clark, Andrew, 'Degree System of the
  University', 46, 49
Clarke, John, at Roanoke, 124, 131
Clarke, William, at Oxford, 40
Clavius, 110
Cleaver, William (d. 1815), principal
  of Brasenose, 18
Clerke, Agnes M., 'Life of Harriot',
  30-1, 364, 460, 472

Clerke, Francis, priest, executed, 321
Clifford, George, earl of Cumberland,
  171, 189, 301; ships for the
  Azores, 177
clocks, 150
Cobham, Lord, *see* Brooke, Henry
Coke, Sir Edward, attorney-general,
  trials: Gunpowder Plot, 350-1;
  Northumberland, 354-6;
  Ralegh, 310, 312-16, 321
Coldwell, John, bishop of Salisbury,
  177, 289, 290
Cole, William, Vice-chancellor, Oxford,
  38
Collado, Luys, on artillery, 259
Collins, John, mathematician, 8-9;
  correspondence, 9, 12
colonisation: administration, 116-17,
  118-19, 137; exploration,
  115, 135-7, 140; military
  preparations, 115-16; reports
  on, 145-7; sites for, 136-7, 141
colonists, skills required of, 116;
  see also Ireland; Roanoke I.
comets: (1585), 151; Halley's (1607),
  15, 16, 27, 393-7, 416-17;
  (1618), 15, 16, 27, 449, 453
Commission for Causes Ecclesiastical
  (1594), 190; interrogatory,
  190-1; evidence, 191-6,
  199-200
Commission for escheated lands (1586),
  Ireland, 161
commodities: American, 146-7;
  Caribbean, 126
Common Law, 312, 313
compasses, 84, 149, 376
Compton, William, earl of Northampton, 444
conic sections, 27
Constable, Marmaduke, Roanoke
  colonist, 122
constellations, 27
Cope, Sir Walter, 'Certayne briefe
  remembrances . . . 1613', 423
Copernicus, Nicholaus, 15, 27, 45, 92,
  243, 361; *De revolutionibus*,
  421; theory of planetary motion,
  393-4
Copley, Anthony, 304
copper, 136; ornaments, 131n
Corano, Antonio, theologian, 56-8
Cork, county, 156, 157

Corbet, Richard, bishop of Norwich, 414-15, 418; *Certain Elegant Poems* (1647), 416-17
Cornbury, Viscount, *see* Hyde, Henry
Cotton, William, bishop of Exeter, 289
Cranmer, Thomas, archbishop of Canterbury, 184
Cresswell, Joseph, S.J., 341
Croatoan I., N. Car., 130
cross-staff, 17, 86, 88, 125, 395, 396; use of, 90-1
Cumberland, earl of, *see* Clifford, George
Currituck Sound, N. Car., 137

Daniel and Susannah, 312
Danvers, Sir Charles, 202, 203, 204, 205
Danvers, Henry, Lord Danvers, 204-5
Danvers, Sir John, 202, 204
Darcy, Sir Francis, 293
Dartmouth, Devon, *Madre de Deus* at, 187-8
Dasemunkepeuc, Indian village, 139
Davis, John, curate of Motcombe, 192
Davis, John, navigator, 91; *The seamans secrets* (1595), 318
dead-reckoning, 84
declination, 17
Dee, Dr. John, 62, 74n, 75, 80, 87, 92n, 150n, 201; as conjuror, 180
Dekker, Thomas, dramatist, 467n
Delavale, Robert, pursebearer to 9th earl, 295n
Delaware, University of: copies of Harriot MSS at, 33, 36
Democritus, 361
Dench, John, churchwarden, 193
Derby, earl of, *see* Stanley, Ferdinando
'De reflexione corporum rotundorum', 261, 451-2
Descartes, René, philosopher, 10; *Discours de la méthode* (1637), 11, 12, 13, 381
'De stella Martis', 27
Devereux, Dorothy, countess of Northumberland (formerly Lady Perrot), 244-5, 296, 299, 342, 346, 352, 390-1; death, 452; pension, 292; property, 225, 410
Devereux, Penelope, Lady Rich, 224, 299, 391

Devereux, Robert, 2nd earl of Essex, 175, 178, 204, 291, 296, 298-9, 346, 358, 390, 444, 447; naval expeditions, (1596), 229; (1597), 233-4; plot against Queen, 203, 205, 328
Devereux, Walter, 1st earl of Essex, 390
Devonshire, earl of, *see* Blount, Charles
dialectic, at Oxford, 43
Digby, Sir Everard, 328; conspirator, 350; executed, 351
Digby, Sir Kenelm, 63
Digges, Leonard, 92n, 150n, 247
Digges, Thomas, 114n, 246, 252, 259n; *Pantometria* (1571), 247-8; extracts, 248-9
Diophantes, mathematician, 110
disease: among Indians, 150-1; treatment of, 438n, 441
'Doctrine of Nautical triangles Compendious', 88, 91, 318
Dolman family, of Shaw, 465, 466-7n
Dominica I., Leeward Is., 126
Doncaster, Viscount, *see* Hay, James
Douglas, John, 229
Drake, Sir Francis, 60, 171, 183; circumnavigation, 117; lectureship in navigation, 72; rescues Roanoke colonists, 135, 141-3, 155, 157; at Azores (1591), 164n
Dudley, Robert, earl of Leicester, 159, 179; Chancellor of Oxford, 38, 43, 45, 62; and Corano, 56-7
Dudley, Sir Robert, 228
Dungarvan, Co. Waterford, 161
Durham House, London, 81, 223, 304; angular position, 239-40; Harriot's chamber in, 82, 237; H. working at, 86, 89, 226, 229, 234, 238, 263

Early English Text Society, 28
earth, orbit of, 27
East Indies, rutter, 229
eclipses, 17
Edinburgh Philosophical Journal, 21
Edinburgh Review, 21
Edward III, king of England, statute, 312
Edward VI, king of England, 226; statutes, 312

Edwards, Edward, *Life of Raleigh* (1868), 448
Egerton, Thomas, Lord Ellesmere, lord chancellor, 354, 356
Egremont, Lord, *see* Wyndham, Sir George
elements and qualities, 268-9, 272-3
Elizabeth I, queen of England, 159, 226, 292; death, 300; funeral, 451; proclamation against priests (1591), 179; relations with Ralegh, 81, 156-7, 175-8, 233, 291; succession to, 296-7; support for voyages, 76, 117, 189
Elizabeth, daughter of James I, 418, 419
Elizabethan garden, Roanoke I., 34-5
Elks, Timothy, tutor, 344, 365, 371, 406n
Emden, C.S., *Oriel Papers* (1948), 53-4
Ent, Sir George, physician, 8
Epicurus, 242, 361
equinox, 27
Ericksen, John, 387
Ernest II, of Saxe-Coburg-Gotha, 15
Erskine, Sir Thomas, captain of the guard, 304
Espejo, Antonio de, *El viaie que hizo Antonio de Espeio* (1586), 201
Essex, earls of, *see* Devereux
Essex County Records Office, 115
Essex House, London, 291, 333, 339, 343, 365
Exeter, earl of, *see* Cecil, Thomas
Euclid, *Optica et catoptria*, ed. Pena (1604), 420, 421

Fawkes, Guy (*alias* John Johnson), 329, 330, 339, 350; executed, 351
Felton, –, receiver for 9th earl, 338
Fernandes, Simão (Fernandez, Simon), pilot, 76, 118, 124, 129
Ferrers, Henry, 339
Fever, John, basketmaker, 123
fire works, 150
fish weirs: Indian, 139; Irish, 166
Fitzjames, John, at Trenchard dinner party, 195, 196
Fleet prison, 390

Fleming, Sir Thomas, chief baron of exchequer, 354
Fletcher, –, lawsuit with Warner (1596), 227
Floyer, William, agent for Ralegh, in Ireland, 157, 158, 165
Forest, Henry, paymaster to 9th earl, 210
Forman, Simon, *The groundes of the longitude* (1591), 318, 319
Fortescue, Sir John, 354
forts: at Puerto Rico, 126-7; at Roanoke I., 137-40
Fotherley, Thomas, disburser for 9th earl, 337
Fox, John, *Book of martyrs*, 49n
Francis, Sir Edward, steward of Petworth, 216n, 337, 344, 429
Frobisher, Martin, N.W. passage voyages (1576-8), 74
Fuller, Thomas, *Worthies*, 445n

Galen, 441, 442
Galileo Galilei, 16, 25, 35, 45, 167, 249, 397, 398; and Jupiter's satellites, 16-17; *Siderius nuncius*, 401-2
Ganz, David, astronomer, 122
Ganz, Joachim (Doughan Gannes), Roanoke colonist, 121-2
Garibal, –, and Harriot MSS, 9
Garnet, Henry, S.J., 329
Garter ceremony (1593), 210
Gassendi, Pierre, 15
Gatehouse prison, 340, 427, 444, 445, 448
Gemma Frisius, 93
geometry, 27, 44
Ghetaldi, Marino, *Apollonius redivivus* (1607), 420, 421n, 422; *Promotus Archimedes*, 392n, 400
Gilbert, Adrian, 382; Ralegh bequest, 235, 236
Gilbert, Sir Humphrey, 74-6; academy, 78-9; charter (1578), 75; voyages: (1578), 76-7; (1583), 79-80; *Discourse*, 75
Gilbert, Sir John, 188
Gilbert, William, 387, 388; *De magnete*, 282, 319
globes, 1, 370, 375, 462
Gloucester Hall, Oxford, 61, 64
Godyer, Sir Henry, 407n

gold, 138, 387-8; alchemical, 272-3, 286; symbol, 285
Golden Grove, Carmarthenshire, 412
Gondomar, Diego Sarmiento de Acuña, count of, 431
Goold, Alice, and daughter, 236
Gorges, Sir Arthur, 304, 317n, 360
Gotha observatory, 15
Gowry conspiracy, 332, 333
grammar at Oxford, 43
Granganimeo, an Indian, 133
Grant, John, conspirator, 350; executed, 351
gravity, 27, 265, 317, 380-2; rate of fall, 263-5, 266(fig.), 267
Great Bear (star), 395
Green, J.R., *History of the English People*, 328-9
Greenway, Oswald, S.J., 329
Greenwich, 302
Grene, Giles, steward to 9th earl, 302, 339
Grenville, Sir Richard, 164; death, 164n, 171; plans for Ireland, 156, 158; voyages to Roanoke, 118-20, 125-8, 131, 135; return to England, 134, 155
Gresham College, London, 79, 360, 379
Greville, Sir Fulke, 43
Grey, Arthur, Lord Grey of Wilton, lord deputy, 159
Grey, Thomas, Lord Grey of Wilton, 304, 311, 317n, 321-2, 326, 374-5
Griffin, Rowland, 123
Guayanilla Bay, Puerto Rico, 125, 126
Guggenheim Memorial Foundation, 31
Guiana, charts of, 231; *see also* maps voyages to: (1594), 218; (1618), 442, 447; (1595), 86, 88, 91; financing of, 218-19, 228; preparations, 200, 218; return, 227
Gunpower Plot (1605), 327-31, 349-50, 355; Harriot's involvement in, 340-1, 346

Hakluyt, Richard, of the Middle Temple, 59
Hakluyt, Richard, of Oxford, 74, 76, 229, 360, 375; association with Harriot, 60-1, 71-2, 80;

at Oxford, 58-60
Discourse of Western Planting (1584), 60, 113-14, 123-4; *Principall navigations* (1589), 59, 60, 104, 121, 134, 144, 155; *Principal navigations* (1598-1600), 102n, 144, 171, 319
Hall, Rupert, *Ballistics in the Seventeenth Century* (1952), 249
Halley, Esmond, 17; *see also* comets
Hampton Court, 301
Hancock, Edward, secretary to Ralegh, 305, 306
Hancocke, John, clergyman, 191
Hannelius, 27
Harington, John, 1st Baron Harington, 418-19
Harington, John, 2nd Baron Harington, 418-19, 462, 468; books lent by Harriot, 420-2; death, 422; eulogy, 422-3
Hariot, Sir John, clergyman, 466
Harrington, J.C., archaeologist, 34
Harriot (Harriottes), John (uncle), 40, 52, 465, 466
Harriot, Thomas, 233, 356; correspondence, with R. Cecil, 346; with Privy Council, 348-9; *see also* Aylesbury; Kepler; Mayerne
education, at Oxford, 40, 54, 55(fig.), 56, 374; handwriting, 163
illness, 386, 425-7, 430-1, 453; symptoms, 199, 438-40; treatment, 440-1, 456-9; death, 1, 24, 147n, 476; burial, 30, 472; memorial, 30-1, 474-5
will, 2-3, 7, 24, 69, 165-7, 287n, 324, 383, 425, 460-70, 472; discovery of, 29-31, 460
income: bequest from Ralegh, 236-8; pension from 9th earl, 67, 209-11, 216, 292, 326, 362-4, 377; property, 212-14
religious beliefs, 58, 68, 122, 439, 441-2; atheist, 186, 187, 191, 193, 194, 197, 199, 316; conjuror, 180, 320; juggler, 182, 185, 320;
in Ireland, 157-8, 160, 162-5;

Harriot (*cont.*)
  in N. Carolina, 120n, 122, 135,
    137, 139, 155-6, 426; survey,
    131; voyages to, 105-7, 125-9;
    attitude to Indians, 140, 151-4;
    see also Carolina Algonquian
    language
  books, 3, 453, 469; containing
    references to, 201, 282n,
    318-20; MSS, 3; deposited at
    Petworth, 7, 469-70; search
    for, 7-9; discovery of (1784),
    14-15; proposals to publish,
    15, 18-19, 469
  works: *Arcticon*, 86, 88-9, 95;
    Artis Analyticae Praxis, 4, 6,
    9, 10, 12, 33, 362, 366, 367,
    372; *Briefe and true report*, 28,
    34, 60, 121, 134, 374; editions,
    143-4, 319; extracts, 144-50,
    152-6
  See also Durham House; Gunpowder
    Plot; Syon House
Harriotes, John, servant to Dolman,
    52, 465, 466
Harriots, John, executor to T. Harriotts,
    52
Harriottes, John (cousin), 52, 465
Harriots, Thomas, of Oxford, smith,
    51, 466; will, 51-2
Harriot's walk, Roanoke I., 35
Harris, Christopher, 221
Harrison, G.B., *A Jacobean Journal*,
    350-1
Harrison, William, topographer, 44
Hart, John, orthographer, 109-10
Hart, Peter, servant to Ralegh, 323
Harvey, Gabriel, *Pierces supererogation*
    (1593), 201, 318, 319
Harvey, Sir George, lieut. of the Tower,
    323, 324, 325
Harvey, Richard, *Theologicall discourse
    of the lamb of God* (1590),
    318, 319
Harvey, William, physician, 8, 360,
    362, 366
Hatton, Sir Christopher, lord chancel-
    lor, 161, 175
Hawarde, John, of the Middle Temple,
    354, 356
Hawkins, Sir John, comptroller of the
    navy, 188
Hawley, Francis, vice-admiral, Dorset,

190, 196, 197
Hawthorne, Gilbert, preacher, 323
Hay, James, Viscount Doncaster, 444,
    447, 471-2
Hele, John, sergeant-at-law, 310-11
Heneage, Sir Thomas, vice-chamberlain,
    210; letter, 188
Henry V, king of England, 225
Henry VIII, king of England, 225-6
Henry, son of James I, 173, 350,
    418-20, 468; death, 422, 433
Henry, Cape, Virginia, 137
Herbert, Edward, Lord Herbert of
    Cherbury, 8-9
Herbert, Sir John, 354
Hercules Club, 28
Hermetic tradition, 271
Herr, Richard, 'Solar rotation
    Determined from Thomas
    Harriot's Sunspots Obser-
    vations' (1978), 35
Hill, Christopher, *Intellectual Origins*
    (1969), 42, 64; extract, 310
Hill, Nicholas, philosopher, 361, 364
Hipparchus, 93
Hippesley, John, gentleman of the
    horse, 339, 369; pension, 372
Hippocratic oath, 442
Hispaniola, 128
Historical Manuscripts Commission,
    Sixth Report, 26-7, 29
Holecroft, Robert, of Middlesex,
    122
Holinshed, Raphael, *Chronicles* (1577),
    44; (1587), 77, 104, 121,
    318; of *Ireland*, 161
Holroyd-Smyth family, of Molanna,
    166
Hood, Thomas, *Use of . . . the crosse
    staffe and Iacob's staff* (1592),
    201, 318, 319
Hooke, Robert, *Micrographia* (1665),
    384
Hooker, John, 161
Hornsby, Thomas, Savilian professor
    of astronomy, 14
horoscopes, 338, 339-40, 341, 343-4,
    356; by Harriot, 343-4, 345,
    355
Horsey, Sir Ralph, 190, 194-7
Horsmanden, —, tutor of Algernon
    Percy, 365, 376
Horwood, Alfred J., report on Harriot

MSS at Petworth, 26-7, 37
House of Commons, Bill (1584),
    106-7
Howard, Charles, Lord Howard of
    Effingham, lord high admiral,
    171, 172, 184, 188, 301; earl
    of Nottingham, 354, 415
Howard, Henry, earl of Northampton,
    204, 304-5, 306, 354; and
    Ralegh trial, 310, 314
Howard, Lord Thomas, 190
Howard, Thomas, Viscount Howard of
    Bindon, 190, 196, 301
Howard, Thomas, earl of Suffolk, 310
Hues (Hughes), Robert, 282n, 373-5,
    451; epitaph, 375-6; executor,
    2, 468-9; Magi, 65-6, 360,
    364; pension from 9th earl,
    363, 365n, 374, 375, 376,
    377; *Tractatus de globis* (1594),
    201, 318, 319, 360, 361, 362,
    375; tutor to Algernon Percy,
    376-7, 379
Hulton, Paul and Quinn, D.B., *American
    Drawings of John White*, 128-9
Humphrey, duke of Gloucester, 42
Hussey, William, churchwarden, 192
Hutton, Charles, *Mathematical and
    Philosophical Dictionary* (1796),
    18, 20
Hyde, Edward, earl of Clarendon,
    lord chancellor, 8, 9
Hyde, Henry, Viscount Cornbury, 9
Hyde, Robert, of Sherborne, 194
hydrostatic balance, 381

Ignis experiment, 279, 281, 286
impacts, theory of, 261-3, 451
Inca Empire, 201
Inchiquin Map, 162
Indians: attitude of colonists to,
    115-16; of N. Carolina, 133;
    eating habits, 154, 457; religion,
    153; importance of tobacco,
    147-8; drawings of, *see* White,
    John; language, *see* Carolina
    Algonquian
Ingram, −, of the custom house, 407n
Ingram, Christopher, clerk of works,
    295, 467
instruments, 1, 72, 149, 238n, 240n
Ireland, 156-64; colonists, 119, 158,
    164; maps, 157, 162; *see also*

Lismore; Molanna; Munster
iron, 281
Ironside, Ralph, clergyman, 193;
    conversation with Ralegh,
    192, 194, 197, 198; relation
    of disputation, 195-6
Isleworth church, Middlesex, 462,
    470

James I, king of England, 350, 450;
    attitude to Ralegh, 303-4,
    321-2, 340; correspondence,
    see Cecil, R.; Percy, H., 9th
    earl; horoscope, 338, 339-40,
    341, 343; treatise, on Gun-
    powder Plot, 331; on tobacco,
    147n; visit to Syon, 301-3
James VI, king of Scotland, 204n,
    296-7; *see also* James I, above
James, duke of York, 8
James, Dr. Francis, chancellor of
    London diocese, 194, 196,
    197
James, Thomas, keeper Bodleian L., 63
Jefferys, Nicholas, clergyman, 192-3
Jessop, John, clergyman, 191-2
Jesuits, 179
Joanes, David, 371
Jobson, Francis, cartographer, 162
John, Dr. −, surgeon, 323, 429
Jones, Inigo, 407
Jupiter (planet), 285; observation of
    satellites, by Galileo, 402;
    by Harriot, 16-17, 27, 402-3,
    429; by Lower, 403, 405

Kalmar, Martin, 35; *Thomas Hariot's
    De reflexione*, 262n
Kargon, Robert H., 35; *Atomism in
    England*, 360-1
Kellett, Christopher, painter, 465
Kelton, Thomas, receiver for 9th earl,
    209n, 369
Kendall, −, Roanoke colonist, 119,
    120n
Kendall, Abraham, navigator, 282n
Kepler, Johannes, 1, 16, 45, 396,
    400, 401; correspondence with
    Harriot, 29, 385-8, 397, 427-8;
    observation of comets, 17;
    Astronomiae Novae, 388;
    Visier Büchlein, 385
Kerrycurrihy, Co. Cork, 158

Kett, Francis, clergyman, 180
Kettle, Dr. Ralph, 63
Keyes, Robert, conspirator, 350; executed, 351
Keymis, Lawrence, 67, 68, 219, 314; death, 443; voyage to Guiana (1596), 230-1, 232; *Relation of the second voyage to Guiana* (1596), 232-3, 318, 319
Kilcolman, Co. Cork, 159
Knollys, William, Lord Knollys, 354
Kyd, Thomas, dramatist, 66-7, 184, 189; letters, 185-6

Lacey, Robert, *Sir Walter Ralegh* (1973), 448
Lane, Ralph, 119-20, 127, 167, 145; governor of Roanoke I. (1585-6), 118-19, 121, 131, 134-5, 137-40, 142-3, 318
Lane, Sir William, overseer at Tower, 344, 354
lapides, 275(fig.), 277-8, 281, 282; significance of, 283-4
Laski, Count Albertus, 62
latitude, determination of, 87, 93
Laurency, Matthew de, 307
Law of God, *see* Canon Law
lead line, for soundings, 84
Lee, Sidney, 209n, 364
Lefranc, Pierre, *Sir Walter Ralegh écrivain*, 196, 197
Leibniz, Gottfried Wilhelm, 249
Lenox, James, book collector, 30
lenses, 32
Lismore Castle, Co. Waterford, 156; records from, 157, 164; surveys of estates, 163
Littleton, Stephen, conspirator, 349
lodestone, 149, 382
logarithms, 26, 163n, 360, 366; tables, 404
Lohne, Johannes A., Harriot studies, 33, 35, 238n, 384, 428
London, 70-1; Harriot in, 71-4, 200; schools, 73-4; ships for Azores (1591), 177; *see also* Tower
London, bishops of, *see* Aylmer, J.; Vaughan, R.
London, Great Fire of (1666), 30, 474
London, History of Science Museum, copies of Harriot MSS in, 33

London Bridge, 351
longitude, 93; determination of, 150n
Lookout, Cape, N. Car., 129, 136
Lore, Peter van, 323
Lorkin, Thomas, 448
Low Countries (Netherlands), maps of, 296; Northumberland's embassy to, 295, 369, 370; expenses, 296
Lower, Alexander, 64
Lower, Dorothy, 410, 411
Lower, Sir Nicholas, 410n
Lower, Penelope, 410; marriage, 410-11
Lower, Thomas, 410, 411
Lower, Sir William, M.P., 4, 25; biography, 388-91; death, 410, 423; correspondence with Harriot, 391-3, 398-401, 404-6; and Gunpowder Plot, 340, 347-8; observations, of Halley's comet, 17, 395; of Jupiter, at Syon, 403, 408-9, 421
Lucretius, 242, 361
Luddington, Thomas, Roanoke colonist, 122
Lynnhaven Bay, Virginia, 137
Lynley, Paul, 370

Macclesfield, George Parker, 2nd earl of, astronomer, 25
Macmillan, Harold, 32
Magdalen College, Oxford, 38
magnetism, 282
Manganin's Ephemerides, 180n
Mannourie, —, physician, 444n, 447
Manteo, an Indian, 105, 106, 112, 113, 129, 133
maps, 1, 85, 227, 462; bought for 9th earl, 296, 370-1; of Guiana, 228, 230; of Ralegh's Irish estates, 108n, 162
Margaret (sister of Henry VIII), 224
Markham, Sir Griffin, 304, 317n, 321-2
Marlowe, Christopher, dramatist, 67, 359; atheism, 180-1, 183-6, 189; death, 181
Marlowe (Marloe), Edmund, 103, 104, 229; 'Ars Naupegica', 99
Mars (planet), 17, 281
Marshall, Christopher, customs official, 123

Martin, Richard, of the Middle Temple, recorder of London, 407n
Martyr, Peter, *De orbe nouo* (1587), 60n, 80, 318
Mary, queen of Scots, 358
Mary Tudor, queen of England, statute, 312
Maskelyne, Nevil, astonomer royal, *Nautical Almanac*, 14
mathematics, at Oxford, 43; in navigation, 85, 87; schools for, 73-4; Harriot's work on, 92-4, 200-2, 241-2; studies of, 33-5, 87-8
matter, density of, 382
Maunder, Henry, messenger, 181
Mawle, Robert, agent in Ireland, 157
Mayerne, Sir Theodore Turquet de, physician, 436n; to Harriot, 432-3, 441, 449, 457, 459, 467; letters from Harriot, 58n, 435-7(figs.), 438-41; notes on illness, 433-4
Melindes, *see* Menéndez
Mellis, John, schoolmaster, 73
Menatonon, Indian chief, 138, 140
Mendoza, Bernardino de, ambassador, 76
Menéndez de Valdes, Diego, governor of Puerto Rico, 128
mercury, 272, 277-9, 283, 286; symbol, 285
Meres, John, bailiff of Sherborne, 221, 222, 237, 289, 324
meridional parts, tables of, 87
metals, *see* minerals
metaphysics, at Oxford, 44
Metcalf, Edmund, clerk of the kitchen, 302
meteorology, 387, 388
minerals, 136, 138, 285
mirrors, 150n
Mogeley (Mogeely) Map, 162-3
Molanna Abbey, Co. Cork, 157, 160; census, 164-5; history of, 165-6; survey, 162, 166
Molyneux, Emery, globe maker, 375
Moneado, Hugo de, Armada captain, 171
Monatliche Correspondenz, 396
Monteagle, William Parker, Lord, 329, 332, 333
Montucla, J.F., *Histoire des math-*

ématiques, 13
moon, 35, 394; observations, by Galileo, 17, 402; by Harriot, 150n, 397-8, 428-9; by Lower, 399
moon map, 407
Moray, Sir Robert, 8
More, Sir Francis, 303
More, Richard, *The carpenters rule* (1602), 318
Mornay, Sir Robert, 228
Mountjoy, Baron, *see* Blount, Charles
Mudge, Thomas, horologist, 14
Mulcaster, Richard, schoolmaster, 109
Munster: colonisation of, 156-7; devastation in, 161; grants of land in, 156, 161; Ralegh's lands in, 160, 161-2; accounts for, 470; census taken, 164
music, at Oxford, 44
Myrtle Grove, Youghal, 156, 160

Nashe, Thomas, dramatist; *Christs teares over Jerusalem*, 186-7; *Pierce Penilesse*, 186, 318, 319
National Library of Ireland, 164n
National Maritime Museum, Greenwich, 162
natural philosophy, at Oxford, 44
Naunton, Penelope, 411
Naunton, Sir Richard, 410-11, 413, 445n; *Fragmenta regalia*, 389n
naval tactics, 172-3
navigation, 34, 87; coastal, 83-4; oceanic, 84-5; training for, 72-3, 78-9
Nedham, George, of Keswick, 121
Newbury (Newberry), Berkshire, 467n
Newton, Isaac, 9, 249
Newtown in Kilmore, *see* Ballynoe
Nonius (Pedro Nunes), 95; sea ring, 90
Norman, Thomas, clergyman, 193-4
Northampton, earls of, *see* Compton, William; Howard, Henry
North Pole, elevation of, 89, 93
Northumberland, duke and earls of, *see* Percy
Northwest Passage, 74-5
Norton, Robert, engineer, 361
Norton, Sir William, of Southampton, 303
nose, description of, 455
Nottingham, earl of, *see* Howard, Charles

Nugent, Edward, Roanoke colonist, 140

O'Brien, Murrough (d. 1577), 159
Ocracoke, N. Car., 129
Olbers, Heinrich William Mathias, on comets, 17-18, 396
Oldcastle, Hugh, teacher of arithmetic, 73
Oldenburg, Henry, secretary Royal Society, 8-9
optics, 25, 150n, 238, 383-4, 397, 421, 428
Oriel College, Oxford, 40, 52, 53
Orinoco River, 200, 223, 231, 358
Otho, L. Valentin, 421
Oughtred, William, mathematician, 9, 10, 12
Oxford, 40-1
Oxford, earl of, *see* Vere
Oxford Botanical Garden, 205n
Oxford Philosophical Society, 9
Oxford University: course of study, 42-5; dress, 46; dispensations, 48-9; disputations, 48; matriculation, 38-40, 47, 64; New Statutes, 43-5
Oxford University Press: publication of Harriot papers, 18, 20, 21, 24; letter from Zach (1786), 15-16

Palomar, Mt., California, 35
parabolic motion, 259, 260(fig.), 261
parallaxis of the staff, 91
Parker, Captain, –, 229
Parmenius, Stephen, poet, 74
Parsons, Robert, S.J. (Philopater), 189; *Responsio*, 179-80
Payne, Robert, canon of Christ Church, 10-11
pearls, 136, 138
Peele, George, dramatist, 67, 209n; *The honour of the Garter*, 210n, 369
Pell, John, mathematician, 7, 9, 49, 107, 366-7, 373
Pemisapan (Wingina), Indian chief, 135, 139; death, 140
Pena, Joannes, editor, 421
Percy, Algernon, 10th earl of Northumberland, 7, 225, 292, 344, 358, 365, 372n; education, 376

Percy, Allen, 339, 352, 395; pension, 292
Percy, Sir Charles, 296; pension, 292
Percy, Dorothy, Viscountess Lisle, 468, 471
Percy, Henry, 4th earl of Northumberland, 333
Percy, Henry, 8th earl of Northumberland, 167
Percy, Henry, 9th earl of Northumberland, 2, 62, 63, 171, 175; character, 205, 207-9; children, 224-5; death, 7; education, 168; family, 167-8; gambling, 170, 218; Garter knight, 67, 209-10; hospitality, 202-4, 367-8; household, 368-70; houses, *see* Essex; Petworth; Syon; library, 32, 296, 360, 361, 370-1; livery, 368; marriage, 224; portraits, 205; privy councillor, 301; religion, 199;
correspondence, with R. Cecil, 206; with James VI, 297-8, 298-9, 299-300; with Privy Council, 333-4
Harriot's patron, 6-7, 10, 29, 156, 202, 204, 223, 227, 291, 360, 361, 364-5, 367; H. papers in custody of, 2-3; H. bequest to, 462, 463
implicated in Gunpowder Plot, 329-33, 406n; interrogatories, 336-9, 344-6; trial in Star Chamber, 352-7; imprisonment, *see* Tower of London
See also Low Countries; Ralegh, Sir Walter
Percy, Henry, son of 9th earl, 377
Percy, Sir Hugh Algernon, 10th duke of Northumberland, 32, 226n, 475
Percy, Sir Jocelyn, 296; pension, 292
Percy, Josceline, 11th earl of Northumberland, 15
Percy, Richard, 202, 203
Percy, Thomas, 7th earl of Northumberland, 167, 362
Percy, Thomas, constable of Alnwick, 297, 352, 353, 356, 406n, 427; conspirator, 330, 332, 333, 336-9; description, 334; death, 335-6, 351

Percy Society, 28
Perham, Sir Edward, 447
Perrot, Sir John, lord deputy, 389-90
Perrot, Penelope, wife of Wm Lower, 389, 390, 391
Perrot, Sir Thomas, 224, 389-90
perspective glasses (cylinder; trunks), 149, 399, 401, 402
Peto, Franciscan, 227-8
Petworth House, Sussex, 169n, 205, 367, 369, 471; Harriot papers at, 7, 15, 20, 22, 26-7, 37
Philipson, Thomas, principal St. Mary's Hall, 53, 54, 61
Phillips, Sir Edward, master of the Rolls, 220
Philosopher's Stone, 273, 277, 284, 285, 406
philosophy, at Oxford, 43
phlebotomy, 457-8
pinnace, 126, 131
Pitiscus, *Trigonometria*, 404
plague, 306, 372
planetary motion, 393-4
planets, 1, 19, 269-71, 400; symbols, 285
Plat, Sir Hugh, *The jewell house of art and nature* (1594), 318
Plate, River, rutter of, 229
Playfair, John, mathematician, 21
Pleura, –, de pharmacist, 440
Plymouth, Eng., 76
Polaris, 86, 93, 94
Pomeiok, Indian village, 131; drawing of, 133
Popham, Sir John, lord chief justice, 310, 313, 315, 316-17, 320, 354, 356, 401
Portland, Dorset, 171, 191
Portsmouth, Eng., 157
Portsmouth, N. Car., 129
Powell, –, of Balliol, 18, 19
Powell, William S., on Roanoke colonists, 119n, 120
Powton, Edmund, cofferer to 9th earl, 210n, 211, 216, 293, 295n, 352, 371
Prague, 385, 387
Prideaux, –, Roanoke colonist, 119, 120n
prisms, 384
privateering, 99, 113
Privy Council, 181, 183

projectiles, 27
projections, 87; stereographic, 85
Protheroe, John, 4, 25, 401, 410; biography, 412; bequest from Harriot, 383, 462-3; correspondence with 9th earl, 412-13; executor for Harriot, 2, 3, 9, 31, 366, 399, 413, 467, 469, 472; will, 413-14; wife, *see* Vaughan, Elinor
Prutenic tables, 92
Ptolemaic system, 393
Puckering, Sir John, lord keeper of the great seal, 67, 185
Puerto Rico, 125, 126, 127
Purbachius, astronomer, 15
Pygott, Richard, principal St. Mary's Hall, 38, 40, 53, 54, 61

quadrants, 92
'Queen Elizabeth's Academy', 78-9

Radcliffe Observatory, Oxford, 14
radius astronomicus, 92n, 94
rain, experiment with, 82-3
rainbow, 384, 385, 386, 387, 428
Ralegh, Carew, 191, 323; atheist, 191-2, 193, 195, 197; ships for the Azores, 177; voyage (1578), 76-7
Ralegh, Damerei (son of Sir Walter), 178
Ralegh, Sir Walter, 299-300, 375; character, 168-9; courtier, 176; marriage, 177-8; portrait, 169; religious beliefs, 58, 195-6, 197-8, 199; testimony on Gunpowder Plot, 334; will (1597), 234-8, 324; houses, *see* Durham; Sherborne; wife, *see* Throckmorton, Elizabeth
correspondence, with R. Cecil, 178-9, 228; with James I, 298, 300; with Lady Ralegh (1603), 305-6, 322
promoter of American colonisation charter (1584), 81, 104, 118, 123, 124, 156; *see* Roanoke I.; in Ireland, 81, 104, 156-66; *see also* Munster; Youghal
Harriot in household of, 80-1, 82, 173; working for, 218-19,

Ralegh, Harriot in household of
    (*cont.*)
    223, 232, 289–90, 321, 324,
    470; Northumberland's links
    with, 168–70, 203
  arrested (1603), 304–5; attempted
    suicide, 305, 396; indictment,
    307, 311; defence, 312, 315;
    trial, 310–15; judgement, 315–
    17; imprisonment, *see* Tower of
    London; re-trial (1618), 444;
    speech, 444; execution, 423,
    443, 445; descriptions of,
    443–6; 448; Harriot's notes
    on, 446–8
  voyages: (1578), 76–7; (1595),
    86, 88, 91; (1596), 229; (1597),
    233–4
  works: *Discouerie of . . . Guiana*,
    233; *Historie of the world*
    (1614), 29, 358, 363; extract,
    121–3; *Report . . . of the fight
    about the . . . Açores*, 164n, 171
Ralegh, Walter (son), 234, 235, 236–7,
    289; death, 442
Raymond, George, captain *Lion*,
    118, 124, 130
Read (Reid), Alexander, physician,
    337, 431, 453–4; *Chirurgical
    Lectures of Tumors and Vlcers*,
    359, 361–2, 455–9; *Description
    of the Body of Man*, 454;
    Manual of the anatomy, 454–5
Recorde, Robert; *Grounde of artes*, 74;
    Vrinall of physick, 438
reflection of bodies, 27
Reformation, in Oxford, 41–2
refraction, 24–5, 392n; Harriot's work
    on, 17, 150n, 238, 380–1, 384,
    428; sine law of, 385; table of,
    386, 387
Regiomontanus, 15
Reinhold, Erasmus, 92
Reynolds, Dr. John, president Corpus
    Christi, 62
Rheticus, *Opus Palatinum*, 420, 421
rhetoric, at Oxford, 43
rhumbs, 27, 88, 201, 375, 423
Rigaud, Stephen Jordan, 25n
Rigaud, Stephen P., Savilian professor
    of geometry, 399, 460; reports
    on Harriot MSS, 14n, 21–6,
    29; *Harriot's Astronomical

Papers*, 23; extracts, 23–4, 25–6
Rigaud, S.P. and Stephen J., *Cor-
    respondence of Scientific
    Men of the Seventeenth Century*
    (1841), 9n, 25
Roanoke I., 130(fig.), 133(fig.); col-
    onists, 120–3, 464; names,
    120n; colony (1585), 118,
    119n, 124, 129, 130–4, 426
Roanoke River (Moratico), expedition,
    137–8, 140
Robertson, Abraham, Savilian pro-
    fessor, 18; report on Harriot's
    MSS, 19–20, 21, 35
Robins, (Robbyns), Arthur, surveyor,
    162
Roche, John, 94–5; 'Thomas Harriot's
    Astronomy', 92n, 287n, 407
Rookwood, Ambrose, conspirator, 350;
    executed, 351
Roxo Bay, Puerto Rico, 127
Royal Exchange, London, 1, 73
Royal Institution Journal, 21
Royal Society, London, 14; search for
    Harriot MSS, 7–9, 12; Rigaud's
    paper on 'Harriot's Astronomical
    Observations' read to, 22
Royal Society of Berlin, *Astronomical
    Ephemeris*, 16
Royden, Matthew, poet, 67, 68, 185n,
    186, 359; *Willobie his Avisa*,
    360
Rukeyser, Muriel, *Traces of Thomas
    Hariot*, 233, 242, 473n
Russe (Rowse), Anthony, Roanoke
    colonist, 120n, 123
rutters, 83–4, 85, 227, 228–9

Sackville, Thomas, earl of Dorset, lord
    treasurer, 354
saddle, 169, 170
St. Bridget, Order of, 225
St. Christopher's Church, London,
    Harriot buried in, 29, 460n,
    462, 470, 472; memorial plaque
    in, 30, 69, 472–4
St. Croix (Santa Cruz), Virgin Is., 126
St. Leger, Sir Warham, provost-marshal
    of Munster, 158
St. Mael-Anfaidh, 165
St. Mary Magdalen, Oxford, 41
St. Mary's Hall, Oxford, 38, 40, 51–3,
    65, 373, 374

St. Mary's (the Virgin) Church, Oxford, 38, 40

St. Olave's parish, London, 73

St. Paul's Cathedral, London, 73

St. Paul's churchyard, 68, 186, 351

Salisbury (Sarum), bishops of, *see* Coldwell, John; Ward, Seth

salt, at Puerto Rico, 127-8

Sancroft, William, archbishop of Canterbury, 448

Sanderson, William, merchant, 228, 375; lawsuit v. Ralegh estate, 218-19; counter suit, 220-2

Sandys, Sir Arthur, 317n

San German, Puerto Rico, 127

Santa Cruz, Álváro de Bazan, marquis of, 172

sassafras, 136, 138, 139, 147

Saturn (planet), 285

Savilian Chair of Astronomy, Oxford, 45

Scaliger, Joseph Justus, *Cyclometria* (1593), 201; (1594), 201-2, 318

Scarburgh, Sir Charles, physician, 8

Scarlett, Francis, clergyman, 194

'School of Night', 359

School Street, Oxford, 41, 47

sea ring, 88; use of, 90

Seaton, Ethel, 'Thomas Hariot's Secret Script', 108, 109, 283

Secotan, Indian village, 131, 135, 153; drawing of, 133

Seymour, Edward, duke of Somerset, 226

Shakespeare, William, sonnets, 203; *Love's Labour's Lost*, 359

Shelbury, John, 323; Ralegh executor, 218, 220, 222

Sheller, John, servant, 464, 465

Sherbourne Castle, Dorset, 176-7; Ralegh at, 189, 191, 223, 227; title to, 177, 288-91, 321

shipbuilding, 34; Harriot's notes on, 96-7, 99-100, 103-4

shipping: Dutch, 99-100; English, 100; French, 100; Spanish, 127

ships: *Adventure*, 101; *Anne Aucher*, 76; *Bark Raleigh*, 105; *Dorothy*, 105, 118; *Dreadnought*, 101; *Elizabeth*, 118, 126, 127, 128; *Due Repulse*, 229; *Falcon*, 76; *Hope of Greenway*, 76;

Lion (*Red Lion*), 118; *Madre de Deus*, 102, 187-9, 204; *Merhonour*, 101; *Prince Royal*, 103; *Repulse*, 101; *Revenge*, 164n, 177; *Roebuck*, 118, 177, 187, 236; *Tiger*, 117-18, 120, 125-9, 133; *Vanguard*, 101; *Warspite*, 229; *Watts*, 233

ship's company, 97, 98(fig.), 99

ship's tonnage, calculation of, 101-3

Shirley, Anthony, adventurer, 66

Shirley, (Frederick) John, canon of Canterbury, 32

Shotton, Timothy, rutters, 229

Shrewsbury, Gilbert Talbot, 7th earl of, 354

Sidney, Henry, lord deputy, 159

Sidney, Sir Philip, 43, 176, 204, 468; *Astrophel and Stella*, 224, 391

Sidney, Robert (d. 1626), earl of Leicester, 468

Sidney, Sir Robert, Viscount Lisle, 462; executor, 30, 467-8, 472

silver, symbol for, 285

Sion College, London, 4, 25, 29, 107, 108, 472n; library, 283

Skelton, a horse, 170

Skiko, an Indian, 138, 139, 140

smallpox, 150

Smith, Robert, Ralegh executor, 218, 220

Smith, Sir Thomas, secretary of state, 109, 342

Smythe, Sir John, 114n

Snedall, Hugh, 219

Snedall, Margaret, 219

Snell, Willebrord, 25, 27, 381; *Apollonius Batavus* (1608), 420, 421n, 422

Sockett, Rev. Thomas, 399n

solstices, 17, 27

Spain, 152; ships of, 100, 171-3; soldiers in W. Indies, 126, 127-8; threat to English colonies, 136, 141

Spenser, Edmund, poet, in Ireland, 158-9

spherical triangles, 317n

Stafford, Edward, Roanoke colonist, 119, 120n, 137

Stanhope, Sir John, Lord Stanhope of Harrington, 310, 354

Stanley, Ferdinando, 5th earl of Derby, 359, 361

Stapleton, Robert, paymaster to 9th earl, 216n, 369-70

Statuta pro Scholaribus, Oxford, 43-5

Stevens, Henry, studies of Harriot, 27-31, 441n; trs Torporley title page, 5; *Thomas Harriot and his associates*, 6n, 31, 448, 460; extracts, 28, 29, 446-7

Stevens, Henry N., 28n, 31, 460

Stevin, Simon, mathematician, 110

Stifel, —, mathematician, 110

Stock, Richard, clergyman, 422; eulogy, 422-3

Strout, Eugeny and Moore, P., 'First Maps and Drawings of the Moon', 35

Star Chamber, Court of, 350, 352-7

Stow, John, *Annals* (1631), 352, 353; *Survey of London* (1633), 473-4

Strathmann, Ernest, *Sir Walter Ralegh, a Study in Elizabethan Skepticism*, 198

Streete, John, 335-6

Strozzi, Pietro, death at Azores, 172

Stuart, Lady Arabella, 224, 307, 358

Stukeley, John, Roanoke colonist, 119, 131

Stukeley, Sir Lewis, vice-admiral of Devon, 444, 447

sulphur, 272, 277-9, 281, 283, 286

sun, 16; eclipse of (1585), 125, 151; haloes, 385; regiment of, 88, 92, 93, 94

sun spots, 16, 19, 27, 55, 383, 403-4, 407-9, 419-20

Supremacy, Oath of, 352n, 353

surplus of the horizon, 91

Sussex, Robert Radcliffe, earl of, 341

symbols: algebraic (Cossic), 110; phonetic, 109-10, 111(fig.)

Syon House, Isleworth, 24, 25, 29, 225-6, 303, 369, 471, 475; angular position, 239-40; waterworks, 263, 293, 294(fig.), 295

Harriot's house at, 226, 291, 293, 295, 365; searched, 342; H. working at, 226, 238-9, 264, 276, 326, 380, 391, 417; library, 296, 420-1, 453, 462-3

Talbot, John, servant to Ralegh, 323

Tanner, Robert, *Brief treatise . . . of the sphere* (1592), 201, 318

Tartaglia, Niccolo, 249; *Concerning the arte of schooting*, 246, 247; *La nova scientia*, 245, 252

Taylor, E.G.R., navigation studies, 34, 72, 81, 89, 150n

Taylor, Henry, clerk of kitchens, 301

telescopes (instruments): used by Galileo, 401-2, 407; used by Harriot, 24, 26, 29, 35, 150n, 238n, 287n, 383, 397-8, 428; bequest of, 1, 32, 463; *see also* perspective glasses

Templemichael Castle, Co. Cork, 158

Terra experiments, 274, 275(fig.), 276-8, 280-1, 286

Thames, River, 70-1

Theodosius, of Tripoli, *De sphaera*, ed. Pena (1558), 420, 421

Thorpe, Roger, retainer, 368

Three Magi, 65, 68, 360, 362-4, 377; pensions for, 378(fig.)

Throckmorton, Anna, 178

Throckmorton, Arthur, 177, 178, 237, 290, 324

Throckmorton, Elizabeth (Lady Ralegh), 218, 219, 223, 323; inheritance, 235, 237, 289; letters from Ralegh, 305-6, 322; marriage, 177-8, 187

Throgmorton Plot, 167

Thynne, John, of Longleat, 72-3

Tichbourne, Sir Benjamin, sheriff, 321

tide table, 84

tilt boat, 131

time glass (sand glass), 84, 99

tobacco, 147-8, 168, 193, 209, 382, 433; pipe, 183

Tooke, Christopher, lens grinder, 24, 326, 382, 397, 408-9, 423; bequest from Harriot, 383, 462-3, 464-5

Torporley, Nathaniel, 23, 25, 62, 72, 340, 355, 361, 364; Harriot bequest, 383, 462-3; executor, 2, 3, 68, 469; implicated in Gunpowder Plot, 342-4; pension from 9th earl, 363, 399; Sion College papers, 29, 107-8, 283

'Analytical Corrector', 5-6; *Diclides coelometricae* (1602), 319
Tower Hill, London, 369
Tower of London, 355-6, 379; report on, 325-6; Northumberland in, 15, 344, 351-2, 359-60, 362, 364; release, 15, 470-2; Ralegh in (1592), 178, 189; (1603), 323, 325-6, 363-5
Townson, Robert, dean of Westminster, 444, 446, 448
trajectories, 254-5, 256(fig.), 257(fig.), 258-9
Traventi farm, Carmarthenshire, 391, 192
treason, penalty for, 317, 350-1
Trenchard, Sir George, 197; dinner party, 192, 193; account of, 195-6
triangles, 27
trigonometry, 85; tables, 421
Trinidad, W. Indies, 91, 231
Trinity College, Oxford, 66; library, 63
Turner, Peter (d. 1614), physician, 283, 429-30, 432
Turner, Samuel, 430; letter to Harriot, 432, 436, 440
Turner, William (d. 1568), botanist, 429
Tyrone, Hugh O'Neill, earl of, 285

Uden, Grant, *Eight Horses for My Coach*, 471n
Unitarianism, 184
University College, Oxford, 38
Unton, Henry, at Oriel, 53
urinal, 438n, 440

vacuum, 387-8
Valdes, Pedro de, with Armada, 171
Van Dyke, portrait of 9th earl, 205
variation of the compass, 88, 89, 125; calculation of, 94, 229
Vaughan, Elinor, 412, 414
Vaughan, John, 1st earl of Carbery, 412
Vaughan, John, Roanoke colonist, 119, 137
Vaughan, Richard, 2nd earl of Carbery, 9
Vaughan, Richard, bishop of London, 354
Vaughan, Walter, of Llanelly, 413

vector analysis, 259
Venus (planet), 383
Vere, Edward de (d. 1604), earl of Oxford, 171
Vere, Sir Francis, 207, 229, 295, 370
Vere, Henry de (d. 1625), earl of Oxford, 444, 471
Vieta, François, 1, 10, 13, 26, 110, 405; *Algebra nova* (1591), 3, 12, 400
Virginia (N. Carolina), 132(fig.); exploration, 135-9; fauna 148-9; flora, 136, 147, 148, 149; voyages to: (1584), 104-5; (1585), 125, 130(fig.)
Vitellio, 387, 388

Waad (Wade), Sir William, 310; lieut. of Tower, 324-5, 332, 351, 354; report, 325-6
wages, 210
Wales, 414; Northumberland property in, 410, 412-13
Wallace, W.A., of Co. Mayo, research on Ralegh in Ireland, 157; on Harriot, 160; on H's symbols, 108n, 109
Wallis, John, Savilian Professor of Geometry, support for Harriot, 9-13; 'Recapitulation of Particulars', 13; *Treatise of Algebra*, 10, 12-13
Wallop, Sir Henry, 120n
Walsingham, Frances, Countess of Essex, 176
Walsingham, Sir Francis, 176
Walsingham, Thomas, of Kent, 181
Wanchese, an Indian, 105, 106, 112, 113
Ward, Seth, bishop of Salisbury, 199, 367, 430
Warner, Walter, 2, 62, 66, 68, 72, 186, 373, 451; ed. *Artis Analyticae Praxis*, 4, 6, 10-11, 379; named as a Magi, 65, 360, 362-4; retainer of 9th earl, 67, 210n, 216, 239, 296, 365, 367-71, 377; pension, 7, 362, 363, 367-8, 371-2
Warner, William, poet, 359
Warton, Thomas, *History of English Poetry*, 66
watch (chronometer), 14

Waterford, county, 156, 157
Waters, David W., *Art of Navigation*, 34, 93
waterworks, 380; *see also* Syon
Watson, William, priest, 304; executed, 320
Wheatley, –, apothecary, 467
Whetcomb, Elizabeth, housewife of Sherborne, 194n
White, John, artist, 34, 122n; colonist in Ireland, 157–8, 160–7; in Roanoke, 131, 135, 137; voyages, 105, 125
 drawings, 30, 61, 121, 126, 128–9, 137, 149, 154–5; published, 145; surveys, 162; handwriting, 162, 163
White, Rowland, letter to Mornay, 228
White, William, Roanoke colonist, 122
Whitlock, Edmund, retainer 9th earl, 331, 334, 339, 347, 406n
Whittle, –, vicar of Forthington, 195
Whittlesey, Robert, engraver, plan of Oxford, 39(fig.)
Wight, I. of, 77
Williams, David, lawyer, 122–3
Williams, John, sheriff of Dorset, 190, 196, 197
Williams, Sir Roger, 114n
Winchester, Ralegh trial at, 307, 310–17, 371, 443, 444; executions at, 321
Windebank, Sir Thomas, letter to R. Cecil, 342–3
Windsor, 210, 301
Wingina, Indian chief, 129, 137, 138, 139, 151; *see also* Pemisapan
Winter, Robert, conspirator, 349–50; executed, 351
Winter, Thomas, conspirator, 350; executed, 351
Witelo, *Opticae Thesaurvs*, 238
Withington, –, vice-chancellor of Oxford, 57
Wococon, N. Car., 129, 131, 133
Wood, Anthony à, antiquary, 30, 41, 49, 199, 367; *Annals*, 41–2, 375; *Athenae Oxonienses* (1691), 51, 53, 61–2, 65, 66, 68, 363, 431, 472n
Worcester, Edward Somerset, 4th earl of, 354

Worthe, Sir Robert, of Essex, 303
Wotton, Sir Edward, Lord Wotton, 310, 354
Wren, Matthew, Royal Society, 8
Wright, Edward, mathematician, 87, 231, 282n
Wright, Thomas, 66
Wright-Molyneux globe (1592), 201
Wriothesley, Henry, 3rd earl of Southampton, 202–3, 204, 358, 471
Wycliffe, Thomas, cofferer to 9th earl, 169, 227, 293, 337
Wycliff, William, reciever general, 211, 212, 216, 370n
Wyndham, Chalres Henry, Lord Leconfield, 31–2
Wyndham, George O'Brien, 3rd earl of Egremont, 15, 20
Wyndham, Henry, 2nd Lord Leconfield, 31–2
Wyndham, John Edward Reginald, 1st baron Egremont, 6th baron Leconfield, 32
Wyndham, John Max Scawen, 2nd baron Egremont, 7th baron Leconfield, 33
Wytfliet, Cornelis van, *Descriptiones Ptolemaicae augmentum sive occidentalis* (1597), 319
Wyvel, Sir Marmaduke, 303

Yates, –, Harriot's brother-in-law, 40
Yates, Thomas (nephew), 465, 466
Yates, Frances: 'Giordano Bruno's Conflict with Oxford', 41, 42; *Study of 'Love's Labour's Lost'*, 360
Yates, William, 466
Yong, Andrew, pursebearer to 9th earl, 169
Youghal, Co. Cork, 160, 166; Ralegh in, 156–7, 159–60
Young, Henry, 183, 185

Zach, Franz Xavier, Baron von Zach, 15–16, 22–3, 395, 396; and Harriot MSS at Petworth, 14, 20–1, 24, 29, 33, 398–9; *Monatliche Correspondenz*, 1n, 17
Zodiac, signs of, 283
Zouche, Edward, Baron Zouche of Harringworth, 354